9/11: THE ULTIMATE TRUTH

Books by **Laura Knight Jadczyk**

Amazing Grace – An Autobiography of the Soul

The Secret History of the World

High Strangeness

The Wave – Books 1-6

911: The Ultimate Truth

Second Revised Edition

Laura Knight-Jadczyk
Joe Quinn

With
Signs of the Times Editors
Scott Ogrin
Henri Sy

Preface by
Pentagon Strike Creator
Darren Williams

Red Pill Press
2009

Third Edition
Copyright 2002-2009, Laura Knight- Jadczyk
Research Sponsored by Quantum Future Group, Inc.
P.O. Box 4322, Boulder, CO 80306
ISBN 1-897244-45-6

Portions of this book were published in 2002 as *The Occult Significance of 9/11*

Printed in Poland

TABLE OF CONTENTS

Acknowledgements

We are indebted to the many people around the world who have been working on uncovering the truth about 9/11 whose work we draw from in the first part of this book. In particular, we would like to acknowledge the work of Thierry Meyssan and his team at Réseau Voltaire for the books *9/11 The Big Lie* (*L'Effroyable imposture*) and *Pentagate,* and the work of the fine folks at www.physics911.net.

In the days following September 11, 2001, as we pondered the question *cui bono*, or "who benefits?", the answer that began to emerge as the obvious solution was "Israel". Nevertheless, we assumed the facts on the ground described by the mainstream media were pretty much what had happened in logistical, physical terms. It was only after reading *9/11 The Big Lie* that we saw that there was a mountain of evidence to indicate that the official story did not stand up to careful forensic scrutiny either in the hard data or in the naming of the culprits.

We would also like to recommend David Ray Griffin's *The New Pearl Harbor* as an introduction to a critical analysis of what really happened on September 11, 2001. Griffin holds a carefully circumspect position in his analysis of the flaws in the official story, yet by piling up point after point where the official story collapses against the facts, he leads his readers to the inescapable conclusion that there must have been state-sponsorship of the attacks. However, having taken the case that far, Griffin does not attempt to speculate on what might really have happened that day. Nevertheless, it is an excellent primer for those who still accept the fairy tale told by the mainstream American media.

We would also like to acknowledge the work of Dave McGowan, Killtown for his Pentalawn pages, and The Center for Cooperative Research.

Finally, and most important of all, we would like to thank Andrew M. Lobaczewski for his amazing work and timely input.

PREFACE

Darren Williams

Typing "9/11 conspiracy" into a popular internet search engine returns over 200,000 hits, just one indication that the events of September 11, 2001 are some of the most controversial in recent history.

The Signs of the Times *Pentagon Strike Presentation* was created following two-and-a-half years of research into the events of 9/11. The attack on the Pentagon was selected as the subject of the presentation due to the overwhelming evidence contradicting the "official story" presented by the United States Government and subsequently promulgated worldwide by mainstream media organisations.

Drawing on her exhaustive research into the events of 9/11, in addition to over 30 years of research covering a multitude of fields, Laura Knight-Jadczyk and Signs of the Times' *9/11: The Ultimate Truth* presents an in-depth and often shocking exposé of the how and the why of the 9/11 attacks and the implications they hold for the entire human race.

9/11: The Ultimate Truth begins with a detailed examination of the evidence for each of the events of 9/11 in turn, focusing on the Pentagon attack in particular, and presents a convincing hypothesis of what really happened to each of the flights on that day. For the first time ever, the authors reveal the possibility of an Israeli double-cross that saw the Neo-con plans take an unexpected and dramatic turn of events as the day unfolded.

Laura's narrative then leads the reader from the events of 9/11 into a labyrinth of Counter Intelligence cover-ups, Mind Programming, Ethnic Specific Weapons and Jewish and Christian "end times" prophecy, until we are brought face to face with "the most dangerous idea in the world". What at first might appear to the reader as intriguing, yet seemingly discontinuous threads, Laura skillfully weaves into a millennia-long panorama that will startle the reader in its implications.

In any given situation, our ability to effect real change in our lives, and therefore on our planet, is limited only by our ability to recognise truth from lies. In essence, the question, "what can anyone do?" can only be answered if one has a sufficiently objective knowledge base. It is in this respect, at a time when the world population is perched on the edge of an abyss, that the truth unveiled in Laura Knight-Jadczyk and Signs of the Times' *9/11: The Ultimate Truth* may yet earn itself a place in history as one of the most important books ever written.

It is indeed a testament to the ability and resolute will of the authors, and the quality of the analysis presented, that what was once consigned to the realm of "conspiracy" and subjective theory now exists as part of the visible reality.

This inspirational work holds enormous potential for the future of the human race. Whether or not that potential is realised will be determined by the choices made by each and every individual who reads and sincerely considers its message.

Darren Williams *is the author of the Flash animation* Pentagon Strike, *the powerful exposé of the inconsistencies in the official story of what happened at the headquarters of the U.S. military on the morning of September 11, 2001.* Pentagon Strike *has been seen by over half a billion people around the world. It can be found at www.pentagonstrike.co.uk.*

INTRODUCTION TO THE
SECOND, REVISED EDITION

For this second edition of *9/11: The Ultimate Truth*, we have made small revisions to Part One to include some recent work and incidents, such as the non-event in May when the U.S. government made a heroic effort to release two tapes shot by security cameras at the Pentagon. The tapes included nothing of importance, and, if anything, underline the fact that the explosion at the Pentagon is the weak link of the entire 9/11 affair, a point we made in the first edition of this book and will continue to insist upon.

The attacks on those who point to the missing plane, American Airlines Flight 77, as *the weak link* have continued to grow in number and intensity since the book was published. Unfortunately, not only are these attacks coming from those openly defending that absurd "conspiracy theory" known as the official story, but they are also even more vicious when spouting from the mouths and through the keyboards of those who call themselves members of the so-called "9/11 Truth Movement".

We have also revised a large portion of Part Two in order to include our latest research into Ashkenazi genetics, a controversial question that is at the heart of the on-going criminal actions of the State of Israel in Gaza and Lebanon as we write (July 2006). The genocide of the Palestinians, be it through starvation, attrition, the uprooting of ancient olive groves and the razing of houses, or the open warfare of this latest re-colonization of Gaza, reveals the conscienceless inhumanity of the leaders of Israel. The destruction of Lebanon as revenge for the capture by Hezbollah of two Israeli soldiers illegally occupying Lebanese soil, another incidence of collective punishment, is but confirmation that Israeli leaders have no conscience, no capacity to emphatize with the pain and suffering of other human beings.

They are obviously not alone.

The silence of the rest of the world in the face of such horrors clearly shows that this conscienceless inhumanity doesn't stop at the borders of the Zionist state. A cancer speads across the globe, a cancer that eats away at conscience. There exists a form of human devoid of conscience, the psychopath, and it appears as if the values, of lack of them, indicative of psychopathic thought are becoming ever more widespread and are infecting ever-greater portions of the world population.

This infection can become epidemic because the psychopath is an invisible enemy that is found in all races, speaking all languages, worshipping every god, and, sadly, directing most if not every country, multinational, Supreme Court, media outlet, and police force, to mention but a few of the positions of power to which they gravitate and from which they impose their pathological view of the world.

The first edition of this book introduced the ideas of Polish psychologist Andrew W. Lobaczewski to the world. His book, *Political Ponerology*, has now been published by Red Pill Press. Although excerpts of that work that help us understand 9/11 will be found in Part Two, it should be read in its entirety as a companion volume to this work. It is a clinical dissection of the workings of the rule of the psychopath, called the *Pathocracy* by Lobaczewski. If evil exists in our world, a strong case can be made that it manifests through the psychopath. Moreover, associations of psychopaths are formed to carry out their work. As Lobaczewski explains, psychopaths recognize each other and are able to work together to achieve common goals. Such associations when seen in the larger picture of history can give a scientific foundation to the study of what is now derided with the term "conspiracy theory".

If our analysis of 9/11 is correct, the attacks on the World Trade Center and the Pentagon on September 11, 2001 mark the opening volley of the final act of a plan set in motion long, long ago, the subjugation of the society of normal people, to use Lobaczewski's term, to the Pathocrats, that is, the psychopaths who are seeking to create a world in their image.

This book is our analysis of how we got here and the danger we, the ordinary people of our planet, face at the hands of the pathocrats who feel compelled to annihilate us to ensure their own survival.

[Note: Images used in this book are available in color for online viewing at <http://www.signs-of-the-times.org/signs/9-11_pics.htm>. We have also created an online page of links to all web sources cited in this book at <http://www.signs-of-the-times.org/signs/9-11_links.htm>.]

Introduction

> It must be remembered that the first job of any conspiracy, whether it be in politics, crime or within a business office, is to convince everyone else that no conspiracy exists. The conspirators' success will be determined largely by their ability to do this. – Gary Allen, *None Dare Call It Conspiracy*

Within hours of the September 11, 2001 attack, the blame was being laid at the doorstep of Osama bin Laden's cave in the mountains of Afghanistan. We were told that 19 Arab men, mostly Saudi nationals, were the hijackers, and for some obscure reason, Saudi National Hijackers being the culprits justified the 2003 invasion and occupation of Iraq.

This troubling inconsistency was not sufficient, however, to dissuade a majority of American citizens from believing that Saddam Hussein was also somehow involved in the 9/11 attacks, despite the fact that there has *never been any evidence* of a link between Osama and Saddam, while there *is* a mountain of evidence that there was no love lost between the secular Hussein and the religious zealot bin Laden. Furthermore, there has *never been any proof* offered that any of the 19 men accused of the hijackings were even on the planes that day, not to mention the fact that *some of them are actually still alive* according to international news reports.[1]

The Bush administration provided no proof of the existence of the weapons of mass destruction that it claimed Saddam was preparing to use against the U.S., or might *prepare* to use against the U.S., or might *think* about creating in order to prepare to use against the U.S. We now know, to the contrary, that he had no weapons of mass destruction, nor did he have the means of creating them due to years of international sanctions that had already reduced Iraq to a state of military and economic impotency.

We confront here a strange and frightening problem: What can lead so many people to believe a story for which there is not only *no* evidence, but in fact, the preponderance of evidence points in a different direction? How can so many people be wrong? Within this book, we will present a scientific study that will answer this question.

In the spring of 2002, after the publication of Thierry Meyssan's book, *9/11 The Big Lie*, many readers of our website[2] deluged us with emails asking what we thought about the evidence that a Boeing 757 did *not* hit the Pentagon.

---

[1] http://news.bbc.co.uk/1/hi/world/middle_east/1559151.stm
[2] http://www.sott.net

Up to that moment in time, there was no question in our minds that the physical events of 9/11 happened exactly as described by the media and the Bush Administration. Of course, we had certain ideas as to *who* might be behind those events, but the important point is that we did not question the 'facts on the ground'—the physical logistics—of the event.

Certainly, because this was our belief, we began to search for data with something of a bias. I[3] was quite certain that the "no-Boeing" theory was a "psy-ops"[4] program designed to set up people who were asking "whodunnit" so that when the "proof of the Boeing" hitting the Pentagon was finally un-veiled, everyone who suspected an "inside job" would look completely stupid and all related conspiracy theories would be thoroughly squashed. In that way, all other questions—mainly *cui bono*—would be silenced. In fact, I ex-pected such a revelation any day as the "No Boeing" theory raced around the globe via the internet and Meyssan's book became a best-seller. I began to wonder what was really going on when the "big revelation designed to make everybody look stupid and stop asking questions" never happened. Could it be possible that there was *no* proof that a Boeing 757 hit the Pentagon? What were they waiting for?

I also must admit that I did not consider it within the realm of possibility that such a "switch" could have been perpetrated upon the American public, *much less the media.*[5] Surely no criminal element within our own government would be crazy enough to fake a terrorist attack on the Pentagon and try to pass it off as a Boeing and expect to get away with it! What a lunatic idea! And yet, as I continued to dig through the piles of information, both pro and con, it was beginning to look as though that was exactly what had happened.

But that idea was so crazy, so impossible, so unbelievable that — like most other average people — I wanted to resist it tooth and nail. And certainly there *seemed* to be many good reasons to resist such an idea, the main one being: how could such a theorized "conspiracy" actually exist?

The term "conspiracy theory" has been used in a derisive way for so long now that the mere pronouncing of the words acts to turn off the thinking ca-pacities of the average citizen of Western nations. The "conspiracy theory" of history has been dismissed repeatedly and pejoratively by U.S. politicians and the media.

---

[3] Laura Knight-Jadczyk

[4] Intelligence organization operations to convey selected information and indicators to audiences to influence their thinking, emotions and behavior.

[5] I admit to being somewhat naïve. I knew the media could be "swayed" this way or that by government or corporate influence, but I was not yet ready to think that it could be as completely controlled as has been demonstrated since 9/11. I do want to mention that I have a friend who is a program director for a major radio station in the U.S. He visited us one evening in late 2000 and said that he was concerned that "something was up". He had noted that nearly all the radio stations in the U.S. were being bought up by a single company and all the programs were going to be "canned".

I find that to be curious. And when I am curious, I go looking for an answer. The first thing I thought about was the fact that the word "conspiracy" evokes such a strong reaction in all of us—me included. Nobody wants to be branded as a "conspiracy theorist". It just isn't "acceptable". It's "un-scientific" or it's evidence of mental instability. Right?

In fact, I think that the very reading of the word even produces certain physiological reactions: a slight acceleration of the heartbeat and perhaps a quick glance around to make sure that no one is watching while you simply read the word silently.

I asked myself *why*, why does this word evoke such an instantaneous emotional reaction? Have *you* ever wondered why it stimulates such a strong "recoil"? After all, it is only a word. It only describes the idea of people in "high places" thinking about things and doing things that manipulate other people to produce benefits for themselves. There's nothing untrue about that! It is, in fact, the truest thing about our world. The act of conspiring is an ancient and well-documented part of history. In the Bible, Cain conspired to kill Abel; the sons of Jacob conspired to sell their brother into slavery; Judas conspired to betray Jesus, Brutus et al. conspired to 'do in' Julius Caesar. The instigators of the American Revolution were conspirators.

In 1934, Irénée du Pont and William S. Knudsen (president of General Motors) conspired with friends of the Morgan Bank to effect a *coup d'etat* against Franklin D. Roosevelt. They had a mercenary army of terrorists and the only reason they were undone was because they approached Gen. Smedley Butler to lead the coup. Butler didn't like Roosevelt's "New Deal"; he was, however, a decent human being. He immediately informed on the conspirators. Roosevelt knew that arresting the conspirators would create a worse crisis in the midst of the depression, so instead he decided to leak the story to the press which downplayed it as a "ridiculous rumor" even though it was the absolute and terrifying truth. However, knowing that they were unmasked, the plotters left the country. Congress appointed a special commission to investigate the matter, but we can surmise that powerful pressure was put on the committee to not come up with the truth "officially". The congressional committee dragged the process out for *four years* and finally issued a report for "restricted circulation" only. The report stated that "certain persons made an attempt to establish a fascist organization in this county" and added that the committee "was able to verify all the pertinent statements made by General Butler".[6]

Journalist Jim Marrs writes:

> The fact that this attempted overthrow of the government is not mentioned in history texts illustrates the deficiency of this nation's public education in such matters, thanks to a mass media more concerned with "Mickey Mouse" topics than investigative news. It is ironic that today the Disney empire includes many news media organizations.

---

[6] Charles Higham, Trading with the Enemy: An Expose of the Nazi-American Money Plot 1933-1949 (New York : Delacorte Press, 1983), 99.

In the preface to their book *Fifty Greatest Conspiracies of All Time*, authors Jonathan Vankin and John Whalen point out The 'Disney' version of history could just as easily be called the '*New York Times* version' or the 'TV news version' or the 'college textbook version'. The main resistance to conspiracy theories comes not from the people on the street, but from the media, academia, and government—people who manage the national and global economy of information.[7]

In 2005, the *New York Times* version was openly exposed for the Disney-esque nature of its reporting; reporter Judith Miller spent 85 days in jail and the assistant to the Vice President, I. Scooter Libby was indicted for "lying" about "leaking" the identity of CIA agent, Valerie Plame. Considering the situation that Roosevelt found himself in and how it was managed and then ridiculed by the press, one has to wonder what was really behind the "Plamegate" scandal.

Richard M. Dolan studied at Alfred University and Oxford University before completing his graduate work in history at the University of Rochester, where he was a finalist for a Rhodes scholarship studying U.S. Cold War strategy, Soviet history and culture, and international diplomacy. (The same subjects on which Condoleezza Rice is supposed to be an "expert"). He has written about "conspiracy" in the following way:

> The very label [conspiracy] serves as an automatic dismissal, as though no one ever acts in secret. Let us bring some perspective and common sense to this issue.
>
> The United States comprises large organizations—corporations, bureaucracies, 'interest groups', and the like—which are conspiratorial by nature. That is, they are hierarchical, their important decisions are made in secret by a few key decision-makers, and they are not above lying about their activities. Such is the nature of organizational behavior. 'Conspiracy', in this key sense, is a way of life around the globe.
>
> Within the world's military and intelligence apparatuses, this tendency is magnified to the greatest extreme. During the 1940s, [...] the military and its scientists developed the world's most awesome weapons in complete secrecy....
>
> Anyone who has lived in a repressive society knows that official manipulation of the truth occurs daily. But societies have their many and their few. In all times and all places, *it is the few who rule*, and the few who exert dominant influence over what we may call *official culture*. [...] All elites take care to manipulate public information to maintain existing structures of power. It's an old game.
>
> America is nominally a republic and free society, but in reality an empire and oligarchy, vaguely aware of its own oppression, within and without. I have used the term 'national security state' to describe its structures of power. It is a convenient way to express the military and intelligence communities, as well as the worlds that feed upon them, such as defense contractors and other underground, nebulous entities. *Its fundamental traits are secrecy, wealth, independence, power, and duplicity.*
>
> Nearly *everything of significance* undertaken by America's military and intelligence community in the past half-century has *occurred in secrecy*. The undertaking to build an atomic weapon, better known as the Manhattan Project, re-

---

[7] Jim Marrs, *Alien Agenda* (New York: Harper Collins, 1997), 570-571.

mains the great model for all subsequent activities. For more than two years, *not a single member of Congress even knew about it* although its final cost exceeded two billion dollars.

During and after the Second World War, other important projects, such as the development of biological weapons, the importation of Nazi scientists, terminal mind-control experiments, nationwide interception of mail and cable transmissions of an unwitting populace, *infiltration of the media and universities*, secret coups, secret wars, and assassinations all took place far *removed not only from the American public, but from most members of Congress* and a few Presidents. Indeed, several of the most powerful intelligence agencies were themselves established in secrecy, unknown by the public or Congress for many years.

Since the 1940s, the U.S. Defense and Intelligence establishment has had more money at its disposal than most nations. In addition to official dollars, much of the money is undocumented. From its beginning, the CIA was engaged in a variety of off-the-record 'business' activities that generated large sums of cash. The connections of the CIA with global organized crime (and thus de facto with the international narcotics trade) has been well established and documented for many years. Much of the original money to run the American intelligence community came from very wealthy and established American families, who have long maintained an interest in funding national security operations important to their interests.

In theory, civilian oversight exists over the U.S. national security establishment. The President is the military commander-in-chief. Congress has official oversight over the CIA. The FBI must answer to the Justice Department. In practice, little of this applies. One reason has to do with secrecy. [...]

A chilling example of such independence occurred during the 1950s, when President Eisenhower effectively lost control of the U.S. nuclear arsenal. The situation deteriorated so much that during his final two years in office, Eisenhower asked repeatedly for an audience with the head of Strategic Air Command to learn what America's nuclear retaliatory plan was. What he finally learned in 1960, his final year in office, horrified him: half of the Northern Hemisphere would be obliterated.

If a revered military hero such as Eisenhower could not control America's nuclear arsenal, nor get a straight answer from the Pentagon, how on earth could Presidents Truman, Kennedy, Johnson, or Nixon regarding comparable matters?

Secrecy, wealth and independence add up to power. Through the years, the national security state has gained access to the world's most sophisticated technology, sealed off millions of acres of land from public access or scrutiny, acquired unlimited snooping ability within U.S. borders and beyond, conducted overt or clandestine actions against other nations, and prosecuted wars without serious media scrutiny. Domestically, it maintains influence over elected officials and communities hoping for some of the billions of defense dollars.

Deception is the key element of warfare, and *when winning is all that matters, the conventional morality held by ordinary people becomes an impediment.* When taken together, the examples of official duplicity form a nearly single totality. They include such choice morsels as the phony war crisis of 1948, the fabricated missile gap claimed by the air force during the 1950s, the carefully managed events leading to the Gulf of Tonkin resolution....

The secrecy stems from a pervasive and fundamental element of life in our world, that *those who are at the top of the heap will always take whatever steps are necessary* to maintain the status quo.

[S]keptics often ask, 'Do you really think the government could hide [anything] for so long'? The question itself reflects ignorance of the reality that *secrecy is a way of life in the National Security State*. Actually though, the answer is yes, and no.

Yes, in that cover-ups are standard operating procedure, frequently unknown to the public for decades, becoming public knowledge by a mere roll of the dice. But also no, in that [...] information has leaked out from the very beginning. It is impossible to shut the lid completely. *The key lies in neutralizing and discrediting unwelcome information, sometimes through official denial, other times through proxies in the media.*

[E]vidence [of conspiracy] derived from a grass roots level is unlikely to survive its inevitable conflict with official culture. And acknowledgement about the reality of [conspiracies] will only occur when the official culture deems it worthwhile or necessary to make it.[8]

Indeed, the very fact that this is one of many books presenting the case for government involvement in 9/11 is clear evidence that this particular conspiracy has certainly *not* succeeded, or at least not to the extent that the conspirators would have liked. The problem however, lies in the fact that the conspirators have key people in positions of power that enable them to continue to act as they please and as if there is no conspiracy, without fear of repercussions. If you control the military, most of the media, and the judiciary, there isn't much that ordinary people—who just want to live their lives with as little pain as possible—are going to risk to oppose you.

Now, think about the word "conspiracy" one more time and allow me to emphasize the key point: *From a historical point of view, the **only** reality is that of conspiracy*. Remember: Secrecy, wealth and independence add up to power; deception is the key element of warfare (the tool of power elites), and *when winning is all that matters, the conventional morality held by ordinary people becomes an impediment*. Secrecy stems from a pervasive and fundamental element of life in our world; that *those who are at the top of the heap will always take whatever steps are necessary to maintain the status quo, i.e. their position of power and their drive to get what they want.*

And how do they do that? By 'official culture'. Exactly how this works is one of the subjects we are going to cover in this book.

I recently had an exchange with Robin Ramsay, Editor of *Lobster* magazine, allegedly the "primo" conspiracy mag. The context of the exchange was related to one of his recent 'Konspiracy Korner' pieces published in *Fortean Times*. He wrote:

...there is widespread agreement on the pro-conspiracy side that whatever struck the Pentagon, it was not Flight 77.

---

[8] Richard Dolan, *UFOs and the National Security State*, Revised Edition (Hampton Roads, 2002).

Ramsay then informs the reader of *Fortean Times* that Christopher Kelly from the U.S. Armed Forces Institute of Pathology has stated that, "What some experts have called 'the most comprehensive forensic investigation in U.S. history' ended on November 16 with the identification of 184 of the 189 who died in the terrorist attack on the Pentagon."

Ramsay dismisses the "conspiracy theorists" by writing:

> "Of course, it must be faked", say many conspiracy buffs. And yes, it's possible that there is no Christopher Kelly; or that he is a stooge for 'the conspirators'; or that dcmilitary.com is so in thrall that it is willing to run a fabricated report. But none of this is likely.

Did you catch that? All of the most likely things in the world, in terms of real conspiracies, which do exist as we all well know, Robin Ramsay, supposedly the "conspiracy expert", has just dismissed as though considering them is a sign of a feeble mind! The most troubling fact of all is that the 'Official Version' gleaned from the news reports and information released by government officials does not stand up to even the most cursory scrutiny which Ramsay could have learned had he taken the time to peruse it. Contrary to the claims of Christopher Kelly cited above by Robin Ramsay, there never was a complete 'forensic analysis'. Well, let me correct that: very probably there was some sort of a 'forensic analysis', but there was no *forensic investigation* prior to that analysis!

After writing a rather long email to Robin Ramsay that included a lot of chunks of material from our research and the research of others, Mr. Ramsay wrote back:

> Ultimately it comes down to how you see the world. The kind of conspiracy you are describing, or implying, is inconceivable to me: too big, too complex, too likely to go wrong or be discovered, ever to be mounted. What you are describing [...] is vastly much bigger—and more complex and more dangerous—than any known mind control/psy ops project. And there is no evidence for it. [...]
>
> Those—like you—who argue for a U.S. state conspiracy are proposing a massive, multi-agency conspiracy of a kind which has never been seen before. All the U.S. state agencies hate each other and barely co-operate, engage in endless turf wars. The kind of inter-agency operation you are proposing simply has never existed in peace time. It is inconceivable to me that such a group could be got together. And this is probably the main reason that the official U.S. state organisations and politicians have never taken the conspiracy theories seriously. They know how the U.S. state operates and thus dismiss this idea at the outset. (And the official inquiry into 9/11 is full of examples of the hostility between state agencies.) In reality, when the planes hit the towers a large slice of the U.S. military and intelligence bodies immediately thought of Bin Laden. And they have never had a good reason to change their minds—not least because Bin Laden and his various cohorts have admitted—boasted of—doing it.[9]

---

[9] Robin Ramsay, personal correspondence.

Robin Ramsay, in short, suffers from the very malady identified by Richard Dolan: ordinary morality which cannot conceive of the true reality of conspiracy and conspirators. Remember:

> From a historical point of view, the **only** reality is that of conspiracy. Secrecy, wealth and independence add up to power; deception is the key element of warfare, (the tool of power elites), and when winning is all that matters, the conventional morality held by ordinary people becomes an impediment. Secrecy stems from a pervasive and fundamental element of life in our world, that those who are at the top of the heap will always take whatever steps are necessary to maintain the status quo...

Undoubtedly, Robin Ramsay's remarks are "on target", all things being considered to be equal. But this is where we encounter the problem: based on close and careful scientific observation, all things are *not* equal. More than that, there is the mountain of evidence—much of it circumstantial but so compelling that it would be accepted in a court of law—that there *is* such a gigantic conspiracy, and that the "power elite" (individuals who may be completely unknown to us since the highest level movers and shakers in the political and corporate world may only be their pawns) are somehow, at the top of the heap, controlling everything beneath them including the governments of various countries.

Boy, does that ever sound crazy! But before you reject such an idea out of hand, let me explain my remark that "all things are not equal". In this book, we are going to present scientific research that demonstrates how it is possible for such a conspiracy to exist in our reality based on little known 'natural laws'. This research was done in secret by scientists experiencing such a reality in Eastern Europe before, during, and after World War II. The story of this group of scientists and their research has never been publicly revealed though certainly, individuals among the Neocons were aware of it and suppressed it, as we shall see. Indeed, the work undertaken by these scientists and the results they reached provide more than enough evidence to show that a 9/11 conspiracy is not only possible but very likely.

But we are getting ahead of ourselves. First, let's go back to...

9/11 GROUND ZERO

On September 14, 2001—just two days after the Terrorist Attacks—I[10] read a curious article on a Russian News Site[11] that caught my attention and left me feeling strangely uneasy. It was an interview with a former Russian high official and specialist in *Russian secret services* which was translated for us by a reader who sent it in, and I am going to reproduce it as I read it with underlinings and other emphases that I have added to show those points that struck me as most interesting:

---

[10] Laura Knight-Jadczyk
[11] www.strana.ru

Acts of terrorism carried out on 11 September in America, and their consequences are commented upon in an interview with Andrey Kosyakov, former assistant to the chairman of the Russian Congress, *a specialist in International Security*.

Q: What suggests that terrorism in the USA was planned well in advance?

A: First, the conspirators *possessed the professional skill to fly an aircraft*. There had to be at least four of them with substitutes on hand in the event one of them failed. There is a high probability that the hijacking of an aircraft will fail, thus there had to be stand-by hijackers and/or pilots in this eventuality.

In the second place, all participants in the operation were ready to sacrifice themselves, and such individuals are not easy to find.

Finally, the *departure times* of the aircraft from four different points were *coordinated minute by minute*. This means that the *routes and timing were known well in advance*, and these particular flights were selected specifically for their routes and schedule.

All of this is *sufficiently complicated* to necessitate a long period of planning.

Q: And how long, in your opinion, would it take to plan something like this? How large an organization would it require? Could, for example, the Red Army carry out such an operation? Some analysts say that *only a National organization* could do this.

A: As far as the time of preparation is concerned, it would require months. And *such an organization must be very powerful.*

But, the participation of a National organization, such as a government of a country, is very doubtful.

I assure you that National resources have not been used here.

No secret service would risk their operatives in this way. They spend a lot of time and money training their agents. However, if President Bush had been the target, then one would suspect a secret service of some organization. But here, the target was different: civilians.

As for the Red Army, it doesn't fit for one simple reason: it consists of mainly Orientals and it is too easy to distinguish Japanese from Americans.

Q: So, what do you conclude from all this?

A: You see, analyzing this situation, I was struck by one significant fact: it is known that there were telephone calls from the plane. One of the calling persons was a professional journalist. And yet, not one of the calling individuals said that they were being hijacked by "Moslem terrorists". There was, apparently, nothing unusual about the appearance of the hijackers. There was no attempt to describe them. No one said: "Moslem terrorists have hijacked the plane", which would have logically been the first comment by this journalist *if* it was apparent that the hijackers were "foreign". *There was obviously nothing unusual about them in terms of appearance, accent, pronunciation, or other similar factors.*

Q: But, secret organizations could hide these things, couldn't they?

A: All these calls were private. And even the FBI was not able to suppress the fact that these calls took place. So, the conclusion which comes to mind, is that *the external appearance of the hijackers was in no way different from the other passengers*. Only in such cases would the communicants identify the hijackers in a shorthand way. *This suggests that the hijackers were European in appearance.*

There is also the suspicious fact that the conspirators left a huge "clue" in the leased automobile at the airport with a copy of the Koran and instructions for flying a plane in Arabic.

Now look, not one organization claimed responsibility. This means that the terrorists want to hide their identity.

With every other aspect of total control and professionalism, *how could they make such a mistake?*

This does not compute with all the rest of the perfection of the operation.

All this says that the criminals want to create a false track.

In this way, the secret services have been induced very cleverly to look for "Moslem terrorists".

Q: But indeed the practice of self-sacrifice is typical to the Moslem culture?

A: You are completely right. But who told you that those who died were not Muslims?

This way we can narrow the radius of our search.

On the basis of this information which we have, by analysis, we may come to the conclusion that those who did it were Americans or Europeans who were followers of radical Islam.

They were manipulated so that the true criminals will be thus spared for follow-up actions.

It is completely clear that this is a multi-phase operation.... *it seems that the target is precisely America; precisely civilians.*

Q: But, we remember that some analysts were claiming that if George Bush was in the White House on September 11, then the aircraft would have been aimed at the White House instead of the Pentagon.

A: This is highly improbable. In that case the White House or the Pentagon, but not peaceful population would be the *first* targets.

Indeed after a first successful terrorist act, the chances of success for the rest fall.

You see that the last action did fail in the crash of the aircraft in Pittsburgh. *It was most certainly shot down.* However hard it is to admit, this was the correct thing to do.

So it is clear that the main targets are civilians.

There is this formula that is part of the mentality of terrorists: the civilian population in the democratic countries are responsible for the actions of their government. The terrorists accept and use this formula. Therefore, the next terrorist acts will follow the same pattern. Obviously, they will occur on Wednesday or Thursday of next week. Why? I don't want to explain the terrorist's logic. But it is based on a certain sense of the "rightness" of the thing.

But I would like to repeat this: the fact that no terrorists are claiming responsibility, tells us that they will kill again and again until the next stage of global conflict is achieved. This is precisely the goal of these actions. Only then will they reveal their identity in order to get followers.

Q: How could the special services of the USA fail to detect such a terrorist act?

A: I will give two examples. Half a year ago Israeli reconnaissance carried out studies through the use of aerial targets for conducting terrorism.

It is certain that the Americans had access to these studies. But it seems to not have entered their minds to apply this information in defensive ways.

And other—in March of 1991 in our office sat Korzhakov, and we told him about the situation leading to the September government coup. We predicted that everything would occur in September. Everything actually occurred, exactly following our scenario, only it happened one month earlier: August. No one paid any attention. This means that when there are predictions of scenarios that seem to be improbable, no one takes them seriously, especially the secret services. That is why Putin says that what is needed is a union of all secret services of all nations.

Q: What is the probability that the American secret services will succeed in finding the leader of this operation, or that they simply will present to society a fake?

A: Very high. There are people, there are apartments where they were located, which means, there are traces, certainly. Following these traces, one may find the leader.

Q: And who this? Bin Laden?

A: Hardly.

Yes, there was the interception of his conversation with someone, where they reported to him the destruction of two targets. This was seen as indirect confirmation of his participation. But he is not an ideologist. He is too well known. And *the one who organized all of this is too smart to be noticed.*

Ever.

Now, remember, this interview with an intelligence expert took place just a few days after the 9/11 attacks. He was analyzing based on the publicly available information, but it struck me that he was overemphasizing some points, as though to give hints. Several points in this article started me to thinking.[12] Those points are as follows: the attacks were carried out against civilians, targets that are highly symbolic to the ordinary American. In other words, it was intended to make every single American full of fear and outrage so that whoever came along as a "strong man" pointing a finger at culprits and declaring that he was going go after them, would be able to do anything he wanted to do. And that is exactly what George W. Bush did.

The Russian intell guy said that it was obvious that the attacks were carried out by a very "powerful organization" that *wishes to blame Muslims*—to create a false trail—for these attacks. He contradicted himself later when he said they must be radical Muslims (though probably European). And he also noted that, because the attacks were so carefully planned, it was obvious that the planners would be too smart to be noticed—and certainly much too smart to leave clues lying about such as passports and "how to fly" videos in Arabic.

---

[12] As we will make clear in Part 1 of this book, there are many assumptions in this interview that our subsequent research has shown to be doubtful, such as the physical presence of the accused hijackers on any of the planes. The nineteen men accused of this crime were likely patsies chosen to take the fall by the real masterminds, much as Lee Harvey Oswald was blamed for the killing of JFK or Sirhan Sirhan for the murder of RFK.

Indeed, the passports and videos were dead giveaways to the fact that they were planted so as to falsely blame the act on Islamic terrorists.

After reading through all of his giving and taking away of clues, the thing that struck me rather forcibly was the question *"[h]ow could the special services of the USA fail to detect such a terrorist act?"*, when considered in light of what else he said: *"Israeli reconnaissance carried out studies through the use of aerial targets for conducting terrorism"*, followed by his assertion that, *"It is certain that the Americans had access to these studies"*.

So, I began to think about what this intelligence guy was saying a bit more deeply despite the fact that he confidently assured his interviewer that no "national service" did this, as though to say, "of course, a national service did this!".

This assessment struck me as one of the more intelligent bits of commentary about the 9/11 attacks to come out *at the time*, emerging through the hysterical rants about Osama and those nasty Muslims like a small island of sanity.

What I found to be most interesting was exactly *who* was most vigorously pointing the finger at Radical Islam: a veritable Greek Chorus led by a former cheerleader, our own George Bush, and the Warmongers.

Another astute bit of commentary comes from Musa Keilani writing for *The Jordan Times*:

> Jordan is fully committed to fight both terrorism and Osama Ben Laden whose followers are still being prosecuted this week for their attempt to sabotage and carry out attacks in Amman. Yet, many of us still feel with the Saudi foreign minister who brought out the names of five Saudis wanted by the American FBI while they died years ago before the anti-Arab hysterical witch hunt started.

> But some questions are still being raised amid the U.S. effort against 'international terrorism'.

> We in Jordan have had several narrow escapes from the nefarious plots hatched by Ben Laden and would welcome any initiative that would remove the lingering fears of continued conspiracies against our national security and stability. As such, the Jordanians' commitment to a genuine international campaign against terrorism, in all its forms and shapes, *including the state-sponsored style practiced by Israel*, is unwavering.

> Veterans who have spent a lifetime studying intelligence operations assert that *the attacks could not have been carried out by any 'Arab or Islamist' group without involvement of highly-placed 'insider' networks in the U.S. institutions.*

> These veterans are indeed best placed to assess intelligence operations, particularly in the United States, because the very focus of their professional work was the U.S. and they have acquired intimate knowledge of how the intelligence community works in the U.S. They include, among others, Mikhail Magrelov, a long-standing intelligence specialist and deputy chairman of the Russian Federation Council Foreign Affairs Committee, Yevgeny Kozhokin, director of the state-run Russian Institute for Strategic Studies (RISS), and Andrei Kosyakov, formerly assistant to the chairman of the subcommittee of the Supreme Soviet of Russia, in charge of monitoring the activity of the intelligence services.

Doubts over the U.S. assertions that the attacks had an 'Arab and Islamist' link in the form of Ben Laden have also been raised by former government veterans and diplomats in Europe who argue that Washington should not jump to the conclusion that the Saudi dissident was responsible for the attacks and try to sell it to the world; the U.S. should focus more on homegrown terrorism in its investigations.

The overall argument of the Russian intelligence experts is that a yet-to-be-identified but powerful and influential organisation could have been behind the operation, and this group may have little in common or may not have any links with Arabs and Muslims.

The experts argue that an organisation controlled by someone like Ben Laden could not have orchestrated the attacks that required the involvement of at least 100 to 150 dedicated people living within the U.S., dozens of them with extraordinary skills in flying, absolute familiarity with the U.S. civil aviation system, emergency procedures and routines, high-level communication expertise and strategic planning, as well as the ability to evade intelligence surveillance. Such hi-tech minds with military precision and coordination could only belong to a group much more sophisticated than the largely ragtag operatives of any Third World country or organisation whose erstwhile operations have involved, at best, slamming explosives-laden trucks into buildings.

The argument and mainstream belief that no American would carry such a heinous crime of destruction in a suicide operation as that of Sept. 11 is immediately countered by the Oklahoma bombing of 1995. Timothy McVeigh was framed for that bombing in the same way that several other patsies have been used in high profile murders and bombings over the course of the past 50 years. *The reality, which is backed up by solid evidence, is that the Oklahoma bombing was carried out by a rogue group within the U.S. intelligence community* who have infiltrated a wider network of Pure American (Anglo-Saxon) militants which includes active and retired military officers and Green Beret colonels.

The truth about the group that McVeigh was involved with was deliberately suppressed, the experts argue, pointing out that McVeigh had equally strong suicidal feelings when he insisted on being executed. Furthermore, there was also a visible but unexplained anxiety on the part of the authorities in Washington to see that his mouth was sealed with death without delay.

Among the many questions raised by the experts are:

- How was it possible for an 'Arab or Islamist group' to find 'suicidal' professionals in the art of flying with precision and who could command a large civilian aircraft with such precision as to inflict maximum damage?

- How did the 'emergency procedures' fail to go into effect in a few minutes after the hijacked planes deviated from their predetermined flight path?

- How did the hijacked planes manage to remain in air for between 55 minutes and 80 minutes?

- Why did the hijacked passengers who spoke with family members from aboard the planes did not bother to mention anything about the way the hijackers looked? ('The appearance of the hijackers in no way distinguished them from all the other passengers.... This supports the supposition that hijackers looked European in outward appearance', says one of the experts.)

- Why and how could the brains behind such a meticulously planned operation allow 'extra big leads!!' to be left behind, like a traceable rented vehicle filled with the Holy Koran and flying manuals in Arabic that clearly establish an Arab link to the attacks?

- How did the 'Arabs and Muslims' who the U.S. says carried out the attacks manage to evade attention from the alert intelligence agencies of the U.S. for the several months it would require to plan the operation?

The argument here is that almost every Arab or Muslim living in or entering the U.S. with the slightest trace of links with militancy has come under very close scrutiny of the country's investigating and intelligence agencies. It is virtually impossible for such a large number of Arabs and Muslims to have evaded investigation and to have managed to take part in an operation of this magnitude and which involves such high-sensitive areas as aviation security.

All indications at this point in time are that accusing Arabs and Muslims of carrying out the attacks is very convenient for many interested groups and serves more than one purpose. Moreover, *it is an exercise that shifts attention from the real authors of the assault.*[13]

When we look at the fact that, from the very beginning, this event has been compared to Pearl Harbor, we have to wonder if this is a sort of "signature"?

I remember back in 1986 when I came across the documented evidence that the attack on Pearl Harbor was known to the United States well before it happened, I was shocked. Not only did the government do nothing to prevent it, they did not even warn those who were going to be attacked. The loss of American lives was horrendous. And the blame lies on the doorstep of the *leaders of America.* There is even evidence that they deliberately manipulated the situation, at the highest levels, to ensure that the attack would take place.

Why?

Well, to get the United States into the war, of course. War is big business. Whenever you have a slow economy, a little warmongering is always the answer. In ancient times, it was the business of the day: go to war, kill the men, capture the women and the wealth of the enemy, go home when you have spent it all and gotten tired of the women, and then go out and do it over again. Even Herodotus understood this to be the reason for war. And human beings haven't changed at all—at least not those who seek power positions.

Is it possible that the government of our country had an inkling that the events of 9/11 were going to happen?

After examining all the evidence available, indeed, that seems to be true.

And if so, is it possible that they did nothing?

Again, that seems to be true as well. When they did finally wake up from their war games and school reading classes, the only thing they did was the exact opposite of trying to get to the bottom of the matter, trying to find the real culprits. Instead, they went after the false flag clues that were left to lead

---

everyone astray and denied anyone the right to question the conclusions that they propagandized so vigorously.

Well, sure, such clues might lead the average citizen astray. They might not be aware of what are called "false flag operations". They aren't educated in the ways of intelligence and don't know about all the evil manipulations that go on in the world of spy vs. spy.

But surely, the President of the Greatest Nation on Earth is not going to be taken in by such blatant nonsense as a "how to fly" video in Arabic or the fortuitous discovery of the passport of alleged lead hijacker Satam Al Suqami that miraculously escaped the Flight 11 crash and the WTC collapse to be found on a Manhattan street, is he?[14]

Apparently so.

So here we have an administration not acting when and how it ought to act, *either before or after the attack.*

Is this a coincidence? Or is it evidence of complicity?

In the four years since September 11, 2001, we read endless discussions of U.S. government complicity spreading like wildfire over the web, followed by books and videos analyzing in great detail all available video footage of the attacks, and the official story. We read the results of published information in the mainstream media that punched holes in that official version. Dozens, then hundreds, and now thousands of commentators of greater or lesser prestige simply do not believe in the "failure of intelligence" that is the administration's answer to why and how George and Co. got caught with their pants down. Many, many people are certain that the government not only knew about the attack, but that they condoned it for their own nefarious purposes—or that they even participated—and that the 9/11 attacks were the equivalent of a new Pearl Harbor or even Hitler's Reichstag fire.

So, we have two opposing forces here: the administration's official conspiracy theory supported by the Zionist controlled (for the most part) mass media, against a growing percentage of the population that claims that there was no failure of intelligence, that the government deliberately condoned or even participated in this attack, and that it is part of a planned schedule to impose a One World Government on all of us, to abridge our freedoms, and entrap us in a fascist state.

On their side, George Bush and his administration say that we have to accept some new, restrictive laws to make us "safe" (never mind that the intelligence was available, and it was the government that failed to heed the intelligence and make America safe). They say we must make some significant changes in the way the country does business, and most definitely, we need a little war here and there to level things out again (not to mention the economy). And all of the Joe Sixpack's of the world may be buying it. All the grandmother Sally Stock-market-investors are sitting at home, glued to Fox News on their televisions, glad that Uncle Sam has taken charge here,

---

[14] http://abcnews.go.com/sections/us/DailyNews/WTC_MAIN010912.html

bombed the Afghanis, given Saddam a major spanking, and is actively wiping out the Iraqis and anybody who ever helped them, meanwhile passing all the laws necessary to ensure the safety of their great nation. Never mind if that includes moving to a cashless society, implanting micro-chips under the skin so that everyone will be trackable, and wiretapping the private phone and Internet conversations of millions of Americans so as to ensure that they aren't committing terrorist acts on their lunch break.

There's a saying attributed to Franklin Roosevelt: "In politics, nothing happens by accident, if it happens, you can bet it was planned that way." Maybe he really said it, maybe he didn't. Whether he did or not, anyone who studies history deeply can figure out that it comes pretty close to the truth. I[15] also once had a conversation with a fellow who was trained in military intelligence and he told me that one of the first rules of intelligence gathering is to observe the situation *as it is* and extrapolate to who will gain from it: *cui bono*. So these two principles were uppermost in my mind as I was considering all the data. Clearly, the attacks on 9/11 are "political events".

The situation at present is a bit complex. But we notice that it has only become complex *after* the fact. It is only the wild speculations and constant playing of agendas and counter-agendas that have tended to obscure the basic essentials of the matter. There are groups that go on and on about a "flash of light" that was emitted between the two airliners that crashed into the WTC, and this (according to them) proves there was some sort of missile fired. That's an interesting idea, but it really doesn't even make it to "theory" status because there are other possible explanations for such a flash, including a discharge of electricity between the plane and the building as soon as it is close enough to be "grounded" or a video artefact due to the different fields in a video image.

There are groups that make a big deal about supposed "pods" under the aircraft that hit the WTC. We can pretty easily dispose of that one by carefully examining photos of the underside of that particular type of aircraft.

Then, there's the group that takes the cake, in my opinion: the "hologram" people. That is about the silliest thing going. That is not to say that I don't think that hologram technology does exist and that it might be used in a number of ways, but I don't think that holograms photograph too well since they are produced by light and there are the endlessly repeating videos of the planes crashing into the World Trade Center Towers.

So, let's go back to ground zero of the present situation and look at the event itself, *by itself*, and ask the first important question: *Who benefits?*

It's easy to see that the Military-Industrial Complex in America has been the primary beneficiary along with Zionist Israel. Actually, the two are almost one creature, so it's hard to think of them as separate entities. It could be suggested that, by focusing the anger of the citizens of the United States against the Muslims, Israel has powerful backing for their expansionist goals,

---

[15] Laura Knight-Jadczyk

and with much of the MIC (Military-Industrial Complex) in their pockets, they have the money to do what they want to do—the money of the American tax payer, we should add. On this point, consider the fact that at a meeting in the Pentagon *on September 10, 2001*, Secretary of Defence Donald Rumsfeld admitted that the Pentagon could not account for *2.3 trillion dollars.*[16]

> According to some estimates we cannot track $2.3 trillion in transactions," Rumsfeld admitted.

> $2.3 trillion—that's $8,000 for every man, woman and child in America. To understand how the Pentagon can lose track of trillions, consider the case of one military accountant who tried to find out what happened to a mere $300 million.

> "We know it's gone. But we don't know what they spent it on," said Jim Minnery, Defense Finance and Accounting Service. [17]

Keep in mind that up to August of 2004 only 144 billion dollars had been pledged to the war in Iraq so that 2.3 trillion is a lot more money than has been spent on the whole "Shock and Awe" show to date. At the time, 2.3 trillion dollars was the equivalent of six annual Pentagon budgets.

> One day after Rumsfeld's admission of Sept. 10, this mother-of-all-scandals in the making disappeared from the corporate media's vision. For good.

> The comptroller who arrived at the figure, Dov Zakheim, was a primary author of the infamous Project for a New American Century manifesto of September 2000, "Rebuilding America's Defenses." This detailed a manic plan for U.S. military domination of the world and re-ordering of the Middle East, observing that this process might require a "new Pearl Harbor" before Americans were willing to pay the costs.

> And what was Zakheim's explanation for the missing 2.3 trillion? His testimony to the House Budget Committee (July 11, 2002) begins as follows:

> Mr. Zakheim: *First of all, I should say that very often, although the numbers seem large, it's not because we really don 't know what happened with the transactions. The problem has tended to be that we just didn't record them properly....*

> Right. Money never disappears off the face of the earth. It always ends up somewhere. It's just the destinations sometimes are not recorded properly.[18]

GETTING DOWN TO BRASS TACKS

The September 11, 2001 attacks on the World Trade Center were followed live on television by hundreds of millions of people around the world. Everyone was shocked by the horror of the attack. TV networks broadcast the videos of the attacks over and over again with very little reporting since no one really knew what to say; it was just too shocking and unexpected. All the while the attack was being shown repeatedly, there was no explanation of the events because no one, we are told, knew any details. No one, that is, except

---

[16] http://www.defenselink.mil/speeches/2001/s20010910-secdef.html

[17] http://www.freerepublic.com/focus/fr/620276/posts

[18] http://www.911truth.org/article.php?story=20050825010121987

the FBI who released the names of all 19 hijackers within a week of the attacks and claimed that they were connected to Bin Laden and al-Qaeda, a name that quickly surfaced on 9/11 as the principal and sole plausible candidate as culprit, even if they have never claimed responsibility. In fact, we note that a number of video tapes and written messages, allegedly from Bin Laden, have been released over the years since the 9/11 attacks, yet it was not until two days before the 2004 Presidential election that the FBI was able to provide a tape in which Osama appeared to take responsibility for the 9/11 attacks. Coincidence? Hardly. Previous tapes that were released were clearly faked, with claims that the translations, carried out by FBI translators, have inaccurately translated Bin Laden's words. One video tape in particular, made public on December 13, 2001,[19] featured a man who was so obviously *not* Osama Bin Laden that it was hard to imagine that the U.S. or Israeli intelligence authors of the tape actually believed they would get away with it.

During the next few days bits and pieces of information were released to the press by government officials, reports were issued and retracted, and most news focus was concentrated on the frenzy of rescue efforts. The focus of this reporting very quickly turned to the collapse of the twin towers of the World Trade Center, pushing aside any mention of events at the Pentagon. This is extremely curious when you consider that an attack on the command center of the U.S. military might be considered far more improbable and shocking than an attack on an unprotected skyscraper. We believe that this sidelining of the attack on the Pentagon, from the very beginning, was an early clue as to the true character of the attack.

Over the next few months, more information was released in bits and pieces, but again, few people were paying any attention to the data because, by then, the shock had turned into terror. Osama and Saddam were Muslim, Osama did this evil deed, and Saddam—Osama's good buddy, or so we were told — was planning even worse with his Weapons of Mass Destruction.

The meta-facts are that just under 2,750 people died in America on September 11, 2001, and as a result, the United States invaded Afghanistan and Iraq, killing hundreds of thousands more human beings, including killing or permanently maiming many thousands of its own citizens. The official U.S. military casualty figures from Iraq, at just under 3,000 as we write, are most certainly false given that American deaths that happen in military hospitals outside of Iraq are not counted as part of the official casualty figures. Observers have estimated the true total may be close to 8,000[20] U.S. military deaths, nearly three times the number killed in September 2001, and this

---

[19] http://www.whatreallyhappened.com/osamatape.html
[20] As of May 13, 2006, Aljazeera estimates more than 12,000 American deaths. They state that, in addition to those who die *outside* of Iraq, troops not killed by direct enemy fire and those who are not American citizens are not included in the official count. See: http://www.aljazeera.com/me.asp?service_ID=11372

doesn't include the 200,000[21] Iraqis who have lost their lives but who the U.S. does not deem important, or human, enough to be counted.

The events of 9/11, however, are still a confusing morass of contradiction that has only been exacerbated by the so-called official 9/11 Report that used the American intelligence agencies as a scapegoat for the clear evidence of government complicity.

Nevertheless, the public of the United States has been, for the most part, accepting of the "official culture" version of the attacks. The claim that "National Security" requires the authorities to conceal much of the data about this crime is accepted almost without question. It is actually quite amazing how *little* the average American really knows about the events of that day even if you restrict your definition of "events" to what was reported by the media.

The most troubling fact of all is that the Official Version gleaned from the news reports and information released by government officials does not stand up to even the most cursory scrutiny.

What bothers us most of all is, considering the fact that the attacks on 9/11 were about the most audacious crime in American history; *there was no proper forensic investigation.* There was no Sherlock Holmes on hand to use his magnifying glass and his great knowledge of different kinds of cigarette ash; there was no Hercule Poirot called in to exercise his little gray cells; there was no Columbo bumbling about with his seemingly innocuous questions that annoy the heck out of the perpetrators. (This was also the case with the assassination of JFK. The crime scene was so thoroughly violated before a proper investigation took place that there was no possibility of finding the facts.)

You would think that, in the alleged greatest and most powerful nation on Earth that the investigation would have been the most thorough and scientific ever conducted.

But that isn't the case, administration claims to the contrary notwithstanding.

Although the terror attacks of September 11 were clearly criminal acts of mass murder, no effort was made to preserve the integrity of the crime scenes and the essential evidence was disposed of like garbage. Former New York City Mayor Rudolph Giuliani, the so-called "Prince of New York", hired two large British construction management firms to oversee what many experts consider to be massive *criminal destruction of evidence.* The editor-in-chief of *Fire Engineering* magazine, William A. Manning, issued an urgent call to action to America's firefighters at the end of 2001, calling for a forensic investigation and demanding that the steel from the site be preserved to allow investigators to determine what caused the collapse, to no avail. Ironically, one of the firms involved in the clean up job at the WTC complex was a company by the name of "Controlled Demolition".

Both the independent 9/11 Commission and federal authorities have stated that of the four devices that could have recorded the final moments of the

---

[21] This figure reported in 'Audits of the Conventional Wisdom', a project of the Center for International Studies at MIT. http://web.mit.edu/CIS/pdf/Audit_6_05_Roberts.pdf

Flights that crashed into the WTC towers—a cockpit voice recorder (CVR) and flight data recorder (FDR) from the two planes—*none* were ever found in the wreckage.

However, as reported by the Philadelphia Daily News in October of 2004,[22] two men who worked extensively in the wreckage of the World Trade Center claim they helped federal agents find three of the four black boxes from the jetliners that struck the towers on 9/11.

New York City firefighter Nicholas DeMasi stated that he escorted federal agents on an all-terrain vehicle in October 2001 and helped them locate three of the four devices.

His account is supported by a volunteer, Mike Bellone, whose efforts at Ground Zero have been chronicled in the *New York Times* and elsewhere. Bellone said he assisted DeMasi and the agents and that he saw a device resembling a "black box" in the back of the firefighter's ATV.

The black boxes—actually orange in color—could have provided valuable new information about the worst terror attack to ever take place on American soil, but then, maybe the data didn't fit the official story.

The devices are built to survive an impact of enormous force—3400 G's— and a fire of 1100 degrees Celsius for one hour, considerably higher than official estimates of the World Trade Center blaze that reached, at the very most, 800 degrees.

Federal aviation officials themselves have remarked that the World Trade Center attacks seem to be the only major jetliner crashes in the history of aviation where the black box devices were *never* located. Coincidence, or conspiracy?

The two black boxes for Flight 93 were also found. However, they were deemed too severely damaged, and it isn't known if the data could be recovered. Again, the 9/11 crashes would be *the first time in history that black boxes did not survive an air crash.* Many months after the attacks, the FBI revealed that they were able to extract the contents of the boxes from Flight 93, but they chose to release only select quotes from the recordings.[23]

The two black boxes for Flight 77 were also found according to FBI Director Robert Mueller, but they only contained information on altitude, speed, headings and other information and the voice recorder contained "nothing useful".[24] We suppose we will just have to take his word on that.

Just for the exercise, let's assume that the conspiracy theorists are correct and the government is lying and covering up the truth of the attacks on 9/11, either in whole or in part. Without any real evidence, without any real impartial investigation, what do we have to go on?

Admittedly, we do not have much left other than to observe the behaviors of all the parties before, during and after the event. But even though we have

---

[22] http://www.pnionline.com/dnblog/extra/archives/001139.html

[23] http://news.bbc.co.uk/1/hi/world/americas/1543564.stm

[24] http://www.cbsnews.com/stories/2002/02/25/attack/main501989.shtml

very little in the way of forensic evidence, we can still assert with the great detective Sherlock Holmes: "when you eliminate the impossible, whatever remains—however improbable—must be the truth!"

Contrary to those who claim that no real passenger jets were used in the attacks at all, that it was all a hologram, it seems rather clear that actual commercial jets hit the twin towers of the World Trade Center exactly as described by the many witnesses and as confirmed by government officials. It was on film, and we simply cannot refute that in our opinion. It happened, and everyone saw it; again and again and again and again.

But that does not mean that a commercial Boeing 757 hit the Pentagon.

Why do I say that?

Because the fact that large commercial jets were *seen* to hit the World Trade Center, over and over again on TV could very easily have "conditioned" the public to believe that the same type of craft hit the Pentagon when they were told that this was the case by government officials, backed up by "witnesses" most of whom just happened to be government officials.

Brain studies show that what is *suggested* during a period of pain or shock becomes *memory*. The brain sort of "traps" the ideas being assimilated at times of pain and shock into permanent "synaptic patterns of thought/memory".

The conditions surrounding the events of 9/11 were perfect for creating specific impressions and "memories"—manipulation of the minds of the masses by shocking events and media spin.

So, since we have video images of commercial jetliners hitting the World Trade Center towers , it is certain that this is what happened. The issue of the collapse of the buildings is different and most certainly does suggest prior planning to ensure that the buildings would not survive the impact, and that the collapse would be dramatic and shocking.

It is to these and other questions that we will turn in Part One of this book. Part Two takes up the question from an altogether different and original perspective, one extending back many thousands of years. It concerns the role of the three monotheistic religions in the unfolding tragedy in the Middle East, trying to understand why it seems just a little too convenient that these three religions should be at the heart of a conflict that could ignite a war that may well annihilate both the Jewish and the Arab populations of the region. Part Two also includes startling evidence about why and how monstrous conspiracies can and very definitely *do* exist.

Ladies and gentlemen, fasten your seatbelts.

PART 1: 911

911

One commentator on the internet wrote:

> Among the speculations being made by observers were ideas that the CIA was somehow involved in the 9/11 attack. Recent discoveries [...] bring that same sure but murky sense of the CIA's presence leading up to the attack. Perhaps another operation gone very sour.
>
> We also have the recent arrest and expulsion, although this is officially denied in Washington, of a large Israeli spy ring.... Spy rings as large as this one simply do not operate in a place like the United States without the CIA being aware of them. Apparently, there is a serious question whether Mossad, the Israeli intelligence service, told the U.S. what it knew before September 11. At any rate, we know the aftermath of the attack certainly has tipped the balance to favor Mr. Sharon's bloody-minded way of seeing the world. [...] Americans, for a second time, may have been the unintended victims of their own agency's dirty work.[25]

As readers may be aware, there are already many books and articles, both in print and on the internet, that make a convincing case that the 9/11 attacks were an inside job, or, at the very least, could not have been carried out solely by a rag-tag bunch of Islamic terrorists operating out of a cave in Afghanistan. While this community of 9/11 researchers, often referred to as the "9/11 Truth Movement", agree on most of the major points of evidence that strongly suggest a government conspiracy, the one bone of contention that has apparently divided them concerns the events surrounding the attack on the Pentagon.

While most sincere 9/11 researchers agree that both Flight 11 and Flight 175 did indeed hit the WTC towers, and that it really was Flight 93 that ended its journey in the Pennsylvanian countryside, the question as to what exactly hit the Pentagon remains in dispute.

While we freely admit that the details of the attacks on the WTC and the fate of Flight 93 present many potential smoking guns pointing to U.S. and Israeli government complicity or direct involvement in 9/11, it is our belief that the attack on the Pentagon constitutes at least one of the real Achilles' heels of the conspirators. For this reason it comes as no surprise to us that there appears to be a concerted attempt, by what we suspect to be government Counter Intelligence operatives, to loudly declaim and discredit the idea that something other than Flight 77 hit the Pentagon that bright September morning in 2001.

---

[25] John Cluckman, "Footprints in the Dust", CounterPunch, March 11, 2002, http://www.counterpunch.org/chuckmanfootprints.html

Mike Ruppert, former LA police officer and owner of the website "From the Wilderness", rose to fame in the 9/11 truth movement with the publication of his exhaustive tome, *Crossing the Rubicon*, an extremely well-researched analysis of the many gaping holes in the official government story of the 9/11 attacks and the reason they occurred. However, in his book, *Ruppert states that, while he is quite convinced that it was not Flight 77 that hit the Pentagon, he refuses to include the subject as part of his overall case for conspiracy because of the implications, i.e. if Flight 77 did not hit the Pentagon, then what happened to Flight 77?*

Ruppert balks at the idea of offering an answer to this question to his readers because *he believes most people would be unable to accept it.* But let's be clear here, in the context of 9/11 being the work of a faction of the U.S. government and military, the answer to the question—"if Flight 77 didn't hit the Pentagon, what happened to it?"—is quite obvious: Flight 77 and its occupants (or the majority of them as we shall later explore) were flown to a specific destination and "disposed of" by the conspirators. On the one hand Ruppert is sure that his readers can accept the fact that U.S. government officials participated in the slaughter of the passengers on Flights 11 and 175 and the occupants of the WTC towers, yet he is equally sure that the *same readers* would be *unable* to accept the idea that the same government officials played a part in disposing of the passengers of Flight 77 in a much less imaginative way.

Unlike Ruppert and others, we are not inclined to shrink from facing the highest probable truth, regardless of how unsavory that reality may turn out to be. As for the suggestion that it is inconceivable that the U.S. (or any other government) would murder its own citizens when need dictates, we refer readers to any of the historical precedents that show that certain individuals within previous U.S. administrations have not hesitated to sacrifice the lives of U.S. citizens in order to further some political or personal goal.

Consider, for example, the fact that in the early 1960's *the U.S. Joint Chiefs of Staff drew up and approved plans to launch a secret and bloody wave of terrorist attacks against their own country in order to trick the American public into supporting an ill-conceived war they intended to launch against Cuba.*

Code named 'Operation Northwoods', the plan, which had *the written approval of the Chairman and every member of the Joint Chiefs of Staff, called for innocent people to be shot on American streets; for boats carrying refugees fleeing Cuba to be sunk on the high seas; for a wave of violent terrorism to be launched in Washington, D.C., Miami, and elsewhere, by agents of the U.S. government. Innocent people would be framed for bombings they did not commit; planes would be hijacked.* Using phony evidence, *all of it would be blamed on Castro,* thus giving this little cabal of warmongers the excuse, as well as the public and international backing, they needed to launch their war.

It should be especially noted that *the plan was developed and approved **without** the awareness of then President Kennedy*. This fact alone should provide readers with some insight into the distinct possibility that the real source of political and military power in the U.S. does not necessarily rest in the hands of the President and the Executive branch as most ordinary citizens have been lead to believe, which then begs the question: who really is in control of the U.S., and does anyone know who these people are and what their agenda is?

While *Operation Northwoods* was not actually implemented, previous and later U.S. governments concocted several other equally *diabolical schemes that called for the sacrificing of the lives of American citizens,* and unlike Operation Northwoods, these schemes *were* carried through to their brutal conclusion. We need mention only the attack on Pearl Harbor, where historical documents now prove beyond doubt that the Roosevelt administration had not only been forewarned of the Japanese attack plans, but actually provoked and enticed the Japanese Navy into attacking the sitting ducks at Pearl Harbor. Roosevelt's goal, of course, was to manufacture enough public outrage to facilitate a U.S. entrance into WWII. (Because of their mutual defense agreements, war with Japan automatically meant war with Germany.) Overwhelming evidence from government documents clearly shows that FDR had advance knowledge of the Japanese attack and allowed it to happen so that he could drag the U.S. into the war.[26] The lives of over 2,400 American citizens were sacrificed for the power-lust of the few.

It should be noted that Roosevelt acted under intense Zionist pressure. Patriotic Americans such as aviator Charles Lindbergh saw this and tried to warn the American people that Zionist media influence was intending to drive us into another World War. Said Lindbergh:

> I am not attacking the Jewish people. But I am saying that the leaders of both the British and the Jewish races, for reasons which are as understandable from their viewpoint as they are inadvisable from ours, for reasons which are not American, wish to involve us in the war.[27]

For those that may still be harboring some doubts about the willingness of any government, especially that of the United States, to sacrifice their citizens for the "higher good" (and let us never forget that in their minds, it is always for some "higher good" that they believe we, the great unwashed, would be incapable of understanding), we suggest a careful consideration of the events surrounding the sinking of the USS Maine, the sinking of the Lusitania and the Gulf of Tonkin incident for more clear-cut evidence that it is not only foolish but potentially life-threatening to maintain any illusions about what our government officials would or would not do.

For any 9/11 researchers to base their refusal to discuss the "no plane at the Pentagon" theory on the assertion that the American and world public could

---

[26] Robert Stinnett, *Day of Deceit.*
[27] Charles Lindbergh's Speech in Iowa. September 11, 1941. Interesting date, yes?

never accept the idea that the U.S. government would murder 64 American citizens is misinformed at best and disingenuous at worst. The simple fact is that the people that carried out the 9/11 attacks did much more than murder the 64 U.S. citizens on Flight 77, they murdered over 2,700 U.S. citizens in the World Trade Center that day, and used the 9/11 event as justification to pursue their imperial war of aggression, murdering hundreds of thousands innocent Afghan and Iraqi citizens in the process and killing or permanently maiming tens of thousands of Americans.

If there is one quote that sums up the present situation as regards the reality of 9/11 and the inability of many people to accept that reality, it is the words of former U.S. President Herbert Hoover, who is reported to have said, "The individual is handicapped by coming face to face with a conspiracy so monstrous he cannot believe it exists."

DETAILS OF THE EVENTS OF 9/11/2001

Flight 77 took off at 8:20 a.m. from Washington's Dulles International airport.

> The pilot had his last routine communication with the control tower at 8:50 a.m. "At 9:09 a.m., being unable to reach the plane by radar, the Indianapolis air controllers warned of a possible crash", the Washington Post reported. Vice-President Dick Cheney would later explain that the terrorists had, "turned off the transponder, which led to a later report that a plane had gone down over Ohio, but it really hadn't". [Meet the Press, NBC, September 16, 2001]

On September 12 it was learned that the transponder had been cut off at about 8:55 a.m., rendering the plane invisible to *civilian* air controllers. During this period of invisibility, the plane was said to have made a U-turn back to Washington. This is, of course, an assumption. The information that the plane turned around has no known source.

The problem is that turning off the transponder, under the conditions that prevailed that day, would have been the best way of raising an alert.

The procedures are very strict in the case of a problem with a transponder, both on civilian and military aircraft. The FAA regulations describe exactly how to proceed when a transponder is not functioning properly: the control tower should enter into radio contact at once with the pilot and, if it fails, immediately warn the military who would then send fighters to establish visual contact with the crew [See FAA regulations].[28]

The interruption of a transponder also directly *sets off an alert* with the military body responsible for air defenses of the United States and Canada, NORAD.

The transponder is the plane's identity card. An aircraft that disposes of this identity card is immediately monitored:

---

[28] http://faa.gov/ATpubs

"If an object has not been identified in less than two minutes or appears suspect, it is considered to be an eventual threat. Unidentified planes, planes in distress and planes we suspect are being used for illegal activities can then be intercepted by a fighter from NORAD." [NORAD spokesman][29]

See also "Facing Terror Attack's Aftermath",[30] *Boston Globe September 15, 2001*, where you will read:

Snyder, the NORAD spokesman, said its fighters *routinely* intercept aircraft.

It is important to note that in the years prior to 9/11, hundreds of planes of all shapes and sizes lost contact with, or were otherwise unresponsive to, air traffic control. In *every case* where contact could not be re-established, U.S. Air Force jets were immediately and automatically scrambled as per the long-standing orders. In fact, in the 12 months prior to 9/11, this automatic procedure was triggered flawlessly a total of 67 times, and *every time* U.S. air force jets reached the unresponsive plane *within 15 minutes*.

So what happened on 9/11?

How could it have been possible that not one U.S. military jet was scrambled in time to reach any of the four planes? Remember, Flight 77 hit the Pentagon *one hour and twenty five minutes after* Air traffic controllers in New York were aware that Flight 11 had been hijacked, yet NORAD did nothing until after all four planes were well beyond help.

Even allowing for the official claim of a "breakdown in communications", considering the conditions that prevailed on September 11, 2001, by turning off the transponder at 8:56 a.m. the "terrorists" on Flight 77 actually gave the alert at least forty minutes before the plane struck the Pentagon, and this alert ought to have been taken very seriously!

Three F-16's at Langley AFB, Virginia (130 miles from the Pentagon), were ordered to get airborne at approximately 9:30 a.m. The pilots were Major Brad Derrig, Captain Craig Borgstrom, and Major Dean Eckmann, all from the North Dakota Air National Guard's 119th Fighter Wing stationed at Langley.[31] If the assumed NORAD departure time is correct, the F-16s would have had to travel slightly over 700 mph to reach Washington before Flight 77 does. The maximum speed of an F-16 is 1,500 mph. Even traveling at 1,300 mph, these planes could have reached Washington in six minutes— well before Flight 77 hit the Pentagon. Yet it is claimed they were *accidentally directed over the Atlantic Ocean instead*, and reached Washington about 30 minutes later. Remember, this was at a point during the day when all necessary personnel in the U.S. government and NORAD were fully aware that they were under attack by hijacked airliners.

Andrews Air Force Base is just a few miles from the Pentagon and has two fighter wings, yet no orders were given to scramble any planes from this base until long after Flight 77 had hit the Pentagon.

---

[29] http://www.airforce.dnd.ca/athomedocs/athome1e_f.htm
[30] http://emperors-clothes.com/9/11backups/bg915.htm
[31] http://www.cooperativeresearch.org/timeline/2002/ap081902c.html

The U.S. government-sponsored 9/11 Commission (certainly not an "independent" body given that the Chairman, Thomas Keane, is a cousin of President Bush) summed up the reasons why America's military defense structures failed to thwart the attacks:

> On 9/11, the defense of U.S. air space depended on close interaction between two federal agencies: the Federal Aviation Administration (FAA) and North American Aerospace Defense Command (NORAD). Existing protocols on 9/11 were unsuited in every respect for an attack in which hijacked planes were used as weapons.

As we have seen, this claim is untrue. The protocols to quickly intercept suspect craft were long-established and had worked flawlessly in the past.

> What ensued was a hurried attempt to improvise a defense by civilians who had never handled a hijacked aircraft that attempted to disappear, and by a military unprepared for the transformation of commercial aircraft into weapons of mass destruction.

Again, this is not true. Whether or not the craft was hijacked was irrelevant for air traffic controllers. What *was* relevant was that the aircraft were unresponsive and/or had turned off their transponders. In such a case, the long-standing procedures are activated, NORAD is contacted and jets are scrambled, without fail.

> A shoot down authorization was not communicated to the NORAD air defense sector until 28 minutes after United 93 had crashed in Pennsylvania. Planes were scrambled, but ineffectively, as they did not know where to go or what targets they were to intercept. And once the shoot down order was given, it was not communicated to the pilots. In short, while leaders in Washington believed that the fighters circling above them had been instructed to "take out" hostile aircraft, the only orders actually conveyed to the pilots were to "ID type and tail".[32]

Yet again this statement flies in the face of the Commission's own findings. As we shall see, Transport Secretary Mineta testified to the Commission that VP Cheney had apparently given a shoot down order for Flight 77 sometime before 9:20 a.m. while he sat in the Presidential Emergency Operating Center in the White House.

Ultimately, the 9/11 Commission concluded that, due to many factors (a considerable number of which have no apparent explanation or none that the Commission was willing to investigate fully), it was a catastrophic breakdown in communication that had lead to the hijackers unchallenged success. But do such massive and unprecedented failures happen all by themselves? Surely someone was responsible?

In certain regions, air traffic controllers have radar, called "primaries", that are able to detect movement in the air while the radar they normally use are called "secondaries" and are limited to recording signals emitted by the transponders of airplanes which tell them the registration, altitude, etc. Turning off the transponder permits an aircraft to vanish from these "secondary"

---

[32] http://www.9/11commission.gov/report/911Report_Exec.htm

radar. Such an aircraft will only appear on "primary" radar. According to the FAA, the air traffic controllers did not have access to primary radars in Ohio.

See "Pentagon Crash Highlights a Radar Gap", where you will read:

> The airliner that slammed into the Pentagon on Sept. 11 disappeared from controllers' radar screens for at least 30 minutes—in part because it was hijacked in an area of limited radar coverage. [...]

> The aircraft, traveling from Dulles International Airport to Los Angeles, was hijacked sometime between 8:50 a.m. — when air traffic controllers made their last routine contact with the pilot — and 8:56, when hijackers turned off the transponder, which reports the plane's identity, altitude and speed to controllers' radar screens.

> The airliner crashed into the Pentagon at 9:38 a.m., about 12 minutes after controllers at Dulles sounded an alert that an unidentified aircraft was headed toward Washington at high speed.

> The answers to the mystery of the aircraft's disappearance begin with the fact that the hijacking took place in an area served by only one type of radar, FAA officials confirmed. Although this radar is called a "secondary" system, it is the type used almost exclusively today in air traffic control. It takes an aircraft's identification, destination, speed and altitude from the plane's transponder and displays it on a controller's radar screen.

> "Primary" radar is an older system. It bounces a beam off an aircraft and tells a controller only that a plane is aloft—but does not display its type or altitude. The two systems are usually mounted on the same tower. Primary radar is normally used only as a backup, and is usually turned off by controllers handling aircraft at altitudes above 18,000 feet because it clutters their screens.

> All aircraft flying above 18,000 feet are required to have working transponders. If a plane simply disappears from radar screens, most controllers can quickly switch on the primary system, which should display a small plus sign at the plane's location, even if the aircraft's transponder is not working.

> But the radar installation near Parkersburg, W. Va., was built with only secondary radar—called "beacon-only" radar. That left the controller monitoring Flight 77 at the Indianapolis center blind when the hijackers apparently switched off the aircraft's transponder, sources said.[33]

The only effect then of turning off the transponder at that precise point was to make the plane invisible to *some civilian* aviation authorities. One wonders how the "terrorists" knew that this act would make them invisible to only the civilian air traffic controllers and why they felt confident that being visible to only military ATCs would not lead to immediate interception. Again, under the conditions prevailing that day, and as a general routine, turning off the transponder should have brought the aircraft to the direct attention and scrutiny of the Military Defense Systems of the United States automatically. It is therefore a near certainty that, at all times, it was visible and monitored by the military.

---

[33] http://www.washingtonpost.com/ac2/wp-dyn?pagename=article&contentId=A32597-2001Nov2&notFound=true

According to the statement of General Myers, the military waited three quarters of an hour—knowing that airliners had been hijacked and flown into the World Trade Center—before ordering fighters to take off [Senate hearing, September 13, 2001].

Two days later, on September 15, NORAD issued a contradictory press release. It said that it *hadn't been informed* of the hijacking of Flight 77 until 9:24 a.m. and had then immediately given orders to two F-16's to take off from Langley, 105 miles from the Pentagon, instead of Andrews, only 10 miles from the Pentagon. They were in the air by 9:30, much too late... the object that impacted the Pentagon arrived at 9:37 a.m.

This version puts all the blame on the FAA for waiting. But this is implausible due to the established procedures that were *automatic* and had worked flawlessly 67 times in the previous 12 months!

If we were to theoretically accept NORAD's claim, then the question that needs to be asked, considering all that was known at that claimed "late moment" of awareness—that two aircraft had crashed into the WTC and the United States was "under attack"—is: why were fighter jets sent instead of a missile?

The fact is, independently of the interception of Flight 77, the crisis situation that existed that day demanded maximum air defense protection over Washington. This activity would have fallen to Andrews Air Force Base, just as General Eberhart, CO of NORAD had already activated the SCATANA plan and had taken control of the New York airspace in order to position fighters there.

For the military, from the moment they were alerted of Flight 77's disappearance, which was, indeed, *the moment the transponders were turned off*, and not when the FAA supposedly got around to calling them, it was not a question of speculating that they were dealing with a mechanical failure. The facts on the ground were rather precise: shortly after two airliners were flown into the WTC towers, the transponder of another plane was cut off and the pilot failed to respond to radio contact. The job of the military could not have been clearer: shoot down the plane that was claimed to be headed for Washington.

These facts show clearly that the U.S. military had no intention of shooting down whatever was heading for the Pentagon despite the menace it represented.

On September 16, 2001, Dick Cheney tried to justify the military's failure by claiming that the shooting down of a civilian airplane would be a "decision left up to the President". He played on the sympathy of the American people, saying that the President just couldn't take such a decision hastily because "the lives of American citizens were at stake".

Yet the reality of the situation is that Bush was one of the last to know about the 9/11 attacks. In fact, tens of millions of people in the U.S. and around the world knew that New York was under attack before the American "Commander in Chief". Or so the official story would have us believe.

When Flight 11 hit the first WTC at 8:46 a.m., President Bush's motorcade was crossing the John Ringling Causeway on the way to Booker Elementary school.[34]

Not long thereafter, then Press Secretary Ari Fleischer, who was riding in another car in the motorcade and talking on his cell phone, exclaimed, "Oh, my God, I don't believe it. A plane just hit the World Trade Center". This call took place "just minutes" after the first news reports.[35]

Congressman Dan Miller also says he was told about the crash just before meeting Bush at Booker elementary school at 8:55 a.m.[36]

Some reporters waiting for Bush to arrive also learned of the crash just minutes after it happened. While we might expect that the Commander in Chief of the Armed Forces and President of the USA would be one of the first to know about the crash, the official story remains that Bush was not told about the first plane attack until after he arrived at the school. On page 17 of his book *A Pretext For War*, author James Bamford comments:

> Despite having a secure STU-III phone next to [Bush] in the Presidential limousine and an entire national security staff at the White House, it appears that the President of the United States knew less than tens of millions of other people in every part of the country who were watching the attack as it unfolded.

So we see that Cheney's claim that part of the reason for the failure by America's defence apparatus to respond effectively to the attack was due to the difficult decision that confronted the President is a moot point since it is claimed that the President was not even informed of the attacks until *after* the first plane had hit the WTC.

Official accounts would have us believe that Bush simply thought that Flight 11's impact on the North Tower of the WTC was an accident and continued with his book reading in a Florida classroom:

> "I was concentrating on the program at this point, thinking about what I was going to say. Obviously, I felt it was an accident. I was concerned about it, but there were no alarm bells."[37]

Yet over *40 minutes earlier*, at about 8.20 a.m., it was claimed that Boston's Logan Airport had received a call from Flight 11 attendant Amy (Madeline) Sweeney stating that the aircraft had been hijacked. Somewhere between 8.13 a.m. and 8.21 a.m. Flight 11's transponder was turned off prompting Boston flight control manager Glenn Michael to say later, "We considered it at that time to be a possible hijacking".[38]

[34] http://www.washtimes.com/national/20021008-21577384.htm

[35] http://web.archive.org/web/20021004153618/http://www.abqtrib.com/archives/news02/091002_news_draper.shtml

[36] http://www.sarasotamagazine.com/Pages/hotstories/hotstories.asp?136

[37] http://www.washtimes.com/national/20021007-85016651.htm

[38] http://www.boston.com/news/daily/12/attacks_faa.htm

In any case, Cheney's claims are disingenuous. He equated the interception of the aircraft with the decision to shoot it down.

Interception is merely establishing visual contact, giving instructions with wing movements etc., and being *ready* to take action. A shoot down means that the fighters are already positioned to receive the order.

Further, it is incorrect that this decision to place fighter jets in a position to take action can only be made by the President. The interception of a suspect civilian aircraft by fighters is *automatic* and does not require any kind of political decision making by the President. It should have taken place on September 11 when the transponder was cut off. The fighters should have taken off immediately—unless they were ordered to "stand down". Furthermore, by September 11, 2001 the ability to give a shoot down order was not limited to the President but shared also by the Secretary for Defense.

Again, let me reiterate the fact that Flight 77 was invisible *only to civilian* aviation authorities. The fact that the transponders were turned off *automatically alerts military air defense.*

The New York Times reported:

> During the hour or so that American Airlines Flight 77 [was] under the control of hijackers, up to the moment it struck the west side of the Pentagon, military officials in [the Pentagon's NMCC were] urgently talking to law enforcement and air traffic control officials about what to do.[39]

MSNBC stated:

> [A]lthough the Pentagon's NMCC reportedly knew of the hijacking, NORAD reportedly was not notified until 9:24 a.m. by some accounts, and not notified at all by others.[40]

While ABC News tells us:

> Brigadier General Montague Winfield, commander of the NMCC, the Pentagon's emergency response center, later said: 'When the second aircraft flew into the second tower, it was at that point that we realized that the seemingly unrelated hijackings that the FAA was dealing with were in fact a part of a coordinated terrorist attack on the United States'.[41]

However, Winfield wasn't actually at the NMCC during the 9/11 crisis.[42] Captain Charles Leidig was in command of the National Military Command Center (NMCC), "the military's worldwide nerve center". Telephone links were established with the NMCC located inside the Pentagon (but on the opposite side of the building from where the explosion will happen), U.S. Strategic Command, theater commanders, FEMA agencies and the Canadian military command center.

An Air Threat Conference Call was initiated and it lasted for eight hours. At one time or another, President Bush, Vice President Cheney, Defense Sec-

[39] http://www.wanttoknow.info/010915nytimes11

[40] http://www.msnbc.msn.com/id/5233007/]

[41] http://abcnews.go.com/onair/DailyNews/sept11_moments_1.html

[42] http://www.cooperativeresearch.org/timeline/2004/independentcommission061704b.html

retary Rumsfeld, key military officers, leaders of the FAA and NORAD, the White House, and Air Force One were heard on the open line. NORAD command director Captain Michael Jellinek claimed this happened "immediately" after the second WTC hit.[43]

However, the 9/11 Commission concluded it started nearly 30 minutes later, at approximately 9:29 a.m. Brigadier General Montague Winfield, who later takes over for Leidig, said, "All of the governmental agencies that were involved in any activity going on in the United States at that point, were in that conference". While the call continued right through the Pentagon explosion, the impact was allegedly not felt within the NMCC.[44]

However, despite being in the Pentagon, Defense Secretary Rumsfeld didn't enter the NMCC or participate in the call until 10:30 a.m.

And so we see that the one man who, officially, could issue a shoot down order (other than the President who was still reading a book on goats to children in Florida) decided not to enter the crisis meeting at the NMCC that began 40 minutes before the Pentagon was hit.

Just to close the book on Cheney's allegations that only the President could order a shoot down, the 9/11 Commission interviewed Transportation Secretary Norman Mineta:

> Mr. Hamilton: We thank you for that. I wanted to focus just a moment on the Presidential Emergency Operating Center. You were there for a good part of the day. I think you were there with the Vice President. And when you had that order given, I think it was by the President, that authorized the shooting down of commercial aircraft that were suspected to be controlled by terrorists, were you there when that order was given?
>
> Mr. Mineta: No, I was not. I was made aware of it during the time that the airplane [was] coming into the Pentagon. There was a young man who had come in and said to the Vice President, "The plane is 50 miles out. The plane is 30 miles out." And when it got down to, "The plane is 10 miles out," the young man also said to the Vice President, "Do the orders still stand?" And the vice President turned and whipped his neck around and said, "Of course the orders still stand. Have you heard anything to the contrary?" Well, at the time I didn't know what all that meant. And...
>
> Mr. Hamilton: The flight you're referring to is the...
>
> Mr. Mineta: The flight that came into the Pentagon.
>
> Mr. Roemer: So when you arrived at 9:20, how much longer was it before you overheard the conversation between the young man and the vice President saying, "Does the order still stand?"
>
> Mr. Mineta: Probably about five or six minutes.
>
> Mr. Roemer: So about 9:25 or 9:26. And your inference was that the vice President snapped his head around and said, "Yes, the order still stands." Why did you infer that that was a shoot-down?

[43]

http://web.archive.org/web/20041009173402/http://www.aviationnow.com/content/publication/a
wst/ 20020603/avi_stor.htm

[44] http://911research.wtc7.net/cache/pentagon/attack/abcnews091102_jenningsinterviews.html

Mr. Mineta: Just by the nature of all the events going on that day, the scrambling of the aircraft and, I don't know; I guess, just being in the military, you do start thinking about it, an intuitive reaction to certain statements being made.[45]

So what are we to understand from these comments? Well, from the testimony of Mr. Mineta, we see that VP Cheney had given an order at some point *prior* to 9:20 a.m., at least 18 minutes before the plane is alleged to have struck the Pentagon. Mr. Mineta claimed to the 9/11 Commission that he assumed that the order was a shoot down order, but if this is true, why was this order from the Vice President not quickly conveyed along the chain of command to the necessary parties? Clearly such an order would have rendered obsolete any confusion over whether or not to scramble jets in the first place. So why were no Air Force Jets scrambled from nearby Andrews AFB?

Mr. Mineta stated that he did not hear the order itself but assumed, given the situation in hand, that it was a shoot down order for Flight 77.

But what if it wasn't?

Why would the unnamed official feel the need to ask Cheney if a shoot down order still stood? The danger had certainly not passed by 9:25 a.m. when Mineta heard the exchange. By then everyone knew that "America was under attack", *so who would query a shoot down order from the Vice President?* It seems much more plausible that the order that was being questioned was something akin to a "stand down" order. This would explain the obvious confusion on the part of the unnamed official and his compulsion to ask if the order still stood, even as he watched the obviously hijacked aircraft wing its way towards the Pentagon. It might also better explain Cheney's vexed response of, "Of course the orders still stand. Have you heard anything to the contrary?". It would also explain, of course, why no jets were scrambled and why the 9/11 attacks in general were so successful.

Interestingly, four months prior to 9/11 on May 8, 2001, Bush announced a new Homeland Security initiative:

Cheney to Oversee Domestic Counterterrorism Efforts

President Bush May 8 directed Vice President Dick Cheney to coordinate development of U.S. government initiatives to combat terrorist attacks on the United States.

"I have asked Vice President Cheney to oversee the development of a coordinated national effort so that we may do the very best possible job of protecting our people from catastrophic harm. I have also asked Joe Allbaugh, the Director of the Federal Emergency Management Agency, to create an Office of National Preparedness. This office will be responsible for implementing the results of those parts of the national effort overseen by Vice President Cheney that deal with consequence management. Specifically it will coordinate all federal programs dealing with weapons of mass destruction consequence management within the Departments of Defense, Health and Human Services, Justice, and Energy, the Environmental Protection Agency, and other federal agencies. The Office of National Preparedness will work closely with state and local govern-

---

[45] http://www.9/11commission.gov/archive/hearing2/9/11Commission_Hearing_2003-05-23.htm

ments to ensure their planning, training, and equipment needs are addressed. FEMA will also work closely with the Department of Justice, in its lead role for crisis management, to ensure that all facets of our response to the threat from weapons of mass destruction are coordinated and cohesive."[46]

On the morning of 9/11 then, Vice President Dick Cheney was directly responsible for coordinating federal preparedness for international terrorist attacks on U.S. soil.

Mr. Mineta also testified that the FAA was very much in contact with NORAD right from the moment that the transponder on the very first flight, Flight 11, was switched off at 8:20 a.m., a full hour and 18 Minutes **before** the Pentagon was hit!

> "The FAA was in touch with NORAD. And when the first flight from Boston had gone out of communications with the air traffic controllers, the air traffic controller then notified, I believe, Otis Air Force Base about the air traffic controller not being able to raise that American Airlines flight."

Let's recap the events to that point according to the official story.

FLIGHT 11

At 8:20 a.m. a flight attendant on Flight 11 phoned Boston Logan airport reporting that the aircraft has been hijacked. For some reason that has never been explained, no one in Boston contacted NORAD as per the *long-standing and automatic protocols* until over 20 minutes later, 6 minutes before Flight 11 ploughed into the WTC North Tower.

ABC reported:

> There doesn't seem to have been alarm bells going off, [flight] controllers getting on with law enforcement or the military. There's a gap there that will have to be investigated.[47]

However, as per the testimony of Transport Secretary Mineta, NORAD suspected that Flight 11 had been hijacked as soon as communication with it was lost at 8:20 a.m. and Boston air traffic controllers *did* notify Otis AFB. Yet somehow, for some reason, NORAD did nothing.

Officially, pilots at Otis AFB received a call from Boston Flight control at 8:34 a.m. informing them of the situation. The pilots were reported to be sitting in their aircraft for over 5 minutes. *They did not get official clearance to take off until 8:46 a.m., the exact time that Flight 11 hit the WTC North Tower.* There has been no explanation as to why ATC at Boston did not inform Otis AFB immediately at 8:20 a.m. and no explanation for *the delayed order to scramble the jets until after Flight 11 had been transformed into a ball of flames in Manhattan.*

Also at 8:34 a.m., Boston flight control attempted to contact an Atlantic City, New Jersey, air base to send fighters after Flight 11. For decades, the air

---

[46] http://www.usembassy.it/file2001_05/alia/a1050801.htm
[47] http://abcnews.go.com/sections/us/DailyNews/wtc_ticktock010914.html

base had two fighters on 24-hour alert status, but this changed in 1998 due to budget cutbacks. The flight controllers did not realize this, and apparently tried in vain to reach someone. Two F-16's from this base were practicing bombing runs over an empty stretch of the Pine Barrens near Atlantic City. Only eight minutes away from New York City, they were not alerted to the emerging crisis.

Shortly after the second WTC crash at 9:03 a.m., the same two F-16's were ordered to land and were refitted with air-to-air missiles, then sent aloft. However, the pilots re-launched more than an hour after the second crash. They were apparently sent to Washington, but did not reach there until almost 11:00 a.m.

After 9/11, one newspaper questions why NORAD *"left what seems to be a yawning gap in the midsection of its air defenses on the East Coast—a gap with New York City at the center".*[48]

Had these two fighters been notified at 8:37 a.m. or before, they could have reached New York City before Flight 11.

FLIGHT 175

At 8:43 a.m. NORAD was notified by Boston flight control that another flight, Flight 175, had been hijacked.[49] Yet no orders were given at this time to scramble any aircraft. Later, *the 9/11 Commission ignored the testimony of New York flight controller Dave Bottoglia that he was aware that Flight 175 was hijacked at this time and had notified NORAD,* claiming instead that NORAD was unaware that Flight 175 had been hijacked until 9:03 a.m., the approximate time that it crashed into the WTC South Tower.

One of the main excuses offered by the National Military Command Center (NMCC) and the Department of Defense for their failure to thwart the 9/11 attacks was that the 4,000 other planes in America's skies on the morning of September 11, 2001 made the task almost impossible. *Yet what is not pointed out is that, of those 4,000 planes, the 4 hijacked planes were the ONLY ones that were not transmitting a transponder signal, making them stick out like sore thumbs on any **military** radar screen.*

FLIGHT 77

The last radio contact with Flight 77 occurred at 8:50 a.m. At 8:56 a.m. its transponder was turned off. Somewhere between these two times the plane was "hijacked". *The New York Times* reported:

[48] http://www.northjersey.com/page.php?qstr=eXJpcnk3ZjczN2Y3dnFlZUVFeXkyNjMmZmdiZWw3Zjd2cWVlRUV5eTY0NTk1MDUmeXJpcnk3ZjcxN2Y3dnFlZUVFeXk5

[49] http://web.archive.org/web/20020615115751/http://www.norad.mil/presrelNORADTimelines.htm

During the hour or so that American Airlines Flight 77 [was] under the control of hijackers (8:56 a.m.), up to the moment it struck the west side of the Pentagon, military officials in [the Pentagon's NMCC were] urgently talking to law enforcement and air traffic control officials about what to do.[50]

Despite this assertion, and the fact that it is backed up by transport Secretary Mineta's testimony that Cheney had given an order to shoot down Flight 77 sometime before 9:20 a.m., the 9/11 Commission accepted testimony from some that NORAD was not notified until 9:24 a.m. and from others that NORAD was not notified at all.[51]

Pentagon spokesman, Lieutenant-Colonel Vic Warzinski claimed the military had not been expecting such an attack. This is not credible. Even though the transponder had been turned off, the Pentagon knew full well where that aircraft was. Communications between civilian air traffic controllers and the various federal authorities functioned perfectly as they had on many previous occasions.

In fact, not only had the FAA Command Center set up a teleconference with FAA facilities in the New York area by 8:40 a.m., but a communication line was also opened with the Air Traffic Services Cell, a military cell which had been created by the FAA and the Defense Department to coordinate priority aircraft movement during warfare or emergencies. This cell is staffed by Pentagon employees, and while it is usually only staffed three days per month for refresher training, September 11 just happened to be one of those days.[52]

Even more coincidentally, the cell had been given a secure terminal and other hardware just weeks earlier which had supposedly "greatly enhanced the movement of vital information".[53]

FLIGHT 93

According to NORAD's *initial statement, Flight 93 was hijacked at 9:16 a.m.,* yet they were unable to say when the FAA notified them of the hijacking or how the FAA knew. Flight 93 is the only flight where NORAD could not at least supply this time of notification of hijacking.[54]

Despite this, the 9/11 Commission concluded that *the hijacking of Flight 93 began at 9:28 a.m.* saying only that the original statement by NORAD was incorrect without giving any explanation as to how or why such an error was made.[55]

At this same time, Cleveland flight controllers *noticed Flight 93 climbing and descending in an erratic way,* and shortly thereafter *screams and shouts of 'get*

---

[50] http://www.wanttoknow.info/010915nytimes11

[51] http://www.msnbc.msn.com/id/5233007/

[52] http://www.freerepublic.com/focus/f-news/592509/posts

[53]
http://web.archive.org/web/20020917072642/http://www.aviationnow.com/content/publication/a wst/ 20020603/avi_stor.htm

[54] http://www.cnn.com/2001/US/09/16/inv.hijack.warning/

[55] http://web.archive.org/web/20040617211819/http://www.msnbc.msn.com/id/5233007/

out of here' were heard by controllers over the cockpit transmission. Arabic voices are also heard. At this point contact was lost with Flight 93. Yet despite this, we are told that *no one notified NORAD.*[56]

According to the 9/11 Commission, at 9: 36 a.m. Cleveland flight control specifically asked the FAA Command Center whether someone had requested the military to launch fighters toward Flight 93. Cleveland offered to contact a nearby military base. The Command Center replied that FAA personnel well above them in the chain of command have to make that decision and were working on the issue.[57]

This single fact suggests that somewhere along the chain of command someone was preventing the implementation of standard procedures taken in respect of suspect aircraft, which is the immediate scrambling of fighter jets.

At about 9:36 a.m. Flight 93 made a 180 degree turn and headed back to Washington.[58]

Still no fighters were scrambled.

From 9:30 a.m. until Flight 93 "crashed" several passengers were *alleged* to have made calls to their family members and to phone operators specifying that a hijacking was taking place.

According to NORAD, Flight 93 crashed at *10:03 am.* However, *a seismic study* authorized by the U.S. Army to determine when the plane crashed concluded that the crash happened at *10:06:05.* [59]

Furthermore, according to a CNN report, the cockpit voice recording of Flight 93 was recorded on a 30-minute reel which started at 9:31am and ended at 10:02 am, with the last minute of recording apparently missing. This fact led some victim's family members to wonder if the tape had been tampered with.[60]

So what exactly happened in that last minute before Flight 93 hit the ground in Pennsylvania?

Several eyewitness reports of the crash of Flight 93 attest to the presence of a white unmarked military-style jet over-flying the crash scene.[61]

The mayor of Shanksville, the closest town to where Flight 93 "crashed" stated:

"I know of two people—I will not mention names—*that heard a missile*", Stuhl said. "They both live very close, within a couple of hundred yards... This one fellow's served in Vietnam and he says he's heard them, and he heard one that day." The mayor adds that based on what he knows about that morning, military F-16 fighter jets were "very, very close".[62]

---

[56] http://members.fortunecity.com/seismicevent/msnbctransponder.html#
[57] http://www.msnbc.msn.com/id/5233007/
[58] http://europe.cnn.com/2001/US/09/12/plane.phone.call/
[59] http://www.mgs.md.gov/esic/publications/download/911pentagon.pdf
[60] http://inn.globalfreepress.com/modules/news/article.php?storyid=470
[61] http://news.independent.co.uk/world/americas/story.jsp?story=323958
[62]
http://web.archive.org/web/20011116093836/http://dailynews.philly.com/content/daily_news/local/ 2001/11/15/SHOT15c.htm

Another eyewitness stated that he heard *two loud bangs* before watching the plane take a downward turn of nearly 90 degrees.[63]

It is also a matter of record that the debris of the crash was strewn across an area of approximately 8 miles.[64] Ask yourself: how could parts of a commercial jet that allegedly hit the ground intact be 8 miles from the crash site? Consider also the following from a news photographer who was on the scene within minutes and talked to Fox news:

Fox News reporter: It looks like there's *nothing there, except for a hole in the ground.*

Photographer Chris Konicki: Ah, basically that's right. The only thing you can see from where we were, ah, was a big gouge in the earth and some broken trees. We could see some people working, walking around in the area, but from where we could see it, there wasn't much left.

Reporter: Any large pieces of debris at all?

Konicki: Na, there was nothing, nothing that you could distinguish that a plane had crashed there.

Reporter: Smoke? Fire?

Konicki: Nothing. It was absolutely quiet. It was, uh, actually very quiet. Um, nothing going on down there. No smoke. No fire. Just a couple of people walking around. They looked like part of the NTSB crew, walking around looking at the pieces.

Reporter: How big would you say that hole was?

Konicki: Eh...from my estimates I would guess it was probably about *20-15 feet long and probably about 10 feet wide.*[65]

Flight 93 'crash' crater

[63] http://www.newsnet5.com/news/956371/detail.html
[64] http://archives.cnn.com/2001/US/09/13/penn.attack/
[65] http://www.youtube.com/watch?v=JZekosYOmXc

Somerset County Coroner Wallace Miller, who was one of the first people to arrive at the crash site, said it looked as if someone took a scrap truck, dug a 10-foot ditch and dumped trash into it. Miller said there was nothing visible of human remains and that it was as if the plane had "stopped and let the passengers off before it crashed."[66] He said that the most eerie thing about the site was that he hadn't seen a "single drop of blood."[67] Miller said he was stunned at how small the crater was. "I stopped being coroner after about 20 minutes," Miller said, "because there were *no bodies there*." It should be noted that Miller has made it clear that he does not support any "conspiracy theories" about 9/11 or the "crash" of Flight 93.

These facts are clearly consistent with Flight 93 having been shot down and that the claimed crash site was the area where just a section of the broken apart plane, probably the largest, hit the ground. Of course, if Flight 93 was shot down and did not crash as claimed by the U.S. government and 9/11 Commission, not only does this pose serious questions about the authenticity of the alleged phone calls made by passengers to the effect that they were going to try and "do something" to take control of Flight 93 from the hijackers, but it throws all other facets of the official story of what happened on 9/11 into doubt.

In the one hour and thirty minutes from the time authorities had become aware of the first plane hijacking to the time that Flight 93 "crashed" in Pennsylvania, the official story claims that the FAA, NORAD and the Presidential Emergency Operating Center (PEOC) *all failed* to organise the effective scrambling of a single fighter jet to confront the "hijackers". Not only that, but over the course of the day, air traffic controllers and employees of the FAA failed a total of 16 times to follow (or to have implemented) the automatic and long-standing procedures in which they were all well-versed.

And let us just remind readers once more, in the 12 months leading up to 9/11, procedures for the interception by military aircraft of suspect airplanes had been implemented flawlessly 67 times. On every occasion fighter aircraft had visual sighting of the suspect aircraft within 15 minutes of notification.

THE ROLE OF THE MILITARY

There are five extremely sophisticated anti-missile batteries in place to protect the Pentagon from an airborne attack. These anti-missile batteries operate *automatically*.

At 9:25 a.m., the control tower at Dulles airport observed an unidentified vehicle speeding towards the restricted airspace that surrounds the capital [*Washington Post*, September 12, 2001]. The craft was heading toward the White House.

---

[66] http://www.post-gazette.com/headlines/20011015newsmaker1015p2.asp
[67] http://www.pittsburghlive.com/x/pittsburghtrib/s_90823.html

"All of a sudden, the plane turned away. [...] This must be a fighter. This must be one of our guys sent in, scrambled to patrol our capital and to protect our President.... We lost radar contact with that aircraft. And we waited. [...] And then the Washington National controllers came over our speakers in our room and said, 'Dulles, hold all of our inbound traffic. The Pentagon's been hit'."
[Danielle O'Brien, ABC News, October 24, 2001]

The Army possesses several very sophisticated radar monitoring systems. The PAVE PAWS system is used to detect and track objects difficult to pick up such as missiles flying at very low altitudes. PAVE PAWS *misses nothing occurring in North American airspace.* "The radar system is capable of detecting and monitoring a great number of targets that would be consistent with a massive SLBM (Submarine Launched Ballistic Missile) attack. The system is capable of rapidly discriminating between vehicle types, calculating their launch and impact points."[68]

Thus, contrary to the Pentagon's claims, the military knew very well that an unidentified vehicle was headed straight for the capital. Yet, the military did not react, and the Pentagon's anti-missile batteries did not function.

Why?

We come back to the issue of Transponders.

Military aircraft and missiles possess transponders which are much more sophisticated than those of civilian planes. These transponders enable the craft to declare itself to the *electronic eyes* watching American airspace as either friendly or hostile. An anti-missile battery will not, for example, react to the passage of a friendly missile, so that in battlefield conditions, it is ensured that only enemy armaments and vehicles are destroyed.

*Thus, it seems that whatever hit the Pentagon **must** have had a military transponder signalling that it was "friendly",* i.e. *it would take an American military craft to penetrate the defenses of the Pentagon,* or the anti-missile batteries would have been *automatically* activated. Considering all aspects of the problem suggests that the systems *were* operational... and the object that hit the Pentagon was "read" by the anti-missile batteries as "*ours*".

Strangely, the *entire* responsibility for air defense is attributed to NORAD, and that is simply not the truth.

The previously-mentioned National Military Command Center, located in the Pentagon, centralizes all information concerning plane hijackings and directs military operations. The NMCC was in a state of maximum alert on the morning of September 11. The highest military authority of NMCC is the Chairman of the Joint Chiefs of Staff. On September 11, General Henry Shelton fulfilled this role. However, Shelton was conveniently en route for Europe, somewhere over the Atlantic. Thus, his job fell to his deputy, *General Richard Myers,* who was also conveniently hobnobbing with Senator Max Cleland at the time of the attacks. We have also noted that Secretary of Defense Donald Rumsfeld strangely chose *not* to join his colleagues at the

---

[68] http://www/pavepaws.org/ and http://www.fas.org/spp/military/program/track/pave paws.htm

NMCC crisis meeting being held in the Pentagon on the morning of 9/11, opting instead to stay in his office nearby until the Pentagon was hit.

In short, the answers to what happened on that day devolve to claimed technical failures, coordination problems, temporary incapacity, absence of commanders, transfer of responsibility, and so on.

Even if we were to accept such an implausible excuse, we are still left with the problem of *why the automatic systems in place did not work.*

USA Today reported:

NORAD had drills of jets as weapons

In the two years before the Sept. 11 attacks, the North American Aerospace Defense Command conducted exercises simulating what the White House said was unimaginable at the time: hijacked airliners used as weapons to crash into targets and cause mass casualties.[69]

One of the imagined targets was the World Trade Center! Yet despite this fact, the Bush administration, most notably then National Security Advisor Condoleeza Rice, claims that they were completely unprepared for the 9/11 attacks *because the idea of someone hijacking commercial airliners and flying them into buildings was never thought possible.* Does this mean that Condi was lying?

Take your time, no hurry.

On November 3, 2000 a U.S. military website reported:

The fire and smoke from the downed passenger aircraft billows from the Pentagon courtyard. Defense Protective Services Police seal the crash sight. Army medics, nurses and doctors scramble to organize aid. An Arlington Fire Department chief dispatches his equipment to the affected areas.

Don Abbott, of Command Emergency Response Training, walks over to the Pentagon and extinguishes the flames. The Pentagon was a model and the "plane crash" was a simulated one.[70]

Yet still we are asked to believe the Bush administration when they say that they could never have anticipated the 9/11 attacks because they never imagined it? The reality, it seems, is that not only did a faction of the U.S. government anticipate the attacks; they had a direct hand in *facilitating* them.

One of the explanations for why things went so wrong on the fateful day is that on the morning of 9/11 at least five "Training Exercises" were in progress. Each and every one, and others we may not yet know of, were under the control of Vice President Dick Cheney. The 9/11 Commission has accepted testimony from various officials implicated in the 9/11 "failures" that *it was just a case of bad luck or coincidence* that these exercises were taking place at the

---

[69] http://usatoday.printthis.clickability.com/pt/cpt?action=cpt&title=USATODAY.com+-
+NORAD+had+drills+of+jets+as+weapons&expire=&urlID=9961878&fb=Y&url=http%3A%2
F%2Fwww.usatoday.com%2Fnews%2Fwashington%2F2004-04-18-
norad_x.htm&partnerID=1660
[70] http://www.mdw.army.mil/news/Contingency_Planning.html

time. Taken together with all other conditions, that has to be one of the most extraordinary coincidences of all time. The exercises we know of included:

1) *Military Exercise, Northern Vigilance*: Transferred most of the combat ready interceptors and possibly many AWACS from the northeast into northern Canada and Alaska. This explains, in part, why there were only eight combat interceptors in the northeast on 9/11. The calculated effect of this war game was to *take USAF fighters away from the Eastern seaboard* and avoid the eventuality that a gung-ho fighter pilot might attempt to thwart the attacks.

2) *Non-Military Biowarfare Exercise, Tripod II:* FEMA arrived in NYC on September 10, 2001 to set up the command post for FEMA, New York City and Department of Justice on Manhattan's pier 29. The effect and obvious benefit to the conspirators of this exercise was to have FEMA employees already on the ground when the WTC towers were hit in order to *manage the fall out of information* in the immediate aftermath of the attacks.

3) *Wargame Exercise, Vigilant Guardian:* This exercise *simulated hi-jacked planes* in the northeast sector. The 9/11 Commission *made only mention* of this single exercise and *lied* about its purpose. The commission said its purpose was to intercept Russian bombers. The effect of this war game was also to *take USAF fighters away from the Eastern seaboard* and avoid the eventuality that a gung-ho fighter pilot might attempt to thwart the attacks.

4) *Wargame Exercise, Vigilant Warrior:* This exercise *simulated hi-jacked planes in the northeast sector* and was essential to the conspirators in order to control (delay) the relaying of information about the "hijacked" aircraft in order that they could complete their mission.

5) *Wargame Exercise, Northern Guardian*: This exercise *simulated hi-jacked planes in the northeast sector* and was also essential to the conspirators in order to control (delay) the relaying of information about the "hijacked" aircraft in order that they could complete their mission.

Again we note that these exercises can be observed to be precisely designed to facilitate the attacks on 9/11. If, as we are expected to believe, these exercises just happened to be scheduled on the day when a gang of Arab Terrorists, working out of a cave in Afghanistan, were actually planning the exact types of attacks, it was either the most extraordinary coincidence of all time, or someone "in the know" passed the information on to said "Muslim Extremists", an issue that has never been addressed. The most reasonable explanation is, of course, that these exercises on that date, coming in conjunction with the attacks themselves, demonstrate clear U.S. Government complicity.

As a result of these exercises, at the time of the real hijackings there were as many as 22 "hijacked aircraft" on NORAD's radar screen. Some of these drills were "Live Fly" exercises where actual aircraft, likely flown by remote control, were simulating hi-jacked aircraft. Some of the drills electronically added the hi-jacked aircraft into the system. All this as the real hijackings began! NORAD offered these exercises, at least five in all, as an explanation for the apparent failure of U.S. military command and the FAA to prevent the attacks, suggesting it couldn't tell the difference between the seventeen bogus blips and the four actual hi-jacked aircraft blips. While such a claim may sound plausible enough to the average citizen, it is in reality very hard to believe, particularly given that, on December 9, 2001, the Toledo Blade reported the following:

> Deep inside a mountain (Cheyenne) in Colorado, members of the North American Aerospace Defence Command (NORAD) are at full battle staff levels for a major annual exercise that tests every facet of the organization. *Operation Northern Vigilance*, planned months in advance, involves deploying fighter jets to locations in Alaska and northern Canada.
>
> Everything is going as planned when Capt. Mike Jellinek arrives for his 6 a.m. shift. The Canadian will be overseeing the crew staffing a crucial post inside the mountain—NORAD's command centre.
>
> Whether it's a simulation or a real-world event, the role of the centre is to fuse every critical piece of information NORAD has into a concise and crystalline snapshot.
>
> An hour into his shift, something unscripted happens. NORAD's Northeast Air Defence Sector (NEADS), based in Rome, N.Y., contacts the mountain.
>
> The Federal Aviation Administration has evidence of a hijacking and is asking for NORAD support. This is not part of the exercise.
>
> In a flash, Operation Northern Vigilance is called off. *Any simulated information, what's known as an "inject", is purged from the screens.*
>
> Someone shouted to look at the monitor displaying CNN.
>
> 'At that point, we saw the World Trade Center, one of the towers, smoke coming out of it. And a minute later, we watched the live feed as the second aircraft swung around into the second tower', says Jellinek.[71]

So we see that a NORAD employee involved in the training exercises made it clear that *there was no problem whatsoever with purging the simulated "injects" from the radar screen,* leaving only the real "hijacked" planes that were *clearly identifiable by the fact that they were not emitting a transponder signal.*

As per the report, the FAA contacted NORAD, and this "purging" occurred *a few minutes before the second plane* impacted the WTC south tower at 9:03 a.m., by which time Flight 77's transponder had already been switched off, and *Flight 93 was not even "hijacked" until some 15 minutes later!* Of course, we are still left with the nagging question as to why NORAD was contacted by the FAA about "hijacked airliners" some 10-15 minutes *after* Flight 11 had already been transformed into a ball of flames in the North Tower of the WTC at 8:46 am.

Let's look now in more detail at some of the most glaring evidence for a conspiracy on 9/11.

Reuters news agency was first on the scene of the Pentagon attack. Based on the information they gathered there *from eyewitnesses,* they announced that the Pentagon had suffered damage from a *helicopter explosion. Associated Press confirmed this* with Democratic Party consultant, Paul Begala.

---

[71] http://www.ringnebula.com/northern-vigilance.htm

2:41:05 p.m. "The Pentagon is being evacuated in expectation of a terrorist attack. It is believed a fire has broken out in the building." – *TCM Breaking News* (9/11/01)[72]

2:47:43 p.m. "There are reports that a helicopter has crashed into the Pentagon. An eyewitness said that they saw the helicopter circle the building and after it disappeared behind it, an explosion occurred." – *TCM Breaking News* (9/11/01)[73]

2:52:26 p.m. "Paul Begala, a Democratic consultant, said he witnessed an explosion near the Pentagon *shortly after two planes crashed into World Trade Centre*. 'It was a huge fireball, a huge, orange fireball', Begala said. He said another witness told him a helicopter exploded." – *TCM Breaking News* (9/11/01)[74]

Shortly after the attack on the Pentagon, *the Department of Defense said* that a plane was involved. Suddenly, *new* "eyewitnesses" came forward that *contradicted the first ones,* and these new "eyewitnesses" now supported the "official version".

Fred Hay, assistant to Senator Bob Ney, was the first to claim that he saw a Boeing aircraft fall as he was driving down the highway next to the Pentagon. *Senator Mark Kirk* claimed that he was leaving the Pentagon parking lot after *breakfast with Donald Rumsfeld,* and he declared that a large plane had crashed into the Pentagon.

It was several hours before the Chairman of the Joint Chiefs of Staff, General Richard Myers, declared that the "suicide plane" was the Boeing 757, AA Flight 77 which had taken off from Dulles airport in Washington D.C. bound for L.A., and which had been lost to air traffic controllers at 8:55 a.m.

The air traffic controllers said that, at 8:55 a.m., the Boeing Flight 77 descended to 29,000 feet and did not respond to their instructions. Its transponder then went silent. They assumed electrical failure. (!) The pilot was not responding to them, but—according to them—apparently was able to intermittently turn on his radio which allowed them to hear a voice with "a strong Arab accent" threatening him. The plane then made a turn "back toward Washington" and after that, all trace was lost. Keep in mind that not one of the civilian air traffic controllers saw this "turn back", because there was no transponder by which they could track it. It is just a claim that was made *after the fact.*

The air traffic controllers notified FAA headquarters that a hijacking was suspected. The FAA staff said that, in the midst of the panic of that day, they just thought this message was another notification concerning the second plane that hit the WTC. It was only a half hour later that they realized it was, in fact, a third plane. That is to say, at about 9:24 they knew they had a third problem:

---

[72] Please note that the times given correspond to the time the events were reported in Ireland (5 hours ahead of EST). http://archives.tcm.ie/breakingnews/2001/09/11/story23297.asp

[73] http://archives.tcm.ie/breakingnews/2001/09/11/story23298.asp

[74] http://archives.tcm.ie/breakingnews/2001/09/11/story23300.asp

"General Richard Myers, vice chairman of the Joint Chiefs of Staff, said that, prior to the crash into the Pentagon, military officials had been notified that another hijacked plane had been heading from the New York area to Washington. He says he assumed that hijacked plane was the one that hit the Pentagon, though he could not be sure."   -TCM Breaking News (9/11/01)[75]

On September 13, General Myers was unable to give a report to the Senate on defensive measures taken to intercept this Boeing. Based on his testimony, the Senate Armed Services Committee determined that no attempt at interception had taken place.

NORAD immediately jumped up and said "Not so!". They issued a press release the next day stating that it only received the warning of the third hijacking at 9:24 and had most definitely immediately ordered two F-16's from Langley AFB in Virginia to intercept Flight 77. But, they claimed that the Air Force did not know its location and went in the wrong direction! Apparently, a military transport taking off from Andrews Air Force base happened to spot the Boeing by chance, but by then it was too late. Keep in mind that a plane with a turned off transponder is *always visible to military radar.*

A Boeing 757-200 measures 155 feet long and has a wingspan of 125 feet. Fully loaded, it weighs up to 90 tons and cruises at 560 miles per hour. So, this last claim above is simply not plausible. We are expected to believe that the U.S. military radar system could not locate a Boeing within a range of only a few dozen miles? The military radar of the most powerful nation on earth? And further, that said Boeing—a flying whale—could outmaneuver and elude two fighter jets?!

It is known that the security arrangements that protect Washington were revised after a plane managed to land on the White House lawn in 1994. It is also known that those security arrangements, while mostly secret, include the above mentioned five batteries of anti-aircraft missiles installed on top of the Pentagon and fighters stationed at Andrews Air Force Base. Yet, we are expected to believe that "the Pentagon simply was not aware" that a hijacked Boeing was headed its way; that "no one expected anything like that here"?

Essentially, we are being asked to believe that the headquarters of the most powerful and militarized nation on earth had been helpless to defend itself even in the midst of the most elaborate military exercises dealing with the exact problem faced on that day ever held in the United States!

Among the various news reports of an initial explosion before or at the same time as the main aircraft impact was the claim that a truck bomb[76] (others claimed a helicopter[77]) had exploded. The fact is that there was a diesel generator stationed just to the right of the impact point in front of the Pentagon[78] that was part of the Pentagon refurbishment project. Diesel generators

[75] http://archives.tcm.ie/breakingnews/2001/09/11/story23360.asp

[76] http://history.amedd.army.mil/memoirs/soldiers/responding.pdf

[77] http://www.guardian.co.uk/wtccrash/story/0,1300,550486,00.html

[78] http://www.pjstar.com/services/news/sept11/js/g96217a.html

usually have a large fuel tank located somewhere nearby to power them. Photos taken moments after the impact show an already burning fire to the right of the main impact site that is emitting a dense cloud of black smoke.

This black smoke is consistent with burning fuel (diesel), which continued to burn long after the flames and smoke from the main impact had died down. This fact lends credence to the eyewitness reports of some kind of an explosion a few seconds before or at the same time as the main impact.

If Flight 77 struck the Pentagon, we would expect there to be a major and prolonged fire from the thousands of gallons of aircraft fuel that Flight 77 was carrying. But in the case that another smaller aircraft was used, the lack of burning aircraft fuel would be evident. It is our contention therefore that the conspirators detonated the oil truck bomb just before or at the moment of impact in order to augment the aircraft explosion claim (complete with thousands of gallons of fuel) and also to provide *a literal smoke screen* in an attempt to hide the fact that Flight 77 was not involved in the attack. This is one of two "primer" explosions that occurred and which were reported at the time in the mainstream news. The second primer explosion *occurred at the White House*[79] and was designed as a preparation for an attack on that building, an attack that the Bush gang had been told to expect. Of course, one might have thought that, by now, Bush, Cheney et al. would be old and wise enough not to believe everything they are told. We will discuss this aspect later.

CNN correspondent Jamie Mcintyre reporting from the Pentagon lawn about an hour after the attack had this to say:

> "From my *close up inspection, there is no evidence of a plane having crashed anywhere near the Pentagon.* [...] *There are no large tail sections wing sections, fuselage, nothing like that anywhere around which would indicate that the entire plane crashed into the side of the Pentagon.*"[80]

Strangely enough, the reports of odd happenings at the Pentagon kept coming in until late in the day:

---

[79] http://www.nih.gov/news/NIH-Record/10_02_2001/story01.htm
[80] http://thewebfairy.com/911/pentagon/

4:05:16 p.m. "*A second aircraft* has crashed into the Pentagon building. It is not known whether this plane was that which was hijacked from Boston airport a short time ago, the fourth such plane to be used in this major attack on the U.S. *Earlier, a small plane had slammed into the building and set it ablaze.*" – TCM Breaking News (9/11/01)[81]

4:17:03 p.m. "Part of the Pentagon building outside Washington has collapsed. It had been *hit by two planes* apparently hijacked by terrorists in Boston earlier today." – *TCM Breaking News* (9/11/01)

6:40:29 p.m. "Fighter jets are patrolling the skies above Washington after a jet hijacked by terrorists struck the Pentagon. An aircraft has crashed on a helicopter landing pad near the Pentagon, and the White House. The Pentagon has taken a direct hit from an aircraft. The nerve centre of the U.S. military burst into flames and a portion of one side of the five-sided structure collapsed when the plane struck.

"*Secondary explosions* were reported in the aftermath of the attack and great billows of smoke drifted skyward towards the Potomac River. Authorities immediately began deploying troops, including a regiment of light infantry. General Richard Myers, vice chairman of the Joint Chiefs of Staff, says that prior to the crash into the Pentagon, military officials had been notified that another hijacked plane had been heading from the New York area to Washington. *He says he 'assumed that hijacked plane was the one that hit the Pentagon, though he could not be sure'.*" – *TCM Breaking News* (9/11/01)

Members of the press were kept away from the scene for the ostensible reason that they might "hinder rescue operations". However, the Associated Press obtained photos taken by a private individual from a nearby building.

It is due to those photos—taken by a private individual while the news services were banned from the area—that the biggest questions about the strike on the Pentagon have been raised.

After all of this confusion, it was finally announced that, according to officials, the explosion at the Pentagon was caused when American Airlines Flight 77, a 100 ton Boeing 757 commercial airliner, crashed at ground level into the only section of the building that was being renovated to be more "blast resistant" and which housed the smallest number of employees. Flight 77 was allegedly hijacked by five Arab Islamic terrorists on an apparent suicide mission killing all 64 people on board. Officials claimed that the flight recorders from Flight 77 and the remains of all but one of the 64 passengers on board were found at the crash scene.

Now, let us pause for a moment to think about this. First of all, we should consider the alleged "mindset" of terrorists who would want to inflict the most damage possible on their selected target. Certainly, if a fundamentalist Islamic terrorist organization managed to get hold of a plane, and then get it into range of the Pentagon, the "heart of the Great Satan", as they refer to the United States, they are going to want to go out in a blaze of glory that will be celebrated in legend for years to come! What a strike! Imagine! Being able to completely destroy the nerve center of the hated "Satan"!

---

[81] http://archives.tcm.ie/breakingnews/2001/09/11/story23320.asp

Already, these alleged terrorists have managed to destroy the "commercial symbol" of the United States, or so we are told, and now we are informed that they had other objects in their sights—the symbol of the United States' Military Supremacy.

But somehow, they bungled it. Somehow, with all the skills they are claimed to have had, evidenced by the way that infamous Flight 77 swooped down on the Pentagon like a giant bird of prey going after a running rabbit, American Airlines Flight 77, a 100 ton Boeing 757 commercial airliner that could have almost completely destroyed the entire Pentagon, crashed at ground level into the *only section of the building* guaranteed to produce the least damage and the fewest casualties.

And here we find ourselves in the midst of a double conundrum; for not only did the alleged hijackers of Flight 77 go to extraordinary lengths to inflict the least damage possible on the Pentagon, the alleged pilot of Flight 77 couldn't even fly!

Flight instructors at the Scotsdale, Arizona flight school where alleged Flight 77 hijacker pilot Hani Hanjour trained, claimed that he was a completely incompetent pilot. CBS News reported:

> Months before Hani Hanjour is believed to have flown an American Airlines jet into the Pentagon, managers at an Arizona flight school reported him at least five times to the FAA. They reported him not because they feared he was a terrorist, but because his English and flying skills were so bad... they didn't think he should keep his pilot's license.
>
> "I couldn't believe he had a commercial license of any kind with the skills that he had." – Peggy Chevrette, Arizona flight school manager[82]

Despite these facts, the U.S. government insists that Hanjour was an "expert pilot", simply because *only* an expert could have executed the incredible flying maneuvers required to steer a 757-200 across several lanes of traffic avoiding trucks, lamp-posts and trees and then hit the Pentagon at ground height.

This leads us to the obvious question: if these were really five Arab terrorists on a suicide mission to take down the hated Satan, and they were so skilled as to have pulled off all the stunning feats of that day, how did they bungle their chance for what would have been the greatest coup in Muslim Extremist history? How did they bungle so badly by using their fantastic flying skills to hit the part of the Pentagon that was the *least occupied* and the *most fortified*?

That is the "fact on the ground".

Just consider this: in order to cause the greatest damage to the Pentagon, the plane should obviously have dived right into the Pentagon's roof. The building is a pretty big target; it covers a surface area of 29 acres, making it an easy "hit". Instead, what actually happened makes no sense at all from the perspective of Islamic terrorists—we are assuming real, "freedom-hating" terrorists here as the Bush Administration has assured us they were—who now have their chance to do some real damage: they chose to strike a single

---

[82] http://www.cbsnews.com/stories/2002/05/10/attack/main508656.shtml

facade, the height of which was only 80 feet instead of getting a bull's eye on that 29 acre target. Terrorists that can fly a 757 like a barrel racer rides a horse, and they appear to have used their alleged flying expertise to inflict the least damage possible?!

Perplexing, is it not?

The alleged Boeing, purported to be in the hands of Islamic Fundamentalists who, with burning hatred in their heart of the United States and "its freedoms", steered said *flying whale* with unerring accuracy into a flight path as though they were going to land on the Pentagon lawn. While remaining horizontal, this amazing Boeing, we are told, came down almost vertically and struck the Pentagon at the height of the ground floor. What is more, it managed to do this without even ruffling the grass of the Pentagon's immaculate lawn. And then, despite its weight and forward momentum, the flying whale only destroyed a *small section* of the first ring of the building.

What is more, these deadly terrorists with race car driving skills *sacrificed their lives* to hit the Pentagon in such a way that only a small section was damaged, and it happened to be a section that was undergoing renovation and many of the offices of that section were unoccupied! You would think that if one is going to sacrifice one's life for something, like "burning hatred in their hearts for Mom, Apple Pie and the American Way", they would have wanted to get more bang for their buck.

Well, there's actually another very interesting thing about the section of the Pentagon that was hit: the Navy's brand new Command Center was destroyed. According to *Aviation Now*:

> *Vice Adm. Darb Ryan*, chief of naval personnel, was in his office at the Navy Annex about halfway between Trapasso's home and the Pentagon. Having learned that New York had been attacked, he was on the telephone recommending the evacuation of the Pentagon "when out of the corner of my eye I saw the airplane" a split second before it struck.

Ryan was overheard reporting some of the initial damage assessment, which included spaces belonging to the chief of naval operations (CNO), the Navy's tactical command center on the D-ring, an operations cell and a Navy intelligence command center. These included up to four special, highly classified, electronically secure areas. Many of the *enlisted sailors* involved were *communications technicians with cryptology training who are key personnel in intelligence gathering and analysis.* Some personnel were known to be trapped alive in the wreckage.

Other navy personnel confirmed the admiral's initial assessment and said the dead "numbered around 190", including 64 on the aircraft. Among them was Lt. Gen. Timothy Maude, who was in the Army support and logistics section. Many others were *Navy captains, commanders* and *lieutenant commanders* with offices between the fourth and fifth corridors (the western wedge of the Pentagon). The Navy's special operations office, which oversees classified programs, had moved out of the spaces *only a few days before.* All but one of the senior Navy flag officers were out of the building.

Early press reports claimed 800 deaths at the Pentagon, yet Donald Rumsfeld did not correct this grossly exaggerated figure on September 12 when the true death toll of 125 was certainly known.

> "Up to 800 people may have died Tuesday when a hijacked commercial airliner was crashed into the Pentagon, officials said. The more than 20,000 civilians and military men and women who work in the Pentagon streamed into the surrounding parking lots, driven by blue and white strobe alarm lights and wailing sirens." – CNN (9/12/01)

> "125 people were killed on the ground at the Pentagon. An additional 59 perished aboard American Airlines Flight #77. We do not count the five terrorists. Approximately 63 people were wounded/injured in the attack." – DOD

The shock of the impact was felt throughout the entire building. 125 people in the Pentagon lost their lives, to which should be added the alleged 64 people aboard the Boeing which can carry 269 passengers. In other words, *it was almost empty.*

We could go on, but there are many other sources that cover the details of that day in very competent ways not to mention the dozens of sources that only add to the confusion. At the present moment, we are of the opinion that a Boeing 757 most definitely did *not* hit the Pentagon, that the object that struck the Pentagon *was* different from the commercial jetliners that were clearly seen to fly into the World Trade Center Towers.

Now, let's move on to the "how they did it" question.

How Did They Do It?

I once spoke at length with an individual who served in the Persian Gulf conflict. His job was to "program" missiles—*very* smart ones. Even though it was his job, he was completely astonished at their capabilities. He said, "They can be programmed to go down the street just above the ground, turn right or left at a cross street, and hit the designated building at the exact floor, even the exact window, that you tell them to hit"! My jaw dropped and he then said that he was exaggerating, but only a little, and he was describing it this way just to emphasize for me the capability of modern guidance systems.

Now, that's amazing. That was also back in the early 1990s.

But let's make this perfectly clear: *We do not believe that it was a missile alone that hit the Pentagon.*

The point of mentioning the smart missiles in use during Gulf War I is to bring up the subject of the *guidance system* that was available even at that time. We notice in the above reports that the circumstances of the strike even led some witnesses to describe what hit the Pentagon as a helicopter, but there were so many reports of a plane that we should hypothesize that it was a plane-like object, even if it was a plane that could "fly like a helicopter".

Once I realized that the description of the smart missile maneuvers exactly fit what happened at the Pentagon, the question that occurred to me was: *Could such a guidance system be used in a plane?* Even commercial jetliners? If they could do this with missiles back in the 1990s, what have they done in the more than ten years since with such a system?

> Radar shows Flight 77 did a downward spiral, turning almost a complete circle and dropping the last 7,000 feet in two-and-a-half minutes. The steep turn was *so smooth,* the sources say, it's clear there was no fight for control going on. And the complex maneuver suggests the hijackers had better flying skills than many investigators first believed.[83]

Consider now something called the "Universal Replacement Autopilot Program" or URAP.[84] The diagram below, showing what the program can do when it is installed as the guidance system of an aircraft, is included in the paper published on this interesting technology.

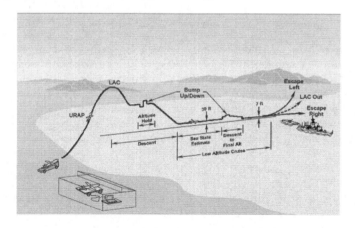

[83] http://www.cbsnews.com/stories/2001/09/11/national/main310721.shtml
[84] http://www.dtic.mil/ndia/air/bruns.pdf

A system designed to be installed in guided missiles or *unmanned aircraft*. There are two flight options available to the operator of an aerial vehicle with such a device installed: programmed flight and manual flight. In either flight mode the operator maintains full control over the vehicle and its trajectory including the ability for "instant recovery" from any unexpected divergence from the flight path, control over any payloads that the vehicle is carrying, "mission selection" (i.e. the mission can be aborted at any time) "manual takeover" (if programmed flight has been chosen) and "return to automatic" (if manual flight has been chosen) not to mention a host of other options to control just about every aspect of the vehicle and its trajectory.

The capabilities of the "Universal Replacement Autopilot" guidance system seem to describe very well the behavior of the alleged anomalous 757 that struck the Pentagon.

As we have seen from the news reports, the *very first descriptions*—before the stories began to change to support the "official" announcements— repeated that something *smaller than a 757 was seen to strike the Pentagon*.

> "I was convinced it was a missile. It came in so fast it sounded nothing like an airplane", said Lou Rains.[85]

> "It just was amazingly precise", Daryl Donley, another commuter, said of the plane's impact. "It completely disappeared into the Pentagon."[86]

> "The plane came in at an incredibly steep angle with incredibly high speed", said Rick Renzi.[87]

This certainly creates some confusion. What can we make of it? Can the early witnesses be trusted more than the ones who came forward later, after having watched the shocking impact of commercial jetliners on the World Trade Center, over and over and over again on television and after hearing the repeated assurances that a Boeing hit the Pentagon as well, or having been "set up" to be witnesses?

We must certainly consider that it is altogether possible that such repeated exposure to the WTC event by the media could create certain synaptic maps of the event that were then overlaid on the Pentagon event by simple suggestion. This method of psychological priming, and its effect on the accuracy of memory is discussed by Dennis Howitt in *Forensic and Criminal Psychology*.[88]

One of the ramifications is, of course, that many of the witnesses who later said they saw a commercial airliner are, in fact, convinced that that is what they saw, although we do not discount the possibility that a certain number of them are lying to protect their jobs or because they are being paid to spread disinformation, or because they are part of the conspiracy. Remember the early reports of a helicopter, a truck bomb, small planes, etc., that were then followed by "official reports" or reports from government authorities that it

[85] http://www.space.com/news/rains_september11-1.html

[86] http://www.delawareonline.com/newsjournal/local/2001/09/12terrorspreadsto.html

[87] http://www.pittsburgh.com/partners/wpxi/news/pentagonattack.html

[88] http://www.signs-of-the-times.org/signs/forum/viewtopic.php?pid=2607#p2607

was Flight 77, after which more "eyewitnesses came forward" with new and different stories that supported the "official versions".

One of our researchers looked into this problem and wrote:

> Some witnesses said they saw a commuter plane, and others like Army Captain Lincoln Liebner (who may have had an agenda), said he saw a large American Airlines passenger jet. Now such confusion at any accident scene is understandable. What is more, with the craft going 460 mph, added to the shock of it all, it was probably hard to tell what they really saw.

> Of the things that didn't make sense however were the many reports that *the object hit the ground*, when *we know from the photos that it didn't*. Something that was supposed to be as big as a 757 was certainly flying low enough to clip light poles yet it didn't scrape the ground? Something is wrong with that picture.

> Some eyewitnesses even claimed they saw people on the plane and faces in windows!

The many confused descriptions—confused even while declaring it to be a commercial jet—lead us to believe that as long as they could see it with their eyes, it registered as being a passenger plane of some sort. And, even though the propaganda machine tells us that it was supposed to be a huge plane, it was obvious from the descriptive terms used by the witnesses—and by the evidence on the ground—that this was not the case, even if the "impression" was. The descriptions, when taken all together, are full of cognitive dissonance. What we do notice was those who did *not see* the plane, but were still close by and experienced something of the effects of the event had most peculiar "impressions" related to the sound.

> "At that moment *I heard a very loud, quick whooshing sound* that began behind me and stopped suddenly in front of me and to my left. In fractions of a second I heard the impact and an explosion. *The next thing I saw was the fireball.*"[89]

Steve Patterson, 43, said he was watching television reports of the World Trade Center being hit when he saw *a silver commuter jet* fly past the window of his 14th-floor apartment in Pentagon City:

> The plane was about 150 yards away, approaching from the west *about 20 feet off the ground*, Patterson said. He said the plane, which *sounded like the high-pitched squeal of a fighter jet*, flew over Arlington cemetery so low that he thought it was going to land on I-395.

> It was flying so fast that he couldn't read any writing on the side. *The plane, which appeared to hold about eight to 12 people*, headed straight for the Pentagon but was flying as if coming in for a landing on a nonexistent runway, Patterson said.

> "At first I thought 'God, there's a plane truly misrouted from National,' Then this thing just became part of the Pentagon. […] I was watching the World Trade Center go and then this. What's next?"

> He said the plane, which *approached the Pentagon below treetop level*, seemed to be flying normally for a plane coming in for a landing other than going very fast for being so low."

---

[89] http://www.space.com/news/rains_september11-1.html

Then, he said, he saw the Pentagon "envelope" the plane and bright orange flames shoot out the back of the building.[90]

In the above report, we not only have a witness who says the plane looked like a "silver commuter jet", he also said that the plane *sounded* like the "high-pitched squeal" of a fighter jet.

"*I was right underneath the plane*", said Kirk Milburn, a construction supervisor for Atlantis Co., who was on the Arlington National Cemetery exit of Interstate 395 when he said he saw the plane heading for the Pentagon.

"I heard a plane. I saw it. I saw debris flying."[91]

Here he said he saw the plane heading for the Pentagon, and *because he saw it* he also said, "I heard a plane. I saw it. I saw debris flying".

What he said next, however, is not in keeping with a 757: "I guess it was hitting light poles", said Milburn. "It was like a *whoosh whoosh*, then there was fire and smoke, then I heard a *second explosion.*"

Notice that the witness says, "I *guess* it was hitting the light poles". One suspects that he couldn't see it if he was guessing. What is most interesting is that he said, "It was like a WHOOSH whoosh, then there was fire and smoke, then I heard a *second explosion*".

Two early, primary witnesses have described a sound of a "whoosh"! The second one, when he couldn't see it, said it was like a "WHOOSH whoosh", just like the other man who couldn't see it, but then he has also told us that he saw a plane and heard a plane. But what he described was most definitely *not* a 757 flying low over his head.

A 757, under *no* circumstances makes a sound of "whoosh", and if the "whoosh" sound was being made by the hitting of light poles, it is a certainty that if a 757 was doing it, you would not hear the "whoosh" of hitting light poles over the roar of the jet engines. If there's a 757 right overhead that's hitting light poles, and it's going 460 mph, it would not be "whooshing"! Anyone that has ever spent any time at the end of an international airport runway knows that the sound of a large commercial jet flying low overhead would be more accurately described as a deafening ROAR!

In short, if a 757 was low enough to hit light poles, it should have blown the witnesses' eardrums out along with everything else in the engine's way, not to mention the fact that the jet blast can literally blow cars off the road.

Another problem with this part of the story is the following comments from a resident of the DC area:

"I live in the DC area, and the street lights are not very tall. In fact DC is a very 'treed' city. Many of the trees are taller than the lamp posts. [...] If the wings of a 757 were hitting the lamp posts, the engines would be driven into the ground, provided that the plane was in a straight and level position."

---

[90] http://www.washingtonpost.com/wp-srv/metro/daily/sep01/attack.html
[91] Ibid.

The exhaust of those huge engines—that would necessarily be *scraping the ground if they are hitting light poles*—is like a supersonic cannon! The vortex and power of the exhaust would have produced an experience that is unmistakable—impressive beyond words—and hard to forget.

There are two engines on a 757 and they hang lower than the plane fuselage itself.

The interested reader can go to the Boeing website[92] to learn about the jet engine specs, exhaust velocity contours, and so forth. According to CBS News:

> [S]ome eyewitnesses believe the plane actually hit the ground at the base of the Pentagon first, and then *skidded into the building*. Investigators say that's a possibility, which if true, crash experts say may well have saved some lives.[93]

Of course, "officials" have not explained how, in such a case, the Pentagon lawn was left untouched by the *skidding* 82 ton aircraft.

Look again at the photo taken just a few seconds after impact.

---

[92] http://www.boeing.com/assocproducts/aircompat/753sec6.pdf (assuming the information has not been scrubbed by the time you read this, as so much data on the internet has been removed since 9/11).
[93] http://www.cbsnews.com/stories/2001/09/11/national/main310721.shtml

This is the photo that the U.S. government claims shows that a 155 feet long, 44 foot high (at the tail) Boeing 757-200 crashed into the Pentagon.

Our question: *Where is it?*

Look at the cable spools that are positioned just to the right of the impact point (the dark objects in front of the fireball from this view). The spools are approximately 6 feet high and are sitting no more than 20 feet from the Pentagon façade.

Again; where is the plane?

Consider a to-scale image of a 757 placed in the hole caused by the collapse of the burning building some time after initial impact.

The main damage caused was limited to the first ring of the Pentagon.[94] As can be seen from the image, only about 50% of the length of a 757 actually fits into this space. What we would naturally expect to see in the previous photo of the "moment of impact", is, at the very least, some of the remainder of the fuselage, or debris of the wings and the tail of the plane spread across the Pentagon lawn.

But in reality, what do we see?

No trace, whatsoever, of a Boeing 757. No trace, whatsoever, of Flight 77.

---

[94] Remember, the façade collapsed about twenty minutes after the impact.

Among the theories that arose in an attempt to explain these glaring problems with the official story was the U.S. government suggestion that the aircraft was pulverized instantly when it impacted the reinforced façade of the building—never mind that this contradicts the "skidding" theory which, as CBS News said, "according to crash experts, may well have saved some lives". Later, we were asked to consider the possibility that the aircraft melted with the exception of one pristine, if mangled piece of the fuselage that fortuitously was blown onto the Pentagon lawn.

As Thierry Meyssan and his colleagues pointed out in their in-depth analysis of the Pentagon crash, *Pentagate*,[95] *not even the U.S. Department of Defense claims that this part comes from Flight 77.*

---

[95] Thierry Meyssan, *Pentagate* (Londong: Carnot Publishing Ltd., 2002).

At this point, it is instructive to note that, despite the fact that Flight 11 and 175 were completely swallowed by the towers, exposed to massive explosions from the aircraft fuel and finally suffered the destructive force of the collapse of the towers, reports from 'ground zero' at the WTC stated that *entire rows of aircraft seats with bodies in them were discovered in the debris*. Such remains are commonly found at the sites of aircraft crashes, yet at the Pentagon, we are asked to believe that no discernible remains were left. No luggage, no wings, no seats, no sizeable body parts. All that remained of Flight 77 was **one** small turbofan from **one engine** and one small piece of fuselage that looked like it *might* fit an AA commercial aircraft. The rest, we are told, "disintegrated".

Who do these people think they are kidding?

Consider the composite image of the façade of the Pentagon below, where we are asked to believe the ill-fated Flight 77 struck. Note that, while the graphic of the plane has obviously been added, the image of the Pentagon is true to life.[96] Other than the 16 x 24 ft. hole, for the most part, what we see can be termed blast damage: a chunk of the façade has fallen off, many windows have been blown out (although many remain intact) and there is smoke damage to a large area. What is very obviously missing, however, is any trace of the wings or the 44 ft. tall tail stabilizer of a 757 having struck the façade. Look at the façade of the building. Look at the damage, realise that there were little or no large parts of a 757 found anywhere at the site, and ask yourself: could a 757 have crashed here?

That just leaves the matter of the body parts that were allegedly identified and which somehow managed to escape the 2500+ °C fire that we are told melted 100 tons of aircraft metal. Surely if a plane is "vaporized" then the occupants would be vaporized too? Nevertheless, the U.S. government maintains that they were able to identify all of the passengers on Flight 77, *using fingerprints no less*!

---

[96] See the website http://0911.site.voila.fr/index11.htm for an excellent photographic analysis of the Pentagon event.

The initial hole made by the aircraft was *at the very base of the Pentagon wall*. The *only* way that a 757 could have made this hole would be if it had been *sliding on its belly*, which of course would have left very clear marks in the Pentagon lawn. Look again the picture of the collapsed Pentagon façade above. Do *you* see any evidence of a large commercial airliner having slid along the Pentagon lawn?

A series of photographs taken by an official federal photographer at the Pentagon crash site show what appears to be an easily identifiable piece of a small-diameter turbofan engine.

If the government wants to prove that a Boeing 757-200 crashed into the Pentagon, why is no one willing or able to identify which part from which engine this is?

The photographs were taken by Jocelyn Augustino, a photographer for the Federal Emergency Management Agency (FEMA), at the Pentagon crash site on September 13, 2001. The round piece appears to be less than 3 feet in diameter and is propped up against what appears to be part of the engine housing and thick pieces of insulating material.

A Boeing 757 has two large engines, which are about 9 feet in diameter and 12 feet in length. A Rolls Royce RB211-535 engine, used on 757 aircraft, has a fan tip diameter of 78.5 inches. Nothing this large is to be seen in the FEMA photographs. The photo ID numbers are 4414 and 4415 and can be seen on-line.[97]

For those who say a smaller plane or unmanned drone, such as a Global Hawk, was involved in the Pentagon attack, identifying the piece in the photo could prove what kind of aircraft hit the building.

The Global Hawk is a singe-engine drone that uses a Rolls Royce Allison engine hand-built in Indianapolis, Indiana. The AE3007H engine has a diameter of 43.5 inches. The *unmanned* Global Hawk, using a satellite guidance system, is capable of landing *within 12 inches of its programmed destination*.

---

[97] www.photolibrary.fema.gov/photolibrary/advancedsearch.do

Several investigators suggested that the disk was from the auxiliary power unit (APU) mounted in the tail section of a Boeing 757.

Christopher Bollyn of *American Free Press* undertook the task of trying to find out what exactly this disk was. He called Honeywell's Aerospace division in Phoenix, Ariz., where the GTCP331-200 APU used on the 757 aircraft is made:

"There's no way that's an APU wheel", an expert at Honeywell told AFP.

The expert, who cannot be named, added: "That turbine disc—there's no way in the world that came out of an APU".

Bollyn then contacted John W. Brown, spokesman for Rolls Royce (Indianapolis), asking if the disk was from a Rolls Royce manufactured engine, perhaps the AE3007H used in the Global Hawk. Brown's response was:

"It is not a part from any Rolls Royce engine that I'm familiar with, and certainly not the AE 3007H made here in Indy."

Next Bollyn called Pratt & Whitney who manufactures parts of the 757's turbofan jet engines:

"If the aircraft that struck the Pentagon was a Boeing 757-200 owned by American Airlines, then it would have to be a Rolls Royce engine", Mark Sullivan, spokesman for Pratt & Whitney, told AFP.

Bollyn then contacted John W. Brown, spokesman for Rolls Royce once more, to inform him that the Pratt & Whitney spokesperson had stated that it must be a piece of a Rolls Royce engine. At this point Brown balked and asked who at Pratt & Whitney had provided the information.

Asked again if the disc in the photo was a piece of a Rolls Royce RB211-535, or from the AE 3007 series, Brown said he could not answer.

Bollyn then *asked Brown if he was actually familiar with the parts of an AE 3007H, which is made at the Indiana plant: "No", Brown said. "I don't build the engines. I am a spokesman for the company. I speak for the company."*

Bollyn states:

Rolls Royce produces the RB211-535 engines for American Airlines 757-200 aircraft at a plant in Derby, England. Martin Johnson, head of communications at Rolls Royce in Derby, said he had followed the story closely in *American Free Press* and had also been notified in advance by Rolls Royce offices in Seattle and Indianapolis.

However, rather than address the question of the unidentified disc, Johnson launched a verbal attack on this reporter for questioning the government version of events at the Pentagon on 9/11. "You are the only person in the world who does not believe that a 757 hit the Pentagon", Johnson said. "The idea that we can have a reasonable conversation is beyond your wildest dreams", Johnson said and hung up the phone.[98]

The conclusion then is that the engine disk in the FEMA photos is probably *too small to be part of a 757 engine and it is definitely **not** a part of a 757's*

---

[98] http://www.americanfreepress.net/10_10_03/Controversy_Swirling/controversy_swirling.html

APU. So what is it? It could very well be part of a Global Hawk AE3007H engine. To date however, no one has been able to confirm or disprove this.

Because the Global Hawk is a *surveillance drone*, the engine is contained in a heavily insulated housing designed to be *extremely quiet*. This corresponds with eyewitness reports. *American Free Press* asked eyewitness Steve Riskus, who said he was within 100 feet of the aircraft, what he heard. He said he *"did not recall hearing anything".* As noted previously, if a 757 or jet fighter flew at high speed 100 feet from an eyewitness the sound would be deafening.

The important thing is, if you have ever seen a 757 up close, the main words you will use—even if it passes you at 460 mph—are "humongous", or "gigantic"—words along that line. You will also—even at a distance—be overwhelmed by the noise of the jet engines. Yet, over and over again, even those who later *named* the object that hit the Pentagon as a "commercial airliner" used descriptive terms that are quite different from those that would have been used if a real 757 had been the impacting object. This could easily be a consequence of the "memory making" process mentioned earlier.

The fact is, until the spin control machine had done its work, except for a few government officials, most of the witness' descriptive terms are more in keeping with descriptions of *something other than a Boeing 757.*

Witnesses who saw only one plane fall into two distinct groups, each seeing a different plane, on a different path, at different altitude, with different sound, at different speeds. *A third set of witnesses saw two planes approach the Pentagon and one of these veer away.*

Many heard a jet; others heard a missile (all military men). Those near Flight 77 as it came over the cemetery, saw it and *heard it pass silently* (no engine); whereas those near the killer jet which came by the freeway and knocked down the lamp posts *heard its loud scream as it put on speed* to reach the wall as an airliner flew over it.

Nevertheless, again we say, we do *not* think it was a missile that struck the Pentagon: *we are certain that it was a plane*—it had wings—it knocked over poles on the incoming trajectory, and it maneuvered "like a smart missile". Furthermore, we know that there is a "guidance system" that has the capability of doing exactly what this object was described to have done even if the system was loaded into something other than a missile. *The average cruise missile is far too small* (about 20 feet long with a wingspan of just 8 feet) to be a realistic contender for the Pentagon plane *and is therefore ruled out.*

One problem with the idea that it was an UAV like the Global Hawk that impacted the Pentagon is how to explain the damage that *was* inflicted not only to the façade but to 3 rings of the Pentagon. Whatever hit the Pentagon created a hole of approximately 15 feet across in the façade and extensive damage to the first floor of the first ring (as evidenced from previous photographs) which eventually collapsed. While the size of the hole and the limited overall damage is not consistent with a Boeing 757, neither is it consistent with an aircraft the size of a Global Hawk.

The Global Hawk is 44 feet long with a wingspan of 115 feet and a tail height of 15 feet and, *alone*, it could not have caused the damage to the Pentagon.

One of the most intriguing aspects of the Pentagon attack was the round hole that was left in ring C.

Bizarrely, the U.S. government claims that an engine of a 757 made this hole, yet as we have seen, remains of the engine of the aircraft that hit the Pentagon were found at the *front* of the building and possibly in the first ring that sustained the main force of the impact, *not* in the third ring where clearly *something else* must have punched out this hole. Whatever it was, it had enough force to breach the main reinforced steel concrete outer wall and then travel some 250 feet, *passing through five other double-brick walls on the way*. In fact, Terry Mitchell, Chief of the Office of the Assistant Secretary of Defense

(Public Affairs) was one of the first on the scene at this "punch out" point. In a DOD news briefing about the reconstruction of the Pentagon he stated:

"This is a hole in—there was a punch-out. They suspect that this was where a part of the aircraft came through this hole, *although I didn't see any evidence of the aircraft down there.*"

Yet later in the same briefing when referring to the same hole he stated:

"This pile here *is all Pentagon metal. None of that is aircraft whatsoever.* As you can see, they've punched a hole in here. This was punched by the rescue workers to clean it out". [99]

So which was it? Was the hole punched out by some part of the aircraft or by rescue workers? Look again at the picture of the hole. We don't need the contradictory statements of Mr. Mitchell to conclude that the hole was punched out from the inside, yet how could it have been "punched out" by rescue workers when there are *scorch marks* at the top of the hole *on the outside*? Did the rescue workers punch out this hole when the fire was still raging inside?

Hardly likely. Limiting air flow is part of fighting a fire. You don't make holes to let in more air while you are trying to extinguish a fire.

Dare we suggest that the OASD chief was lying that day? He changed his story because the "official" version of events did not include the idea that part of the aircraft made that hole, because it is inconceivable that any part of a 757 could have done so.

So what did?

While the Global Hawk is an unmanned reconnaissance plane, an article from 2002 on the Center for Defense Information (CDI) web site stated that initial designs for the craft included the possibility for it to carry "three to six missiles". [100]

Eyewitness to the Pentagon attack and Pentagon worker Don Perkal was on the scene within minutes:

"Even before stepping outside *I could smell the cordite.* Then I knew explosives had been set off somewhere."

He also stated:

"Hundreds of F.B.I., Secret Service and Defense Department plainclothes investigators were deployed in the parking lot, *recording witness statements.*"[101]

Another eyewitness, Gilah Goldsmith said:

"We saw a huge black cloud of smoke", adding that it *smelled like cordite,* or gun smoke. [102]

---

[99] http://www.defenselink.mil/transcripts/2001/t09152001_t915evey.html

[100] http://www.cdi.org/missile-defense/uav.cfm

[101] http://www.mcsweeneys.net/2001/09/19perkal.html We would like to note here that this gave the FBI and other intell agencies a list of names and the capability of "leaning" on witnesses to ensure that they would say what they were "supposed" to say.

[102] http://web.archive.org/web/20021116175404/http://www.jewishsf.com/bk010921/usp14a.shtml

Witnesses inside the Pentagon, mostly military men, described *a shockwave and a blast*. The problem is that *only explosives create a shockwave*; there is no shockwave from a crash and fire. *The Washington Post* ran a story where it was stated:

> Air Force Lt. Col. Marc Abshire, 40, a speechwriter for Air Force Secretary James Roche, was working on several speeches this morning when he felt the blast of the explosion at the Pentagon. His office is on the D ring, near the eighth corridor, he said. "It shot me back in my chair. There was a huge blast. *I could feel the air shock wave of it*", Abshire said. "I didn't know exactly what it was. It didn't rumble. It was more of a direct smack."[103]

Donald R. Bouchoux, 53, a retired Naval officer, Great Falls resident, Vietnam veteran and former commanding officer of a Navy fighter squadron, was driving west from Tysons Corner to the Pentagon for a 10 a.m. meeting. He wrote:

> "At 9:40 a.m. I was driving down Washington Boulevard (Route 27) along the side of the Pentagon when the aircraft crossed about 200 yards (should be more than 150 yards from the impact) in front of me and impacted the side of the building. There was an enormous fireball, followed about two seconds later by debris raining down. *The car moved about a foot to the right when the shock wave hit.*"

John Bowman, a retired Marine lieutenant colonel and a contractor, was in his office in Corridor Two near the main entrance to the south parking lot. "Everything was calm", Bowman said. *"Most people knew it was a bomb.* Everyone evacuated smartly. We have a good sprinkling of military people who have been shot at."[104]

Stars and Stripes reporter Lisa Burgess was walking on the Pentagon's innermost corridor, across the courtyard, when the incident happened. "I heard two loud booms—one large, one smaller, and *the shock wave threw me against the wall*", she said.[105]

Lon Rains, an editor of Space.com, was also an eyewitness to the Pentagon attack. He commented:

> "In light traffic the drive up Interstate 395 from Springfield to downtown Washington takes no more than 20 minutes. But that morning, like many others, the traffic slowed to a crawl just in front of the Pentagon. With the Pentagon to the left of my van at about 10 o'clock on the dial of a clock, I glanced at my watch to see if I was going to be late for my appointment. At that moment I *heard a very loud, quick whooshing sound* that began behind me and stopped suddenly in front of me and to my left. In fractions of a second I heard the impact and an explosion. The next thing I saw was the fireball. *I was convinced it was a missile.* It came in so fast *it sounded nothing like an airplane.*"[106]

---

[103] http://www.washingtonpost.com/wp-srv/metro/daily/sep01/attack.html
[104] http://www.dcmilitary.com/army/pentagram/6_37/local_news/10380-1.html
[105] http://www.pstripes.com/01/sep01/ed091201i.html
[106] http://www.space.com/news/rains_september11-1.html

While these testimonies are intriguing, eyewitness accounts of any major incident, particularly one as shocking as the Pentagon attack, are notoriously unreliable. Yet the fact remains that, even without them, the actual observable damage at the Pentagon leads us to conclude that some kind of explosive charge or hardened warhead was used to do the damage. A warhead that was very probably carried and released just seconds before impact, by an unmanned Global Hawk aircraft painted up in AA colors, complete with fake windows, just for good measure.

There were at least *four video cameras capable of recording the attack on the Pentagon.* One was on the roof of the Sheraton Hotel, a second was at a gas station across the road from the Pentagon itself, the third belonged to the Virginia Department of Transportation and was stationed on route 27, which the aircraft flew over. The fourth was the Pentagon's security camera stationed at the opposite one end of the façade from where the plane struck.

The footage from the cameras at the Sheraton, the gas station and on route 27 were confiscated by the FBI and have never been released.

The first footage made available to the public was that recorded by one of the Pentagon's two security cameras.

The image below shows the first still from the first video footage of the Pentagon attack released by the U.S. government. According to the U.S. government, it shows an approaching Boeing 757 in the upper right hand corner.

Sep. 12, 2001, 17:37:19   plane

If we think back to the images and video footage of Flight 11 and Flight 175 hitting the WTC towers, we remember that we all saw both large Boeing

767 airplanes, as clear as day, even though they were flying at over 500 mph and were over 1,000 feet up in the air when they struck the WTC Towers. This provides us with an excellent guide on how such commercial aircraft appear at that distance. The side of the Pentagon is 971 feet long and the plane in the footage is no more than 750 feet (250 yards) from the camera that is stationed near the opposite end of the Pentagon. Remember the indelible images of those huge planes flying into the World Trade Center towers? Even at that distance, even with the size of the WTC towers, the image and size of the aircraft that was burned into our minds from having seen the tapes replayed endlessly is awe-inspiring.

So, look again at the image from the Pentagon Security camera of the plane approaching the building.

Again we must ask the question: where is the Boeing 757-200 in this image?

Next time you are at an airport, take five minutes and go and look at some planes on the runway. Pick out a large passenger jet that is approximately 750 feet away, preferably one in the process of taking off or landing. Take a picture of it. Then think about this image from the Pentagon Security camera again and ask yourself.

Where *is* that Boeing 757?!

Now look at a close up.

Do you see a Boeing 757-200 in this picture?

If a Boeing 757 really did hit the Pentagon, it would stick out like, well... like a Boeing 757 in this footage, *but the simple and obvious fact is that there is no Boeing 757 there.*

In fact, there is no plane of *any* description in the footage released by the Pentagon.

Note that the time stamp displays a date and time of *September 12 at 5:37:19 p.m.* The DOD *has offered no reason for this discrepancy.* In the footage, the progression of seconds jumps from 19, where it starts, to 21 and then on to 22 and 23 where it ends.

What is clear from the *3 seconds of footage* is that one second and an undetermined number of frames have been cut from the film.

No explanation has ever been offered by the DOD or the U.S. government as to why this video footage has clearly been "doctored", why one second and several frames have been removed—frames that would likely show just what it was that struck the Pentagon.

What we do see in the above image is a stream of white smoke that is *en-*

tirely inconsistent with a commercial jet aircraft at ground level and much more in line with the trail left by a missile launch, even if we keep repeating that something *more* than a "missile" struck the Pentagon.

In May 2006, the Pentagon released what it (and many mainstream news sites) claimed was additional (grainy) video evidence of "Flight 77 hitting the Pentagon". No great analysis of the "evidence" was needed since there was precious little new data. The "evidence" comprised the same images as we have discussed above and additional footage from that camera showing the aftermath of the impact and explosion, and footage from a second security camera at more or less the same location. This second camera footage was new, and it is claimed that in this footage the "nose cone" of "Flight 77" can be seen. After the "nose cone" appears from the right of the frame, there is nothing more to seen other than the same explosion as can be seen in the first camera footage. Essentially then, the "nose cone" is meant to be further, and we assume conclusive, "proof" from the U.S. government that "Flight 77 hit the Pentagon". Below is an image of this "nose cone":

I don't know what else to say other than, "do they really think we are so stupid?" The bottom line is this: The U.S. government claims that Flight 77 hit the Pentagon on 9/11, yet the only videos of the event that they are prepared to release, appear to confirm what we have been saying all along: there is *no Boeing 757 in this video footage.*

The facts are the following: the FBI is in possession of *at least* four tapes, from cameras at different locations that would clearly show what hit the Pentagon. The FBI (on instruction from the federal government) continues to refuse to release all of these videos and chooses instead to release footage form just two videos from Pentagon security cameras. These cameras show 'something' that in no way matches the description of a large Boeing 757. Consider the below image into which a fake, yet correct-to-scale Boeing 757 has been inserted. If a Boeing 757 really did hit the Pentagon, why do we not see something like this in the Pentagon security camera footage?

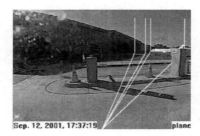

Conclusion? A Boeing 757 did not hit the Pentagon, and for some reason, the U.S. government is very reluctant to show the public what did hit.

As it happens, a correspondent of one of the authors[107] had an interesting encounter on a train that goes along with the story about the military transport plane that so "luckily" spotted the "Boeing". In his own words:

> "I met a gentleman that was of Jamaican descent who said he was an artist by trade. He was heading back home to Washington. I have no reason to doubt the man's story as he seemed very sincere and told it 'as a matter of fact'.

> "He said that when he heard on the radio of his car about the WTC event that the tension around the capital was rising, he was on his cell phone talking to other people while he drove. *He was in viewing distance of the Pentagon at the time of the attack and he saw two planes in the air,* one of them being a 'small commuter type jet' but he didn't ID the other plane. He said *it was this smaller plane that hit the Pentagon,* so it could have been laced with explosives and remote controlled in by that other plane (there were reports of a C-130 in the area)."

Summing up the eyewitness reports and the available photographic evidence, we see that *there is nothing that supports the official story's claim that Flight 77 hit the Pentagon* except the claims of the Bush Administration who

---

[107] Laura Knight-Jadczyk

have repeatedly been exposed as liars and manipulators, and the later "eye-witness reports" of people whose names and addresses were immediately compiled into a list by the FBI, Secret Service, and other intell units on the scene.

The early eyewitness reports that came out before the official story began to be trumpeted via the media are consistent with the object having been a plane much smaller than Flight 77, such as a drone loaded with explosives. The reports were made before "damage control" was firmly in place, and this damage control either served to influence and change people's perceptions, or compelled them to change their stories. The reports that it was a commercial jet only emerged later—hours later, even.

The claim that Flight 77 hit the Pentagon is extremely suspect for another reason: as previously noted, there is *no proof* that the plane that disappeared from radar over Southern Ohio actually "turned around" and headed back for Washington. A *Washington Post* article discusses the thirty minutes of complete radar invisibility. The report says, in part:

> The aircraft, traveling from Dulles International Airport to Los Angeles, was hijacked sometime between 8:50 a.m.—when air traffic controllers made their last routine contact with the pilot—and 8:56, when hijackers turned off the transponder, which reports the plane's identity, altitude and speed to controllers' radar screens. The airliner crashed into the Pentagon at 9:38 a.m., about 12 minutes after controllers at Dulles sounded an alert that an unidentified aircraft was headed toward Washington at high speed. [...]
>
> *With no signal on their radar screens, controllers did not realize that Flight 77 had reversed direction.*
>
> At 9:09 a.m., unable to reach the plane by radio, the Indianapolis controller reported a possible crash, sources said.
>
> The first time that anyone became aware an aircraft was headed at high speed toward Washington was when the hijacked flight began descending and entered airspace controlled by the Dulles International Airport TRACON facility, an aviation source said.
>
> The first Dulles controller noticed the fast-moving plane at 9:25 a.m. Moments later, controllers sounded an alert that an aircraft appeared to be headed directly toward the White House. It later turned and hit the Pentagon.[108]

The report from the *Washington Post* also contradicts other reports which said that the radios transmitted sounds of voices with Arabic accents making threatening sounds.

---

[108] http://www.washingtonpost.com/ac2/wp-dyn?pagename=article&node&contentId=A32597-2001Nov2

"Unlike at least two of the other aircraft, whose pilots apparently held radios open so controllers could hear the hijackers, there was only silence from Flight 77."

However, one must take the other stories of hijacker voices with a grain of salt. There is no proof that the 19 Arab men alleged to have committed this crime were ever on the planes.

THE NEXUS OF FANTASY AND REALITY

What then are we to make of the many calls that were alleged to have been made by passengers of the doomed flights citing "Arab hijackers", most notably the call by the wife of former Solicitor General Bob Olson, Barbara Olson? (We'll get back to her later.) Firstly, it has been effectively demonstrated scientifically that it is extremely difficult to make cell phone calls from above 8,000 feet. Almost all the alleged cell phone calls were claimed to have been made from well above this height. We aren't going to discard the idea that some cell phone calls did make it through, but expert opinion within the wireless telecom industry casts serious doubt on the likelihood that many of the calls could have been made. According to Alexa Graf, a spokesman of AT&T, commenting in the immediate wake of the 9/11 attacks:

> "It was almost a fluke that the [9/11] calls reached their destinations... From high altitudes, the call quality is not very good, and most callers will experience drops. Although calls are not reliable, *callers can pick up and hold calls for a little while below a certain altitude*".[109]

In 2004, *Aviation Week* magazine described how a U.S. phone company and AA were attempting to develop the technology to allow commercial aircraft passengers to use their cell phones in-flight:

> Qualcomm and American Airlines are exploring [July 2004] ways for passengers to use commercial cell phones in-flight for air-to-ground communication. In a recent 2-hr. proof-of-concept flight, representatives from government and the media used commercial Code Division Multiple Access (CDMA) third-generation cell phones to place and receive calls and text messages from friends on the ground.

---

[109] http://wirelessreview.com/ar/wireless_final_contact

For the test flight from Dallas-Fort Worth, the aircraft was equipped with an antenna in the front and rear of the cabin to transmit cell phone calls to a small in-cabin CDMA cellular base station. This "pico cell" transmitted cell phone calls from the aircraft via a Globalstar satellite to the worldwide terrestrial phone network.[110]

Needless to say, this technology was not available to the passengers of the doomed 9/11 flights. Despite this, Ted Olson claimed that his wife made two calls from Flight 77 telling of the "Arabs" conducting the hijacking:

> "She [Barbara] had trouble getting through, because *she wasn't using her cell phone*—she was *using the phone in the passengers' seats*", said Mr. Olson. "I guess she didn't have her purse, because *she was calling collect*, and she was trying to get through to the Department of Justice, which is never very easy." [...] "She wanted to know 'What can I tell the pilot? What can I do? How can I stop this?'"

The problem with this account is, if Mrs. Olson had neither her cell phone nor her credit card with her, she could not possibly have made a call to anyone because a credit card is required before *any* connection from the satellite phones in airline passenger seats can be made.

The 9/11 Commission yet again, completely overlooked all of these facts. We aren't saying that Barbara Olson did not call her husband, but we will come to that issue soon.

So if some of the calls could have been real, and some could have been faked, how can that be?

Consider a 1999 report in the *Washington Post* entitled, "When Seeing and Hearing Isn't Believing", where it was stated:

> "Gentlemen! We have called you together to inform you that we are going to overthrow the United States government." So begins a statement being delivered by Gen. Carl W. Steiner, former Commander-in-Chief, U.S. Special Operations Command.

> At least the voice sounds amazingly like him.

> But it is not Steiner. It is the result of voice "morphing" technology developed at the Los Alamos National Laboratory in New Mexico.

> By taking just a 10-minute digital recording of Steiner's voice, scientist George Papcun is able, in near real time, to clone speech patterns and develop an accurate facsimile. Steiner was so impressed, he asked for a copy of the tape.

> Steiner was hardly the first or last victim to be spoofed by Papcun's team members. To refine their method, they took various high quality recordings of generals and experimented with creating fake statements. One of the most memorable is Colin Powell stating, "I am being treated well by my captors."

> *"Once you can take any kind of information and reduce it into ones and zeros, you can do some pretty interesting things"*, says Daniel T. Kuehl, chairman of the Information Operations department of the National Defense University in Washington, the military's school for information warfare.

---

[110] http://www.aviationnow.com/avnow/

Digital morphing — voice, video, and photo — has come of age, available for use in psychological operations. PSYOPS, as the military calls it, *seek to exploit human vulnerabilities in enemy governments, militaries and populations to pursue national and battlefield objectives.*

To some, PSYOPS is a backwater military discipline of leaflet dropping and radio propaganda. To a growing group of information war technologists, *it is the nexus of fantasy and reality. Being able to manufacture convincing audio or video, they say, might be the difference in a successful military operation or coup.*[111]

"The nexus of fantasy and reality" indeed. Given the scope and depth of the conspiracy with which we are dealing, it is entirely possible that the cell phone calls that were made from the planes on 9/11—*if* those reporting them are sincere and believe they received such calls—were actually the result of a 'real time' application of this *voice morphing technology.*

Who could forget the rousing reports of the "soldier citizens" on Flight 93 who courageously decided to "do something" about the hijackers with the words "let's roll"?

One of those involved was Mark Bingham, a California PR executive. According to his mother, Bingham called her to tell her that his flight had been hijacked. Bizarrely however, the very first words that Bingham said to his mother, with whom he was very close by all accounts, were, "Hi Mom, this is Mark Bingham."[112]

The only other words he said before hanging up were, "I love you".[113]

Now think about this: Why would anyone use their full name when calling their mother?? Would you, in a similar circumstance, call your mother and announce your full name? Really stop and think about it a moment. Could this small and seemingly innocuous detail in fact, be an example of one of the many flaws in the cover-up plans of the conspirators?

Since we keep facing this type of thing, over and over again, on that day of "incredible coincidences" that are off the scale of mathematical probability, it's time to stop thinking about "coincidences", and amazing flukes, and violations of the laws of physics, and start thinking about what really happened on 9/11: a *coup d'état.*

The bottom line is, there are just too many problems with the Pentagon attack that indicate that it could not have been a Boeing 757 that ploughed into the building. This leads us to the most interesting questions.

If it was not a Boeing 757 that hit the Pentagon, why is the Bush administration so assuredly declaring that it was, and attacking anyone who questions that story with the slur of "conspiracy theorist", rather than providing the evidence that it was Flight 77 for the public to examine themselves? We notice that very few items of so-called "conspiracy theory" have rattled the "Bushes" quite like our *Pentagon Strike* Flash did. The *Pentagon Strike* video

[111] http://www.washingtonpost.com/wpsrv/national/dotmil/arkin020199.htm
[112] http://www.markbingham.org/legend.html
[113] http://www.guardian.co.uk/september11/story/0,11209,610356,00.html

came out on August 23, 2004. Probably nobody really noticed it at that point, but it hit a chord of response in the hearts of millions of people around the world. They began to madly download and forward it to their friends and relatives. Latest stats on how many people have viewed it to date are over 500 million!

Apparently it even landed in the email box of the Editor of the *Washington Post*, which is why Carol Morello sent me[114] an email asking for an interview. Or so she said. My suspicion was that the Post was instructed to do "damage control", albeit oh, so gently!

Now, look at this mini-timeline:

August 23, 2004: Pentagon Strike Video which propagates wildly for a month.

September 21, 2004: First contact by Carol Morello of the *Washington Post*

October 7, 2004: *Washington Post* article[115]

October 19, 2004: George Bush visits New Port Richey[116]—a previously unscheduled "whistle-stop" on his campaign trail. NPR just happens to be my hometown.

It was an interesting situation to know that if they hadn't seen the *Pentagon Strike* before, certainly George and Dick, Karl and the gang were watching it after the *Washington Post* wrote an article about it.

My initial feeling was that Dubya's visit to my little home town—certainly of *no* importance on the campaign trail—was deliberately done to send a message to me. Fact is, my daughter's ex-boyfriend wrote to tell her that he had been among those selected to shake the hand of George W. himself! Now, how's that for a coincidence?

As to exactly what Carol Morello wrote to me, here is the pertinent passage which is actually quite revealing:

A couple of editors here saw the video/film, and I was asked to find out what I could about it.

As you can imagine, we continue to have an intense interest on the attack on the Pentagon and the people who were affected.

I've just begun reporting, so it would be premature to tell you what "perspective" my story would have. My initial impressions are that *the questions and theories expressed in the video got a spurt of attention in early 2002, after the publication of a best selling book in France, then the furor died down for a while, and now they have re-emerged with the extraordinarily wide dissemination of this video on the Internet.*

The 911 Commission report appears to have done little to dampen the controversy. I hoped to speak to you about how and why you posted it on your web site, what kind of response you've received and what you think about it. [...]

Notice that she attributes the resurgence of interest in the "Pentagate" problem to the *Pentagon Strike* video.

Can we say "damage control"?

---

[114] Laura Knight-Jadczyk
[115] http://www.washingtonpost.com/wp-dyn/articles/A13059-2004Oct6.html
[116] http://www.sptimes.com/2004/10/20/Decision2004/A_George_Bush_kind_of.shtml

And if there is damage control, then that means there is damage.

Up to this point in time, the only acknowledgement the administration ever gave to such issues was to refer vaguely and dismissively to "conspiracy theories". Now, suddenly, it seems that dealing with the "conspiracy theories" in a direct manner was seen to be imperative. "9/11: Debunking the Myths"[117] came out in *Popular Mechanics Magazine* in March of 2005, just five months after the *Washington Post* article. That's pretty fast work!

Under the tutelage of Editor-in-Chief Jim "Oh look, a tank!" Meigs, *Popular Mechanics* assembled a team of researchers, including "professional fact checkers" (impressive, eh?) to debunk the 16 most common claims made by conspiracy theorists about 9/11.

Unsurprisingly, the PM editors claim that, in the end:

> [W]e were able to debunk each of these assertions with hard evidence and a
> healthy dose of common sense. We learned that a few theories are based on
> something as innocent as a reporting error on that chaotic day. Others are the
> byproducts of cynical imaginations that aim to inject suspicion and animosity
> into public debate.

In fact, a careful analysis of the article shows that at most, just three of the sixteen claims could have been the result of "reporting error", forcing us to assume that, in the razor-like, emotionally unclouded cerebrum of Jim Meigs, at least 13 of the conspiracy claims about 9/11 are the result of "cynical imaginations aiming to inject suspicion and animosity into public debate".

The sad fact is that, while *Popular Mechanics* claims to be interested in understanding what really happened that day, their rebuttal of sixteen of the most common claims by so-called "conspiracy theorists" about 9/11 isn't worth the $3.57 of server space that it has so far cost them to publish it.

If there is one glaring hole in the arguments put forward by 9/11 conspiracy "debunkers", it is the fact that such people have *never* come up with a reasonable argument to explain *why*, in the wake of 9/11, so many obviously intelligent citizens became gripped by the uncontrollable urge to continually waste their time recklessly and fecklessly "injecting suspicion and animosity into public debate" for no apparent reason. It really is a mystery. Maybe they're trying to take over the world or something.

On the other hand, it doesn't take a degree in psychology to understand the primary motivations of the conspiracy debunkers.

You see, the very last thing that many Americans (and others) *want* to believe is that their government would attack its own people. For 9/11 "debunkers", logic and intellect have *no* part to play in investigating the question of what really happened on 9/11. It's pure emotion all the way.

In the beginning, on the morning of September 11, 2001, we were all united in our emotional reactions: shock, horror, grief (and not to forget: jubilation from a bunch of Israeli Mossad agents and former Israeli Prime Minister Netanyahu). As the emotion subsided, most went on with their lives, but a

---

[117] http://www.popularmechanics.com/science/defense/1227842.html?page=1&c=y

few stood on, brows furrowed, scratching their heads. After considerable
digging and research, it became obvious that the official story did not satisfactorily answer all of the questions, and the fact that officials were refusing
to answer those outstanding questions, gave rise, logically enough, to a "conspiracy theory". Not long thereafter, the debunkers stepped in, *not* because
they had the answers to the outstanding questions, but because it was their
job to act like they had their emotional buttons severely poked by the fact that
someone was saying that their government was lying!

Sadly, the editors at *Popular Mechanics* are no different, and their little
fear-inspired rebuttal of 9/11 conspiracy theories is of little actual use to *anyone*, least of all to those who really do want to know the truth of 9/11. Far
from approaching the matter with an open mind (which is crucial in any attempt to find the truth), it is clear that *Popular Mechanics'* "professional fact
checkers" *began* with the premise that the U.S. government was *not* lying
about the main events of 9/11, *despite all of the evidence to the contrary.*
From there, the objectivity and integrity of their research went sharply down-
hill as they busied themselves with hunting down the *very same sources that
provided the official story* to confirm that the official story was in fact correct. Apparently, in "debunkerland", it is completely reasonable to ask U.S.
government representatives to testify that the U.S. government is squeaky
clean and then present that evidence as "fact". It is also kosher, we assume, to
have a murder suspect double as a credible expert defense witness in his own
murder trial.

For those of you who have looked unemotionally at the events of 9/11, it is
not unusual to be left wondering how those members of the U.S. government
who were clearly complicit in the murder of 2,750 of their own citizens can
remain so smug and seemingly self-assured. To find the answer we need look
no further than the Jim Meigs of this world.

You see, it is people like Meigs who lack any love or appreciation for the
truth and worship only their subjective, psychopathic view of the world that
make it so easy for big government to commit big crimes. At present there
are millions of Americans and others around the world who, aided by the
years of psychopathic social conditioning and media mind programming,
drew a very clear line around what they would and would not believe about
their government and country. Most of what was inside the line was "feel
good" stuff about "greatest democracy on earth" and other jingoistic nonsense, with perhaps a few admissions that "sometimes bad things happen"
and "not everyone is a saint". This mindset provided (and continues to provide) a perfect opportunity for psychopathic U.S. politicians to literally get
away with murder of which most of the U.S. public refuse to believe they
were, and are, capable. The result is that, for all intents and purposes, today
there are two Americas:

1. The America of the average American citizen which is little more than a
psychopathically manipulated, government-provided dream world.

2. The real America of the corrupt politicians and the select few who run the country, and much of the rest of the world.

Luckily for the select few, the elite at the top that wish to maintain control of the masses, this second, real America just happens to lie outside of what many ordinary Americans are willing or able to believe is possible. Lest anyone think otherwise, the setting up of any accusation against government as being the domain of "conspiracy nuts" is not the result of pure coincidence. Conspiracy theories are as old as the first lie ever told and the subsequent attempts by the liar to avoid exposure. "Am I my brother's keeper?" Most people think that "conspiracy theories" are made up by "conspiracy theorists", but the term "conspiracy theory" is most often used by those people who have most to gain from the ridicule of the allegations that are directed at them. The tactic has been used to such great effect over the years that certain high crimes committed by government have become the touchstone by which all other "conspiracies" are measured.

Take the folks at *Popular Mechanics*. In dealing with 9/11 they simply couldn't resist referencing that other most despicable crime committed by a U.S. government—but of course, to them it just another "theory":

> Don't get me wrong: Healthy skepticism is a good thing. Nobody should take everything they hear--from the government, the media or anybody else--at face value. But in a culture shaped by Oliver Stone movies and "X-Files" episodes, it is apparently getting harder for simple, hard facts to hold their own against elaborate, shadowy theorizing.

Did you catch it? The reference to Oliver Stone can mean only one thing: Jim's "fact checkers" contacted the CIA, and they told him straight up that some bullets really can do magic things.

So far, we have been generous to the people at *Popular Mechanics*. We have assumed that they are simply well-intentioned but misguided souls. However, it appears that there is a more sinister, and dare we say it, "conspiratorial" side to *Popular Mechanics'* "innocent" debunking of 9/11 conspiracy theories. You see, it turns out[118] that one of the main contributors to the article is one Benjamin Chertoff, a cousin of the new Department of Homeland Security Chief Michael Chertoff. *American Free Press'* Christopher Bollyn, who dug up the information, also claims that Ben Chertoff's mother was a Mossad agent.[119] While there is, as of yet, no evidence of any working relationship between the two, it is certainly noteworthy that the cousin of the current Homeland Security Chief (who, in his previous incarnation as head of the Justice Department's criminal division was instrumental in the release of obvious Israeli spies before and after 9/11) happens to be behind a high-profile attempt to debunk 9/11 conspiracy theories.

So if you happen to stop by and read the sorry article in question, don't be fooled or intimidated by the word "science" in big bold letters on the *Popular*

---

[118] http://www.rense.com/general63/bellchert.htm
[119] http://www.etherzone.com/forum/index.php/topic,3280.msg35630.html#msg35630

Mechanics page. In Europe, McDonald's drink cups have the words "I'm loving it" emblazoned across them in various languages, regardless of what you put in them.

Credit by association or juxtaposition is one of the oldest tricks in the book of mass mind programming. Just because "they" say it, doesn't make it so. This simple, logical statement is a salient lesson for us all in these heady days where disinformation masquerades as truth and even "innocent" fun-loving "boys with toys" have become obedient workers in the lie factory.

According to another 9/11 researcher:

> The editors of *Scientific American* followed in the footsteps of *Popular Mechanics* in exploiting a trusted brand in order to protect the perpetrators of the mass murder of 9/11/01. The column by Michael Shermer in the June, 2005 issue of *Scientific American*, titled *Fahrenheit 2777*, is an attempt to deceive the magazine's readers into dismissing the overwhelming evidence that 9/11 was an inside job without ever looking at that evidence. More specifically, Shermer attempts to inoculate readers against looking at the decidedly scientific refutation of the official story....

> Shermer's column exhibits many of the same propaganda techniques as the ambitious feature article in the March issue of *Popular Mechanics* by Benjamin Chertoff, for which Shermer professes admiration:

> "The single best debunking of this conspiratorial codswallop is in the March issue of *Popular Mechanics*, which provides an exhaustive point-by-point analysis of the most prevalent claims."

> Comparing the two attack pieces is instructive. Both pieces mention a similar range of issues, with Shermer adding Jewish conspiracy rumors and UFOlogists to the mix. Both employ the following three deceptive techniques, but with different emphasis.[120]

Shermer uses an array of deceptive methods to persuade the reader that challenges to the official story of the 9/11 attack are worthy only of ridicule and should not be scrutinized. His primary technique is to use hoaxes and unscientific ideas to "bracket" the valid ideas from which he seeks to shield the reader. That Shermer went to such great lengths to thoroughly misrepresent the painstaking, scientific, evidence-based work of many researchers is a testament to the success of the *Pentagon Strike* video! It really stepped on a sore toe.

And that tells us something important, the same thing Carol Morello of the *Washington Post* wrote about the *Pentagon Strike* video:

> "...the questions and theories expressed in the video got a spurt of attention in early 2002, after the publication of a best selling book in France, then the furor died down for a while, and now they have re-emerged with the extraordinarily wide dissemination of this video on the Internet."

We notice that *never*, in any of the two major "debunking" articles that followed fast on the heels of the *Pentagon Strike* video, was our website mentioned. Other books, other researchers, other websites *were* mentioned, but

---

[120] http://911research.wtc7.net/essays/pm/index.html

the *deliberate avoidance* of *Signs of the Times*—the origin of the *Pentagon Strike*—was conspicuous.

In *Thirteen Techniques for Truth Suppression* by David Martin, author of *America's Dreyfus Affair*, we read:

> Strong, credible allegations of high-level criminal activity can bring down a government. When the government lacks an effective, fact-based defense, other techniques must be employed. The success of these techniques depends heavily upon a cooperative, compliant press and a mere token opposition party.
>
> *Dummy up.* If it's not reported, if it's not news, it didn't happen.
>
> *Wax indignant.* This is also known as the "how dare you?" gambit.
>
> *Characterize the charges as "rumors" or, better yet, "wild rumors".* If, in spite of the news blackout, the public is still able to learn about the suspicious facts, it can only be through "rumors".
>
> *Knock down straw men.* Deal only with the weakest aspect of the weakest charges. Even better, create your own straw men. Make up wild rumors and give them lead play when you appear to debunk all the charges, real and fanciful alike.
>
> *Call the skeptics names like "conspiracy theorist," "nut," "ranter," "kook," "crackpot," and of course, "rumor monger."* You must then carefully avoid fair and open debate with any of the people you have thus maligned.
>
> *Impugn motives.* Attempt to marginalize the critics by suggesting strongly that they are not really interested in the truth but are simply pursuing a partisan political agenda or are out to make money.
>
> *Invoke authority.* Here the controlled press and the sham opposition can be very useful.
>
> *Dismiss the charges as "old news."*
>
> *Come half-clean.* This is also known as "confession and avoidance" or "taking the limited hang-out route." This way, you create the impression of candor and honesty while you admit only to relatively harmless, less-than-criminal "mistakes." This stratagem often requires the embrace of a fall-back position quite different from the one originally taken.
>
> *Characterize the crimes as impossibly complex and the truth as ultimately unknowable.*
>
> *Reason backward, using the deductive method with a vengeance.* With thoroughly rigorous deduction, troublesome evidence is irrelevant. For example: We have a completely free press. If they know of evidence that the Bureau of Alcohol, Tobacco, and Firearms (BATF) had prior knowledge of the Oklahoma City bombing they would have reported it. They haven't reported it, so there was no prior knowledge by the BATF. Another variation on this theme involves the likelihood of a conspiracy leaker and a press that would report it.
>
> *Require the skeptics to solve the crime completely.* For example: If Vince Foster was murdered, who did it and why?
>
> *Change the subject.* This technique includes creating and/or reporting a distraction.

The timing of these articles—immediately following the wild popularity of the *Pentagon Strike* video—is too "coincidental" to not be connected. Again we point out: debunkers are sent in only when damage control is needed. And damage control is only needed when it is thought that there *might* be damage.

That means that the *Pentagon Strike* is understood clearly, in the minds of the perpetrators, to be the weak link in their chain of lies. Debunkers are sent in *not* to give answers to the outstanding questions, but to push the emotional buttons of the public, to reassure people who really want "a reason to believe" that their government is not lying to them.

Why would George Bush and his gang be so resistant to an *impartial* investigation? (The official investigation cannot be considered impartial. See David Ray Griffin's book *The 9/11 Commission Report: Omissions and Distortions.*)

Why was all the evidence of the crime scene immediately destroyed even though the government claims that "their experts" were taking care of everything and doing a "full forensic investigation"?

Why can't we see the various films of the event that certainly exist from numerous security cameras in the area?

Why is the public denied full access to *all* the information about the crime? After all, if the perpetrator of a crime has been identified—as the Bush Administration certainly claims is so—there should be nothing about the crime scene that would need to be withheld in order to catch the criminal, right?

If there is so much *certainty* about the perpetrators, why not let the public know all the details that prove the perfidy of the guilty?

If Islamic Fundamentalists with burning hatred in their hearts for the Great Satan, the United States, had (or have) the ability to pull off something on the scale of the attacks of September 11, *where's the beef?* Show us! Inspire us to stand behind the government in going out and taking care of such evildoers! If their claims are true, it could only help the Administration's case to release the evidence, right?

So why all the stonewalling, all the back-pedalling, debunking and secrecy? If actions are undertaken in good faith with the honest purpose of discovering the truth, there is no need for carefully guarded secrecy. In such circumstances, *only the guilty seek the darkness of secrecy to hide their crimes.*

The whole thing has been so "managed", so quickly "figured out" and cleaned up and put away, that it stinks to high heaven of a "sales job".

Can it be that the public has been "sold" an answer—the answer that the Bush Administration wants them to believe and has arranged, with the complicity of the mass media, to out-shout any other explanation? And if they can't out-shout them, to smear them, to marginalize them, to defame them, to out them, and perhaps, even to murder them?

Many citizens of the United States did not seem to have any problem at all believing that some crazed Islamic fundies hijacked four planes in the Most Powerful Nation on Earth, flew them around for extended periods of time, flew two of them into the World Trade Center Towers, and that North America's entire air defense simply failed. So why stonewall on the evidence?

But, let's assume that's what happened. Let's also give the Administration the benefit of the doubt about their hurried naming of the perpetrators and their too quick destruction of the crime scene.[121] Let's assume that their experts did handle everything well, and they just have some psychological need for secrecy, or that there *is* some compelling reason to stonewall a proper investigation.

We are still faced with the sticking point here: hypothesizing that somebody went to the trouble to arrange for a couple big jets to hit the World Trade Center, and the public was shown the films of these jets hitting said buildings over and over again, *why was the attack on the Pentagon so "different" in scope and evidence, most particularly the absence of repeatedly showing the attack on television?*

Why can't we see the surveillance videos of the same type of commercial jet hitting the Pentagon?

We are stuck with a marvellous conundrum. If no 757 hit the Pentagon, why is the government claiming it did? After all, if they can sell the rest of the flimsy story, and if something *other* than Flight 77 hit the Pentagon, there is no reason they couldn't have cooked up a story to back up that fact. If Osama bin Laden, from his cave in Afghanistan, could so "coincidentally" do the *real* thing on the very day that all the military exercises simulating hijacked airliners were being run so that his operation was hidden from the U.S. defense under that smokescreen, there is no reason to not propose that he could also have gotten his hands on some kind of military craft to strike the Pentagon.

Let's assume that it *was* a smaller or different type of plane that hit the Pentagon. No matter who was behind the events, if they did not use a 757 to strike the Pentagon, *why?*

If they (whoever "they" are) were able to commandeer large airliners for the WTC, why not use one for the Pentagon? Certainly, if it was Osama and gang, they would probably prefer the flying whale option to do the most damage (we've already made note of the fact that, as Burning Fundies, they failed miserably when they hit the Pentagon, doing so little damage), unless, of course, they actually wanted to deliver a nuke or some other type of charge, in which case a military type craft would have been preferable.

Now here we are going to go in a couple of different speculative directions, so bear with us.

When we just sit back and look at the situation on that day, turn off the noise, the claims and counter-claims, there is one thing that strikes us again and again as the single major difference between the strikes on the WTC towers and the Pentagon: the differences in *the extent of the destruction.*

In intell parlance, that is what *is*. Those are the "facts on the ground".

---

[121] The remains of the central core and floors of the Twin Towers were carted away and shipped to China as scrap before investigators had time to analyse the evidence. The reader might want to ask him/herself, "in whose interest was it to clean up the evidence before it could be analyed?"

Referring back to the rules of intell gathering, "if it happens, it was planned that way". So, let's ask a question: could there be a reason for this? In other words: *cui bono?*

The first thing we notice when we compare the two events—that is, the attack on the Towers and the attack on the Pentagon—is that the World Trade Center towers were *totally destroyed,* and there was enormous loss of life (even if that is not completely explained by the impact of two jetliners, which we will get to further on), while the Pentagon only had a small hole, and the collapse of a section that was not even fully occupied because it was still under construction. We have already noted this supreme failure on the part of the suicidal "Islamic Fundies" who could plan such an extraordinary operation and yet do such limited damage to the Pentagon, the "heart of the Great Satan".

So, let us speculate that doing limited damage to the Pentagon was *intended.* Total destruction of the WTC as opposed to minimal destruction and damage, or "targeted" destruction of a small, specific area of the Pentagon, was also intended.

We can also speculate with some confidence that doing limited damage to the Pentagon was undoubtedly *not* the objective of Fundamental Islamic Terrorists who were ostensibly giving up their lives to strike at the heart of the "Great Satan" with a burning hatred for the United States and its freedoms. They certainly would want to do as much damage as possible.

So the first logical conclusion—based on the facts on the ground—is that it was not Islamic terrorists striking at the heart of the Great Satan behind the attack on the Pentagon.

We must then ask the question: Why a strike on the Pentagon at all? Why would the conspirators want to totally destroy one target—where civilians were the main victims—and only partly destroy another where one would think that crazed Islamic Fundies would want to do the most damage?

What could that reason be?

What immediately comes to mind is this one of the oldest tricks in the criminal play book: *self-inflicted injury as an alibi.* This strategy is so old that it is one of the first things criminal detectives consider when beginning their investigations. There are cases across the board of people falsely claiming to be the victims of crimes—insurance fraud is a good example—and this tactic is a favourite of psychopaths. It is also pure Machiavelli and as old as time. The story of Joseph being sold into slavery comes to mind once again. Not only did the guilty brothers claim that he was killed by wild animals, they took his coat and smeared blood on it to make the point.

This bit of speculation leads us to the possible answer as to *why* a different type of craft might be used in the strike on the Pentagon: *the necessity for precision so as to inflict an exact amount of damage, no more, no less.*

So let us theorize that *precision* was the *major concern* in the strike on the Pentagon, and that is why a different attack device was utilized.

Which brings us back to the idea of *a plane that had onboard smart missile guidance system—a system that can guide its carrier to literally turn corners and hit the target with such precision that "it is amazing"*.

Theorizing that precision was a major concern—precision of the type that can hit an exact window on a designated floor and do an exact and designated amount of damage—we arrive at the idea that such precision and limitation was *essential* for some reason.

The fact is that the buildings that represent not only America's status in the world, but also America's ability to maintain that status—i.e. its military organization—were hit by alleged terrorists. The emotional reaction of the masses of citizens was that the U.S. not only had a right to strike back with all its power, but also that it *must*. That is also "what *is*". The masses of pedestrian thinkers do not look at the possibility of a self-inflicted wound being an alibi.

But that brings us back to the problem of why—assuming it was done with something other than a commercial jet—it could not be claimed that Osama did even that? It would have been so easy to do!

Since no claim was made that Osama got his hands on a military (or other) craft in an attempt to deliver a warhead to the Pentagon, and since the damage was so limited and so minimized even in publicity terms, we have to look elsewhere for the solution to this problem.

What if there was someone—or something—in the Pentagon that someone wanted to destroy?

We notice that the Navy lost its new command center.

We wonder, of course, if the Navy ONI was one agency that had not been compromised by the Neocon invasion of Washington. Could that be one of the reasons that the Naval Command Center was destroyed? Consider the following:

> "It's easy to imagine an infinite number of situations where the government might *legitimately give out false information*", the Solicitor-General, *Theodore Olson*, told the court on Monday. "It's an unfortunate reality that the issuance of incomplete information and even *misinformation* by government may sometimes be perceived as necessary to protect vital interests."[122] (emphasis ours)

Al Martin's book *The Conspirators* is a secret history of the late 20th century and an uncensored version of what really goes on in the back rooms of realpolitik brokers and gofers. In his book, Al writes that contrary to popular belief, ONI is *the most powerful U.S. intelligence agency*:

> "The ONI already had a deep existing covert illegal structure. They had a mechanism before the CIA even existed. They had contacts in foreign intelligence services and in foreign governments that the CIA never could have hoped to obtain.

> "The only people the CIA wouldn't step on to accomplish their aims was ONI. They would easily subvert an FBI or DEA investigation, but never ONI, because they were frightened of them....

---

[122] http://story.news.yahoo.com/news?tmpl=story&u=/020323/79/1ao0k.html

"ONI is where the real deep control is. It's where the real deep secrets are kept. That was what ONI always did the best. Keeping secrets. Accumulating secrets. Warehousing secrets for the purposes of control."

When I asked him "what secrets?" he replied, "one thing I can tell you is the ONI was instrumental in dethroning former Mexican President Louis Portillo. Portillo got very friendly with George Bush and the CIA, and *ONI had never aligned with the Bush faction.* I know what people think, but that's not true. From what I can tell, it has never been aligned, but has always been hostile to that Eastern Country Club Bush Cabal and their friends in the CIA. The Bill Casey faction is the George Bush-Allen Dulles Faction".[123]

We notice that George H. W. Bush was a Navy man—a pilot—but that the ONI never admitted him to their club. In 1945 George H. W. Bush and 44 other agents from the OSS joined what was then known as the Super program, which later became the CIA. We ought to also note that the CIA is taking the "blame" for 9/11, which is actually a very good cover. It could very well indicate that the CIA is, in fact, more involved in the conspiracy than we are led to believe.

So we can speculate, therefore, that the targeting of the ONI offices in the Pentagon on 9/11 was an act of internal warfare against the ONI, either by some section of the U.S. intelligence agencies, or by Israeli intelligence. Not a very nice idea, is it? That the United States has been taken over by a *coup d'état,* that the secrets of the ways and means of keeping "American Freedoms" may have been destroyed in the WTC and in a few selected rooms of the Pentagon.

Basically, the self-inflicted, limited damage hypothesis has actually split into two lines of thinking: that of alibi, and that of intentional murder, which may, in fact, just be two sides of the same coin.

If we consider the alibi conjecture, we include the idea that precision was necessary to insure the safety of *certain* occupants of the building. If you inflict an injury on yourself to allay suspicion, you don't want to make a mistake and blow your head off!

In short, one line of this split hypothesis proposes that a number of the conspirators were *in the Pentagon at the time it was hit,* or that certain *targets* were in the building, and this was the reason for a different "mode of attack"—a precision strike. And it is possible that both objectives could be served with a precision strike.

We notice that Newsweek coyly mentions that:

On Sept. 10 [...] a group of top Pentagon officials suddenly canceled travel plans for the next morning, apparently because of security concerns.[124]

San Francisco mayor Willie Brown was warned off flying that day as well.[125]

---

[123] http://www.almartinraw.com/uri1.html
[124] http://www.msnbc.com/news/629606.asp?cp1=1
[125] "Early Warning - State Department memo warned of terrorist threat" Phillip Matier, Andrew Ross, Chronicle Staff Writers, SFGate.com, Friday, September 14, 2001

If what we have theorized is true, it's not likely that they cancelled their travel plans because they might get on the wrong jet—after all, according to them, they didn't know about a possible terrorist attack—but rather to assure that they would be in place for their alibi—or their destruction. We would be very interested to know who those guys were.

Without data we can't answer these questions, but the fact is, with either of these two lines of conjecture, we still face the same dilemma: if Flight 77 did not hit the Pentagon, if it was a different type of craft, why could it not be claimed that Osama did even that? It would have been so easy to do! It would have painted Osama and the Islamic fundies in such evil colors that the whole world would have gone after them, including France and Russia! What's more, imagine the publicity value of the miraculous preservation of the Pentagon from an evil nuke strike by that clever Osama, holed up in his underground fortress with unlimited resources to outfox the entire United States military and intell services!

But nope, assuming that this theory is correct, for some reason, the obvious thing to do—show *all* the evidence and still blame Osama—was *not* done. We will return to this question.

Since the publication of our *Pentagon Strike* Flash presentation mentioned above, we have been inundated with emails from some of the over *500 million people* that have seen it to date. By far the most common question we are asked is: *if it wasn't Flight 77 that hit the Pentagon, then what happened to the **real** Flight 77 and its occupants?*

We will return to this question later, although it should be clear to the attentive reader at this point that this is the central mystery, but first, in order to approach this problem with sufficient data and mental coolness, the reader might wish to first consider:

WHAT REALLY HAPPENED TO FLIGHT 93?

We have already presented some information that supports the likelihood that Flight 93 was shot down, yet this still leaves the question as to *why* Flight 93 was shot down. If, as now seems clear, the terrorist attacks of 9/11 were in fact carried out by a faction of the U.S. government,[126] and assuming that the order to shoot down Flight 93 was given by the conspirators themselves, why would they shoot down an aircraft that was essentially on a covert mission? If they shot this flight down, why were the other three flights left to complete their missions? (Assuming they actually *did* complete their missions.) Surely the drama of the "hijacking" of Flight 93 was not deliberately planned to have such an inauspicious ending being harmlessly scattered across the Pennsylvania countryside?

In the context of 9/11 as an inside job, it seems much more likely that Flight 93 was originally meant to attack a fourth high-profile American

---

[126] We'll look at Israeli involvement below.

landmark; most likely the White House. In fact, in the midst of the confusion on the morning of 9/11, *there were reports of fire and an explosion at the White House.* Meyssan writes in *The Big Lie*:

> On 11 September, at 9:42 am, ABC broadcast live images of a fire that had broken out in the White House annex, the Old Executive Building. The television network contented itself with showing a fixed shot of plumes of black smoke escaping from the building. No information has ever leaked out concerning the origin of the blaze, or its exact scale. No one has had the presumption to blame the fire on a kamikaze plane. A quarter of an hour later, the Secret Service took Dick Cheney from his office and ordered the evacuation of the White House and its annex.

It is entirely possible that these reports[127,128] were accurate and, just like the report of the initial explosion at the Pentagon, a bomb or incendiary device of some sort had been detonated at the White House in anticipation of the attack by Flight 93. Perhaps the explosion was supposed to coincide with the crash of Flight 93 into the building, and a glitch caused the explosive to go off earlier, or the glitches on Flight 93 caused a failure of the plane to arrive on schedule.

So why shoot it down? The most plausible reason is that the real mission of Flight 93 was compromised in some way, and the decision was taken to prematurely end its active participation in the attack. Dave McGowan closes his article on Flight 93 thusly:

> Assuming that some General somewhere didn't get the hare-brained notion that it was actually his duty to defend the country against these attacks, why would a plane be shot down that was for all intents and purposes on a covert mission for the very people who would have ordered the downing of the aircraft?

> If this were the case, then there would be only one reason for shooting the flight down: to destroy any and all evidence in the event that the mission became compromised for any reason.

> And how, you may wonder, might the mission be compromised?

> One possible scenario could be if, say, the passengers were able to disarm the hijackers and take control of the plane.

> That would conceivably leave dozens of *eyewitnesses to what really happened* on those planes that fateful day. The contents of 'black boxes' can be suppressed quite easily; a parade of eyewitnesses, particularly eyewitnesses rightly viewed as American heroes, is another matter entirely.

> As disturbing as it may be to contemplate, the answer to the question of what really happened to flight 93 could be that it *was shot down precisely because the passengers were able to overpower the hijackers,* or at least were making an attempt to do so. It could be that the very heroism for which they have been cynically praised by the Bush regime may have earned them a summary execution.[129]

We agree, with the one proviso that we suggest the possibility that there were *no hijackers* on the planes. What would have happened if the plane had landed safely with no hijackers on board?! Talk about compromising a mission!

---

[127] http://www.pbs.org/newshour/extra/features/july-dec01/bombing_background.html
[128] http://tinyurl.com/s92lf
[129] http://davesweb.cnchost.com/wtc5.html

The official version of events holds that all four flights were hijacked by Arab terrorists, yet there are a host of reasons why this is extremely unlikely. Not least among these is the fact that none of the alleged pilots had shown the aptitude to master control of a single-engine Cessna much less a large commercial airliner as reported by flight instructors at the flying schools were they alleged "learned to fly", added to the fact that a number of the alleged hijackers are reportedly alive and well and were nowhere near a plane on that fateful morning. The fact that so few members of the public are aware just how difficult it is to fly such a large aircraft greatly helped in the successful dissemination of this unlikely scenario.

Equally unlikely is that, armed only with box cutters, four or five hijackers on each flight could have successfully subdued trained pilots and crew and dozens of passengers. In fact, the term "box cutter" is not entirely accurate, at least for Flight 11.

According to the British *Telegraph* newspaper,[130] the only weapons that the would-be hijackers on that flight had were individual razor blades that they had smuggled onto the plane hidden in wash bags in their hand luggage. The hijackers then used these razor blades, we are told, to fashion "deadly knives" by *attaching them to flimsy plastic credit cards*, of all things, which they then used to cow the 11 crew and 81 passengers of Flight 11. We are not told exactly what they used to attach the blades to the credit cards, perhaps it was scotch tape, or super glue or bubble gum. But there you have it: a conspiracy theory if we ever heard one!

Of course, some passengers, on at least one of the flights, allegedly claimed that the "hijackers" had a bomb, yet is it credible that a hijacker who couldn't get anything more threatening than a razor blade on-board had somehow smuggled a bomb aboard unseen?

We are also expected to believe that these improvised and surely ineffective weapons were later used to "stab" and kill Daniel Lewin, *an ex-member of the Israeli Defense Force's Sayeret Matkal, a top-secret counterterrorist unit*, and two flight attendants.[131]

According to the official story, it was by pure chance that Lewin was given a seat directly in front of and directly behind two of the hijackers. An Israeli counter-terrorist expert on a hijacked flight with Islamic terrorists sitting in the seats directly in front of and behind him—who could have imagined it?! Of course, one wonders about his status as an "ex-member," and therefore, his expendability.

Now think about this: There was a total of ninety-two passengers and crew on Flight 11. Five slightly-built "hijackers" jumped up with razor blades taped (or bubble-gummed) to credit cards, and managed to kill three people, subdue the rest, and overpower the pilots. Could ninety-two people, who surely had many items in their hand luggage or as part of the aircraft's

[130] http://www.telegraph.co.uk/news/main.jhtml?xml=/news/2001/09/16/watt16.xml
[131] http://www.upi.com/inc/view.php?StoryID=06032002-121706-8744r

equipment that they could have used as weapons, not have overcome five men with razor-blades precariously attached to credit cards!?

We are further asked to believe that, without the aid of any navigational instruments, the untrained hijackers were able to pinpoint their targets from 35,000 feet in the air. Anyone that has ever been on a commercial airliner and looked out the window at the ground below will understand just how unlikely this proposition is.

The official story further stretches the boundaries of belief by suggesting that, somehow, on all four planes, the hijackers were able to stand up, subdue the passengers, bypass the crew, break into the cockpit, overpower the pilots and turn off the transponders, all before the pilots were able to send a distress signal that the flight was being hijacked (a procedure that takes about three seconds to complete).

Another troubling discrepancy is the fact that, on all four "hijacked" flights, none of the names of the alleged hijackers appear on the publicly released *official passenger lists* of those flights. In the case of Flight 77 the names of the hijackers did not even appear on the autopsy list provided by the Armed Force Institute of Pathology.[132]

Flight attendant on Flight 11 Madeline Amy Sweeney allegedly called Boston ATC to report the hijacking. The only problem being that, while the FBI claims that there were five hijackers on Flight 11, Ms. Sweeney allegedly described only four. In addition, a BBC article states that the seat numbers she gave were different from those allegedly registered in the hijackers' names.[133] Efforts have been made by independent researchers to get the final flight manifests from these planes, but all such requests have been refused.[134]

There is also the problem of how exactly the 19 alleged hijackers got onto the flights in the first place. To check in and board a flight in the U.S. some form of photo ID is required. The name on the ID must match the name on the ticket and the photograph on the ID must match the face of the holder. If none of the alleged hijackers are recorded as having been on the flights, how does anyone know that there actually were any hijackers on the flights? Where did the FBI get the names, dates of birth and photographs of the 19 alleged hijackers that were published on the FBI website within two weeks of the attacks?

As a *Time Magazine* article, in the aftermath of the attacks, reported:

> U.S. officials are investigating whether the hijackers had accomplices deep inside the airports' "secure areas".[135]

---

[132] http://www.sierratimes.com/03/07/02/article_tro.htm
[133] http://news.bbc.co.uk/1/hi/world/americas/1556096.stm
[134] For more detail on the official flight manifests, and the many unexplained official accounts, see David Ray Griffin's *The 9/11 Commission Report: Omissions and Distortions* (Olive Branch Press, 2005).
[135] http://www.time.com/time/nation/article/0,8599,175953,00.html

Billie Vincent, a former FAA security director, also suggested that the hijackers had inside help at the airports:

> "These people had to have the means to take control of the aircrafts. And that means they had to have weapons in order for those pilots to relinquish control. Think about it, they planned this thing out to the last detail for months. They are not going to take any risks at the front end. They knew they were going to be successful before they started… It's the only thing that really makes sense to me."[136]

Not long after these names were published, at least *seven of the "hijackers" loudly and publicly stated that they were still alive as reported by the BBC in September of 2001*:

> FBI Director Robert Mueller acknowledged on Thursday that the identity of several of the suicide hijackers is in doubt. [137]

Despite this, the same 19 "hijackers" remain on the FBI website to this day!

There is also a problem with alleged chief hijacker Mohammed Atta. In *September of 2002* Atta's father went public with the claim that his son was still alive on September 12, 2001:

> "As I saw the picture of my son," he said, "I knew that he hadn't done it. *My son called me the day after the attacks on September 12th* at around midday. We spoke for two minutes about this and that."[138]

In fact, former Attorney General John Ashcroft went on record, and stated in no uncertain terms, that the United States government has no idea who the hijackers were,[139,140] which, of course, begs the question as to how they know who to retaliate against.

It took the CIA over three years to come up with a video tape of Osama[141] allegedly accepting responsibility for the 9/11 attacks. Prior to this, bin Laden had steadfastly denied that he was in any way involved.[142] Of course, the timing of the video could not have been any better for the Bush administration: October 29, 2004, just three days before the U.S. Presidential election, which, given the reports of serious voting irregularities in Ohio and elsewhere, would appear to have been the second time that the Bush camp stole the Presidency.

Former CBS NEWS anchorman Walter Cronkite summed up the reality of the situation during an interview on CNN in October 2004 when he stated:

> "I am inclined to think that Karl Rove, the political manager at the White House, who is a very clever man, he probably set up bin Laden to this thing."

136
http://web.archive.org/web/20011009220602/www.miami.com/herald/special/news/worldtrade/digdocs/002594.htm
[137] http://news.bbc.co.uk/2/hi/middle_east/1559151.stm
[138] http://www.guardian.co.uk/september11/oneyearon/story/0,12361,784541,00.html
[139] http://transcripts.cnn.com/TRANSCRIPTS/0109/28/se.20.html
[140] http://www.globalsecurity.org/military/library/news/2001/09/mil-010913-usia18.htm
[141] Refer back to the voice and videotape morphing technology on this item.
[142] http://www.taipeitimes.com/News/us/archives/2001/09/17/103315

Unsurprisingly, interviewer Larry King did not ask Cronkite to elaborate on the provocative election-eve observation.[143]

It may come as a surprise to many to realize that, while Osama bin Laden appears on the FBI's website of most wanted people, he is not wanted in connection with the 9/11 attacks. When questioned by an internet journalist in June 2006 about this strange fact, an FBI spokesperson stated: "The reason why 9/11 is not mentioned on Usama Bin Laden's Most Wanted page is because the FBI has no *hard evidence* connecting Bin Laden to 9/11."[144]

THE THREE TOWERS

Designed originally as part of an urban renewal project, the Twin Towers were one of New York's best-known landmarks, rivaling the Statue of Liberty and the Empire State Building. In the early 1960's, David Rockefeller, *then president of Chase Manhattan Bank* and grandson of oil magnate John D. Rockefeller, enlisted his brother Nelson Rockefeller, *then governor of New York*, to build the WTC complex. As Eric Darton, author of *Divided We Stand: A Biography of New York City's World Trade Center* states, "The trade centre got built through a combination of a giant banker and a political giant."

Oddly enough however, the Rockefellers were never the official owners of their creation. The complex was built by the New York Port Authority, a bi-state government agency, which appears to have owned the complex from the beginning until just 2 months before the 9/11 attacks when, for the first time ever, it was sold to Larry Silverstein, a private property developer, for $3.2 billion on a 99 year lease. Silverstein is a former leader of the *United Jewish Appeal*, the largest Zionist organization dedicated to raising money and support for Israel. Lewis Eisenberg is the former chairman of the New York Port Authority and the man who personally supervised the negotiations that delivered the 99-year lease to Silverstein. 'Coincidentally', Eisenberg is also a former leader of the *United Jewish Appeal*.

Since 9/11, Silverstein has been involved in legal attempts to get $7 billion in insurance for the destruction of the WTC towers. In late 2004, Silverstein was tentatively awarded $2.2 billion. However, the ruling keeps open the possibility that Silverstein could eventually receive as much as $6.4 billion for his trouble.

The impossibility of the WTC Towers collapsing from the impact of aircraft impact and fire has been well documented. In fact, many structural engineers have expressed their shock and surprise at the fact that the towers

---

143

http://www.google.co.uk/url?sa=t&ct=res&cd=3&url=http%3A//www.whatreallyhappened.com/binladen_cronkite.html&ei=JMUhQ7yFJJ6kiAKuy6ydAw
[144] http://www.teamliberty.net/id267.html

collapsed as a result of the aircraft impacts or fire. The towers were in fact deliberately designed to be able to withstand the impact of a large commercial aircraft!

Frank A. Demartini, on-site construction manager for the World Trade Center, who died in the 9/11 attacks, spoke of the resilience of the towers in an interview recorded on January 25, 2001:

> *"The building was designed to have a fully loaded 707 crash into it.* That was the largest plane at the time. ***I believe that the building probably could sustain multiple impacts of jetliners*** because this structure is like the mosquito netting on your screen door—this intense grid—and the jet plane is just a pencil puncturing that screen netting. It really does nothing to the screen netting."[145]

The centers of the WTC towers were built with large steel beams extending from the foundations up to the top of both buildings. These beams are the skeleton of the buildings to which each floor is attached via trusses.

The core was designed to support the entire weight of the buildings several times over. Far more than a mere "service core", it comprised 47 steel box columns tied together at each floor by steel plates, similar to the 52" deep spandrel plates that tied the perimeter columns together. The largest of these core columns were 18" x 36", with steel walls 4" thick near the base, tapering in thickness toward the top, and anchored directly to the bedrock.

The official government reason given for the collapse of the twin towers is that structural failures occurred on the impacted floors due to infernos of 800°C. Yet, as reported in the *South Bend Tribune* on November 22, 2004:

> A laboratory director from a South Bend firm has been *fired for attempting to cast doubt on the federal investigation into what caused the World Trade Center's twin towers to collapse* on September 11, 2001. Kevin R. Ryan was terminated Tuesday from his job at Environmental Health Laboratories Inc., a subsidiary of Underwriters Laboratories Inc., the consumer-product safety testing giant.
>
> Ryan wrote that the institute's preliminary reports suggest the WTC's supports were *probably exposed to fires **no hotter than 500 degrees***—only half the

---

[145] http://www.freepressinternational.com/wtc_11152004_manager_88888.html

1,100-degree temperature needed to forge steel, Ryan said. That's also much cooler, he wrote, than the 3,000 degrees [Fahrenheit] needed to melt bare steel with no fire-proofing.

'This story just does not add up,' Ryan wrote in his e-mail to Frank Gayle, deputy chief of the institute's metallurgy division, who is playing a prominent role in the agency investigation. *'If steel from those buildings did soften or melt, I'm sure we can all agree that this was certainly not due to jet fuel fires of any kind, let alone the briefly burning fires in those towers.'*[146]

In February of 2005, an electrical fire in Madrid's 8th tallest building (350 feet) burned for *18 hours*. While the building also had a core of steel beams, it was naturally much less sturdy than the 1,300 feet tall WTC towers. [147]

At the peak of the Madrid fire, the temperature reached 800°C. Despite this, *only after 18 hours* did six upper floors collapse, and when they did, as one might expect, they collapsed *around* the core steel beams that they were attached to. Of course, unlike the WTC towers, the Madrid building did not suffer any initial damage to its core beams.

According to Tomasz Wierzbicki, director of the Impact and Crashworthiness Laboratory at M.I.T., the aluminum wings and the planes' fuselage would have been almost instantly shredded into pieces the size of an adult's fist, with the engines and other heavy parts continuing to the core. But by working out the amount of energy involved, Dr. Wierzbicki and a student, Liang Xue, determined that *at most only half of the inner columns could have been broken or severely mangled.*[148]

---

[146] http://inn.globalfreepress.com/modules/news/article.php?storyid=1059
[147] http://news.scotsman.com/latest.cfm?id=4127075
[148]

http://www.nytimes.com/2001/11/11/nyregion/11COLL.html?ex=1126584000&en=be2140f5f59 3be38&ei=5070&pagewanted=2&ei=1&en=6e7e84802c73aed6&ex=1006447757&oref=login

Obviously then, after the initial impact of the planes into the WTC towers, the steel core beams were still able to support the weight of the upper floors and the towers remained standing. The fact is that after the initial impact and fireball, *the fires in both WTC towers burned for a relatively short period of time* (South tower 56 minutes, North tower 85 minutes) and *were diminishing in intensity all the time* as is evidenced by the thick black smoke that issued from the towers—evidence of an *oxygen-starved fire* and, therefore, a *relatively cool fire*.

So the WTC core beams were damaged by the impact of the planes, but not badly enough that the beams could not support the upper floors, and the resulting fires burned at approximately 500 degrees for about an hour each. *Then, for no apparent or explicable reason, both towers fell into their own footprints.*

Anyone that has watched the footage of the WTC collapse cannot but remark on the surprising way in which the towers fell. It was as if *the steel cores* of the buildings, the 'skeleton' that holds them up, *suddenly disappeared* and the body of the buildings were left to collapse straight down with nothing to resist them but thin air. This brings us to the other "Achilles' heel" of the official government version of what happened on 9/11.

The footage of the collapse of the 1,300 ft. WTC towers has been played and replayed *ad nauseum* and is etched in all of our minds. If by some miracle you have not seen the footage, it is freely available on the various memorial DVDs of the 9/11 attacks. It is also available for download from our web site.[149] I strongly suggest that you avail yourself of a copy and study the collapse of both towers. What you will see is that from the start point of the collapse until there is nothing but fresh air where the towers used to be, *about 10 seconds elapse*. Physicists tell us—based on repeated experiments since the time of Galileo and his famous Leaning Tower of Pisa experiment—an object in 'free fall' i.e. falling through thin air, will take a specific amount of time to reach the ground. The laws of gravity dictate that a 5-ton SUV, for example, and a 1 lb rock, given that their relative densities are so much higher than the resistance presented by the surrounding air, will take approximately the same time to reach the ground when dropped from the same height. The time, t, required for an object to fall from a height, h, (in a vacuum) is given by the formula $t = \operatorname{sqrt}(2h/g)$, where g is the acceleration due to gravity. Thus an object falling from the top of one of the towers (taking $h = 1306$ feet and $g = 32.174$ ft/sec2) would take 9.01 seconds to hit the ground. Of course, this is in a vacuum, with no air present. Allowing for the resistance of the air we would have to add on a few seconds. Yet according to the government's 9/11 Commission report,[150] the south tower collapsed *in 10 seconds flat. But,* as we all saw, the collapse of the south tower 'pancaked' through the 75 lower floors of the tower. *Those undamaged floors below the impact zone would have offered resistance that is thousands of times greater than air.* What time

[149] http://www.signs-of-the-times.org/signs/south_tower_collapse.mpeg
[150] http://www.9-11commission.gov/report/911Report.pdf

might we allow for the section above the impact point that collapsed to pass through each floor? 1 second each floor? If so, then the collapse should have taken 75 + 10 seconds, or over 1 minute and 20 seconds.

For the sake of argument, let's allow just a half second delay in the collapse provided by each 'pancaked' floor.[151] In this case it should have taken 37.5 + 10 seconds. But let's be really charitable and suggest that each floor below the impact point offered just $1/10^{th}$ of a second resistance to the section that first began to 'pancake' on the lower floors. In this case the collapse should have taken 7.5 + 10 seconds for a total of 17.5 seconds. Yet this is not what happened. As the official 9/11 report states and as we all saw, *the towers collapsed in just 10 seconds!*

How can this be possible? The *only* explanation is that the floors below the impact point *offered no resistance whatsoever* allowing the building to fall in 'free fall' with only fresh air as resistance. The only way that *this* could have occurred is if the support offered by the steel core beams was in some way undermined. The most obvious way to undermine the steel core beams of the WTC tower would seem to be via the techniques employed by demolition experts to take down buildings and have them fall into their own 'footprint'—which is exactly what happened to the WTC towers. However, in the case of the WTC towers there are several factors that point to something other than standard technology being used to demolish towers.

For anyone that has seen a controlled demolition, the fact that explosives are used is very evident, with plumes of dust and debris being ejected and a series of resounding 'booms' of explosive charges detonating just before the building falls. What appear to be small explosions were observed below the collapse point. Notice the anomalous "puffs" of explosive smoke to the right and in the center front of the building, below the collapsing wave in the photo below.

---

[151] For a scientific analysis of this problem that gives a conservative estimate of a 30.6 second required collapse time, see: http://janedoe0911.tripod.com/BilliardBalls.html

If we hold to the official version, these 'squibs' have no obvious explanation. They do, however, fit very well with what we would expect to see in a planned demolition. Added to this are the many reports from firefighters and civilians who reported hearing and witnessing explosions going off inside the building before the towers collapsed.[152] These reports were finally released by the City of New York, i.e. the U.S. government, after a prolonged campaign by families:

> "*We thought there was like an internal detonation, explosives, because it went in succession, boom, boom, boom, boom, and then the tower came down…* It actually gave at a lower floor, not the floor where the plane hit." *Firefighter Edward Cachia.*

> "There was just an explosion in the south tower. *It seemed like on television when they blow up these buildings.* It seemed like it was going all the way around like a belt, all these explosions." *– Firefighter Richard Banaciski.*

> "I saw a flash, flash, flash at the lower level of the building. *You know like when they demolish a building?*" *– Assistant Fire Commissioner Stephen Gregory*

> "*It was like a professional demolition where they set the charges on certain floors* and then you hear 'Pop, pop, pop, pop, pop'." *– Paramedic Daniel Rivera.*

Among the reports of explosions throughout the building there were many reports of explosions in the basement areas of the towers. For example, janitor William Rodriguez reported that he and others felt an explosion below the first sub-level office at 9:00 am, after which co-worker Felipe David, who had been in front of a nearby freight elevator, came into the office with severe burns on his face and arms yelling, "Explosion! Explosion! Explosion!"[153] Rodriguez's account was corroborated by José Sanchez, who was in the workshop on the fourth sub-level. Sanchez said that he and a co-worker heard a big blast that "sounded like a bomb," after which "a huge ball of fire went through the freight elevator".[154]

Engineer Mike Pecoraro, who was working in the sixth sub-basement of the North tower, said that after an explosion he and a co-worker went up to the C level, where there was a small machine shop. "There was nothing there but rubble," said Pecoraro. "We're talking about a 50 ton hydraulic press— gone!" They then went to the parking garage, but found that it was also gone. Then on the B level, they found that a steel-and-concrete fire door, which weighed about 300 pounds, was wrinkled up "like a piece of aluminum foil." Having seen similar things after the terrorist attack in 1993, *Pecoraro was convinced that a bomb had gone off.*[155]

152

http://www.nytimes.com/packages/html/nyregion/20050812_WTC_GRAPHIC/met_WTC_histories_01.html

[153] http://www.arcticbeacon.com/24-Jun-2005.html

[154] http://www.arcticbeacon.com/12-Jul-2005.html

[155] http://www.chiefengineer.org/article.cfm?seqnum1=1029

What are we to make of these reports, from dozens of witnesses, that explosions were going off throughout the WTC towers? Particularly, how do we explain the reports of massive explosions in the *basement areas* of both towers where we assume there were no hidden jetliners? In the immediate aftermath of the collapses of the towers, a company was employed by the City of New York to begin the clean up. In an act that can only be described as criminal negligence at the scene of a crime, this company *immediately* began to collect the steel beams, most of which had been inexplicably reduced to 30 ft. sections, and ship them off to Asia to be melted down. What was the name of this company? Why, *Controlled Demolition Incorporated* (CDI)[156] of course! When asked about the collapse of the towers, Mark Loizeaux, the head of CDI, which calls itself "the innovator and global leader in the controlled demolition and implosion of structures," stated:

> "If I were to bring the towers down, I would put explosives in the basement to get the weight of the building to help collapse the structure."[157]

Is this getting strange enough for you yet? Perhaps most interestingly of all is the fact that, many weeks after the collapse, *still molten metal* was discovered by removal teams in what used to be the basement levels of the WTC towers. This same Mark Loizeaux of CDI, affirmed that "hot spots of molten steel were found at the bottoms of the elevator shafts of the main towers, **down seven basement levels**." Adding to the mystery is the video footage of what appears to be *molten metal* falling out of the impact area of the South tower immediately before the tower collapsed.[158] (This footage is dramatic and powerful, so do take a few moments to watch it.)

As reported in the November 29, 2001 edition of *The New York Times*, while some engineers said that a combination of an uncontrolled fire and the structural damage *might* have been able to bring the buildings down, Dr. Jonathan Barnett, professor of fire protection engineering at the Worcester Polytechnic Institute said that uncontrolled fire and the structural damage *would not explain steel members in the debris pile that appear to have been partly evaporated in extraordinarily high temperatures.*[159]

Think about that for a while.

Authorities found evidence that some of the massive steel core beams had partly *evaporated!* Evaporating steel beams? The temperature required to evaporate steel is somewhere in the region of 2,860 degrees centigrade, much higher than the 500-800 degrees centigrade proposed for the WTC fires.

It is an established fact (and agreed to as fact by the 9/11 Commission itself) that the jet fuel in the planes and the office fixtures that provided further

[156] http://www.controlled-demolition.com/
[157] http://www.americanfreepress.net/09_03_02/NEW_SEISMIC_/new_seismic_.html
[158] http://video.google.com/videoplay?docid=-2991254740145858863&q=cameraplanet+9%2F11
[159]
http://www.underreported.com/modules.php?op=modload&name=News&file=article&sid=1148

fuel for the fires burned intensely for just 10-15 minutes but nevertheless could *not* have reached the 1,500 degrees centigrade required for the core steel beams of the towers to have melted. Added to this we have the surpassingly strange fact that a large percentage of the material of the towers (plastics, concrete, steel, etc.) was apparently turned literally to dust *as the towers fell*. If we take a piece of concrete and drop it from several hundred feet onto the ground, would we expect it to turn to dust?! How can we explain this? How can the Bush government explain this? Are they going to? Are they going to explain how the laws of physics were somehow suspended on September 11, 2001, only in New York and only in the area of the WTC complex?

If we are to believe the official claim that the towers fell as a result of a 'pancake' effect, not only would we expect most of the material to remain in sizeable chunks, but we would also expect to see most of the 47 large core steel beams still standing as the floors pancaked *around* them. At the very least we would expect to see chunks of steel beams that were hundreds of feet in height/length. Yet, that is not what we saw. What we saw was the almost complete disintegration of the WTC towers into either dust or relatively small chunks of steel and masonry ready to be immediately hauled or swept away. Needless to say, none of these facts fit with the official story that the planes or the resulting fires caused the towers to collapse.

SO WHAT *DID* CAUSE THE COLLAPSE OF THE WTC TOWERS?

Professor of Physics Steven E. Jones at Brigham Young University in Provo, Utah posits that the most likely explanation is that some form of thermite reaction was employed. Thermite reactions are caused by the mixture of aluminium metal and the oxide (rust) of another metal, usually iron, and an external ignition source and are used in industry to cut and melt steel. They are also used in thermite grenades and bombs that have been used in combat as incendiary devices, *able to burn through heavy armor or other fireproof barriers.* The result of a thermite reaction is a temperature of 2,500 degrees centigrade that, when employed on metals such as steel, results in the liquification of said metal. However, given the apparently *instantaneous* undermining of these massive steel columns, we may not be dealing with ordinary, publicly available thermite compounds.

In his analysis, Professor Jones makes a brief reference to "nanoaluminum" and "superthermites". In January 2005 the magazine *Technology Review*, a publication of the *Massachusetts Institute of Technology* (MIT) ran a story entitled *Military Reloads with Nanotech*. In the article, the U.S. military's latest research and development of 'nanotech' weapons was discussed:

Smaller. Cheaper. Nastier. Those are the guiding principles behind the military's latest bombs. The secret ingredient: nanotechnology that makes for a bigger boom.

Nanotechnology is grabbing headlines for its potential in advancing the life sciences and computing research, but the Department of Defense (DoD) found another use: a new class of weaponry that uses energy-packed nanometals to create powerful, compact bombs.

With funding from the U.S. government, Sandia National Laboratories, the Los Alamos National Laboratory, and the Lawrence Livermore National Laboratory are researching how to manipulate the flow of energy within and between molecules, a field known as nanoenergentics, which enables building more lethal weapons such as "cave-buster bombs" that have several times the detonation force of conventional bombs such as the "daisy cutter" or MOAB (mother of all bombs).

Researchers can greatly increase the power of weapons by adding materials known as superthermites that combine nanometals such as nanoaluminum with metal oxides such as iron oxide, according to Steven Son, a project leader in the Explosives Science and Technology group at Los Alamos.

"The advantage (of using nanometals) is in *how fast* you can get their energy out," Son says.

Son says that the chemical reactions of superthermites are faster and therefore release greater amounts of energy more rapidly.

"Superthermites can increase the (chemical) reaction time by a thousand times," Son says, resulting in a *very rapid reactive wave.*

Son, who has been working on nanoenergetics for more than three years, says that scientists can engineer nanoaluminum powders with different particle sizes to vary the energy release rates.

The U.S. Army Environmental Center began a program in 1997 to develop alternatives to the toxic lead that is used in the hundreds of millions of rounds that are annually fired during conflicts and at its training ranges. Carpenter says that although bullets using nanoaluminum are ready to be field tested, the government has been slow implement the technology.

However, researchers aren't permitted to discuss what practical military applications may come from this research.[160] (emphasis ours)

Professor Jones concludes:

[S]ubstantial evidence supporting the current conjecture that some variation of thermite (e.g., solid aluminum powder plus Fe2O3, with possible addition of sulfur) was used on the steel columns of the WTC Tower to weaken the huge steel supports, not long before explosives finished the demolition job. Roughly 3,000 pounds of RDX-grade linear-shaped charges (*which could have been pre-positioned by just a few men*) would then suffice in each Tower and WTC 7 to cut the supports at key points so that gravity would bring the buildings straight down. The estimate is based on the amount of explosives used in controlled demolitions in the past and the size of the buildings. Radio-initiated firing of the charges is implicated here. Using computer-controlled radio signals, it would be an easy matter to begin the explosive demolition near the point of entry of the planes in the Towers.

---

[160] http://www.technologyreview.com/articles/05/01/wo/wo_gartner012105.asp?p=1

Consider the image below of the wreckage of the WTC towers:

Do you notice anything? Look at the steel beam directly behind the fire-fighter in the middle of the picture. Does that look like a steel beam that buckled under pressure? What about the evidence of melting on the front edge of the beam? Is that curious? What seems clear from this image is that the beam was very precisely and deliberately cut, or rather, melted.

It is certainly very plausible then to suggest that "superthermite", with its ability to almost instantly generate temperatures of 2,500 degrees centigrade and thereby instantly liquefy steel (and possibly many other materials, although we are not allowed to know) could well have been used to effect the demolition of the WTC towers. Such a suggestion is certainly more plausible than the official conspiracy theory version of events.

However there is still a problem: the thermite theory does not explain how the thousands of tons of concrete and other items in the towers were literally pulverized into dust almost instantaneously. Joe Casaliggi, a firefighter with Engine 7 commented:

> "You have two 110-story office buildings: you don't find a chair, you don't find a telephone, a computer. [[…]] The biggest piece of a telephone I found was half a keypad, and it was this big (holds up thumb and forefinger). *The buildings collapsed to dust.*"[161]

Dr. Charles Hirsch, the chief medical examiner dealing with 9/11, informed relatives of 9/11 victims not to expect remains of their loved ones to be found since most bodies had been "vaporized" (his own word).[162] This was the finding of the chief medical examiner at the WTC site. How can anyone explain

---

[161] http://st12.startlogic.com/~xenonpup/collapse%20update/Engine-7.htm
[162] http://www.firehouse.com/news/2001/12/4_APmissing.html

that people, human beings, caught in a building collapse were completely "vaporized", turned to dust, just like the concrete and fixtures of the WTC towers?

Most investigators point to evidence of "explosives" and "squibs" in video footage of the collapse of the two towers, yet to effect the complete destruction of so much concrete and office material and human beings, a massive quantity of explosives would surely have been required, and such a quantity is simply not evident in the available footage. As has been suggested by Professor Jones, an advanced and publicly unknown form of "superthermite" was probably used to cut the steel core beams of the WTC towers, which leaves open the possibility that other similarly advanced and publicly unknown technology was used to disintegrate the concrete that constituted the body of the towers. It this case, it would not be responsible or wise for us to theorize about what specific device or technique was used to turn the towers to dust, however, we *will* say that 'light' and "EM pulse" weapons have been developed in the past 20 years by the U.S. and Israeli military that are capable of 'invisibly' destroying hardened targets.[163,164] To that we will add that part of the prepping of the WTC towers could have included the planting of 'conductors' to effect the propagation of such an induced wave throughout the buildings and thereby causing the vaporization of concrete and of fixtures and human bodies alike.

All that remains to complete the picture of how and why the WTC towers collapsed then is for the U.S. government to explain to the world how 'al-Qaeda' managed to obtain large quantities of superthermite compounds, acquire the specialized knowledge to successfully plan the demolition of two massive skyscrapers, and gain access to both WTC towers in the months prior to 9/11 to prepare the towers for demolition. I will not, however, be holding my breath for any such disclosure.

Any analysis of the collapse of the WTC towers would not be complete without mention of the fact that there were not two but *three* buildings in the WTC complex that suffered catastrophic failures and collapsed into their own footprints on the morning of September 11, 2001. The third building to undergo such a collapse was WTC 7, a 47-story 600 ft. skyscraper that housed then mayor of New York Rudolf Giuliani's Office of Emergency Management (OEM) also known as "the bunker". The building was also home to offices of the CIA, the U.S. Secret Service, the IRS and the Securities and Exchange Commission[165] (among others).

Guiliani's OEM, which was built in 1999 on floor 27 of WTC 7, was designed to coordinate responses to various emergencies, including natural disasters like hurricanes or floods, and *terrorist attacks*. The 50,000 square foot center had reinforced, bullet-proof, and bomb-resistant walls, its own air sup-

[163] http://en.wikipedia.org/wiki/Tactical_High_Energy_Laser
[164] http://www.defenseindustrydaily.com/laser_em_weapons/index.php
[165] http://www.cnn.com/SPECIALS/2001/trade.center/tenants1.html

ply and water tank, and three backup generators powered by a 6,000 gallon diesel tank. Many people were more than a little surprised therefore when Guiliani announced that he would build his terror attack response center in the shadow of two landmark towers that were themselves considered prime 'terrorist' targets. In fact, around the time that Giuliani decided to place his emergency command center in WTC 7, the North American Aerospace Defence Command (NORAD) was *conducting exercises simulating hijacked airliners used as weapons* to crash into targets and cause mass casualties. One of the targets was the WTC.[166] Guiliani's decision to place a key emergency response center at the site of a predicted future 'terrorist attack' was therefore difficult to understand.

According to news reports,[167] Guiliani's team were in "the bunker" in WTC 7 when the first WTC tower collapsed. At this point, the building was evacuated and a temporary OEM was set up at the NYPD's command post two blocks north, at 75 Barclay Street.

At about 5 p.m. that afternoon, WTC 7 inexplicably collapsed despite the fact that it had suffered only superficial damage from the falling twin towers earlier that morning. WTC 7 was approximately 350 feet from the nearest twin tower (the North tower) and was separated from it by WTC 6. Consider the image below taken some time in the afternoon of September 11, 2001. WTC 7 is the tall building in the background.

Notice that, while severely damaged by falling debris, even the buildings that were *adjacent* to the twin towers did not collapse as a result of falling debris or fire. So why did WTC 7 collapse? No one seems to know. A government FEMA investigation into the collapse of WTC 7 stated:

---

[166] http://www.usatoday.com/news/washington/2004-04-18-norad_x.htm
[167] http://www.newyorkmetro.com/nymetro/news/sept11/features/5270/

The specifics of the fires in WTC 7 and how they caused the building to collapse ["official theory"] remain unknown at this time. Although the total diesel fuel on the premises contained massive potential energy, **the best hypothesis [fire/debris-damage-caused collapse] has only a low probability of occurrence. Further research, investigation, and analyses are needed to resolve this issue.** (FEMA, 2002, chapter 5)

Essentially FEMA's conclusion was that, while two small fires were observed burning in WTC 7, there is no explanation as to how these fires were started or how they could possibly have caused the complete and uniform implosion of the building. Remember that no planes struck WTC 7, so there was no aircraft fuel involved, only small office fires with paper, wood and plastics as fuel for these small fires.

As noted by the FEMA report, further research, investigation, and analyses are needed to resolve this issue, yet no such research or investigation has been undertaken, at least not by any credible official government body. For its part, the official 9/11 Commission, that was tasked with a *thorough investigation* of the 9/11 attacks, did not even mention the collapse of WTC 7. I highly recommend that you watch a clip of the collapse of WTC 7.[168] Like the Twin Towers, it is hard to describe the collapse of WTC 7 as anything other than a very obvious controlled demolition.

In a September 2002 PBS documentary called "America Rebuilds," in reference to World Trade Center Building 7, Larry Silverstein, who had recently acquired the complex, stated:

"I remember getting a call from the, er, fire department commander, telling me that they were not sure they were gonna be able to contain the fire, and I said, 'We've had such terrible loss of life, maybe the smartest thing to do is pull it'. And they made that decision to pull and we watched the building collapse."[169]

Silverstein's comment appears to be an admission that collapse of WTC 7 was indeed the result of a deliberate controlled demolition, but to prepare a building for demolition via standard procedures, particularly one the size of WTC 7, often requires several weeks. Are we to believe that the planning and placing of explosives to demolish WTC 7 was completed in a matter of hours on 9/11? If WTC 7 was deliberately demolished with carefully placed explosives of some description, then we must conclude that the demolition was planned a considerable amount of time *before* 9/11.

According to a report in the National Institute of Standards and Technology,[170] the alarm system in WTC 7 was placed on "test" status for a period of eight hours on the morning of September 11. This ordinarily happened during maintenance or other testing, and resulted in any alarms received from the building being ignored. We know that WTC 7 housed offices of the U.S. Secret Service. We also know that WTC 7 was evacuated just after the first

---

[168] Video clip can be downloaded here: http://www.signs-of-the-times.org/signs/wtc7_collapse.mpg
[169] http://en.wikipedia.org/wiki/Larry_Silverstein
[170] http://wtc.nist.gov/progress_report_june04/chapter1.pdf

Twin Tower collapsed at approximately 10:00 am. It is interesting to note then that official reports tell us that a Secret Service agent named Craig Miller perished in the rubble of building 7. What was Mr. Miller doing in WTC 7 seven hours after it had been evacuated and when, if we are to believe Mr. Silverstein, it had been prepared for imminent demolition? Did no one inform Craig Miller that the building was set to go down?

Why was the alarm system of WTC 7 switched off and rendered ineffective on the morning of 9/11? What was the origin of the two small fires that erupted in WTC 7? What was the source of the molten metal that was found flowing underneath the rubble of WTC 7 (and the Twin Towers) many weeks after it collapsed? These unanswered questions surrounding the bizarre collapse of WTC 7 simply add further fuel to the raging fires of serious doubts that exist about the official U.S. government conspiracy theory of what happened on September 11, 2001.

Finally, let me reiterate that, until 9/11, no steel-beam high-rise building had ever before (or since) completely collapsed due to fire. However, every year, hundreds of high-rise buildings undergo complete and nearly symmetrical "implosions" as a result of pre-positioned explosives, otherwise known as controlled demolitions.

ISRAELI INVOLVEMENT

We now come to the numerous threads indicating Israeli involvement in the organization of the 9/11 attacks.

There is much evidence to warrant an in-depth investigation of the role played by agents of Israel in the 9/11 attacks. Yet the ubiquitous, tiresome, and completely baseless threat of being labelled "anti-Semitic" for criticising the actions of the Israeli government effectively prevents all but the most courageous from following these leads.

First of all, we notice that two of the three 9/11 airports were serviced by one Israeli owned company, ICTS. ICTS, under its subsidiary Huntleigh International (which ICTS acquired in 1999) sells security, ticketing, check-in and passenger screening services to Boston's Logan airport and New Jersey's Newark airport from which Flights 175, 11 and 93 departed on the morning of 9/11. ICTS was *not*, however, involved in Washington's Dulles airport from which Flight 77 departed.

The interesting thing about ICTS is that it is a Netherlands-based aviation and transportation security firm that is headed by "former [Israeli] military commanding officers and veterans of government intelligence and security agencies."[171] Imagine that! A company owned by Israeli intelligence agents was handling security and passenger screening at the airports where the alleged hijackers just strolled on to the planes! But it gets better. The owner and President of ICTS is an Israeli named Menahem Atzmon. Atzmon, just

---

[171] http://www.mathaba.net/0_index.shtml?x=534550

happens to be a good friend of current Israeli prime minister Ehud Olmert. In fact, Atzmon is such a good friend of Olmert that he was involved in a financial scandal involving forged receipts for donations to the 1988 Likud campaign with Olmert back in 1997 when Atzmon was co-treasurer of the Likud party, and you can't get much friendlier than that! As you can see, we are dealing here with a very murky web, where our ability to accept events as mere "coincidences" is stretched to the limit.

It is important to note that during the months prior to the WTC attack, many people in America and Europe were withdrawing their support for Israel and there was a growing feeling of dis-ease among the peoples of many countries that Israel was simply going too far in its persecution of the Palestinians. Everyone was getting tired of the constant harassment, the constant attacks against anyone who said a single word against Israel's political ambitions; who—if they did not support every single thing said and done by Israel—were flamed as "anti-Semitic".

In short, despite the Holocaust Guilt Industry, Israel was losing its grip on the collective guilt of the world; sympathies were turning against them, and toward the beleaguered Palestinians.

During the Clinton years, significant efforts had been made to bring the plight of the Palestinian people and the need for a just solution to the Middle East conflict to the attention of the international community. While Israel had successfully scuppered the Camp David peace talks by making demands that they knew the Palestinian people, and therefore Arafat, could not accept, Israel was finding itself increasingly isolated and increasingly pressured to make the concessions that peace required.

Once 9/11 happened, all bets were off.

On September 10, 2001, the *Washington Times* ran an article entitled, "U.S. troops would enforce peace under Army study", which detailed the findings of an elite U.S. Army study center plan devised for enforcing a major Israeli-Palestinian peace accord that would require about 20,000 well-armed troops stationed throughout Israel and a newly created Palestinian state. The most interesting aspect of the report was the mention of a 68-page paper by the Army School of Advanced Military Studies (SAMS) drafted to analyse the daunting task facing any international peacekeeping force if Israel and the Palestinians ever reached a peace agreement backed by the United Nations.

In the report, we are told that:

> [T]he School for Advanced Military Studies is both a training ground and a think tank for some of the Army's brightest officers. Officials say the Army chief of staff, and sometimes the Joint Chiefs of Staff, ask SAMS to develop contingency plans for future military operations. During the 1991 Persian Gulf war, SAMS personnel helped plan the coalition ground attack that avoided a strike up the middle of Iraqi positions and instead executed a 'left hook' that routed the enemy in 100 hours.

> The exercise was undertaken by 60 officers dubbed 'Jedi Knights,' as all second-year SAMS students are nicknamed. *The SAMS paper* attempts to predict

events in the first year of a peace-enforcement operation, and sees possible dangers for U.S. troops from both sides. It *calls Israel's armed forces a '500-pound gorilla in Israel.'* Well armed and trained. Operates in both Gaza [and the West Bank]. *Known to disregard international law to accomplish mission.* Very unlikely to fire on American forces. Fratricide a concern especially in air space management.'

Of the Mossad, the Israeli intelligence service, the SAMS officers say:
'Wildcard. Ruthless and cunning. Has capability to target U.S. forces and make it look like a Palestinian/Arab act.'[172]

Hmmm... We suppose that the Bush Gang didn't read that particular item of intell. They were too busy reading the "cooked intell" that said Saddam Hussein had weapons of mass destruction or was going to have them or was thinking about planning to have them, or... well, you get the idea.

Alone, the quote from the Army School wouldn't mean much, but when added to the other evidence of Israeli spy rings, Israeli companies providing security at the airports, it does seem to support the idea that Mossad may indeed have been deeply involved in the 9/11 attacks on the World Trade Center and, perhaps, even the Pentagon, and that the Bush Cabal was not only complicit in ordering the U.S. military and intelligence services to "stand down", but that they were directly involved in the plot.

According to ABC news, alleged chief hijacker Mohammed Atta was financed by "unnamed sources in Pakistan". According to *Agence France Presse* and the *Times of India,* an official Indian intelligence report informs us that the 9/11 attacks were *funded by money wired to Mohammed Atta from Pakistan, by Ahmad Umar Sheikh, under orders from Pakistani intelligence chief General Mahmoud Ahmad.* The report said:

> The evidence we have supplied to the U.S. is of a much wider range and depth than just one piece of paper linking a rogue general to some misplaced act of terrorism.[173]

Guess where General Mahmoud Ahmad was on the morning of September 11? Why in the U.S. of course!

Guess what he was doing?

Why, the good general just happened to be having breakfast with Florida's senator, Bob Graham—the then esteemed chairman of the Senate Intelligence Committee. Also present at the breakfast was Pakistan's ambassador to the U.S. Maleeha Lodhi and Representative *Porter Goss* (Goss is a 10-year veteran of the CIA's clandestine operations wing and was appointed by Bush Jr as CIA director until his resignation under the shadow of a scandal). *There were other members of the Senate and House Intelligence committees present also.*[174]

---

[172] *Washington Times,* September 10, 2001.

[173] http://globalresearch.ca/articles/CHO206A.html

[174] http://www.washingtonpost.com/ac2/wp-dyn?pagename=article&node=&contentId=A36091-2002May17&notFound=true

Don't you find it the least bit curious that so many darned bizarre things get done in Florida or in connection to Florida? After all, it was in Florida that Bush stole the 2000 election. Florida seems to be a "safe zone" for all kinds of nefarious activities because Bush's brother, Jeb, is governor there. It also looks like the Bush Reich have the Florida Senator in their pocket, and even if he votes against any of the legislation desired by the Bush Gang, you can bet it is all for show: good cop, bad cop, S.O.P.

The day after the 9/11 attacks, then former Israeli Prime Minister, Benjamin Netanyahu, when asked what he thought about the event, stated that it was "very good for Israel".

Indeed it was.

The spin that was immediately put on the events of September 11 created much-needed sympathy and vindication for the "war on Arab terrorism" that Israel claims it has been silently fighting for many years. Again we must ask, who had the motive *and* the capability to carry out the 9/11 attacks, and who stood to benefit the most?

Just hours after the attacks, intelligence analyst George Friedman[175] proclaimed Israel as the primary beneficiary. "The big winner today, intended or not, is the state of Israel", wrote Friedman, who said on his Internet website at stratfor.com adding: "There is no question that the Israeli leadership is *feeling relief.*" Again we come back to the question that all serious criminal investigators begin with—"Who benefits?"

The fact is, there exists much evidence, conveniently overlooked by certain 9/11 investigators, to strongly suggest that agents of Israel were deeply involved in the events surrounding the 9/11 attacks. For example: There is the fact of the existence of the Israeli spy ring, as exposed, surprisingly, by Fox News' Carl Cameron. In the four part series aired on Fox News in December 2001, Cameron reports many interesting facts such as:

> Two Israeli companies *Amdocs* and *Comverse InfoSys* (now called Verint), manage just about every aspect of the US telephone system.
>
> *Amdocs is responsible for billing and records for almost all phone calls in the U.S.* Cameron states: Amdocs has contracts with the 25 biggest phone companies in America, and more worldwide. The White House and other secure government phone lines are protected, but *it is virtually impossible to make a call on normal phones without generating an Amdocs record of it.*
>
> In recent years, the FBI and other government agencies have investigated Amdocs more than once. The firm has repeatedly and adamantly denied any security breaches or wrongdoing. But sources tell Fox News that in 1999, the super secret National Security Agency, headquartered in northern Maryland, issued what's called a *Top Secret sensitive compartmentalized information report, TS/SCI,* warning that *records of calls in the United States were getting into foreign hands, in Israel, in particular.*

---

[175] http://www.stratfor.com/about-stratfor/executive-team/george-friedman.php

Investigators don't believe calls are being listened to, but the data about who is calling whom and when is plenty valuable in itself. An internal Amdocs memo to senior company executives suggests just how Amdocs generated call records could be used. 'Widespread data mining techniques and algorithms. [...] combining both the properties of the customer (e.g., credit rating) and properties of the specific 'behavior'.' Specific behavior, such as who the customers are calling.[176]

Note the comment that, "the White House and other secure government phone lines are protected". Well, it just so happens that *Comverse InfoSys provides the wiretapping equipment and software for U.S. law enforcement agencies.* Cameron tells us:

Every time you make a call, it passes through the nation's elaborate network of switchers and routers run by the phone companies. Custom computers and software, made by companies like Comverse, are tied into that network to intercept, record and store the wiretapped calls, and at the same time transmit them to investigators.

The manufacturers have continuing access to the computers so they can service them and keep them free of glitches. This process was authorized by the 1994 Communications Assistance for Law Enforcement Act, or CALEA. Senior government officials have now told Fox News that while CALEA made wiretapping easier, it has led to *a system that is seriously vulnerable to compromise, and may have undermined the whole wiretapping system.*

Indeed, Fox News has learned that Attorney General John Ashcroft and FBI Director Robert Mueller were both warned Oct. 18 in a hand-delivered letter from 15 local, state and federal law enforcement officials, who complained that 'law enforcement's current electronic surveillance capabilities are less effective today than they were at the time CALEA was enacted.'

Comverse insists the equipment it installs is secure. But the complaint about this system is that the wiretap computer programs made by Comverse have, in effect, a back door *through which wiretaps themselves can be intercepted by unauthorized parties.*

Adding to the suspicions is the fact that in Israel, Comverse works closely with the Israeli government, and under special programs, gets reimbursed for up to 50 percent of its research and development costs by the Israeli Ministry of Industry and Trade. But *investigators within the DEA, INS and FBI have all told Fox News that* to pursue or even suggest Israeli spying through Comverse is considered career suicide.

To this last comment we have to ask: just what level of power do Israeli interests wield in the halls of power in the U.S. that any investigation into Israeli spying activities on U.S. soil against U.S. intelligence agencies can be so completely quashed? Would this constitute a level of power and control that would allow those interests to carry off a terrorist attack like 9/11 and have it blamed on "Arab terrorists"? Remember the U.S. School for Advanced Military Studies assessment of the Israeli Mossad: "Wildcard. Ruthless and cunning. *Has capability to target U.S. forces and make it look like a Palestinian/Arab act.*"

---

[176] http://tinyurl.com/ftekt

Cameron goes on to tell us that *a group of 140 Israeli spies were arrested prior to September 11, 2000 in the U.S. as part of a widespread investigation into a suspected espionage ring run by Israel inside the U.S.*

U.S. Government documents refer to the spy ring as an *"organised intelligence-gathering operation"* designed to *"penetrate government facilities"*. Most of those arrested had served in the Israeli armed forces—but military service is compulsory in Israel and a number also had an intelligence background. *Many were posing as art students.*

These spies were spread out across the U.S., *usually living close to suspected Arab terrorist cells*. One group was living just a few blocks away from alleged chief "hijacker" Mohammed Atta in Hollywood, Florida. Cameron reports that, according to intelligence sources within the U.S., *a number of the terrorist cells that they had been watching changed their activities and routines immediately after having covert taps put on their communications by U.S. intelligence agents.*

Now think about this. You have a group of at least 140 Mossad agents and/or their accomplices running around the U.S. with apparent impunity prior to 9/11 conducting a "spying" operation that is designed to "penetrate government facilities". You have two Israeli companies that control the entire U.S. telephone and wiretapping technology that are suspected of passing sensitive information to Israel. You have U.S. intelligence agencies realising that, on a number of occasions, terrorist suspects that they had sought to wiretap and survey immediately changed their telecommunications processes and began acting much differently as soon as the, supposedly secret, U.S. initiated wiretaps went into place. Then recall who has access to the wiretapping system information: Comverse, an Israeli company.

But it doesn't end there.

On the morning of September 11 and just as the WTC towers were crumbling, five Israelis were caught doing the "happy dance" as they videotaped the Twin Towers fall and over two thousand American civilians die. The now infamous "Dancing Israelis" were spotted by a woman who called the police, who then contacted the FBI. The five were apprehended in a moving company van, which contained $4,700 in cash, *box cutters* and recently taken photographs, *one image showing a hand flicking a lighter in front of the destroyed buildings* as if mocking the event. Investigators said that:

"There were maps of the city in the car with certain places highlighted. [...] *It looked like they're hooked in with this. It looked like they knew what was going to happen."*

The driver of the van later told the arresting officers:

"We are Israeli. We are not your problem. Your problems are our problems. The Palestinians are the problem."

Did this most interesting comment give the world a tantalising glimpse into the *real* reason for and, at the same time, reveal the co-conspirators—or even perpetrators—of the 9/11 attacks??

The five were detained for two months during which time at least two were identified as active Mossad agents. They were subjected to polygraph tests which one of them resisted for ten weeks before *failing*.[177]

Now ask yourself: What questions might have been asked of this person during the test? We will probably never know, but we can speculate that he was probably asked direct questions about his involvement in the WTC attacks, and he, as a Mossad agent working for the state of Israel, was found to be lying.

After being released and deported to Israel, the five appeared on an Israeli television show where they made the following telling remark:

> *"The fact of the matter is we are coming from a country that experiences terror daily. Our purpose was to document the event."*

This remark begs the question: How can you document an event if you do not know beforehand that it is going to happen?

Another interesting detail was the fact that an Israeli instant messaging company, *Odigo*, received a warning about the WTC attacks two hours before the first plane hit the WTC; this warning originated in Israel.[178]

As reported by ex-Mossad agent Victor Ostrovsky,[179] the Mossad has a history of creating and supporting radical Islamic groups for its own purposes, and as Seymour Hersh, veteran investigative journalist writing in *The New Yorker* on October 8, pointed out:

> [M]any of the investigators believe that some of the initial clues about the terrorists' identities and preparations, such as flight manuals, *were meant to be found*.

The fact that Israeli interests possess vastly disproportionate power in the U.S. was highlighted by Congressman Jim Moran (Democrat of Virginia), speaking at a 2003 public forum in his congressional district, and reported in the *New York Times* of March 15, 2003,[180] where he stated:

> "If it were not for the strong support of the Jewish community for this war with Iraq, we would not be doing this. The leaders of the Jewish community are influential enough that they could change the direction of where this is going, and I think they should."

By "Jewish community", Moran was certainly not talking about the average Jewish American or the average Jew in Israel, but rather the *leaders of the Jewish political and industrial communities, the Israeli lobby groups in the U.S. such as AIPAC, the ADL and the self-proclaimed 'Zionist' leaders.* In short, we are talking about people who *claim* to be acting in the interests of ordinary Jews but who, in reality, are manipulating the Jewish people and their history to achieve their own self-serving goals. Of course, we should not forget that many of the so-called Washington neocons and high-level Penta-

---

[177] http://www.larouchepub.com/other/2001/2849isr_spies_911.html
[178] http://www.haaretzdaily.com/hasen/pages/ShArt.jhtml?itemNo=77744&contrassID=/has%5C
[179] Victor Ostrovsky, *By Way of Deception* (Toronto: Stoddart, 1990).
[180] http://www.cnn.com/2003/ALLPOLITICS/03/14/moran.remarks/

gon staff, all of whom are instrumental in forming American foreign policy, hold dual American and Israeli citizenship.

That the Israel lobby in America essentially dictates American foreign policy was highlighted in March 2006 by John Mearsheimer, Professor of Political Science at Chicago University, and Stephen Walt, Professor of International Affairs at the Kennedy School of Government at Harvard, in a paper entitled simply *The Israel Lobby*.[181] The paper created a significant political storm immediately after its release, and the cries of anti-Semitism from the Israel lobby served only to back up one of the theses of Walt and Mearsheimer's paper: that any public claims that Israel wields an inordinate amount of power in Washington are effectively silenced by the exercising of the very same power of the Israel lobby. To the dismay of many people who hoped that the paper would open up debate on the highly secretive relationship between Washington and Tel Aviv, most mainstream news outlets played up the Israel lobby's screams of anti-Semitism and ignored the actual details of Walt and Mearsheimer's hard-hitting research that exposed the co-opting of American foreign policy by the state of Israel.

All of these facts are indisputable and constitute just the tip of the iceberg of what is clearly deep involvement by the agents of the state of Israel in not only the 9/11 attacks but the formulation of American foreign policy, and any domestic policies that impinge on foreign policy.

And so, there it was: after those nasty Islamic fundies attacked America, Israel had the biggest bully on the global block on their side. With the repeating rants of how evil Muslims are, how fanatical they are, how cruel and unusual they are, the rest of the world had better fall in line with Israel's thinking and help them find the "final solution" for Palestine and those other 'A-rabs'.

Shades of Nazi Germany going after the Jews?

Thus we see that *the main beneficiary of 9/11 was Israel*. It was clearly not any Arab nations of the Middle East, which, already marginalised and demonized by Western states, could ill-afford to provide the U.S. and Israel with renewed *carte blanche* to label them as "terrorist supporters" and summarily invade and occupy their lands.

See Iraq and Iran for examples of the first two nations, who had nothing to do with 9/11, to experience just such a backlash.

Logic would also suggest that any *real* Islamic terror groups also had nothing to gain by carrying out any major attack on America. Such groups claim that their main goal is to protect Muslim people from the kind of oppression that they have been subjected to for many years by Western nations, in particular Israel. Yet we are asked to believe that these 'defenders of Islam' were unaware that attacking the U.S. would obviously provide justification for a massive increase in this very same oppression?

---

[181] http://www.lrb.co.uk/v28/n06/mear01_.html

Have Iraqi Muslims benefited from 9/11? What about the 86 million in Iran? Who are these 'terrorists' that claim to be acting in their name?

None of it makes any sense, and when something makes no sense, we must endeavour to make sense of it and this can only be done by asking questions such as *cui bono*.

We can also make a good case for the claim that the 9/11 attacks did not benefit the U.S. either. Bush's approval ratings in 2006, mainly because of the "war on terror", are at an all time low, the lowest of any American President—ever—and the 9/11 attacks appear to have initiated the rapid process of the political and economic destruction of the United States.

Again we state, the only entity to fully benefit from the 9/11 attacks, with no 'down side', is the state of Israel, or at least the people who control the state of Israel and appear to have a very specific plan for its future.

The Pentagon Strike and Israel

At the beginning of our analysis of the 9/11 attacks, we stated that the attack on the Pentagon constituted one of the "Achilles' heels" of the entire 9/11 conspiracy. The reason we have formed this opinion is very simple: while we all saw repeated footage of Flight 11 and Flight 175 crash into the WTC towers, and we all saw the wreckage of Flight 93 and have several eyewitness testimonies that a commercial airliner did indeed crash in Pennsylvania, no one has seen any footage of Flight 77 hitting the Pentagon, and the government studiously *refuses* to release any of the footage that they have that would show conclusively if it was Flight 77 or not.

More importantly, and here we present the defining argument for the "no plane at the Pentagon" argument, there is *no* evidence of a Boeing 757 having struck the Pentagon on 9/11. Think about it. The *only* primary evidence that Flight 77 hit the Pentagon is the word of U.S. government and military officials and the alleged phone call of Barbara Olson that she could *not* have made. Also, both the Olsons were high level members of the Bush Cabal. That, of course, is one of the reasons that some people might argue that it *was* Flight 77 that hit the Pentagon. Why would the Bush Cabal sacrifice one of its own? How could they persuade Ted Olson to go along with lying about a phone call from his wife in order to give support to the story that Flight 77 hit the Pentagon, when his wife was lost in the attack? Well, we will come to that.

Imagine for a moment that we have found a unique human being who is completely unaware of the 9/11 attacks. Imagine further that this person is somewhat knowledgeable about aircraft disasters, crash scenes and the effects of explosives. Imagine that we can go back in time and place this person at the Pentagon and give them unhindered access to the crash scene. Imagine finally that the only thing we tell this person is that some kind of flying object struck the Pentagon.

In such a case, after having examined the evidence, the very *last* thing that such a person would conclude would be that a large commercial aircraft like a 757 caused the damage to the Pentagon? Why? Because there is absolutely *no* evidence to support such a conclusion.

Thinking a little more deeply about the matter, we realise that, even in the event that evidence for the obvious controlled demolition of the WTC towers were to be publicly revealed and accepted, the U.S government could plausibly claim that 'al-Qaeda' somehow managed to plant explosives in the buildings, that this evidence had somehow been overlooked due to "incompetence" in the 9/11 investigation. Pursuing the deliberate controlled demolition of the Twin Towers will not ever bring any of the conspirators to justice. The Pentagon attack, however, is a very different matter. If it were ever to be publicly revealed that it was not Flight 77 that hit the Pentagon, there is simply no way that the U.S government could continue to claim that "al-Qaeda did it" because they would *have to explain what happened to Flight 77 and its passengers*. It is for this reason that the "no plane at the Pentagon" theory has been the target of official direct attack and debunking when nothing else about 9/11 even raises the eyebrow of the conspirators. And here we can include government shills masquerading as 9/11 investigators.

Five years have passed since the 9/11 attacks, and the controversy still rages. Many Americans are becoming more and more disenchanted with their President and his government. Subtle hints are emerging that many, perhaps over 50% of Americans do not believe the official version of the attacks and are more than a little suspicious that their government may well have played a part. Despite this, the mainstream press in the U.S. continues to propagandize the "Party Line" and to bow down to the demands of big business and big government, refusing to bring truth to the people.

Most of the 2,752 people that died on September 11, 2001 were ordinary American civilians. There remain serious questions about how and why those people died. Their families, and all American citizens have a right to the truth about 9/11 and the U.S. government in concert with the media refuses to give it to them or gives them nothing but lies and confusion mixed with truth so as to confuse and exhaust the average person who just wants to keep a roof over their head and put food on the table.

What is lacking in the many independent books and analyses of the 9/11 attacks that have been published in such proliferation over the past five years is a concise outline—a theory, if you will—that fits the evidence, of *what may well have happened that day*. To rectify this glaring omission, we would like to propose the following step-by-step breakdown of the events of that day, as we have been able to reconstruct it.

Obviously, even our scenario cannot be a definitive account because so many lies have been told, and so much data has been hidden or destroyed, that the best anyone can do is to carefully consider *all* that is available, and then formulate a working hypothesis based on logic, science, deep digging, common sense, and an objective understanding of the resources available to, and the true nature of, the people that were likely involved: psychological deviants in positions of power.

Our scenario is a plausible account, much more plausible than the crazy conspiracy theory that blames it on Osama in a cave and 19 guys—most of whom couldn't fly a kite much less a 757—and which led to the equally incomprehensible decision to destroy Saddam and Iraq to exact revenge!

First, let us state that the *specific planning* for the 9/11 attacks probably began *at least* six or seven years prior to the events themselves. This time was needed to maneuver the conspirators, active and passive (of which there were probably hundreds), into the correct positions within the armed forces, government, and civilian agencies to enable the successful completion of the operation. This maneuvering also included the setting up and/or infiltration of businesses (the Israeli airport security and telephone companies for just a few examples) that were also to play key roles. This time frame was also needed to develop the "Muslim terror" threat in the public awareness and to select and deploy the patsies who would ultimately be labeled as the "hijackers".

However, there are strong indicators that the ideological infrastructure has been in place—and active—a lot longer than six or seven years. Since Gulf War I, instigated by George I, effectively turned Iraq into a "straw man", that was thought to be easy to "knock down" with a quick "Shock and Awe", we might also plausibly suggest that the designs on Iraq were put on the table some years before that event, that is to say, in the 1980s. Still other indicators of the ideology afoot in the U.S. that breeds such conspiracies are the "*Northwoods Plan*", and *the assassination of John Kennedy*, not to mention the puerile nonsense called "Monicagate" that included the deep involvement of ex-U.S. solicitor general Ted Olson and his TV-pundit wife, Barbara.

Now, just in case you think that this is way too "conspiracy-minded," we are going to give you a concrete example here.

In a recent issue of Vanity Fair (June, 2006), journalist Craig Unger wrote about the investigation into the so-called Plamegate Affair in an article entitled *The War They Wanted, The Lies They Needed*. The editorial synopsis of the article states:

> The Bush administration invaded Iraq claiming Saddam Hussein had tried to buy yellowcake uranium in Niger. As much of Washington knew, and the world soon learned, the charge was false. Worse, it appears to have been the cornerstone of a highly successful "black propaganda" campaign with links to the White House.[182]

Based on Unger's research, this "black propaganda campaign" was conceived and put into action years ago with many players. The article gives us a good idea of just how complex and long running these conspiracies can be and is recommended reading.

---

[182] http://www.vanityfair.com/features/general/articles/060606fege02

THE SETUP

It will come as no surprise to our regular readers to learn that the 'Muslim terror threat' as defined by the American government is a phenomenon manufactured mainly by Israeli, British and American intelligence agencies. The group that has come to be known as "al-Qaeda" is officially recognised as being a remnant of the Russian Afghan war in the late 1970's when the CIA, using *Saudi intelligence* as a go-between, funneled arms and funds to fundamentalist Islamic groups to counter the Russian invasion of Afghanistan, which itself was provoked by U.S. government meddling in Afghanistan which threatened Russian influence in the region.

Throughout the 1980's and 1990's, U.S. and Israeli intelligence agencies carefully developed this 'base' (al-Qaeda means 'the base' in Arabic) of disaffected Islamic radicals into the modern-day 'al-Qaeda'. In an effort to cement the "reality" of the Islamic terror threat, several false flag terror attacks were carried out by agents of the Israeli and American government during the 1990's including the bombing of the U.S.S. Cole and several bomb attacks on American embassies. Evidence was planted to incriminate "Islamic terrorists" including, but not limited to, false claims of responsibility by previously unheard of "Islamic terror groups".

To state it bluntly, al-Qaeda *does not and never has existed in the form claimed by Western governments*. However, that is not to say that *real* Islamic terrorists did not exist, or that the response of the Bush Administration to the events of 9/11 has not bred a whole new generation of *real* Islamic terrorists. (Readers are encouraged to do their own research to verify the truth of this statement, an excellent starting point being the *BBC*-aired documentary *The Power of Nightmares*[183]).

Let us begin then with our reconstruction of the events of September 11, 2001.

THE PREPARATION

During the years prior to 9/11, members of the Israeli Mossad operate a large network of agents (including Sayanim[184]), who are involved in setting

---

[183] http://www.informationclearinghouse.info/video1037.htm

[184] Writes Selwyn Manning in *The Scoop* (Apr. 22, 2004): Mossad insiders, now on the outside, say the Mossad has just 30 to 37 case officers called katsas operating at any one time. The Mossad is able to function on a low number of core katsas due to a loyal Jewish community outside Israel. The loyalists are networked via a system of *sayanim*, or volunteer Jewish helpers. Sayanim loyalists are usually Jewish, live outside of Israel, and are often recruited via Israeli relatives. There are reportedly thousands of sayanim around the world. Their role will be specific to their professions: A loyalist in the travel industry could help Mossad obtain documents. Sayanim offer practical support, are never put at risk, and are certainly not privy to classified information. A sayan in the tenancy business would find accommodation, financiers, doctors, civil servants, care-givers employed caring for the severely disabled—all have a part to play without knowing the complete or bigger picture, and will remain silent due to loyalty to the cause. Katsas in charge of active sayanim will visit once every three months involving both face-to-face meetings and numerous telephone conversations. "The system allows the Mossad to work with a skeleton

up the attacks, which include handling the Middle Eastern 'al-Qaeda' patsies. These agents and their superiors are also involved in conducting surveillance on the individuals in the U.S. government and federal agencies that will be directly involved in the immediate response to the attacks. They employ tactics that include blackmailing and assassination to ensure that as little as possible is left to chance. Additionally, with the Israeli control of the telephone and computer network infrastructure of the U.S., it is also very likely that any selected member of the U.S. government can be individually targeted for blackmail and/or control so that virtually every function of the U.S. government is under the control of Israel.

Several "trial runs" of the attacks in the form of military exercises were probably carried out in the years and months prior to September 11 in order to fully understand the workings of the various agencies involved, with a view to co-opting their ability to respond effectively as described above. At the same time, several new operations centers were created that would allow the conspirators to control the key area of air traffic control. (See the previously-mentioned Air Traffic Services Cell for an example.)

The key conspirators most likely include very few publicly-known members of the U.S. military or government executive branch, but are rather made up of high-level members of the Israeli government and particularly the Israeli intelligence agency *Mossad*. Those publicly-known members of the U.S. government and military such as Dick Cheney, Donald Rumsfeld, etc., the *apparent* power brokers of American politics, were also in on the plot, but the Israeli contingent were planning a special surprise for them, as we shall see.

At some point prior to September 11, 2001, four commercial aircraft, two Boeing 757's and two Boeing 767's were fitted with software that allowed them to be remotely commandeered by the conspirators. The aircraft were also fitted with hidden video equipment that allowed the conspirators to view events in the cabins of the aircraft in real time. *The ventilation systems in all four aircraft were fitted with canisters containing a fatal analgesic gas mixture that could be activated automatically.* We refer readers to the October 2002 hostage crisis in a Moscow theatre for evidence of the effects of this type of gas.[185]

While it is possible that these modifications to the aircraft could have been made covertly, there also exists the possibility—suggested by other researchers—that duplicate aircraft were used, although we consider it unlikely.

For example: there is evidence to suggest that there were two Flight 11's that left Boston the morning of 9/11. Flight 11 was an institution at Logan Airport. It was American Airlines' early morning transcontinental flight *for years*. Its departure was scheduled *regularly* for 7:45 a.m. at *Terminal B,*

---

staff. That's why, for example, a KGB station would employ about 100 people, while a comparable Mossad station would need only six or seven." [According to *The Scoop*'s source - Ed.]
http://www.scoop.co.nz/mason/stories/HL0404/S00176.html
[185] http://en.wikipedia.org/wiki/Moscow_theatre_siege

Gate 32 as it apparently was on September 11, as the *New York Times* radio transcript reports.[186] Despite this longstanding "institution" of a flight, the official version of events states Flight 11 left from *Gate 26* which is repeated by many press reports.[187] That could be simply a reporting error.

Another most interesting detail is that, despite the official story, *Flight 77 was not scheduled to fly* and was not recorded as actually having flown from Washington Dulles airport on September 11, 2001![188]

The U.S. government's *Bureau of Transportation* documents details things such as flight number, tail number, destination airport, scheduled departure time, etc. about *every commercial flight in the USA*. A search of The U.S. Government's Bureau of Transportation Statistics shows no Flight 0077 listed on *September 11, 2001*. A search for all American Airlines scheduled flights departing from Washington Dulles International Airport on *September 10, 2001* showed Flight number 0077 to have been scheduled and did depart.

A search of the full list of American Airlines scheduled flights departing Dulles on *September 9, 2001* shows American Airlines Flight number 0077 is on this list as well. The list for *September 8, 2001* also included American Airlines Flight number 0077.

Curiously, the full list of American Airlines scheduled flights departing from Dulles on *September 12, 2001*, the day after the attacks, show American Airlines Flight number 0077 is on the schedule, even though all flights had been cancelled.

Why was Flight 77 omitted from the Gov list on 9/11? Were any of the other hijacked aircraft similarly omitted from these government lists?

A search for all United Airlines scheduled flights departing from Boston Logan International Airport on September 11, 2001 showed that *Flight 0175 is listed* and did indeed depart. A search of the full list of United Airlines scheduled flights departing from Newark, New Jersey Airport on September 11, 2001—United Airlines *Flight 0093* is listed as a scheduled flight which departed for San Francisco. A search of the full list of American Airlines scheduled flights departing from Boston, Massachusetts Airport on September 11, 2001 shows United Airlines *Flight 0011* is listed as a scheduled flight and departed for Los Angeles International Airport.

So, again, why wasn't Flight 0077 on the Gov Flight list? Was it an administrative error or oversight or was it due to Flight 0077 not being actually scheduled to fly at all on the morning of September 11, 2001? Is it possible

---

[186] http://www.nytimes.com/2001/10/16/national/16TEXT-FLIGHT11.html?ex=1126411200&en=2da859e407225ee9&ei=5070&ex=1071378000&en=4b6 d66a63bf99b3a&ei=5070 "*7:45:48* - Ground Control 1: American eleven heavy Boston ground *gate thirty two* you're going to wait for a Saab to go by then push back."

[187] http://www.washingtonpost.com/ac2/wp-dyn/A38407-2001Sep15 "American Airlines Flight 11 had backed away from *Gate 26 of Terminal B* at Boston's Logan Airport and was rolling toward the runway for a six-hour flight to Los Angeles."
http://www.telegraph.co.uk/news/main.jhtml?xml=/news/2001/09/16/watt16.xml

[188] http://www.apfn.net/Messageboard/03-26-05/discussion.cgi.24.html

that this is a "glitch" in the plans? An item that indicates that American Airlines Flight 77—as the "institution" it was—never left the ground on 9/11? It is certainly curious.

Furthermore, by some bizarre "glitch in the system", the Bureau of Transportation has *Flight 93 actually arriving at its destination in San Francisco at midday on 9/11* (the scheduled arrival time was 11:14 am). Normally, any emergency landing or crash would be denoted on the BTS database as a 'diversion'.[189]

There is also a report that the passengers that boarded and died on United Airlines Flight 93 were originally meant to board UA Flight 91 to the same destination but due to a "crack in the windshield" of Flight 91 the passengers were transferred to Flight 93. Given the fact that Flight 93 had just 33 passengers and all of Flight 91's passengers were transferred to Flight 93, we wonder if there were *any* passengers booked on Flight 93 in the first place.[190] Not only that, but Tuesday September 11, 2001 was *the first time that Flight 93 flew the Newark to SF route on a Tuesday.*

In short, the possibility of duplicate, "modified aircraft" which were brought out of the hangar to be utilized on September 11 is plausible, and the Gov statistics might very well be "glitches" in the plans that indicate such "switching". Whatever happened we know that raising a smokescreen via dispensing false or confusing information—as we see above—might be part of the plan, simply to divert and confuse. But again, it is unlikely that any unnecessarily complicated maneuvers were implemented because each additional "step" in the plan is another stage at which something can go wrong. It is more likely that all of the above is intended to confuse and obfuscate and that the simplest approach was taken: fit out the already existing planes with the required equipment and just follow "normal procedures."

On September 13, then Attorney General John Ashcroft, in a briefing on the 9/11 attacks, stated that a total of 18 hijackers had been involved in the attacks.[191] In the same briefing, FBI Director Robert Mueller stated that all of the hijackers were "ticketed passengers".[192]

This poses a problem because, of the four hijackers alleged to be on Flight 77, none had received any training on how to fly a Cessna much less a 757. To resolve this issue, the following day on September 14, the FBI added pilot hijacker Hani Hanjour to the list of hijackers on Flight 77.[193]

But arbitrarily adding another hijacker to the list was not as simple as it might seem, because, of course, *Hanjour's name was not on the manifest*, which led the *Washington Post* to speculate that he did not have a ticket, which not only contradicted FBI Director Mueller's statement that the hijack-

[189] http://www.thoughtcrimenews.com/flight93notscheduled.htm

[190] http://rsjames.com/newsletters/2001/14-10-26-2001-13-14.txt

[191] http://www.chron.com/disp/story.mpl/front/1046473.html

[192] http://www.globalsecurity.org/military/library/news/2001/09/mil-010913-usia18.htm

[193] http://www.cnn.com/2001/US/09/14/fbi.document/

ers were "ticketed passengers", but also raised the impossible question of *how anyone can get on a commercial flight without a ticket.*[194]

Several news sites published unofficial lists of all the people on board the hijacked airlines. These lists are very curious because the numbers do not add up. Take for instance Flight 11. The list has 86 passengers onboard, including five hijackers, plus 11 crew members, a total of 97; but there only were 92 people total on board the plane according to all accounts. *The numbers only work if you subtract the five hijackers.* The other passenger lists also have too few names, by up to five people.[195] It is obvious from these items that the conspirators could not control everything, but they have managed quite effectively to deflect the public's attention away from these things by demonizing "conspiracy theorists" who point out the problems. That in itself suggests the guilt of those who do not want these issues examined. After all, if real Islamic terrorists did all these things, we would certainly want to know how and these details are crucial evidence.

PREPPING THE WTC

On several occasions prior to 9/11, the conspirators, possibly disguised as engineers, or NYC officials, entered the WTC North and South Towers and WTC 7. The 'work' carried out involved preparing the towers for demolition including the planting of 'charges' of some sort that would eventually bring the buildings down. WTC worker Scott Forbes has testified that on the weekend before the 9/11 attacks, there was a power down in the WTC South tower, allegedly to carry out maintenance on the electrical cabling in the building:

"On the weekend of 9/8/2001 - 9/9/2001 there was a 'power down' condition in WTC tower 2, the south tower. This power down condition meant there was no electrical supply for approx 36 hrs from floor 50 up. I am aware of this situation since I work in IT and had to work with many others that weekend to ensure that all systems were cleanly shutdown beforehand [...] and then brought back up afterwards. The reason given by the WTC for the power down was that cabling in the tower was being upgraded.

"Of course without power there were no security cameras, no security locks on doors and many, many 'engineers' coming in and out of the tower. I was at home on the morning of 9/11 on the shore of Jersey City, right opposite the Towers, and watching events unfold I was convinced immediately that something was happening related to the weekend work."[196]

[194] http://www.washingtonpost.com/wp-srv/nation/graphics/attack/hijackers.html
[195] http://www.cnn.com/SPECIALS/2001/trade.center/victims/AA11.victims.html
[196] http://www.rense.com/general63/wte.htm

THE BIG DAY ARRIVES

7:59 a.m. (14 minutes after its scheduled **7:45 a.m.** departure time) American Airlines Flight 11, specially modified with remote guidance system and gas canisters, takes off from Boston's Logan airport with 92 passengers and crew and *no* hijackers aboard.

8:14 a.m. (16 minutes after its scheduled departure time) United Airlines **Flight 175**, specially modified with remote guidance system and gas canisters, takes off from Boston's Logan airport with 65 passengers and crew and *no* hijackers aboard.

8:13 - 8:21 a.m. Flight 11 transponder is turned off.

8:20 a.m. (10 minutes after its scheduled departure time), American Airlines **Flight 77**, specially modified with remote guidance system and gas canisters, takes off from Dulles airport Washington with 64 passengers and crew and *no* hijackers on board.

8:42 a.m. (41 minutes after its scheduled departure time), United Airlines **Flight 93**, specially modified with remote guidance system and gas canisters, takes off from Newark International Airport, New York, with 33 passengers and crew and *no* hijackers on board.

With the exception of Flight 93, not long after the pilots reach cruising altitude, they switch on the autopilot—which they do not know is a the "Universal Replacement Autopilot Programme" (URAP)—and a silent, colorless, odorless gas is released into the cockpit and the cabin via the ventilation system. Within minutes all occupants of the planes are beginning to slump over as they fall into unconsciousness. Not long thereafter, the gas begins to cause respiratory seizure and the passengers and crew quietly suffocate to death.

Communications systems on the planes are overridden giving the conspirators exclusive access to and control over all incoming and outgoing communications from the planes. Of course, in reality, there will be no *real* communications coming from any of the flights.

With the activation of the URAP, new flight plans are now being followed by the aircrafts' computers.

Flight 11's new trajectory will take it through the airspace occupied by floor 89 of the WTC North tower.

Flight 175 is programmed to fly through the airspace of floor 75 of the WTC South tower.

8:46 a.m. Flight 175 Changes Transponder Signal but Remains Easily Traceable.

8:46 a.m. Flight 11 completes its pre-programmed missions and hits the WTC North Tower.

8:48 a.m. CNN begins showing WTC crash footage.

8:50 a.m. Last radio contact with Flight 77 is received.

8:55 a.m. George W. Bush arrives at Booker Elementary School.

8:56 a.m. Flight 77 Transponder Signal Disappears. Flight 77 disappears from radar screens.

9:00 a.m. VP Cheney watches the WTC crash on television.

9:03 a.m. Flight 175 completes its pre-programmed mission and hits the WTC South Tower while millions watch it live on television. Condoleezza Rice goes to Cheney's office where she meets Richard Clarke, and Wolfowitz continues a routine meeting; Rumsfeld stays in his office; Dubya stays in the classroom.

9:05 a.m. Richard Clarke recommends evacuating the White House. Rice notes the Secret Service wants them to go to the bomb shelter below the White House, and as Clarke leaves, he sees Rice and Cheney gathering papers and preparing to evacuate.

9:06 - 9:16 a.m. Bush reads a goat story to the children at Booker Elementary School in Florida.

9:12 a.m. Renee May, a flight attendant on Flight 77 allegedly uses a cell phone to call her mother.

9:16 - 9:29 a.m. Bush allegedly works with his staff on a speech.

9:20 a.m. Barbara Olson is said to call from Flight 77 but the account is full of contradictions.

9:27 a.m. Ted Olson calls the Justice Department's control center to relate his wife Barbara's call from Flight 77.

9:27 a.m. Flight 93 passenger Tom Burnett allegedly calls wife, Deena, and mentions a bomb, knives and a gun. "He spoke quickly and quietly" according to his wife. The original versions of this conversation appear to have been censored. The call wasn't recorded, but Deena's call to 9/11 immediately afterward was. In that call she states, "They just knifed a passenger and there are guns on the plane". Deena said later, "If he said there was a gun on board, there was". This is the first of over 30 additional phone calls by passengers inside the plane.

9:29 a.m. Bush makes an already scheduled speech at Booker Elementary and announces a "Terrorist attack on our country". The speech occurred at exactly the time and place publicly announced beforehand making it clear that Bush—nor anyone else—considered himself to be a terrorist target. This is the last seen of Bush until the evening of September 11.

9:30 a.m. Radar tracks "Flight 77" as it closes within 30 miles of Washington, "moving from the northwest to the southwest". There are accounts that VP Cheney is told at 9:27 a.m. that radar is tracking Flight 77, 50 miles away from Washington. The 9/11 Commission says the plane wasn't discovered until 9:32 a.m.

9:30 a.m. The Secret Service finally rush Bush out of Booker Elementary School. A Sarasota police officer recalls that immediately after President Bush's speech, "The Secret Service agent [runs] out from the school and [says] we're under terrorist attack we have to go now."

9:30 - 9:37 a.m. Langley fighters fly *East* toward the ocean instead of north toward Washington. There are varying accounts that they were ordered to Washington, New York, Baltimore, or nowhere. In 2003 testimony, NORAD Commander Major General Larry Arnold explains that the fighters head over the ocean because NORAD is "looking outward" and has to have clearance to fly over land. Yet, the *BBC* reports that just before takeoff at 9:24 a.m., the pilots are specifically told that Flight 77 may have been hijacked and they had a cockpit signal indicating that they were in an emergency wartime situation. All accounts concur that, for whatever reason, the fighters go *East*.

9:34 a.m. Bush's motorcade heads for the Sarasota-Bradenton airport. A year later, Chief of Staff Andrew Card said, "As we were heading to Air Force One, we did hear about the Pentagon attack, and we also learned, what turned out to be a mistake, but we learned that the Air Force One package could in fact be a target."

9:35 a.m. Treasury Department evacuates; Pentagon does not.

9:36 a.m. Reagan Airport flight control instructs a military C-130 that has just departed Andrews Air Force Base to intercept Flight 77 and identify it. Pilot said, "When air traffic control asked me if we had him in sight, I told him that was an understatement—by then, he had pretty much filled our windscreen. Then he made a pretty aggressive turn so he was moving right in front of us, a mile and a half, two miles away. I said we had him in sight, then the controller asked me what kind of plane it was. That caught us up, because normally they have all that information. The controller didn't seem to know anything." He reported that it was either a 757 or 767 and its silver fuselage meant it was probably an American Airlines plane. They told us to "turn and follow that aircraft". Remarkably, this is the same C-130 that was 17 miles from Flight 93 when it later "crashed" in Pennsylvania.

9:36 a.m. Flight 93 turns around and files a new flight plan with a final destination of Washington. Radar shows the plane turning 180 degrees. The new flight plan schedules the plane to arrive in Washington at 10:28 a.m.

9:36 a.m. Flight 77 turns and disappears from radar. Just before radar contact is lost, FAA headquarters is told, "The aircraft is circling. It's turning away from the White House."

9:37 a.m. Flight 77 crashes into the Pentagon.

9:37 a.m. Witnesses claim that they see a military cargo plane near Flight 77. One witness says the military cargo plane was flying directly above the plane that hit the Pentagon "as if to prevent two planes from appearing on radar". As the craft descended toward the Pentagon, the military transport veered off to the West. The account of the pilot of the C-130 differs from the on-the-ground eyewitnesses. Interviewed later, he said, "with all of the East coast haze, I had a hard time picking him out." He also said that, just after the explosion, "I could see the outline of the Pentagon", implying by these statements that he was *not* nearby at all.

9:37 a.m. VP Cheney telephones Bush and tells him that the White House has been "targeted" and urges him to "stay away".

9:39 a.m. Jim Miklaszewski states on *NBC News*, "Moments ago, I felt an explosion here at the Pentagon".

9:40 a.m. FBI confiscates film of Pentagon crash "within minutes", says gas station employee. The security film on top of a hotel near the Pentagon was also confiscated.

9:40 a.m. Flight 93 transponder signal turned off; flight still closely tracked.

9:42 a.m. Passenger Mark Bingham calls his mother... "Hi Mom, this is Mark Bingham."

9:45 a.m. Bush aides debate "where to go" with Bush.

9:55 a.m. Langley Fighters receive vague order to "protect White House".

9:55 a.m. Air Force One takes off, destination unknown, with no fighter escort.

9:56 - 10:40 a.m. Air Force One flies in circles while "Bush and Cheney and the Secret Service argue." The journalists onboard reported that the television reception for a local station remained generally good. So, one might think that Air Force One was circling over Florida, or at least over the Gulf of Mexico adjacent to Florida.

9:57 a.m. Passengers begin the attempt to regain control of Flight 93.

9:58 a.m. A man dialed emergency 9/11 from a bathroom on Flight 93 and says "we're being hijacked", and then reports an explosion and white smoke. The line then goes dead. The mentions of smoke and explosions on the recording of his call are now denied. The person who took the call is not allowed to speak to the media.

9:59 a.m. the South tower of the WTC, which was hit 17 minutes *after* the North tower and sustained a less-direct impact, collapses.

9:59 a.m. White House finally requests "Continuity of Government" Plans, Air Force One escort, and fighters for Washington.

10:00 a.m. Flight 93 transponder is turned back on and remains on for about 3 minutes.

10:00 - 10:15 a.m. Bush and Cheney claim to have been conferring on shoot down orders. There is no documentary evidence for this call. Even the 9/11 Commission was skeptical of this account.

10:00 - 10:30 a.m. Rumsfeld says that he returned from the Pentagon crash site around 10 a.m. He claimed to have made one or two calls in his office, one of which was to the President. Essentially, his whereabouts during this period are actually quite problematical.

10:03 - 10:10 a.m. Flight 93 "crashes". A Seismic study says the crash occurred at 10:06:05 a.m.

10:00 - 10:15 a.m. Cheney is told that Flight 93 is still headed for Washington and he orders it shot down. It is claimed that the plane had already crashed before this happened.

10:06 a.m. Witnesses see Flight 93 "rocking" its wings as it slowly descends.

10:06 a.m. Fighter plane seen trailing Flight 93. A second plane, described "as a small, white jet with rear engines and no discernible markings", was seen by at least six witnesses. Shortly after 9/11, an unnamed New England flight controller ignores a ban on controllers speaking to the media; he claims "that an F-16 fighter closely pursued Flight 93..." Ernie Stuhl, the mayor of Shanksville: "I know of two people—I will not mention names—that heard a missile. They both live very close, within a couple of hundred yards... This one fellow's served in Vietnam and he says he's heard them, and he heard one that day."

Flight 93 apparently started to break up before it crashed because debris was found far away from the crash site. Debris fields are found two, three, and eight miles away from the main crash site.

10:15 a.m. The section of the Pentagon that had been hit by the unknown aircraft collapses.

10:28 a.m. the North WTC tower, hit 17 minutes before the South tower, collapses.

10:30 a.m. Acting Joint Chiefs of Staff Chairman Richard Myers enters the NMCC. There are discrepancies in the testimonies about where, exactly, he was, and these remain unresolved. In his own testimony, he fails to mention where he was or what he was doing from the time of the Pentagon crash until about 10:30 a.m.

10:30 a.m. Missing Rumsfeld finally enters NMCC after being missing for 30 minutes that are unaccounted for.

10:32 a.m. Vice President Cheney reportedly called President Bush and told him that Air Force One was a target. A later account calls the threat "completely untrue", and says Cheney probably made the story up to reinforce the reason that Bush was "unavailable".

10:35 a.m. Bush heads for Louisiana on Air Force One.

10:55 - 11:41 a.m. Fighter escort finally reaches Air Force One. One report says this occurred at 10 a.m. and another says it happened at 10:41 a.m. The *St. Petersburg Times*, after interviewing people who had been on Air Force One, concluded that the fighter escort from Texas arrived between 11:00 and 11:20. Why fighters did not reach Air Force One earlier is not clear.

11:00 a.m. Customs head, Robert Bonner, claimed later that he identified all 19 of the hijackers by running the passenger manifests through the system used by Customs. However, for two days, the FBI believed there were only 18 hijackers. (This, along with BBC reports of where the hijackers were allegedly sitting, is an example of the apparently inconsistent or perhaps even entirely fabricated points of the official story.)

11:30 a.m. Media speculation that al-Qaeda is responsible promoted by General Wesley Clark.

11:30 a.m. Two congressmen, Dan Miller and Adam Putnam, who are on Air Force One, are summoned to meet with the President. Bush tells them about the "threat" and points to the fighter jet escort outside.

11:45 a.m. Air Force One lands at Louisiana Air Force Base. Bush remains in this location for approximately one hour recording a brief message and talking on the phone. Supposedly, these phone conversations consist of arguments with Dick Cheney and others over where he should go next.

12:58 p.m. "A few minutes before 1 p.m.", Bush agreed to go to Nebraska. It is alleged that this was due to "credible terrorist threats" on his life which prevented his return to Washington.

1:02 p.m. Donald Rumsfeld calls for WAR.

1:30 p.m. Air Force One leaves Louisiana for Nebraska.

2:00 p.m. An F-15 fighter pilot, Major Daniel Nash, returns to base after chasing Flight 175 and patrolling the sky over New York. He reports that, when he gets out of his plane, "he [is] told that a military F-16 had shot down a fourth airliner in Pennsylvania..."

2:50 p.m. Bush arrives in Nebraska, Offutt Air Force Base. Bush stays on the plane for about ten minutes before entering the United States Strategic Command bunker at 3:06 p.m. where he begins a video conference meeting with Cheney, Rice, Rumsfeld, Armitage, Tenet, Mineta, Clarke, and others. Bush begins the meeting by saying, "I'm coming back to the White House as soon as the plane is fueled. No discussion." The meeting ends at **4:15** p.m.

4:00 p.m. CNN blames bin Laden for attacks.

4:10 p.m. WTC 7 is burning.

4:30 p.m. WTC 7 area evacuated.

4:33 p.m. Air Force One leaves Nebraska heading for Washington.

5:20 p.m. WTC building 7 collapses; the first modern, steel-reinforced high-rise to collapse "because of fire". The building's leaseholder, Larry Silverstein said in a PBS documentary, that the decision was made to "pull it", a term that implies deliberate demolition. However, building demolition takes a considerable period of preparation—even weeks.

6:54 p.m. Bush returns to the White House.

7:00 p.m. Secretary of State, Colin Powell, returns from Peru.

8:30 p.m. Bush gives third speech of the day; declares the Bush Doctrine: "We will make no distinction between the terrorists who committed these acts and those who harbor them."

9:00 p.m. Bush meets with the full National Security Council and then later with a smaller group of key advisers. They declare that Osama bin Laden is behind the attacks. He announces, "I want you all to understand that we are at war and we will stay at war until this is done. Nothing else matters. Everything is available for the pursuit of this war. Any barriers in your way, they're gone. Any money you need, you have it. This is our only agenda". When Rumsfeld points out that international law only allows force to prevent future attacks and not for retribution, Bush yells, *"No. I don't care what the international lawyers say, we are going to kick some ass."*

10:49 p.m. Attorney General Ashcroft tells members of Congress that there were three to five hijackers on each plane armed only with knives.

11:30 p.m. Bush writes in his diary: "The Pearl Harbor of the 21st century took place today."

Now that we have a pretty good "bird's eye view" of the official events of the day, let's zoom in a bit.

ZOOM

Flight 77's role in the 9/11 attacks is somewhat problematic. As we have already noted, there were many conflicting accounts in the initial hours after the Pentagon was hit.

After all of this confusion, it was finally announced that, according to officials, the explosion at the Pentagon was caused when American Airlines Flight 77, a 100 ton Boeing 757 commercial airliner, crashed at ground level into the only section of the building that was being renovated to be more "blast resistant" and which housed the fewest number of employees in it. Flight 77 was allegedly hijacked by five Arab Islamic terrorists on an apparent suicide mission killing all 64 people on board. Officials claim the flight recorders from Flight 77 and the remains of all but one of the 64 passengers on board where found at the crash scene.

The strongest "evidence" that it was Flight 77 that crashed into the Pentagon was the testimony of Bush Administration member, Ted Olson, who claimed that his wife, a passenger on the flight, called him and gave him the inside info about what was going on. So let's take a moment to zoom in even closer and discuss:

THE SAGA OF BABS AND TED

Ted and Barbara Olson were long time members of the Bush Cabal, deeply involved in numerous nefarious activities both known and unknown.

A passenger on Flight 77, Barbara Olson, allegedly called her husband, Theodore (Ted) Olson, who was Solicitor General at the Justice Department.[197] Ted Olson was in his Justice Department office watching WTC news on television when his wife called. *A few days later*, he said:

> "She told me that she had been herded to the back of the plane. She mentioned that they had used knives and box cutters to hijack the plane. She mentioned that the pilot had announced that the plane had been hijacked." [*CNN*, 9/14/01]
>
> He tells her that two planes have hit the WTC. [*Daily Telegraph*, 3/5/02]
>
> She feels nobody is taking charge. [*CNN*, 9/12/01]

---

[197] http://www.sfgate.com/cgi-bin/article.cgi?file=/chronicle/archive/2004/07/23/FLIGHTS.TMP

He doesn't know if she was near the pilots, but at one point she asks, "What shall I tell the pilot? What can I tell the pilot to do?" [*CNN*, 9/14/01]

Then she is cut off without warning. [*Newsweek*, 9/29/01][198]

Ted Olson's recollection of the call's timing is extremely vague, saying it "must have been 9:15 [a.m.] or 9:30 [a.m.]. Someone would have to reconstruct the time for me." [*CNN*, 9/14/01]

Other accounts place it around 9:25 a.m. [*Miami Herald*, 9/14/01; *New York Times*, 9/15/01 (C); *Washington Post*, 9/21/01][199]

The call is said to have lasted about a minute. [*Washington Post*, 9/12/01][200]

By some accounts, his message that planes have hit the WTC comes later, in a second phone call. [*Washington Post*, 9/21/01][201]

In one account, Barbara Olson calls from inside a bathroom. [*Evening Standard*, 9/12/01] [202]

In another account, she is near a pilot, and in yet another she is near two pilots. [*Boston Globe*, 11/23/01][203]

Ted Olson's account of how Barbara Olson made her calls is also conflicting. Three days after 9/11, he said, "I found out later that she was having, for some reason, to call collect and was having trouble getting through. You know how it is to get through to a government institution when you're calling collect." He said he doesn't know what kind of phone she used, but he has "assumed that it must have been on the airplane phone, and that she somehow didn't have access to her credit cards. Otherwise, she would have used her cell phone and called me." [*Fox News*, 9/14/01][204]

Why Barbara Olson would have needed access to her credit cards to call him on her cell phone is not explained. However, in another interview on the same day, he said that she used a cell phone and that she may have been cut off, "because the signals from cell phones coming from airplanes don't work that well." [*CNN*, 9/14/01][205]

Six months later, he claimed she called collect, "using the phone in the passengers' seats." [*Daily Telegraph*, 3/5/02]

However, it is not possible to call on seatback phones, collect or otherwise, without a credit card, which would render making a collect call moot. Many other details are conflicting, and Olson faults his memory and says that he "tends to mix the two [calls] up because of the emotion of the events."

[198] http://www.msnbc.com/news/635771.asp

[199] http://www.startribune.com/stories/484/703150.html

[200] http://www.washingtonpost.com/ac2/wp-dyn/A14365-2001Sep11

[201] http://www.startribune.com/stories/484/703150.html

[202] http://www.cooperativeresearch.org/timeline/2001/eveningstandard091201.html

[203] http://www.boston.com/news/packages/underattack/news/planes_reconstruction.htm

[204] http://www.cooperativeresearch.org/timeline/2001/foxnews091401.html

[205] http://www.cooperativeresearch.org/timeline/2001/cnn091401c.html

Larry King's interview with Ted Olson

KING: Did she sound terrified, anxious, nervous, scared?

OLSON: No, she didn't. She sounded very, very calm.

KING: Typical Barbara.

OLSON: In retrospect, enormously, remarkably, incredibly calm. But she was calculating—I mean, she was wondering, "What can I do to help solve this problem?" Barbara was like that. Barbara could not have not done something.

KING: What's going through you?

OLSON: My—I am in—I guess I'm in shock. And I'm horrified because I really—while I had reassured her that I thought everything was going to be OK, I was pretty sure everything was not going to be OK. I, by this time, had made the calculation that these were suicide persons, bent on destroying as much of America as they could.

KING: Did you hear other noises on the plane?

OLSON: No, I did not. At one point, when she asked me what to say to the pilot, I asked her if she had any sense for where she was. *I had, after the first conversation, called our command center at the Department of Justice to alert them to the fact that there was another hijacked plane and that my wife was on it* and that she was capable of communicating, even though this *first phone call* had been cut off.

So I wanted to find out where the plane was. She said the plane had been hijacked shortly after takeoff and *they had been circling around,* I think were the words she used. She reported to me that she could see houses. I asked her which direction the plane was going. She paused—there was a pause there. I think she must have asked someone else. She said I think it's going northeast.

KING: Which would have been toward the Pentagon?

OLSON: Depending upon where the plane was,..

KING: Dulles...

OLSON: Dulles is west of the Pentagon. So east of Dulles is the Pentagon. And this plane had been in the air for, I think, over an hour. So I don't know where she was when she called.

KING: They didn't do any direct flight right to the Pentagon.

OLSON: No, no. Her plane took off at 8:10. Its impact with the Pentagon must have been around 9:30 or so. You will probably be able to reconstruct that or have that information as to the time of the impact.

KING: How does the *second conversation* end?

OLSON: We are—we segued back and forth between expressions of feeling for one another and this effort to exchange information. And then the phone went dead. I don't know whether it just got cut off again, because the signals from cell phones coming from airplanes don't work that well, or whether that was the impact with the Pentagon.

It was not—*I stayed glued to my television.* I did call the command center again. Someone came down so I can impart this information and also to be there in case she called again. But it was very *shortly thereafter that news reports on the television indicated that there had been an explosion of some sort at the Pentagon.*

KING: Did you immediately know then that's what it was?

OLSON: I did. I mean I didn't want to. I did and I didn't want to, but I knew. But *it was a long time before what had happened at the Pentagon—or it seemed like a long time—before it was identified as an airplane. Then the first report that I heard was that it was a commuter plane, and then I heard it was an American Airlines plane.*

I called some people, I guess maybe just because I had to share the dread that was living with me. I called my mother and I called my son. I said I didn't think—I thought that—I was hoping that it wasn't true, but I was very worried. I did not want them to see something on television and hear her name.

KING: Your son was Barbara's stepson, right?

OLSON: Yes. I also tried to call my daughter, who was her stepdaughter.

KING: Did you hear from the President or the attorney general?

OLSON: Oh, yes, I did. *I heard from the President.* Well, *he was in the air.* I can't tell you exactly what time of day that was on the 11th. I also heard from the *attorney general.* I also heard from the *Vice President* and many other of our officials of government. And of course, scores of other people, including you and your wife and...

KING: How are you—as you look at yourself, and looking at you now, how were you able—and everybody, I'm sure, is saying this—to *handle this so well?*

OLSON: I think—I haven't talked to people that they call grief counselors or anything like that. But I think that *people are in shock for a considerable period of time.* That's why you're advised, I mean, not to make important decisions, not to do things that don't make sense. That's why people gather around. That's why friends show up at your home. That's why people go with you wherever you go just to be able to talk to you and insulate you from the emotions that are so— packed so strongly in your body.

KING: By the way, was the President comforting?

OLSON: I thought the President was wonderfully comforting.

KING: To you on the phone?

OLSON: Yes, he was, enormously. *We couldn't speak long. This was during the day of the crisis.* And I didn't—*I hadn't expected him to call,* because he is the President of the United States. We know now—he knew then there were thousands of victims and terrible devastation and *crisis and the potential of further dangers to the structure of our government, meaning the institutions of our government and the leadership of our government.* I am deeply indebted to him that he had the time to call. He was very comforting. He is a very compassionate man.

KING: The audience of the show knows her so well. But a lot of the time they saw Barbara as harsh, Barbara very strongly opinionated, very conservative, maybe even more conservative than you, Ted.

OLSON: I don't know about that. But I think that's, it's interesting that you use that word opinionated, because Barbara mentioned once that she thought she was opinionated. And I said, "Barbara, you're not opinionated, you just have opinions."

KING: You told me about one thing last night, which just tore Shawn and my heart out. When you finally went to bed on Tuesday night, the end of this harrowing day, you find a note.

OLSON: Yes.

KING: What was it?

OLSON: Barb—I left the home a little before 6:00, as I said. And Barbara left not long thereafter to catch the plane. And it was my birthday. And when I finally went to bed, it was after 1:00 on—now it was September 12. There was a note that Barbara had written to me on the pillow, saying, "I love you. When you read this, I will be thinking of you and I will be back on—I will be back Friday."

There were a few more words than that, but I just, that was a—extraordinarily special and very much like Barbara. And I'm grateful that she did that.

KING: Thank you, Ted, our hearts are with you.

OLSON: Thank you, Larry.

KING: Ted Olson, solicitor general of the United States. He did that earlier for broadcast tonight."[206]

I have italicized a few of Ted's remarks for emphasis, but there are two particular remarks that I would like to put together here:

"[I]t was a long time before what had happened at the Pentagon—or it seemed like a long time—before it was identified as an airplane. Then the first report that I heard was that it was a commuter plane, and then I heard it was an American Airlines plane."

"I heard from the President. Well, he was in the air. I can't tell you exactly what time of day that was on the 11th. [...] We couldn't speak long. This was during the day of the crisis. And I didn't—I hadn't expected him to call, because he is the President of the United States. We know now—he knew then there were thousands of victims and terrible devastation and crisis *and the potential of further dangers to the structure of our government, meaning the institutions of our government and the leadership of our government....* I also heard from the attorney general. I also heard from the Vice President and many other of our officials of government."

Now, let's think about this for a few moments while keeping the voice morphing technology in mind when we consider phone calls from airplanes. It's not that they can't happen, but the ones that supposedly happened that day were often so bizarre as to challenge credulity.

Looking back at the testimony of the C-130 pilot above, we can see that it is contradictory, and no facts can be established from that. If we hold the phone call from the flight attendant on Flight 77 as being possibly suspect, then we are left with this: the evidence that it was Flight 77 that hit the Pentagon rests entirely on the *later* testimony of government officials who most certainly might have an agenda. What is more, the *main* proof that Flight 77 hit the Pentagon, the single event that clinches it according to the official story, was the famous "phone call" from Barbara Olson to her husband—a phone call that *could not have happened as described!*

Let us now return to the fact that the main mystery surrounds the fact that the government will not release the security videos that obviously would

[206] http://www.cooperativeresearch.org/timeline/2001/cnn091401c.html

show what hit the Pentagon. The whole matter could be settled right here and now with those videos.

Let me repeat: there is no reason to *not* release the videos even if a different craft was used to strike the Pentagon, because, after all, a terrorist attack is a terrorist attack no matter what kind of plane they use, right? If you have control of the media—as is most certainly the case here, and has been used to good effect to conceal or marginalize the truth about 9/11—then even if the government is complicit in the attacks on 9/11, they could spin whatever happened any way they wanted to as they have done so far.

If, according to the conspiracy theory of the current administration, Osama bin Laden had the resources to set up the hijacking of commercial jets to hit the World Trade Center, there is no reason he could not also have had the resources to get his hands on a fancy guided drone plane, or even a smaller jet, or anything similar for that matter. It would have been just as easy to lay it at Osama's door. That is to say, if Osama can be blamed for hitting the WTC with a couple of commercial jets, there is no reason he can't be blamed for hitting the Pentagon with something else.

In other words, no matter what it was—a Boeing 757 or a kite with a nuke attached to its tail—there is no reason the Powers That Be could not spin it to their advantage.

So why won't they release the security camera tapes?

If it was Flight 77, why can't we see it?

If it was something else, why can't we see it?

Heck, the American people are pretty accepting of explanations. There's no reason they wouldn't accept that Osama and gang could get hold of something else and fly it into the Pentagon. After all, Osama was said to have a massive underground hideout with missiles and a small army and about everything else. There's no reason why he couldn't also have been accused of getting his hands on a Global Hawk!

So again, and again, and again: why can't the American People *see what hit the Pentagon*?

It clearly is not because of concern for the families of the victims and their grief. After all, the videos of the planes flying into the WTC were shown over and over and over and over again until the entire world was whipped into a frenzy of grief and rage.

Surely, assuming that the theory of direct complicity of Bush and Co. is correct, if the conspirators were setting this thing up as long as we think they were, they would have prepared the craft that hit the Pentagon very carefully and there would be nothing about it that would arouse suspicion or reveal their identify, right? Then they could just haul out the videos and show them around the world and blame Osama, right?

But something isn't quite right about the Pentagon Strike. And whatever it is, it has something to do with the "missing time" of Dick Cheney, Don Rumsfeld, and the flying in circles and "arguing" on the phone that George

Bush did on that day *and* the strange testimony of Ted Olson that confirmed that Flight 77 hit the Pentagon.

Where did the body parts come from that were so quickly identified as those of the passengers of Flight 77 that allegedly hit the Pentagon? Body parts that survived from a massive aircraft that was claimed to have vaporized almost instantly?

The question about what happened to the passengers of Flight 77 leads us to the core of the mystery. If it was Flight 77 on the video, just show it and settle it. If it wasn't Flight 77 on the surveillance videos, why must the Bush Cabal *insist* that it was, even if they could just as easily have revealed that Osama had, in addition to hijacking three commercial jets, flown a guided drone into the Pentagon, or anything else? They could even explain a U.S. military plane being flown into the Pentagon by claiming that Osama owned one and painted it up to look like a U.S. craft.

Indeed, this small item is a terrible problem. It suggests that if the surveillance videos of what hit the Pentagon were shown, it would reveal the truth. And whatever truth that is, the Powers That Be will fight to the last gasp to conceal it.

We must dig deeper, it seems, for the solution to this problem.

Let's consider the fact that it seems obvious that George Bush, Dick Cheney, and Don Rumsfeld, *in no way*, felt threatened by the events of that day. Their insouciance demonstrates that said "terrorists" were terrifying everybody but them. We can look at the little stories about Cheney and Bush being worried that Air Force One was a target as "window dressing". After all, if you are going to play the victim, at some point you have to put on the victim act. They are smart enough to know that they had to act at least a little bit like they were concerned, even if they didn't manage to pull it off very well.

But what also seems obvious is that something strange was going on during the period of time George Bush was flying around in circles, burning up the phone lines to Cheney, Rumsfeld and... Ted Olson? Yes indeedy.

After all, it was right at that time that George, Dick and Don ought to have been putting on their "victim" act. But the facts are that all of them "went missing" at a very crucial time and the key to the whole Pentagon mystery must lie in that fact.

So, the question that I think needs to be asked, based on the strange behavior of Bush, Cheney and Rumsfeld on that day, is this: even if they were complicit in setting up an exercise that provided a smoke screen for the 9/11 attacks to be executed by someone else, is it possible that Flight 77 was *not* part of the plan, as far as they were aware?

It seems pretty certain that an attack on the Pentagon by *some* means *was* part of the plan: witness the blasé behavior of Cheney and Rumsfeld even to the extent of Rumsfeld sitting in his office with Rep. Christopher Carter, making a prediction: "Believe me, this isn't over yet. There's going to be another attack, and it could be us." That was at 9:37 a.m., one minute before the Pentagon was hit.[207] Can you imagine Cheney and the gang—including Ted Olson—being privy to the fact that the plane selected was the very one that Babs was on? Remember the report that several government officials cancelled their plans to fly on that day. Why didn't Babs? Do we think that she and her husband Ted, after their faithful service to the neocons, were not "in" on the plans?

In any event, the point is that these guys were not the least bit afraid, not the least bit ruffled, and they were actually hard pressed to even pretend to be shocked and afraid.

But something happened that changed all that. Notice this little bit of timing:

9:16 a.m. - 9:29 a.m. Bush is happily working on the speech he has to give in a few minutes. Never mind that "America is under attack", nothing is more important than Bush's speech at Booker elementary.

9:20 a.m. Barbara Olson is said to have called from Flight 77 but the account is full of contradictions.

9:27 a.m. Ted Olson allegedly calls the Justice Department's control center to relate his wife Barbara's call from Flight 77.

9:29 a.m. Bush makes his scheduled speech without a care in the world even if he is announcing that, "America is Under Attack".

Pay close attention to these next three items:

9:29 a.m. Pentagon Command Center begins high level conference call.

9:30 a.m. Three Langley fighters go airborne, but they fly _due East_.

9:30 a.m. Suddenly, the Secret Service remember their job and hustle Bush out of the School and witnesses later state that they had the impression that there _was_ a threat to the President at that point. That was one short speech!

9:34 a.m. Bush's motorcade heads for the Sarasota-Bradenton airport.

9:35 a.m. Treasury Department evacuates; Pentagon does not.

9:36 a.m. Flight 93 turns around, files a new flight plan with a final destination of Washington. Radar shows the plane turning 180 degrees. The new flight plan schedules the plane to arrive in Washington at 10:28 a.m.

9:36 a.m. Flight 77 turns and disappears from radar. Just before radar contact is lost, FAA headquarters is told, "The aircraft is circling. It's turning away from the White House".

9:37 a.m. Flight 77 allegedly crashes into the Pentagon.

9:37 a.m. VP Cheney claims that he telephoned Bush to tell him that the White House has been "targeted" and urges him to "stay away".

9:40 a.m. FBI confiscates film of Pentagon crash "within minutes", says a gas station employee. The security film on top of a hotel near the Pentagon was also confiscated.

9:40 a.m. Flight 93 Transponder signal turned off; flight still closely tracked.

9:42 a.m. Passenger Mark Bingham calls his mother...

---

[207] Another account puts Rumsfeld's "I've been around the block a few times. There will be another event" comment two minutes before the first WTC crash at 8:46 a.m.

9:42 a.m. ABC broadcasts live images of a fire in the Old Executive Building, an annex of the White House.

9:45 a.m. Bush aides debate "where to go" with Bush.

9:55 a.m. Langley Fighters receive vague order to "protect White House".

9:55 a.m. Air Force One takes off, destination unknown, with no fighter escort.

9:56 - 10:40 a.m. Air Force One flies in circles while "Bush and Cheney and the Secret Service argue".

10:00 - 10:15 a.m. Bush and Cheney claim to have been conferring on shoot down orders. There is no documentary evidence for this call. Even the 9/11 Commission was skeptical of this account.

10:00 - 10:30 a.m. Rumsfeld says that he returned from the Pentagon crash site around 10 a.m. He claimed to have made one or two calls in his office, one of which was to the President. Essentially, his whereabouts during this period is actually quite problematical.

Notice that the entire flavor of the events changes right after Ted Olson called the Justice Department to report his wife's "call." Notice that almost immediately, Bush is suddenly perceived to be "in danger" and notice the jets that were scrambled and ordered to fly *due east*. Now, remember what Ted Olson said in his interview quoted above?

> "…it was *very shortly thereafter that news reports on the television indicated that there had been an explosion of some sort at the Pentagon*."

> "…*it was a long time before what had happened at the Pentagon—or it seemed like a long time—before it was identified as an airplane. Then the first report that I heard was that it was a commuter plane, and then I heard it was an American Airlines plane.*"

> "…*I heard from the President.* Well, *he was in the air.* I can't tell you exactly what time of day that was on the 11th. I also heard from the *attorney general.* I also heard from the *Vice President.*"

> "…*We couldn't speak long. This was during the day of the crisis.* And I didn't—*I hadn't expected him to call…*"

> "…he knew then there were thousands of victims and terrible devastation and *crisis and the potential of further dangers to the structure of our government, meaning the institutions of our government and the leadership of our government.*"

What if Ted Olson was telling the truth—or at least part of the truth—in these words? After all, as an attorney he would know that the best liars are those that stick closest to the truth?

Here's a scenario for the reader to consider.

There were in fact two event plans for the 9/11 attacks—the plan as relayed to the American conspirators and the *real* plans known only to the key members of the plot—the Israeli contingent. In the murky world of international politics, one should never fully trust anyone, even those with whom you temporarily share a common goal. As such, Bush, Cheney et al. were told by the Israeli organizers of 9/11 that three planes would be "hijacked", two of them flown into the WTC towers, another into the Washington Monument where a lot of innocent civilians would be killed, while two smaller light aircraft packed with explosives would be flown into the Pentagon and the White House to create a "cover" for the conspirators. These latter craft would be of a type that would fit with Osama's alleged arsenal and the much-publicized light aircraft training received by the patsy "hijackers".

The *real* plan, however, was somewhat different and involved an "insurance" aspect that the Israeli contingent could later use to ensure full compliance of the Bush Administration with Israeli wishes. After all, if Mossad was going to stick its neck out and help the Bush gang effect a *coup d'état*, they needed insurance that Bush and Co. would never turn on them if the going got rough and too many questions were asked.

From the available data, we suggest that, from the point of view of the Bush contingent, that Flight 77 was never meant to part of the 9/11 attacks.

Let's zoom in again: By 8:55 a.m. the pilots of Flight 77 are aware that their plane has been "hijacked" by persons unknown and they have verified that they are no longer in control of the aircraft. Not long thereafter, a call is routed to Barbara Olson's seatback satellite phone. The voice on the other end is one she knows, and the message is a deadly serious one. She is informed that the two men in the seats beside her have been assigned to her and that if she wants to live, she should follow their instructions to the letter.

Barbara is told by her handlers that she should call her husband, Ted, which she duly does. But the message she delivers is not that Flight 77 has been hijacked by Arab terrorists. No, indeed, it is much worse than that. As Ted said:

"[The President knew] the potential of *further dangers to the structure of our government,* meaning the institutions of our government and *the leadership of our government.*"

The ball was no longer in the court of the Bush Cabal; they had been checked and mated. They had formed an unholy alliance with masters of deception, whose only rule was "do unto others before they do unto you". In short, Barbara is "insurance". Just because the perpetrators of the 9/11 attack have the cooperation of the Bush Cabal, it doesn't mean that they trust them. They want insurance. And now they have it.

Not long after Barbara hangs up the phone to Ted, she notices that her "handlers" are putting on gas masks. They hand one to her which she meekly places over her mouth and nose. They are sitting virtually alone in first class. As the analgesic gas is released, the other 63 passengers behind them and the pilots and crew fall unconscious.

Not long after the gas is released into the cabin of Flight 77, the URAP that has been activated switches off the transponder at about 8:56 a.m making the craft invisible to civilian air traffic control. Flight 77 continues westward and then bears north towards Wright Patterson landing about 40 minutes later at almost the same time that something *else* hits the Pentagon.

Around the time that Flight 77's transponder is switched off, a specially modified Global Hawk UAV (unmanned aerial vehicle) equipped with a "shaped charge" warhead and a secondary Depleted Uranium warhead takes off from a ship off the *Eastern coast* of the U.S. That is why the scrambled jets were ordered to fly east. It was not a mistake, it was "negotiation time."

At 9:35 a.m. the specially fitted global hawk approaches the controlled Washington airspace from the Northwest and the batteries of anti-aircraft defense systems "read" the intruder as "ours", because it *is*. Air traffic controllers at Washington's Dulles Airport pick up the aircraft using primary radar as a blip on their screens, only the aircraft's position, altitude and speed can be read. The global hawk is traveling at almost 500 miles per hour prompting flight controller Todd Lewis to say:

> "My colleagues saw a target moving quite fast from the northwest to the southeast.
> So she—we all started watching that target, and she notified the supervisor.
> However, nobody knew that was a commercial flight at the time. Nobody knew
> that was American 77. […] I thought it was a military flight."[208]

Danielle O'Brien, the Dulles flight controller said to be the first to spot the blip, comments on the speed and maneuverability of the approaching craft and opines that it must be "one of ours" (a USAF jet). The global hawk initially over-flies the immediate area of the Pentagon only to carry out a 270 degree turn with a steep descent from several thousand feet as it zeroes in on the Pentagon. Descending further to just above ground level as it gets within 200 feet of the Pentagon's west façade, the missile carrying the shaped charge is unleashed. In the initial explosion the global hawk's lightweight carbon-fibre-epoxy composite wings are completely destroyed, while the 5 feet wide, 44 feet long aluminum fuselage is torn into relatively small pieces. The shaped charge punches holes through three rings of the Pentagon, and the remote controlled nuke comes to rest. There isn't much time to make a decision, so the Bush Cabal thinks fast and decide to make the best of a bad situation. They even see how they can turn it to their advantage. After all, Barbara Olson is an attractive public figure and if she is thought to have been a victim, no one will ever suspect the perpetrators of sacrificing one of their own. Of course, the evidence that a Global Hawk hit the Pentagon and that Barbara Olson is still alive is firmly in the hands of the Israeli contingent: insurance.

The negotiations having already been completed, Cheney and Rumsfeld send special agents out immediately to confiscate the videos of the Pentagon and the cover-up machine goes into operation.

At about the same time as the global hawk impacts the Pentagon, Flight 77 is landing by remote control at Wright Patterson AFB. Barbara Olson and her two handlers step off the plane, the only ones to do so, and are met and moved to a secure location. The remaining dead passengers and crew are removed from Flight 77 by a "clean up" crew. Body parts are removed and later that day taken to the Pentagon to be found and identified. The remaining body parts are incinerated.

---

[208] http://www.aldeilis.net/aldeilis/content/view/310/107/

Flight 77 is literally taken apart in a private hanger at Wright Patterson and later taken "piecemeal" to a secure location.

Barbara Olson currently resides in one of the many extensive secure locations somewhere on the planet. Her husband, Ted Olson, who as Solicitor General was instrumental in preventing the Supreme Court from ordering a recount of votes in the 2000 election and ensuring the Presidency for George Bush, possibly is allowed to meet with her regularly. And the Bush Cabal will defend to the death the claim that Flight 77 hit the Pentagon against *all* evidence to the contrary. It was, after all, a decision made under pressure when the other side held all the cards.

MORE EVIDENCE FOR A *COUP D'ÉTAT*

While Thierry Meyssan became famous for his work establishing that Flight 77 did not hit the Pentagon in his books *The Big Lie* and *Pentagate*, he also presents evidence in *The Big Lie* that supports the theory we are proposing here. His analysis is presented in Chapter Three, "Moles in the White House". Meyssan sees the negotiations as an apparent *coup de palais*, while we think it was intense discussions between the Bush Administration and their Israeli "friends" who had just delivered a rather big surprise.

Meyssan tells the following story:

At 9:42 a.m., ABC broadcasts live images of a fire in the Old Executive Building, an annex of the White House. About fifteen minutes later, Secret Service agents command Cheney to vacate his office in the White House and take cover in the Presidential Emergency Operations Cover, in the basement under the West Wing. According to Ari Fleischer, then the press secretary for Bush, the Secret Service had received a message from the attackers that they planned to destroy Air Force One and the White House. Information from Fleischer and Karl Rove, according to reports cited by Meyssan, "raised questions about possible domestic leads, whereas the pro-war propaganda wants to see only foreign enemies."[209]

Indeed, the information that the attackers had conveniently phoned the Secret Service to warn them that the White House and Air Force One were targets, has been convenient scrubbed from the official account. Even though the bin Ladens and the Bushes were business partners, it is a little hard to believe that Osama would have been chatting with George from his cave in Afghanistan. If the attackers were phoning, given the scenario we have outlined above, it was likely to have to do with their trump card, the double-cross and hostage taking of Barbara Olson.

The hypothesis that the people behind the attacks were not hiding out in Afghanistan is backed up by reports carried in *The New York Times* that indicated that those responsible for the attacks "had established the credibility of

---

[209] Thierry Meyssan, *The Big Lie* (London: Carnot Publishing Ltd., 2002), 43.

their call by using the Presidential identification and transmission codes".[210]
Meyssan continues:

> And more astonishing still, *World Net Daily*, citing intelligence officers as its
> sources, said the attackers also had the codes of the Drug Enforcement Agency
> (DEA), the National Reconnassance Office (NRO), Air Force Intelligence (AFI),
> Army Intelligence (AI), Naval Intelligence (NI), the Marine Corps Intelligence
> (MCI) and the intelligence services of the State Department and the Department of
> Energy. Each of these codes is known by only a very small group of officials. No
> one is authorized to possess several of them. Also, to accept that the attackers
> were in possession of them supposes either that there exists a method of cracking
> the codes, or that moles have infiltrated each of these intelligence bodies.[211]

But this is not all of the evidence that suggests that there were negotiations
going on during the day of September 11 between the "partners" of the attacks. A look at Bush's flight plan between leaving Florida and arriving in
Nebraska is also instructive. If the perpetrators had the authentification and
transmission codes, the only way for Bush to override them was to be physically present at Stategic Command headquarters at Offhut in Nebraska. That
explains the destination. But how to explain that Air Force One was flying at
a low level and in a zigzag pattern that necessitated a stopover at Barkdale for
refuelling? Evasive measures were used because there was a real fear of attack on the plane. Flying at low altitudes consumes more fuel so AF1 made a
pitstop at Barkdale. Another curious fact is that while on the ground at both
bases, before entering shelter, Bush was being protected against possible
sniper fire. Are we to believe that Osama had suicide snipers positioned near
these bases? Or, after being extremely lax about Bush's safety between 8:45
and 9:30, had the Secret Service obtained new information that Bush was in
real danger?

We must also consider, as Meyssan points out, that the apparent threat to Bush
had been removed by the time he flew back to Washington in the evening.

Does that suggest that Bush had been negotiating with someone during that
time, and that after the successful conclusion of the negotiations, he knew he
was safe?

Needless to say, any mention of the fire at the White House or the phone
calls to the Secret Service, including the authentification and transmission
codes, has disappeared from the official story of 9/11.

Meyssan closes his chapter by summing up:

> Let's summarize the elements available to us. A fire breaks out in the White
> House annex. Responsibility for the attacks is claimed during a phone call to the
> Secret Service. The attackers issue demands, or even an ultimatum, and estab-
> lish their credibility by using the Presidency's own transmission and authentifi-
> cation codes. The Secret Service initiates the Continuity of Government proce-
> dure and puts the principal political leaders in shelters for safekeeping.
> President Bush negotiates during the afternoon and calm is restored by evening.

---

[210] Meyssan, *The Big Lie*, 44.
[211] Ibid.

The attacks were thus not ordered by a fanatic who believed he was delivering divine punishment, but by a group present within the American state apparatus, which succeeded in dictating policy to President Bush. Rather than a *coup d'état* aimed at overthrowing existing institutions, might it not involve instead the seizure of power by a particular group hidden within those institutions?[212]

And now we have a good idea of who that group is.

THE PROBLEM WITH FLIGHT 93

After following its normal flight plan towards Cleveland, and at approximately 9:40 a.m. Flight 93's transponder is remotely switched off and a new flight path is initiated via the URAP that will see it plough into the Washington Monument and the Mall where thousands of innocent civilians will be waiting for their date with destiny—but it will never arrive there. As yet, the pilots of Flight 93 are unaware that their aircraft is now under the control of the automatic URAP, believing that the autopilot is still guiding the plane along its normal intended path. As Flight 93 climbs further, an anomalous "misfiring" occurs in the air pressure sensitive mechanism that should have activated the analgesic gas. No gas is released and the passengers and crew remain sitting comfortably in their seats, fully awake and aware.

Alarmed by this apparently disastrous "mechanical glitch", the "technician" sitting in front of the screen quickly calls his superiors to inform them of the matter in hand. The order is given to go to "plan B" and to verify that control can still be exerted over the aircraft. The URAP is set to "manual takeover" and the technician attempts to perform some basic maneuvers to confirm that the URAP is still functional in this mode. It may also have been an attempt to set off the canisters of gas, if they had been set to go off according to a change of pressure in the cabin.

As reported by MSNBC:

> Cleveland flight controller Stacey Taylor recalls, "I hear one of the controllers behind me go, 'Oh, my God, oh my God,' and he starts yelling for the supervisor. He goes, 'What is this plane doing? What is this plane doing?' I wasn't that busy at the time, and I pulled it up on my screen and he was climbing and descending and climbing and descending, but very gradually. He'd go up 300 feet, he'd go down 300 feet."[213]

The "automatic" control and the ability to have Flight 93 fly into the White House has been fatally compromised because the pilot and passengers were not dead.

Previously, at about 9:00 a.m. Ed Ballinger, a flight dispatcher for United Airlines, sent messages one by one to the 16 transcontinental flights he is covering, including Flight 93, warning them of the first WTC crash and of the risk of a hijacking. These erratic and independent maneuvers of their air-

---

[212] Meyssan, *The Big Lie*, 49.

[213] http://members.fortunecity.com/seismicevent/msnbctransponder.html

craft alert the pilots of Flight 93, Jason Dahl and LeRoy Homer, that something is seriously wrong. Aware of the fact that commercial aircraft can be remotely controlled, the pilots conclude that this is in fact what is happening and decide to take back control of the plane. Denied any chance to communicate effectively with Air Traffic Control or the outside world by the conspirators, the pilots decide that rather than continue on the long trek to San Francisco, the best course of action is to turn around and manually pilot the 757 towards Washington Dulles airport which, given the nature of the events that were transpiring, they reasonably assume will be one of the safest parts of U.S. airspace. As reported by several news sites, it was around this time that *Flight 93 did indeed log a new Flight plan for Washington Dulles.*[214]

Yet even as the two pilots of Flight 93 are discussing their options, an unmarked white F-15 jet with two AMRAAM missiles slung under its wings is preparing to take off from a remote corner of Olmsted AFB in Pennsylvania.

Just before 10:00 am, as Flight 93 is heading towards the Pennsylvania border, the F-15 comes within 10 miles of Flight 93 and launches its missiles at the Boeing. Both missiles target the heat signatures given off by the 757's engines. On impact, the war heads detonate, knocking a large chunk off one engine, seriously damaging the other and blowing a hole in the fuselage and scattering passenger bodies, luggage and debris into the air.

As originally officially reported, at 9:58 a.m., passenger Edward Felt dials emergency 9/11 from a bathroom on Flight 93 stating: "We're being hijacked"[215] and reports an explosion and white smoke after which the line goes dead.[216] The mention of smoke and explosions on the recording of his call are now denied by the FBI. The person who took the call is no longer allowed to speak to the media.[217] (It should be noted that, at this point, Flight 93 was at a low enough altitude that a phone call could be made.)

Flight 93 has been fatally damaged, but the pilots and crew do not give up. The plane is severely damaged and is going down, yet the pilots, and possibly two passengers who have pilots licences, are fighting to maintain control.

The damage from the missiles to Flight 93's electronics causes the URAP to go off line and the Boeing's transponder comes back for a few moments[218] before Flight 93 definitively ends its journey in field near Shanksville Pennsylvania. As Flight 93 struggles to stay aloft, the cockpit voice recorder gives definitive proof of the real cause of the crash:

---

[214] http://www.guardian.co.uk/wtccrash/story/0,1300,575518,00.html

[215] http://www.canoe.ca/CNEWSAttack010916/16_week-sun.html

[216]

http://web.archive.org/web/20011223160242/http://abclocal.go.com/kgo/news/091101_nw_terrorist _attack_united.html

[217]

http://www.mirror.co.uk/news/allnews/page.cfm?objectid=12192317&method=full&siteid=50143

[218] http://members.fortunecity.com/seismicevent/msnbctransponder.html

As reported by CNN:

Near the end of [Flight 93's] cockpit voice recording, loud wind sounds can be heard.[219]

As reported in the UK Mirror:

Sources claim the last thing heard on the cockpit voice recorder is the sound of wind—suggesting the plane had been holed.[220]

Sometime after 9:57 a.m. (just a few minutes before the plane hits the ground) at the end of the cockpit voice recording the sounds of the passengers and or pilots are heard in unaccented English to say: "Give it to me!" "I'm injured", and then something like "roll it up" or "lift it up" is heard.[221]

Yet to no avail. Flight 93 hits the ground somewhere between 10:03 a.m. and 10:06 a.m. Part of one of the engines is found about a mile away from the main crash site, the only reasonable explanation being that it somehow "detached" while the plane was still high in the air. Debris, and possibly body parts, are found by locals up to 8 miles from the crash site and paper is reported to have been still floating in the air for an hour after the impact.[222]

As previously noted, at least five eyewitnesses report a "small, white jet with rear engines and no discernible markings", flying low and in erratic patterns, not much above treetop level, over the crash site within minutes of the United flight crashing.

Of course, the simple truth is that, after Flight 93 developed its "glitches" and the pilots were attempting to bring the plane and passengers home safe and sound, there was simply no way that the conspirators could allow the occupants of the plane to survive and tell their stories.

On the one year anniversary of 9/11, George and Laura Bush attended a memorial ceremony at the Flight 93 "crash" site.

---

[219] http://www.cnn.com/2002/US/04/19/rec.flight.93.families

[220]

http://www.mirror.co.uk/news/allnews/page.cfm?objectid=12192317&method=full&siteid=5014
3

[221] http://msnbc.msn.com/id/3080117/

[222]

http://web.archive.org/web/20021028201123/http://news.independent.co.uk/world/americas/stor
y.j sp?story=323958

Considering all of the evidence that points to members of the Bush administration being guilty of the cold-blooded and needless murder of the 44 passengers and crew of Flight 93, the above image should leave readers in no doubt as to the extent of the arrogance, hypocrisy and callousness with which the current leaders of the United States pursue their insane, megalomaniacal agenda.

Meanwhile, back in Washington, agents acting on behalf of the Bush contingent had started a fire at the White House in anticipation of the impact of the "Osama special", the small light aircraft they had been told to expect. The many references in media reports in the aftermath of the attacks that the Bush gang were expecting an attack on the White House and references to a fire at the White House are evidence of this. Of course, this attack never came, forcing the Bush gang to hurriedly cover it up.

From a strategic point of view, the attack on the White House that never came was a smart maneuver that helped to sow doubt and confusion among the Bush gang, not to mention making them look like a bunch of scared and incompetent buffoons and leaving the proverbial sword of Damocles hanging over their heads.

In short, while Bush was flying around, or better said, "running scared" that day, during that period of awful silence when no one knew where the Commander in Chief was, or what he might be doing, or what terrible thing was going to happen next, it is quite likely that he *was* on the phone to Ted Olson, among many others, and that some very fast damage control was being discussed, all the while the conspirators were having it shoved in their faces that they were *not* as smart as they thought they were.

Speculating further about the possible existence of national level satellite photos in the hands of someone with whom the Bush Cabal has had to negotiate, we can then move to the suggestion that, once these negotiations were satisfactorily concluded, the plan was resumed to utilize Flight 77, as the "plane that hit the Pentagon" with the agreement and complicity of Ted Olson who had been so "comforted" by the phone call from the President, and his "late" wife Barbara Olson.

After this step was taken, the hangman's noose was sprung: from that moment on, the video footage of what really struck the Pentagon had to be concealed at all costs. If it were to be released and the truth revealed, impossible questions about the fate of Flight 77 and its occupants and the phone calls they made would immediately arise and the entire operation would be exposed for what it is: a murderous attack on the United States' citizens by masters of deception with the complicity of their own government.

If our speculative line is correct, it means that the Bush Cabal have been hoisted on their own petard and are being controlled, blackmailed, or otherwise held to a certain "line" by *some other group* so that this information will not be released. The main question is, of course, who is it and what is this other group demanding? Based on simple observation, nothing but the total destruction of the United States is going to satisfy them, along with a radical reshaping of the Middle East along Israeli lines that will necessarily involve a major war in which a significant percentage of Middle Eastern peoples, Jews and Arabs alike, will likely perish. Given the Iraqi quagmire that the U.S. has *apparently* willingly entered into, a quagmire that seems increasingly likely to lead to the fall and discrediting of America from it position as "world leader", it is eminently reasonable and logical to suggest that they are only doing so under some form of duress.

We think that the scenario that we have outlined is much more plausible than the story floated by the Bush Administration to cover it up. What, in fact, could be more outlandish than the idea that 9/11 was carried out by 19 Arab terrorists armed only with box cutters, guided by a crazy recluse from a cave in Afghanistan? That's your choice: toxic gas, computer-controlled aircraft, and an air defense system that was commanded to stand down while greedy neocons were entrapped by their own arrogance, or Arabs with box cutters, and the largest failure of NORAD and the greatest number of insane coincidences one could possibly imagine conveniently falling on the one day they were needed.

It's your call.

To believe the conspiracy theory the government has promoted about 9/11, you need to believe that everything that could go wrong, did go wrong; that the system that had worked perfectly 67 times in the previous twelve months for intercepting aircraft somehow, at the most crucial moment in U.S. history, failed.

In short, the Greatest Military Machine on earth was obliged to declare itself the most incompetent in order to cover up a truly horrific crime. Thousands of lives of U.S. citizens were lost on that day, thousands more American, Afghani, and Iraqi lives have been lost in the years since, and no one has been held accountable. At the same time, Draconian laws curtailing American freedoms have been passed to "make America Safe". The fact is, if the systems *already in place* had not been ordered to stand down, there would not have been an attack on the WTC Towers, much less the Pentagon. If U.S. political leaders were really interested in protecting the American people, the systems in place would have worked, and there would have been no need for the Patriot Act.

In the five years since the images of planes exploding in the windows of the World Trade Center were engraved in our psyches, the movement of people who doubt the official story of 9/11 has grown. There are now many websites devoted to the question. But how many Americans are willing to look the facts in the face and confront the truth: the "attack" of 9/11 was an inside job with help.

Half a million people marched in New York in 2003 and again in Washington in 2005, against George Bush. They were angry that he has brought on war, deficit, tax cuts for the rich, surging unemployment and the most anti-democratic loss of rights ever seen in the USA. But how much coverage did these (and other) marches get in the media?

Moreover, even if they are in the streets protesting against the abuses and lies that are known, how many of those 500,000 people know how bad the situation really is? How many are willing to consider that Israeli Intelligence, with the help of a group of people in the Bush government, may very well have organised and staged the attacks on the World Trade Center and the Pentagon in order to justify a "war on terror", that is, a war on the peoples of the Middle East? This war began in Afghanistan and has continued into Iraq. It looks now as though the administration is ready to take on Iran and eventually Syria, the countries named in a 1996 report prepared for Israeli PM Netanhayu by members of the neo-con cabal. *Eretz Israel*, these lands are called; the land God gave the Jews; and they want it all.

This abbreviated collection of data (believe me, there is a ton of material out there on this subject) does seem to support the idea that Mossad may, indeed, have been responsible for the 9/11 attacks on the World Trade Center and that the Bush Reich was not only complicit in ordering the U.S. military and intelligence services to "stand down", but that they were directly involved in the plot as the evidence of the link between Bob Graham and Mahmoud Ahmad demonstrates not to mention the saga of Babs and Ted.

And, of course, though each group is playing the other as in Spy vs. Spy, there are many things that Israel ought to consider in the volatile climate of burgeoning criticism of Israel around the world, a climate that could become full-blown anti-Semitism if Israel continues its ruthless aggression. But then again, we notice that the Israeli government and its intelligence agencies are actively promoting the idea that "a new wave of anti-Semitism" is sweeping Europe, an idea that serves to immediately quell any criticism of the inhuman policies of the Israeli government in the Middle East and around the world. Never mind that Bush and Co., and American Intell organizations have been stirring the pot for years. Just as people were "angry" and wanted an "answer" to 9/11, what kind of answer will be given when the heat is turned up on the Bush Reich? Is it not likely that Bush and friends would sacrifice their Israeli friends before taking the fall themselves? Just imagine what would happen if, suddenly, all the fingers pointed to Israel and Mossad as the masterminds of Global Terrorism?

In our research, it became abundantly clear to us that the events of September 11 were planned by those who not only had the motive, means, and opportunity to carry out the plan, but also were best placed to manage the consequences stemming from it, as well as managing the flow of information. What was also evident was that the question "who benefits?" had to be asked from a completely different perspective than simple diplomatic or foreign relations would allow. It became evident that the agenda was much more than just that of Israel wanting to get support for a war against the Palestinians or the Americans helping Israel because they wanted to gain control of oil in Iraq or opium trade and pipelines in Afghanistan. We realized that the events of September 11 were masterminded by those who were in the best position to manage the consequences and to obtain the benefits. It was clear that this was not *just* Israel, though Israel may have been manipulated to participate because of its own tunnel-vision as well as particular conditions created by the events of World War II. Also, it was clear that the desired benefits were seen to be something altogether different.

It appears that the events of September 11 were planned years in advance, with the groundwork being carefully laid by a propaganda campaign orchestrated to convince the public that the United States has a plausibly sophisticated nemesis with the motive, means, and opportunity to perpetrate a devastating act of terror against Americans: Arab terrorism.

It also seems that the whole show was orchestrated using proxy agents and operative planners who are not only sufficiently distanced and compartmentalized from the true masterminds (to create a condition of "plausible deniability"), but have been set up as patsies with evidence that has been carefully laid to incriminate them at the proper time.

As we have said, the real guilt must be sought among those who are in the best position to manage the flow of information as well as to reliably benefit from the new world order that is being created. When we take a broad view of the problem, we first see that the right-wing Israeli agenda benefits greatly from world opinion being turned against "Arab terrorists" and by extension, the Palestinians. At the same time, there are those who seek to accuse the Jews—as a whole—of a plan for global domination, by gaining control of the Middle Eastern oil and thereby controlling the world. Unfortunately, since Israel itself may very likely be destroyed in the process they will not be the ones who benefit. The only ones who will benefit are the political and corporate elites of the United States, the United Kingdom, the European Union and the expatriate "Zionists", who claim to act in the best interests of the Jewish people—also, as it happens, the very parties orchestrating the global war on terrorism.

In short, it appears that someone is using the Jews—the nation of Israel—to play the patsy in the final episode of the "Final Solution".

There are those commentators of the political and global scene who would like to think that this is merely a conspiracy of rich and powerful people who "see it as their moral duty" to establish a One World Government and to whom a unified world government is the most logical way to manage the affairs of the world. It is absurd to assign the motive to a perception of a moral duty, or even a logical approach to managing world affairs. That is nonsense in the face of the facts and when considering history. Historically, whenever such strategies have been attempted as a panacea for society's ills, they have resulted in nothing but backwardness and decay not to mention horrific environmental destruction and decline of health, most generally inflicted on the working classes, the base upon which all power rests. Said working classes then, invariably, rise up like a mindless beast and destroy the very rulers that claimed to be acting in their best interests.

And this brings us, finally, to the necessity for identifying the real agenda being manifested here: the ultimate secret behind the events of 9/11.

PART 2: THE ULTIMATE TRUTH

Into the Labyrinth

The most successful tyranny is not the one that uses force to assure
uniformity but the one that removes the awareness of other possibilities,
that makes it seem inconceivable that other ways are viable,
that removes the sense that there is an outside.
Allan Bloom – *The Closing of the American Mind*

The "core" of the 9/11 event can only be reached with a more or less spiraling
approach. In this sense, it is very much like a labyrinth—which is an entirely
appropriate metaphor—and we will follow the threads that lead from one
item to another, finally arriving at the center, facing the monster, and then
hopefully finding our way out again.

Curiously, after exploring this labyrinth, we will come to see that whether
or not 9/11 was orchestrated by the U.S., by Israel, or by Osama bin Laden, is
secondary to the ultimate secret. On this level, it is more important that the
event happened than who actually came up with the idea.

Since we have established the likelihood that Israeli interests are a large
part of the motivations for the 9/11 attacks, we need to take a look at Israel
itself.

The current nation of Israel is a completely artificial and arbitrary construction that came about as the result of political maneuvering leading to the Balfour Declaration in the early part of the 20th century.

The Balfour Declaration was a letter from British Foreign Secretary Arthur
James Balfour, to Lord Rothschild (Walter Rothschild, 2nd Baron Rothschild), a leader of the British Jewish community, for transmission to the Zionist Federation, a private Zionist organization:

Foreign Office

November 2nd, 1917

Dear Lord Rothschild,

I have much pleasure in conveying to you, on behalf of His Majesty's Government, the following declaration of sympathy with Jewish Zionist aspirations which
has been submitted to, and approved by, the Cabinet.

"His Majesty's Government view with favour the establishment in Palestine of a
national home for the Jewish people, and will use their best endeavours to facilitate
the achievement of this object, it being clearly understood that nothing shall be
done which may prejudice the civil and religious rights of existing non-Jewish
communities in Palestine, or the rights and political status enjoyed by Jews in any
other country."

I should be grateful if you would bring this declaration to the knowledge of the Zionist Federation.

Yours sincerely,

Arthur James Balfour[223]

At the time, most of the area of Palestine was still under the control of the Ottoman Empire, and the borders of what *would* become Palestine had been outlined as part of the May 16, 1916 Sykes-Picot Agreement[224] between Britain and France.

One of the main Jewish figures who negotiated the granting of the declaration was Dr. Chaim Weizmann, the leading spokesman for organized Zionism in Britain. During the first meeting between Chaim Weizmann and Balfour, in 1906, the Unionist leader was impressed by Weizman's personality. Balfour asked Weizmann why Palestine—and Palestine alone—could be the basis for Zionism. "Anything else would be idolatry", Weizmann protested, adding: "Mr. Balfour, supposing I were to offer you Paris instead of London, would you take it?" "But Dr. Weizmann", Balfour retorted, "we have London", to which Weizmann rejoined, "That is true, but we had Jerusalem when London was a marsh."[225]

Weizmann was a chemist who managed to synthesize acetone via fermentation. Acetone is needed in the production of cordite, a powerful propellant explosive needed to fire ammunition without generating tell-tale smoke.

---

[223] http://en.wikipedia.org/wiki/Walter_Rothschild%2C_2nd_Baron_Rothschild

[224] The Sykes-Picot Agreement of May 16, 1916 was a secret understanding between the governments of Britain and France defining their respective spheres of post-World War I influence and control in the Middle East. The boundaries of this agreement still remain in much of the common border between Syria and Iraq. The agreement was negotiated in November 1915 by the French diplomat François Georges-Picot and British Mark Sykes. Britain was allocated control of areas roughly comprising Jordan, Iraq and a small area around Haifa. France was allocated control of South-eastern Turkey, Northern Iraq, Syria and Lebanon. The controlling powers were left free to decide on state boundaries within these areas. The area which subsequently came to be called Palestine was for international administration pending consultations with Russia and other powers.

This agreement is viewed by many as conflicting with the Hussein-McMahon Correspondence of 1915–1916. The conflicting agreements are the result of changing progress during the war, switching in the earlier correspondence from needing Arab help to subsequently trying to enlist the help of Jews in the United States in getting the US to join the First World War, in conjunction with the Balfour Declaration, 1917. The agreement had been made in secret.

The agreement was later expanded to include Italy and Russia. Russia was to receive Armenia and parts of Kurdistan while the Italians would get certain Aegean islands and a sphere of influence around Izmir in southwest Anatolia. The Italian presence in Anatolia as well as the division of the Arab lands was later formalized in the Treaty of Sèvres in 1920.

The Russian Revolution of 1917 led to Russia being denied its claims to parts of the Ottoman Empire. At the same time Lenin released a copy of the confidential Sykes-Picot Agreement as well as other treaties causing great embarrassment among the allies and growing distrust among the Arabs.

The agreement is seen by many as a turning point in Western/Arab relations, as it negated the promises made to Arabs through T.E. Lawrence for a national homeland in the Syrian territory in exchange for their siding with British forces against the Ottoman Empire.

[225] B. Dugdale, *Arthur James Balfour, Vol I.* (1939), 326-327.

Germany had cornered supplies of a major source of acetone, calcium acetate and other pre-war processes in Britain were inadequate to meet the increased demand in the Great War. A shortage of cordite would have severely hampered Britain's war effort. The Minister for Munitions David Lloyd-George, who became Prime Minister shortly after, was grateful to Weizmann and also supported him. Balfour asked what payment he would like in return for the use of his process. Weizmann responded, "There is only one thing I want. A national home for my people." He eventually received both payment for his discovery and a role in the history of the origins of the state of Israel.

In his November, 2002 interview with the *New Statesman* magazine, the UK Foreign Secretary, Jack Straw, has blamed Britain's imperial past for many of the modern political problems, including the Arab-Israeli conflict.

"The Balfour declaration and the contradictory assurances which were being given to Palestinians in private at the same time as they were being given to the Israelis—again, an interesting history for us, but not an honourable one," he said.[226]

Let's take a closer look at what Weizmann said: Balfour asked Weizmann why Palestine—and Palestine alone—could be the basis for Zionism. "Anything else would be idolatry." "Mr. Balfour, supposing I were to offer you Paris instead of London, would you take it?" "But Dr. Weizmann", Balfour retorted, "we have London", to which Weizmann rejoined, "That is true, but we had Jerusalem when London was a marsh."

As it happens, that is not the truth. But also, as it happens, that fiction of the great land of Israel that was given to the Jews by God Almighty himself is a widespread belief among the three main monotheistic religions that dominate the world today.

In my book, *The Secret History of the World*, I examine the question of the so-called "history of the Jews" in some detail. This material is also published on our website.[227] In *Secret History* I wrote:

> One might think that the Laws of Probability would mandate that, without any intelligent input, 50% of the time the events in our world would lead to benefits for mankind. In a strictly mechanical way, life in our world ought to have manifested a sort of "equilibrium." Factoring in intelligent decisions to *do good* might bring this average up to about 70%. That would mean that humanity would have advanced over the millennia to a state of existence where good and positive things happen in our lives more often than "negative" or "bad" things. In this way, many of the problems of humanity would have been effectively solved. War and conflict would be a rarity, *perhaps 70 percent of the earth's population* would have decent medical care, a comfortable roof over their heads, and sufficient nutritious food so that death by disease or starvation would be almost unheard of. In other words, human society would have "evolved" in some way, on all levels.

[226] "British Empire blamed for modern conflicts", http://news.bbc.co.uk/2/hi/europe/2481371.stm (November 5, 2002).
[227] http://www.cassiopaea.org/cass/biblewho1.htm

The facts are, however, quite different.

More than 840,000,000 people on the Earth suffer from hunger. That's about *three times the population of the entire USA*. This is chronic, persistent hunger, which kills 24,000 people *every day*, or over 8 million human beings each year. Three out of four who die from starvation are younger than five years old. How can "evolved" human beings accept that fact as "normal?"

According to the *Historical Atlas of the Twentieth Century*, during the past 100 years there have been approximately 2 billion deaths (including civilians) resulting from war, tyrannical governments, and man-made famine. When these figures are broken down into deaths caused by Communism vs. Capitalism, they are almost equal, with the figures slightly higher for Capitalism which may surprise some people who believe that the Capitalistic system is the "right" one. "By their fruits you shall know them."

Turning to mortality statistics that are *not* related to war and famine, we find that it is a bit difficult to get an actual number because the statistics are nearly always expressed in terms of percentages rather than in hard population numbers. One gets the feeling that the actual count is so frightening that this approach is used for the express purpose of avoiding having to face the facts. One thing we do know is that deaths from cardiovascular diseases and stroke are the leading cause of death in 31 of the 35 Western Hemisphere countries that report disease related mortality statistics. The highest of these mortality rates are found in the *English-speaking* Caribbean, USA, Canada, Argentina, Chile and Uruguay. Mortality rates from these causes are increasing in the Central American and Latin Caribbean regions as they come more and more under the sway of Western capitalism. Again, "By their fruits you shall know them."

What we are talking about above are the "quiet" statistics, from our present reality. They are quiet because nobody ever makes a big deal about them. The headlines of our newspapers do not trumpet them on the front page where they rightly belong. Even now it is easy to forget that there were 65 million deaths from WWII alone and that deaths from disease and starvation continue as a quiet, steady, drumbeat of increasing mortality behind the blaring headlines of school shootings, sensational murder trials, and little Cuban boys who become the center of international custody disputes.

I don't think that one single person on this planet will disagree that they want a better life for themselves and their children; and most of them will add that they do not presently have the capacity to make it a reality. Except for a very small minority of very sick people, I don't think anybody really likes to see misery and suffering, disease and death and despair, in any context. And again we must ask: if these things are so detestable to human beings at large, if so many people are working and thinking and praying to improve the conditions of our world, why isn't it happening?

Seekers of Spiritual Verity—a large number of whom could be considered "Intelligentsia"—are always aware of these things, and they are asking, "What is the origin of all the misery and suffering? Does it just happen? Do people and only people cause others to suffer? Is it that God is good, but allows bad things to happen?"

"Don't forget the power of prayer," we are told by our religious leaders, or "positive thinking," as the New Age gurus tell us. The only problem is, prayers and positive thinking do not seem to have improved the world very much on the occasions when it is certain that nearly every human being was praying for a certain outcome.

Jesus promised: "If any two of you shall agree and ask... it shall be done." (Matt 18:19) That's a promise. What do you want or need? Just ask!

But it doesn't work and we see it!

Over sixty million people died because God didn't do what everybody thought he should do. C.S. Lewis struggled with this issue in the latter part of his life. He saw clearly that, before World War II, practically every human being on the planet was praying—to Jesus, God the Father, the Virgin Mary, Allah, Buddha and whoever else you can name or mention, so all the bases were covered—that this terrible thing would not happen. The memory of the previous "Great War" was still fresh in the mind of mankind. They remembered the horrible carnage and vowed, *never again!*

In the end, after the mightiest cry of prayer in human memory, rising from the earth, *almost one-third of the world was uninhabitable and sixty-five million human beings were dead.* Are we to think that this was God's answer to prayer? It certainly doesn't give us much hope for the "power of positive thinking."

Think about it.

And here I would like to point out the interesting fact that the three major monotheistic religions extant in the world today are all based, essentially, on a single religion, Judaism.

Think about that for a moment.

When researching religious matters, one always comes across prophecy and miracles. It seems that those who are to be kept in fear of the Lord need an unequivocal sign from time to time. Miracles and visions can sway whole armies. We can think of the battle cry "Allah Is Great!" and the claim of the salvific blood of Christ that was held up as a shield against the Saracens. We should also be reminded of the mandate of Yahweh to "utterly destroy" just about everybody who wasn't hanging out with Joshua and his gang. Such "visions" go back into our primeval past. Around 5,000 BCE, the divine Ishtar was said to have appeared to Enme-Kar, the ruler of Uruk, telling him to overthrow the city of Aratta. But, at the moment, we are mostly concerned with visions in the context of the Bible since it is the Bible that underpins the beliefs of a staggering number of human beings on planet earth at the present time, including their "revised forms" in the New Age and Human Potential movement.

Hans Conzelmann, Professor of New Testament Studies at Tottingen admitted that the Christian community continues to exist because the conclusions of the critical study of the Bible are largely *withheld* from them. Joachim Kahl, a graduate in theology of Phillips University, Marburg, noted:

The ignorance of most Christians is largely due to the scanty information provided by theologians and ecclesiastical historians, who know two ways of concealing the scandalous facts of their books. They either twist reality into its exact opposite or conceal it.

Dr. Johannes Lehman, co-translator of a modern edition of the Bible remarked:

> The evangelists are interpreters, not biographers; they have not illuminated what had grown dark with the passage of generations, but obscured what was still light. They have not written history, but made history. They did not want to report, but to justify.

The "original texts" that are so often referred to in theological hairsplitting do not exist. What *do* exist are transcripts that originated between the fourth and tenth centuries. And these are transcripts of transcripts, some fifteen hundred of them, and not one of them agrees with another. More than eighty thousand variations have been counted. There does not exist a single page of the "original texts" without contradictions. The most prominent of them, the *Codex Sinaiticus*, has been found to contain sixteen thousand corrections, which can be traced back to seven correctors. These correctors made their "corrections" because each one understood the verses differently, and they transformed the functions according to what they perceived to be the needs of the time.

Dr. Robert Kehl of Zurich writes:

> Frequently the same passage has been 'corrected' by one corrector in one sense and immediately 'recorrected' in the opposite sense by another, depending entirely on which dogmatic view had to be defended in the relevant school. At all events, a completely chaotic text and irremediable confusion has already arisen owing to individual 'corrections,' but even more so to deliberate ones.

Father Jean Schorer, for many years spiritual adviser to the Cathedral of Saint-Pierre, Geneva, concluded that the theory of the divine inspiration of the Bible is in such contradiction with the most basic, elementary knowledge base of normal human reason, and is so obviously refuted by the Bible itself, that only ignorant persons would defend it, while only people completely devoid of any kind of culture would believe it.

Dr. Robert Kehl writes in *Die Religion des modernen Menschen*:

> Most believers in the Bible have the naive credo that the Bible has always existed in the form in which they read it today. They believe that the Bible has always contained all the sections, which are found in their personal copy of the Bible. They do not know—and most of them do not want to know—that for about 200 years the first Christians had no 'scripture' apart from the Old Testament, and that *even the Old Testament canon had not been definitely established in the days of the early Christians*, that written versions of the New Testament only came into being quite slowly, that for a long time no one dreamed of considering these New Testament writings as Holy Scripture, that with the passage of time the custom arose of reading these writings to the congregations, but that even then no one dreamed of treating them as Holy Scriptures with the same status as the Old Testament, that this idea first occurred to people when the different factions in Christianity were fighting each other and they felt the need to be able to back themselves up with something binding, that in this way people only began to regard these writings as Holy Scripture about 200 CE.

The fact is, in examining this matter, we find nothing of "God Almighty" or the "Holy Ghost" in the Bible at all. That's the plain fact, and a lot of people in the "business" of religion know it.

Nevertheless, our institutions of higher learning generally have a special faculty allotment for the teaching of theology, *financed by the taxpayer*, whether Christian or Jew. One assumes that the students who study this theology are also given exposure to other studies, such as math, languages, science, and so forth. The question then becomes: what kind of strange distortion, what incomprehensible corruption takes place in the minds of human beings, so that they so completely separate their academic knowledge from what they hear preached at them from the pulpit?

What kind of brainwashing can so effectively cause the simplest of facts to be forgotten?

How does this happen?

It is literally staggering to a logical, intelligent human being that the fairy tale of the Bible—as God's word—has endured so long. There is nothing to which we can compare this in the entire seven thousand years of human history of which we are aware. Calling it all a "pack of lies" seems rather harsh, but it is increasingly evident that it is certainly intentionally misleading, and, in that case, what shall we call it?

Christian theologians claim that the teachings of Jesus (which is the established religious dogma) are unconditionally valid. Rudolf Augstein asks:

> With what right do the Christian churches refer to a Jesus who did not exist in the form they claim, to doctrines which he did not teach, to an absolute authority which he did not confer, and to a filiation with God which he never laid claim to? [228]

Naturally, all of these problems have led to many interesting theological solutions. It is amazing how creative true believers can be when faced with facts that this or that idea they have held for a long time is no longer tenable.

Nowadays, the presence of widespread sharing of information relating to anomalous appearances of what are now being called "aliens" has naturally led to the identification of Jesus with the "interstellar astronaut" theory. Jesus is an "alien."

Dr. Vyatcheslav Saitsev of the University of Minsk claimed that Jesus came from outer space. His idea was that Jesus was a representative of a higher civilization, and that this is the explanation of his supernatural powers. He noted: "In other words, God's descent to Earth is really a cosmic event."

Meanwhile, the *Holy Blood, Holy Grail* guys and Dan Brown with his *DaVinci Code* are busy cooking up a "divine bloodline." At the same time, we have a host of true 'New Age' believers around the planet preaching the gospel of those cute and helpful Grays, and the reptilian Lord who really loves us and never did anything to humanity except teach them all about how to be civilized.

---

[228] Rudolf Augstein, *Jesus Menschensohn* (Munich, 1972).

Simultaneously, we have what is claimed to be a "gradual revelation" plan going on via the government and its space program, and now a big push by George Bush and the Fundamentalists of both Christian and Zionist tendencies to try to institute what can only be described as a One World Government under the rule of the U.S.

We have a right to ask: what the heck is really going on? What does it mean to talk about the "New Jerusalem" when, in point of fact—as I demonstrate, backed by the facts, in *Secret History*—anything and everything that had to do with the Old Jerusalem was lies and disinformation issuing from the spokesmen of that crafty Yahweh/Jehovah guy with control issues?

The reality seems to be that Judaism, Christianity and Islam were specifically designed and created just to produce a particular situation that is desirable to someone at a certain point in time, and again, we see the same operation being run on humanity in the present day as the New Age—Human Potential movement.

When we step back from the situation, the one thing that we see is that prophecy is at the center of the Judaeo-Christian-Islamic tradition. The prophets of these religions claimed to be in direct contact with the Creator of the Universe, and this creator seems to have been singularly "personal" in the sense of having personal traits, whims, likes and dislikes. His prophets are, naturally, privileged messengers, receiving his divine revelations, and these revelations divide mankind into those who believe them and those who don't. Naturally, those who don't are damned.

Judaism, Christianity, Islam, and their New Age offshoots, are the chief proponents of the many End of the World scenarios with which we are most familiar. Scenarios about the end times originate mostly in the body of apocalyptic, eschatological writings of the New and Old Testaments. It is in the final book, "Revelation", that most striking and symbolic representations about the end of the world are said by many to be depicted.

It is a difficult work to comprehend. Probably no other piece of writing in history has been examined more thoroughly and interpreted more widely. It is the end-of-the-world legend, a doomsday tale on moldy bread with virtual reality special effects in abundance. It is the inspirational fountainhead for mad prophets, spittle spewing, pulpit-pounders, apocalyptic Enochian magicians, fanatical true believers, grade-B moviemakers, and knaves and snake-oil salesmen of every form and sort.

It is also, as it happens, at the root of the present global crises with Israel at the center.

So, turning our attention once again to Israel, we notice that the claim to Israel is based on the claim that God Almighty gave the land to the Jews via Moses. Let's look at that with a selected excerpt from *The Secret History of The World*:

WHO WROTE THE BIBLE AND WHY?

The problem with the subject of the Bible and History is that there are so many fields that can contribute data—archaeology, paleontology, geology, linguistics, and so forth—these types of things provide *data*, which are discarded in favor of "wishful thinking". On the other side we have mythology and history. They are, unfortunately, quite similar because, as it is well known, the "victors write history." And people are prone to do many evil deeds in difficult situations, which they later wish to cover up in order to present themselves in a more positive light for posterity.

The oldest extant texts of parts of the Old Testament in Hebrew are those found at Qumran which date only to two or three centuries before Christ. The oldest version before the Qumran texts were discovered was a *Greek* translation from about the same period! The earliest complete *Hebrew* text dates *only from the tenth century CE*! Something is wrong with this picture.

It is generally believed from textual analysis that a very small part of the Old Testament was written about 1000 BCE and the remainder about 600 BCE. The Bible, as we know it, is the result of many changes throughout centuries and is contradictory in so many ways we don't have space to catalog them all! There are entire libraries of books devoted to this subject, and I recommend that the reader have a look at the material in order to have some foundation upon which to judge the things I am going to say.

Biblical scholars generally date Abraham to about 1800 - 1700 BCE. The same scholars date Moses to 1300 or 1250 BCE. However, if we track the generations as listed in the Bible, we find that there are only seven generations between and including these two patriarchal figures! Four hundred years is a bit long for seven generations. Allowing 35 to 40 years per generation, places Abraham at about 1550 BCE and Moses at about 1300 BCE. This obviously means that there are a few hundred years not accounted for in the text. Tracking back to Noah, using the generations listed in the Bible, one arrives at a date of about 2000 to 1900 BCE—about the time of the arrival of the 'Indo-Europeans' into the Near East. The geological and archaeological records do not support a cataclysm at that time, though what could be described as a global discontinuity of cataclysmic elements is supported right around 12,000 years ago. In this case, we have lost 8,000 years, give or take a day.

In a more general sense, using the Bible as historical source material presents a number of very serious problems, most particularly when we consider the "mythicization" factor. There are many contradictions in the text that cannot be reconciled by standard theological mental contortionism. In some places, events are described as happening in a certain order, and later the Bible will say that those events happened in a different order. In one place, the Bible will say that there is two of something, and in another it will say that there were 14 of the same thing. On one page, the Bible will say that the Moabites did something at a specific time, and then, a few pages later, it will say that the Midianites did exactly the same thing at exactly the same time! There is even an instance in which Moses is described as going to the Tabernacle before Moses built the Tabernacle! (I guess Moses was a time traveler!)

There are things in the Pentateuch that pose other problems: it includes things that Moses could not have known if he lived when he is claimed to have lived. And, there is one case in which Moses said something he could not have said: the text gives an account of Moses' death, which it is hardly likely that Moses described. The text also states that Moses was the humblest man on earth! Well, as one commentator noted, it is not likely that the humblest man on earth would point out that he is the humblest man on earth!

All of these problems were taken care of for most of the past two thousand years by the Inquisition, which also took care of the Cathars and anybody else who did not follow the Party Line of Judaeo-Christianity.

For the Jews, the contradictions were not contradictions; they were only "apparent contradictions"! They could all be explained by "interpretation"! (Usually, these interpretations were more fantastic than the problems, I might add.) Moses was able to "know things he couldn't have known" because he was a prophet! The medieval biblical commentators, such as Rashi and Nachmanides, were *very* skillful in reconciling the irreconcilable!

In the 11th century, a real troublemaker, Isaac ibn Yashush, a Jewish court physician in Muslim Spain, mentioned the distressing fact that a list of Edomite kings that appears in Genesis 36 named a few kings who lived long after Moses was already dead. Ibn Yashush suggested the obvious, that someone who lived after Moses wrote the list. He became known as "Isaac the Blunderer."

The guy who memorialized clever Isaac this way was a fellow named Abraham ibn Ezra, a 12th century rabbi in Spain. But ibn Ezra presents us with a paradox because he also wrote about problems in the text of the Torah. He alluded to several passages that appeared not to be from Moses' own hand because they referred to Moses in the third person, used terms Moses would not have known, described places that Moses had never been, and used language that belonged to an altogether different time and place than the milieu of Moses. He wrote, very mysteriously, "*And if you understand, then you will recognize the truth. And he who understands will keep silent.*"

So, why did he call Ibn Yashush a "Blunderer"? Obviously because the guy had to open his big mouth and give away the secret that the Torah was not what it was cracked up to be, and if the truth got out, lots of folks who were totally "into" the Jewish mysticism business would lose interest. And keeping the interest of the students and seekers after power was a pretty big business in that day and time. More than that, however, we would like to note that *the entire Christian mythos was predicated upon the validity of Judaism,* being its "New Covenant", and even if there was apparent conflict between Jews and Christians, the *Christians most desperately needed to validate Judaism and its claim to be the revelation to the "chosen people" of the One True God.* It was on that basis that Jesus was the Son of God, after all. In short, it could even be said that Christianity created Judaism in the sense that it would have faded to obscurity long ago if there had not been the infusion of validating energy at the end of the Dark Ages.

In 14th century Damascus, a scholar by the name of Bonfils wrote a work in which he said *"And this is evidence that this verse was written in the Torah later, and Moses did not write it."* He wasn't even denying the "revealed" character of the Torah, just making a reasonable comment. Three hundred years later, his work was reprinted with this comment edited out!

In the 15th century, Tostatus, Bishop of Avila, also pointed out that Moses couldn't have written the passages about the death of Moses. In an effort to soften the blow, he added that there was an "old tradition" that Joshua, Moses' successor, wrote this part of the account. A hundred years later, Luther Carlstadt commented that this was difficult to believe because the account of Moses' death is written *in the same style as the text that precedes it.*

Well, of course, things were beginning to be examined more critically with the arrival of Protestantism on the world stage and the demand for wider availability of the text itself. The Inquisition and assorted "Catholic Majesties" tried, but failed, to keep a complete grip on the matter. But, it's funny what belief will do. In this case, with the increase in literacy and new and better translations of the text, "critical examination" led to the decision that the problem was solvable by claiming that, yes, Moses wrote the Torah, but editors went over them later and added an occasional word or phrase of their own!

Wow. Glad they solved that one!

A really funny thing is that the Catholic Index blacklisted one of the proponents of this idea of editorial insertions, who was only trying to preserve the *textus receptus* status of the Bible. His work was put on the list of "prohibited books"! Those guys just kept shooting themselves in the foot.

Well, finally, after hundreds of years of tiptoeing around this issue, some scholars came right out and said that Moses didn't write the majority of the Pentateuch. The first to say it was Thomas Hobbes. He pointed out that the text sometimes states that this or that is so *to this day.* The problem with this is that a writer describing a contemporary situation would not describe it as something that has endured for a very long time, "to this day."

Isaac de la Peyrère, a French Calvinist, noted that the first verse of the book of Deuteronomy says, *"These are the words that Moses spoke to the children of Israel across the Jordan..."* The problem was that *the words meant to refer to someone who is on the other side of the Jordan from the writer.* This means that the verse amounts to the words of *someone who is **West** of the Jordan at the time of writing, who is describing what Moses said to the children of Israel on the **East** of the Jordan.* The problem is exacerbated because Moses himself was never supposed to have been in Israel in his life.

De la Peyrère's book was banned and burned. He was arrested and told that the conditions of his release were conversion to Catholicism and recanting his views. Apparently he perceived discretion as the better part of valor. Considering how often this sort of thing occurred, we have to wonder about the "sanctity" of a text that is preserved by threat and torture and bloodshed.

Not too long after this, Baruch Spinoza, the famous philosopher, published what amounted to a real rabble rousing critical analysis. He claimed that the problem passages in the Bible were not isolated cases that could be solved one by one as "editorial insertions," but were rather a pervasive evidence of a third person account. He also pointed out that the text says in Deuteronomy 34 *"There never arose another prophet in Israel like Moses..."* Spinoza suggested, quite rightly, that these were the words of a person who lived a long time after Moses and had had the opportunity to make comparisons. One commentator points out that they also don't sound like the words of the "humblest man on earth!" [229]

Spinoza was really living dangerously because he wrote: *"It is [...] clearer than the sun at noon that the Pentateuch was not written by Moses, but by someone who lived long after Moses."*[230] Spinoza had already been excommunicated from Judaism; now, he was in pretty hot water with the Catholics and Protestants! Naturally, his book was placed on the "prohibited books" list, and a whole slew of edicts were issued against it. What is even more interesting is that an attempt was made to assassinate him! The lengths to which people will go to preserve their belief in lies are astonishing.

A converted Protestant who had become a Catholic priest, Richard Simon, undertook to refute Spinoza and wrote a book saying that Moses wrote the core of the Pentateuch, but there were "some additions." Nevertheless, these additions were clearly done by scribes who were *under the guidance of God or the Holy Spirit*, so it was okay for them to collect, arrange and elaborate on the text. It was still God in charge here.

Well, you'd think the Church would know when it was ahead. But, nope! Simon was attacked and expelled from his order by his fellow Catholics. *Forty refutations* of his work were written by Protestants. Only six copies of his book survived burning. John Hampden translated one of these, getting himself into pretty hot water. He "repudiated the opinions he had held in common with Simon [...] in 1688, probably shortly before his release from the tower."[231]

In the 18th century, three independent scholars were dealing with the problem of "doublets," or stories that are told two or more times in the Bible. There are two different stories of the creation of the world. There are two stories of the covenant between God and Abraham. There are two stories of the naming of Abraham's son Isaac, two stories of Abraham's claiming to a

---

[229] Richard Elliot Friedman, *Who Wrote the Bible* (New York: Harper & Row, 1987).
[230] Quoted by Friedman.
[231] Ibid.

foreign king that his wife is his sister, two stories of Isaac's son Jacob making a journey to Mesopotamia, two stories of a revelation to Jacob at Beth-El, two stories of God changing Jacob's name to Israel, two stories of Moses getting water from a rock at Meribah, and on and on.

Those who simply could not let go of the *a priori* belief that Moses wrote the Pentateuch, tried to claim that these doublets were always complimentary, not repetitive or contradictory. Sometimes they had to really stretch this idea to say that they were supposed to "teach" us something by their contradictions that are "not really contradictions."

This explanation, however, didn't hold up against another fact: in most cases one of the two versions of a doublet would refer to the deity by the divine name, Yahweh, and the other would refer to the deity simply as "God," or "El." What this meant was that there were two groups of parallel versions of the same stories, and each group was almost always consistent about the name of the deity it used. Not only that, there were various other terms and characteristics that regularly appeared in one or the other line of stories, and what this demonstrated was that *someone had taken two different old source documents and had done a cut and paste job on them to make a "continuous" narrative.*

Well, of course, at first it was thought that one of the two source documents must be one that Moses had used as a source for the story of creation and the rest was Moses himself writing! But, it was ultimately to be concluded that both of the two sources had to be from writers who lived *after* Moses. By degrees, Moses was being eliminated almost entirely from the authorship of the Pentateuch!

Simon's idea that scribes had collected, arranged and elaborated on the *textus receptus* was, finally, going in the right direction.

I would like to note right here that this was not happening because somebody came along and said, "Hey, let's trash the Bible!" Nope. It was happening because there were *glaring problems,* and each and every researcher working on this throughout the centuries was struggling mightily to *retain* the *textus receptus* status of the Bible! The only exception to this that I have mentioned in this whole chain of events is our curious guy Abraham ibn Ezra, who *knew* about problems in the text of the Torah in the 12th century and enjoined others to silence! Remember what he said? "*And if you understand, then you will recognize the truth. And he who understands will keep silent.*" What do we see as the result of this silence? Over eight hundred years of Crusades, the Inquisition, and general suppression, and in our present day, the wars between the Israelis and Palestinians based on the claim that Israel is the Promised Land, and that it "belongs" to the Jews. Which brings us to another startling bit of information.

The great Jewish scholar, Rashi de Troyes (1040-1105), makes the astonishingly frank statement that the Genesis narrative, going back to the creation of the world, *was written to justify what we might now call genocide.* The

God of Israel, who gave his people the Promised Land, had to be unequivocally supreme so that neither the dispossessed Canaanites nor anyone else could ever appeal against his decrees.[232] Rashi's precise words were that God told us the creation story and included it in the Torah "*to tell his people that they can answer those who claim that the Jews stole the land from its original inhabitants. The reply should be; God made it and gave it to them but then took it and gave it to us. As he made it and it's his, he can give it to whoever he chooses.*"

The fact is, the Jews are still saying this, with the support of many Christian fundamentalists whose beliefs are being pandered to by George Bush and his purported Christian cronies for their own imperialist and economic motives.

This leads us to another interesting point: the establishing of "one god" over and above any and all other gods, is an act of violence no matter how you look at it. In *The Curse of Cain*, Regina Schwartz writes about the relationship between Monotheism and Violence, positing that *Monotheism itself is the root of violence*:

> Collective Identity, which is a result of a covenant of Monotheism, is explicitly narrated in the Bible as an invention, *a radical break with Nature*. A transcendent deity breaks into history with the demand that the people *he* constitutes obey the law <u>he</u> institutes, and first and foremost among those laws is, of course, that they *pledge allegiance to him, and him alone*, and that *this is what makes them a unified people* as *opposed* to the 'other,' as in *all other people* which leads to violence. In the Old Testament, vast numbers of 'other' people are obliterated, while in the New Testament, vast numbers are colonized and converted for the sake of such covenants.[233]

Schwartz also writes about the idea of the "provisional" nature of a covenant: *that it is conditional*. "Believe in me and obey me or else I will destroy you." Doesn't sound like there is any choice, does there? And we find ourselves in the face of a pure and simple Nazi Theophany.

In the 19th century, Biblical scholars figured out that there were not just two major sources in the Pentateuch; there were, in fact, *four*. It was realized that the first four books were not just doublets, but there were also triplets that converged with other characteristics and contradictions leading to the identification of another source. Then, it was realized that *Deuteronomy was a separate source altogether*. More than that, there was not just the problem of the original source documents, there was also the problem of the work of the "mysterious editor."

Thus, after years of suffering, bloodshed and death over the matter, it was realized that somebody had "created" what Westerners know as the Old Testament by assembling four different source documents in an attempt to create a "continuous" history, designated at different times as Torah, as well as additional "edited" documents. After much further analysis, it was concluded

---

[232] Geoffrey Ashe, *The Book of Prophecy* (London: Blandford, 1999), 27.

[233] Regina M. Schwartz, *The Curse of Cain* (Chicago: The University of Chicago Press, 1997).

that most of the laws and much of the narrative of the Pentateuch were not even part of the time of Moses. And, that meant that *it couldn't have been written by Moses at all*. More than that, the writing of the different sources was not even that of persons who lived during the days of the kings and prophets, but were evidentially products of writers who lived toward the end of the biblical period!

Many scholars just couldn't bear the results of their own work. A German scholar who had identified the Deuteronomy source exclaimed that such a view *"suspended the beginnings of Hebrew history not upon the grand creations of Moses, but upon airy nothings."* Other scholars realized that what this meant was that *the picture of biblical Israel as a nation governed by laws based on the Abrahamic and Mosaic covenants was completely false.* I expect that such a realization may have contributed to a suicide or two; it most definitely led to a number of individuals leaving the field of Theology and textual criticism altogether.

Another way of putting their conclusions was that the Bible claimed a history for the first 600 years of Israel that probably never existed. It was all a lie.[234]

Well, they couldn't handle this. After years of being conditioned to believe in an upcoming "End of the World," with Jehovah or Christ as saviors of the chosen during this dreaded event, the terror of their condition, *that there might not be a "savior,"* was just too awful to bear. So along came the cavalry—Julius Wellhausen (1844-1918)—to the rescue.

Wellhausen synthesized all of the discoveries so as to *preserve the belief systems of the religious scholars.* He amalgamated the view that the religion of Israel had developed in three stages with the view that the documents were also written in three stages, and then he defined these stages based on the content of the "stage." He tracked the characteristics of each stage, examining the way in which the different documents expressed religion, the clergy, the sacrifices and places of worship as well as the religious holidays. He considered the legal and narrative sections and the other books of the Bible. In the end, he provided a "believable framework" for the development of Jewish history and religion. The first stage was the "nature/fertility" period; the second was "spiritual/ethical" period; and the last was the "priestly/legal" period. As Friedman notes: *"To this day, if you want to disagree, you disagree with Wellhausen. If you want to pose a new model, you compare its merits with those of Wellhausen's model."*[235]

I should also note at this point that even though Wellhausen was trying to save the buns of Judaism and Christianity from the fire, he was not appreci-

---

[234] Of course, by now the reader has realized that it is not really a "lie," properly speaking. It is just a highly mythicized account of the doings of some people in a certain historical context. But after the mythicization, and the imposition of the belief in the myth as the reality, as well as the passage of a couple of thousand years, figuring out who is who and who really did what is problematical at best.

[235] Friedman, op. cit., 26-7.

ated in his own time. A professor of Old Testament, William Robertson Smith, who taught at the Free Church of Scotland College at Aberdeen, and who was the editor of the *Encyclopedia Britannica*, was *put on trial* before the church on the charge of *heresy* for promoting the work of Wellhausen. He was cleared, but the tag "the wicked bishop" followed him to his grave.

Nevertheless, analysis of the Bible has proceeded. The book of Isaiah was traditionally thought to have been written by the prophet Isaiah who lived in the eighth century BCE. As it happens, most of the first half of this book fits such a model. But, chapters 40 through 66 are apparently written by someone who lived about 200 years later! This means that, in terms of "prophecy," it was written *after the fact.*

New tools and methods of our modern time have made it possible to do some really fine work in the areas of linguistic analysis and relative chronology of the material. Additionally, there has been a veritable archaeological frenzy since Wellhausen! This archaeological work has produced an enormous amount of information about Egypt, Mesopotamia, and other regions surrounding Israel, which includes clay tablets, inscriptions on the walls of tombs, temples and habitations, and even papyri. Here we find another problem: in all the collected sources, both Egyptian and west Asian, there are virtually *no* references to Israel, its "famous people" and founders, its Biblical associates, or anything else *prior to the 12th century BCE.* And the fact is, for 400 years after that, *no more than half a dozen allusions can be deduced.* And they are questionable in context. Yet the fundamentalist Orthodox Jews cling to these tattered references like straws in the hands of a drowning man. Oddly, the fundamentalist Christians just simply close off any awareness to the entire matter by the simple expedient of the execution of the 11th commandment: thou shalt not ask questions!

The problem of the lack of outside validation of the existence of Israel as a sovereign nation in the area of Palestine finds correspondence in the Bible itself. The Bible displays absolutely no knowledge of Egypt or the Levant during the 2nd millennium BCE. The Bible says nothing about the Egyptian empire spreading over the entire eastern Mediterranean (which it did); there is no mention of the great Egyptian armies on the march (which they were); and no mention of marching Hittites moving against the Egyptians (which they did); and especially no mention of Egyptianized kinglets ruling Canaanite cities (which was the case).

The great and disastrous invasion of the Sea Peoples during the second millennium is not even mentioned in the Bible. In fact, Genesis described the Philistines *as already settled in the land of Canaan at the time of Abraham!*

The names of the great Egyptian kings are completely absent from the Bible. In other places, historical figures that were not heroic have been transformed by the Bible into heroes as in the case of the Hyksos Sheshy (Num. 13:22). In another case, the sobriquet of Ramesses II is given to a Canaanite general in error. The Egyptian king who was supposed to assist Hosea in his rebellion of 2 Kings 17:4 has "suffered the indignity" of having his city given as his name. The Pharaoh Shabtaka turns up in the Table of Nations in Genesis 10:7 as a Nubian tribe!

The errors of confirmed history and archaeology pile higher and higher the more one learns about the actual times and places, so that the idea that comes to mind again and again is that *the writers of the Bible must have lived in the 7th and 6th centuries BCE, or later*, and knew almost nothing about the events of only a few generations before them. Donald B. Redford, Professor of Near Eastern Studies at the University of Toronto, has published extensively on archaeology and Egyptology. Regarding the use of the Bible as an historical source, he writes:

> For the standard scholarly approach to the history of Israel during the United Monarchy amounts to nothing more than *a bad attack of academic 'wishful thinking'*. We have these glorious narratives in the books of Samuel and 1st Kings, so well written and ostensibly factual. What a pity if rigorous historical criticism forces us to discard them and not use them. Let us, then, press them into service—what else have we?—and let the burden of proof fall on others. [...]
>
> While one might be unwise to impute crypto-fundamentalist motives, the current fashion of treating the sources at face value as documents written up in large part in the court of Solomon, arises from an equally misplaced *desire to rehabilitate the faith and undergird it with any arguments, however fallacious*. [...]
>
> Such ignorance is puzzling if one has felt inclined to be impressed by the traditional claims of inerrancy made by conservative Christianity on behalf of the Bible. And indeed *the Pentateuch and the historical books boldly present a precise chronology that would carry the Biblical narrative through the very period when the ignorance and discrepancy prove most embarrassing.* [...]
>
> Such manhandling of the evidence smacks of prestidigitation and numerology; yet it has produced the shaky foundations on which a lamentable number of "histories" of Israel have been written. Most are characterized by a somewhat naive acceptance of sources at face value coupled with failure to assess the evidence as to its origin and reliability. The result was the reduction of all data to a common level, any or all being grist for a wide variety of mills.
>
> Scholars expended substantial effort on questions that they had failed to prove were valid questions at all. Under what dynasty did Joseph rise to power? Who was the Pharaoh of the Oppression? Of the Exodus? Can we identify the princess who drew Moses out of the river? Where did the Israelites make their exit from Egypt: via the Wady Tumilat or by a more northerly point?
>
> One can appreciate the pointlessness of these questions if one poses similar questions of the Arthurian stories, without first submitting the text to a critical evaluation. Who were the consuls of Rome when Arthur drew the sword from the stone? Where was Merlin born?
>
> Can one seriously envisage a classical historian pondering whether it was Iarbas or Aeneas that was responsible for Dido's suicide, where exactly did Remus leap over the wall, what really happened to Romulus in the thunderstorm, and so forth?

In all these imagined cases none of the material initially prompting the questions has in any way undergone a prior evaluation as to how historical it is! *And any scholar who exempts any part of his sources from critical evaluation runs the risk of invalidating some or all of his conclusions.* [...]

Too often "Biblical" in this context has had *the limiting effect on scholarship by implying the validity of studying Hebrew culture and history in isolation.* What is needed rather is a view of ancient Israel within its true Near Eastern context, and one that will neither exaggerate nor denigrate Israel's actual place within that setting.[236] (emphasis ours)

Please take careful note of Redford's comment: "any scholar who exempts any part of his sources from critical evaluation runs the risk of invalidating some or all of his conclusions." The seriousness of this cannot be understated. You see, people have died by the millions because of this book called The Bible and the beliefs of those who study it. And they are dying today in astonishing numbers for the same reasons!

In the end, *if* those who read and/or analyze this book and come to some particular belief about it are wrong, and they then impose this belief upon millions of other people, who are then influenced to create a culture and a reality based upon a false belief, and in the end, it is wrong, what in the name of God is going on? (No pun intended!)

The problem with using the Bible as history is the lack of secondary sources. There is considerable material from the various ancient libraries prior to the 10th century BCE, "grist for the historian's mill," but these sources fall silent almost completely at the close of the 20th dynasty in Egypt. Thus, the Bible, being pretty much the only source that claims to cover this particular period, becomes quite seductive; never mind that the archaeology doesn't really "fit," or can only be made to fit with a large helping of assumption or closing of the mind to other possibilities.

But, might there be a *reason* for this silence of other sources? That's one good question about "what is."

The person who is using the Bible as history is forced, when all emotion is taken out of the picture, to admit that he has no means of checking the historical veracity of the Biblical texts. As Donald Redford noted above, the scholars who admit, when pressed, that rigorous historical criticism forces us to discard the Biblical narratives, *nevertheless will use them* saying "what else do we have?"

Again, I ask: why?

In older times, we know that the many books written about the Bible as history were inspired from a fundamentalist motivation to *confirm the religious "rightness" of Western Civilization.* In the present time, there is less of this factor involved in Biblical Historical studies. Nevertheless, there is still a tendency to treat these sources at "face value" by folks who ought to know better!

---

[236] Donald B. Redford, *Egypt, Canaan, and Israel in Ancient Times* (Princeton: Princeton University Press, 1992), 301, 258, 260-1, 263.

I could go on about this in some detail, but I think everyone reading this is with me here in having a clue about what I am saying, even if they don't agree. But, the point is, again: "Who wrote the Bible and *why*?"

We come back to that curious assertion of Rashi's that *the Genesis narrative was written to justify genocide.* If we put that together with Umberto Eco's implication in his book, *The Search for The Perfect Language,* that validation of the Hebrew Bible was supported by early Christian scholars primarily to validate Judaism, which was necessary in order to then "validate" Christianity as the "one true religion", we begin to get the uneasy feeling that we have been "had." What this amounts to is that we are all "Christian" so that the "rights" of the Jews, the unappealable decrees of Jehovah/Yahweh, could be "inherited" by the Christian Church as instituted for political reasons by Constantine! Nevertheless, by the very act of validating Judaism, and "creating" Christianity in the form of the Egyptian religion, the Western world, in its greed for power, may very well have taken a tiger by the tail.

During this very period when the New Testament came into being, (incorporating some older texts, based on internal evidence, but highly edited and mostly a "cut and paste" job), we find the Western world in the midst of the dark ages from which, again, very few secondary sources survived.

Isn't that strange?! The Old Testament is written about a Dark Age, though a few hundred years after it, and the New Testament is written about a Dark Age, also a few hundred years after it. Both of them incorporate some probably valid stories though mostly they are edited, cut and pasted, with a lot of glossing and interpolation from the perspective of a definite "political" agenda.

Do we see a pattern here? Could there be a reason?

At the end of it all, what we observe is a basically *Draconian, monotheistic system in place over most of the globe.* It is the wellspring from which nearly every aspect of our society is drawn. It has been the justification for the greatest series of bloodbaths in "recorded" history.

Could there be a reason for this?

Considering this, one would think that the knowledge of who wrote the Bible, and when they probably did it, would be considered crucial to anyone who wishes to be better equipped to make decisions of faith and belief *upon which every aspect of their lives may depend.*

As we have already discovered, what began as a search for answers about the puzzling contradictory passages in the Pentateuch led to the idea that Moses didn't write them. This then led to the discovery that several widely divergent sources were combined into one, and that even this was done at different times, in different ways. Each of the sources is clearly identifiable by characteristics of language and content. New breakthroughs in archaeology and our understanding of the social and political world of the time have helped enormously in our understanding of the milieu in which this document was created. Because, in the end, the Bible's history is really the history of the Jews, and it looks like the history of the Bible is a history of lies and deceptions.

In the Bible, the story of the unification of the tribes of Israel under David, followed by the great reign of Solomon, followed by schism in the reign of Solomon's son Rehoboam, is the central theme. The "hope of Israel" is based on the idea of reunification of Judah and Israel under a Davidic king. Of course, all of this is based on the giving of the land to the Children of Israel when they were "brought out of Egypt" by the hand of God during the Exodus to begin with. Moses represents the divinely inspired leader who revealed the god of the patriarchs to the nation as the "Universal Deity." Does the testimony of the spade support the Exodus on either side of the story?

The Exodus story describes how a nation enslaved grows great in exile and then, with the help of the Universal God, claims its freedom from what was then the greatest nation on earth: Egypt.

Powerful imagery, yes? Indeed! So important is this story of liberation that fully four-fifths of the central scriptures of Israel are devoted to it.

The fact is: two hundred years of intensive excavations and study of the remains of ancient Egypt and Palestine have failed to support the Exodus story in the context in which it is presented.[237]

THE EXODUS CONSPIRACY AND THE BALFOUR AGREEMENT

All of the above would seem to be just "old history" and not relevant to us now except for an extraordinary incident that has received very little attention and which may very well bear strongly on the conditions prevailing over the world today.

In November 1922, a momentous discovery—unlike any other before or since—was to change our understanding of the ancient world: the intact tomb of the 18th dynasty pharaoh, Tutankhamum was discovered by Howard Carter. It is in the context of this discovery that the above mentioned extraordinary—but little noted—incident occurred; an incident that conceals a secret that could literally change the face of our history and our present world view:

> Let [the reader] imagine how they appeared to us as we looked down upon them from our spy-hole in the blocked doorway, casting the beam of light from our torch—the first light that had pierced the darkness of the chamber for three thousand years—from one group of objects to another, in a vain attempt to interpret the treasure that lay before us. [Carter and Mace, *The Tomb of Tut.Ankh.Amen*, I, p. 98][238]

These are Howard Carter's thoughts after he first set eyes on Tutankhamun's final resting place, sometime around two o'clock on Sunday 26 November 1922.

---

[237] Redford, op. cit.
[238] Quoted by Andrew Collins, Chris Ogilvie-Herald, *Tutankhamun and the Exodus Conspiracy* (London: Virgin Books, 2002).

[Carter, Lett's No. 46 *Indian and Colonial Rough Diary 1922*, entry for Sunday, 26 November, the Griffith Institute, Ashmolean Museum, Oxford.]

Yet what the British Egyptologist fails to disclose in his written testimony is that he went on to enlarge the spy hole and climb inside, without waiting for official permission to do so. This fact is recorded in a draft article on the events leading up to the great discovery by Lord Carnarvon dated Sunday 10 December 1922, which was in fact a variation of an article that appeared in *The Times* of London on Monday, 11 December. It provides a more realistic spin on what transpired that all-important day in the Valley of the Kings when he, Carter, Pecky Callender and Lady Evelyn Herbert reached the sealed doorway between the entrance passageway and the Antechamber. [...]

So why the apparent deception? Why did Carter claim to have entered the Antechamber for the first time a day later than he actually did? The answer would *appear* to be petty politics. Article 3 of the digging concession officially issued to Lord Carnarvon in 1915 (and renewed annually) made it clear that the 'Permittee', i.e. Howard Carter on behalf of Carnarvon, should 'give notice at once' to the chief inspector of the Antiquities Service for Upper Egypt at Luxor of the discovery of any tomb or monument. At the time the position of chief inspector was held by the British Egyptologist Reginald 'Rex' Engelbach, who had been kept informed of all developments at the tomb, and only two days beforehand, on Friday, the 24th, had 'witnessed part of the final clearing of rubbish from the [first] doorway'.

Yet on this day Engelbach had been the bringer of bad tidings, for he informed Carter and Carnarvon that Pierre Lacau, the director-general of the Antiquities Service, wished them to know that he, Engelbach, or one of his colleagues should be present at the opening of any chamber found. This was despite the fact that Article 4 of the digging concession asserted that 'the Permittee himself shall be reserved the privilege of opening the tomb or monument discovered, and of being the first to enter therein.' [...]

In the end, and, as we shall see, Carnarvon, Lady Evelyn and Callender, pressed ahead and entered the tomb. Yet, since their actions would have been seen as a breach of Article 3 of the digging concession, there was no way that they could admit to entering the tomb without having first notified Engelbach. [...]

Aside from Lord Carnarvon's typewritten draft article on the events leading to the discovery of the tomb, as well as an earlier handwritten version of the same article and a few careless whispers by the British aristocrat, the group's unofficial entry into the Antechamber managed to escape public notice for more than seventy years. It was finally brought to the attention of the world with the publication in 1978 of a sensational book entitled *Tutankhamun—The Untold Story*, written by Thomas Hoving, a former head of New York's Metropolitan Museum of Art. [...]

Yet the group's indiscretions went far beyond simply entering the Antechamber without official permission, for there is now indisputable evidence to show that sometime between Tuesday 28 November and Thursday 30 November 1922, the four of them breached the sealed doorway in the north wall of the Antechamber and explored the king's inner sanctum. This, it must be stressed, was almost *three months before the official opening* of the Burial Chamber when Carter and

Callender broke down the doorway[239] in front of a distinguished group of invited guests on Friday 16 February 1923 (not Friday 17 February, as is recorded incorrectly by Carter and Mace in their book—an error repeated again and again in modern accounts of the discovery of the tomb).

The first inklings of this greater transgression on the parts of Carter and Carnarvon came to light with the publication in 1972 of a book entitled *Behind the Mask of Tutankhamen*, penned by the historical writer Barry Wynne. Having gained the trust and respect of the sixth Earl of Carnarvon (1898-1987), who wrote a testimonial for the book, Wynne was able to draw from the slowly fading memories of the ageing aristocrat for a more personal account of his father's life and times. In addition to this, Wynne examined the diaries of the fifth earl's half-brother, the Hon. Mervyn Herbert (1881-1929), who was present at the official opening of the Burial Chamber.

Mervyn's diary and the testimony of other individuals in a position to know the facts (and conceal them) indicate that Carter and Carnarvon did, indeed, enter the tomb long before the "official" opening. As the story goes and as most people know it, when the tomb was officially opened it was a sensation, and some weeks afterward, Lord Carnarvon died supposedly from blood poisoning after he had nicked a mosquito bite while shaving leading to the "legend of the Curse of King Tut." There may be more to this than meets the eye, as we are about to learn.

The discovery of the tomb of Tutankhamen and all its details are not what concern us here. We are more interested in the fact that this discovery led eventually to a legal battle between Howard Carter and the Egyptian government. This dispute was so bizarre and aroused so much emotion that it deserves a bit of scrutiny considering the fact that the extraordinary incident occurred in response to this litigation. But first, let's take a look at Howard Carter himself, the litigant.

HOWARD CARTER

Howard Carter was born on March 9, 1874 in Kensington, London, the youngest son of eight. He grew up in the county of Swaffam, North Norfolk, England with no formal education although his father, Samuel Carter, an artist, trained him in the fundamentals of drawing and painting. Although Howard Carter developed a well above average skill, he had no ambition to continue the family business of painting portraits of pets and families for the local Norfolk landowners. Instead, Howard Carter sought the opportunity to go to Egypt and work for the Egyptian Exploration Fund as a tracer, a person who copies drawings and inscriptions on paper for further studying. In October of 1891 at the age of 17, Howard Carter set sail for Alexandria, Egypt, which was his first journey outside of Britain.

---

[239] The doorway had been carefully repaired so as to appear to be unbreached.

In 1892, Carter joined Flinders Petrie, at el-Amarna. Flinders was a strong field director and one of the most credible archaeologists of his time. Petrie believed Carter would never become a good excavator, but Carter proved him wrong when he unearthed several important finds at the site of el-Amarna, the Capital of Egypt during the sovereignty of Akhenaten. Under Petrie's demanding tutorage, Carter became an archaeologist, while keeping up with his artistic skills. He sketched many of the unusual artifacts found at el-Amarna.

Carter was appointed Principle Artist to the Egyptian Exploration Fund for the excavations of Deir el Babri, the burial place of Queen Hatshepsut. This experience allowed him to perfect his drawing skills and strengthen his excavation and restoration technique. In 1899, at the age of 25, Carter's hard work paid off, when he was offered the job of First Chief Inspector General of Monuments for Upper Egypt by the Director of the Egyptian Antiquities Service, Gaston Maspero. Carter's responsibilities included supervising and controlling archaeology along the Nile Valley.

Carter's employment at the Egyptian Antiquities Service came to an end in an unfortunate incident between the Egyptian site guards and a number of drunken French tourists. When the tourists became violently abusive to the guards, Carter allowed the guards to defend themselves. The French tourists, enraged, went through some high officials including the Egyptian Consul General Lord Cromer and called for Carter to make a formal apology. Carter refused, standing by his belief that he made the right decision. The incident gave Carter a bad name and caused him to be posted to the Nile Delta town of Tanta, a place with very little archaeological involvement. This forced Carter to resign from the Antiquities Service in 1905.

From 1905-1907, Carter sustained a hard existence after resigning from the Antiquities Service. He had to make a living by working as a commercial watercolorist or sometimes a guide for tourists. In 1908 Carter was introduced to the fifth Earl of Carnarvon by Gaston Maspero.

Carter became the Supervisor of the Excavations funded by Carnarvon in Thebes and by 1914 Carnarvon owned one of the most valuable collections of Egyptian artifacts held in private hands. However, Howard Carter had still more ambitious aspirations. He had his eye on finding the tomb of a fairly unknown pharaoh at the time, King Tutankhamun. After various clues to its existence had been found, Carter tore up the Valley of the Kings looking for Tutankhamun's burial place, but season after season produced little more than a few artifacts. He worked in the field with Lord Carnarvon in the west valley at the tomb of Amenophis III in 1915 and in the main valley from 1917-1922. Carnarvon was becoming dissatisfied with the lack of return from his investment and, in 1922, he gave Carter one more season of funding to find the tomb. [240]

---

[240] Rachel Frisk,
http://www.mnsu.edu/emuseum/information/biography/abcde/carter_howard.html

A biography of Howard Carter, written by Egyptologist, T.G.H. James, former Keeper of Egyptian Antiquities at the British Museum, draws on a wide variety of hitherto unexamined source materials. James' portrait of Howard reveals a complex man who was moody, brooding, stubborn, and—to understate the matter—undiplomatic. He had few close friends and was, apparently, driven with bulldog-like persistence to accomplish whatever he had set his mind to do. He was careful, meticulous and had a gift for organization as well as boldness and courage. It is said that on more than one occasion he tracked and confronted tomb robbers, and he thrived in an environment that offered little in the way of comfort and was, at times, even quite dangerous. The man that we come to know is one whose work is his master and mistress, and he never suffered fools gladly.

It was the discovery of King Tut's Tomb—an intact royal burial—in the Valley of the Kings that ensured Howard Carter's name would go down in history. Instantly, he was an international celebrity honoured by some, and vilified by others. What is curious is that, in the end, he was a sad, disillusioned man whose success—which was due solely to his own drive and diligence—did not bring any reward or happiness. His last years were marked by poor health and when he died on March 2, 1939, there were very few attendees at his funeral.

But let us turn to the events of 1924, almost a full year has passed since the death of Lord Carnarvon, Carter's patron.

OVER TUT'S DEAD BODY

Upon the discovery of the fabulous treasures of King Tut, it appears that many old disputes between Howard Carter and the bureaucracy, as well as old enemies came to a head. The Egyptian government—apparently motivated by extreme paranoia that will only be understandable further on—insisted that the pharaoh's treasures should remain in the care of Egyptian curators. The press was employed by both sides as guns to fire off their broadsides against one another. As a result of the press coverage, ordinary Egyptians thought Tutankhamen's treasures should be used to pay off the national debt while Howard Carter kept saying that he just wanted to handle the artifacts in the most scientific way possible. Everybody had a different agenda for the remains of King Tut. But through it all, there was a most evident current of a breakdown in trust between Carter and officialdom.

The battle began when, after months of handling the dig, at one point, Carter had invited quite a number of visitors to the excavation site, even though prior agreements with the Egyptian government stipulated that only those persons associated with the dig could be present. Carter had asked Sa'ad Zaghloul, Under-Secretary of State to the Ministry of Public Works, to grant entrance permits to the English and American wives of his assistants. Zaghloul refused the request. Carter insisted that the ladies be admitted to join their husbands, at which point they were prevented from entering by Egyptian authorities. Insulted, Carter closed down and locked up the excavation site. Zaghloul responded by stationing an armed guard at the tomb to prevent even Carter from entering.

In retrospect, it seems quite obvious that this little contretemps was engineered specifically to get Carter out of the way. Certainly, the request was an innocuous one that should have readily been granted and certainly, Carter's character was well known to Zaghloul who must have predicted what Carter would do in response.

Carter proceeded to Luxor, where he published a notice in the local hotels that said:

> Owing to impossible restrictions and discourtesies on the part of the Public Works Department and its Antiquity Service, all my collaborators, in protest, have refused to work any further upon the scientific investigations of the discovery of the tomb of Tutankhamen. I, therefore, am obliged to make known to the public that immediately after the Press view of the tomb this morning between 10 a.m. and noon, the tomb will be closed and no further work carried out.

The press went wild and after some scathing reviews of the actions of the Egyptian officials, negotiations between Carter and the Egyptian government opened but soon collapsed. Carter was not a happy camper, saying:

> This was only the culminating point of a series of acts of unwarrantable interference on the part of the government since work was resumed in October, which, in their cumulative effect, have tended to render scientific work at the tomb increasingly difficult.

The *Times of London* reported Carter's criticism of the Antiquities Department:

> The exclusive right of your Department to the tomb does not commence until I have had sufficient time to examine the tomb and take such notes as I judge necessary. As you are doubtless aware, I so far have had time to examine but a small part of the contents of the tomb, and the opportunity to examine and make notes on the rest is a fundamental right, which I will not give up.[241]

The pro-British press in Egypt naturally supported Carter's claims against the Egyptian government. The Egyptian *Gazette* opined that the real issue for Carter was *not* the question over sequestration rights but the Egyptian government's constant interference to the detriment of science and history.[242]

The Egyptian *Gazette* further argued that the Egyptian government had previously transferred the license at the death of Lord Carnarvon to his wife Almina, which required the government to be responsible for protecting the archaeologists from any unnecessary interruptions; however, the Ministry of Public Works had only managed to hinder Carter and his team.[243]

---

[241] *Times of London*, February 14, 1924.
[242] *Egyptian Gazette*, February 16, 1924.
[243] Ibid.

Le Journal du Caire, the pro-French newspaper, described Carter as "obstinate" and "incomprehensible" and said further that Carter was only "pretending" that he was a victim being persecuted by tyrants.[244]

Al-Siyasa, a local Egyptian paper declared that the government should have avoided a confrontation over the visitation of workers' wives to the tomb:

> The incident makes us laugh indeed, because the arrangements made in regard to it have been unworthy of these who made them. Why did the Minister of Public Works refuse Mr. Carter's demand to permit the wives of his collaborators to visit the Tomb several days before other people? It is not natural for the wives of the Ministers to hear the important news of the Ministry before they become known to the public? And even if it is natural would it not be an act of courtesy to agree to the ladies' visit. What patriotic interests and national dignity required the refusal of the request? To tell the truth, the Minister of Public Works was too strict where strictness was not required.

Egyptian Prime Minister Sa'ad Zaghloul Pasha issued a statement in response that was supposed to 1) clarify the government's position in regards to Carter's nationality; 2) assuage nationalist sentiment as well as 3) placate foreign public opinion:

> Not at any moment has our action been influenced by Mr. Carter's nationality. On the contrary, because of that nationality and our sincere desire that nothing should happen to trouble the friendly relations between the two countries, the Egyptian Government has never ceased to display much consideration and quite special sympathy for Mr. Carter, and I can assure you that if the concession-holder had been an Egyptian we would not have treated him with as much consideration.[245]

In the middle of all these accusations and counter claims, the Egyptian *Gazette* reminded its readers that the granite lid to Tutankhamen's sarcophagus was still hanging precariously above the tomb and mummified remains of the late pharaoh. Should the ropes holding the lid in place give way under the strain, it would come crashing down and destroy the most valuable treasure of all.[246] The same paper then reported that the deadlock between the Egyptian government and Howard Carter had forced the Egyptian government's decision to procure the services of other, more amicable, archaeologists, said experts within the archaeological community having already been contacted. This report also urged the Egyptian government to remove the danger of the dangling lid post-haste, after which they could train their own Egyptian archaeologists in Europe who could then return to manage the excavation without worrying that Carter was going to be absconding with any of the artifacts.

Again, it seems obvious that the minor dispute over the wives' attendance at the tomb was merely a diversion.

On February 14, 1924, when Carter arrived at the tomb to inspect the condition of the locks, he encountered Habeeb Affandi, the local inspector for the

---

[244] *Le Journal du Caire*, February 16, 1924.
[245] *Times of London*, February 22, 1924.
[246] *Egyptian Gazette*, February 18, 1924.

Antiquities Department, who denied him access to the tomb. Habeeb Affandi explained that he was under direct orders from Cairo to forbid anyone from visiting the tomb.

The French journal, *Le Temps,* explained that after careful deliberation, it had been decision of the Director of the Antiquities Department, M. Pierre Lacau, to place a guard at the tomb and bar Carter's entry.[247] It was disturbing to many in the archaeological community that Carter who, after thirty years of hard work and dedication, finally realized his ambition of uncovering the lost tomb, and was now prohibited from entering the tomb.

Since the negotiations had broken down between the Egyptian government and Carter, rumors in Egypt predicted that a settlement could only be achieved in court. In the meantime, it was predicted that the government would reopen the tomb to finish the job originally begun by Carter. At the same time, the Egyptian *Gazette* opined that the Egyptian government was incapable of properly supervising the excavation:

> It seems obvious that were such a course attempted Mr. Carter would immedi-
> ately apply to the Courts for an injunction to restrain the Government, but, apart
> from that, the task would be an impossible one for the Government, which has
> not in its employ a single official competent to undertake the work.[248]

On February 18, 1924, the *Times* of London reported that the Ministry of Public Works was interested in resolving the dispute with Carter; however, should the negotiations falter it had no compunction in appropriating the tomb and continuing the work of its own volition.[249]

In retrospect, it almost seems as though the press was scripting and direct-ing the events for the participants. It is therefore not a surprise that the next day, Howard Carter filed suit against the Egyptian government. In his legal action, Carter affirmed:

> I have initiated proceedings in the Mixed Courts for the protection of the objects
> contained in the tomb. If the director of the Antiquities Department will express
> regret for having insulted the ladies who had been invited by the Countess of
> Carnarvon to visit the tomb on Wednesday, after the visit of journalists, and if
> he undertakes to make no opposition of such kind as might provoke an incident,
> I will open the tomb a second time for a period of ten days in conformity with
> the agreement of February 8, Article 8 of which has been contravened by you.[250]

In Britain, a Member of Parliament, Ormsby Gore, in the House of Com-mons, proposed that the British government contact the American govern-ment in order to jointly protest the poor treatment of British and American archaeologists by the Egyptian Minister of Public Works. Member of Parlia-

---

[247] *Le Temps*, February 17, 1924.
[248] *Times of London*, February 19, 1924; *Egyptian Gazette*, February 18, 1924.
[249] *Times of London*, February 19, 1924.
[250] *Egyptian Gazette*, February 21, 1924.

ment MacDonald blocked this proposal because he believed that the British government should avoid such involvement *at that time*.[251]

On February 20, M. Pierre Lacau, Director General of Antiquities, revoked Carter's excavation permit and Egypt dispatched guards to Luxor. Lacau argued that Carter had voluntarily abandoned his work at the site and was averse to reopen it, in violation of Article 13 from their contract dating to 1915. In response to this maneuver, Carter initiated a second lawsuit in the civil chamber of Cairo's Mixed Courts without delay, requesting admittance to the tomb. He wanted to work, but another motivation was that the executors to Lord Carnarvon's estate were also seeking ownership of half the artifacts discovered, in accordance with Article 11 of the same contract. In the same court proceeding, Carter demanded a writ prohibiting the Egyptian government from entering the tomb. His claim was that the Egyptians would do irreversible damage to the tomb and its contents.

That same day, the Egyptian government published a ministerial *arrêté*, canceling the concession to Lady Carnarvon. This action incensed Carter, as it was obviously designed to do. He requested permission to return to the tomb for the sole purpose of securing the relics and protecting them from any damage, stating, "I should be given the opportunity of taking measures to protect the contents of the tomb and the laboratory during the suspension of work."[252]

On February 21, 1924, M. Pierre Lacau, the director general of the Antiquities Department, in an obvious effort to grandstand for the press, departed Cairo for Luxor, ostentatiously inviting Carter to join him at the tomb the next day. Lacau declared to the press that his intention was to "guarantee the safety of the sarcophagus since Carter was unable to properly secure it" before locking up the tomb; another obvious attempt to send Carter over the edge.

Carter—not surprisingly—refused to assist Lacau, declaring that it would be "improper for him to participate in such a venture with court action beginning the following day".

On February 22, 1924, without Carter present, Lacau had Egyptian workmen saw off the padlocks which Carter had placed on the tomb's entrance and replaced them with his own locks. He then entered the tomb and successfully lowered the granite lid without damaging it.[253]

Meanwhile, the Egyptian government was ready to issue a new digging concession to Almina, the Countess of Carnarvon. The stated reason was that Egypt believed that the concession had operated well under Lord Carnarvon but had deteriorated under Carter, and it granted the license to Lady Carnarvon rather than Carter. This was another obvious poke at Carter, whose fuse was known to be short. Almina, the Countess of Carnarvon, defended Carter—or ridiculed him—depending on your point of view:

---

[251] This most likely related to the powder keg issues of Britain having sold out the Arabic world via the Balfour Declaration.

[252] *Egyptian Gazette*, February 21, 1924.

[253] *Le Temps*, February 24, 1924. *Times of London*, February 23, 1924.

The discovery of the tomb has been dogged by bad luck and bad temper. [...] Howard Carter stands before the archaeological world as a partly wronged, partly foolish figure. He has done all the hard work and done it well, but the government of Egypt handed him a rope and persuaded him to hang himself.[254]

Legal proceedings began in Cairo on February 23, 1924. The writ served on Morcos Bey Hanna, Minister for Public Works, maintained that both Lord Carnarvon *and* Howard Carter held the concession to excavate the Valley of the Kings. This license from the Egyptian government provided for the excavation of the valley and preservation of artifacts. Carter requested that the Court designate him as the sequestrator of the tomb of Tutankhamen and the relics held within.

The Egyptian *Gazette* described the scene in the courtroom as something reminiscent of a performance at the Royal Opera House. Egyptians—mainly university students[255]—packed the courtroom on the first day of the trial. Most of them came to demonstrate *against* Howard Carter and throughout the proceedings, the Judge[256] had to bang his gavel repeatedly and admonish the crowd in order to have enough quiet in the courtroom to continue the proceedings. There were other gangs of students protesting outside of the court, showing their support for the Egyptian government. Judge Crabitès finally had to request a police detachment in order to continue the proceedings. Certainly, Crabitès aggravated the already tense situation by creating a disturbance himself by visiting the tomb,[257] and Egyptian nationalists called for him to recuse himself because he was a friend of Carter's.

---

[254] *New York Times*, February 22, 1924.

[255] One is reminded of various COINTELPRO actions in the US and elsewhere, that utilized paid university students as "bodies" and clappers in various contexts and venues because they are always looking for some way to make a little extra money.

[256] Judge Pierre Crabitès was born in the French Quarter of New Orleans, Louisiana, February 17, 1877. His father was a wealthy French immigrant, and his mother was a Virginian. His family connections helped him when President Taft nominated Crabitès to a seat on the Mixed Courts of Egypt in 1911, and he sat on the bench in Cairo for the next twenty-five years, rendering decisions on many important cases, including the case for the sequestration rights to the tomb of the Pharaoh Tutankhamen. His career as a judge on the Mixed Courts coincided with a period of British dominance over Egypt, and his anti-British sentiments thus evolved during his stay in Egypt. These anti-British feelings ultimately barred his appointment to the Mixed Courts' Court of Appeals and later hindered his work for the OSS.
After serving on the Mixed Courts for twenty-five years, Crabitès took up a post lecturing on law at Louisiana State University. When not busy teaching, Crabitès spent much of his time giving speeches on popular subjects in the 1930s, such as politics and the war. President Roosevelt appointed Crabitès as the American delegate to the Montreaux Convention, which resolved to slowly phase out the Mixed Courts. Crabitès finally realized his goal of obtaining a foreign service post when he accepted a job working for the OSS and Colonel Bill Donovan; however, his anti-British sentiments continued to haunt him when he returned to the Middle East, and he was subsequently transferred from Egypt to Iraq. Unfortunately, Crabitès died soon after his arrival in Iraq on 10 October 1943, in Baghdad. [Brian Parkinson, Doctoral Thesis, Department of History, Florida State University, August 4, 2005]

[257] Newspaper clipping, Mss. 73-85, Scrapbooks 1919-1939 (Crabitès Collection, University of New Orleans, New Orleans, LA). *Le Journal du Caire*, February 25, 1924.

Carter withdrew his case against the Egyptian government on February 29, 1924 believing that he had no chance of winning. In early March, both parties consented to external arbitration in lieu of a lengthy civil trial. Shortly afterward, the incident took place that concerns us intensely.

It was the spring of 1924, and all was lost to Carter. [...] The concession issued to Almina, Countess of Carnarvon, had been revoked and a fierce court battle to reverse this decision had ended in mayhem. [...]

Carter came to believe that there was only one recourse left open to him: to seek the assistance of the British Consulate at the Residency in Cairo. He considered that the High Consul and the other British diplomats posted there were in a position to apply pressure on the Zaghlul regime in order to get the Antiquities Service to issue a new [digging] concession. Previously, Egypt's High Commissioner, General Allenby, had offered his support for Carter's cause and had even given the impression that he backed in full his struggle against governmental interference.

Yet now Allenby was conveniently unobtainable,[258] and so, before his departure for England via Venice on 21 March, Carter decided that he would pay the British Consulate a visit in order to determine exactly what the position was with regard to his claims of unfair dismissal. With his temper frayed, Carter was in no mood for quiet discussions: he wanted the consulate's full support forthwith and nothing less would do.

Inside the Residency, Carter was led into the office of an official, where he began sounding off his grievances, fully expecting him to sympathise with his predicament and offer some means of resolving the problem. Although the British official did indeed sympathise with Mr. Carter, he also made it clear that the consulate could do nothing to influence the decisions of the Egyptian government and the Antiquities Service. It was simply beyond British jurisdiction.

Carter, never the best tempered of men, was incensed by this attitude and flew into a rage. Heated words were exchanged. Carter spoke of the total inadequacy of the department and the imbecility of its staff before exclaiming that:

> ...unless he received complete satisfaction and justice, he would publish for the whole world to read the documents that he found in the tomb giving the true account according to the Egyptian Government of the exodus of the Jews from Egypt.

Realising the potential damage that such revelations might have on the delicate situation existing between Britain and Egypt, and being aware also of the growing Arab hostility towards the establishment of a Jewish homeland in Palestine, the British official lost his temper. Without thinking, he forsook his code of di-

---

[258] On November 2, 1917, two days after General Edmund Allenby's Egyptian Expeditionary Force took Beersheba from the Ottoman Turks and prepared to march north toward Jerusalem, the British government announced an entirely different rationale for the campaign: [The Balfour Declaration.]

Five weeks later, Allenby's army took Jerusalem. For two days after the actual conquest, the general's arrival was meticulously planned. ... Christian armies were returning to the city for the first time since the Crusades. Allenby arrived at Jaffa Gate riding a white horse, with the pomp of a king. Then, before he entered the Old City, he dismounted and walked. A standard account of the general's reason: His Savior had entered this city on foot, and so would he.

plomacy and let fly at Carter a half-full inkwell that stood on his desk. Carter ducked just in the nick of time to avoid injury, leaving the projectile to bounce wildly off the wall—the resulting mess making it necessary for the whole room to be redecorated. Eventually, both men calmed down 'and an adjustment was made so that Carter was silenced and the threat never materialised.'

From Andrew Collins' notes on the above account:

Carter's confrontation with a British official in Cairo has come down to us through the memoirs of Lee Keedick, president of the Keedick Lecture Bureau and Carter's lecture agent in the U.S., yet the identity of the official is not at all clear. Keedick records Carter as having said that he confronted the 'British Vice Royal of Egypt', but after Egypt's independence in 1922 that office no longer existed. This fact seems to have been acknowledged by Thomas Hoving, for, in his book *Tutankhamun – The Untold Story*, he draws upon Keedick's memoirs but states that the official with whom Carter had his row was the vice-consul. Quite how Hoving reaches this conclusion seems unclear. While on the other hand TGH James in his book *Howard Carter: The Path to Tutankhamun* says it was General Sir Edmund Allenby, who served as Egypt's High Commissioner from 1919 until his retirement in 1925. Yet there is nothing in Keedick's notes to indicate that this was indeed the case.

According to the 'Foreign Office List and Diplomatic and Consular Year Book' for 1924, the vice-consul during the spring of 1924 was a Captain TC Rapp. The authors have identified him as Sir Thomas Cecil Rapp (1893-1984), who spent most of his life as a diplomat in various postings around the world. Rapp's own memoirs, from 1920-52, are located in the Private Papers Collection of the Middle East Centre at St. Antony's College, Oxford. The authors could find no reference in them to the reported meeting with Howard Carter during this period. However, Rapp's memoirs relating to his term in Cairo amount to no more that seventeen or so pages and one would not expect, in so short an account, for the confrontation to have been recorded. Although not in the above context, Rapp does mention meeting Carter shortly after Carnarvon's death when he was attending to the 'formalities' for the transfer of his body to England. It is possible that Keedick, not being a man of politics, misunderstood the intricacies of the British forms of political office, but until further research can shed more light on with whom exactly Carter had his confrontation, the official's identity remains a mystery.

Carter's diary notes that on 3 March 1924 he had an appointment at 08:30 at 'The Residency' in Cairo, where the offices of the High Commissioner and the High Consul were located. Plausibly it was during this meeting that the exchange occurred, since no other appointment at the Residency is recorded in his diary between January 1924 and 21 March 1924 when Carter left for England via Venice to prepare for his spring tour of North America.[259] (emphasis ours)

Returning to the general timeline of the Tut Tomb Scandal: Shortly after Carter withdrew his case and had the alleged encounter cited above, M. Pierre Lacau staged the official opening of Tutankhamen's tomb, another move obviously designed to bait Carter. The Egyptian government invited hundreds to attend the ceremony on March 5, 1924, including eminent Egyptologists,

---

[259] Collins and Ogilvie-Herald, op. cit.

senior officials, diplomats, and other notables. The Egyptians intended the opening ceremony to be a largely ceremonial function, but it quickly metamorphosed into a nationalist demonstration. Supporters of Zaghoul Pasha, numbering in the thousands, lined the route to cheer their hero, awaiting his arrival at Luxor. Students spread out along the road from Cairo to Luxor just for a glimpse of their own champion, student MP Hassan Yassin. British newspapers denounced the spectacle as a political maneuver undertaken by the Egyptian government with no relevance to the preservation of the artifacts.

On March 7, 1924, the Egyptian *Gazette* published an opinion piece railing against the Egyptian government's conduct during the Tutankhamen affair. All along, the Egyptians had intimated that they merely sought to safeguard the tomb for the sake of posterity. The Egyptian *Gazette* challenged this notion, for were it sincere, then why had the Egyptian government compromised the objects in the tomb by admitting visitors:

> In fact, it is difficult to avoid the conclusion that in this miserable affair they are behaving in a willfully hostile and provocative manner.[260]

This article declared that what the government was really interested in was the promotion of hostility and animosity between Egyptians and the British. A root cause of the enmity between the two groups was the failure of Egyptians to cope with foreigners scavenging for their native treasures. The Egyptian *Gazette* denounced Egyptians for disregarding the hard work of foreigners who discovered their national monuments, and so on.

Almost immediately following the withdrawal of his initial lawsuit and the failure of his appeal to the British government for help, Carter instituted a new action, including Sir John Maxwell[261] and Almina, the Countess of Carnarvon as litigants. Sir John Maxwell and Lady Carnarvon were the executors of the estate of Lord Carnarvon and had previously been in line to receive a share of the tomb loot but, for the sake of trying to reassure the Egyptian government of their good intentions had publicly and legally renounced all claims to anything in the tomb. Carter then persuaded American archaeologist, Dr. James Breasted, to act as a third party referee in the ongoing negotiations between the Egyptian government and the Carnarvon trustees.

Maxwell—not surprisingly considering his background—behaved in a way designed to antagonize the Egyptian government against Carter, at one point even referring to said government as "rapacious bandits," and nearly causing a riot thereby. Carter himself was said to have been out of control by this time and his friend, Judge Crabitès, tried to find a way to elicit from him the behavior and arguments that would help his case. Meanwhile, another attempt was made to come to an out-of-court agreement, this time by the

---

[260] *Egyptian Gazette*, March 7, 1924.
[261] Among the many items in Maxwell's CV is the following: During World War I, Irish revolutionaries declare their independence and seize Dublin; Maxwell is appointed Commander-in-Chief, Military Governor of Ireland shortly after, and crushes the rebellion for which he gains the name "Bloody Maxwell".

Americans, but that was so badly bungled that the judge wrote a letter to the American Minister, Howell, reproving him for bowing under Egyptian pressure to the detriment of American prestige in the region. He compelled Howell to send a stern message to the Egyptians so that "the new Egyptian Parliament would not labor under the false impression that having become independent, Egypt's new Ministry could flout America with impunity."[262]

Finally, on March 12, 1924, Judge Crabitès handed down his verdict in the case for the appointment of Carter as the sequestrator for Tutankhamen's tomb, ruling in favor of Howard Carter and the trustees of Lord Carnarvon on all points. In rendering his decision, Judge Crabitès said that the judgment was one for all of mankind, not in opposition to Egypt or in favor of Howard Carter.[263]

A few days later, the Egyptian government filed an appeal in the court at Alexandria. A Judge Eeman presided over the case. The Egyptian government vituperatively attacked Carter, Sir John Maxwell, and the Countess Carnarvon, claiming that they were exploiters who commercialized their discovery. The government argued that the tomb was within the state's domain and that revocation of their license and taking control of the tomb were administrative actions, beyond the jurisdiction of the Mixed Courts.[264]

The Court of Appeals adjourned long enough for the Procurator General M. van der Bosch to compose a decision. When parties returned to court on March 30, the procurator general explained that Egypt's protests concerning the legitimacy of Howard Carter's attorney did not even apply to the case since Howard Carter and the trustees of Lord Carnarvon relinquished their claim to property within the tomb, there was no argument over the second claim in the case, possession of the objects; therefore, there was no cause to appoint a sequestrator for the tomb!

Judge Eeman then overturned Judge Crabitès's earlier conclusion in support of Howard Carter and the trustees of Lord Carnarvon and ruled in favor of the Egyptian government, ruling that the Mixed Courts lacked jurisdiction in the affair and said it was one for the Egyptian government to resolve.

End of subject, discussion, case and story.

THE EXODUS CONSPIRACY

Just what the heck really happened here?

It's as obvious as the nose on an elephant that Howard Carter was a lamb being thrown to the wolves.

Did Carter's threats to expose the truth about the Exodus have anything to do with the attitudes of the various players throughout the proceedings recounted above? Can those attitudes reveal anything to us?

---

[262] Hoving, *Tutankhamun*, 307.

[263] *New York Times*, March 13, 1924. Clive Hardy, "From Praline to Pyramid," *The Courier* (September 15-17, 1977), 12.

[264] *New York Times*, March 20, 1924.

Andrew Collins examines the issue of whether or not it was possible that items were removed from the tomb of Tut and hidden away, including written documents—papyri—and it seems that the circumstantial evidence—including conflicting descriptions of what did or did not happen, when and how, made by the concerned parties—does, indeed, point in that direction. Further to that, the find of a cache papyri *was openly discussed* when the tomb was first opened!

> Ever since the opening of the tomb in November 1922, Tutankhamun's 'missing' papyri have been the subject of both rumour and speculation by newspapermen and historical writers... On Tuesday 28 November 1922, Lord Carnarvon dispatched a letter to his friend and colleague the philologist Alan H. Gardiner describing the contents of the tomb. If we look at what it said, we can see that it refers quite specifically to the discovery of papyri:
>
>> The find is extraordinary. It is a cache and has been plundered to a certain extent but even the ancients could not completely destroy it. After some slight plundering the inspectors shut it again. So far it is Tutankhamon—beds, boxes and every conceivable thing. *There is a box with a few papyri in*—the throne of the King the most marvellous inlaid chair you ever saw...[265]
>
> The discovery of papyri is alluded to in another letter written by Carnarvon in connection with the opening of the tomb, this time to Sir Edgar A Wallis Budge, the Keeper of Egyptian and Assyrian Antiquities at the British Museum. On Friday 1 December 1922, he wrote:
>
>> One line just to tell you that we have found the most remarkable 'find' that has ever been made, I expect, in Egypt or elsewhere. I have only so far got into two chambers [a little short of the truth here], but there is enough in them to fill most of your rooms at the B.M. (upstairs); and there is a sealed door where goodness knows what there is. I have not opened the [innumerable] boxes, and don't know what is in them; *but there are some papyrus letters*, faience, jewellery, bouquets, candles on ankh candlesticks. All this is in [the] front chamber, besides lots of stuff you can't see.[266, 267]

The issue of the papyri also received media attention. Arthur Merton, the official Times of London correspondent dispatched bulletins from Luxor every day and on November 30, 1922, while listing many of the treasures of the tomb, he stated

> ...one of the boxes contained rolls of papyri which are expected to render a mass of information.

As late as Sunday, December 17 of 1922 Carnarvon was still saying that they had discovered papyri in the tomb. On a trip back to England, he was interviewed by the London Times and quoted as saying:

---

[265] Letter from Lord Carnarvon to Alan H. Gardiner, dated November 28, 1922, quoted in Reeves and Taylor, *Howard Carter: Before Tutankhamun*, 141.
[266] Budge, Tutankhamen: Amenism, Atenism, and Egyptian Monotheism, xviii-xix.
[267] Collins and Ogilvie-Herald, op. cit.

One of the boxes contains rolls of papyri which may be expected to shed much light on the history of the period, and other papyri may be discovered in other of the boxes which have yet to be examined.[268]

So, for at least two weeks, the subject of the papyri and the potential for finally having some light shed on the history of the period was bandied about quite openly and undoubtedly, many people were waiting breathlessly for these revelations, including the Egyptian government.

Collins suggests that Carnarvon discussed the papyri with Gardiner on his return to England. A telegram from Carnarvon to Gardiner from early December of 1922, though the specific day is not stated, was quoted by Vandenberg in *The Forgotten Pharaoh* on page 125. Apparently, it was a request for Gardiner to "undertake the philological work in connection with the papyrus find in the antechamber to the tomb."

Based on the fact that no papyri have ever been produced, it may be assumed that Carnarvon took the papyri back to England with him. Gardiner did *later* join the team until things began to go South vis-à-vis the Egyptian government, but by this time, the public face of it was that his duties only included making translations of inscriptions found on the walls and artefacts. We also note that it was only after Carnarvon's untimely and unusual death that Carter claimed that the find of papyri was a "misidentification."

Collins has collected the evidence and testimony and makes a quite convincing case that a significant cache of papyri was indeed found in Tut's tomb. British Egyptologist Nicholas Reeves was so fascinated by the idea that papyri might have been found in the tomb that he wrote a paper on the subject. In the end, he concluded that inscriptional materials that *should have been there were conspicuous by their absence.*

Reviewing the events, we notice that it was only after Carnarvon's trip back to England where he undoubtedly met with Gardiner that, suddenly, the whole idea of papyri disappeared, was covered up, shushed, explained away, denied and forgotten.

Judging by the attitude of the Egyptian government toward Carter as evidenced in the legal issues, rumors that important items had been—or were being—removed from the tomb may have circulated widely; how could they not after the subject of the missing papyri had been discussed in major newspapers? Carter later addressed the issue by saying that anything that was thought to have been papyri actually turned out to be rolls of linen. One wonders how experienced Egyptologists such as Carter and Carnarvon could have made such an error. It's clear that the Egyptian government wasn't buying it either.

All in all it was a very bizarre and confusing series of events that suggests many things going on behind the scenes and putting the clues together, it all seems to focus on the papyri that were claimed to have been found, then were disavowed after Carnarvon traveled to England. This leads to a most interest-

---

[268] *The Times*, December 18, 1922, 14.

ing story recounted by Andrew Collins which we include for the purpose of giving some background on the type of man the Earl was and just what he may or may not have done regarding said alleged papyri.

The Curse of King Tut

[…] The fifth Earl of Carnarvon […] was deeply influenced by spiritualism and the occult. He was also an active member of the London Spiritual Alliance. On numerous occasions Carnarvon organised séances in the East Anglia Room at Highclere Castle. Present would be his daughter Lady Evelyn Herbert, the politician and lawyer Sir Edward Marshall Hall KC;[269] Lady Cunliffe-Owen and, when in the country, Howard Carter.

In his published memoirs the sixth Earl of Carnarvon says that his father became 'keenly interested in the occult' as he and Howard Carter waited restlessly for hostilities to cease during World War One. Moreover, he recalls attending one of these séances organised by his father. It occurred during a month spent with the family following his return from military duty with the 7th Hussars in Mesopotamia in the late spring of 1919, when Carter was also present.

He remembers how, in the company of his sister Lady Evelyn, he proceeded to the East Anglia Room, where his father, along with Howard Carter, Louis Steele, 'a brilliant photographer domiciled in Portsmouth', and Helen Cunliffe-Owen were readying themselves for the psychic session.

When everyone had settled down, Steele began to utter some form of 'incantation' that sent Lady Cunliffe-Owen into a trance in which she *began speaking Coptic*. By 'Coptic' he presumably meant the language used by the original inhabitants of Egypt, as opposed to the Greek immigrants, in the wake of Alexander the Great's celebrated entry in 332 BCE. […]

The sixth earl records that *only Howard Carter understood Lady Cunliffe's strange utterances*, and afterwards she had no recall whatsoever of what had been said.

The sixth earl goes on to say that Lady Evelyn was then placed in a similar trance, 'but she was so overcome by the experience that she *had to go into a nursing home* in London for a fortnight's rest'. […]

These are the words of the sixth Earl of Carnarvon, a greatly respected British aristocrat who moved in high society circles before his death in 1987. That he believed these events took place does not seem to be in doubt, as they are recorded in his published memoirs. However, exactly what transpired at Highclere Castle that night in 1919 is probably lost for ever. All that the authors have been able to ascertain is that the sessions did indeed take place in the East Anglia Room, something that is looked on with some embarrassment by the tour guides, reflecting perhaps the feelings of the present-day Carnarvon family. Indeed, when the authors visited Highclere and met the future 8th Earl of Carnarvon in August 2001, special permission had to be gained to enter the East Anglia Room, which is currently out of bounds to the general public. They were

---

[269] Wikipedia: Sir Edward Marshall-Hall (Brighton, 1858-1927) was an English barrister who had a formidable reputation as an orator. He successfully defended many notorious murderers and became known as "The Great Defender". John Mortimer, creator of Rumpole of the Bailey, dramatised many of Marshall-Hall's cases in a radio series starring ex-*Doctor Who* star Tom Baker.

finally able to enter the room, used today as a dressing room for wedding parties, in the company of Tony Leadbetter, the godson of Lady Almina Herbert, the fifth earl's wife. He insisted that she loathed the séances and would have nothing to do with them, since they frightened her greatly. [...]

The Rebirth in Egypt

Lord Carnarvon's interest in the occult was not unique for his era. Many wealthy, well-to-do people in British society shared a belief in the omnipotent powers of ancient Egypt. To them this distant land, beneath the hot desert sun, was an exotic paradise, where the ancient gods still lived on in the invisible world. These very humanlike deities were seen not simply as the product of the superstitious fears of a bygone race, but as the power and motivation behind the great civilisation that built the Great Pyramid and flourished for nearly 3,000 years before its decline at the time of the Roman Empire.

With the spread of spiritualism from the United States to Europe in the mid-1800s, the idea of communicating with perceived celestial intelligences suddenly became more acceptable. And, if an American Indian chief or a Chinese philosopher could act as a spirit guide, then so could long-dead Egyptian spirits and even the gods and goddesses of that wonderful country. More significantly, the revival in the mystic powers of ancient Egypt was embraced by a number of occultists of the era, who felt some kind of sympathetic connection with this unseen world. More importantly, *it was the influence of one such mystic that may well have convinced Lord Carnarvon that his destiny was linked inextricably not only with coming events connected with the resurrection of the Amarna age in popular consciousness, but also with the opening of the tomb of Tutankhamun.*

We speak of 'Cheiro' (pronounced ki-ro), alias Count Louis le Warner Hamon (1866-1936), the world-renowned fortune-teller and palmist of Irish birth, who during the late Victorian period read palms, cast horoscopes and made psychic predictions for the rich and famous. His first client is said to have been *Arthur James Balfour*, the future Conservative Prime Minister and the signatory on the so-called Balfour Declaration of 1917.

From the 1890s onwards, Hamon attracted an elite clientele both at his Indian-style salon in London's trendy Bond Street, and while on his travels abroad. The list is mind-boggling, and apparently included, among others, Mark Twain, Sarah Bernhardt, the British statesman Sir Austin Chamberlain, the writer Oscar Wilde and the Dutch dancer and spy Mata Hari, with whom he became a close acquaintance. Sir Ernest Shackleton, the explorer of the Antarctic, went in disguise to his Bond Street address in order to test him, but was told, correctly, that he would not return from a second expedition. When Field Marshal Horatio, *Lord Kitchener*, the hero of the Sudan, turned up to see Hamon he was informed that his death would come at sea. He was to die when his cruiser, HMS Hampshire, struck a mine and sank in the North Sea, off the Orkney Isles, in June 1916.

As Hamon's reputation as a fortune-teller grew, he was introduced to more and more clients of distinction. Among them was the King of Italy, Humbert I, whom he met in Rome in 1900 and predicted correctly that he would be dead within three months. Another was the Shah of Persia, whom he met in Paris that same year. Hamon informed him that his life was in grave peril, prompting the shah's police guard to foil an assassination attempt by an anarchist.

Most famous of all Hamon's clients was Edward VII, for whom he predicted the exact date of his coronation in August 1902 and subsequent death in 1909. Through the British king he was introduced to other members of the royal family, for whom he cast horoscopes and made predictions. It was also through Edward VII that Hamon came to meet Tsar Nicholas II of Russia, about whom he predicted that around '1917 he will lose all he loves most by sword or strife in one form or another, and he himself will meet a violent death'. So intrigued was the Tsar by this prediction that in late 1904, on a visit to St Petersburg, Hamon was invited to dine with him at the Summer Palace. During his stay Gregori Rasputin came to meet Hamon one afternoon in January 1905. As with the Tsar, he predicted that Rasputin would suffer 'a violent end within a palace. You will be menaced by poison, by knife, and by bullet. Finally I see the icy waters of the Neva closing above you'. It goes without saying that both Rasputin and the Tzar were to lose their lives in the manner prescribed.

Marshall Hall QC

It is certainly not the place here to extol any further the apparent predictions of Count Louis Hamon, alias 'Cheiro', whatever their basis in truth. Yet what is significant to the story behind the discovery of Tutankhamun's tomb is that the author Barry Wynne in his 1972 book *Behind the Mask of Tutankhamun* claimed that Lord Carnarvon was one of Hamon's clients. Indeed, it is recorded that in 1899 Hamon had cause to ask the Earl of Carnarvon's close friend and lawyer, Sir Edward Marshall Hall QC, to defend him. […]

Since Marshall Hall was one of the participants in the séances that took place at Highclere Castle, it seems reasonable to assume that by this time Hamon had become a personal acquaintance of the Earl of Carnarvon. This should be borne in mind as we review the strange psychic warning that Hamon sent to Lord Carnarvon shortly after the discovery of the tomb of Tutankhamun.

Cheiro's Warning

Later he would claim that it had been delivered to him in the form of automatic writing by Meketaten, one of Akhenaten's daughters, whose mummified hand he believed he had been given by an elderly Egyptian guide at the Temple of Karnak in the mid-1880s. Yet, regardless of its original source, the unnerving nature of the message must have sent a chill down the British aristocrat's spine, for, according to Hamon,

> It was to the effect that on his arrival at the tomb of Tut-Ankh-Amen *he was not to allow any of the relics found in it to be removed or taken away*. The ending of the message was 'that if he disobeyed the warning he would suffer an injury while in the tomb—a sickness from which he would never recover, and that death would claim him in Egypt'.

Rightly or wrongly, Hamon sent the warning message to Lord Carnarvon at Highclere, which was received by him *shortly after his return from Egypt in mid-December 1922*. He was said to have 'read it over to one of his companions, the Hon. Richard Bethell, and to a close friend of Admiral Smith Dorrien, whose letter relating these facts I have still in my possession'. Apparently, Carnarvon was 'deeply impressed by the warning', yet responded with the words,

> 'If at this moment of my life all the mummies in Egypt were to warn me I would go on with my project just the same.'

Yet Hamon goes on to reveal that it was *'common knowledge what happened'*
next, for, according to him, 'Lord Carnarvon took numerous relics out of the
tomb and sent them on to England. He would probably have taken still more if
the Egyptian Government had not interfered'.

This outrageous claim made in Hamon's autobiographical work *Real Life Sto-*
ries, published in 1934, must have infuriated not only the fifth earl's friends and
family, but also the entire Egyptological community, including Howard Carter,
who had completed his clearance of the tomb just two years beforehand. Yet,
whatever Hamon's source was for this information, it proved to be staggeringly
accurate, for [...] there is overwhelming evidence to show that Carnarvon and
Carter did indeed illegally remove art treasures from the tomb.

Ridiculous stories

That a warning of the sort described by Hamon was received by his lordship
around the time of the discovery of the tomb is confirmed by the sixth earl's
memoirs, which tell us:

> Upon the news of the discovery of the tomb he [Hamon] had written to
> my father warning him not to become involved. This matter preyed on
> my father's mind and he decided to consult his own clairvoyant, Velma.

[...] Having explained the contents of the communication from Hamon, the
palmist took hold of his hands and pointed out a fairly long lifeline, which was
thin at the centre with ominous spots that might indicate death at this point in
his life. Similar combinations in other areas of the hand led Velma to advise:

> 'I do see great peril for you [...] Most probably—as the indications of
> occult interest are so strong in your hand—it will arise from such a source.'

According to the writer Barry Wynne, in his 1972 book *Behind the Mask of*
Tutankhamun, Carnarvon's reply to this second warning was somewhat jocular:

> 'Whatever happens I will see to it that my interest in things occult never
> gets so strong as to affect either my reason or my health.'

A second meeting with Velma

[...] Whatever his final thoughts, Carnarvon is known to have returned to
Velma for a second meeting before his departure for Egypt in January 1923. We
are told that on this occasion, when Velma took his hands, the ominous spots
noted before had, if anything, enlarged. As Wynne penned with a sense of
drama, 'In particular, the spot on the Life Line seemed perilously close to the
earl's present age.'

[...] The sixth Earl of Carnarvon, in his memoirs, also provides details of his father's visits to see Velma, and confirms that on the second occasion the seer and
palmist warned him against returning to Egypt lest disaster strike.

Lord Carnarvon departed for Egypt in the company of Lady Evelyn in mid
January, and was back in the Valley by Wednesday, the 31st. He examined the
treasures removed from the Antechamber inside the nearby tomb of Seti II,
which was being used as a laboratory, and in the days that followed hung
around Tutankhamun's tomb receiving invited guests and visitors. [...]

As we know, it was around the time of the official opening of the Burial Chamber [Friday, February 16, 1923] that Lord Carnarvon became ill and, exactly as
Arthur Weigall had flippantly remarked, he was to be dead just over six weeks
later. Yet strange stories are told about his final night on earth. Amid the fever-

ish delirium that accompanied the final stages of his illness, he is reported to have said over and over again, 'A bird is scratching my face. A bird is scratching my face'.

The Fifth Earl of Carnarvon died on April 5, 1923. Eleven months later, Howard Carter was threatening the British government with the revelation of the truth about the Exodus and the origin of the Jews.

As the reader probably noticed, the players in the above story are members of the same circles involved with the Balfour Declaration. This document was the ultimate achievement of very intense negotiations between prominent Zionists and British politicians (formerly known as statesmen). The deal was revolting at its most basic level: in exchange for Zionist help in getting the U.S. to enter World War I, the Zionists were promised Palestine. But more than that, the Zionists claim on Palestine was based on their whole religion shtick, Moses and the Exodus and that it was all a great miracle and God Almighty gave the land to them.

But what if the real story, the papyri in the tomb of King Tut, said something that would blow that whole claim out of the water? That seems to be the only reason for suppression of what Howard Carter referred to as "the true account according to the Egyptian Government of the exodus of the Jews from Egypt". It also makes sense of what Lord Carnarvon said in response to the warning from Hamon:

'If at this moment of my life all the mummies in Egypt were to warn me I would go on with my project just the same.'

The question is: who was doing the suppressing and why?

Collins' theory is that Carnarvon, once he knew what he had, tried to "sell" the documents to the Zionists in order to get more money to continue his dig. He points out that, before the commencement of the 1922-23 digging season, Carnarvon was experiencing financial troubles already, and after the discovery of the tomb, realized he was facing at least another 5 years of work that needed a great deal of money. Collins also establishes the fact that Carnarvon's wife was the illegitimate daughter of Alfred de Rothschild (apparently a well known "secret" and openly admitted by the family) and that she had inherited a great deal of money on the death of Alfred in 1918, but was rapidly spending it on her own projects which did not include archaeology (or, apparently, psychic séances!). And so, Collins suggests something akin to "blackmail" on the part of Carnarvon:

Faced with such a daunting prospect [5 more years of digging], and aggrieved by the vast fortune that Almina and his children had been left by her father, is it possible that Carnarvon's financial frustration led him to concoct some kind of plan? Did it involve the papyrus documents found in the tomb? From Carter's outburst in the offices of the British High Consul in Cairo we know that the contents of the supposed papyri found in the tomb exploded the accepted version of the Exodus story, and thus would have been of extreme embarrassment to Zionists worldwide. Is it possible therefore that the Earl of Carnarvon intended to try to persuade certain leading Zionist Jews that he had at his disposal ancient

Egyptian documents that, owing to their highly sensitive nature, were best kept private? Thus in order to ensure that they never reached the public domain, and to compensate for the archaeological irregularities on the parts of himself and Howard Carter, did he suggest some kind of financial remuneration? The plan could have been as simple as that, and if this was the case then to whom might it have been directed?[270]

At this point we need to remember that the Balfour Declaration was addressed to Lionel Walter de Rothschild, a cousin of Carnarvon's wife. Walter had worked closely with Chaim Weizmann for the cause of Zionism and at the celebration of this great event at the Covent Garden Opera House on December 2, 1917, Walter told the audience that the Balfour Declaration was the greatest event that had occurred in Jewish history for the last 1800 years.

Collins then speculates that Carter, perplexed by the British government's refusal to put pressure on the Egyptian government, stormed into the offices of the British High Consul and made his threat.

Well, we agree that Carter might have been frustrated and might have thought that his government could do something, but we don't really think it was quite that simple considering all the evidence. Carnarvon and Carter trying to sell the secret to the Zionists on their own initiative and then just covering it up all by themselves by saying "Oops, sorry, there were no documents" doesn't fly. It is clear from examining the history of the legal fight between Egypt and Carter that the Egyptian government had a major burr under its saddle and some intense pressures were being brought to bear on various entities from various directions, and Carter's wants in the matter were of minimal importance whether he fully understood that or not. There is also the fact that the Egyptian government of the time was entirely beholden to the British government, which makes us wonder if it really was the Egyptian government that was thwarting Carter's progress, or their masters in Whitehall.

Let's look again at what Carter is reported to have said that undoubtedly relates to the alleged missing papyri:

> ...unless he received complete satisfaction and justice, he would publish for the whole world to read the *documents that he found in the tomb* giving the true account according to the Egyptian Government of the exodus of the Jews from Egypt.

What exactly did Carter mean and why did he think that this threat would persuade the official in question to support him? The fact that he was able to say this to a British official—a very particular one at that, no doubt—and that the official would *know what he was talking about*, and would then be able to persuade him to calm down and keep quiet, even in the face of possibly losing his access to the tomb of King Tut—his life's work—suggests some tremendous political clout behind the suppression. It's hard to imagine Carter being persuaded to suppress such information and go away quietly otherwise. One even wonders if the sudden and mysterious death of Carnarvon might

---

[270] Collins and Ogilvie-Herald, op. cit., 275.

not have been part of the "persuasion" to silence? We don't think for a minute that there was any "Curse of Tutankhamun," but if Carnarvon wanted to reveal the information to the world and could not be trusted not to do so at some point, that would surely be sufficient reason to get rid of him. Then, all the nonsense about the "Curse of King Tut" that circulated in the press so wildly would make even more sense.

Except for confiding in Lee Keedick on his lecture tour in America which followed his loss of the court case (at which point, the highly emotional Carter was still undoubtedly feeling quite angry and resentful), he apparently didn't talk about it again. But that makes one wonder why Carter himself didn't meet with some untimely accident? Is a clue to be found in the fact that he claimed to the British official that he would "publish" the documents as though he still had access to them, or copies? If that is the case, perhaps those copies still exist somewhere.

In any event, we don't think that Carnarvon and Carter were involved in some kind of cheap blackmail against the Zionists. It is far more likely that the cover-up was instituted and carried out by the British government because they had plans for the Jews and getting them back in Israel was important either for imperialist reasons, or "religious" reasons, or both.

What one has to ask is this: what kind of human beings, knowing that an entire civilization is being controlled by a particular religion and its offshoots, i.e. Judaism, Christianity and Islam, and that those systems of belief were at the root of most of the conflict on the planet, would cover up a document that might put to rest millennia-old questions about the founding events of said religion?

It is clear from Carter's reported outburst to the British Government official that the content of the papyri was information that would put the entire Biblical story of the origins of the Jews and the "gift of the land" by God Almighty into question. The cover-up suggests that this information would also have put into question the justification for the establishment of a modern state of Israel. At that particular moment in time, when the world's media was focused on Howard Carter, he could certainly have carried out this threat, and it would have been an explosion heard around the world.

But somehow, that British official was able to calm him down and convince him to suppress what he knew.

One thing that this little episode does tell us is that the "real story of the Exodus" occurred around the Amarna age.

> In all likelihood it began during the co-regency between Amenhotep III and Akhenaten, when the deposed priesthoods and the Egyptian people as a whole became scared that in abandoning the old gods there would be a terrible price to pay. [...]
>
> Thus when a plague began sweeping across Egypt's northern empire towards the end of Akhenaten's reigh it was deemed just punishment for Egypt having not supplicated the gods for some thirteen years. Yet nothing was done until after control of the country had been transferred from Akhenaten's city at Tell el-

Amarna to either Memphis or Thebes, which did not occur until the reign of the boy-king Tutankhamun. [...] [By this time, numerous members of the royal family had succumbed to the plague, Akhenaten and Nefertiti had disappeared, and other mysterious events that are still not explained took place.]

Under Tutankhamun, control of the empire was placed in the hands of Aye, the priest and vizier, and Horemheb, the king's Deputy and Regent, who was in charge of all military affaires. Through the influence of the latter some effort would appear to have been made to convince the king that the only way to rid the land of the plague was to round up those responsible and expel them from the Two Lands. This meant the 'polluted' priests and followers of the Aten. [271]

The plague mentioned, and the other troubling events of the time are strong evidence for these events being tied to the eruption of Thera. This would upset a lot of archaeologists.

During the Late Bronze Age, the Aegean volcanic island of Thera erupted violently, spreading pumice and ash across the eastern Mediterranean and triggering frosts as far away as what is now California. The Theran town of Akrotiri was completely buried. Tsunamis up to 12 meters high crashed onto the shores of Crete, 110 kilometers to the south, and the cataclysm may ultimately have sped the demise of Crete's famed Minoan civilization. For nearly 30 years, archaeologists have fought over when the eruption took place. Those who rely on dates from pottery styles and Egyptian inscriptions put the event at roughly 1500 B.C., whereas radiocarbon experts have consistently dated it between 100 and 150 years earlier.

Now, two new radiocarbon studies claim to provide strong support for the earlier dates. [272]

I would like to insert here an excerpt from my book *The Secret History of the World* which discusses the problem of the Exodus and the identities of the individuals involved.

LET MY WIFE — ER, PEOPLE — GO!

As it happens, there is one significant story in the Bible that is claimed as "history" that *does* have external verification in the records of Egypt in the form of the "rest of the story." This story is that of Abram and Sarai in Egypt. In fact, this story is one of the very problematical "triplets." The story goes:

Genesis 12:10 And there was a famine in the land: and Abram went down into Egypt to sojourn there; for the famine was grievous in the land.
12:11 And it came to pass, when he was come near to enter into Egypt, that he said unto Sarai his wife, Behold now, I know that thou art a fair woman to look upon:
12:12 Therefore it shall come to pass, when the Egyptians shall see thee, that they shall say, This is his wife: and they will kill me, but they will save thee alive.
12:13 Say, I pray thee, thou art my sister: that it may be well with me for thy

---

[271] Collins and Ogilvie-Herald, op. cit., 263.
[272] "New Carbon Dates Support Revised History of Ancient Mediterranean", *Science* 312, (April 28, 2006).

sake; and my soul shall live because of thee.

12:14 And it came to pass, that, when Abram was come into Egypt, the Egyptians beheld the woman that she was very fair.

12:15 The princes also of Pharaoh saw her, and commended her before Pharaoh: and the woman was taken into Pharaoh's house.

12:16 And he entreated Abram well for her sake: and he had sheep, and oxen, and he asses, and menservants, and maidservants, and she asses, and camels.

12:17 And the *Lord plagued Pharaoh and his house with great plagues* because of Sarai Abram's wife.

12:18 And Pharaoh called Abram and said, What is this that thou hast done unto me? why didst thou not tell me that she was thy wife?

12:19 Why saidst thou, She is my sister? so I might have taken her to me to wife: now therefore behold thy wife, take her, and go thy way.

12:20 And Pharaoh commanded his men concerning him: and they sent him away, and his wife, and all that he had.

13:1 And Abram went up out of Egypt, he, and his wife, and all that he had, and Lot with him, into the south.

13:2 And Abram was very rich in cattle, in silver, and in gold.

In all of Egyptian history, nothing is as mysterious as the strange life of Akhenaten and the odd appearance and equally mysterious disappearance of his queen, Nefertiti, whose name means: "a beautiful woman has come." We notice in the above account that the "the Lord plagued Pharaoh and his house with great plagues because of Sarai." This reminds us of the plagues at the time of the Exodus. We also notice that the pharaoh told Abraham, "take your wife and go." This strangely mirrors the demand of Moses: "Let my people go."

The timing of this event is also important, and I think that we can nail it down to the time of the eruption of the Thera Volcano on the island of Santorini[273] around 1600 BCE, which happens to be the time that the entire Earth experienced a disruption recorded in ice cores, and brought the Bronze Age world to an end. It was very likely also the time when many refugees from many areas of the Mediterranean all showed up in Palestine—including Danaan Greeks—to form the mixed ethnic groups from which the later Jewish peoples evolved.

There is evidence that the eruption of Thera coincided generally with the ejection of the Hyksos from the Nile Delta. There is also evidence that many of the king list segments that are currently arranged in a linear way may have represented different dynasties in different locations, *some of which ruled simultaneously* exactly as Manetho has told us. In particular, there is evidence that the 18th dynasty overlapped the Hyksos kings to some considerable extent. This is important to us at present because of the fact that the story of Abraham and Sarai in Egypt is mirrored by the story of Akhenaten and his Queen, Nefertiti. The earliest document that describes the time of the Hyksos is from the Temple of Hatshepsut at Speos Artemidos that says:

---

[273] Island group in the Aegean Sea 200 km southeast of Greece.

Hear ye, all people and the folk as many as they may be, I have done these things through the counsel of my heart. I have not slept forgetfully, (but) I have restored that which had been ruined. I have raised up that which had gone to pieces formerly, since the Asiatics were in the midst of Avaris of the Northland, and *vagabonds* were in the midst of them, *overthrowing that which had been made*. They ruled without Re, and he did not act by divine command down to (the reign of) my majesty.[274]

The expulsion of the Hyksos was a *series* of campaigns which supposedly started with Kamose who was king in Thebes (Egypt). He unsuccessfully rebelled against the Hyksos. His son Ahmose was finally successful in pushing the Hyksos out. An army commander named Ah-mose records in his tomb the victory over the Hyksos. He says:

When the town of Avaris was besieged, then I showed valor on foot in the presence of his majesty. Thereupon I was appointed to the ship, 'Appearing in Memphis.' Then there was fighting on the water in the canal Pa-Djedku of Avaris. Thereupon I made a capture, and I carried away a hand. It was reported to the king's herald. Then the Gold of Valor was given to me. Thereupon there was fighting again in this place. [...] Then Avaris was despoiled. Then I carried off spoil from there: one man, three women, a total of four persons. Then his majesty gave them to me to be slaves. Then Sharuhen was besieged for three years. Then his majesty despoiled it.[275]

Note that Avaris was besieged, there is no mention of how Avaris was taken, and there is no burning of Avaris claimed. What is more, the archaeological evidence shows that Avaris was not destroyed in a military engagement. The likelihood is that, after years of unstable relations with the Southern Egyptian dynasty, *Avaris was abandoned due to the eruption of Thera.*

This exodus from Egypt by the Hyksos, many of whom fled to Canaan, was part of their history. In fact, there were probably many refugees arriving in the Levant (Israel, Jordan, Syria) from many places affected by the eruption and the following famine. When the descendants of the refugees were later incorporated into a tribal confederation known as Israel, the story became one of the single events they all agreed upon. In this respect, they all did, indeed, share a history.

The fact is, other than the expulsion of the Hyksos [and the expulsion of the adherents of the Aten] there is no other record of any mass exit from Egypt. Avaris was on the coast, and thus closer to the effects of the volcano. Naturally, the Egyptians of Thebes saw the expulsion of the Hyksos as a great military victory, while the Hyksos themselves, in the retelling of the story, viewed their survival as a great salvation victory. This seems similar to other events recorded in ancient history where both sides claim a great victory.

---

[274] ANET 1969, 231; James Breasted, *Ancient Records of Egypt,* 1906-7, reprinted 1988, 5 Vols. (London: Histories & Mysteries of Man Ltd., 1988), 122-26; Shanks, Hershel, "The Exodus and the Crossing of the Red Sea, According to Hans Goedicke", *Biblical Archaeology Review* 7:5 (September/October 1981), 49.
[275] ANET 1969, 233.

The editors of the Bible created their history by inserting segments of the *Book of Generations*, so that retellings of stories that occurred during the same time period suddenly looked like they'd happened over many hundreds or even thousands of years. In other words, the stories' *"horizontal" arrangement in time became a vertical arrangement.* What happened to many peoples suddenly happened to the "chosen" people. What is more, the stories that were passed from group to group about a single individual and series of activities were often "personalized" to that specific group according to the idea of mythicization discussed in *Secret History*.

The way we need to think about these matters is to consider first the facts as we can discover them, and then see if *any* of the stories of the Bible fit to those facts in any way, *disregarding entirely the manufactured genealogies and "historical timeline" of the Bible* as it is presented in the Bible.

The Bible is supposed to be the history of a long series of eponymous founders. The different versions of the stories, assembled from the different tribes, were arranged in a vertical timeline across centuries, with the insertion of genealogies, most of which were uncertain and repetitious if not actually invented for the purpose. Even so, I have suggested, there is one story of a series of interactions situated in one frame of time reference that can be extracted from these stories that *is* recorded in both Egyptian history and the Bible so accurately that the two sides of the story fit together like a hand in a glove. What is more, as I have suggested, understanding this event, this connection of a real historical event that is reported both in the Bible, and in Egyptian records, is the key to unlocking the entire puzzle.

What does all of this mean?

Basically, as I show in more detail in my book, *The Secret History of the World*, we can speculate that Abraham and Moses were one and the same person and the event had nothing to do with the "enslavement" of the Israelites, but rather the enslavement of the Egyptians by the bringers of a strange new god—the Aten—by a couple of mysterious visitors: Abram and Sarai, one of whom was taken to be the wife of the Pharaoh Akhenaten, while her brother/lover lurked in the background making himself rich by manipulating the gullible pharaoh. No doubt it was a great con-job while it lasted, but when the volcano at Santorini erupted and the plague spread, the Middle Eastern grifters saw that their gig was up and they flew the coop; incestuous Nefertiti did the midnight flit with Abraham/Moses and the rest is history—or at least was fraudulently represented as history.

In any event, it seems that the papyri giving the true story of the Exodus—and many other matters—have a high probability of actually having been found in the tomb of King Tut. It seems that these papyri were spirited away to England and that philologist and Egyptologist Alan H. Gardiner was involved in translating the documents. It's clear that, at first, Carnarvon and Carter intended to record the existence of the documents for the Egyptian government, and the evidences for this are the numerous mentions of them in letters and newspaper accounts of the time.

Yet it was after Carnarvon's trip back to England and his meeting with Gardiner when the translation was undoubtedly accomplished, that everything changed. The highly explosive nature of the content of the documents made it impossible to record them officially, and the Egyptian government took note and then took steps.

Gardiner and Carnarvon moved in circles that made them aware of the highly controversial nature of the revelations, and it is likely that they immediately took the matter to the highest levels of the British government.

Perhaps Carnarvon had scruples about the suppression of the information, and his silence could not be guaranteed, and that may have led to his convenient removal at an early stage. Carter may have noted this and had his own suspicions about it. Certainly Carnarvon must have told him something. This could very well have contributed to his extremely emotional and erratic behavior throughout the entire episode. He may have concocted his "insurance plan" and claimed that he had copies of the documents when, in fact, he did not. Or maybe he did. We don't know.

The end result of this maneuver is the existence of the State of Israel based on lies, deception and fraud that took place 3,600 years ago and was then covered up again in the present day. A truly bizarre state of affairs if it is true (as it seems highly probable to be).

Though the illegal giving of Palestine to the Zionists is often presented as an "imperialist gesture," that Britain wanted friendly Jews in Palestine to further their political goals, it also seems to be true that the obsession of certain powerful individuals with Biblical prophecy was influential as well.

CHRISTIANS AND ZION

Donald Wagner, professor of religion and Middle Eastern studies at North Park University in Chicago and executive director of the Center for Middle Eastern Studies, wrote this commentary, the second in a series of five on Christian Zionism, for the Lebanese newspaper *The Daily Star*:

> The British have had a long-term fascination with the idea of Israel and its central role in biblical prophecy that dates back to their earliest recorded literature. The Epistle of Gildas (circa. 6th century CE) and the Venerable Bede's Ecclesiastical History (735 CE) both saw the British as "the new Israel," God's chosen people, who were destined to play a strategic role despite repeated invasions by their Nordic neighbors. In the British perception of being an elect, these battles were understood in the context of Israel's battles against the Philistines, Babylonians and others.
>
> A clear resurgence of such themes was evident in the 16th century, perhaps influenced by the Protestant Reformation and its emphasis on the Bible and varied interpretations of its texts, now that Rome had lost its control over the new clergy and theologians. One of the early expressions of fascination with the idea

of Israel was the monograph *Apocalypsis Apocalypseos*, written by Anglican clergyman Thomas Brightman in 1585. Brightman urged the British people to support the return of the Jews to Palestine in order to hasten a series of prophetic events that would culminate in the return of Jesus.

In 1621, a prominent member of the British Parliament, attorney Henry Finch, advanced a similar perspective when he wrote: "The (Jews) shall repair to their own country, shall inherit all of the land as before, shall live in safety, and shall continue in it forever." Finch argued that based on his interpretation of Genesis 12:3, God would bless those nations that supported the Jews' return. However, his idea did not find support from fellow legislators.

While these writers cannot be classified as Christian Zionists, they might be viewed as proto-Christian Zionists, as they prepared the way for those who would follow. Gradually their views receded, but the turbulence following the American and French revolutions provoked significant feelings of insecurity across Europe. As the anxiety rose in the run-up to the centennial year at the beginning of the 19th century, prophetic speculation concerning Jesus' return and related events was in the air.

During the decade that followed the year 1800, several Christian writers and preachers began to reflect on the events leading to Jesus' would-be imminent return, among them Louis Way, an Anglican clergyman. Way taught that it was necessary for the Jews to return to Palestine as the first stage prior to the Messianic Age, and he offered speculation as to the timing of Jesus' second coming. Within a short period of time, Way gained a wide readership through his journal *The Jewish Expositor*, and counted many clergymen, academics and the poet Samuel Taylor Coleridge as subscribers.

A number of influential proto-Christian Zionists emerged in the generation that followed Way. John Nelson Darby (1800-81), a renegade Irish Anglican priest, added several unique features to Way's teachings, including the doctrine of "the Rapture," whereby "born again Christians" would be literally removed from history and transferred to heaven prior to Jesus' return. Darby also placed a restored Israel at the center of his theology, claiming that an actual Jewish state called Israel would become the central instrument for God to fulfill His plans during the last days of history. Only true ("born again") Christians would be removed from history prior to the final battle of Armageddon through the Rapture—based on his literal interpretation of 1 Thessalonians 4:16.

Darby's extensive writings and 60-year career as a missionary consolidated a form of fundamentalism called "premillennialism" (Jesus would return prior to the Battle of Armageddon and his millennial rule on earth). Darby made six missionary journeys to North America, where he became a popular teacher and preacher. The premillennial theology and its influence on Christian fundamentalism and the emerging evangelical movement in the United States can be directly traced to Darby's influence.

Christian Zionism is the direct product of this unusual and recent Western form of Protestant theology. Found primarily in North America and England, it is now exported around the globe via satellite television, the internet, best-selling novels such as the *Left Behind* series, films and a new breed of missionaries. These unique doctrines were found among fringe movements in Christianity throughout the ages, which most Catholic, Eastern Orthodox and Protestant churches regarded as extreme and marginal, if not heretical.

One of the influential British social reformers to be influenced by premillennial theology was Lord Shaftesbury, a conservative evangelical Christian who was intimately linked to leading members of the British Parliament. In 1839, Shaftesbury published an essay in the distinguished literary journal the *Quarterly Review*, titled "The State and Restoration of the Jews," where he argued: "(T)he Jews must be encouraged to return (to Palestine) in yet greater numbers and become once more the husbandman of Judea and Galilee." Writing 57 years before Zionist thinkers Max Nordau, Israel Zangwill and Theodor Herzl popularized the phrase, Shaftesbury called the Jews "a people with no country for a country with no people." The saying was curiously similar to that of the early Zionists, who described Palestine as "a land of no people for a people with no land." Gradually, Shaftesbury's views gained acceptance among British journalists, clergy and politicians.

One of the most important figures in the development of Christian Zionism was the Anglican chaplain in Vienna during the 1880s, William Hechler, who became an acquaintance of Herzl. Hechler saw Herzl and the Zionist project as ordained by God in order to fulfill the prophetic scriptures. He used his extensive political connections to assist the Zionist leader in his quest for an international sponsor of the Zionist project. Hechler arranged meetings with the Ottoman sultan and the German kaiser, but it was his indirect contacts with the British elite that led to a meeting with the politician Arthur Balfour. That meeting in 1905 would eventually lead to Balfour's November 1917 declaration on a Jewish homeland, which brought the Zionists their initial international legitimacy. Balfour's keen interest in Zionism was prepared at least in part by his Sunday school faith, a case put forth by Balfour's biographer and niece, Blanch Dugdale.

Then-British Prime Minister David Lloyd-George was perhaps even more predisposed to the Zionist ideology than Balfour. Journalist Christopher Sykes (son of Mark Sykes, co-author of the Sykes-Picot Agreement of 1916), noted in his volume, *Two Studies in Virtue,* that Lloyd-George's political advisers were unable to train his mind on the map of Palestine during negotiations prior to the Treaty of Versailles, due to his training by fundamentalist Christian parents and churches on the geography of ancient Israel. Lloyd-George admitted that he was far more familiar with the cities and regions of Biblical Israel than with the geography of his native Wales—or of England itself.

British imperial designs were undoubtedly the primary political motivation in drawing influential British politicians to support the Zionist project. However, it is clear that the latter were predisposed to Zionism and to enthusiastically supporting the proposals of Herzl and leading Zionist officials such as Chaim Weizmann due to their Christian Zionist backgrounds. Balfour's famous speech of 1919 makes the point:

> "For in Palestine we do not propose even to go through the form of consulting the wishes of the present inhabitants of the country. […] The four great powers are committed to Zionism, and Zionism, be it right or wrong, good or bad, is rooted in age-long traditions, in present needs, in future hopes, of far profounder import than the desires and prejudices of 700,000 Arabs who now inhabit that ancient land."

The phrases "rooted in age-long traditions" and "future hopes" were perhaps grounded in Balfour's British imperial vision, but they were also buttressed by his understanding of Bible prophecy, which undergirded his bias toward the Zionist project as well as his grand designs for Britain's colonialist policy.[276]

BIBLE AND SWORD: US CHRISTIAN ZIONISTS DISCOVER ISRAEL

Donald Wagner continues his analysis in the third in a series of five articles on Christian Zionism, for *The Daily Star*:

The first lobbying effort on behalf of a Jewish state in Palestine was not organized or initiated by Jews. It occurred in 1891, when a popular fundamentalist Christian writer and lay-preacher, William E. Blackstone, organized a national campaign to appeal to the then-president of the United States, Benjamin Harrison, to support the creation of a Jewish state in Palestine.

Blackstone gained notoriety through his 1882 national bestseller *Jesus is Coming*, his summary of end-of-time premillennial doctrines. He saw a need to politically support the Jewish people after hearing horrifying stories of the pogroms in Russia. Blackstone appealed to multimillionaire friends such as oil magnate *John D. Rockefeller*, publisher Charles B. Scribner and industrialist *JP Morgan* to finance advertisements and a petition campaign that were carried in major newspapers from Boston to the Mississippi. Aside from wealthy financiers, Blackstone also received support from most members of the *U.S. Senate and House of Representatives and the chief justice of the Supreme Court*. Despite powerful backing, his appeal went nowhere.

There is little record of significant political backing for the Zionist cause after Blackstone's initiative, as fundamentalists began to withdraw from political activity following the Scopes trial and battles over evolution. However, after a 50-year hiatus, gradual change began occurring after World War II. Two post-war developments galvanized conservative Christians—the establishment of Israel in 1948 and the Cold War. A previously small and marginalized school of Biblical interpretation called "premillennialism" began to assert itself within the larger evangelical Protestant community. Israel and the Cold War were usually linked by premillennial preachers and authors who interpreted them using selected prophecy texts. According to their prophetic timetable, as the end of history approached an evil global empire would emerge under the leadership of a mysterious world leader called the "Antichrist" and attack Israel, leading to the climactic Battle of Armageddon. Israel was understood by conservative Christians to be at the center of these Biblical events, and thus commanded unconditional financial and spiritual support.

When Israel captured Jerusalem and the West Bank (not to mention Gaza, Sinai and the Golan Heights) in the June 1967 Arab-Israeli war, conservative Christians sensed that history had entered the latter days. L. Nelson Bell, the father-in-law of evangelist Billy Graham and editor of the influential journal *Christianity Today*, wrote in July 1967:

---

[276] Donald Wagner, professor of religion and Middle Eastern studies at North Park University in Chicago and executive director of the Center for Middle Eastern Studies. Second in a series of five on Christian Zionism, written for *The Daily Star*.

"That for the first time in more than 2,000 years Jerusalem is now in the hands of the Jews gives the students of the Bible a thrill and a renewed faith in the accuracy and validity of the Bible."

Premillennialism gained popularity through a flurry of books and the activities of radio evangelists and television preachers. For example, Hal Lindsay's *The Late, Great Planet Earth*, which became one of the bestselling books in history. Lindsay's message popularized the premillennialist narrative for a generation of Americans, placing Israel at its historical center. *Lindsay also developed a consulting business that included several members of the U.S. Congress, the CIA, Israeli generals, the Pentagon and the then-governor of California, Ronald Reagan.*

With the American bicentennial in 1976, several trends converged in America's religious and political landscape, all pointing toward increased U.S. support for Israel and a higher political profile for the religious right. First, fundamentalist and evangelical churches became the fastest growing sector of American Christianity, as mainline Protestant and Roman Catholic branches saw a decline in their members, budgets and missions.

Second, Jimmy Carter, an evangelical from the "Bible Belt," was elected president of the United States, giving increased legitimacy to evangelicals as *Time* magazine confirmed when it named 1976 "the year of the evangelical."

Third, following the 1967 war, Israel gained an increased share of U.S. foreign and military budgets, becoming the "western pillar" of the U.S. strategic alliance against a Soviet incursion into the Middle East, particularly after the revolution in Iran (sponsored by the U.S.) took the country out of the U.S. orbit. It is during this period that AIPAC and other pro-Israel organizations started shaping U.S. foreign policy.

Fourth, the Roman Catholic Church and mainstream Protestant denominations began to develop a more balanced approach to the Middle East, bringing them closer to the international consensus on the Palestine question. Pro-Israel organizations interpreted this shift as being anti-Israeli and, in turn, began to court conservative Christians. Marc Tannenbaum of the American Jewish Committee captured this sentiment well when he told the *Washington Post*: "The evangelical community is the largest and fastest-growing bloc of pro-Jewish sentiment in this country."

The fifth development was the victory of Menachem Begin and the right-wing Likud coalition in the Israeli election of 1977. Begin's Revisionist Zionist ideology that mandated establishing an "iron wall" of Israeli domination, and his policy of annexing Arab land, accelerating construction of Jewish settlements in the Occupied Territories and militarizing the conflict with the Arab world, all found ready support within the American Christian right. Likud's tactic of employing Biblical names for the West Bank (Judea and Samaria) and Biblical arguments to defend its policies ("God gave us this land") found resonance with fundamentalist Christians.

A surprising development, and arguably the lynchpin in forging the fundamentalist Christian-Zionist alliance, occurred in March 1977, when Carter inserted the clause "Palestinians deserve a right to their homeland" into a policy address. Immediately, the pro-Israel lobby and the Christian right responded with full-page ads in major U.S. newspapers. Their text stated: "The time has come for evangelical Christians to affirm their belief in biblical prophecy and Israel's divine right to the land." The text concluded with a line that took direct aim at Carter's statement: "We affirm as evangelicals our belief in the promised land to the Jewish people. [...] We would view with grave concern any effort to carve out of the Jewish homeland another nation or political entity."

The advertising campaign was one of the first significant signs of the Likud's and the pro-Israel lobby's alliance with the Christian right. It redirected conservative Christian support from Carter, a Democrat, to the Republican right. Jerry Strober, a former employee of the American Jewish Committee, coordinated the campaign and told *Newsweek* magazine: "The evangelicals are Carter's constituency and he (had) better listen to them. [...] The real source of strength the Jews have in this country is from the evangelicals."

By the 1980 elections, the political landscape had shifted, both in the Middle East and in the U.S. The Iranian hostage crisis helped ensure Carter's defeat against his Republican rival, Ronald Reagan. However, it was not the only factor: An estimated 20 million fundamentalist and evangelical Christians voted for Reagan and against Carter's brand of evangelical Christianity that failed the test of unconditional support for Israel.

The power of the pro-Israel Republicans became a prominent feature during the Reagan years, with the president leading the way. *On at least seven public occasions Reagan expressed belief in a final Battle of Armageddon.* During one of his private conversations with AIPAC director Tom Dine, Reagan said: "You know, I turn back to your ancient prophets in the Old Testament and the signs foretelling Armageddon, and I find myself wondering if – if we're the generation that is going to see that come about." The conversation was leaked to the *Jerusalem Post* and picked up across the U.S. on the AP wire. *This stunning openness displayed by an American president with the chief lobbyist for a foreign government indicated the close cooperation that had developed between the administration and Israel.*

A little-known feature of the Reagan White House was the series of seminars organized by the administration and the Christian right with assistance from the pro-Israel lobby. These sessions were designed to firm up support for the Republican Party, and, in turn, encourage AIPAC and Christian Zionist organizations to advance their respective agendas. Participation by the Christian right in gala dinner briefings at the White House reads like a Who's Who of the movement, including author Hal Lindsay, Jerry Falwell, the head of the Moral Majority, and evangelist Pat Robertson, as well as Tim LeHaye (co-author of the influential *Left Behind* series) and Moral Majority strategist Ed McAteer. State Department official Robert McFarlane, one of those implicated in the Iran-Contra scandal, led several briefings. Quietly working in the background was another Christian fundamentalist, Marine Colonel Oliver North.

Begin developed a close relationship with leading fundamentalists, such as Falwell, who later received a Learjet from the Israeli government for his personal travel and in 1981 was honored with the Jabotinsky Award in an elaborate ceremony in New York. When Israel bombed Iraq's Osirak nuclear reactor in 1981, Begin made his first telephone call to Falwell, asking him to "explain to the Christian public the reasons for the bombing." Only later did he call Reagan. Falwell also converted former Senator Jesse Helms from a critic of Israel into one of its staunchest allies in the U.S. Senate, where he chaired the influential Foreign Relations Committee.

Late in the Reagan administration, a number of scandals in the Christian right began to erode its public support. Pat Robertson's ineffective run for the presidency in 1988 led to a decline in fundamentalist political fortunes. Resilient as ever, the pro-Israel lobby was able to somewhat reassert itself with the election of another Bible-toting Southern Baptist president, Bill Clinton, despite his liberal social agenda. However, Christian Zionist influence did decline after the Reagan presidency, though it would return with renewed vigor after the tragedy of September 11, 2001.[277]

Rapturing Red Heifers and Rivers of Blood

Of course, Zionism and Christian Zionism make little sense if the entire foundation of Judaism is based on a lie and that lie has been covered up by those with imperialist agendas. The problem is, even those without imperialist agendas can be so attached to their belief system that no matter how much evidence is provided that it is based on lies, they will cling to it desperately and declare that all the "proofs" are just being provided to "test their faith." A closed mind that is chained and locked is a terrible thing to see.

The reader may want to pick up copies of Gershom Gorenberg's book, *The End of Days: Fundamentalism and the Struggle for the Temple Mount*,[278] and *Forcing God's Hand: Why Millions Pray for a Quick Rapture and Destruction of Planet Earth*,[279] by Grace Halsell.

Gershom Gorenberg is an associate editor and columnist for *The Jerusalem Report*, a regular contributor to *The New Republic*, and an associate of the Center for Millennial Studies at Boston University. He lives in Jerusalem, where he has spent years covering the dangerous mix of religion and politics.

Grace Halsell served President Lyndon Johnson as his speech writer for three years. She covered both Korea and Vietnam as a journalist. She was the author of 14 books, including, *Prophecy and Politics: Militant Evangelists on the Road to Nuclear War*.

The facts that these two authors, one Christian and one Jewish, bring forward are that the *Armageddon theology of the New Christian Right* is being propagated by numerous TV evangelists, including Pat Robertson and Jerry Falwell, along with Hal Lindsey's widely read *The Late Great Planet Earth*, and Tim LaHayes' *Left Behind* series. This theology is influencing millions of human beings worldwide to not only believe that the world is going to end soon, but that it is their duty to hasten the event in any way they can. It is in

---

[277] Donald Wagner, professor of religion and Middle Eastern studies at North Park University in Chicago and executive director of the Center for Middle Eastern Studies. Third in a series of five on Christian Zionism, written for *The Daily Star*.

[278] Gershom Gorenberg, *The End of Days: Fundamentalism and the Struggle for the Temple Mount* (Oxford University Press, 2000).

[279] Grace Halsell, *Forcing God's Hand: Why Millions Pray for a Quick Rapture and Destruction of Planet Earth* (Amana Publications, expanded and revised edition, 2003).

this context that we gain greater understanding of the politics of George W. Bush, though both of these books were written long before Bush effected his first *coup d'état* in 2000.

Halsell interviewed fundamentalists, all of whom believed that it is their duty to fulfill the biblical prophecy of fighting World War III, preparatory to Christ's Second Coming. Most disquieting is her discussion of *an alliance of the New Christian Right and militant Zionists who share a common belief and enthusiasm for a global holocaust.* Alarming, too, is the extent of the political influence of the above mentioned tele-evangelists, the Israeli lobby and the fact that the policies of George W. Bush are largely subject to his alleged belief in the inevitability of a God-willed nuclear war. We suspect that Bush, behind the scenes, is not truly Christian, even in his own mind, but rather follows the ideas of Machiavelli which posit that a leader must *appear* to be religious in order to induce the masses who are believers to follow him. On the other hand, Bush and much of Congress may very well believe in this Armageddon Theology.

Both Gorenberg and Halsell detail and document the history of the alliance between militant Zionism and Christian fundamentalism and expose the purpose of the alliance which is the return to Israeli control of all of Palestine and the rebuilding of the Temple in Jerusalem, on the site where the Al-Aqsa mosque and the Dome of the Rock now stand. For the religious Zionist, these actions are the prerequisite to the Messiah's *first* coming. For the Christian fundamentalists, it is prerequisite to Armageddon and Messiah's *second* coming. Reclamation of Israel from the Palestinians who have lived there for over 5000 years, and establishing Jewish hegemony, including the use of nuclear weapons (Armageddon) are seen as events to be earnestly desired and supported.

Armageddon is seen by Christian fundamentalists as "nuclear and imminent", waiting only for proper orchestration from American political leaders. We should note that there are somewhere between 40 and 50 million such Christian fundamentalists in the U.S. (some estimates go as high as 75 million). The Zionists, naturally, do *not* include Armageddon in their messianic aspirations. This conflict of interests at a higher level is exposed in Gorenberg's book.

Gorenberg's book was written before 9/11 and, in this sense, was extremely prescient. The reader who wishes to understand what is at the root of the current conflict that threatens to engulf our planet will find his history of those 35 disputed acres of the Temple Mount to be crucial. Gorenberg makes clear what is at the root of the volatile relationships between Arabs, Jews and Christians in Israel. He pays special attention to carefully documenting and analyzing the actions and beliefs of fundamentalist groups in all three religions.

Jewish messianists and Christian millennialists both believe that building the Third Temple on the site where both Solomon's and Herod's temples are alleged to have stood is essential for their respective prophetic scenarios to take place, (never mind that they seem to both be using each other and each believe that the other is just a dumb tool). The Muslim believers fear that efforts to destroy Al-Aqsa mosque, to make way for the Third Temple, will prevent fulfillment of the prophecy about Islam's Meccan shrine migrating to Jerusalem at the end of time. Gorenberg calls the Temple Mount "a sacred blasting cap".

As far-fetched and delusional as this may sound to the average fair-weather Church, Synagogue or Mosque goer, it would be a mistake to underestimate the hypnotic effects that the idea of a personal 'savior' have on those people who seem to be 'tailor made' to fall prey to such manipulative honeyed promises of 'eternal happiness'. Did any of us really think that among the 6.5 billion people on the planet, none would take the prophecies of manufactured religion at face value and clamour for their fulfillment at the 'appointed time'?

The problem is that, based on the best scholarly research, the facts are that there probably never was a *first* "Temple of Solomon", and the Old Testament is *not* a true "history of the Jews". So, the question is: if Islam is predicated on two previously "manufactured" religions, what does that say about the faith of the Islamic fundamentalists?

The fact remains: There is an alliance between America and Israel in the war on Islam. They are both determined to establish Israeli control over Jerusalem and rebuild the Temple where the Dome of the Rock now stands, and the Palestinians are in the way. This is the core issue behind the current "War on Islam", disguised as a "War on Islamic Terrorists" or as it was later called, "War on those who hate our freedoms and Western civilization". And just as Christians and Jews are quite willing to sacrifice their own people for this monstrous agenda, so too are a certain percentage of fundamentalist Muslims. But to really get a grip on the explosive situation, we have to lay the major share of the blame for "Islamic terrorism" in the current day where the power has resided for a very long time—in the West, the Christian West:

> "There's a new religious cult in America. It's not composed of so-called 'crazies' so much as mainstream, middle to upper-middle class Americans. They listen—and give millions of dollars each week—to the TV evangelists who expound the fundamentals of the cult. They read Hal Lindsey and Tim LaHaye. They have one goal: to facilitate God's hand to waft them up to heaven free from all trouble, from where they will watch Armageddon and the destruction of Planet Earth. This doctrine pervades Assemblies of God, Pentecostal, and other charismatic churches, as well as Southern Baptist, independent Baptist, and countless so-called Bible churches and mega-churches. At least one out of every 10 Americans is a devotee of this cult. It is the fastest growing religious movement in Christianity today." – *Dale Crowley Jr., religious broadcaster, Washington D.C.*[280]

The "Rapture of the Church" is an idea popularized by John Darby, a nineteenth-century British preacher. The word "Rapture" describes the joy of the

---

[280] Cited in Halsell, 5.

believers while the rest of humanity is facing apocalyptic terror—seven years' worth—before God's kingdom on earth is established.

Tim LaHaye—with his ghost-writer Jerry B. Jenkins—has produced a series of books that seek to make that terror real, to depict the "Rapture" in the world of jumbo jets and iPods.

LaHaye's books are *real* to people living in frightening times. For the true believer, LaHaye's books are not just accurate descriptions of how it is all going to actually happen, they provide satisfyingly delicious scenarios of being proven *right*. The non-believers are treated to long and drawn-out descriptions of what is going to happen to them on earth after the Rapture.

One of the key elements of the "Rapture" theory is the Antichrist. This individual signs a seven-year peace treaty with Israel—which includes rebuilding the Temple. Jews are expected to unanimously support this project and Muslims also will agree to move the Dome of the Rock to "New Babylon".

The rebuilding of the Temple in Jerusalem is required in the scenario because the Antichrist must desecrate it half way through the Tribulation which is supposed to include war, earthquakes, and locusts. All of this is to be *hoped for* as a necessary preliminary to establishing God's kingdom on Earth.

The theory demands something else: *that Jews will convert to Christianity in masses* so that they can then become "witnesses" or converters of more gentiles. Darby's theory insists that God's promises to the people of Israel must be read literally as applying to literal Jews. Therefore, the Jews *will* convert (because it is in the eschatological screenplay).

At the "End of the World", the believers of three faiths will watch the same drama, but with different programs in their hands. In one, Jesus is Son of God; in another he is Muslim prophet. The Jews' messiah is cast in the Muslim script as the *dajjal*—another name for the Antichrist, the deceiver predicted by Christian tradition. The infidels in one script are the true believers of another. If your neighbor announces that the End has come, you can believe him, even if he utterly misunderstands what is happening.

It makes sense: *Christianity's scriptwriters reworked Judaism and Islam rewrote both.* David Cook notes that from the start, apocalyptic ideas moved back and forth between the faiths; the global village is older than we realize. *Some of the early spokesmen of Islamic apocalyptic thinking were converted Jews and Christians; they arrived with histories of the future in their saddlebags.*

What's more, a story's end is when the truth comes out, the deceived realize their mistake. *The deep grievance at the start of both Christianity and Islam is that the Jews refused the new faith—so the Jews must appear in both religions' drama of the End, to be punished or recognize their error.*

And the setting of the End is also shared. The crucial events take place in or near Jerusalem. After all, the script began with the Hebrew prophets, for whom Jerusalem was the center not only of their world but of God's, and everyone else worked from their material. Isaiah's announcement of the End of Days comes directly after he laments that the 'faithful city [has] become a harlot'. That sets up the contrast: In the perfected age, 'the mountain of the Lord's house shall be established as the top of the mountains' and 'out of Zion shall go forth the law'.

The messiah's task is to end the Jews' exile and reestablish David's kingdom—in his capital.

Christianity reworked that vision. Jesus, says the New Testament, was not only crucified and resurrected in the city, he ascended to heaven from the Mount of Olives—and promised to return there. Without the Jews' national tie to the actual Jerusalem, Christians could allegorize such verses. The Jerusalem of the end could be built on other shores, and countless millennial movements have arisen elsewhere. But the literal meaning is there to be reclaimed, particularly in a time of literalism, such as our own.

Most striking of all is Islam's adoption of the same setting. For Muslim apocalyptic believers, Jerusalem is the capital in the messianic age. At the end of time, say Muslim traditions, the Ka'ba—Islam's central shrine in Mecca—will come to Jerusalem. The implication is that in Islam, speaking of the apocalypse at least hints at Jerusalem—and *a struggle over Jerusalem alludes to the last battle.*

Curiously, academic experts often say that Islam assigns scant space to apocalypse. In the religion's early centuries, believers attributed a vast body of contradictory traditions to the Prophet. Early Islamic scholars winnowed the sayings, establishing which were most reliable. Meanwhile, Islam became the faith of an empire, and it was time to talk softly of overthrowing the given order. So the authors of books containing the "most accurate" traditions, the pinnacle of the canon, said little of the End. *'High' Islam appears un-apocalyptic.*[281]

Thus, we see that, for those Christians who believe in Armageddon Theology, the only thing to do is to promote the well-being of Israel with money, arms, and other kinds of support, so that the Temple can be rebuilt; never mind that it is going to be desecrated and that Israel is supposed, in the scenario, to be utterly destroyed in the process of establishing God's kingdom! What a double-cross!

I've listened to Muslim sheikhs explain how verses in the Koran foretell Israel's destruction, and to American evangelical ministers who insist on their deep love for Israel and nevertheless eagerly await apocalyptic battles on Israel's soil so terrible that the dry river beds will, they predict, fill with rivers of blood. I also came to realize that the center of my story had to be the Temple Mount. What happens at that one spot, more than anywhere else, quickens expectations of the End in three religions. And at that spot, the danger of provoking catastrophe is greatest. [...]

Melody, the cow that could have brought God's kingdom on earth, or set the entire Middle East ablaze, or both, depending on who you ask, has her head stuck between the gray bars of the cowshed and is munching hay and corncobs. [...]

Melody's birth in August 1996 seemed to defy nature: Her mother was a black and white Holstein. In fact, [Gilad Jubi, dairyman of the Kfar Hasidim agricultural school] says he'd had trouble breeding the dairy cow, and finally imported semen, from Switzerland, he thinks, from a red breed of beef cattle. But 'red' cows are normally splotched. An entirely crimson one is extraordinary: The *Mishneh Torah,* Moses Maimonides twelfth-century code of Jewish law, records

---

[281] Gorenberg, op. cit., 44-45.

that just nine cows in history have fit the Book of Numbers' requirements for sacrificing as a 'red heifer'. Yet the rare offering was essential to maintaining worship in the Temple in Jerusalem. *The tenth cow, Maimonides asserts, will arrive in the time of the messiah. That's when Jewish tradition foresees the Third Temple being built on the Temple Mount.* [...]

Finding a red heifer is one precondition to building the Temple. Another, it's generally assumed, is removing the Dome of the Rock from the Temple Mount. [...]

The next day, a newspaper broke the story. [Adir Zik, an announcer on the settler's pirate radio station known for his fiery rhetoric] spoke about the red heifer on his radio show. The madness about Melody had begun. [...] Press photographers arrived. The rabbi, sans calf, appeared on national TV. The *Boston Globe*'s man did a story, and other American correspondents followed. [...] A CNN crew made a pilgrimage to the red heifer, as did crews from ABC and CBS, and from Japan, Holland, France.

If much of the world's media reported on Melody in a bemused tone, as a story about the strange things people believe, not everyone saw the cow as a joke. On the opinion page of the influential Israeli daily *Ha'aretz*, columnist David Landau argued that the security services should see the red heifer as a 'four-legged bomb' potentially more dangerous than any terrorist. Landau [...] understood the expectations of building the Temple that the cow could inspire among Jewish religious nationalists, and its potential for inciting war with the Muslim world. 'A bullet in the head', he wrote, 'is, according to the best traditions, the solution of security services in such cases...'

Too shrill? As Landau alluded, the nameless agents of Israel's Shin Bet domestic security force, caught off guard by the assassination of Prime Minister Yitzhak Rabin in November 1995, had underestimated the power of faith in the past. At Kfar Hasidim, Melody was moved from the cowshed to 'solitary confinement' in the school's petting zoo, where she could be kept slightly safer from the visitors arriving daily. A dog was posted to guard her. It couldn't guard against sprouting white hairs [which Melody did, disqualifying her and saving her from being turned into cow toast].

Unquestionably, the reactions to Melody seem bizarre. But there are three very solid reasons for the fears and hopes she engendered: the past, the present, and most of all the future.

Numbers 19 is one of the most opaque sections in scripture. A red heifer, 'faultless, wherein is no blemish, and upon which never came a yoke', is to be slaughtered, and its body burned entirely to ash. Paradoxically, this sacrifice must be performed outside the Temple, yet the heifer's ash becomes the key to the sanctuary: It alone can cleanse a man or woman tainted by contact with human death.

For, says the biblical text, anyone who touches a corpse, or bone, or grave, anyone who even enters the same room as a dead body, is rendered impure, and must not enter the Temple. Yet proximity to death is an unavoidable part of life, and sacrifice was how Israelites served God. So to free a person of impurity, says Numbers, mix the heifer's cinder with water, and sprinkle the mixture on him. As Jewish tradition read those verses, the heifer really had to be faultless. Two white hairs would disqualify it. The rarest possible beast was essential to purify a priest who'd attended his own father's burial, or to allow any Israelite who'd been in the presence of a corpse to share in the sacrificial cult. [...]

The last ashes of the last red heifer ran out sometime after the Romans razed the Temple in Jerusalem in the year 70. *Every Jew became impure* by reason of presumed contact with death which, practically speaking, didn't matter much because there was no sanctuary to enter and *sacrifice had ceased being the center of Judaism.* The tenth heifer logically belonged to the imagined time of the messiah because a rebuilt temple also did.

Except that today, the absent ashes of the red heifer have a new function. They are a crucial factor in the political and strategic balance of the Middle East.

Over nineteen hundred years have passed since the Temple's destruction, but its location—give or take a few crucial meters—is still a hard physical reality. [...] In principle, Temple Mount remains the most sacred site in Judaism. [...]

But the Mount itself isn't in ruins. As Al-Haram al-Sharif, the Noble Sanctuary, it is the third-holiest site in Islam. [...] A glance at the Mount testifies that any effort to build the Temple where it once stood—the one place where Jewish tradition says it can be built again—would mean removing *shrines sacred to hundreds of millions of Muslims, from Morocco to Indonesia.* An attempt to dedicate even a piece of the enclosure to Jewish prayer would mean slicing that piece out of the Islamic precincts.

On June 7, 1967, the third day of the Six-Day War, Israeli troops took East Jerusalem, bringing the Temple Mount under Jewish rule for the first time in almost 2,000 years. Israel's leaders decided to leave the Mount, Al-Haram al-Sharif, in Muslim hands. The decision kept the ingredients for holy war apart, just barely. [...]

Yet a separation made by the civil government would not have worked without a hand from Jewish religious authorities. From the Six-Day War on, Israel's leading rabbis have overwhelmingly ruled that *Jews should not enter the gates of the Mount.* One of the most commonly cited reasons [...] is that under religious law, every Jew is presumed to have had contact with the dead. *For lack of a red heifer's ashes, there is simply nothing to be done about it: no way for Jews to purify themselves to enter the sacred square, no way for Judaism to reclaim the Mount, no way to rebuild the Temple.* Government officials and military leaders could only regard the requirement for the missing heifer as a stroke of sheer good fortune preventing conflict over the Mount. [...]

In 1984, the Shin Bet stumbled onto the Jewish settler underground's plot to blow up the Dome of the Rock. One of the group's leaders explained that among the "spiritual difficulties" that kept them from carrying out the attack was that it is forbidden to enter the Temple Mount because of impurity caused by contact with the dead—that is, *they lacked the ash of a red heifer.* In a verdict in the case, one judge wrote that if the plan had been carried out, it would have 'exposed the State of Israel and the entire Jewish people to a new Holocaust'.

The danger hasn't gone away: The Temple Mount is potentially a detonator of full-scale war, and a few people trying to rush the End could set it off."[282]

---

[282] Gorenberg, 6-13.

According to Gorenberg, between a fifth and a quarter of all Americans are evangelicals (up to 75 million people). In Latin America, the number of Protestants subscribing to these beliefs has climbed from 5 million in the late sixties to 40 million in the mid-nineties. "One reason for the rise [was] the campaign of John Paul II against the leftist faith of liberation theology. Denied a tie between religion and hope for a better world, Latin American Catholics have been more open to the catastrophic hopes of premillennialism."

South Korea's apocalyptically oriented Protestants have gone from 15 percent of the total population to 40 percent during the seventies and eighties.

The stereotypical image of the apocalyptic believers as tramps on street corners carrying signs saying, "The End is Nigh", no longer stands. Today's adherents of the Rapture theory wear suits in boardrooms and stride the corridors of power.

> Reverend Irvin Baxter, a Pentecostal minister from Richmond, Indiana, made Melody the cover story in his *Endtime* magazine, which provides 'World Events from a Biblical Perspective', then published a follow-up article when he was able to come and visit himself. To his 40,000 Christian subscribers, he explained Maimonides' view that the tenth red heifer would be offered in the messiah's time—and then noted that under the diplomatic schedule then in effect for the Oslo accords, 'the final status of Jerusalem and the Temple Mount is to be settled by May of 1999. It's in 1999 that Melody will be three years of age...'

> In other words, the calf, the medieval Jewish sage, and the Israel-PLO peace agreement all proved that the Temple would be in place for the End Times to begin by the millennium's end.

> Televangelist Jack Van Impe likewise noted that, 'scripture requires the red heifer be sacrificed at the age of three', and asked breathlessly, 'Could Melody's ashes be used for Temple purification ceremonies as early as 2000?'[...]

> [In] 1999, I [Gorenberg] dropped in at the offices of the *Al-Aqsa Association* [...] to see Ahmad Agbariay [who] is in charge of the association's efforts to develop the mosques at Al-Haram al-Sharif. [...] The Jews, he told me, 'intend to build the Third Temple'.

> Was there a target date? I asked.

> 'All I know is that three years ago they said a red heifer had been born [...] and that in three years they'd start building. Three years will be up in August 1999'. [...]

> *The folks with the cow have a star role on the stage of the End.* [...]

> [Rabbi Chaim Richman, a proponent of Religious Zionism] asserts that human beings are acting to bring the world's final redemption. Jews returning to their land and building a state is a piece of that. [...]

> Reverend Clyde Lott knows cows. [...] Knowledge of what rabbis want in a cow has come more recently. [...] At the end of the 1980s, Lott recalls, 'there was a wave of prophecy preaching going through Mississippi, and the question was when is Israel going to build the Temple'. For that, Lott knew, a red heifer was needed. [...] The question weighed on him for months. Until one day, when he was working in the field and a piece of equipment broke down and Lott got in his car to head for town, the car took him instead to the state capital of Jack-

son, where he strode uninvited into the office of Ray Manning, international trade director for the State of Mississippi. [...] The bizarre meeting eventually produced a letter to the agriculture attaché at the U.S. embassy in Athens, responsible in his specialty for the entire Middle East.

Manning explained that he'd been approached by a cattle producer who'd made this offer: "Red Angus cattle suitable for Old Testament Biblical sacrifices, will have no blemish or off color hair, genetically red... also excellent beef quality."

What Lott did has a logic. Cattle-raising today is biotech. It was his life's work. But did it mean anything? Lott isn't the only technical person pulled to the vision of Temple-building because it promises that a technical skill is essential to the world's salvation. Nor is he the only one in our technological age to read the Bible itself as a tech manual, installation instruction for the final, fantastic upgrade of the universe. [...]

Lott's name was getting out, people who'd never met him were inspired by his plan, in one significant swath of American society he was not nuts but cold sane. [...]

The 'restoration of Israel'—the term Christians concerned with the End have used for generations to refer to the prophesied return of the Jews to their land—must also, he decided, be the 'restoration' of Israel's livestock industry."[283]

In 1994, Rabbi Richman visited Lott in Mississippi where he was shown four heifers. One caught his attention and he examined it for fifteen minutes or so. Then he declared, "You see that heifer. That heifer is going to change the world". It was the first cow in 2000 years to satisfy Numbers 19. Lott had "proved he could deliver". However, Richman wanted a heifer born in Israel to insure that it was "legally unblemished".

Lott gave up his family farm. At a Nebraska ranch, he began raising Red Angus bred to the highest standards, which means, he explains, 'marbling in the meat, white flakes through the flesh... easy calving, hardiness... longevity'. To further the effort, the Association of Beef Cattle Breeders in Israel set up a professional board whose members included Lott, Richaman, and several Israeli Agriculture Ministry officials. [...]

In the spring of 1998, Canaan Land Restoration of Israel, Inc., a nonprofit body dedicated to bringing cattle to Israel, was established, with pastors scattered from California to Pennsylvania as officers and advisory board members. Lott appeared at churches, raising funds, and on Christian TV. Donation cards, adorned with sepia photos of grazing cows, allowed supporters to sponsor the purchase of '1 red heifer – $1,000.00', a half-heifer or quarter, or 1 air fare (1 cow) at $341. A fundraising letter exhorted, 'Remember, Gen 12:2-3: 'I will bless those who bless you, and whoever curses you, I will curse', a verse often cited by evangelicals as a reason to support Israel. [...]

Guy Garner [...] pastor of the Apostolic Pentecostal Church of Porterdale, Georgia [gave up his tire sales business] to commute to Israel to handle Canaan Land's affairs. [...] The cows, Guy stresses, are 'a giveaway to the Jewish people'. The growers get them and the calves they produce free of charge, with just two obligations: After a number of years they must provide Canaan Land with

[283] Gorenberg, 16-24.

the same number of young cows as they received originally. And, along the way, Canaan Land has the right to examine every newborn calf, and to take any it judges to be "special"—likely to qualify as a red heifer and speed establishment of the Temple. […]

Yet who is supposed to reap the real benefit of bringing red heifers to Israel? Garner's certainty he is helping Israel is sincere. But he has humbly cast himself as a bit character in an Endtime drama whose script is somewhat rougher on Jews than on born-again Christians. In fact, the Christians will safely exit to the wings, while on stage, the Jews will find themselves at the center of the apocalypse. […] 'It's not a pleasant thing to think about', Garner says glumly, 'but God's going to do what He's going to do'. […]

[Lott says] *'God has been waiting for six thousand years* to share with mankind to prove to the world who He is. And he's chosen people just like us to be a part of the greatest Endtime plan that mankind could ever have experienced'.[284]

In 1998, Rabbi Richman broke his connections to Canaan Land after learning that Lott had been filmed at a Florida church *talking about converting the Jews to Christianity*. Gorenberg notes that this was symbolic of the state of the much wider alliance between the Christian Right and Israel. It is "an alliance in which each side assumes that the other is playing a role it doesn't understand itself, in which each often regards the other as an unknowing instrument for reaching a higher goal".

Richman speaks astringently of the 'doormat theology' of Christians who see Israel as a stepping-stone to an apocalypse from whose horrors only Christians will be saved. […] On the Christian side are those who want to 'bless' Israel, and provide it with what they believe is the fuse for Armageddon. And perhaps also to convert the Israelis, another "blessing" since only the converted will make it through the Last Days. […]

In letters after the breakup [of Richman and Lott] Richman said that, 'the Temple Institute has its own plans with regard to red heifers.' […]

Prophecy, Guy Garner explains, is 'history written in advance'. He's not unusual in thinking so.[285]

The question we need to ask is: *Why does faith look for a finale?* What power does this idea hold over humanity? Why can't modern people put the religions of Judaism, Christianity and Islam in the museum of religious concepts alongside Zeus and Ishtar?

Gorenberg proposes a partial answer: A true believer in God (be he Jew, Christian or Muslim), is highly invested in both the power and goodness of his god. God *must* be good. And for an individual raised in a particular faith, who had no choice about his social, cultural and religious conditioning, this necessity for god to be good has very deep roots in his or her psyche. Being convinced that the "faith of our fathers" is *good,* is natural and powerful.

---

[284] Gorenberg, 25-28.
[285] Gorenberg, 28-29.

But, here is the rub: bad things happen in this world that do *not* fit with the concept of a *good* and All-Powerful god. Therefore, to be a believer means to exist in a state of dissonance that must be resolved.

Human beings struggle with this problem daily; trying to find answers that will solve the issues of death, disease and destruction; trying to fit their experiences with their faith in a good God. Gorenberg gives an example of a clergyman who preaches endless sermons about men whose lives were saved because they gave to charity, when the fact in the background was that his own daughter died of cancer at the age of twenty.

And so, the most daring idea of all is to assert that the world is broken and needs to be fixed. Of course, God—being omnipotent and omnipresent—*must* know that the world is broken, and being good, he plans to fix it someday. And so, the answer of the millennialist is "desperately honest": there *is* something wrong with the creation of the Good and All-Powerful God, and in the same moment, the despair about the situation, the cognitive dissonance of the Good God who lets bad things happen—is rejected because *God is going to make everything alright.*

Naturally, your vision of the repair will depend on what you think is broken.
[…]
The picture of God's kingdom follows accordingly, but there is also the matter of how badly broken things are, of whether God acting through men and women is already fixing the world, or whether there is no choice but to wait for the Repairman to come to smash and break down and rebuild the world the way He always meant it to be.

Throughout their growing up years, people are told that when something good happens, that is god acting, and when something bad happens, that is Satan who got in the door because the person's faith wasn't strong enough. With that kind of conditioning, it's no wonder that people are powerfully invested in maintaining the "goodness" of their god. To insist that a messiah or saviour is "yet to come" is, essentially, a rejection of now, of responseability. The Millennialists hang on to their beliefs for dear life because the alternatives are to either accept the world as it is, and reject the "good god hypothesis", or to abandon the world completely, both of which would bankrupt their faith.

The power of Millennialism is enormous! The problem that the religions face, however, is how to keep that hope burning, keep dangling that carrot, without letting it explode in their faces. Because, when people give signs to know when the Time has come, and others discover that the signs have been fulfilled and that the day is near, and others say the day *is* here, the irresistible force of enthusiasm inevitably smashes into immovable reality: The world doesn't end.

And it's nothing but rivers of blood everywhere. Every time.

"God does not look on all of His children the same way", said Dr. John Walvoord, President of Dallas Theological Seminary, mentor to Hal Lindsey.

God, he tells me, had plans for Jews and Christians, but not for the others—
unless they became Christians. God, he said, had a heavenly plan for Christians,
and an earthly plan for Jews.

And, I ask, the earthly plan for Jews?

"To re-create Israel."[286]

What is not widely reported, but is well known among these fundamentalists circles is that, *once Israel has done what the Christians want it to do:* re-
create itself and re-build the Temple, then *they are finished.* Those that do not
convert will be destroyed. It's that simple. Christians can love and support
Jews now, encouraging them and praising them and sending them money and
everything they need to "get the job done". However, once that is accomplished, do not think for a minute that this love and support will continue as
long as the Jews remain Jews.

In early 1999, members of a Denver, Colorado dispensationalist group called
Concerned Christians were arrested by Israeli police, handcuffed, jailed as common criminals and deported back to the States. Israeli police accused them of
planning a 'bloody apocalypse' to hasten the Second Coming of Christ. It was
suggested that they plotted the destruction of Jerusalem's most holy Islamic
shrine.

In a fervent wish to replace the mosque with a Jewish temple, the Denver cult
members are no different from other dispensationalists who believe God wants
this done. As I learned from Christians on a Falwell-sponsored tour, they hold
this idea quite sacred. A retired Army major named Owen, who lives in northern
Nebraska, seems typical.

I spent much time with Owen, a widower, who is slightly built and about five
feet, five inches tall. He stands erect and has a pleasant smile. Well dressed and
with a full head of sandy hair, he looks younger than his age. He had served in
Europe during World War II and later for a number of years in Japan. One day,
as I am walking alongside Owen, our group moves toward the old walled city.
As we enter Damascus Gate and pass along cobblestone corridors, I easily
imagine Jesus having walked a similar route. In the midst of a rapidly changing
environment, the old walled city, guarding layer-upon layer of history and conflict, provides the stellar attraction for tourists and remains home for 25,000
people. As the Palestinian Muslim Mahmud had told me earlier, throughout its
long history, Jerusalem has been predominantly and overwhelmingly Arab.

We approach Haram al-Sharif, or Noble Sanctuary, which encloses the Dome of
the Rock and Al-Aqsa Mosque — sites which I had visited earlier with Mahmud. Both these edifices, on raised platform grounds, generally are called simply 'the mosque' and represent Jerusalem's most holy Islamic shrine.

We stand on lower ground below the mosque and face the Western Wall, a 200-
foot-high and 1,600-foot-long block of huge white stones, believed to be the
only remnant of the second Jewish temple.

'There' our guide said, pointing upward toward the Dome of the Rock and Al-
Aqsa mosque — 'we will build our Third Temple. We have all the plans drawn
for the temple. Even the building materials are ready. They are hidden in a se-

---

[286] Halsell, op. cit., 46-47.

cret place. There are several shops where Israelis work, making the artifacts we will use in the new temple. One Israeli is weaving the pure linen that will be used for garments of the priests of the temple.' He pauses, then adds:

'In a religious school called Yeshiva Ateret Cohanim the Crown of the Priests — located near where we are standing, rabbis are teaching young men how to make animal sacrifice.'

A woman in our group, Mary Lou, a computer specialist, seems startled to hear the Israelis want to return to the rites of the old Solomonic sacrificial altar of the temple.

'You are going back to animal sacrifice?' she asks. 'Why?'

'It was done in the First and Second Temples,' our Israeli guide says. 'And we do not wish to change the practices. Our sages teach that neglecting to study the details of temple service is a sin.'

Leaving the site, I remark to Owen that our Israeli guide had said a temple must be rebuilt on the Dome of the Rock site. But he said nothing about the Muslim shrines.

'They will be destroyed,' Owen tells me. 'You know it's in the Bible that the temple must be rebuilt. And there's no other place for it except on that one area. You find that in the law of Moses.'

Did it seem possible, I ask Owen, that the Scripture about building a temple would relate to the time in which it was written — rather than to events in the current era?

'No, it is related to our era', Owen says. 'The Bible tells us that in the End Times the Jews will have renewed their animal sacrifice.'

In other words, I repeat, a temple must be built so that the Jews can resume their animal sacrifice?

'Yes', said Owen, quoting Ezekiel 44:29 to prove his point.

Is Owen convinced that Jews, aided by Christians, should destroy the mosque, build a temple and reinstate the killing of animals in the temple — all in order to please God?

'Yes', he replies. 'That's the way it has to be. It's in the Bible'.

And does the building of the temple, I ask, fit into any time sequence?

'Yes. We think it will be the next step in the events leading to the return of our Lord. As far as its being a large temple, the Bible doesn't tell us that. All it tells us is that there will be a renewal of sacrifices. And Jews can do that in a relatively small building.'

Isn't it atavistic, I ask, to go back to animal sacrifice? And what about a multitude concerned with animal rights in our modern age?

'But we don't care what they say. It's what the Bible says that's important', Owen stresses. 'The Bible predicts a rebuilding of a temple. Now the people who are going to do it are not Christians but Orthodox Jews. Of course the Old Testament made out a very specific formula for what the Jews must follow regarding animal sacrifice. They can't carry it out without a temple. They were observing animal sacrifice until 70 A.D. and when they have a temple they will have some Orthodox Jews who will kill the sheep or oxen in the temple, as a sacrifice to God.'

As Owen talks of reinstating animal sacrifice — a step he feels necessary for his own spiritual maturity — he seems to block from his awareness the fact that Muslim shrines stand on the site where he says God *demands* a temple be built.

That evening, after dinner, Owen and I take a long walk. Again, I voice my concerns about the dangers inherent in a plot to destroy Islam's holy shrines.

'Christians need not do it', Owen says, repeating what he told me earlier. 'But I am sure the shrines will be destroyed'.

But, I insist, this can well trigger World War III.

'Yes, that's right. We are near the End Times, as I have said. Orthodox Jews will blow up the mosque and this will provoke the Muslim world. It will be a cataclysmic holy war with Israel. This will force the Messiah to intervene.' Owen speaks as calmly, as softly as if telling me there'd be rain tomorrow.

'Yes', he adds, as we return to our hotel. 'There definitely must be a third temple.'

Back home in Washington, D.C. [...] I talked with Terry Reisenhoover, a native of Oklahoma, who told me he raised money to help Jewish terrorists destroy the Muslim shrines.

Reisenhoover—short, rotund, balding and a Born Again Christian blessed with a fine tenor voice—told me he frequently was invited during the Reagan administration to White House gatherings of dispensationalists, where he was a featured soloist.

Reisenhoover spoke freely to me of his *plans to move tax-free dollars from American donors to Israel.* In 1985 he served as chairman of the American Forum for Jewish-Christian Cooperation, being assisted by Douglas Krieger as executive director, and an American rabbi, David Ben-Ami, closely linked with Ariel Sharon.

Additionally, Reisenhoover served as chairman of the board for the Jerusalem Temple Foundation, which has as its sole purpose the rebuilding of a temple on the site of the present Muslim shrine. Reisenhoover chose as the foundation's international secretary *Stanley Goldfoot.* Goldfoot emigrated in the 1930s from South Africa to Palestine and became *a member of the notorious Stern gang,* which shocked the world with its massacres of Arab men, women and children. Such figures as *David Ben-Gurion denounced the gang as Nazis and outlawed them.*

Goldfoot, according to the Israeli newspaper *Davar,* placed a bomb on July 22, 1946, in Jerusalem's King David Hotel that destroyed a wing of the hotel housing the British Mandate secretariat and part of the military headquarters. *The operation killed some 100 British and other officials* and, as the Jewish militants planned, hastened the day the British left Palestine.

'He's a very solid, legitimate terrorist', Reisenhoover said admiringly of Goldfoot. 'He has the qualifications for clearing a site for the temple.'

Reisenhoover also said that while Christian militants are acting on religious fervor, their cohort *Goldfoot does not believe in God or sacred aspects of the Old Testament.* For Goldfoot, it's a matter of Israeli control over all of Palestine.

'It is all a matter of sovereignty', Goldfoot deputy Yisrael Meida, a member of the ultra right-wing Tehiya party, explained. 'He who controls the Temple Mount, controls Jerusalem. And he who controls Jerusalem, controls the land of Israel.'

Reisenhoover told me he had sponsored Goldfoot on several trips to the United States, where Goldfoot spoke on religious radio and TV stations and to church congregations. Reisenhoover helped me secure a tape cassette of a talk Goldfoot made in Chuck Smith's Calvary Chapel in Costa Mesa, California. *In soliciting donations for a temple, Goldfoot did not tell the Christians about plans to destroy the mosque.*

Reisenhoover had given me several names of persons who knew Stanley Goldfoot, among them George Giacumakis, who for many years headed the Institute for Holy Land Studies, a long established American-run evangelical school for studies in archaeology and theology. On one of my visits to Jerusalem, I made an appointment with Giacumakis, a Greek American with dark eyes and cultivated charm.

Might he, I asked, after we had visited casually over coffee, help me arrange an interview with Goldfoot?

'Oh, no', Giacumakis responded, dropping his head into both hands, as one does on hearing a disaster. 'You don't want to meet him. He goes back to the Irgun terrorist group!' Raising his head and waving an arm toward the King David Hotel, he added, 'Stanley Goldfoot was in charge of that operation. *He will not stop at anything.* His idea is to rebuild the temple, and if that means violence, then he will not hesitate to use violence.'

Giacumakis paused, then assured me that while he himself did not believe in violence, 'If they do destroy the mosque and the temple is there, that does not mean I will not support it'

It was also Terry Reisenhoover who helped me get acquainted with the Reverend James E. DeLoach, a leading figure in the huge Second Baptist Church of Houston. After we had talked a few times on the telephone, DeLoach volunteered he would be in Washington, D.C. He came by my apartment, at my invitation, and I set my tape recording running — with his permission.

'I know Stanley very, very well. We're good friends', he said. 'He's a very strong person.'

Of Reisenhoover, DeLoach said, 'He's very talented — at raising money. *He's raising $100 million.* A lot of this has gone to paying lawyers who gained freedom for 29 Israelis who attempted to destroy the mosque. It cost us quite a lot of money to get their freedom.'

And how, I ask, did he and the others *funnel the money from U.S. donors to the aid of the Jewish terrorists?*

'We've provided support for the Ateret Cohanim Yeshiva.'

The Jewish school, I asked, that prepares students to make animal sacrifice?

'Yes,' he agreed.

And Christian donors are paying for that?

'It takes a lot of training,' he said. Then, quite proudly: 'I've just hosted in my Houston home two fine young Israelis who study how to do the animal sacrifice in the temple to be built'."[287]

---

[287] Halsell, 63-69.

Indeed, the Torah devotes a lot of words to animal sacrifice, yet Judaism has survived without such barbarity for nearly two thousand years.

> Sometime during the Roman siege of Jerusalem, Yohanan ben Zakkai escaped the city and established a new center of Jewish learning in the town of Yavneh. Ben Zakkai was a revolutionary posing as protector of tradition. Before, the ram's horn had been blown on Rosh Hashanah only in the Temple; he ruled that it could be blown elsewhere. He did not say the same of sacrifices. His successors instituted prayers that took the place of burnt offerings, in part by praying for the Temple's restoration. [...]

> In nostalgia, Jews idealized the Temple; it stood for a lost utopia where God and human beings enjoyed a perfect relationship, a lost childhood. Its destruction symbolized loss of innocence. Judaism became a religion of the intellect, with study as the central religious act. It superseded sacrifices by remembering them. The modern denominations of Reform and Conservative Judaism altered their liturgy to diminish that memory. Except that sometimes a culture's old memory can come suddenly back to life, like a recessive gene that has waited generations.

> For its part, Christianity regarded the razing of the Temple as proof that God had moved his covenant from the old Israel who'd rejected Jesus to the new Israel of the Church. Second-century Christian philosopher Justin Martyr lumped sacrifices together with the Sabbath, circumcision, and all the other commandments that, he said, were irrelevant after Jesus. Besides, Christians argued, Jesus' crucifixion was the last atonement by blood—a thesis that both accepted the idea of sacrifice (even human sacrifice) and rejected it.[288]

A pamphlet for tourists tells us:

> The beauty and tranquility of Al-Aqsa Mosque in Jerusalem attracts thousands of visitors every year. Some believe it was the site of the Temple of Solomon, peace be upon him [...] or the site of the Second Temple [...] although no documented historical or archaeological evidence exists to support this.[289]

There is something to be said for this as the reader will know from reading my series "Who Wrote the Bible".[290] Archaeologists have been digging up the "Holy Land" since the nineteenth century and, so far, there has been not a shred of evidence to support the "Temple of Solomon" story, nor much of anything else in the Bible "as history".

Nevertheless, Temple Mount *is* standing there, taking up nearly a sixth of the walled Old City of Jerusalem. It is certainly true that Herod built a Temple in the vicinity that replaced the earlier temple built by Jews returning from exile in the fifth century B.C. Those, in turn, claimed that they were building the Temple on the spot where the former "Temple of Solomon" had stood. As we discover in *Who Wrote the Bible*, the so-called "Temple of Solomon" was very likely a pagan Temple that had existed for some time in Jerusalem and had fallen into disrepair and was restored by King Hezekiah as part of his religious reform project.

---

[288] Gorenberg, 68-69.
[289] Gorenberg, 70.
[290] http://www.cassiopaea.org/cass/biblewho1.htm

But, even the Temple Mount is a matter of stories and not facts. Medieval philosopher Moses Maimonides says that not only was Adam born where the altar stood, but Cain and Able made their sacrifices there and Noah did the same after the flood (never mind that he supposedly landed on Mt. Ararat in Turkey). Abraham was told to go to "Mount Moriah" to sacrifice his son Isaac, and Mount Moriah is where the Second Book of Chronicles informs us Solomon built the Temple. As noted in *Who Wrote the Bible*, Second Chronicles is a late rewrite of Jewish royal history and it is altogether likely that the redactor took the name "Moriah" and assigned it to where the Temple that was refurbished stood in order to affirm its sanctity.

Another curious point that Gorenberg makes is the fact that the word "Jerusalem" occurs hundreds of times in the Bible, but *not* in the Torah. The closest is "Salem", possibly an early, pagan name for the city. Archaeologists tell us that Jerusalem was a sacred center long before the alleged time of David and Solomon. The Temple was supposedly built on a "threshing floor", which may indicate that the religion practiced in the region, and the temple that actually stood there already, was devoted to fertility gods and goddesses.

In our own more recent history, Christian Spaniards who conquered Cordoba turned its Great Mosque into a cathedral and the Ottoman sultan who vanquished Constantinople in 1453 converted the church of Hagia Sophia to a mosque. Central Asia's oldest standing mosque in Bukhara, north of Afghanistan, stands on layers that archaeologists have shown reveal the prior existence of both a Zoroastrian temple and a Buddhist temple.

The temple that was in Jerusalem—which was *not* Solomon's—was destroyed in 586 B.C. by the Babylonians. Seventy years later, the returning exiles were tasked with building a new Temple "on the site" of the old one. The big question is: after so many years, did they actually build on the right spot? Did they even know what was the place where the former temple in Jerusalem stood? For that matter, is what is now known as Jerusalem really the place that was known as Jerusalem before the exile? Gorenberg points out that it's hard to understand why any city stood there at all. "It's on the edge of a desert; the soil is rocky; the sole spring is grade C; the trade routes cross to the north."

It seems that the "temple" built by the returning exiles from Babylon was little more than a human-built *platform* on top of the mountain, achieved by moving a lot of earth to accommodate the crowds that came to witness the sacrifices. It was on this earthwork platform that Herod built the temple that remains in the memory of the Jews.

Josephus described Herod as, "brutish and a stranger to all humanity. He married the last princess of the Hasmonean dynasty and murdered her and her sons and another of his sons by a different wife. But he certainly did build the most magnificent temple that Jerusalem had ever seen—probably the *only* "Jewish" temple that ever existed. The purpose of the temple, according to various sources, was to make money. The building project attracted pilgrims by the thousands—"customers for faith, the only product Jerusalem has ever had to sell".

Herod's temple didn't last long. It was razed in the summer of 70 CE by Titus and sixty years later, the emperor Hadrian rebuilt the city as "Aelia Capitolina, dedicated to Jupiter, Juno, and Minerva". It is very likely that the "Wailing Wall" so revered by Jews as the last remnant of Herod's Temple, is actually part of the Temple of Jupiter built by Hadrian.[291]

Nevertheless, the troops of the caliph Umar, second commander of the faithful after Mohammed, conquered Aelia Capitolina in 638. At that time, the city's Christian patriarch, Sophronius was asked to show him where the Temple had formerly stood. A Byzantine account tells us that, when the patriarch saw Umar there, he knew the world was ending (but remember, at that time the idea of rebuilding the temple was not part of the Christian theology), and so he pointed out the mount which had become a heap of rubbish.

Umar cleared away the rubbish and built a mosque that was the forerunner of the Dome of the Rock which was built by Caliph Abd al-Malik ibn Marwan in 691, and stands nearby. The problem is, historians can't really explain why the Caliph wanted to create a "holy site" there since Mecca was already "The Holy Site" of Islam. Gorenberg suggests that the Byzantine building indicates strong Christian influence in its design. It does, in fact, somewhat resembles the later Templar style of church and one might be justified in thinking that there was a strong Islamic influence on the Templars both in terms of architecture as well as esotericism. A clue to this esoteric stream is revealed inside where a mosaic inscription from the Koran addresses "The People of the Book", an Islamic designation for Christians, saying:

> "Do not say things about God but the truth! The messiah Jesus, son of Mary, is indeed a messenger of God... So believe in God and all the messengers, and stop talking about a trinity... Verily God is the God of unity. Lord Almighty! That God would beget a child? Either in the Heavens or on the Earth?"[292]

And, for the Jews, there was also a message in the structure itself: The Dome stands where everyone knew the Temple did, and therefore, it can be seen that Islam is the culmination of Judaism and Christianity.

Many of the popular ideas about the location of the Temple in Jerusalem are due to the work of Sir Charles Warren.

> Lieut.-General Sir Charles Warren was born at Bangor, North Wales, on 7th February 1840. His early education took place at the Grammar Schools of Bridgnorth and Wem, and at Cheltenham College. He then entered the Royal Military College at Sandhurst, and from that passed through the Royal Military Academy at Woolwich and received a commission as lieutenant in the Royal Engineers on 23rd December 1857. After the usual course of professional instruction at Chatham, Warren went to Gibraltar, where he spent seven years, and, in addition to the ordinary duties of an Engineer subaltern—looking after his men and constructing or improving fortifications and barrack buildings—he

---

[291] http://www.templemount.org/
[292] Gorenberg, op cit., 72.

was employed on a trigonometrical survey of the Rock, which he completed on a large scale. He constructed two models of the famous fortress, one of which is now at the Rotunda at Woolwich, and the other at Gibraltar. He was also engaged for some months in rendering the eastern face of the Rock inaccessible by scarping or building up any places that might lend a foothold to an enemy.

On the completion of his term of service at Gibraltar he returned to England in 1865, was appointed Assistant Instructor in Surveying at the School of Military Engineering at Chatham, and a year later his services were lent by the War Office to the Palestine Exploration Fund.

The object of the Palestine Exploration Fund was the illustration of the Bible, and it originated mainly through the exertions of Sir George Grove, who formed an influential committee, of which for a long time Sir Walter Besant was secretary. Captain (afterwards Sir) Charles Wilson and Lieut. Anderson, R.E., had already been at work on the survey of Palestine, and, in 1867, it was decided to undertake excavations at Jerusalem to elucidate, if possible, many doubtful questions of Biblical archaeology, such as the site of the Holy Sepulchre, the true direction of the second wall and the course of the first, second, and third walls, involving the sites of the towers of Hippicus, Phaselus, Mariamne, and Psephinus, and many other points of great interest to the Biblical student.[...]

'It was Warren who restored the ancient city to the world; he it was who stripped the rubbish from the rocks and showed the glorious temple standing within its walls 1,000 feet long, and 200 feet high, of mighty masonry: he it was who laid open the valleys now covered up and hidden; he who opened the secret passages, the ancient aqueducts, the bridge connecting the temple and the town. Whatever else may be done in the future, his name will always be associated with the Holy City which he first recovered.' [...]

It was on his way to Kimberley from Cape Town via Port Elizabeth [...] that he had the late Mr. Cecil Rhodes as his traveling companion. As they were driving over the brown veldt from Dordrecht to Jamestown, Warren noticed that Mr. Rhodes, who sat opposite to him, was evidently engaged in learning something by heart, and offered to hear him. It turned out to be the Thirty-nine Articles of the Church of England. In the diary of this journey, also published in 'Good Words' of 1900, Warren relates, 'We got on very well until we arrived at the article on predestination, and there we stuck. He had his views and I had mine, and our fellow-passengers were greatly amused at the topic of our conversation—for several hours—being on one subject. Rhodes is going in for his degree at home, and works out here during the vacation.'

Sir Charles Warren was later appointed Metropolitan Police Commissioner in London, a post he held at the time of the famous Jack the Ripper murders. Warren never made any statements about who he thought the killer might be but in a report to the Home Office on Oct 17 1888 he wrote, 'I look upon this series of murders as unique in the history of our country'. [293]

Michael Hoffman wrote in 1996:

The most recent Palestinian uprising, this past September, began in the wake of the opening of Jerusalem's 'Hasmonean Tunnel', which runs adjacent to the

---

[293] http://www.casebook.org/ripper_media/rps.spion.html

Haram al-Sharif, Islam's Third Holiest Shrine, is the former site of the Temple of Herod, destroyed in A.D. 70 by Roman legions commanded by Titus.

Though the media repeatedly discounted it at the time, the Palestinians were enraged due to their fear that the opening of the Tunnel was the beginning of the end for the Al-Aqsa Mosque and the start of the rebuilding of the Third Temple, which is the fabled goal to which most of the esoteric secret societies of the West and most especially the orders of Freemasonry, are oriented (indeed, Masonic iconography is obsessed with a rebuilt Temple).

The establishment media, in a remarkable demonstration of the uniformity and power of their monopoly control of large scale communications, were able to stifle any substantial reporting in September, providing evidence that Palestinian fears on this subject had some justification.

In what James Shelby Downard terms a "cryonic process" (after the method by which Walt Disney's mortal remains are supposedly preserved)—the freeze-wait-thaw operation—the truth about the intense concentration of the resources of both esoteric Zionism and esoteric Freemasonry on this "Temple Mount" complex, was frozen while the riots raged. When they subsided, a waiting period ensued as the crisis left the front pages and moved slightly to the rear of the consciousness of the group mind of the masses. After the waiting period, came the thaw, when the truth was taken out of the deep freeze and presented to the public. [...]

The opening of the tunnel in September, 1996, with its ritual bloodshed, a precursor of the sacrificial blood ordained to flow if the Temple is rebuilt, was orchestrated in 1867. It was then that the future General Sir Charles Warren, England's Commissioner of Police and co-conspirator in the occult ritual murder known to history as "Jack the Ripper", had been dispatched on yet another Masonic mission, to lay the groundwork for the rebuilding of the Temple of Jerusalem. And so it was that in 1867, one of England's most important Freemasons, a member of its "research lodge" (*Ars Quator Coronatorum*), "rediscovered" the claustrophobic, 500-yard tunnel.

The "implements" of the old Temple, according to the Talmud, were hidden on the Temple Mount before the destruction of the Second Temple. With Warren's Tunnel now open, the "treasure hunt" begins, as the establishment media admitted, between the lines, during its mid-October "thaw".

In the second week in October, Zionist zealots, involved in crimes of terrorism linked to the hoped-for destruction of Al-Aqsa mosque, suddenly entered stage center from their establishment-imposed positions of obscurity. In the processing of the group mind, chronology is everything. Hence, mid October was the time designated for slowly pulling the curtain back and revealing the actual game afoot. At this juncture the establishment media unveiled Mr. Yehuda Etzion, head of Hai Vekayam, spearhead of the drive to rebuild Herod's Temple upon the ruins of Islam's revered Al-Aqsa mosque. As if on cue, seven Hai Vekayam 'activists' were arrested by Israeli police when they tried to force their way onto the Dome of the Rock in October.

Also on cue, a petition was presented to the Israelis in October, dotting every "i" and crossing every "t" of every Palestinian fear about what the Zionists intend with their "tunnel". The petition, put forth by the Temple Mount Faithful organization, a group financed by deep-pockets Judeo-Churchian fundamentalists in the U.S. and shadowy, international Zionist and Masonic moneybags, calls for the removal of the mosque from the Temple Mount. James Shelby Downard and I have a term for that call: Truth or Consequences via Revelation of the Method. For more on that, interested persons may consult my Truth or Consequences lecture, available on audio-cassette."[294]

With all the things that have happened since 1996, with all that Halsell and Gorenberg have uncovered, Hoffman doesn't sound so nutty, now does he? Fact is, after his expedition, Warren wrote a book entitled *The Land of Promise*, a book arguing that Britain's East India Company should colonize Palestine with Jews. The idea was quite popular in England for two reasons: 1) it promoted British imperial interests and 2) *it fit Bible prophecy*. These two factors would motivate the Balfour Declaration of 1917 in favor of a Jewish Homeland.

Certainly, the British had territorial interests in Palestine, but one cannot ignore the issue of religion and millennialist aspirations about the British. Yes, Imperial logic would say that Britain should take Palestine because it was the gateway to the Ottoman Empire and to Africa as well, but notice what Gorenberg writes:

> On November 2, 1917, two days after General Edmund Allenby's Egyptian Expeditionary Force took Beersheba from the Ottoman Turks and prepared to march north toward Jerusalem, the British government announced an entirely different rationale for the campaign: Foreign Secretary Arthur Balfour sent a letter to British Zionist leader Lord Rothschild, informing him that the cabinet had approved 'a declaration of sympathy with Jewish Zionist aspirations: His Majesty's Government view with favour the establishment in Palestine of a national home for the Jewish people…'.

> Five weeks later, Allenby's army took Jerusalem. For two days after the actual conquest, the general's arrival was meticulously planned. […] Christian armies were returning to the city for the first time since the Crusades. Allenby arrived at Jaffa Gate riding a white horse, with the pomp of a king. Then, before he entered the Old City, he dismounted and walked. A standard account of the general's reason: His Savior had entered this city on foot, and so would he.

> Allenby's action makes sense of the Balfour Declaration: Conquering Jerusalem had to not only be considered strategically, it had to be accomplished "according to prophecy". The British logic was rooted in their fervor for the Old Testament and the hope for the millennium. That logic was derived from the cultic teachings of the Christadelphians and John Darby's premillennialist Plymouth Brethren, as well as the hopes of mainstream Anglicans. It was their desire to convert the Jews and return them to their homeland. Barbara Tuchman writes of these passions about the influential Earl of Shaftesbury, that 'despite all his zeal on the Jews' behalf, it is doubtful if Lord Shaftesbury ever thought of them as a people with their own language and traditions… To him, as to all the 'Israel-for-prophecy's sake school', the Jews were simply the instrument through which Biblical prophecy could be fulfilled. They were *not a people, but a mass Error*

---

that must be brought to Christ in order that the whole chain reaction leading to the Second Coming [...] could be set in motion'.

Neither Balfour nor Lloyd George was a millennialist, but they were products of an England suffused with such belief, and of the ardor it produced for the Old Testament. Balfour defended his declaration to Parliament by arguing that Christendom must not be 'unmindful of the service [the Jews] have rendered to the great religions of the world'. Lloyd George commented that when he discussed Palestine with Weizmann, Zionism's apostle to the British government, Weizmann, 'kept bringing up place names that were more familiar to me than those of the Western front'. The two statesmen could regard restoring the Jews to their land as a British task because English millennialism had made this a reasonable project, even for those who weren't thinking about the millennium. Except that once England actually ruled Palestine, the simple commitment of the Balfour Declaration slammed into the real world.[295]

August 16, 1929 was the day that the Palestine Mandate burst into flames, predictably, as Gorenberg notes. The day before, on the anniversary of the destruction of the Temple, hundreds of Jews had demonstrated along the Western Wall, demanding rights to the spot. A surviving photograph of the demonstrators is interesting because it shows some of them in shorts and regular shoes. Why is this interesting? Because as a sign of mourning on such days, religious Jews do not wear leather shoes on a fast day. This means that the protesters were not demanding rights to the Western Wall for religious reasons, but for nationalistic and territorial reasons. They raised the Zionist flag and sang the Zionist anthem.

So, the next day, Muslim protestors came and beat up the pious Jewish worshippers who had nothing to do with the demonstration of the day before. The following Friday, tensions had increased to such an extent that Arabs began assaulting Jews in the old city, armed with clubs and knives. Within an hour, the attacks had spread to other areas of the city and the British police force was so undermanned it could do nothing.

The violence spread and on the second day (August 24), in Hebron, rioters moved from house to house murdering and looting. Sixty-seven Jews were killed, including a dozen women and three children. Most of the town's Jews were saved by their Arab neighbors.

One historian records that Jews went well beyond self defense. In one instance, in retaliation, Jews broke into a Mosque and destroyed holy books. A Palestinian version of the events tells us that the people of Palestine reacted to the provocation of Jewish religious extremists at the holy site, which seems to be what actually happened.

In a week and a half of terror, 133 Jews and 116 Arabs were killed. From any point of view, the event was a turning point in the struggle for control of Palestine. The fact is that there was, at this early stage, a great opposition of Palestinians to the creation of a Jewish state in Palestine, and it's easy to understand. Palestine was basically "given to the Jews" by Britain. But, many in

---

[295] Gorenberg, op. cit., 84-86.

Britain began to think that the Balfour Declaration's promise of a "national home" for the Jews had been a mistake.

The facts are: two national groups were struggling for one piece of land. One of the groups had been there for a very, very long time, and the other group intended to come and take over what they were convinced was theirs either by right of the British mandate, or by right of their god. The British plan to settle the Jews in Palestine was a disaster and they ran with their tails between their legs, leaving the Palestinians and the Jews to duke it out on their own.

But the fight was not equal. The desire among the Christian West for the Jews to remain in Palestine, to re-create Israel, to re-build the Temple, and to fulfill prophecy was behind the Jewish presence. The Palestinians didn't have a chance from the beginning.

> *Avraham Stern* was a rebel even among rebels, too extreme for the average extremist. A Polish-born Jew who admired Mussolini, he'd been a member of the Irgun Tzva'i Le'umi (National Military Organization), the right-wing Jewish underground in Palestine. In the late '30s, Palestine's Arabs revolted against British rule; attacks on Jews were common. The Irgun rejected the mainstream Haganah policy of restraint and launched revenge attacks on Arabs: gunfire at a bus here, a bomb in a market there, the murder of innocents as payment for the murder of innocents. From there it went on to battling the British, who sought to satisfy the Arabs by restricting immigration even as desperate Jews were trying to get out of Europe. But when World War II broke out, the Irgun declared a truce: Fighting Germany was more important than driving out the British. Such zigzagging wasn't for Stern: In spring 1940, he and his followers left the Irgun to create a more radical group that would keep fighting the British. They robbed banks, tried to assassinate mandatory officials. In Hebrew the group was called Lehi [...] the English called it the Stern Gang, even after police ferreted Stern out in a Tel Aviv apartment in 1942 and shot him dead. The group's new leaders included Yitzhak Yezernitzky, who later changed his name to Yitzhak Shamir and decades later became Israel's prime minister. [...]

> In a newspaper called *The Underground*, Lehi published its eighteen principles of Jewish national renaissance. Number 18 read: "Building the Third Temple, as symbol of the era of the Third Kingdom." After Israeli independence, the group's veterans republished the principles, with an emendation. Now number 18 said: 'Building the Third Temple as a symbol of the era of total redemption'. Historian Joseph Heller explains that "Third Kingdom" sounded too close to 'Third Reich'—a sensitive point since Lehi was stained by having unsuccessfully offered its services to the Axis against Britain in 1941.

> The emendation make the point clearer: 'They were a messianic movement, especially under Stern', says Heller."[296]

Gorenberg tells the story of David Shaltiel who was commander of the Haganah, the Jewish militia-turned army. Shaltiel had been raised in an Orthodox home in Hamburg. He claimed that, "at the age of thirteen he walked out of the synagogue on Yom Kippur and ate pork and waited for God to strike

---

[296] Gorenberg, 91-92.

him down". When nothing happened, he was finished with religion. Shaltiel went on to join the French Foreign Legion and later became an arms buyer for Haganah in Europe. In 1936, the Gestapo arrested him in Aachen. He is said to have been in Dachau and Buchenwald and "another sixteen prisons". Somehow, he was released before World War II began and returned to Palestine where he became a Haganah officer.

In November of 1947, after WWII (which must certainly have profoundly affected Shaltiel), the United Nations (founded at the close of WWII) voted to partition Palestine between a Jewish and an Arab state. You might even say that this vote was a direct result of the events of WWII, and *many people have suggested that there was Zionist complicity in the murder of millions of Jews for the express purpose of generating guilt and sympathy for the Jewish people, to put them in a position of unassailable "moral right" to Palestine.* Indeed, readers may want to pick up a copy of Lenni Brenner's book, *51 Documents: Zionist collaboration with the Nazis* to view a wealth of factual historical evidence that certain 'Zionists' were indeed instrumental in aiding and abetting the Jewish Holocaust as a means to provide justification for a Jewish 'homeland' in Palestine.

In any event, the Arabs were opposed to partition (not a surprise) and were battling Jews even as the British pulled out, leaving Palestine in a shambles.

On May 28, 1948, two weeks after the Zionist leadership proclaimed the establishment of the State of Israel, the Jewish quarter of Jerusalem fell to Jordanian forces.

At dawn on July 17, a U.N. cease-fire was due to go into force. Shaltiel, the guy who had ceremonially eaten pork on Yom Kippur so many years ago, now decided that—before he had to stop fighting upon the execution of the cease-fire—he was going to be a hero and re-take the Old City as his last Hurrah. The Old City didn't have any strategic value, but apparently, its symbolic significance was enormous to the Jews. Shaltiel had the help of the Irgun and Lehi forces, as well as a special explosive charge designed by a physicist.

So confident of victory was Shaltiel that he had a lamb ready to sacrifice on Temple Mount.

Shaltiel died in 1969 and no one knows if he expected the resumption of animal sacrifice as a regular practice, but it is certain that he thought that sacrificing a lamb was the proper way to celebrate the re-taking of Jerusalem. Shaltiel probably would not have contravened David Ben-Gurion's orders not to damage any of the Muslim shrines, had he been successful in his bid to re-take the mount, but the same cannot be said for the commander of the Lehi forces, Yehoshua Zetler. If the attack was successful, he had definite plans to raze the Muslim shrines on the Mount, and he equipped his men with the explosives to do it.

As it happened, the offensive failed. The special bomb made a black mark on the four hundred year old Muslim walls, but didn't even crack them. At 5:00, the cease-fire went into effect.

Yisrael Eldad wrote pornographically of his feelings about that night, later published in a memoir:

> *And the heart imagines: Perhaps it will break out tonight...*
>
> *If only they had a sense of history. Oh, if only! And precisely on this night, the night of the first destruction, the night of the second destruction, precisely on this night if only they burst through and got there—for they are capable of bursting through and getting there... There are enough arms, and there are young men, and there is Jerusalem, all of her desiring it, ready for a dread night like this, if only they would burst through, if only they would get there.*
>
> *To the Wall, to the mourning, to what has been abandoned.*
>
> *To break through and set it all aflame. In fire it fell and in fire it will rise again. To raze it all there, all the sanctified lies and hypocrisy. To purify, purify, purify.*[297]

(Speaking of sanctified lies and hypocrisy, the Old Testament has to be the mother of them all.)

But it didn't happen: the Jewish State was born without the Old City which remained in the hands of the Palestinians who had lived there for 2000 years. Many of them are probably descended from original Jews who converted.

In his 1996 book *Beginning of the End: The Assassination of Yitzhak Rabin and the Coming Antichrist*, Texas pastor John Hagee recalls sitting with his father when news came over the radio that Israel was a new nation. His father told him, "We have just heard the most important prophetic message that will ever be delivered until Jesus Christ returns to earth". For the millennialists, the Balfour Declaration had been exciting, but Israel's "birth" produced absolute frenzies of apocalyptic ecstasy. The prophecies of the Last Days were 'coming true'!

> Except for stories I'd heard in my childhood Sunday School, I knew little or nothing about a Jerusalem where people live everyday lives—where they are born, go to school, get married, have children, at times laugh and celebrate, at other moments cry and mourn. Then, one day, moving to Jerusalem, I began to experience the realities of a people who have always lived there.
>
> I walk the cobblestone streets with an Arab Muslim, Mahmud Ali Hassan, who was born in Jerusalem, bought his first pair of shoes, got his first shave from a barber, was fitted for his first suit of clothes, was married, saw all his children born and watched them grow up—all in the Old Walled City.
>
> With Mahmud, I walk along narrow corridors within one of the few remaining examples in the world of a completely walled town. The walls stand partially on the foundations of Hadrian's Square, built in A.D. 135. They include remains of earlier walls, those of King Herod in 37 B.C, and Agrippa, A.D. 41, and Saladin, 1187. And finally the walls were rebuilt by the Turkish Muslim, Suleiman the Magnificent, in the sixteenth century.

---

[297] Gorenberg, 94-95.

'This Old Walled City throughout its long history has been predominantly inhabited by Arabs,' Mahmud tells me. 'And Arab markets, Arab homes, and Arab religious sites make up about ninety percent of the Old City.'

'As Arabs, we are descendants of an indigenous people, a people who never left Palestine, continually having lived within these old walls', Mahmud continues. 'I can trace my forebears back more than ten generations. And in the case of my father and his father and his father, our families have lived in the same house for the past three hundred years'. [...]

'This is one of the oldest cities in the world', Mahmud reminds me. 'Arabs called Amorites came here four to five thousand years ago. They established this site as a religious foundation to honor their god. And these early Arab worshippers of a god they called Shalem gave us the name of our Holy City, Jerusalem. Then came others of our forebears, the Canaanites from Canaan. They made Jerusalem an early center of worship of the One God. The Canaanites had a king named Melchizedek, and it is written that he also was a priest of God Most High.'

'All this early history predates the arrival of the Hebrews by many centuries... And when a tribe of Hebrews, one of many tribes in the area, did arrive, they stayed for less than 400 years. And they, too, like many before and after, were defeated. And 2000 years ago, they were driven out.'

From Al-Aqsa, we walk a short distance toward the magnificent Dome of the Rock, one of the most beautiful shrines in all the world—often compared in its beauty with the Taj Mahal. [...]

'As Arabs, as Muslims, our quarrel has never been with Jews as Jews, or with the great religion of Judaism. The places that the Jews and Christians revere as holy, we revere as holy. The prophets the Jews and Christians revere as holy, we revere as holy. My point is that everyone in history has borrowed from what went before. No one or no one group has exclusive rights here. There were countless battles over Jerusalem. And the Hebrews were in power here only sixty years'.[298]

---

[298] Halsell, op. cit., 55-57.

A late 1998 Israeli newsletter posted on a "Voice of the Temple Mount" web site, says that its goal is "the liberation" of the Muslim shrines and the building on that site of a Jewish Temple. "Now the time is ripe for the Temple to be rebuilt", says the Israeli newsletter. The newsletter calls upon "the Israeli government to end the pagan Islamic occupation" of lands where the mosque stands. It adds, "The building of the Third Temple is near".

> There remains but one more event to completely set the stage for Israel's part in the last great act of her historical drama. This is to rebuild the ancient Temple of worship upon its old site. There is only one place that this Temple can be built, according to the law of Moses. This is upon Mt. Moriah. It is there that the two previous Temples were built. – Hal Lindsey, *The Late Great Plane Earth*[299]
>
> An anti-Semite "is someone who hates Jews more than he's supposed to." – *TV Evangelist James Robison.*[300]

The Christian Church, throughout most of its history, has been anti-Semitic. With the reformation, however, many Christians turned from anti-Semitism to a new kind of discrimination rampant in the world today: philo-Semitism. This is a stance which views the Jews as practically necessary *as* Jews, because they have a role to play in the salvation of Christians! This "love of Jews" includes within its parameters the complacent sureness that the Jews *are* different and are destined for extinction once they have performed their assigned task.

Certainly, there are personal and political differences among Christians which make a generalization inaccurate and perhaps even dangerous, but the fact remains that many fundamentalists who are leading the "let's help Israel every way we can" and "let's go after the Muslims" charge of the present day have an established history of having taught their followers that Jews were behind all of the world's troubles.

It was after the full horrors of Nazi Germany had been revealed that Western Christianity realized that promoting anti-Semitism, à la *The Protocols of the Elders of Zion,* could be seen as sympathizing with the Nazis. So, those fundamentalists who were blatantly anti-Semitic backed up and regrouped.

With the birth of Israel in 1948, the anti-Semitic Christians changed their tactics. They were still anti-Semitic (still are), but they acted differently on the outside; they became "loving" and "grateful", benign and patronizing toward Jews. Thank goodness the Jews were now doing what they were supposed to do: regather in Israel so Jesus could return and blast them all to smithereens!

As this new appreciation of the Jewish role merged with dispensationalist beliefs, Western Christians became fiercely supportive of the new Jewish state. Nothing must come between Israel and its destiny! Anybody could criticize any other nation in the world, but not Israel. Criticizing France,

---

[299] Cited by Halsell, 72.
[300] Cited by Halsell, 79.

Germany or even the U.S. was just "political". Criticizing Israel was criticizing God Almighty.

At the same time that millennialists proclaim their love for Israel, they frequently reveal that they have no liking for Jews at all.

> Standing, overlooking the Megiddo valley, Clyde, a traveling companion, explained to me that this was the site where Christ would lead the forces of good against evil. 'Two-thirds of all the Jews will be killed', Clyde said, citing Zechariah 13:8-9. Pausing for some math, he comes up with nine million dead Jews. 'For two hundred miles, the blood will reach to the horses' bridles.'
>
> When I express concern over this scenario, Clyde explains, 'God is doing it mainly for his ancient people, the Jews. He's devised a seven-year Tribulation period mainly to purge the Jews, to get them to see the light and recognize Christ as their savior'.
>
> But why, I ask, would God have chosen a people—'God's favorite' as Clyde says—only to exterminate most of them?
>
> 'As I said, God must purge them', Clyde says. 'He wants them to bow down before His only son, our Lord Jesus Christ.'
>
> But a few will be left? To bury their dead?
>
> 'Yes', Clyde tells me. "There'll be 144,000 who are spared. Then they will convert to Christ'.
>
> 'Only 144,000 Jews will remain alive after the battle of Armageddon. These remaining Jews—every man, woman and child among them—will bow down to Jesus. As converted Christians, all the adults will at once begin preaching the gospel of Christ. Imagine! They will be like 144,000 Billy Grahams turned loose at once!' – *Hal Lindsey*
>
> "As long as they don't convert, Jews are 'spiritually blind.'" – *Jerry Falwell*[301]

Traditionally, Jews have been liberal and supportive of liberal agendas. Having known discrimination and racism, they were allied with liberal agendas. However, in 1967, after Israel seized Arab lands that it did not want to relinquish, the Jewish state moved rapidly to the conservative right. American Jews, formerly liberal supporters of the rights of others were persuaded that their number one priority was to support Israel. Under this influence, they also moved rapidly to the right.

The Israeli Right and the Christian Right became strange bedfellows, each with a doctrine centered around Israel and a cult of land. Nathan Perlmutter of the ADL explained why American Jews support the Christian Right in America: First he says, he feels himself a somewhat typical American Jew in that he weighs every issue in life by one measure: "Is it good for the Jews? This question satisfied, I proceed to the secondary issues."

American Jews support Jerry Falwell because he supports the expansionist aims of Israel. Perlmutter knows that evangelical-fundamentalists interpret Scripture as saying all Jews eventually must accept Jesus or be killed. But, meanwhile, he says, "We need all the friends we have to support Israel... If

---

[301] Halsell, 81.

the Messiah comes, on that day we'll consider our options. Meanwhile, let's praise the Lord and pass the ammunition".

Irving Kristol urges American Jews to support such as Falwell telling them that "in the real world" Jews are better off to back the Right, those that are strongly pro-Israel. To be sure, he adds, fundamentalist preachers will say that God does not hear the prayer of a Jew. But, "after all, why should Jews care about the theology of a fundamentalist preacher when they do not for a moment believe that he speaks with any authority on the question of God's attentiveness to human prayer? And what do such theological abstractions matter against the mundane fact that the same preacher is vigorously pro-Israel?"

> Douglas Krieger, an evangelical lay leader of Denver, Colorado, closely connected with Terry Reisenhoover in raising money to eradicate the Al-Aqsa mosque and the Dome of the Rock to rebuild the Temple in Jerusalem, early on urged Israel to work with and totally embrace evangelical-fundamentalist issues in exchange for their support of Israel.

> In a lengthy analysis paper prepared for Israeli and American Jewish leaders, Krieger points out that as a consequence of its wars of aggression, Israel faced two choices: to seek peace by withdrawing from 'territory acquired by war', or to continue reliance upon even greater military strength, i.e. the Christian Right controlled U.S.

> If the Israelis took the second choice, which Krieger urged them to do (as a millennialist he very much wants them to re-take all of Palestine and re-build the Temple), then the Israelis and American Jews would face the danger of an outbreak of anti-Semitism.

> Because of Israel's military seizure of Arab lands, 'a rise of anti-Semitism could possibly surge in the West'. This could be prevented, however, Krieger said, through its alliance with the New Christian Right. He pointed out that Israel could *use* the evangelical-fundamentalists to project through their (the Jews') vast radio and television networks an image of Israel that Americans would like, accept and support.

> Moreover, Krieger said, 'The Religious Right could sell the Americans on the idea that God wanted a militant, militarized Israel. And that the more militant Israel became, the more supportive and ecstatic in its support the U.S. Right would become'.[302]

Militant Zionist Jews and fundamentalist Christians have therefore formed an alliance that embraces the same dogma. *This dogma has nothing to do with spiritual values or living a good life as either a Christian or a Jew.* The alliance is about political power and worldly possessions. It's about one group of people physically taking sole possession of land holy to three faiths, occupied for two thousand years by a people that certainly resist their lands, their rights, and their lives being taken from them. It is a dogma centered on a small political entity—Israel. Both Israeli leaders and the Christian Right make ownership of land the highest priority in their lives, creating a cult re-

---

[302] Halsell, 85.

ligion—and each group is doing so cynically, for their own selfish reasons, expecting the other to be destroyed by their own hubris.

"Dispensational beliefs reduce the complex and diverse societies of Africa, Asia and the Middle East to walk-on roles as allies of Gog in God's great end-time drama... the consensus was clear: prophetic imperatives required the elimination of Arabs not only from (Jerusalem) but from most of the Middle East... They stood in the way of God's promises to the Jews." – *Paul Boyer, When Time Shall Be No More*[303]

"The Evangelical New Right [...] systematically seized control of the leadership of the southern Baptist Convention, the largest Protestant denomination [...] altering long-held theological positions for political advantage." – *Sidney Blumentahal in The New Republic*[304]

"I do not know how many future generations we can count on before the Lord returns." – *James Watt, U.S. secretary of the interior speaking before the House Interior Committee, in an apparent refutation to arguments for conserving natural resources.*[305]

President Reagan represented a dispensationalist view that since "Christ is at the door", spending on domestic issues should not be taken too seriously. "Most of Reagan's policy decisions", said James Mills, a former California state official, were based on his "literal interpretation of biblical prophecies". This led to Reagan's idea that there was "no reason to get wrought up about the national debt if God is soon going to foreclose on the whole world".[306]

George W. Bush apparently has the same view.

Reagan's support of gung-ho neo-conservatives can only be understood in the light of the President's millennialist thinking. "Why waste time and money preserving things for the future? Why be concerned about conservation? It follows that all domestic programs, especially those that entail capital outlay, can and should be curtailed to free up money to wage the War of Armageddon."

The Dispensationalists who preach Armageddon Theology are a relatively new cult—less than 200 years old. There are four main aspects of their belief system:

1) They are anti-Semitic, i.e. anti-Jewish. They profess a fervent love for Israel. Their support of Israel does not, however, arise out of a true love for the Jews and their sufferings. Rather, their 'love and support' is based on their wanting Israel 'in place' for the 'Second Coming of Christ', when they expect most Jews to be destroyed.

2) The Dispensationalists have a very narrow view of God and the six billion people on the planet. They worship a tribal god who is only concerned with two peoples: Jews and Christians, who said tribal God intends to pit against one another for His favor. The other five billion people on the planet are just not on this God's radar except to be killed in the final battle.

---

[303] Halsell, 93.
[304] Halsell, 101.
[305] Halsell, 103.
[306] Halsell, 102.

3) The Dispensationalists are certain right down to their bones that they understand the Mind of God. They provide a scenario, like a movie script, that unfolds with time sequences, epochs or "dispensations" all ending happily with an end-time escapism called the Rapture—for a chosen few like themselves. They appeal to those who want to feel that they are on the "inside" of a "special group" with secret, profound knowledge. This desire for certitude causes millions of the followers of Dispensationalism to trust their leaders to an extraordinary degree.

4) Fatalism is the fourth aspect of Dispensationalists. The world, they say, is getting steadily worse and we can do nothing, so there is no point in doing anything. The teachers teach about the wrath of a vengeful god and declare that God does not want us to work for peace, that God demands that we wage a nuclear war: Armageddon that will destroy the planet.[307]

The frightening by-product of these beliefs is that, since the Cult is in Power in the United States, it is so easy to create the very situations which are described, thus ensuring the fulfillment of the ideas of the Dispensationalists: the Cult that wants to create Armageddon needs five billion people on the planet to go willingly to the sacrificial altar, and Muslims have been chosen to be first.

The nation of Israel, the Jewish people, have suffered so much and so long that they simply do not know who to trust anymore. And now we have individuals who are religious fanatics—Zionists—coming along and doing everything possible to stir up anti-Semitic feelings, calling on all their fellow Jews to unite and congregate in Israel—the Promised Land of their religion—in the same way it has happened over and over again throughout history. Seeing this self-destructive tendency is not only painful, but gives one a feeling of desperation. Not again!

It is very sad because we hear the rumble of revulsion building all around. It is at the root of the growing neo-Nazi thug movement; it is heard even at the supermarket in the checkout line. A current of anger and resentment threading its way into the subconscious minds of non-Jews—that will lay the groundwork for the arising of a new Hitler. Only this time, he won't be just a German dude with the force of the Allies there to stomp him in the dirt. He will raise that ugly cry again, the cry that will be seen as justified by the very actions of Jews themselves, who have walked right into the trap. All the problems will be presented as existing in Jews, in Israel... and he (or they) will present so simple a way to solve these problems: they will point out that the Jews are all gathered in one place (or at least they are all known because they all belong to clubs and synagogues because those kind Zionist folks have been going around gathering them back into the fold), so the 'Final Solution' will be resurrected again. And the whole rest of the human race will not realize that they have been had.

---

[307] Halsell, 113-114. Slightly adapted and rewritten.

Exploring the Labyrinth

Considering the fact that the world is now in the grips of a gang of religious fanatics that believe in the End of the World in literal terms and that it is their duty to 'Initiate the Eschaton', it behoves us to try to figure out just who these people really are and what the truth is. If the true story of the Exodus that was buried with King Tut was so explosive that it would have brought to a halt all the Imperialist aims of Britain and would have cursed forever any Jewish dreams of a homeland in Palestine—a land to which they had no title—and this truth was suppressed—probably one of the greatest crimes against humanity every committed, if not the greatest—then it behoves us to try to find out if there are any traces, any remnants of information we can glean from all the various fields of study available to us in an attempt to put together some idea of what that truth is and what is really going on.

So, this section will consist of just that: a series of turns in the Labyrinth, collecting data, trying to see what fits, trying to find our true history and hopefully, if we can find the truth about the past, if we remember history, we will not be doomed to repeat it, and we will be able to leave the labyrinth unscathed.

Modern Day Manipulations and mtDNA

During the summer of 2003, in all the hullabaloo over the death of Dr. David Kelly, we came across the term "Ethnic Specific Weapons" in an article we published on our news web site "Signs of the Times"[308] that went as follows:

Microbiologists With Link to Race-Based Weapon Turning Up Dead[309]

Exclusive to *American Free Press*
By Gordon Thomas

Dr. David Kelly—the biological warfare weapons specialist at the heart of the continuing political crisis for the British government—had links to three other top microbiologists whose deaths have left unanswered questions.

The 59-year-old British scientist was involved with ultra secret work at Israel's Institute for Biological Research. Israeli sources claim Kelly met institute scientists several times in London in the past two years. [...]

---

[308] http://www.signs-of-the-times.org
[309] http://americanfreepress.net/08_09_03/Microbiologists_With/microbiologists_with.html

There have been persistent reports that the institute is also engaged in DNA sequencing research. One former member of the Knesset, Dedi Zucker, caused a storm in the Israeli Parliament when he claimed that the institute was "trying to create an ethnic specific weapon" in which Arabs could be targeted by Israeli weapons.

We were actually so nonplussed by this article that we didn't quite know what to make of it. But something really bugged us, and the Signs Team decided to take this dangling thread and pull on it. The question was, of course, since all the genetic studies with which we were familiar pointed out the fact that Jews and Arabs are "brothers" (genetically speaking), what in the world were they talking about here? What kind of "Ethnic Specific Weapon" could target Arabs and *not* Jews?

For example, have a look at the graph of the genetic relationships between Jews and their neighbors below.

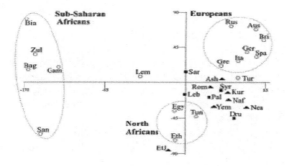

This graph from Michael Hammer's (Uni of Arizona) study. Jews are represented by triangles: Ashkenazim = Ash, Roman Jews = Rom, North African Jews = Naf; Near Eastern Jews = Nea; Kurdish Jews = Kur, Yemenite Jews = Yem; Ethiopian Jews = EtJ; non-Jewish Middle Easterners = Pal, non-Jewish Syrians = Syr, non-Jewish Lebanes = Leb, Israeli Druze = Dru, non-Jewish Saudi Arabians = Sar; Non-Jewish Europeans: Rus = Russians, Bri = British, Ger = Germans, Aus = Austrians, Ita = Italians, Spa = Spanish, Gre = Greeks, Tun = North Africans and Tunisians; Egy = Egyptians, Eth = Ethiopians, Gam = Gambians, Bia = Giaka, Bag = Bagandans, San = San, Zul = Zulu. Tur = non Jewish Turks, Lem = Lemba from south Africa.

Notice, in the above graph, that the lower right corner of the graph is where Near Eastern Jews are positioned. One might therefore theorize that the Near Eastern Jews are, more or less, the most "Jewish" of the Jews in terms of many generations of "Jews" in their family lines. Looking around this cluster, we notice that there are several "families" that are very close, including Yemenite Jews, Druze, North African Jews, *and* Palestinians. On the other hand, the Ashkenazi Jews are not only much closer to Turks, Syrians and Roman Jews, they are quite distant from both the Near Eastern Jews and the Palestinians. I also noted with some considerable interest that *Saudi Arabians are much closer to Europeans and even Ashkenazi Jews than to Palestinians.*

Again the question was: How could an Ethnic Specific Weapon work when we have the idea that just about everybody is related to everybody else to one extent or another, and most particularly, how could anybody have the idea that they could distinguish between Jews and Palestinians genetically?

In recent years, there have been a raft of genetic studies ostensibly focused on issues of "Jewishness". This work has been advanced, to a great extent, by Jewish scientists themselves, so it cannot be considered a venue for anti-Semitism. Nevertheless, in spite of the seeming attempts of Jews seeking to prove that they *are* different from everyone else, there are many voices raised against the issue of Jews as a separate genetic "line". For example:

> Jews are not a race. Anyone can become a Jew—and members of every race, creed and color in the world have done so at one time or another. There is no distinguishing racial physical feature common only to Jews.[310]

> Being Jewish is not a race because Jews do not share one common ancestry or biological distinction. People of many different races have become Jewish people over the years.[311]

Rabbi Harold M. Schulweis explains the nature of Judaism:

> "One of the unique aspects of Judaism is its rejection of Judaism as a biological entity, an inherited spiritual DNA, racial or ethnic. The point is that being a Jew is not a matter of genes and chromosomes. To the contrary, Judaism is the first religion to recognize the 'ger', the stranger who chooses to identify himself with Judaism. Judaism is not rooted in race or clan or in a genetic matter but a religious tradition of choice."[312]

The answer as to "Who is a Jew" that is most often given is that Jews are *a religion and a civilization*, but *not* a race or singular ethnic group. Rabbi Rami Shapiro said, "There is only one response to 'Who is a Jew?' that works: A Jew is one who takes Judaism seriously. One who takes Judaism seriously studies it, argues with it, and lives it".

This, of course, begs the question as to why so many genetic studies are being done by and about Jews, and how does this relate to Ethnic Specific Weapons? Clearly, Jews themselves do not agree on what defines being a Jew, but what confuses the issue even more is the disinformation.

In an article entitled "The Mark of Doom",[313] we find the following comments:

> American scientists have declared that in ten years they will succeed in creating a radically new type of biological weapon. This weapon would be capable of infecting people according to a genetically predetermined marker such as skin color or eye shape. Infection could have a delayed effect or only begin once a certain type of medicine was taken. A recent *closed seminar held by the CIA* was devoted to the topic. The event took place as part of the *Project for the New American Century*. [...]

---

[310] http://www.simpletoremember.com/vitals/Why_Do_People_Hate_The_Jews.htm
[311] http://judaism.about.com/od/abcsofjudaism/a/beingjewish.htm
[312] http://www.vbs.org/rabbi/hshulw/outrchi_bot.htm
[313] http://www.gateway2russia.com/st/art_217290.php

Yet the most terrifying new possibility is the hypothetical biological weapon that could infect people according to genetic markers. Not only would it allow for genocide; it would be created specifically for that purpose. A recent report by the British Medical Association stated that 'the rapid progress in genetics could become the basis for ethnic cleansing on an unheard of scale in the near future'. [...]

Three years ago, ideologues like U.S. Deputy Defense Secretary Paul Wolfowitz and PNAC Director William Kristol were already discussing genetic weapons. They recommended that the Pentagon consider the possibility for using this type of weapon not only to successfully wage war, but also to reconfigure world politics. According to a PNAC report, genetic weapons could completely change the politics of the entire planet: 'cutting-edge biological warfare targeting a certain genotype could turn the reign of terrorism into a politically useful tool'.

According to information from PNAC, Israel has also recently begun to work actively on mutagenic weapons. Israel geneticists confirm that Arabs carry a unique gene that no one else in the world has. This gene forms the basis for the Israeli research, believe American experts. [...]

Fortunately, it is not as easy to create a selective biological weapon as some scientists are claiming. Though it may be possible to create bacteria that multiply only when a person takes a specific medication, the creation of an effective genetic weapon that would not harm the developers themselves seems unrealistic in the foreseeable future. [...]

There is one more reason that is raised as to why this kind of biological weapon is unlikely to be as effective as the ideologues would wish. As Nazi doctor Josef Mengele put it, "Scratch a Frenchman and find an African". Humanity has existed for many millennia. In the context of all our past tribal and intertribal connections, it is not far from the truth to say that *we are all brothers*. "Over the many years of human existence, ethnic groups have intermingled to such an extent that the genetic structures determining ethnic identity have blurred and become difficult to recognize", notes Prozorov.

In the related article, *Politically Desirable, Genetically Unviable,* we find the following:

"You know, there are politicians who set goals for scientists. These goals are often never accomplished, but nonetheless, why not set goals and why not get money for research? Creating genetic weapons is a goal of this kind. In reality, it would be quite difficult to create this kind of weapon. A lot of currently published research is dedicated to the structure of the human genome and the difference between various races. *It has been proven that the differences are very slight*, and scientists have only begun to identify them. [...]

The overwhelming majority of countries, including the U.S. and Russia, signed a convention that prohibits developing, testing, manufacturing, and storing biological weapons. If they begin conducting research and tests, they will be violating this convention and giving other countries an excuse to start this kind of research themselves. [...] Yet *to create viruses that could target only a certain race or people is nearly impossible in my opinion*, at least at the current stage of biology."[314]

Contrast the above with the following from our Ethnic Specific Weapons Supplement:

Ethnic Weapons For Ethnic Cleansing [315]

Greg Bishop
March 2000

[T]his "theoretical possibility" was recognized over 25 years ago, if not before. It was originally brought to the attention of potential customers with the publication of an article in the Military Review of November 1970.

This journal for command-level military personnel was published by the US Army Command and General Staff College in Fort Leavenworth, Kansas. The feature, entitled "Ethnic Weapons", authored by Carl A. Larson, outlines the history, desirability, and possibilities of engineered biological pathogens which would affect only those races which historically have no natural defense against certain "enzyme inhibitors".

Larson is listed as head of the "Department of Human Genetics at the Institute of Genetics, Lund, Sweden", as well as a licensed physician. The Hippocratic oath was apparently not administered in Sweden when Larson received his accreditation. [...]

According to Charles Piller and Keith Yamamoto in their 1988 book Gene Wars, Larson's article was the first time that the subject of ethnically targeted CBWs was broached publicly, and that in "the military's private circles it was old news".

Comment: We learn that the work on such weapons was begun in Nazi Germany. The victims of these weapons were largely Jews. When Larson published his paper in 1970, in 'the military's private circles it was old news', which means it had been discussed for a long time by the U.S. military, most likely with the Nazis brought into the U.S. after World War II via Operation Paperclip. Tests were carried out as far back as 1951 on Blacks working at the Mechanicsburg, PA Naval Supply Depot.

Biowar and the Apartheid Legacy [316]

By Salim Muwakkil, In These Times
June 6, 2003

A two-part story in the Washington Post on April 20 and 21 revealed that biological agents developed by the South African government during its apartheid days have fallen into private hands.

Written by Post reporters Joby Warrick and John Mintz, the piece noted that unique, race-specific strains of biotoxins were available on the world market— for the right price or the right ideology.

[...] The top-secret program that Basson directed was called Project Coast, and it lasted from 1981 to 1993. The South African National Defense Force created

---

[314] Sergei Netesov, Deputy General Director of the Vektor Novosibirsk State Research Center for Bioengineering and Virology, http://www.gateway2russia.com/st/art_217728.php
[315] http://www.excludedmiddle.com/ethnic_weapons.htm
[316] http://www.alternet.org/story.html?StoryID=16095

it at a time when the white-minority regime was under increasing threat by indigenous black South Africans. Daan Goosen, the former director of Project Coast's biological research division, told the Post he was ordered by Basson to develop ways "to suppress population growth among blacks" and to "search for a 'black bomb', a biological weapon that would select targets based on skin color."

[…] The Washington Post even noted, "Goosen says many scientists kept copies of organisms and documents in order to continue work on 'dual-use' projects with commercial as well as military applications."

A May 2002 story on Project Coast in the Wall Street Journal reported that Goosen said he has been 'visited by scores of people looking for 'stuff to kill the blacks.' Race-specific weapons naturally are in hot demand among racists, so it's no surprise that South Africa's race-specific research is highly coveted.

[…] Reported links between Israel's ethnic weapons and South Africa's Project Coast are tentative; some would say tenuous. But the possibility of such links is terrifying, and justifies as much scrutiny as was focused on Iraq's imaginary arsenal.

At this point, the reader may wish to peruse the entire Signs Supplement on Ethnic Specific Weapons[317] so as to understand that the claim that no such weapons are currently available, nor could they even work, is complete disinformation. This work has been going on for a very long time and is, undoubtedly well advanced and may even be being used already!

Our research on this subject, inspired by the Dr. David Kelly affair, was published in August of 2003 and was met with basically dead silence. Nobody even wanted to touch this one. Now, all of a sudden, the issue is popping up here and there, mostly from the disinformation angle.

To continue with our little chronology, the question of what could be used as a "separator" between Jews and Palestinians led us to re-visit all the genetic research we could get our hands on. Our puzzlement grew as we pursued this line and then, slowly, as the pieces began to fit together, that puzzlement turned into horror. It became clear that Ethnic Specific Weapons was just a cover for something else that had nothing at all to do with ethnicity but definitely had everything to do with genetics.

At the present time, it is known that Eastern European Jews have a significant Eastern Mediterranean element which manifests itself in a close relationship with Kurdish, Armenian, Palestinian Arab, Lebanese, Syrian, and Anatolian Turkish peoples. At the same time, there are traces of European (including Western Slavic) and Khazar ancestry among European Jews. Ethiopian Jews mostly descend from Ethiopian Africans who converted to Judaism, but may also be related to a lesser extent to Yemenite Jews. Yemenite Jews descend from Arabs and Israelites. North African Jewish and Kurdish Jewish paternal lineages come from Israelites. The problem with all of these studies is that they fail to compare modern Jewish populations' DNA to

---

[317] http://signs-of-the-times.org/signs/signs_ethnic_supplement.htm

ancient Judean DNA and medieval Khazarian DNA, and they focus on paternal ancestries.

I had a copy of the book *The Seven Daughters of Eve* on the shelf that I hadn't read yet, and decided that it might give me a few clues. It was then that I realized that the answer might lie in mtDNA. And so, I began the search for any genetic studies of Jewish mtDNA. Nicholas Wade writes in "DNA, New Clues to Jewish Roots":

> The emerging genetic picture is based largely on two studies, one published two years ago and the other this month, that together show that the men and women who founded the Jewish communities had surprisingly different genetic histories.
>
> The earlier study, led by Dr. Michael Hammer of University of Arizona, showed from an analysis of the male, or Y chromosome, that Jewish men from seven communities were related to one another and to present-day Palestinian and Syrian populations, but not to the men of their host communities.
>
> The finding suggested that Jewish men who founded the communities traced their lineage back to the ancestral Mideastern population of 4,000 years ago from which Arabs, Jews and other people are descended. It pointed to the genetic unity of widespread Jewish populations and took issue with ideas that most Jewish communities were relatively recent converts like the Khazars, a medieval Turkish tribe that embraced Judaism. [318]

A new study now shows that the women in nine Jewish communities from Georgia, the former Soviet republic, to Morocco have *vastly different genetic histories from the men*. In each community, the women carry *very few genetic signatures* on their mitochondrial DNA, a genetic element inherited only through the female line. This indicates that the community had just a small number of founding mothers and that after the founding event there was little, if any, interchange with the host population. The women's identities, however, are a mystery, because, unlike the case with the men, *their genetic signatures are not related to one another or to those of present-day Middle Eastern populations*.

It was in this last discovery that the skin on the back of my neck began to crawl. Obviously, if Jewish men are related to one another *and* to present-day Palestinian and Syrian populations, the means of producing a "death factor" of so-called "Ethnic Specific Weapons"—by either inclusion or exclusion— might lie in the mtDNA. It occurred to me that it was coincidentally odd that in ancient Israel, the Jewish priesthood was handed from father to son, but at some point, Jewish status came to be defined by *maternal descent*. Nicholas Wade tells us:

> The idea that most or all Jewish communities were founded by Jewish men and local women is somewhat at variance with the usual founding traditions. Most Jewish communities hold that they were formed by families who fled persecution or were invited to settle by local kings.

---

[318] *New York Times*, May 14, 2002.

For instance, Iraqi Jews are said to be descended from those exiled to Babylon after the destruction of the First Temple in 586 B.C. Members of the Bene Israel community of Bombay say they are the children of Jews who fled the persecutions of Antiochus Epiphanus, who repressed the Maccabean revolt, around 150 B.C.

Most of those founding narratives do not have strong historical support. Dr. Lawrence H. Schiffman, professor of Hebrew and Judaic studies at New York University, said the new genetic data could well explain how certain far-flung Jewish communities were formed. [...]

Dr. Shaye Cohen, professor of Jewish literature and philosophy at Harvard, said the implication of the findings and the idea of Jewish communities' having been founded by traders, was 'by no means implausible.'

'The authors are correct in saying the historical origins of most Jewish communities are unknown', Dr. Cohen said. 'Not only the little ones like in India, but even the mainstream Ashkenazic culture from which most American Jews descend'.

In a recent book, 'The Beginnings of Jewishness,' Dr. Cohen argued that far-flung Jewish communities had adopted the rabbinic teaching of the matrilineal descent of Jewishness soon after the Islamic conquests in the seventh, eight and ninth centuries A.D.

One part of the Goldstein team's analysis, that matrilineal descent of Jewishness was practiced at or soon after the founding of each community, could fit in with this conclusion, Dr. Cohen said, if the communities were founded around this time.

The comments about the mtDNA research caught my attention. "A new study now shows that the women in nine Jewish communities from Georgia, the former Soviet republic, to Morocco have *vastly different genetic histories from the men*. In each community, the women carry *very few genetic signatures* on their mitochondrial DNA, a genetic element inherited only through the female line. [...] unlike the case with the men, *their genetic signatures are not related to one another or to those of present-day Middle Eastern populations*." I went to the original research and found the following:

We have analyzed the maternally inherited mitochondrial DNA from each of nine geographically separated Jewish groups, eight non-Jewish host populations, and an Israeli Arab/Palestinian population, and we have compared the differences found in Jews and non-Jews with those found using Y-chromosome data that were obtained, in most cases, from the same population samples.

The results suggest that most Jewish communities were founded by relatively few women, that the founding process was independent in different geographic areas, and that subsequent genetic input from surrounding populations was limited on the female side.

In sharp contrast to this, the paternally inherited Y chromosome shows diversity similar to that of neighboring populations and shows no evidence of founder effects.

These sex-specific differences demonstrate an important role for culture in shaping patterns of genetic variation and are likely to have significant epidemiological implications for studies involving these populations. We illustrate this by presenting data from a panel of X-chromosome microsatellites, which indicates that, in the case of the Georgian Jews, the female-specific founder event appears to have resulted in elevated levels of linkage disequilibrium.[319]

Naturally, I began to tug on this thread to find out exactly who, among Jews, were related to these Eight Founding Mothers. The above cited paper says further:

> Comparison of Y-chromosome and mtDNA patterns reveals a striking contrast between the maternal and paternal genetic heritage of Jewish populations.

> On the Y chromosome, there is no consistent pattern of lower diversity in Jewish communities when compared with their non-Jewish host populations; in two cases, diversity is significantly lower in the Jewish groups; in one case, it is higher; and, in the rest, differences are not significant.

> However, the pattern in the mtDNA is quite different. In each case, the Jewish community has a significantly lower mtDNA diversity than its paired host population. Indeed, every Jewish population has a lower mtDNA diversity than any non-Jewish population. This finding indicates that mistakes in associating particular host populations with Jewish populations would be very unlikely to affect our results. [...]

> When ratios of mtDNA to Y-chromosome diversity were calculated, to standardize the mtDNA results in relation to the other genetic system, the ratio for the Jewish data sets [...] was again found, in all but one case (the Ethiopian Jews), to be less than the ratio for the non-Jewish host. [...]

> Even more striking than this, however, is the high frequency of particular mtDNA haplotypes in the Jewish populations. No host population in our sample has an mtDNA modal frequency greater than 12% (mean 7.7%). In contrast, seven of the Jewish populations have a modal frequency greater than 12% (mean 22.6%), and some of the Jewish groups have much higher frequencies.

> In particular, Moroccan Jews, the Bene Israel, and Georgian Jews have modal frequencies of 27.0%, 41.3%, and 51.4%, respectively, which are all higher than those observed in any of the other populations. Again, this pattern is not seen on the Y chromosome, where the modal frequencies in Jewish populations (mean 15.2%; range 7.4% to 31.2%) are not significantly different from those seen in host populations (mean 13.6%; range 8.1% to 33.3%).

> In most European and Near Eastern populations, the highest frequency mtDNA type is the HVS-1 Cambridge Reference Sequence (CRS). This type occurs at 16%, on average, in Europe, and at 6%, on average, in the Near East. This pat-

---

[319] *Founding Mothers of Jewish Communities: Geographically Separated Jewish Groups Were Independently Founded by Very Few Female Ancestors* by Mark G. Thomas,[1] Michael E. Weale,[1] Abigail L. Jones,[1] Martin Richards,[3] Alice Smith,[2] Nicola Redhead,[2] Antonio Torroni,[5,6] Rosaria Scozzari,[6] Fiona Gratrix,[2] Ayele Tarekegn,[1] James F. Wilson,[2] Cristian Capelli,[2] Neil Bradman,[1] and David B. Goldstein[2] ([1]The Centre for Genetic Anthropology, Departments of Biology and Anthropology; [2]Department of Biology, University College London, London; [3]Department of Chemical and Biological Sciences, University of Huddersfield, Huddersfield, United Kingdom; [4]Bruce Rappaport Faculty of Medicine and Research Institute, Technion and Rambam Medical Center, Haifa, Israel; [5]Dipartimento di Geneticae Microbiologia, Universitàdi Pavia, Pavia, Italy; and [6]Dipartimentodi Geneticae Biologia Molecolare, "LaSapienza" di Roma, Rome - Address for correspondence and reprints: Dr. David Goldstein, Department of Biology, University College London, Gower Street, London WC1E6BT, United Kingdom).

tern is reflected in our data, in that all of the seven European and Near Eastern non-Jewish populations have the CRS as their modal haplotype.

However, only two of the nine Jewish populations have the CRS as their modal haplotype, while, among the other seven, each has a different modal haplotype.

Thus, among the nine Jewish groups there are eight different mtDNA types that are modal with an unusually high frequency.

Apart from the CRS, none of the other Jewish modal haplotypes are represented in the Israeli Arab/Palestinian data set, in contrast to the similarities between Ashkenazic Jews, Sephardic Jews, Israeli Arabs/Palestinian, and Lebanese populations reported for the Y chromosome. [...]

These results therefore suggest that an extreme founder effect has occurred in the maternal but not paternal genetic histories of most Jewish populations.

Greater geographic structuring of the mtDNA than the Y chromosome is an unusual pattern. To assess whether this is specific to the Jewish populations, we also compared mtDNA and Y-chromosome structuring among the host populations. Among the latter populations we found the more usual pattern of greater Y-chromosome differentiation. This demonstrates that the unusual pattern observed among the Jewish populations is not associated with the geographic areas from which they derive but rather with their unique demographic histories. [...]

It would appear that the founder effects on the maternal side have been so severe that mtDNA frequencies in the Jewish populations are very different from those found in any non-Jewish population. The non-CRS modal haplotypes in the Jewish populations are generally rare in the non-Jewish populations. The CRS, on the other hand, is too ubiquitous to allow it to be pinpointed to anything other than a general Eurasian origin. [...]

For example, the most extreme founder effect is seen in the Georgian Jews, of whom 51% possess the same haplotype. The Georgian Jewish modal type is matched by a single individual in the Georgian sample. However, a search of the mtDNA database shows that it also occurs in Syria (2/69 individuals) and Iraq (1/116). One directly derived type is present in two Georgians, but derived types are also found in the North Caucasus (2/208 individuals), Turkey (1/218), Armenia (1/191), and Sicily (1/90). For the Georgian modal haplotype, there is therefore no clear indication of provenance, although an indigenous origin is certainly possible, given the data. [...]

In two cases, however, comparison with the published data does provide some indication of the possible geographic origins of the modal types. The modal type in the Bene Israel is a one-step mutational neighbor of a haplotype present in the Indian sample, as well as being a one-step neighbor of a type previously identified in India. Similarly, the commonest type in the Ethiopian Jewish sample is also present in the non-Jewish Ethiopian sample and occurs in the worldwide mtDNA database only in Somalia. Other high-frequency haplotypes in the Ethiopian Jewish sample are also found almost entirely in Africa. The lack of an indication of a Middle Eastern origin for these haplotypes, on the basis of the Richards database, makes local recruitment a more reasonable explanation in these two cases. [...]

The greatly reduced mtDNA diversity in the Jewish populations in comparison with the host populations, together with the wide range of different modal haplotypes found in different communities, indicates female-specific founding events in the Jewish populations.

Although we cannot be certain whether this occurred immediately after the establishment of the communities or over a longer period of time, a simple explanation for the exceptional pattern of mtDNA variation across Jewish populations is that each of the different Jewish communities is composed of descendants of a small group of maternal founders. After the establishment of these communities, inward gene flow from the host populations must have been very limited. [...]

The differences among the Jewish populations in mtDNA haplogroup frequencies indicates that the Jewish groups formed independently around (at least) eight small, distinct nuclei of women. The severity of these demographic events was sufficiently great to drive an unusual pattern of geographic variation among the Jewish populations.

Although it has been commonly found that Y-chromosome variation shows greater geographic structure than the mtDNA, this pattern is reversed in the Jewish populations, which show greater differentiation for the mtDNA than for the Y chromosome.

Jewish populations therefore appear to represent an example in which cultural practice in this case, female-defined ethnicity has had a pronounced effect on patterns of genetic variation. [...]

The pattern in Ashkenazic Jews is of particular interest. Despite the common opinion that this population has undergone a strong founder event, it has a modal haplotype with a frequency similar to that of its host population (9.0% vs. 6.9%), providing little evidence of a strong founder event on the female side. The possibility remains, however, that present-day Ashkenazic Jews may represent a mosaic group that is descended on the maternal side from several independent founding events. [...]

These results demonstrate that demographic events restricted to only one of the sexes can be of considerable epidemiological significance.

Needless to say, this is an extremely interesting state of affairs, and my guess is that a lot more is known about this research than is currently available to the public. It is almost impossible to speculate about the origins of the "Founding Mothers" of a significant number of Jews, but I am reminded of an old saying that if your son marries, you lose him to his wife's family, and if your daughter marries, you gain a son. Perhaps this is naturally due to the special types of emotional bonds that are formed between women. But, of significant interest here is the issue of what it is that "bottle-necked" these groups of people.

After reading *The Seven Daughters of Eve*, and a host of technical papers on genetics, I finally had a look at Arthur Koestler's *The Thirteenth Tribe*. His theory is that the majority of modern Jews are Ashkenazim, descended from the Khazars, a Caucasian people who had converted to Judaism in the Middle Ages. For a time, Koestler's ideas were vigorously argued—even rejected—but in more recent times, his ideas have been partly vindicated. Ashkenazi Jews have a more significant admixture of Italian, Greek, and

Turkish genes than of Spanish, German, or even Austrian ones as do the Sephardim. This certainly connects them to the Khazars, but does not exclude mixing with the Western "real" Jews of Spain and elsewhere.

There was another issue that popped up during this period: Kevin MacDonald's work. MacDonald ascribes a genetic homogeneity to Jews postulating that Judaism is an "evolutionary group strategy". MacDonald has been generally accused of anti-Semitism and, indeed, anyone with eyes can see that Jews are like everyone else: they come in all colors, shapes and sizes. We realize now, of course, that there is a wide variation in the paternal ancestry, but that there is something truly strange about the maternal ancestry of a significant number of Jews is now quite evident.

The question then became: what is mtDNA and what, precisely, does it do?

To look further into this question, let us return to the death of Dr. David Kelly, the biological warfare weapons specialist who had links to three other top microbiologists who are on the startlingly long list of microbiologists who have died mysteriously in the past few years.

Regular readers of our web site already know that I make unusual connections between things, and this item certainly has been working on me. What it reminded me of was the movie *V*, where the aliens began to target scientists for destruction because they were the only ones capable of figuring out the genetics of the invaders and what might be used as a weapon against them. I know that is a strange connection, but when you try to figure out a reason for the deaths of so many microbiologists in so short a period of time, considering what is happening on the global political stage, you have to start somewhere.

Of course, it wasn't until the death of David Kelly that the clue about Ethnic Specific Weapons turned up, and then it all began to make a sick sort of sense.

The news bytes tell us that Kelly was involved with ultra secret work at Israel's Institute for Biological Research. We are also told that there have been "persistent reports" that the institute is engaged in DNA sequencing research. This last seems to be founded on the fact that a former member of the Knesset, Dedi Zucker, claimed in the Israeli Parliament that the institute was "trying to create an ethnic specific weapon" in which Arabs could be targeted by Israeli weapons.

What does *not* fit in this little scenario is the fact that it was *Israeli sources* making the claim that Kelly met Israeli institute scientists several times in London in the past two years, from which, it seems, the inference was made that Kelly was involved with ultra secret work *for* Israel.

As I have already written, the problem that captured my attention— assuming that Dedi Zucker was letting the cat out of the bag when he said that Israel was "trying to create an ethnic specific weapon in which Arabs could be targeted"—was what kind of "marker" would they use to include or exclude based on *ethnicity*?

There are two points to keep in mind here from our look at genetics. First, studies done from the perspective of the Y chromosome, or the male genetic line, show similarities between Ashkenazi Jews, Sephardic Jews, Israeli Arabs/Palestinian, and Lebanese populations as well as limited genetic connections to European populations.

Second, in *most* European *and* Near Eastern Jewish populations, the highest frequency mtDNA type is the HVS-1 Cambridge Reference Sequence (CRS). This type occurs at 16%, on average, in Europe, and at 6%, on average, in the Near East. All of the seven European and Near Eastern *non-Jewish* populations have the CRS as their modal haplotype.

At that point in time, what was revealed by the genetic studies available to me, suggested that any biochemical weapon specifically designed to take out Palestinians would also take out most of today's Jewry, *and* a large number of Europeans and their descendants, such as many Americans.

Looking at it from the point of view of mtDNA wasn't entirely satisfactory either. Remember the remark: *two of the nine Jewish populations had the CRS as their modal haplotype, including the largest group of modern Jews, Ashkenazim:*

> The pattern in Ashkenazic Jews is of particular interest. Despite the common opinion that this population has undergone a strong founder event, it has a modal haplotype with a frequency similar to that of its host population (9.0% vs. 6.9%), providing little evidence of a strong founder event on the female side.

That meant that the mtDNA as an "excluder" would only work for less than 30 percent of modern Jews—Sephardic Jews—and the remaining 70 percent would be as susceptible to an Ethnic Specific agent as Palestinians. That didn't make a whole lot of sense. Since most of the Zionist Jews are Ashkenazi, why would they create a weapon that would guarantee their own destruction? I kept thinking about Larsen's explication of the possibility of "engineered biological pathogens which would affect only those races which historically have no natural defense against certain enzyme inhibitors".

Of course, I realized that there must surely be a lot more to this issue than was available to the public. Who knows what kind of research goes on in the enclaves of the National Security State?

So there the problem rested as I continued to dig for clues.

Now, let's take a moment to answer the question: what is mtDNA and what, precisely, does it do?

Mitochondria are tiny structures that exist within every cell, though not in the cell nucleus along with the chromosomes. The mitochondria help the cell use oxygen to produce energy. The more active a cell is, the more energy it needs and the more mitochondria it contains. Active cells such as those that make up muscles and neurons can contain as many as a thousand mitochondria.

Each mitochondrion is in a little membranous sac which also contains enzymes for aerobic metabolism, or the burning of fuel that we take in as food.

This "burning" takes place in a "sea of oxygen" which neither produces "flame" nor gives off light, but most definitely produces heat.

The main output of this process is a high-energy molecule called ATP which is needed by the body to run everything from the beating of the heart, to thinking with the cells of the brain.

Right in the middle of each of these little power cells is a tiny piece of DNA that is only sixteen and a half thousand base pairs in length. To compare, the bases in the chromosomes of the nucleus number three thousand million.

Mitochondrial DNA is composed of genetic codes for the oxygen-capturing enzymes that do the work in the mitochondria. Interestingly, many of the genes that control the workings of the mitochondria are found within the nuclear chromosomes. This, of course, reminds us of Larsen's "enzyme inhibitors". An inhibitor that affects "oxygen capturing enzymes"?

There is also something very bizarre about the mtDNA: Mitochondrial DNA forms a circle. As it happens, bacteria and other micro-organisms also have circular chromosomes.

Some experts think that mitochondria were once free-living bacteria that invaded more advanced cells hundreds of millions of years ago. The cells got a boost from being able to use oxygen—a cell can create much more high-energy ATP from the same amount of fuel using oxygen than it can without it—and the mitochondria may have found life within the cell more "comfortable" than outside. Yes, I know this is a really wild explanation, but it gets better. The experts theorize that, very slowly, over millions of years, some of the mitochondrial genes were transferred to the nucleus where they remain. This means mitochondria are trapped within cells and cannot return to the outside even if they wanted to.

This idea is based on the fact that the nuclear chromosomes are littered with broken fragments of mitochondrial genes that can't do anything because they are not intact. Our mtDNA then is the powerhouse of the body, where oxygen capturing enzymes are coded. The mystery as to why parts of mtDNA are attached to nuclear DNA might be easily solved by theorizing that it was once part of the nuclear DNA.

I don't want to speculate too much further on the mtDNA at this point except to suggest that it might be the key to Ethnic Specific biochemical weapons when you consider that its configuration is similar to that of bacteria.

Now, as I mentioned, realizing that Ashkenazi Jews were different in some significant way from Sephardic Jews, I decided to have a look at Koestler's book which presents the theory that Eastern European Jews are descended from the ancient Khazars. Look again at the chart on page 226 to note the position of Ashkenazi Jews relative to other groups according to the male lineage analysis.

Again we notice that the lower right corner of the graph is where Near Eastern Jews are positioned. One might therefore theorize that the Near Eastern Jews are, more or less, the most "Jewish" of the Jews in terms of many generations of "Jews" in their family lines. Looking around this cluster, we notice that there are several "families" that are very close, including Yemenite Jews, Druze, North African Jews, *and* Palestinians. On the other hand, the Ashkenazi Jews are not only much closer to Turks, Syrians and Roman Jews, they are quite distant from both the Near Eastern Jews and the Palestinians.

Naturally, Zionist Jews—most of them Ashkenazi—do not like Koestler's ideas—that the Eastern European Jews were originally Khazars, an Aryan tribe from Central Asia. Obviously, if they aren't "genetically linked" to the original Jews, they don't have a real claim on the land of Israel (as if they had a real claim anyway).

The short version of one of the theories held to by the Ashkenazim themselves is that the Roman Jews are descended from a group of Jews that fled Israel at the time of the diaspora and that some of them migrated up into Eastern Europe, then going even further East and mixing with Turks, forming the Ashkenazi Jews. Another theory is that the Khazars included remnants of original Jews who fled Israel at the time of the Babylonian captivity. When they adopted Judaism in the 9th century, they were just "coming home" so to say. With either of these theories, they retain their "birthright" to Israel upon which the present occupation of Palestine is based.

I can only say that I have read a lot of material on both sides of the question and I find Koestler's research to be original and credible. What is more, there is nothing about the gene flow of the Eastern European Jews that cannot be explained far more completely with his theory than with the "out of Israel at some point" hypothesis. Koestler's ideas explain the anomalies of the Khazar clans as well, when juxtaposed against the Sephardic Jews and their paternal kin, the Palestinians.

Hillel Halkin wrote, in an article entitled *Wandering Jews and Their Genes*:

> Finally, published in last June's Proceedings of the National Academy of Science were the results of a study conducted by an international team of scientists led by Michael Hammer of the University of Arizona and Batsheva Bonné-Tamir of Tel Aviv University. [...]

> Based on genetic samples from 1,371 males [...] its main conclusions are:

> 1. With the exception of Ethiopian Jews, all Jewish samples show a high genetic correlation. [...]

> 3. In descending order after these Middle Easterners, *Ashkenazi Jews correlate best with Greeks and Turks*; then with Italians; then with Spaniards; then with Germans; then with Austrians; and least of all with Russians. [...]

> And on the other hand again: whereas the traditional explanation of East European Jewish origins was that most Ashkenazi Jews reached Poland and Russia from [...] the Rhineland; Rhineland from northern France [...] this version has come under increasing challenge in recent years on both demographic and linguistic grounds.

> Most Jews, the challengers maintain, must have arrived in Eastern Europe not from the west and southwest but from the south and east—that is, via northern

Italy and the Balkans; Asia Minor and the Greek Byzantine empire; the Volga kingdom of the Khazars [...] or a combination of all three.

Now comes the Proceedings of the National Academy of Science report, which appears to bear out this newer version of events. Ashkenazi Jews, it informs us, have a more significant admixture of Italian, Greek, and Turkish genes than of Spanish, German, or even Austrian ones.

In other words, for the Jews to have traveled up through Italy to Eastern Europe, they would have had to mix with Germans or Austrians—but that isn't the case:

Of course, things are not so simple. Even without questioning the study's highly technical procedures, different interpretations could be put on them. It could be argued, for example, that the resemblance of Jewish to Greek and Italian Y chromosomes is traceable to proselytization in the Mediterranean world during the period of the Roman Empire. [...]

What must also be remembered is that Y chromosomes tell us only about males. But we know that in most societies, women are more likely to convert to their husband's religion than vice-versa. [...] If true, this might also explain a number of differences between the Hammer/Bonné-Tamir study and earlier research on the geographical distribution of specific Jewish diseases, blood types, enzymes, and mitochondrial DNA. [...]

This issue is actually so contentious that, after the paper on the Eight Founding Mothers of Judaism was published, Michael Hammer, himself of Ashkenazi heritage, and others, went back to the lab and produced their own "Founding Mother Event of Ashkenazi Jews" paper.

Published on January 14, 2004, the paper, entitled *MtDNA evidence for a genetic bottleneck in the early history of the Ashkenazi Jewish population* tells us the following:

The term 'Ashkenazi' refers to Jewish people of recent European ancestry, with an historical separation from other major Jewish populations in North Africa and the Middle East. The contemporary Ashkenazi gene pool is thought to have originated from a founding deme that migrated from the Near East within the last two millennia. After moving through Italy and the Rhine Valley, the Ashkenazi population presumably experienced a complex demographic history characterized by numerous migrations and fluctuations in population size. During the past 500 years, there was a period of rapid growth culminating in an estimated population size of 8 million Ashkenazi Jews at the outbreak of the Second World War.

Notice that in this most recent research, Hammer is again trying to resurrect the "Up through Italy and the Rhine Valley" idea which is rather thoroughly contradicted by his own earlier research on the paternal ancestry, as Hillel Halkin pointed out. One of the issues of Ashkenazi ancestry is the high frequency of more than *20 known recessive disease alleles*. As any animal breeder knows, this often occurs with inbreeding. Koestler has pointed out that the Khazars—after their conversion—were "more Jewish than the Jews". As converts, they were more zealous in following the "rules" of not marrying outside of their group. After the destruction of the Khazar kingdom, the population of Khazarian Jews was undoubtedly greatly reduced and this accounts not only for a bottleneck, but also for the conditions in which inbreeding would occur, leading to the expression of recessive disease alleles in the gene pool.

Reading Hammer's new paper is almost painful as his efforts to "repatriate" the Ashkenazi Jews are quite transparent. He refers, at the very beginning, to the "Eight Founding Mothers paper" which pretty much left the Ashkenazim out in the cold, Jewishly speaking:

> In a recent study based on mtDNA sequence variation [...] the authors inferred separate maternal founding events for several Jewish populations, with limited subsequent gene flow from surrounding host populations. Interestingly, the Ashkenazi Jewish sample in this study appeared to be an exception to this pattern, showing no strong signal of a founding event. [...]

> To address the question of whether mtDNA from Ashkenazi populations exhibit signs of a genetic bottleneck, we perform a more extensive analysis of mtDNA genetic variation [...] in a sample of 565 Jews from 15 different Ashkenazi communities originating in western and Eastern Europe, and compare these patterns of variation with those of neighboring non-Jewish populations.

> In our analysis, we take advantage of the ability to infer evidence for maternal population bottlenecks on the basis of comparative estimates of mtDNA sequence diversity.

This last paragraph just tells us in Sciencespeak that they intend to "interpret" the data according to their bias; you know, "cook the data".

> The results presented here portray a pattern of highly reduced mtDNA diversity for the Ashkenazi population, an unusually large proportion of mtDNA haplotypes that are unique to the Ashkenazi gene pool, and a reduction in frequency of rare haplotypes and singleton sites compared with Near Eastern populations.

> For example, the three most frequent Ashkenazi haplo-types account for 27.8% of total mtDNA repertoire in our Ashkenazi sample. These Ashkenazi mtDNA haplotypes are virtually absent from surrounding non-Jewish populations and therefore provide a genetic signature of the Ashkenazi maternal gene pool, and bear witness to the strong effects of genetic drift acting on this population.

What Hammer is *not* addressing is the fact that **the maternal gene pool of the Ashkenazim is not related to the maternal gene pool of other Jews**. As Koestler pointed out, the above also bears witness to the self-imposed isolation of Jewish groups among their host populations. They *chose* to live in walled Ghettoes and keep their genes to themselves even if it meant extreme endogamy. In other words, what Hammer et al. are describing is inbreeding. He acknowledges this below:

> This contrasts with the situation in both Near Eastern and European non-Jewish populations, where only a single haplotype (CRS) was found at elevated frequencies (i.e., above 5%).

> There are several periods in the history of Jewish populations when bottlenecks may have occurred, for example: (1) in the Near East before the initial migration to Europe (e.g., 41,500 years ago), (2) during the migrations of Jews from the Near East to Italy after the 1st century A.D., (3) upon establishment of small

communities in the Rhine Valley in the 8th century A.D., and (4) in the 12th century A.D., when migrations took place from western to eastern Europe.

In addition, endogamy in combination with 4100-fold population growth in the last 500 years undoubtedly played a role in shaping patterns of variation in the Ashkenazi gene pool.

While several authors posited that the high frequency of genetic conditions, such as Tay-Sachs disease, is the result of heterozygote advantage, others have argued for an important role of genetic drift. For example, Risch et al. proposed that founder effects resulting from the dynamics of population growth in the 16 - 19th centuries, especially in the northern Jewish Pale of Settlement (Lithuania and Belarus), explain most, if not all of the genetic diseases observed at high frequency in the Ashkenazi population today. This hypothesis was supported by the inference of a recent age of the single founder mutation (B350 years) that causes early-onset idiopathic torsion dystonia.

The much older estimated age of the factor XI type II mutation (B3000 years), which has a high frequency in both Ashkenazi and Iraqi Jewish populations, implies that its frequency is largely independent of the recent demographic up-heavals particular to the Ashkenazi population. [...]

All of the above—and more—is covered rationally and plausibly by Koestler in his book *The Thirteenth Tribe*. Nevertheless, Hammer et al. continue to beat the dead horse of a Near East origin for the Ashkenazi mtDNA gene pool.

The observed mutational frequency peak for the Ashkenazi and Near Eastern non-Jewish populations is similar and consistent with the age of the Pleistocene expansion, which is older than that inferred from the mutational frequency peak for European non-Jews. This is consistent with a Near East origin for a major portion of the Ashkenazi Jewish mtDNA pool.

If the Jewish population bottleneck did begin in the Near East, other Jewish populations from around the world are predicted to harbor similar values of $f0$ and $f1$ in their mismatch distributions. To test this prediction, we examined the mismatch distributions resulting from the data of Thomas et al., which includes samples of the Bukharan, Georgian, Indian, Iranian, Iraqi, Moroccan, and Yemenite Jewish communities. All HVS-1 sequence datasets showed a significantly elevated $f0$ (only Sephardic Jews showed an increase in $f1$) relative to Near Eastern non-Jewish populations. [...] This result implies that global Jewish communities suffered a common bottleneck in the Near East, or independent founder events during the Jewish Diaspora. [...]

Notice in the above that the Sephardic Jews did not fulfill the prediction of the "mismatch theory" above. Also note that this prediction was not tested against anything other than Jewish populations. What if other populations show similar mismatch distributions? But Hammer presses on bravely in his attempt to explain away the fact that Ashkenazim aren't like other Jews in the maternal ancestry:

This suggests the possibility that contemporary Ashkenazi mtDNA diversity may derive, in part, from a small and subdivided ancestral mtDNA gene pool, and is consistent with the hypothesis that some high frequency disease alleles originated before the separation of Jewish communities in the Near East. Indeed, estimates of the age of mutations causing Ashkenazi genetic diseases range from recent times (i.e., during demographic upheavals within Europe in the past 500 years), to times when ancestral Ashkenazi populations were first migrating to and within Europe, to times before Jewish populations migrated out of the Near East. [...]

The combined mtDNA and disease mutation data suggest that Ashkenazi Jewish populations experienced a long period of accentuated genetic drift marked by an early bottleneck, perhaps beginning in the Near East. Prolonged periods of low effective population size can lead to the accumulation of slightly deleterious mutations throughout the genome. Small founder populations derived from large ancestral populations are not always capable of purging these deleterious mutations. This may be the ultimate cause of the segregation of disease mutations in Ashkenazi Jews. However, this explanation does not preclude more proximal causes for the increase in frequency of disease mutations, such as those hypothesized by Risch et al., unequal contribution of a particular segment of the Ashkenazi Jewish community to the explosive population growth occurring in the Pale of Settlement approximately 25 generations ago. Low effective size may have enabled deleterious mutations to become established in the Jewish population, while the recent growth of affected segments of the community amplified these mutations to frequencies sufficiently high to form homozygotes.

In other words, he has described the results of the exact scenario that Koestler has hypothesized—inbreeding of a small, surviving population of Khazars and ghetto-ization of fanatical converts—and still has not managed to provide a single convincing bit of evidence of the origin of the Ashkenazim in the Near East.

The short of it is that Koestler's theory, despite many attempts to deconstruct it, still provides the best answers for the origins of the Ashkenazi Jews: they were Khazars who, for political reasons, converted to Judaism. The interested reader is invited to read Koestler's book with its original research and clear exposition of the links between the Khazars and the Eastern European Jews.

The big question now is: If the Khazars aren't really of ancient Jewish origin and have no real rights to the "Divine Fiat" that gave Israel to the Jews (putting aside for the moment that this was a hoax to begin with), then who were the Khazars and what is behind this bizarre drive of theirs to own Palestine?

The Khazars flourished from the seventh to the eleventh century. This means that they emerged following the reign of the emperor Justinian discussed on our website.[320] The issues surrounding the reign of Justinian, recorded by Procopius, indicate to us that something very strange was going on during that period of history. Procopius describes plagues and what must have been a rain of overhead cometary explosions that threw the Middle East into turmoil and decimated large segments of the population. Shades of the Exodus!

---

[320] http://www.cassiopaea.org/cass/truth_or_lies_7.htm

On August 17, 1999, the Knight Ridder's Washington Bureau published an article by Robert S. Boyd entitled *Comets may have caused Earth's great empires to fall,* which included the following:

> Recent scientific discoveries are shedding new light on why great empires such as Egypt, Babylon and Rome fell apart, giving way to the periodic "dark ages" that punctuate human history. *At least five times during the last 6,000 years, major environmental calamities undermined civilizations around the world.*
>
> Some researchers say these disasters appear to be linked to collisions with comets or fragments of comets such as the one that broke apart and smashed spectacularly into Jupiter five years ago.
>
> The impacts, yielding many megatons of explosive energy, produced vast clouds of smoke and dust that circled the globe for years, dimming the sun, driving down temperatures and sowing hunger, disease and death. The last such global crisis occurred between CE 530 and 540—at the beginning of the Dark Ages in Europe—when Earth was pummeled by a swarm of cosmic debris.
>
> In a forthcoming book, *Catastrophe, the Day the Sun Went Out,* British historian David Keys describes *a 2-year-long winter that began in CE 535.* Trees from California to Ireland to Siberia stopped growing. Crops failed. Plague and famine decimated Italy, China and the Middle East.
>
> Keys quotes the writings of a 6th-century Syrian bishop, John of Ephesus:
>
>> "The sun became dark. [...] Each day it shone for about four hours and still this light was only a feeble shadow."
>
> A contemporary Italian historian, Flavius Cassiodorus, wrote:
>
>> "We marvel to see no shadows of our bodies at noon. We have summer without heat."
>
> And a contemporary Chinese chronicler reported, "yellow dust rained like snow."[321] (emphasis ours)

Dendrochronologist Mike Baillie established that:

> Analysis of tree rings shows that at in 540 CE in different parts of the world the climate changed. Temperatures dropped enough to hinder the growth of trees as widely dispersed as northern Europe, Siberia, western North America, and southern South America.
>
> A search of historical records and mythical stories pointed to a disastrous visitation from the sky during the same period, it is claimed. There was one reference to a "comet in Gaul so vast that the whole sky seemed on fire" in 540-41.
>
> According to legend, King Arthur died around this time, and Celtic myths associated with Arthur hinted at bright sky Gods and bolts of fire.
>
> In the 530s, an unusual meteor shower was recorded by both Mediterranean and Chinese observers. Meteors are caused by the fine dust from comets burning up in the atmosphere. Furthermore, a team of astronomers from Armagh Observatory in Northern Ireland published research in 1990 which said the Earth would have been at risk from cometary bombardment between the years 400 and 600 CE. [...]

---

[321] Robert S. Boyd, "Comets may have caused Earth's great empires to fall", *Knight Ridder Washington Bureau,* August 17, 1999.

Famine followed the crop failures, and hard on its heels bubonic plague that swept across Europe in the mid-6th century. [...]

At this time, the Roman emperor Justinian was attempting to regenerate the decaying Roman Empire. But the plan failed in 540 and was *followed by the Dark Ages and the rise of Islam.*[322]

Apparently this disaster was also followed by the arrival of the Khazars. The question is: *where did they come from?* Well, hopefully we'll be able to track them and find out.

The kingdom of the Khazars has vanished from the map of the world and today many people have never even heard of it. But, in its day the Khazar kingdom, Khazaria, was a major power.

The Byzantine Emperor and historian, Constantine Porphyrogenitus (913-959), recorded in a treatise on Court Protocol that letters addressed to the Pope in Rome, and similarly those to the Emperor of the West, had a gold seal worth two *solidi* attached to them, whereas messages to the King of the Khazars required a seal worth three *solidi*.

In other words, it was clearly understood that *the Khazars were more powerful than the Emperor of the West or the Pope.* As Koestler commented, "This was not flattery, but Realpolitik". How can it be that we are taught about the Byzantine Empire and the rise of the power of the Popes of the Western Empire, and have so little knowledge of an empire that existed at the same time, that was obviously *more powerful than either of them? A Jewish empire, in fact?*

The country of the Khazars was strategically located at the gateway between the Black Sea and the Caspian, acting as a buffer protecting Byzantium against invasions by the barbarian Bulgars, Magyars, Pechenegs, and later the Vikings and Russians. More important than this was the fact that the Khazars also blocked the Arabs from Eastern Europe.

---

[322] Michael Baillie, *Exodus to Arthur* (London: B.T. Batesford Ltd., 1999).

> Within a few years of the death of Muhammad (632 CE) the armies of the Caliphate, sweeping northward through the wreckage of two empires and carrying all before them, reached the great mountain barrier of the Caucasus. This barrier once passed, the road lay open to the lands of Eastern Europe. As it was, on the line of the Caucasus the Arabs met the forces of an organized military power which effectively prevented them from extending their conquests in this direction. The wars of the Arabs and the Khazars, which lasted more than a hundred years, though little known, have thus considerable historical importance. [Professor Dunlop of Columbia University, authority on the Khazars, quoted by Koestler, p. 14]

It is well known that the Frankish army of Charles Martel turned back the Arabs on the field of Tours. Less well-known is that, at the same time, the Muslims were met and held by the forces of the Khazar kingdom.

In 732, the future emperor, Constantine V, married a Khazar princess and their son became Emperor Leo IV, known as Leo the Khazar.

A few years later, probably in 740 CE, the King of the Khazars, his court and the military ruling class *embraced the Jewish faith and Judaism became the state religion of the Khazars*. This came about as a reaction against the political pressure of the other two Superpowers of the day—Byzantium and the Muslims—both of which had the advantage of a monotheistic State Religion which allowed them greater control over their subjects. Not wanting to be subject either to the Pope or the Byzantine Emperor, but seeing the political benefits of state religious controls, the King of the Khazars chose Judaism to be the new State Religion. He clearly saw its advantages as a control system.

The Khazar kingdom held its power and position for most of four centuries during which time they were transformed from a tribe of nomadic warriors into a nation of farmers, cattle-breeders, fishermen, viticulturists, traders and craftsmen. Soviet archaeologists have found evidence of an advanced civilization with houses built in a circular shape at the lower levels, later being replaced by rectangular buildings. This is explained as evidence of the transition from portable, dome shaped tents, to settled lifestyles.

At the peak of their power, the Khazars controlled and/or received tribute from thirty or so different nations and tribes spread across the territories between the Caucasus, the Aral Sea, the Ural Mountains, the town of Kiev, and the Ukrainian steppes. These peoples included the Bulgars, Burtas, Ghuzz, Magyars, the Gothic and Greek colonies of the Crimea, and the Slavonic tribes to the Northwest.

> Until the ninth century, the Khazars had no rivals to their supremacy in the regions north of the Black Sea and the adjoining steppe and the forest regions of the Dnieper. The Khazars were the supreme masters of the southern half of Eastern Europe for a century and a half. [...] During this whole period, they held back the onslaught of the nomadic tribes from the East. [323]

In the timeline of history, the Khazar Empire existed between the Huns and the Mongols. The Arab chroniclers wrote that the Khazars were "white, their

---

[323] Soviet archaeologist M. I. Artamonov, quoted by Koestler, 19.

eyes blue, their hair flowing and predominantly reddish, their bodies large, and their natures cold. Their general aspect is wild".

The Georgians and Armenians, having been repeatedly devastated by the Khazars, identified them as *Gog and Magog*. An Armenian writer described them as having "insolent, broad, lashless faces and long falling hair, like women".

One of the earliest factual references to the Khazars occurs in a Syriac chronicle dating from the middle of the sixth century. It mentions the Khazars in a list of people who inhabit the region of the Caucasus. Koestler recounts that other sources indicate that *the Khazars were intimately connected with the Huns.*

An interesting connection considering the legend that the Huns were a tribe of peoples that descended from Scythian witches who, cast out of their tribes, "mated with devils in the desert."

WHO WERE THE HUNS?

So, let's look at the Huns for a moment.

In 448 CE, the Byzantine Emperor Theodosius II sent an embassy to Attila which included a famed rhetorician by name of Priscus. He kept a minute account not only of the diplomatic negotiations, but also of the court intrigues and goings-on in Attila's sumptuous banqueting hall. He was, in fact, the perfect gossip columnist, and is still one of the main sources of information about Hun customs and habits. But Priscus also has anecdotes to tell about *a people subject to the Huns whom he calls Akatzirs*—that is, very likely, the Ak-Khazars, or "White" Khazars.

The Byzantine Emperor, Priscus tells us, tried to win this warrior race over to his side, but the greedy Khazar chieftain named Karidach, considered the bribe offered to him inadequate and sided with the Huns. Attila defeated Karidach's rival chieftains, installed him as the sole ruler of the Akatzirs, and invited him to visit his court. Karidach thanked him profusely for the invitation and went on to say that "it would be too hard on a mortal man to look into the face of a god. For, as one cannot stare into the sun's disc, even less could one look into the face of the greatest god without suffering injury". Attila must have been pleased with this clever response because he then confirmed Karidach as ruler.

After the collapse of the Hun Empire, the Khazars raided and absorbed numerous tribes of nomadic hordes coming from the East. At this point, the West Turkish kingdom arose, a confederation of tribes ruled by a Kagan, or Khagan. The Khazars later adopted this title for their rulers as well. This "Turkish state" fell apart after a century, but it is important to note that it was only *after* this period that the word Turkish was used in reference to a specific nation, as opposed to its earlier use which simply meant a tribe speaking a Turkic language such as the Khazars and Bulgars. In short, Khazars and Bulgars are, using the older definition, Turks.

So it was that at the time of the cometary disasters that brought on the Dark Ages, the Khazars rose to power. By the first decades of the seventh century, there were three "Superpowers", two of whom had been fighting each other for a century and were seemingly on the verge of collapse. Persia was about to face its doom in the armies of the Khazars, but through its friendship with Khazaria, Byzantium survived.

In 627, the Roman Emperor Heraclius made an alliance with the Khazars so as to defeat his nemesis: Persia. The Khazars provided Heraclius with 40,000 horsemen under a commander named Ziebel, and Heraclius promised him his daughter. The Persians were defeated, which was followed by a revolution and after ten years of anarchy and chaos, the first Arab armies delivered the *coup de grace* leading to the emergence of a new Superpower: the Islamic Caliphate.

In short order, the Muslims conquered Persia, Syria, Mesopotamia, Egypt and surrounded the Byzantine Empire in a half-circle from the Mediterranean to the Caucasus. Between 642 and 652, the Muslims repeatedly penetrated into Khazaria in an attempt to gain a foothold so as to continue their push into Eastern Europe. After a defeat in 652, the Muslims backed off for thirty or forty years and concentrated on Byzantium, laying siege to Constantinople on several occasions. Had they been able to get to the other side, to surround Byzantium from the Khazarian side, it would have been fatal for Europe.

Meanwhile, the Khazars consolidated their own power, expanding into Ukraine and the Crimea, incorporating the conquered people into their empire ruled by the Kagan. By the time of the 8th century, the Khazar Empire was stable enough to actually go on the offensive against the Muslims rather than just holding their position and driving them away repeatedly.

> From a distance of more than a thousand years, the period of intermittent warfare that followed looks like a series of tedious episodes on a local scale, following the same, repetitive pattern: the Khazar cavalry in their heavy armour breaking through the pass of Dariel or the Gate of Darband into the Caliph's domains to the south; followed by Arab counter-thrusts through the same pass or the defile, towards the Volga and back again. [...]

> One is reminded of the old jingle about the noble Duke of York who had ten thousand men; "he marched them up to the top of the hill. And he marched them down again." In fact, the Arab sources speak of armies of 100,000, even of 300,000 men engaged on either side—probably outnumbering the armies which decided the fate of the Western world at the battle of Tours about the same time.

> The death-defying fanaticism which characterized these wars is illustrated by episodes such as the suicide by fire of a whole Khazar town as an alternative to surrender; the poisoning of the water supply of Bab al Abwab by an Arab general; or by the traditional exhortation which would halt the rout of a defeated Arab army and make it fight to the last man: "To the Garden Muslims, not the Fire"—the joys of Paradise being assured to every Muslim soldier killed in the Holy War.[324]

---

[324] Arthur Koestler, *The Thirteenth Tribe* (New York: Random House, 1976), 28.

The giant Islamic pincer movement across the Pyrenees in the west and across the Caucasus into Eastern Europe was halted at both ends at about the same time. As Charles Martel's Franks saved Gaul and Western Europe, so the Khazars saved the Eastern Roman Empire.

At the end of all this was the marriage of the Khazar princess to the heir of the Byzantine Empire in gratitude for defeat of the Muslims. Following this event, of course, was the politically expedient conversion of the Khazars to Judaism already mentioned.

Overnight an entire group of people, the warlike, fanatical Khazars, suddenly proclaimed themselves Jews. The Khazar kingdom began to be described as the "Kingdom of the Jews" by historians of the day. Succeeding Khazar rulers took Jewish names, sent for Jewish scholars from Spain to come and instruct them, settle with them and marry their daughters. During the late 9th Century the Khazar kingdom became a haven for Jews of other lands. But it seems that this process was almost exclusively a question of male Jews—including Kohanim—coming to Khazaria and marrying Khazar women. What does not seem to have happened—or happened only rarely—is the intermarriage of Khazars with Sephardic Jewish women from other European communities of Jews.

Koestler quotes at length from ancient accounts of the Khazars, and I highly recommend this book to the reader not only because it is well researched, but also because it can be quite entertaining reading!

At the height of the Khazar Empire, the main source of royal income was foreign trade. There were enormous caravans that transported textiles, dried fruit, honey, wax, and spices following the Silk Road to and from the East. Arts and crafts and *haute couture* flourished. Slaves and furs were traded by Rus merchants and Vikings coming down the Volga on a north/south trade axis. On all these goods, the Khazars levied a tax of ten per cent. This was added to the tribute paid by the Bulgars, Magyars, and others. Khazaria was cosmopolitan, open to all sorts of cultural and religious influences while, at the same time, using its State Religion to defend itself against the other two ecclesiastical powers in the world.

In short, Khazaria was an extremely prosperous country and this prosperity depended on its military power. Khazaria had a standing army with which it was able to maintain brutal domination over its subject tribes and peoples. Human sacrifice was also practiced by the earlier Khazars—including the ritual killing of the king at the end of his reign. Again, it is astonishing how little this great kingdom is known to our present society.

At the beginning of the ninth century, the Khazars had more or less a tacit "nonaggression pact" with the Caliphate, and relations with Byzantium were friendly. After all, they were family! But, a new cloud was on the horizon: Two centuries earlier, it had been the Arabs and their "Holy War". Now it was the Vikings and their "unholy war" of piracy and plunder:

In neither case have historians been able to provide convincing explanations of the economical, ecological or ideological reasons which transformed these apparently quiescent regions of Arabia and Scandinavia quasi overnight into volcanoes of exuberant vitality and reckless enterprise. Both eruptions spent their force within a couple of centuries but left a permanent mark on the world. Both evolved in this time-span from savagery and destructiveness to splendid cultural achievement. [325]

This is, indeed, a curious thing that Koestler has noted. Of course, we are reminded again of the article quoted above which said:

> Recent scientific discoveries are shedding new light on why great empires such as Egypt, Babylon and Rome fell apart, giving way to the periodic "dark ages" that punctuate human history. *At least five times during the last 6,000 years, major environmental calamities undermined civilizations around the world.*

> Some researchers say these disasters appear to be linked to collisions with comets or fragments of comets such as the one that broke apart and smashed spectacularly into Jupiter five years ago.

> The impacts, yielding many megatons of explosive energy, produced vast clouds of smoke and dust that circled the globe for years, dimming the sun, driving down temperatures and sowing hunger, disease and death. The last such global crisis occurred between 530 and 540 CE—at the beginning of the Dark Ages in Europe—when Earth was pummeled by a swarm of cosmic debris. [326]

That solves the problem of the eruptions in Arabia and the rise of Islam, and we already know that the eruption of Santorini—which may have been related to a swarm of cosmic debris as well—was connected to the "birth of Judaism," so we might also theorize that the "eruption" of the Vikings could have been related to some sort of crisis, localized or otherwise. After all, a Tunguska like event would be all that was needed.

Within a few decades, the Vikings had penetrated all the major waterways of Europe, conquered half of Ireland, colonized Iceland, conquered Normandy, sacked Paris, raided Germany, the Rhone delta, the gulf of Genoa, circumnavigated the Iberian peninsula and attacked Constantinople through the Mediterranean and the Dardanelles, coordinated with an attack down the Dnieper and across the Black Sea. A special prayer was formulated in Christendom: *Lord deliver us from the fury of the Normans.*

Again, Byzantium depended on Khazaria to block the advance of the Vikings.

This branch of norsemen, who were called Rhos or Varangians, originated *from eastern Sweden* and were cousins to the Norwegians and Danes who raided Western Europe.

> These Varangian-Rus seem to have been a unique blend—unique even among their brother Vikings—combining the traits of pirates, robbers and meretricious merchants, who traded on their own terms, imposed by sword and battle-axe.

[325] Koestler, 86.
[326] Boyd, op. cit.

They bartered furs, swords and amber in exchange for gold, but their principal merchandise were slaves.[327]

For a century and a half, trade and diplomacy between the Byzantines and the Khazars and the Rus alternated with war. Slowly but surely, the Vikings built permanent settlements, becoming *Slavonized* by intermingling with their subjects and vassals—the Slavs along the Dnieper who were agricultural and more timid than the "Turks". This mixing of genes and cultures tamed the Rus and turned them into "Russians".

At first, the Rus were friendlier with the Khazars than with the Byzantines. The Rus even adopted the title "Kagan" for their ruler. However, all the while they were having "cultural exchanges" with the Khazars, the Rus were bringing the surrounding Slavs into their own fold. Considering the genetic data, this may be as much due to intermarriage between the Slavonic tribes, as due to conquest. Within a couple of decades, the Rus were receiving tribute from almost half of the former subjects of the Khazars!

When the town of Kiev, on the Dnieper river, passed into Rus hands, apparently without an armed struggle, it was the beginning of the end for Khazaria. There were still large communities of Khazar Jews in Kiev, and later, after the final destruction of Khazaria, they were joined by Khazar refugees.

A tribe called the Magyars now must come under our scrutiny. The Magyars seem to have originated in the forest regions of the northern Urals along with two other tribes, the Vogul and Ostyak. Probably at the time of the cometary bombardment that brought on the dark ages, these tribes were driven out of their forests, and the Magyars attached themselves as willing vassals to first the Huns and then the Khazars. *There is no record of a single armed conflict between the Khazars and Magyars.* Toynbee says that the Magyars "took tribute" on the Khazars' behalf from the Slav and Finn peoples.

At the time of the arrival of the Rus, the Magyars moved across the Don river to its West bank. One might assume, by the fact that they were allies of the Khazars, that they did this with the full permission of the Khazars and that it was intended to act as a check against the advancement of the Rus.

The Khazars compensated the Magyars for their loyalty by giving them a king, the founder of the first Magyar dynasty, and, then, they did something that they apparently had not done up to this point: intermarriage between the Magyar elite and several elite Khazar tribes took place. The Khazar Kagan gave a noble Khazar lady to the new king of the Magyars for his wife. There were no children of this union, but it is assumed that there were also marriages between her retainers and the members of the Magyar court.

At some point during this period, there also seems to have been a rebellion of three Khazar tribes, some of whom fled to the Magyars for refuge. As Koestler puts it: the Magyars received, metaphorically and literally, a blood transfusion from the Khazars. It could even be said that the Khazars became Magyars.

---

[327] Koestler, 89.

Until the middle of the tenth century, both the Magyar and Khazar languages were spoken in Hungary. The result of this double tongue is the mixed character of the modern Hungarian language. Though the Hungarians have ceased to be bilingual, there are still some two hundred loan-words from the Chuvash dialect of Turkish which the Khazars spoke.

There is some evidence to indicate that among the dissident Khazar tribes (the leading one was called Kabar) who de facto took over the leadership of the Magyar tribes, there were Jews, or adherents of a "judaizing religion". Some experts think that this rebellion was, in fact, connected with the religious reforms initiated by King Obadiah of the Khazars. Rabbinical law, strict rules, and other elements of Judaism would certainly have grated on a tribe of steppe warriors.

The alliance of the Magyars and Khazars came to an end when the Magyars crossed the Carpathian mountains and conquered the territory that was to become Hungary. In 862, they raided the East Frankish empire.

> The Magyars seem to have acquired the raiding habit only in the second half of the ninth century—about the time when they received that critical blood-transfusion from the Khazars. The Kabars [...] became the leading tribe, and infused their hosts with the spirit of adventure which was soon to turn them into the scourge of Europe, as the Huns had earlier been. They also taught the Magyars "those very peculiar and characteristic tactics employed since time immemorial by every Turkish nation—Huns, Avars, Turks, Pechenegs, Kumans— and by no other [...] light cavalry using the old devices of simulated flight, of shooting while fleeing, of sudden charges with fearful, wolf-like howling.[328]

In other words: "By way of deception, thou shalt do war."

Thus, the Khazars were instrumental in establishing the Hungarian state, even in becoming the Hungarians. In the tenth century, the Hungarian Duke Taksony invited an unknown number of Khazars to settle in his domains. It is not unlikely that these Khazars were Jews.

SURVIVAL OF THE FITTEST

Let's take a momentary break from the history and look at some present day observations. Steve Jones writes:

> Ashkenazim are *quite distinct from their Mediterranean and Middle-Eastern co-religionists* in the incidence of the disease and in the mutations responsible. [...]

> The genetic family tree of Jews from different parts of Europe shows that they are not a unique group, biologically distinct from other peoples around them. There is, though, evidence of common ancestry that gives Jews at least a partial identity of their own. In most places, there is overlap between the genes of the Jewish population and those of local non-Jews. There has been interchange; sometimes through recent marriage, but more often as a result of mating long ago. [...]

---

[328] Koestler, 103.

The Y chromosomes of Jews are—unsurprisingly—not all the same; the idea of the sons of Abraham is a symbolic one. They do show that many males, some only distantly related to each other, have contributed to the genes of European Jewry. On the average, *most Jewish populations contain more diversity for male lineages than for female* (whose history is recorded in mitochondrial DNA). This means that there has been more invasion of the Jewish gene pool by the genes of non-Jewish men than of women. The Y chromosomes of Jewish men from the Balkans are rather unlike those of other European Jews, perhaps because there was more admixture in this unstable part of the world. [329]

Judit Beres and C. R. Guglielmino write:

Magyars, Jews, Gypsies, Germans, Slovaks, Kuns, Romanians, etc. In this very large study, *Hungarian Jews were found to be highly distinct from all other groups* residing in Hungary. [330]

Bruce Schecter, a Hungarian physicist, paints the following picture of life in Hungary and Budapest at the beginning of the 20th century:

At the turn of the century bankers, merchants, industrialists, artists, and intellectuals thronged the broad boulevards that ring [Budapest] or rode beneath them in Europe's first subway. Between 1890 and 1900 the population of Budapest had increased by more than 40 percent to over three-quarters of a million souls, making it the sixth largest city in Europe. Because of Budapest's lively cafes, boulevards, parks, and financial exchange, visitors called it the 'Little Paris on the Danube'. What would not become apparent for years was that while the cares were doing a booming business, the maternity wards of Budapest were churning out [Jewish] geniuses like a Ford assembly line.

Hungary's economic and intellectual flowering began with the Ausgleich of 1867, which established the dual monarchy with Austria. Under that agreement Hungary achieved something approaching independence from Austria; the Austrian Empire became the Austro-Hungarian Empire. With astonishing rapidity the engines of the industrial age and capitalism would transform Hungary. 'The operators of those mechanisms', writes historian Richard Rhodes, 'by virtue of their superior ambition and energy, but also by default, were Jews'.

Shortly after the establishment of the dual monarchy, discriminatory laws against Jews were repealed, opening to them all civic and political functions. The surge of Jewish immigration followed, paralleling the contemporaneous flood of Jewish immigrants from Russia to New York City.

Political power remained in the hands of the nobility, whose indifference to the gentile non-Hungarian minorities—nearly half the population—would keep a third of the gentiles illiterate as late as 1918, and most of them tied to the land. The Hungarian nobility, unwilling to dirty its hands on commerce, found allies in the Jews. By 1904 Hungarian Jews, who comprised about 5 percent of the population, accounted for about half of Hungary's lawyers and commercial businessmen, 60 percent of its doctors, and 80 percent of its financiers. Budapest Jews were also a dominant presence in the artistic, literary, musical, and

---

[329] Steve Jones, *In the Blood: God, Genes, and Destiny* (Harper Collins, 1996).
[330] Judit Beres and C. R. Guglielmino, "Genetic Structure in relation to the history of the Hungarian ethnic group", *Human Biology* 68:3 (June 1996), 335-356.

scientific life of the country, which caused the growing anti-Semitic community to coin the derogatory label 'Judapest'.

The growing anti-Semitism would in later years cause many of the brightest members of the Hungarian Jewish community to flee their country. Some of the leading scientists and mathematicians, whose ideas and inventions would help form this century, were part of this tide of immigration. Among the better known were Leo Szilard, who was the first person to understand how chain reactions can unleash the power of the atom; John von Neumann, inventor of the electronic computer and game theory; and Edward Teller, the father of the hydrogen bomb. Less well known outside the world of science but equally influential were Theodor von Karman, the father of supersonic flight; George de Hevesy who received a Nobel Prize for his invention of the technique of using radioactive tracers that has had a revolutionary impact on virtually every field of science; and Eugene Wigner, whose exploration of the foundations of quantum mechanics earned him a Nobel Prize.

The list of the great Hungarian scientists could be extended almost indefinitely, but even outside the sciences the prominence of Hungarians is extraordinary. In music it would include the conductors Georg Solti, George Szell, Fritz Reiner, Antal Dorati, and Eugene Ormandy, and the composers Bela Bartok and Zoltan Kodaly. Hungarian visual arts in this century were dominated by Laszlo Moholy-Nagy, who founded the Chicago Institute of Design. Hollywood was even more influenced by the Magyar emigration. Movie moguls William Fox and Adolph Zukor were Budapest-born, as were Alexander Korda and his brothers, Vincent and Theodor, the director George Cukor, and the producer of Casablanca, Michael Curtisz. And of course, Zsa Zsa Gabor and her sisters were Hungarian, as were Paul Lukas and Erich Weiss, better known as Harry Houdini.

Trying to account for what the physicist Otto Frisch called the "galaxy of brilliant Hungarian expatriates", is a favorite activity in scientific circles. The leading theory, attributed to the theoretical physicist Fritz Houtermans, is that, "these people are really from Mars". Andrew Vazxonyi offers a particularly charming version of the extraterrestrial theory. "Well, at the beginning of the century", he says quite seriously, but with a twinkle in his eye, "some people from outer space landed on earth. They thought that the Hungarian women were the best-looking of all, and they took on the form of humans, and after a few years, they decided the Earth was not worth colonizing, so they left. Soon afterward this bunch of geniuses was born. That's the true story".

The actual explanation for Hungary's outpouring of genius is hard to find. Chance certainly played a role. But the strong intellectual values of the Jewish bourgeoisie, combined with the excellent Hungarian educational system, were the fertile field in which the random seeds of genetic chance could flourish.[331]

FIRST CIRCUIT PROGRAMMING – EVEN BETTER THAN RELIGION!

In the 1920s, the Rockefellers and other monied groups made enormous contributions to "education in America", and the preparations for the Hitler drama were underway. When we study history for long enough, we begin to

---

[331] Bruce Schecter, *My Brain is Open* (New York : Touchstone, 1998).

notice a number of "tracks". The first thing we come across is the development of the Aryan supremacy idea of eugenics. We notice that this was picked up in America with funding from the Rockefellers, Carnegies, Merrimans, and other "robber baron" families. We then notice that the Jews were targeted by this "research".

At the same time that the rank and file Jews were being vilified, the Rockefellers were also endowing education and buying the "Jewish brains" and importing them to Princeton to build the bomb, among other things.

This latter event "just happened" to coincide with Hitler's takeover of the German government and the mass expulsion of Jews from German Universities which had, until then, been the seats of higher learning in math and science. Negotiations were begun to get Einstein, who finally agreed to become the second member of the Institute's School of Mathematics. Kurt Godel came, followed by Hermann Weyl, who wanted Von Neumann. In short, overnight, Princeton had become the new Gottingen.

What we basically see in the endowment of Princeton as a mathematical center, and the luring of scientific talent to America, was effectively a "brain drain" on Europe. All the geniuses who were capable of certain, specific things, were being brought to America and settled in Princeton. This produced an almost immediate scientific earthquake. Of course we see that the scientific revolution in America did not begin *after* WWII as many conspiracy theorists would like to believe, but rather before—in the 1920s, to be exact.

Judaism—like all other organised religions on the planet—is little more than a control system and was deliberately imposed on the Jews by a few Middle Eastern psychopaths who first tried their con on the Egyptians before being run out of town. So it is in all times and places. What Judaism was before it was co-opted by these deviants can be discerned by careful textual analysis of the books of the Bible. But believe me, what it became has as much to do with its origins as neocons have to do with the original Republican party or Christianity, as it is practiced, has to do with the teachings of the man around whom the Jesus legend accreted.

However, compared to Christianity and even Islam, Judaism was very effective in preventing Jews from intermarrying with non-Jews. Anyone who suggests that this view of Judaism is "anti-Semitic" might keep in mind that we say the same about Christianity and Islam, so we are an equal-opportunity shooter of sacred cows. We object to all Control Systems. In fact, as we have pointed out, Christianity would not exist if it were not for Judaism, and vice versa. They are very strange bedfellows with Islam, and every now and again one is enabled to glimpse the reality beneath the facade of the power elite who created all three of them and have played one against the other, throughout the millennia, with the masses of normal people caught in the jaws of the trap.

What is the trap? What is the agenda that is promoted most vigorously by the "Zionists"?

We have to realize that the war between the Israelis and Palestinians is based on the claim that Israel is the "Promised Land", and that it "belongs" to the Jews by fiat of God Almighty.

The source of the modern Middle East conflict can be traced to the 19th century and the emergence of "Zionism". The result of Zionist agitation in political circles both in Europe and America over the course of several decades was twofold. First, it led to the idea of creating a "Jewish State". Second, it led to the Holocaust. Yes, I realize that over 60 million human beings were killed in the Holocaust, and only a small percentage of them were Jews. I have also considered the fact that it is very likely that many of the other victims who were not Jews in name, very possibly were peoples who were of "mixed blood", so to say. The real problems, however, began with the creation of the Jewish state, and the repatriation of Jews from all over the world. If, as I have speculated above, there was a psychopathically directed "culling process" in this extermination protocol, then it only makes sense. They created the Jewish Superman and collected them all together in one place.

When one considers that Hitler was determined to follow his protocol for destroying Jews—as well as about anybody else in those areas where Jews had lived for centuries—(even in the face of his impending destruction, and that in the final days of his power, knowing that the Allies were closing in on him, instead of cleaning up the evidence of his monstrous perfidy, he actually ordered an acceleration of the destruction of the Jewish people), it becomes obvious that *this was his clear and singular agenda*, upon which all else he did was predicated.

When one carefully studies Hitler and the Nazi regime, there is a sensation of vertigo that something is dreadfully wrong with this picture that goes far deeper than most commentators and analysts of the situation seem to fathom. Oh, it can all be taken apart and looked at in its separate pieces, and we can see how the German people were in a certain dire situation and Hitler came along and promised to make it all better. We can read psychological profiles of Hitler and come to some idea that the guy had some serious issues. That's all pretty standard.

But still, after reading all the technical details, after all the events are cleaned up and laid out in nice chronological tables, expert after expert will end their discussion just as puzzled as they began. Even when they think that they have an answer for 'why?', they will admit that what they have done is only speculative and that they still have the uneasy feeling that they haven't quite arrived at the answer.

And that is the crux of it: why, oh why, was Hitler damned and determined to destroy the Jews against all human ethics and even logic and good sense? Before you even offer a facile answer, spend 20 or more years poring over the literature and then you will understand why this question nearly drove me crazy. There was *no answer*. And if there was no answer, if such an event was just "random evil" that happened to seat itself in Germany in the third decade of the last century—a civilized and advanced country—then we are all screwed.

All things considered, we come back, again and again, that Hitler's primary agenda was to destroy the Jews. Now where did Hitler even get an idea like that?

We can easily trace the history of the ideas of eugenics and see the "external" view of the matter. The one thing that is difficult to find is where and how the Jews became so determined to be "undesirable", racially speaking.

Essentially, Jewish religious leaders came along and convinced Jews that they were *so* special that they ought not to mingle with other "tribes", and they bought it. One of the great mysteries of Judaism, as many Jews point out, is that you cannot go back three generations in any Jewish genealogy without confronting a "solid wall of belief in Torah". And this leads us directly into the problem: if Judaism is largely fiction, why has it lasted so long?

One of the main aspects of socio-cultural programming is what is called "imprinting". Human beings are born with certain basic behavior patterns built in their DNA. Just as a flower will follow a certain series of steps from the emergence of the seedling to the stage of producing a flower, human beings also develop certain characteristics only at certain times in their growth process. These sequences are something over which we have no control. Konrad Lorenz illustrated this principle with his famous ducks.

Ducks (and humans) are "programmed" at a certain time in their lives to "accept a mother" figure. If the proper mother figure is not there at that moment of "imprinting", whoever or whatever *is* there will be the "mother image" in the mind of the duck. That is to say, when the appropriate (or inappropriate) object of need is presented to the duck at the correct time in its development, the object is labeled "mother" somewhere in the brain, and this label is next to impossible to erase.

Experiments were conducted with ducks which demonstrated that there is a critical age in hours at which a duckling is most responsive to "obtaining and labeling" a mother. Similar studies were done with monkeys. These studies demonstrated that if a monkey has not received motherly stimulation before he is a certain number of weeks old, he will grow up to be cold, aloof, and unfriendly to his own offspring. The curious thing about the monkey experiments was that the sense of touch was more important than the feeding. A fuzzy surrogate with no milk was preferred over a wire surrogate with milk. This demonstrates a high level need for touching and caressing. It also suggests the "mode" of this "mother imprint"—it is sensory. Kinesthetic. It relates to pleasurable feelings of the body—how one is "touched".

Evidence that there is a critical period for the "mother imprint" in the higher animals was emphasized in the monkey experiments. In one instance, the experimenter was not prepared for the arrival of a new baby monkey and had to create a makeshift "surrogate mother" using a ball for the head. This was provided to the baby, while the experimenter worked on a better model with a face. But, it was too late. The baby monkey had already bonded to the faceless mother and turned the face of the new model around so that it was blank. A mother with a face was simply not acceptable because the imprint had already been made.

We are all programmed. Our programs are written in the circuits of our brains by those around us in our formative years, just as their programs were written during their formative years, and so on back into the mists of time. Everyone carries in their genes, it seems, deep archetypes that are very much like a database program just waiting for someone to input data.

The thing is, this database is only open to input for a limited period of time, and whatever data is entered during that time determines how all other data will be evaluated forever after. It will produce over and over again the same response to any set of stimuli that have one or more items that have been organized by the database. Anything that is not found in the database is "discarded".

If the database is not utilized and no data is entered during the period of "readiness", or imprinting, that possibility goes dormant and diminishes.

The higher thinking functions, laid over the deep level archetype database, can be viewed as a kind of software that is linked to the database, and must constantly check with it in order to operate. You could think of it as a word processing program with a fixed dictionary and set of templates, and you can only write in it according to the templates, and you can only use the words that are in the already fixed dictionary.

Since our brains are genetically designed to accept imprint conditioning on its circuits at certain crucial points in neurological development, these critical periods are known as times of Imprint Vulnerability. The imprint establishes the limits or parameters within which all subsequent conditioning and learning will occur. Each successive imprint further complicates the matter, especially if some of these programs are not compatible with others.

Different schools of thought describe these circuits as "stages of development". Some of the earliest work in these concepts has passed into our culture to such an extent that they have become slang terms such as, "Oh, he's just anal-retentive", with very little actual understanding of what is meant by such expressions.

It seems that, according to research, the "older" brain structures—those necessary for basic survival, such as the brain stem—are imprinted in the earliest stages of development, and that the "newer structures", such as the mid-brain and cortex, develop "superimpositions" upon the more primitive imprints. However, the earlier parts of the brain and their imprints form the foundation for the responses to later imprints, and continue to function after the higher thinking modes are developed.

*In other words, if you are traumatized as an infant at a crucial point of Im-
print Receptivity, it doesn't matter if you grow up to be the President of the
United States—you will still be ruled by the imprint.*

The first stage, or circuit, is the oral-passive-receptive, and is imprinted by
what is perceived to be the mother or first mothering object. It can be conditioned by nourishment or threat, and is mostly concerned with bodily security. Trauma during this phase can cause an unconsciously motivated mechanical retreat from anything threatening to physical safety.

In recent times I have given a lot of thought to this particular circuit. Having come to the tentative idea that the whole Judaeo-Christian monotheistic
rant was a major control program, I came face to face with the question: how
and why has it worked so well for so many thousands of years? More than
that, how was it imposed in the first place? I puzzled over this for weeks. I
thought about several things that Friedrich Nietzsche had said that struck me
like thunderbolts of truth, once I was able to really step back and look at the
matter. He wrote:

> The Jews are the most remarkable nation of world history because, faced with
> the question of being or not being, they preferred, with a perfectly uncanny con-
> viction, being at any price; the price they had to pay was the radical falsification
> of all nature, all naturalness, all reality, the entire inner world as well as the
> outer, They defined themselves counter to all those conditions under which a
> nation was previously able to live, was permitted to live; they made of them-
> selves an antithesis of natural conditions—they inverted religion, religious wor-
> ship, morality, history, psychology, one after the other, in an irreparable way
> into the contradiction of their natural values.
>
> [...] Christianity has waged a deadly war against the higher type of man. It has
> put a ban on all his fundamental instincts. It has distilled evil out of these in-
> stincts. It makes the strong and efficient man its typical outcast man. It has
> taken the part of the weak and the low; it has made an ideal out of its antago-
> nism to the very instincts which tend to preserve life and well-being. [...] It has
> taught men to regard their highest impulses as sinful—as temptations. '...What
> is Jewish, what is Christian morality?' Chance robbed of its innocence; unhap-
> piness polluted with the idea of 'sin'; well-being represented as a danger, as a
> 'temptation'. a physiological disorder produced by the canker worm of con-
> science. [Nietzsche, *The Antichrist*]

But, that's not to say that Nietzsche was any paragon himself, with his
mysogynistic, misanthropic rants! He was, in fact, declared insane in 1888.
But then, considering where his ideas were going, is it any wonder? Did he
see something that other people did not, the implications of which were simply too much for him to accept?

In any case, he had a point about Judaism and Christianity (and any and all
other monotheistic, dominator religions).

So, there I was, pondering this and trying to figure out *how* and *why* people
could be so completely taken in by this utter nonsense? How can educated
members of the human race, in this day and age, with all the resources of
knowledge and awareness available to those who have the desire and energy

to search for truth, possibly buy into such myths? It just staggered my mind to think about it. How can such subjectivity prevail over the most evident objective reality?

Well, clearly, something happened so that the strongest and most intelligent minds on our planet—for we know that those of Jewish bloodline are, above all, super-intelligent—were fenced in and placed in a position that has repeatedly endangered their survival as an ethnic group. How was this intellect derailed so effectively?

I went back in my thinking to the whole Jehovah-I AM deal; the Moses story and all that; and went over the details as they are presented in the Bible for clues; and I came up against that most interesting demand of that crafty Jehovah/Yahweh: circumcision—on the 8th day, no less.

What better way to ensure a deep, subconscious, distrust of women—not to mention an overwhelming terror at the very mention of the pain and suffering that might ensue from breaking the monotheistic covenant—the cruel and punishing "mother" image established at the time of Imprint Vulnerability—than whacking a guy's pee-pee when he is interested only in being warm, cozy, and filling his tummy with warm, sweet milk?!

Whoa! Talk about your basic abyssal cunning there!

The first "circuit" is concerned with what is safe and what is not safe. In our society, money is one of the primary items that is intimately tied to survival and biological security. Money represents survival. In addition to that, people who have been traumatized during the imprinting phase of the first circuit tend to view other people in an abstract way. It is "us and them". They also tend to be very easily threatened by disapproval of any sort because disapproval suggests the idea of extinction or loss of food supply. And, finally, those who have been negatively imprinted at this stage tend to have a chronic muscular armoring that prevents proper, relaxed breathing; they are "up tight".

One of the main characteristics of people who are heavily controlled by this circuit, or are "stuck" in this "oral phase", is that when they sense danger of any sort, whether actual or conceptual, *all mental activity comes to a halt.* Such people are chronically anxious and dependent—mostly on religion. They are not able to really understand what other people are feeling or what can happen in the future in regard to relationships, given a certain present situation. They only understand what is happening "now", and they can only feel what *they* feel. They cannot accurately grasp what others feel because they relate to others only as sensory objects.

So we see that, by this simple act of circumcision, the strength of the Jewish bloodline and its potential intellectual ability to "see through" and objectively assess reality, has been "chopped off". Not only do they retreat in terror into their religion, they cannot perceive the effect they are having on others. They cannot even perceive how repellent their acts are to those who are able to see objectively.

Such an act would make it almost literally impossible for a circumcised man to ever climb his way out of the trap. The merest suggestion of threat to his religion, to his belief system, would turn on all the neuro-chemicals that flooded his infant body at the time of the actual event of circumcision, and he would retreat in narcissistic terror to the safety of non-being—or being according to external dictates—religion and the representatives of religion: the priesthood.

Beside the Jews, for years, the AMA (American Medical Association) advocated and urged circumcision of American babies for "hygienic" reasons. There is a distinction between those circumcised ritually on the 8th day, and those circumcised immediately after birth. I know of no study done on human beings like those done on monkeys and ducks, but perhaps the response of the mothers is indicative of the natural moment of Imprint Vulnerability. A study was done and the mothers were asked: "When did you first feel love for your baby?" 41 % said during the pregnancy and 24% said at birth, but 27% said that it was during the first week and 8% said after the first week.

That is, the indicators for when the child might be "vulnerable", if measurable by the indicators of the mothers, suggest that the day of highest susceptibility for the infant first circuit imprint very well might be on the 8th day after birth. This suggests a knowledge of human psychology and physiology that supersedes what we know even now. Much research ought to be done on this matter.

The implications of this, and the importance of circumcision—which is, effectively, a bodily mutilation—to sustain a religion over thousands of years suggests to us that there must be something really important about those genetics for so powerful a lock to have been instituted and put in place to control and manipulate Jewish people and more than that, that somebody figured it out.

As we have noted, circumcision was an Egyptian thing before it was a Jewish thing, and that brings up the question about the fact that archaeologists and other diggers-into-the-past have often noted how "stable" and long lasting the Egyptian culture/religion was for so very long a period of time. Egyptians didn't revolt against their rulers, they were all happy as clams being controlled and directed by their gods (who were their rulers) for millennia. While other nations around them rose and fell, the Egyptians just stayed in their isolated cocoon, doing their thing, marching in the armies of the Pharaoh to conquer most of the known world, giving all to Pharaoh—their divinity in the flesh—until something happened.

Anyway, such speculations aside, there is a very real problem here: as is said, those who do not study history are doomed to repeat it.

We have here an important group of people who have never seemed to be able to extract the lessons of history over and against their own programming. And the truth is, it is likely that it will be mostly the women of Judaism that will be able to grasp the problem, because they haven't been imprinted with the mortal dread of losing their "soul" by abandoning their religion. It will take a powerful intellect to overcome that circumcision imprint. And, as brilliant as a person is, if they don't, they can never be other than a subjective thinker. Ever.

Kevin MacDonald writes in *The Culture of Critique: An Evolutionary Analysis of Jewish Involvement in Twentieth-Century Intellectual and Political Movements*:

> Jews have indeed made positive contributions to Western culture in the last 200 years. But whatever one might think are the unique and irreplaceable Jewish contributions to the post-Enlightenment world, it is naïve to suppose they were intended for the purpose of benefiting humanity solely or even primarily.[332]

I would like to point out that the list of Jewish scientific achievements from the quote above includes atomic bombs and Game Theory. Science, strongly influenced by the important contributions of so many Jewish scientists, has indeed exploded—no pun intended—and it has brought mankind to the edge of self-destruction. Advances in mathematical, physical and computer sciences have brought about "applied game theory", where "wars" are called "games", and to "win the game" is to kill as many people as possible with as little cost as possible.

THOSE WHO FORGET THE PAST

There is still the question hanging as to why our current culture has so little awareness of this vast and powerful Jewish Empire that dominated Eastern Europe and Western Asia for such a long period of time. The answer probably lies in the religious divisions and prejudices erected by the Catholic Church in Rome after the crusades in an effort to hide the perfidy of the destruction of their co-religionists, the Eastern Orthodox Church of Byzantium.

The first non-Arab mention of Khazaria after 965 is a travel report by Ibrahim Ibn Jakub, the Spanish-Jewish ambassador to Otto the Great. He described the Khazars as still flourishing in 973. The Russian Chronicles give an account of Jews from Khazaria arriving in Kiev in 986.

A later mention, in the Russian Chronicle for the year 1023, describes Prince Mtislav marching against his brother Prince Yaroslav with a force of Khazars and Kasogians. Seven years later, a Khazar army is reported to have defeated a Kurdish invading force.

In 1079, the Russian Chronicle says, "The Khazars of Tmutorakan took Oleg prisoner and shipped him overseas to Tsargrad (Constantinople)". Four years later, Oleg was allowed to return to Tmutorakan where "he slaughtered the Khazars who had counseled the death of his brother and had plotted against himself".[333]

---

[332] http://www.csulb.edu/~kmacd/books-Preface.html
[333] The Old Russian Primary Chronicle (which is often translated into English as *Tale of Bygone Years*), is a history of the early East Slavic state, Kievan Rus, from around 850 to 1110 originally

Around A.D. 1100, the Christian saint, Eustratius was a prisoner in Cherson, in the Crimea, and was ill-treated by his "Jewish master", who forced ritual Passover food on him. Koestler emphasizes that the story is probably bunk, but what is important is that it takes a strong Jewish presence in the town for granted.

The last mention of the Khazars in the Russian chronicle is in 1106. About 50 years later, two Persian poets mention a joint Khazar-Rus invasion of Shirwan and speak of Dervent Khazars. At around the same time, there is a "short and grumpy" (Koestler's term) remark made by the Jewish traveler, Rabbi Petachia of Regensburg, who was scandalized at *the lack of Talmudic learning among the Khazar Jews* when he crossed Khazaria.

The last mention of the Khazars *as a nation* is dated around 1245, at which point in time the Mongols had already established the greatest nomad empire in the world, extending from Hungary to China. Pope Innocent IV sent a mission to Batu Khan, grandson of Jinghiz Khan, ruler of the Western part of the Mongol Empire. Franciscan friar, Joannes de Plano Carpini visited the capital of Batu Khan: Sarai Batu, AKA Saksin, AKA Itil, the former city of the Khazars.

After his return, Plano Carpini wrote in his famous history a list of the regions he visited, as well as the occupants. He mentions, along with the Alans and Circassians, the "Khazars observing the Jewish religion".

Then, darkness.

Bar Hebraeus, one of the greatest Syriac scholars, relates that the father of Seljuk (the founder of the Seljuk Turk dynasty), Tukak, was a commander in the army of the Khazar Kagan and that Seljuk himself was brought up at the Kagan's court. He was banned from the court for being too familiar with the Kagan.

Another source speaks of Seljuk's father as "one of the notables of the Khazar Turks". Thus, there seems to have been an intimate relationship between the Khazars and the founders of the Seljuk dynasty. There was an obvious break, but whether it was because of conversion to Islam, or whether conversion to Islam came about because of the break in relations, we cannot

---

compiled in Kiev about 1113. The original work was attributed to a monk named Nestor. Among many sources he used were earlier (now lost) Slavonic chronicles, Byzantine annals of John Malalas and George Hamartolus, native legends and Norse sagas, several Greek religious texts, Russo-Byzantine treaties, oral accounts of Yan Vyshatich and other military leaders. Nestor worked at the court of Sviatopolk II.

In the year 1116, Nestor's text was extensively edited by hegumen Sylvester who appended his name at the end of the chronicle. As Vladimir Monomakh was the patron of the village of Vydubychi where his monastery is situated, the new edition glorified that prince and made him the central figure of later narrative. This second version of Nestor's work is preserved in the Laurentian codex. A third edition followed two years later and centered on the person of Vladimir's son and heir, Mstislav the Great. The author of this revision could have been Greek, for he corrected and updated much data on Byzantine affairs. This latest revision of Nestor's work is preserved in the Hypatian codex.

know. What seems to be evident is that Khazars were absorbed into Hungarians, Turks, and "Mongols." Then, of course, there are the Ashkenazi Jews.

Russian epics and folk tales give us a few scattered bits to consider after the expiration of the official chronicles. They speak of the "country of the Jews" and "Jewish heroes" who fought against Russians and ruled the steppes. Legends from the Middle Ages circulated among Western Jews tell of a "kingdom of the Red Jews":

> The Jews of other lands were flattered by the existence of an independent Jewish state. Popular imagination found here a particularly fertile field. Just as the biblically minded Slavonic epics speak of 'Jews' rather than Khazars, so did western Jews long after spin romantic tales around those 'red Jews', so styled perhaps because of the slight *Mongolian pigmentation* of many Khazars. [334]

Notice Koestler's report above about Rabbi Petachia of Regensburg, who was scandalized at *the lack of Talmudic learning among the Khazar Jews* when he crossed Khazaria around 1150. Even with the lack of learning, strange things were going on among the Khazarian Jews at this time:

> In the twelfth century there arose in Khazaria a Messianic movement, a rudimentary attempt at a Jewish crusade, *aimed at the conquest of Palestine by force of arms*. The initiator of the movement was a Khazar Jew, one Solomon ben Duji, aided by his son Menahem and a Palestinian scribe. *They wrote letters to all the Jews, near and far,* in all the lands around them. [...] They said that the time had come in which God would gather Israel, His people from all lands to Jerusalem, the holy city, and that Solomon Ben Duji was Elijah, and his son was the Messiah.

> These appeals were apparently addressed to the Jewish communities in the Middle East, and seemed to have had little effect, for the next episode takes place only about twenty years later, when young Menahem assumed the name David al-Roy, and the title of Messiah. Though the movement originated in Khazaria, its centre soon shifted to Kurdistan. Here David assembled a substantial armed force—possibly of local Jews, reinforced by Khazars—and succeeded in taking possession of the strategic fortress of Amadie, northeast of Mosul. From here he may have hoped to lead his army to Edessa, and fight his way through Syria into the Holy Land. [...]

> Among the Jews of the Middle East, David certainly aroused fervent Messianic hopes. One of his messages came to Baghdad and [...] instructed its Jewish citizens to assemble on a certain night on their flat roofs, whence they would be flown on clouds to the Messiah's camp. A goodly number of Jews spent that night on their roofs awaiting the miraculous flight.

> But the rabbinical hierarchy in Baghdad, fearing reprisals by the authorities, took a hostile attitude to the pseudo-Messiah and threatened him with a ban. Not surprisingly, David al-Roy was assassinated—apparently in his sleep, allegedly by his own father-in-law. [...]

> His memory was venerated, and when Benjamin of Tudela traveled through Persia twenty years after the event, 'they still spoke lovingly of their leader'. But the cult did not stop there. According to one theory, *the six-pointed 'shield*

---

[334] Koestler, 135.

of David' which adorns the modern Israeli flag, started to become a national symbol with David a- Roy's crusade. [...]

During the half millennium of its existence and its aftermath in the East European communities, this noteworthy experiment in Jewish statecraft doubtless *exerted a greater influence on Jewish history than we are as yet able to envisage.*

Indeed it very well may have. Notice that "Solomon ben Duji, aided by his son Menahem and a Palestinian scribe *wrote letters to all the Jews, near and far,* in all the lands around them. [...] They said that the time had come in which God would gather Israel, His people from all lands to Jerusalem, the holy city."

Prior to this time, apparently, there had been no such thing as a "messianic movement" among Jews that promoted the idea of "returning to Israel." It was an invention of an apparent lunatic who believed that they were all going to be raptured from their rooftops.

Nowadays, the "traditional Jewish understanding" of the messiah is non-supernatural, and is best elucidated by Maimonides in his commentary to tractate Sanhedrin, of the Babylonian Talmud. He writes:

The Messianic age is when the Jews will regain their independence and all return to the land of Israel. The Messiah will be a very great king, he will achieve great fame, and his reputation among the gentile nations will be even greater than that of King Solomon. His great righteousness and the wonders that he will bring about will cause all peoples to make peace with him and all lands to serve him. [...]

Nothing will change in the Messianic age, however, except that Jews will regain their independence. Rich and poor, strong and weak, will still exist. However it will be very easy for people to make a living, and with very little effort they will be able to accomplish very much. [It] will be a time when the number of wise men will increase [...] war shall not exist, and nation shall no longer lift up sword against nation. [...]

The Messianic age will be highlighted by a community of the righteous and dominated by goodness and wisdom. It will be ruled by the Messiah, a righteous and honest king, outstanding in wisdom, and close to God. Do not think that the ways of the world or the laws of nature will change, this is not true. The world will continue as it is. The prophet Isaiah predicted "The wolf shall live with the sheep, the leopard shall lie down with the kid." This, however, is merely allegory, meaning that the Jews will live safely, even with the formerly wicked nations. All nations will return to the true religion and will no longer steal or oppress.

Note that all prophecies regarding the Messiah are allegorical—Only in the Messianic age will we know the meaning of each allegory and what it comes to teach us. Our sages and prophets did not long for the Messianic age in order that they might rule the world and dominate the gentiles, the only thing they wanted was to be free for Jews to involve themselves with the Torah and its wisdom.

This view is accepted by Orthodox Judaism today, but notice the similarity of the ideas to those promoted by the above mentioned Khazarian Jew Solomon ben Duji, and his son Menahem. As it happens, it is very likely that

Maimonides was influenced by this pair since he would have been coming to adulthood at about the same time that these ideas were being promulgated, and he moved in areas and circles where he would surely have heard the stories of the attempt by those Khazarian Jews to re-take Jerusalem and re-establish a Jewish kingdom on Earth.

Maimonides was born March 30, 1135 (died December 13, 1204) in Córdoba, Spain, then under Muslim rule during what some scholars consider to be the end of the golden age of Jewish culture in Spain. Maimonides studied Torah under his father Maimon who had in turn studied under Rabbi Joseph ibn Migash.

The Almohades conquered Córdoba in 1148, and offered the Jewish community the choice of conversion to Islam, death, or exile. Maimonides's family, along with most other Jews, chose exile. For the next ten years they moved about in southern Spain, avoiding the conquering Almohades, but eventually settled in Fes in Morocco, where Maimonides acquired most of his secular knowledge, studying at the University of Fes. During this time, he composed his acclaimed commentary on the Mishnah.

Following this sojourn in Morocco, he briefly lived in the Holy Land, spending time in Jerusalem, and finally settled in Fostat, Egypt, where he was doctor of the Grand Vizier Alfadhil and also possibly the doctor of Sultan Saladin of Egypt. In Egypt, he composed most of his oeuvre, including the Mishneh Torah. He died in Fostat, and was buried in Tiberias (today in Israel).

His son Avraham, recognized as a great scholar, succeeded him as Nagid (head of the Egyptian Jewish Community), as well as in the office of court physician, at the age of only eighteen. He greatly honored the memory of his father, and throughout his career defended his father's writings against all critics. The office of Nagid was held by the Maimonides family for four successive generations until the end of the 14th century.

Although his copious works on Jewish law and ethics was initially met with opposition during his lifetime, he was posthumously acknowledged to be one of the foremost rabbinical arbiters and philosophers in Jewish history. Today, his works and his views are considered a cornerstone of Orthodox Jewish thought and study.

Maimonides was by far the most influential figure in medieval Jewish philosophy. A popular medieval saying that also served as his epitaph states, "From Moshe (of the Torah) to Moshe (Maimonides) there was none like Moshe".

Radical Jewish scholars in the centuries that followed can be characterised as "Maimonideans" or "anti-Maimonideans". Moderate scholars were eclectics who largely accepted Maimonides' Aristotelian world-view, but rejected those elements of it which they considered to *contradict the religious tradition.* [335]

---

[335] http://en.wikipedia.org/wiki/Maimonides

Notice the mention of the fact that Maimonides' ideas were met with opposition and were said to contradict the Jewish religious tradition. One suspects that Rabbi Petachia of Regensburg, who was scandalized at *the lack of Talmudic learning among the Khazar Jews* when he crossed Khazaria around 1150, would also have been scandalized at the work of Maimonides *since it was the lack of Talmudic learning among the Khazar Jews that undoubtedly led to the eruption of the idea of the re-gathering of the Jews to Israel.* We notice that, "Among the Jews of the Middle East, David [the Khazarian Jew who claimed he was the messiah] certainly aroused fervent Messianic hopes", and Maimonides was certainly a Jew in the Middle East at a time that was not long after this madness had taken hold and spread like a disease. It is most ironic that *the idea of Zionism as it exists today, formulated and promoted by Ashkenazi Jews, was originally created by Khazarian Jews over 700 years earlier.*

> In general, the reduced Khazar kingdom persevered. It waged a more or less effective defence against all foes until the middle of the thirteenth century, when it fell victim to the great Mongol invasion. [...] Even then it resisted stubbornly until the surrender of all its neighbors. Its population was largely absorbed by the Golden Horde which had established the centre of its empire in Khazar territory. But before and after the Mongol upheaval, the Khazars sent many offshoots into the unsubdued Slavonic lands, helping ultimately to build up the great Jewish centres of Eastern Europe.
>
> Here, then, we have the cradle of the numerically strongest and culturally dominant part of modern Jewry.[336]

FURTHER BACK IN TIME

Finding the "cradle of the numerically strongest and culturally dominant part of modern Jewry" doesn't really tell us if they were the "Children of Israel." Even if we consider it absurd to just hand the country belonging to a different people for about 2000 years to a different group because they say their God gave it to them, we are interested in finding out if their claims that they are—even from their own point of view—entitled to that land can be true. So, we continue back in time to search for the origins of the Ashkenazim.

Now, we know a great deal about the Khazars in a particular period of history, but we still know nothing about where they came from, which is the burning question. Can they legitimately claim to be Jews genetically, thus having a claim (even if based on a fraudulent history) to Palestine?

We recall that the Georgians and Armenians, having been repeatedly devastated by the Khazars, *identified them as Gog and Magog.* We also recall that the Arab chroniclers wrote that the Khazars were "white, their eyes blue, their hair flowing and predominantly reddish, their bodies large, and their natures cold. Their general aspect is wild".

---

[336] Koestler, 135-137.

It doesn't sound much like the depictions of the Hebrews in the ancient art we are familiar with such as Egyptian, Babylonian, and so on. However, it does sound a lot like the ancient Aryan tribes; they were fierce, with wild, flowing blonde or red hair, cold-natured, yet susceptible to a "furor" that came on them accompanied by great heat. That, of course, reminds us of the genetic issues of mtDNA, mitochondria and their function: the powerhouse of the body that works by virtue of its oxygen-capturing enzymes.

An Armenian writer described them as having, "insolent, broad, lashless faces and *long falling hair, like women*". Again, this description of the Khazars sounds a lot like descriptions of the "long-haired Franks". So, let us look at the Franks and see if we track them back in time and discover anything.

HISTORY OF THE FRANKS

The Franks or the Frankish people were one of several West Germanic federations. The confederation was formed out of Germanic tribes: Salians, Sugambri, Chamavi, Tencteri, Chattuarii, Bructeri, Usipetes, Ampsivarii, and *Chatti*. They entered the late Roman Empire from present central Germany and the Southern Netherlands and settled in northern Gaul where they were accepted as a *foederati* and established a rather long-lasting realm in an area which eventually covered most of modern-day France, the Low Countries, and the western regions of Germany, forming the historic kernel of all these modern countries.

It is conjectured that the Franks came from the East—the area of the Scythians and Khazars—and they met and mingled with the Frisians.

The area that the Frisians originate from was settled as early as 3500 BCE. Yes, that's over 5000 years ago, long before Abraham was allegedly stomping around Israel. There were comings and goings of additional peoples as the archaeological records show, but it seems to be possible to systematically track who was who and who went where by their pottery and other artifacts.

The coming of the Romans to the southern Netherlands in 12 BCE prevented the Frisians from expanding their territory to the south of the Amstel and the Rhine. Around the year 150 BCE, the Frisians also lost the Groningen salt-marshes to the Chatti who had advanced from East Friesland.

A list of place-names compiled in Alexandria by geographer Claudius Ptolameus (Ptolemy) c.150 CE was turned into maps by Europeans in the 15th century. These maps also supply the names of those tribes dwelling along the North Sea coastal regions. The evidence indicates that Saxons lived in southwest Jutland (Ribe and southwards), North Friesland and Ditmarschen—as far as the Elbe. Then we see that between the Elbe and the Weser lived the "greater" Chatti, while the "lesser" Chatti lived in East Friesland. The descriptions given by Ptolemy agree with what has been reconstructed from the archaeological finds.

Depopulation of the Frisian salt-marshes occurred between 250 and 400 CE due to the rising sea levels and flooding and, undoubtedly, the cometary destruction of Europe mentioned above.

The presence of the tribe known as the Chatti has been mentioned by several ancient sources. What I find to be of great interest is that the Hittites were also known as the *Chatti,* and Abraham, the patriarch of the Jews, was said to have been a Hittite; that is to say, an Aryan. I began to wonder if the so-called pejorative characteristics that were historically assigned to Jews might actually be an "Aryan cultural inheritance". It is, after all, the "Salic Law", from the Salian Franks, that deprived women of the rights of inheritance and the position of women was seriously degraded with the imposition of monotheism through Judaism.

Experts note that Frisian Tritzumer pottery has been found in Kent in England. This brings us to consider another fascinating item: the bizarre belief of the ancient Armenians and Georgians that the Khazars were 'Gog and Magog'.

In Genesis, we find the following:

> 10:1 Now these are the generations of the sons of Noah, Shem, Ham, and Japheth: and unto them were sons born after the flood. 10:2 The sons of Japheth; Gomer, and Magog, and Madai, and Javan, and Tubal, and Meshech, and Tiras. 10:3 And the sons of Gomer; Ashkenaz, and Riphath, and Togarmah. 10:4 And the sons of Javan; Elishah, and Tarshish, Kittim, and Dodanim. 10:5 By these were the isles of the Gentiles divided in their lands; every one after his tongue, after their families, in their nations.

It's truly interesting to note that the word "Ashkenaz" is listed as a name of one of great grandsons of Noah, through the "gentile" line. What about the "isles of the Gentiles"?

The only other real mention of Gog and Magog is in a truly weird prophecy given by the prophet Ezekiel:

> 38:1 And the word of the Lord came unto me, saying, 38:2 Son of man, set thy face against Gog, the land of Magog, the chief prince of Meshech and Tubal, and prophesy against him, 38:3 And say, Thus saith the Lord God; Behold, I am against thee, O Gog, the chief prince of Meshech and Tubal: 38:4 And I will turn thee back, and put hooks into thy jaws, and I will bring thee forth, and all thine army, horses and horsemen, all of them clothed with all sorts of armour, even a great company with bucklers and shields, all of them handling swords: 38:5 Persia, Ethiopia, and Libya with them; all of them with shield and helmet: 38:6 Gomer, and all his bands; the house of Togarmah of the north quarters, and all his bands: and many people with thee.

> 38:7 Be thou prepared, and prepare for thyself, thou, and all thy company that are assembled unto thee, and be thou a guard unto them. 38:8 After many days thou shalt be visited: in the latter years thou shalt come into the land that is brought back from the sword, and is gathered out of many people, against the mountains of Israel, which have been always waste: but it is brought forth out of the nations, and they shall dwell safely all of them.

> 38:9 Thou shalt ascend and come like a storm, thou shalt be like a cloud to cover the land, thou, and all thy bands, and many people with thee.

38:10 Thus saith the Lord God; It shall also come to pass, that at the same time shall things come into thy mind, and thou shalt think an evil thought: 38:11 And thou shalt say, I will go up to the land of unwalled villages; I will go to them that are at rest, that dwell safely, all of them dwelling without walls, and having neither bars nor gates, 38:12 To take a spoil, and to take a prey; to turn thine hand upon the desolate places that are now inhabited, and upon the people that are gathered out of the nations, which have gotten cattle and goods, that dwell in the midst of the land.

38:13 Sheba, and Dedan, and the merchants of Tarshish, with all the young lions thereof, shall say unto thee, Art thou come to take a spoil? hast thou gathered thy company to take a prey? to carry away silver and gold, to take away cattle and goods, to take a great spoil?

38:14 Therefore, son of man, prophesy and say unto Gog, Thus saith the Lord God; In that day when my people of Israel dwelleth safely, shalt thou not know it? 38:15 And thou shalt come from thy place out of the north parts, thou, and many people with thee, all of them riding upon horses, a great company, and a mighty army: 38:16 And thou shalt come up against my people of Israel, as a cloud to cover the land; it shall be in the latter days, and I will bring thee against my land, that the heathen may know me, when I shall be sanctified in thee, O Gog, before their eyes.

38:17 Thus saith the Lord God; Art thou he of whom I have spoken in old time by my servants the prophets of Israel, which prophesied in those days many years that I would bring thee against them?

38:18 And it shall come to pass at the same time when Gog shall come against the land of Israel, saith the Lord God, that my fury shall come up in my face. 38:19 For in my jealousy and in the fire of my wrath have I spoken, Surely in that day there shall be a great shaking in the land of Israel; 38:20 So that the fishes of the sea, and the fowls of the heaven, and the beasts of the field, and all creeping things that creep upon the earth, and all the men that are upon the face of the earth, shall shake at my presence, and the mountains shall be thrown down, and the steep places shall fall, and every wall shall fall to the ground.

38:21 And I will call for a sword against him throughout all my mountains, saith the Lord God: every man's sword shall be against his brother. 38:22 And I will plead against him with pestilence and with blood; and I will rain upon him, and upon his bands, and upon the many people that are with him, an overflowing rain, and great hailstones, fire, and brimstone.

38:23 Thus will I magnify myself, and sanctify myself; and I will be known in the eyes of many nations, and they shall know that I am the Lord.

39:1 Therefore, thou son of man, prophesy against Gog, and say, Thus saith the Lord God; Behold, I am against thee, O Gog, the chief prince of Meshech and Tubal: 39:2 And I will turn thee back, and leave but the sixth part of thee, and will cause thee to come up from the north parts, and will bring thee upon the mountains of Israel: 39:3 And I will smite thy bow out of thy left hand, and will cause thine arrows to fall out of thy right hand. 39:4 Thou shalt fall upon the mountains of Israel, thou, and all thy bands, and the people that is with thee: I will give thee unto the ravenous birds of every sort, and to the beasts of the field to be devoured. 39:5 Thou shalt fall upon the open field: for I have spoken it, saith the Lord God.

39:6 And I will send a fire on Magog, and among them that dwell carelessly in the isles: and they shall know that I am the Lord. 39:7 So will I make my holy name known in the midst of my people Israel; and I will not let them pollute my holy name any more: and the heathen shall know that I am the Lord, the Holy One in Israel. [337]

Here, we also need to remember that curious series of events surrounding the establishment of the Old Testament as we know it (more or less) today, the oldest text of which is dated *only to the 10 century*. Recall the story of Isaac ibn Yashush, the Jewish court physician of the 11th century who pointed out that someone who lived after Moses wrote the Edomite king list. He was called "Isaac the Blunderer" by Abraham ibn Ezra, a 12th century rabbi who said, regarding the fact that Moses could not have written the Torah, *"And if you understand, then you will recognize the truth. And he who understands will keep silent."*

Since we now know that Maimonides, the 12th century rabbi whose views are now accepted by Orthodox Judaism was most likely influenced by the above mentioned Khazarian Jew Solomon ben Duji, and his son Menahem, and that they were the source of the ideas of re-taking Jerusalem and establishing a Jewish kingdom on earth, it all begins to make a sick sort of sense. We are also reminded at this moment that the great Jewish scholar, Rashi de Troyes, said that the Genesis narrative, going back to the creation of the world, *was written to justify genocide in the re-taking of Israel.*

Sounds like a conspiracy, doesn't it? *"And if you understand, then you will recognize the truth. And he who understands will keep silent."*

Indeed, the Lord works in mysterious ways! Even when you know how the Bible came to be written, when you begin to understand how the ideas came to be accepted as "holy writ" it makes your skin crawl.

Returning to Gog and Magog, there is another mention in the book of Revelation:

20:7 And when the thousand years are expired, Satan shall be loosed out of his prison, 20:8 And shall go out to *deceive the nations* which are in the four quarters of the earth, Gog, and Magog, to gather them together to battle: the number of whom is as the sand of the sea. 20:9 And they went up on the breadth of the earth, and compassed the camp of the saints about, and the beloved city: and *fire came down from God out of heaven, and devoured them.* 20:10 And the devil that deceived them was cast into the lake of fire and brimstone, where the beast and the false prophet are, and shall be tormented day and night for ever and ever.

---

[337] Such passages are most likely accounts of historical events and are not to be taken prophetically except in the sense that history does tend to repeat itself. With that in mind, it sure sounds like what the currently named Israelis are doing in Israel, doesn't it? Did you notice the references to unwalled cities, and the building of a wall that would be brought down? What about the weird remark "I will turn thee back, and leave but the sixth part of thee, and will cause thee to come up from the north parts, and will bring thee upon the mountains of Israel"? If the Ashkenazim are Gog and Magog, it makes perfect sense. A "sixth part" of them survived the Holocaust and came from the north to Israel… Self-fulfilling prophecy?

This leads to a couple other interesting items in Revelation:

2:8 And unto the angel of the church in Smyrna write; These things saith the first and the last, which was dead, and is alive; 2:9 I know thy works, and tribulation, and poverty, (but thou art rich) and *I know the blasphemy of them which say they are Jews, and are not, but are the synagogue of Satan.*

3:9 Behold, I will make them of **the synagogue of Satan, which say they are Jews, and are not, but do lie**; behold, I will make them to come and worship before thy feet, and to know that I have loved thee.

Apparently, quite a few people knew things back in those times that have been lost to us.

As we noted, depopulation of the Frisian salt-marshes is said to have occurred between 250 and 400 CE due to the rising sea levels and flooding. Later, undoubtedly, the cometary destruction of Europe led to tribes long settled going on the march. Most probably, this is the ultimate reason for the almost total depopulation of the Frisians in North Holland.

As the experts note (though they can't come up with a real reason for it unless they look at the ideas of cometary destruction), this depopulation did not just affect Frisian areas. In the Baltic and northern European coastal regions, the population *retreated to the higher areas inland during the second century CE,* and certainly were on the move when the comets came. So, either there were two periods of depopulation, or only one and the dating is incorrect.

Now, let's have a look at a short excerpt from ethnographer Lev Gumilev's[338] work on *Ethnogenesis and the Biosphere*:

Names deceive. When one is studying the general patterns of ethnology one must remember above all that a real ethnos and an ethnonym, i.e. ethnic name, are not the same thing.

We often encounter several different ethnoi bearing one and the same name; conversely, one ethnos may be called differently. The word 'Romans' (romani), for instance, originally meant a citizen of the polis Rome, but not all the Italians and not even the Latins who inhabited other towns of Latium.

In the epoch of the Roman Empire in the first and second centuries A.D. the number of Romans increased through the inclusion among them of all Italians-Etruscans, Samnites, Ligurians, Gauls, and many inhabitants of the provinces, by no means of Latin origin. […]

A large number of Slavs, Armenians, and Syrians were gradually merged among the Romaic, but they retained the name 'Romans' until 1453, until the fall of Constantinople. The Romaic considered precisely themselves 'Romans', but *not* the population of Italy, where Langobards had become feudal lords, Syrian Semites, (who had settled in Italy, which had become deserted, in the first to third centuries A.D.), the townsmen, and the former colons from prisoners of war of all peoples at any time conquered by the Romans of the Empire became peasants. […]

---

[338] Wikipedia: Lev Nikolayevich Gumilyov (October 1, 1912, St. Petersburg–June 15, 1992, St. Petersburg), better known in the West as Lev Gumilev, was one of the most controversial and popular Russian historians of the 20th century. His unorthodox ideas on the birth and death of ethnoses (ethnic groups) have given rise to the political and cultural movement known as "Neo-Eurasianism".

A third branch of the ethnonym 'Romans' arose on the Danube, which had been a place of exile after the Roman conquest of Dacia. There Phrygians, Cappadocians, Thracians, Galatians, Syrians, Greeks, Illyrians, in short, all the eastern subjects of the Roman Empire, served sentences for rebellion against Roman rule. To understand one another they conversed in the generally known Latin tongue. When the Roman legions left Dacia, the descendants of the exiled settlers remained and formed an ethnos that took the name 'Romanian', i.e. 'Roman', in the nineteenth century.

If one can treat the continuity between 'Romans' of the age of the Republic, and the 'Roman citizens' of the late Empire, even as a gradual extension of the concept functionally associated with the spread of culture, there is no such link even between the Byzantines and the Romans, from which it follows that the word changed meaning and content and cannot serve as an identifying attribute of the ethnos.

It is obviously also necessary to take into consideration the context in which the word—and so the epoch—has a semantic content, because the meaning of words changes in the course of time. That is even more indicative when we analyze the ethnonyms 'Turk', 'Tatar', and 'Mongol', an example that cannot be left aside.

Examples of camouflage. In the sixth century A.D. a small people living on the eastern slopes of the Altai and Khangai mountains were called Turks. Through several successful wars they managed to subordinate the whole steppe from Hingan to the Sea of Azov [i.e. the Khazars].

The subjects of the Great Kaghanate, who preserved their own ethnonyms for internal use, also began to be called Turks, since they were subject to the Turkish Khan.

When the Arabs conquered Sogdiana and clashed with the nomads, they began to call all of them Turks, including the Ugro-Magyars.

In the eighteenth century, European scholars called all nomads '*les Tartars*', and in the nineteenth century, when linguistic classification became fashionable, the name 'Turk' was arrogated to a definite group of languages.

Many peoples thus fell into the category 'Turk' who had not formed part of it in antiquity, for example the Yakuts, Chuvash and the hybrid people, the Ottoman Turks.

The modification of the ethnonym 'Tatar' is an example of *direct* camouflage. Up to the twelfth century this was the ethnic name of a group of 30 big clans inhabiting the banks of the Korulen. In the twelfth century this nationality increased in numbers, and Chinese geographers began to call all the Central Asian nomads (Turkish speaking, Tungus-speaking, and Mongol-speaking), including the Mongols, Tatars. And even when, in 1206, Genghis-khan officially called all his subjects Mongols, neighbors continued for some time from habit to call them Tatars.

In this form the word 'Tatar' reached Eastern Europe as a synonym of the word 'Mongol', and became acclimatized in the Volga Valley where the local population began, as a mark of loyalty to the Khan of the Golden Horde to call themselves Tatars. But the original bearers of this name (Kereites, Naimans, Oirats, and Tatars) began to call themselves Mongols. *The names thus changed places.*

Since that time a scientific terminology arose in which the Tatar anthropological type began to be called 'Mongoloid', and the language of the Volga Kipchak-Turks Tatar. In other words we even employ an obviously camouflaged terminology in science.

But then it is not simply a matter of confusion, but of an ethnonymic phantasmagoria. Not all the nomad subjects of the Golden Horde were loyal to its government. The rebels who lived in the steppes west of the Urals began to call themselves Nogai, and those who lived on the eastern borders of the Jochi ulus, in Tarbagatai and on the banks of the Irtysh, and who were practically independent, because of their remoteness from the capital, became the ancestors of the Kazakhs.

These ethnoi arose in the fourteenth and fifteenth centuries as a consequence of rapid mixing of various ethnic components. The ancestors of the Nogai were the Polovtsy, *steppe Alans*, Central Asian Turks, who survived a defeat by Batu and were taken into the Mongol army, and inhabitants of the southern frontier of Rus, who adopted Islam, which became a symbol at that time of ethnic consolidation.

Thus, the Tatars included Kama Bulgars, <u>Khazars</u>, and Burtasy, and also some of the Polovtsy and Ugric Mishari. The population of the <u>White Horde</u> was the mixture; three Kazakh jus were formed from it in the fifteenth century.

But that is not yet all. At the end of the fifteenth century, Russian bands from the Upper Volga began to attack the Middle Volga Tatar towns, forced some of the population to quit their homeland and go off into Central Asia under the chieftainship of Sheibani-khan (1500-1510). There they were met as fierce enemies because the local Turks who at that time bore the name of 'Chagatai' (after Genghis-khan's second son Chagatei, the chief of the Central Asian ulus), were ruled by descendants of Timur, the enemy of the steppe and Volga Tatars, who ravaged the Volga Valley in 1398-1399.

The members of the horde who quit their homeland took on a new name 'Uzbeks' to honor the Khan Uzbeg (1312-1341), who had established Islam in the Golden Horde as the state religion. In the sixteenth century the 'Uzbeks' defeated Babur, the last of the Timurides, who led the remnants of his supporters into India and conquered a new kingdom for himself there.

So the Turks who remained in Samarkand and Ferghana bear the name of their conquerors, the Uzbeks. The same Turks, who went to India, began to be called 'Moghuls' in memory of their having been, three hundred years earlier, subject to the Mongol Empire.

But the genuine Mongols who settled in eastern Iran in the thirteenth century, and even retained their language, are called Khazareitsy from the Persian word khazar—a thousand (meaning a military unit, or division).

But where are the Mongols, by whose name the yoke that lay on Rus for 240 years is known?

They were not an ethnos, because by Genghis-khan's will Jochi, Batu, Orda, and Sheibani each received 4, 000 warriors, of whom only part came from the Far East. The latter were called 'Kins' and not 'Tatars', from the Chinese name of the Jurchen. This rare name occurred for the last time in the Zadonshchina, in which Mamai was called Kinnish. [339]

---

[339] Lev Gumilev, *Ethnogenesis and the Biosphere* (Progress, 1990).

We realize from the work of Lev Gumilev that names of groups can change in context as well as content. Additionally, language is not always a clue as to origin since languages can be imposed on conquered peoples who then believe that it is their own, or adopted out of necessity.

The point here is that, just because two groups of people speak a similar language, doesn't mean that they are genetically close. The same is probably true for the tribes of the Middle East who came to be known as "Semitic" after the conquest of Sargon, who came down *from the North* and was, most probably, from one of the Aryan steppe tribes. At that time, the Sumerian peoples were developing writing for their agricultural civilization, and this writing was then utilized for the Semitic language of Sargon—the official tongue after the conquest—while the Sumerian language became extinct. The extensive population of Sumerians then came to think of themselves as "Semitic" because they were under the rule of a Semitic elite when, in fact, they weren't—at least not in the terms meant by "Semitic" at that period.

The word "semitic" is somewhat troublesome for a variety of reasons. In linguistic terms, it is well-defined to include ancient and modern versions of Amharic, Arabic, Aramaic, Akkadian, Hebrew, Maltese, Syriac, Tigrinya, etc. The problems arise—as we have seen from the work of Gumilev—when you try to use it for populations, ethnicities, genetics, and so on.

THE MYSTERY OF THE GUANCHES

The Guanches, the original inhabitants of the Canary Islands present us with an interesting clue:

> The original inhabitants of the Canary Islanders referred to themselves as "Canari" long before the Romans arrived. The name appears to have had a similar meaning in both Latin and the native speech, which was a mixed Indo-European language with at least several Latin cognates.

> Previous to the 1st century CE, the Atlantic group was known throughout the Mediterranean World as the Blessed Isles, the Fortunate Isles, the Hesperides, or the Isles of the Blessed. Forgotten for all of classical civilization, they were isolated from outside contact for almost 1,000 years until their rediscovery by Portuguese sailors in the 14th century. The Canari more commonly referred to themselves as Guanches (men) a once civilized race that had slowly degenerated over millennia of interbreeding, while their level of society slid back, quite literally, into the caves. [...]

> Before their virtual elimination, some studies were made of the Guanches, a white people, fair complected and with red, auburn, and occasionally blond hair. Despite their genetically debased condition, they preserved traditions from long gone ages of civilized greatness and still gathered at the ruined stone monuments of their ancestors for special events. Some of these cyclopean walls, called tagora, survive as crumbling rectangular enclosures, circles, and even pyramids.[340]

---

[340] Joseph, Frank, *The Lost Pyramids of Rock Lake* (Lakeville, MN: Galde Press, Inc., 1992).

The Afro-Asiatic language phylum has six distinct branches including Ancient Egyptian, which was known in its last years as Coptic, and which became extinct in the seventeenth century. The other five branches are *Berber*, Chadic, Cushitic, Omotic and *Semitic*.

The Semitic language group is subdivided into an extinct Eastern branch, Akkadian, spoken by Sargon, and a Western branch with two sub-branches, Central and South. The Central group consists of Aramaic, Canaanite, and Arabic. The Southern group consists of South Arabian and Ethiopic. And here is the curiosity: one of the other branches of the Afro-Asiatic language tree is Berber, with sub-branches of *Guanche*—spoken by the original Canary Islanders; East Numidian, which is Old Libyan, and Berber proper.

Now, you ask, what is the problem?

The Guanches and their language.

Some experts tell us that the Guanches must have come from the neighboring African coast long ages before the Black and Arab "invaders" overran it. We are informed that Mauritania was formerly inhabited by the "same ancient Iberian race which once covered all *Western Europe*: a people tall, fair and strong." Spain invaded, and most of the Guanches were wiped out by diseases to which they had no resistance due to their long isolation. It was over a hundred years before anyone attempted to record their language, customs, and what could be remembered of their history. Friar Alonso de Espinosa of the Augustine Order of Preachers, writing in 1580, tells us:

> It is generally believed that these are the Elysian Fields of which Homer sings. The poet Virgil, in the 4th book of the *Aeneid*, mentions the great peak of this island, when he makes Mercury, sent by Jupiter, go to Carthage to undeceive Aeneas, and to encourage him so that he might not abandon the voyage to Italy which he had undertaken.

> It has not been possible to ascertain the origin of the Guanches, or whence they came, for as the natives had no letters, they had no account of their origin or descent, although some tradition may have come down from father to son. [...]

> The old Guanches say that they have an immemorial tradition that sixty people came to this island, but they know not whence they came. They gave their settlement the name "The place of union of the son of the great one."

> Although they knew of God, and called Him by various names, they had no rites nor ceremonies nor words with which they might venerate Him. [...] When the rains failed, they got together the sheep in certain places, where it was the custom to invoke the guardian of the sheep. Here they *stuck a wand or lance in the ground*, then they separated the lambs from the sheep, and placed the mothers round the lance, where they bleated. They believed that God was appeased by this ceremony, that he heard the bleating of the sheep and would send down the rain.

> [...] They knew that there was a hell, and they held that it was in the peak of Teyde [the volcanic mountain], and the devil was Guayota.

> They were accustomed when a child was born, to call a woman whose duty it was, and she poured water over its head; and this woman thus contracted a relationship with the child's parents, so that it was not lawful to marry her, or to treat her dishonestly. They know not whence they derived this custom or cere-

mony, only that it existed. It could not be a sacrament, for it was not performed as one, nor had the evangelic law been preached to them. [...]

The inviolable law was that if a warrior meeting a woman by chance in the road, or in any solitary place, who spoke to her or looked at her, unless she spoke first and asked for something, or who, in an inhabited place, used any dishonest words which could be proved, he should suffer death for it without appeal. Such was their discipline. [...]

This people had very good and perfect features, and well-shaped bodies. They were of tall stature, with proportionate limbs. *There were giants among them of incredible size.* [...]

They only possessed and sowed barley and beans. [...] If they once had wheat, the seed had been lost. [...] They also ate the flesh of sheep, goats, and pigs, and they fed on it by itself, without any other relish whatever. [...] The flesh had to be half roasted because, as they said, it contained more substance in that way than if it was well roasted.

They *counted the year by lunations.* [...] The lord did not marry with anyone of the lower orders, and if there was no one he could marry without staining the lineage, brothers were married to sisters.

They were wonderfully clever with counting. Although a flock was very numerous and came out of the yard or fold at a rush, they counted the sheep without opening their mouths or noting with their hands, and never made a mistake. [341]

I'm sure that the reader can see that even though we have very little to go on, there are a couple of suggestive indicators recorded by the good friar. The first thing we note is the custom of driving a lance into the ground for the sheep to "call the god" which reminds us of a certain story in Genesis:

30:27 And Laban said unto him, I pray thee, if I have found favour in thine eyes, tarry: for I have learned by experience that the Lord hath blessed me for thy sake.
30:28 And he said, Appoint me thy wages, and I will give it.
30:29 And he said unto him, Thou knowest how I have served thee, and how thy cattle was with me.
30:30 For it was little which thou hadst before I came, and it is now increased unto a multitude; and the Lord hath blessed thee since my coming: and now when shall I provide for mine own house also? 30:31 And he said, What shall I give thee? And Jacob said, Thou shalt not give me any thing: if thou wilt do this thing for me, I will again feed and keep thy flock.
30:32 I will pass through all thy flock to day, removing from thence all the speckled and spotted cattle, and all the brown cattle among the sheep, and the spotted and speckled among the goats: and of such shall be my hire.
30:33 So shall my righteousness answer for me in time to come, when it shall come for my hire before thy face: every one that is not speckled and spotted among the goats, and brown among the sheep, that shall be counted stolen with me.
30:34 And Laban said, Behold, I would it might be according to thy word.
30:35 And he removed that day the he goats that were ringstraked and spotted, and all the she goats that were speckled and spotted, and every one that had

---

[341] Alonso De Espinosa, *The Guanches of Tenerife*, trans. Sir Clements Markham (Nendeln/Liechtenstein: Kraus Repring, 1972).

some white in it, and all the brown among the sheep, and gave them into the hand of his sons.

30:36 And he set three days' journey betwixt himself and Jacob: and Jacob fed the rest of Laban's flocks.

30:37 And Jacob took him rods of green poplar, and of the hazel and chesnut tree; and pilled white strakes in them, and made the white appear which was in the rods.

30:38 And he set the rods which he had pilled before the flocks in the gutters in the watering troughs when the flocks came to drink, that they should conceive when they came to drink.

30:39 And the flocks conceived before the rods, and brought forth cattle ringstraked, speckled, and spotted.

30:40 And Jacob did separate the lambs, and set the faces of the flocks toward the ringstraked, and all the brown in the flock of Laban; and he put his own flocks by themselves, and put them not unto Laban's cattle.

30:41 And it came to pass, whensoever the stronger cattle did conceive, that Jacob laid the rods before the eyes of the cattle in the gutters, that they might conceive among the rods.

30:42 But when the cattle were feeble, he put them not in: so the feebler were Laban's, and the stronger Jacob's.

30:43 And the man increased exceedingly, and had much cattle, and maidservants, and menservants, and camels, and asses.

Does this prove that the Guanches were familiar with the Hebrews and their Bible for those many thousands of years of isolation? That the relationship of their language to Berber, a sub-group of Semitic, proves the ancient history of the Hebrews? Not exactly. Considered in context with all the other clues, *it suggests that many of the stories in the Hebrew Bible were taken from much older stories, customs, and so on that actually belonged, as the Semitic language did, to an Aryan people, adopted by peoples we think of as ethnically "Semitic" in modern terms **but who, in ancient terms, were not Semitic at all.***

The languages spoken by many of the tribes of the Eurasian steppes, including the Turkic languages of the Khazars, are also known as Altaic. As a language family, this is still a bit contentious among experts. The Turkic, Mongolian, and Tungusic families do have strong similarities in many ways, but some linguists suggest these are due to intensive borrowing from long contact. To some extent, the Altaic-Turkic languages also resemble the Uralic languages already discussed, such as Finnish and Hungarian. As a consequence, a *Ural-Altaic superfamily* has been suggested: Eurasiatic, in which Indo-European languages would also be included as a "brother" language. This super-family has a parent also which *makes a connect to Amerind languages*, (!) but we won't go into that just now. The short of it is that we can't rely on language to denote a genetic or ethnic affinity over long periods of time, though it can, sometimes, be a clue.

GOG AND MAGOG REPRISE

Let's come back to our problem of Gog and Magog.

We note that the Frisians disappeared from the salt marshes and certainly, by the evidence of pottery, some of them went to England. How does this relate to the belief of the ancient Armenians and Georgians that the *Khazars* were "Gog and Magog."

In Genesis, we read:

> 10:1 Now these are the generations of the sons of Noah, Shem, Ham, and Japheth: and unto them were sons born after the flood. 10:2 The sons of Japheth; Gomer, and Magog, and Madai, and Javan, and Tubal, and Meshech, and Tiras. 10:3 And the sons of Gomer; Ashkenaz, and Riphath, and Togarmah. 10:4 And the sons of Javan; Elishah, and Tarshish, Kittim, and Dodanim. 10:5 By these were the isles of the Gentiles divided in their lands; every one after his tongue, after their families, in their nations.

Notice the remark about "isles of the Gentiles".

In the passage from Ezekiel we notice several of the "sons of Japheth" being named as places:

> 38:1 And the word of the Lord came unto me, saying, 38:2 Son of man, set thy face against Gog, the land of *Magog,* the chief prince of *Meshech* and *Tubal,* and prophesy against him,
> 38:3 And say, Thus saith the Lord God; Behold, I am against thee, O Gog, the chief prince of Meshech and Tubal.

Then later, he mentions the land of Magog in the same breath with "them that dwell *carelessly* in the isles…"

> 39:6 And I will send a fire on Magog, and among them that dwell carelessly in the *isles*…

The only place on the planet that has been called Gog and Magog for any considerable length of time in our recorded history is in England: the Gog Magog hills near Cambridge. We notice immediately that England could definitely fit the description of the "isles of the Gentiles."[342]

Historians suggest that the Gog Magog hills got their name because of the innumerable human bones that have been found there; evidence of a battle so fierce that it reminded the locals of Ezekiel's passage about Gog, king of Magog.

The earliest reference to this name for these hills is in a decree of 1574 forbidding students to visit them or be fined. Nowadays, they are still a trysting area. A map dating from the end of the 16th century also depicts the Gogmagog Hills.

There is a small problem with this explanation: How did the locals know about the prophecy of Ezekiel?

Well, they read the Bible, you say.

---

[342] Curiously, amazing crop circles appeared in a field near to these hills exactly two months before the September 11 attacks on New York.

Did they?

John Wycliff's *hand-written manuscripts* in the 1380s were the first complete Bibles in the English language. They were obviously not widely available.

William Tyndale printed the first English New Testament in 1525/6. One risked death by burning if caught in mere possession of the forbidden book. Only two complete copies of that first printing are known to have survived. Any Edition printed *before 1570* is very rare, most of them were confiscated and burned.

Myles Coverdale and John Rogers, assistants to Tyndale, carried the project forward. The first complete English Bible was printed on October 4, 1535, and is known as the Coverdale Bible.

Considering this timeline, it seems questionable that the locals around the Gogmagog hills should have give such a name to their hills, or that it would have become commonly known to everyone, such that a decree could be published regarding them in less than 40 years after the availability of the Bible. Considering the fact that having or reading the Bible was a crime for most of those 40 years, it is not likely that the local people would have wanted to reveal their knowledge of the name in this way. One would also think that if ancient battle sites were subject to being renamed in this fashion after the release of the English Bible, many other ancient battle sites would have received Biblical names as well. But they didn't.

Even though there is no proof, it seems to be highly probable that the Gogmagog hills were called that *from more ancient times*.

There are two figures of the giants Gog and Magog that strike the hours on a clock at Dunstan-n-the West, Fleet Street, but few people in London seem to know why they are there. Adrian Gilbert writes in his book, *The New Jerusalem*:

> Once more we have to go back to Geoffrey of Monmouth's book, in which there is a story of how, when Brutus and his Trojans arrived in Britain, they found the island sparsely inhabited by *a race of giants*. One of these, called Gogmagog, wrestled with a Trojan hero called Corineus and was eventually thrown to his death from a cliff- top called in consequence 'Gogmagog's Leap'.

> In the 1811 translation into English of *Brut Tysilio*, a Welsh version of the chronicles translated by the Rev. Peter Roberts, there is a footnote suggesting that Gogmagog is a corrupted form of Cawr-Madog, meaning 'Madog the great' or 'Madog the giant' in Welsh. It would appear that with Gog of Magog, the name of a war leader who the Bible prophesies will lead an invasion of the Holy Land at the end of the age.

> In another version of the Gogmagog tale, the *Recuyell des histories de Troye*, Gog and Magog are two separate giants. In this story they are not killed but brought back as slaves by Brutus to his city of *New Troy*. Here they were to be employed as gatekeepers, opening and closing the great gates of the palace.

> The story of Gog and Magog, the paired giants who worked the gates of London, was very popular in the middle ages and effigies of them were placed on the city gates *at least as early as the reign of Henry VI*. These were destroyed in the Great Fire of 1666, but so popular were they that new ones were made in 1708 and installed at the Guildhall. This pair of statues was destroyed in 1940

during the Blitz, the third great fire of London, when the roof and much of the interior furnishings of the Guildhall were burnt. A new pair of the statues was carved to replace them when the Guildhall was repaired after the war.

We should note that the dates of Henry VI are from well before the English Bible was available. The above indicates the existence of the name of Gog Magog in England long before the Bible was available to anyone.

The prophecies of Ezekiel are said to date from sometime around 695-690 BCE, and we would like to consider the question as to where *he* heard the term "Gog, Magog" and what terrible battle was fought in the past that was used as a model for Ezekiel's prediction to which this name was attached?

GOGMAGOG, ARMAGEDDON AND THE TROJAN WAR

As it happens, there are three terms often associated with archetypal battles: Armageddon (Megiddo), Gog Magog, and the Trojan War.

Those of you who have read *Who Wrote the Bible* will recall that the untimely death of the hero—King Josiah—occurred in the valley of Megiddo and that was the end of the story. Note also that this tale is a doublet of the story of the death of King Ahab who was of "The House of David".

Megiddo also features in the story of the deaths of the *sons* of Ahab found in II Kings, chapter 9. This chapter chronicles the death of Jezebel as well. The reason I mention these odd little semi-mythical connections is because I am persuaded that careful examination of Biblical texts compared to many other sources, including hard scientific ones, can assist us in forming at least a vague picture of our true history and this may include the fact that some of the stories of the Old Testament are borrowed from the history of the Northern Peoples, mythicized, and then re-historicized with new names and genealogies added to create the Bible, the so-called "History of the Jews". Those stories did not come into existence in a vacuum and could not have been foisted on the people if there wasn't something in them that resonated with ancient memories handed down orally.

Another point: right away, we notice a homophonic similarity between Megiddo and Magog but is there any kind of connection between Gog, Magog, Troy and Britain? Do these three wars, Armageddon, Gog Magog, and Troy have anything in common that connects us to England?

Well, it's possible. Let's take a look at a startling theory.

WHERE TROY ONCE STOOD

The story of the Trojan War is, in Western Civilization, the greatest non-religious story ever told. It has haunted the western imagination for over three thousand years. "In Troy there lies the scene", Shakespeare said.

The story of Troy is at the bedrock of Western Culture from Homer to Virgil; from Chaucer to Shakespeare to Berlioz to Yeats. We talk about "Trojan

Horses" and "Achilles' Heels" and go on Odysseys and "work like Trojans" and on and on.

The tales of Achilles and Hector, Helen and Paris, and so many other great heroes all assembled into one story have lured a constant stream of pilgrims to the assumed region of Troy for all of that three thousand years; from Alexander the Great to Lord Byron to Heinrich Schliemann, the alleged discoverer of "Troy". The British queen is referred to as the seed of Priam, and it was the fantasy of the Nazis to become the new Achaians, comparing Hitler with Achilles.

Troy has come to stand for all cities because of one tragic event: the siege and destruction and death of all its heroes—all because of a woman. Herodotus tells us that the Trojan War is the root of the enmity between Europe and Asia.

Homer is the starting point of our search for Troy. The Iliad deals with one episode of the war, a few weeks in the tenth year; a small fragment of the vast cycle of stories that dealt with the Trojan War. In classical times a series of epics now only available in fragments, or lost completely, told the rest of the story, drawing on a long and venerable tradition.

The hold that the legend of Troy had on the Greek imagination was such that, based on the story of a violation of Athena's altar at Troy by Ajax of Lokris, the people of Lokris each year sent selected daughters to expiate this sin of their ancestor. They suffered indignities willingly, and it was said that the Trojans had the right to kill them. They lived out their days as slaves, in confinement and poverty. *This custom continued into the 1st century CE* as a testimony to the potency of the legend of Troy.

In the ancient world, it was uniformly believed that the Trojan War was a historical event. Anaxagoras was one of the few who doubted it because he said there was no proof. Herodotus, in the 5th century BCE, inquired of the Egyptian priests as to whether or not the Greek version of the story was true, that is, did they have an alternative record of it, since there were no written records before Homer committed it to writing. We will return to Herodotus' account from the Egyptians later.

Based on the work of Homer, around 400 BCE, Thucydides constructed a "history" of prehistoric Greece. No one knows how much of this was based on deductions from Homer, or derived from other sources that we no longer have. Thucydides wrote:

> We have no record of any action taken by Hellas as a whole before the Trojan War. Indeed, my view is that at this time the whole country was not even called Hellas. [...] The best evidence for this can be found in Homer, who, though he was born much later than the time of the Trojan War, nowhere uses the name "Hellenic" for the whole force.

Thucydides tried to deal with the problem of a story of a great clash of forces that seemed to be contradicted by the evidence of the small sites and relatively primitive nature of the region where Troy was supposed to be. He tells us that, as far as he knew, Mycenaea had always been a village without great importance, while Homer referred to it as a "town with broad streets":

> Many of the towns of that period do not seem to us today to be particularly im-
> posing: yet that is not good evidence for rejecting what the poets and what *gen-
> eral tradition* have to say about the size of the expedition [...] we have no right
> therefore to judge cities by their appearances rather than by their actual power
> and there is no reason whey we should not believe that the Trojan expedition
> was the greatest that ever took place.

So it was that, even in the 5th century BCE, Thucydides has commented on the fact that the only evidence for the Trojan War is the words of poets and "general tradition". The fact is, many present day scholars doubt the existence of a "Mycenaean empire" because the archaeological evidence simply does not support the claims of the story.

Yet, the detailed nature of the descriptions incorporated into the work of Homer suggests that the original works were composed by eye witnesses of a significant conflict. The question that plagues us is: where did that conflict actually take place?

The problem that faces the scholars is this: if you were to remove the place names and read the Iliad, you would *not* think that the writer was talking about the Mediterranean. The text talks about tides, salty, dark, misty seas and a climate of rain, fog and snow. The tall, long-haired warriors traveling overseas in "symmetrical" ships "eager to kill their enemies" remind us more of the Vikings than the Greeks of the classical era. Several of the commanders in the story had Viking-like honorific titles: "Sacker of Cities". It even seems that, since the Greeks themselves could hardly imagine the behavior of these people in the stories, they consigned them to a "heroic age" and some of them to semi-divinity. At the same time this was being done, perhaps the Hebrews were assimilating some of these stories to their own "history," adding genealogies and giving themselves a lineage that was totally fabricated.

The Greek text of the Iliad speaks of "ceaseless rains" in the Trojan plain. The adjective is "*athesphatos*" which means "what even god cannot measure". Such rains are certainly typical of the climate of Northern Europe, but most definitely not typical of Greece or the Mediterranean.

Iman J. Wilkens was intrigued by all of these problems as a schoolboy in Holland. He knew that he was reading a description of an environment much like his own, and not like that of the sunny south. He wondered: could the climate of the Mediterranean have changed so much since then? But even that wouldn't explain the *tides* or the fact that Homer had placed Troy near to Lesbos and the Hellespont, from which Crete and Egypt are just a *few days* voyage by boat. That, of course, raised a question about the Odyssey: how could Ulysses have possibly gotten so terribly lost in the Mediterranean where nearly everything is just a day or two sail away?

The experts answer that Homer's work was obviously just a fantasized version of a historical seed event.

We certainly know that the *written* versions of the Iliad and Odyssey originated in Greece, but do we know for sure that the oral version was about

Greece as we know it today?[343] When we consider the evidence of Lev Gu-milev, do we know that the people of Greece today are the people of Greece in the time of the Odyssey? Just as languages can be adopted, so can myths.

Thucydides noted certain anomalies in Homer's text that may give us a clue. He was surprised that Homer *never* used the word "barbarian" for foreigners or non-Greeks.

More than this, Thucydides remarks that barbarians were living in various parts of Greece and names the Taulentians "of the Illyrian race" living on the shores of the Ionian Gulf. From classical mythology, we know that a certain Galatea had three sons, Galas, Celtus and Illyrius, who founded the three major Celtic peoples: the Gauls, the Celts and the Illyrians. Professor Henry Hubert hypothesized that *the ancient Greeks had been in contact with Celtic culture through the intermediary of the Illyrians*, which seems to be confirmed by Thucydides' remark. What if, during this contact, they received the epics sung by the bards and began to give the place names in the stories to their own settlements? In the manner of mythicization that I have described in *The Secret History of the World*, the Greeks might then begin to believe that the Trojan War had been fought by their own ancestors against an overseas kingdom. One thing is clear from comparing the stories in the Bible to the Greek legends, those stories must have been quite popular everywhere in those days.

There is still another issue. Wilkens writes:

> Quite apart from the difficulty of fitting most places described in the Iliad and the Odyssey into the physical reality of the lands surrounding the Aegean Sea, there is also a problem with the *spiritual* content of Homer's works. Plato had doubts as to their Greek origin and the great philosopher was by no means an admirer of this imaginative poet whose gods, with their jealousies and vengeances, behaved like spoilt children. Plato was particularly worried about the corrupting influence of Homer's poems on the minds of Greek youth, above all because of their "lack of respect" for the gods. He suggested that certain passages of the Iliad and Odyssey should be corrected or even expurgated and if he had been the dictator of his "ideal state", he would have had them burned, thus breaking the chain of transmission of these unique and extremely ancient poems. […]

> Reading the text [of the Iliad and the Odyssey] with an atlas of Greece on one's knees, it is hard to understand the descriptions of many places, or the distances between places, or the sailing directions, or how it was possible to travel or drift in a boat with a head wind. In short, the place names in Greece, the pieces of the puzzle, seem completely jumbled. Once these names are sought in Western Europe, however—and about 90 percent of them can still be found there, far more than in Greece—all the pieces of the puzzle fall perfectly into place and the events described by Homer become entirely logical and comprehensible. […]

---

[343] The same question might be asked about the Bible and Israel and the Jews…

I am certainly not the first to have the impression that the Trojan War must have taken place in Western Europe. As early as 1790, Wernsdorf[344] thought that the stories about the Cimmerians, one of the peoples mentioned by Homer, were of Celtic origin. He had a very precise reason for this: the classical Greek author Aelian mentions them in connection with the "singing" swan, *Cygnus musicus*, which is found in the British Isles and northern Europe, whereas Greece and the rest of Southern Europe knew only the "silent" swan, *Cygnus olor*.

In 1804, M. H. Vosz believed that the Odyssey most probably described certain landscapes in the British Isles and, in 1806, C.J. de Grave arrived at the general conclusion that the historical and mythical background of Homer's works should be sought not in Greece but in western Europe. Towards the end of the nineteenth century, Th. Cailleux wrote that Odysseus adventures had taken place in the Atlantic, starting from Troy, which by a process of deduction he concluded to be near Cambridge in England.[345]

Near Cambridge in England? The Gogmagog hills?

In other words, Wilkens is proposing that there has been a transfer of western European geographical names to the eastern Mediterranean. He suggests that this occurred very late, about 1,000 BCE. My guess is that it began much earlier, after the collapse of the Bronze Age Civilization around 1600 BCE at the same time that another famous "love triangle" was changing history: Akhenaten and Nefertiti/Sarai and Abraham/Moses; we wonder if there is a connection?

With the exception of the Bible, no other works of western literature have been more studied and commented upon than the Iliad and the Odyssey. Considering the fact that the prophet Ezekiel knew the name of a place in England and wrote a description of a battle that certainly appears to be a very early assimilation to the story of Troy, perhaps the Bible and the Iliad have a lot more in common than one would ordinarily suppose? I would like to quote a couple of sections from my book, *The Secret History of The World,* to give us some additional clues:

STONEHENGE AND TROY

Gildas, writing in the sixth century CE, is the first native British writer whose works have come down to us. Nennius, writing about 200 years later, refers to "the traditions of our elders." And Geoffrey of Monmouth praises the works of Gildas and Bede and wonders at the lack of other works about the early kings of Britain saying:

> Yet the deeds of these men were such that they deserve to be praised for all time. What is more, these deeds were handed joyfully down in oral tradition,

---

[344] Gottlieb Wernsdorf, a professor at Dantzig, cited by J. J. Eschenburg in *Manual Of Classical Literature From The German Of J. J. Eschenburg* (Kessinger Publishing, LLC, June 23, 2005).
[345] Iman Wilkens, *Where Troy Once Stood* (Rider, 1990).

just as if they had been committed to writing, by many peoples who had only their memory to rely on.[346]

Perhaps there were other works about early kings of Britain: the Iliad and Odyssey?

In describing the fifty or so years preceding his account of Arthur, Geoffrey of Monmouth tells us about Vortigern and the arrival of the Saxons under the leadership of Hengest and Horsa. Present throughout these events is the presence of Merlin—the British equivalent of Hiram Abiff and Daedalus (the great architects of ancient times playing sidekick to Solomon and Minos respectively) combined. We are also reminded of the unification of Egypt by Narmer, also known as Menes, who also built a great temple to Ptah, who Herodotus and others say was Hephaestus, the volcano/fire god.

What we are interested in here is the fact that *Merlin was credited with building Stonehenge*. For some reason, based on the "oral tradition," Geoffrey of Monmouth connected the mysterious and legendary figure of Merlin to the *prehistoric* monument on the Salisbury plain. The question then is not about the accuracy of Geoffrey's history, but why he made this connection? Was it based on stories in the traditions that he had mentioned and considered to be reliable?

The Stonehenge story told by Geoffrey of Monmouth begins with *a treacherous massacre of the Britons* by Hengest and his Saxons, which took place at a peace conference. The Saxons hid their daggers in their shoes and, at a signal from their leader, drew them and killed all the assembled British nobles except the king. Geoffrey tells us that the meeting took place at the "Cloister of Ambrius, not far from Kaercaradduc, which is now called Salisbury." He later describes this as a monastery of three hundred brethren founded by Ambrius many years before.

As it happens, there is a place called Amesbury about two and a half miles east of Stonehenge, which was originally called Ambresbyrig. This site in no way matches the description of the *Cloister of Ambrius*. The cloister is described as situated on Mount Ambrius, whereas Amesbury is in the valley of the river Avon. Geoffrey tells us that the victims of the massacre were buried in the cemetery beside the monastery, not two and a half miles away. What is more, since it seems that Geoffrey was acting under the pressure of the mythical norm of assimilating current events to the archetype, we then are left free to consider the possibility that this was the site of an ancient and famous massacre and that Stonehenge and the Cloister of Ambrius are one and the same. More than that, we can consider the story of the betrayal at the peace conference to be quite similar to the idea of the "Trojan Horse".

The fact that Geoffrey called the place a "cloister" is a curious choice of words since a cloister is "a covered arcade forming part of a religious or *collegiate* establishment." Stonehenge could very easily have been a "covered cloister" when it was intact and in use. Geoffrey may also have been trying to

---

[346] Geoffrey of Monmouth, *The History of the Kings of Britain*, trans. Lewis Thorpe (1966), 1.

"Christianize" Stonehenge in his references to monastery and monks, though a combination of religion and collegialism was part of the Druidic tradition.

The Saxons gave Stonehenge the name by which we know it today. The Britons called it the *Giant's Dance*, and Geoffrey certainly had a tradition to draw on there if he had wanted to since he begins his history with the adventures of Brutus, a descendant of Aeneas, who, after much traveling and fighting, landed on Britain, which was uninhabited *except for a few giants*. Geoffrey had a reasonable context here in which to place Stonehenge, but he ignored it and instead attributed the building of Stonehenge *to Merlin after the dreadful massacre by the Saxons*. This enabled him to connect his Arthur to the great architect of the monument and all its glories. This suggests to us that there was a solid tradition behind this idea: that Stonehenge was the focal point of a people who had suffered a terrible, terminal disaster. In short, this tradition may reach back into the mists of antiquity.

As W. A. Cummins, geologist and archaeologist, remarks, Geoffrey's tale sounds like a pre-medieval tradition about Stonehenge, possibly even prehistoric, pointing out that Geoffrey was eight and a half centuries closer to the event than we are, so maybe his account is correspondingly closer?

Diodorus Siculus, writing in the first century BCE, gives us a description of Britain based, in part, on the account of the voyage of Pytheas of Massilia, who sailed around Britain in 300 BCE:

> As for the inhabitants, they are simple and far removed from the shrewdness and vice which characterize our day. Their way of living is modest, since they are well clear of the luxury that is begotten of wealth. The island is also thickly populated and its climate is extremely cold, as one would expect, since it actually lies under the Great Bear. It is held by many kings and potentates, who for the most part live at peace among themselves.[347]

Diodorus tells a fascinating story about an island, thought to be Britain, that was obviously of legendary character already when he was writing:

> Of those who have written about the ancient myths, Hecateus and certain others say that in the regions beyond the land of the Celts (Gaul) there lies in the ocean an island no smaller than Sicily. This island, the account continues, is situated in the north, and is inhabited by the Hyperboreans, who are called by that name because their home is beyond the point whence the north wind blows; and the land is both fertile and productive of every crop, and since it has an unusually temperate climate it produces two harvests each year.[348]

This reminds us of the passage in Ezekiel where he mentions the land of Magog in the same breath with "them that dwell *carelessly* in the isles…"

> 39:6 And I will send a fire on Magog, and among them that dwell carelessly in the *isles*…

---

[347] *Diodorus of Sicily*, trans. C. H. Oldfather, Loeb Classical Library, Volumes II and III (London: William Heinemann, and Cambridge, MA: Harvard University Press, 1935 and 1939).
[348] Diodorus, op. cit.

Why should people in the "isles of the gentiles" be described as living carelessly? Is that "carelessly" as in "without cares", or is it carelessly as in not taking sufficient care in some way that led to an incident in which such carelessness became a "marker" for these people? Perhaps a famous blunder of some sort? A peace conference that went terribly wrong? A "Trojan Horse" at the end of a protracted war? A war being fought as a volcano in the Mediterranean was about to erupt and change the climate of the planet for many years to come? A volcano that erupted at the same time that a strange drama including a "love triangle" was taking place in the land we now know as Egypt?

Now, it seems that there is little doubt that Diodorus is describing the same location, but we notice that the climate is so vastly different in the two descriptions that we can hardly make the connection. However, let us just suppose that his description of Britain was based on the climate that prevailed at the time he was writing, and the legendary description of the Hyperboreans was based *on a previous climatic condition* that was preserved in the story. Diodorus stresses that he is recounting something very ancient as he goes on to say:

> The Hyperboreans also have a language, we are informed, which is peculiar to them, and are most friendly disposed towards the Greeks, and especially towards the Athenians and the Delians, who have inherited this goodwill from *most ancient times*. The myth also relates that certain Greeks visited the Hyperboreans and left behind them costly votive offerings bearing inscriptions in Greek letters. And in the same way Abaris, a Hyperborean, came to Greece in ancient times and renewed the goodwill and kinship of his people to the Delians.[349]

Diodorus' remark about the relations between the Hyperboreans and the Athenians triggers in our minds the memory of the remarks of Plato about the war between the "Atlanteans" and the "Athenians" and we are brought back again to the idea of Troy and the mythicization of history. We wonder if the Hyperboreans are the original "Athenians" who may have fled the island at the time of the collapse of the Bronze Age at which time the climate all over the planet was affected. After all, the Greeks are said to be "Sons of the North Wind", Boreas. Herodotus expounds upon the relationship of the Hyperboreans to the Delians:

> Certain sacred offerings wrapped up in wheat straw come from the Hyperboreans into *Scythia*, whence they are taken over by the neighbouring peoples in succession until they get as far west as the Adriatic: from there they are sent south, and the first Greeks to receive them are the Dodonaeans. Then, continuing southward, they reach the Malian gulf, cross to Euboea, and are passed on from town to town as far as Carystus. Then they skip Andros, the Carystians take them to Tenos, and the Tenians to Delos. That is how these things are said to reach Delos at the present time.[350]

---

[349] Ibid.
[350] Herodotus, *The Histories, Book IV*, trans. Aubrey De Selincourt, revised John Marincola (London: Penguin, 1972), 226.

So, we have another connection to the Scythians. The legendary connection between the Hyperboreans and the Delians leads us to another interesting remark of Herodotus who tells us that Leto, the mother of Apollo, was born on the island of the Hyperboreans. That there was regular contact between the Greeks and the Hyperboreans over many centuries does not seem to be in doubt. The Hyperboreans were said to have *introduced the Greeks to the worship of Apollo*, but it is just as likely that the relationship goes much further back. Yes, this is contrary to the idea that culture flowed from south to north, but that's where the clues lead!

Herodotus mentions at another point, when discussing the lands of the "barbarians", "*All these except the Hyperboreans, were continually encroaching upon one another's territory*". Without putting words in Herodotus' mouth, it seems to suggest that the Hyperboreans were not warlike at all.

A further clue about the religion of the Hyperboreans comes from the myths of Orpheus. It is said that when Dionysus invaded Thrace, Orpheus "did not see fit to honor him but instead preached the evils of sacrificial murder to the men of Thrace". He taught "other sacred mysteries" having to do with Apollo, whom he believed to be the greatest of all gods. Dionysus became so enraged, he set the Maenads on Orpheus *at Apollo's temple* where Orpheus was a priest. They burst in, murdered their husbands who were assembled to hear Orpheus speak, tore Orpheus limb from limb, and threw his head into the river *Hebrus* where it floated downstream *still singing*. It was carried on the sea to the island of Lesbos. Another version of the story is that Zeus killed Orpheus with a thunderbolt for *divulging divine secrets*. He was responsible for instituting the Mysteries of Apollo in Thrace, Hecate in Aegina, and Subterrene Demeter at Sparta.[351] And this brings us to a further revelation of Diodorus regarding the Hyperboreans:

> And there is also on the island both a magnificent sacred precinct of Apollo and a notable temple, which is adorned with many votive offerings and is *spherical* in shape. Furthermore, a city is there which is sacred to this god, and the majority of its inhabitants are players on the cithara; and these *continually play on this instrument in the temple* and sing hymns of praise to the god, glorifying his deeds. [...]

> They say also that the moon, as viewed from this island, appears to be but a little distance from the earth and to have upon it prominences, like those of the earth, which are visible to the eye. The account is also given that the god visits the island every **nineteen years**, *the period in which the return of the stars to the same place in the heavens is accomplished,* and for this reason the Greeks call the nineteen-year period the "year of Meton". At the time of this appearance of the god he both plays on the cithara and dances continuously the night through from the vernal equinox until the rising of the Pleiades, expressing in this manner his delight in his successes. And the kings of this city and the supervisors of

---

[351] Robert Graves, *The Greek Myths* (London: Penguin, 1992).

the sacred precinct are called Boreades, since they are descendants of Boreas, and the succession to these positions is always *kept in their family*.[352]

When considering the idea of the god "dancing all night" in the round temple of the Hyperboreans, our mind naturally turns to that most remarkable of incidents in the Bible where David, the great harpist, danced before the Ark of the Covenant—in his underwear, no less![353]

I would like to note also how similar the above story of the Maenads murdering their husbands is to the story of the daughters of Danaus murdering their husbands—sons of Aegyptus—on the wedding night, and how similar both of these stories are to the story of the massacre at the Cloisters of Ambrius attributed still later to Hengist and Horsa. The story of the Maenads adds the spin that it was a religious dispute between sacrificers and those preaching against the evils of sacrifice. Additionally, it is interesting that in the stories of the daughters of Danaus and the Maenads, women have become as deadly as treacherous Helen was to Troy and certainly as deadly as Nefertiti apparently was to Egypt.

Was an original legend later adapted to a different usage, assimilated to a different group or tribe? More than once?

In fact, when you think about it, the stories in the Bible are remarkably similar to the Greek myths with most of the fantastic elements removed, names changed, and genealogies inserted to give the impression of a long history. One could say that the "history" of the Old Testament is merely "historicized myth". And of course, the myths that it was historicized from may have belonged to an entirely different people.

JOSEPHUS: APOLOGIST OR TRAITOR?

Now, let us come back and consider the story of the true history of the Exodus that was alleged to have been found in the tomb of King Tut. We know that the oldest extant Hebrew version of the Old Testament—the Torah and the Prophets and other books—dates only to about the time of the heyday of the Khazar kingdom. We even suspect that the Khazar revival of Judaism is mostly responsible for the texts we now know as the Torah. We know that Maimonides wrote at about the same time. We know that most of the so-called Jewish Talmud also emerged at this time, as well as the Kaballah and other alleged ancient "traditions".

Prior to that, we know that the writing of *some*—very few—of the books of the Bible that we know to have been extant prior to the tenth century CE were written down at about the same time that Homer is said to have written the Iliad and Odyssey. One can notice striking similarities between certain Greek myths and stories in the Bible.[354] Many people assume that this is because the

---

[352] Diodorus, op. cit.

[353] For an in-depth discussion of the Ark of the Covenant, see *The Secret History of The World*.

[354] Numerous examples are given in *The Secret History of the World*.

Greeks borrowed from the Jews. But what if it was the other way around? What if the Greek myths were "mythicized history" that was then taken and "historicized" and mixed in with actual chronicles that were otherwise not terribly exciting, and transformed into a "History of the Jews," complete with genealogies added to give it credibility?

One of our main sources of information about ancient Jewish history, outside of the Bible, is Josephus (c. 37 CE – c. 100 CE) who became known, in his capacity as a Roman citizen, as Flavius Josephus. Josephus was a first century Jewish historian and apologist of priestly and royal ancestry who survived and recorded the Destruction of Jerusalem in 70 CE. His works do give us important insights into first-century Judaism because that is when he lived. The question is: can we rely on him for Jewish history any further back than the Second Temple period (if that)?

Josephus was constantly writing contentious pieces claiming the extreme antiquity of the Jews and Jewish culture and trying to argue for its compatibility with cultured Graeco-Roman thought. Reading his works elicits the feeling that "he protests too much".

Josephus' twenty-one volume *Antiquities of the Jews* reads like a synopsis of the Old Testament. The fact is, the Old Testament could as easily have been written based on Josephus as vice versa! His claim was that various persons had asked him to give an account of Jewish culture, and—as noted—*Antiquities of the Jews* amounts to little more than the Bible stories woven around the many philosophical debates current in Rome at that time as well as repeated insistence on the "Antiquity of the Jews" as well as their "universal significance" to all people. It could be said that the whole "chosen people out of all the nations" shtick originated with Josephus. He claims that Abraham taught science to the Egyptians who in turn taught the Greeks; that Moses set up a senatorial priestly aristocracy which, like that of Rome, resisted monarchy. All the great figures of the Bible are presented as ideal philosophers and leaders.

PLATO ON ATLANTIS

Here we want to stop and consider the alternate claim that had existed since the time of Plato, that the "ancient Greeks" were the ones who taught science to the Egyptians.

Timaeus and *Critias*, written by Plato some time around 360 BCE are the only existing written records that specifically refer to Atlantis—a story of a great and terrible war. The dialogues are conversations between Socrates, Hermocrates, Timaeus, and Critias. Apparently in response to a prior talk by Socrates about ideal societies, Timaeus and Critias agree to entertain Socrates with a tale that is *"not a fiction but a true story"*.

The story is about the conflict between the ancient Athenians and the Atlanteans 9000 years before Plato's time. Knowledge of the ancient times was apparently forgotten by the Athenians of Plato's day, and the form the story of Atlantis took in Plato's account was that Egyptian priests conveyed it to Solon. Solon passed the tale to Dropides, the great-grandfather of Critias; Critias learned of it from his grandfather also named Critias, son of Dropides. Let's take a careful look at the main section of the story, [355] omitting the introduction that describes Solon going to Egypt and chatting up the priests:

> Thereupon one of the priests, who was of a very great age, said: O Solon, Solon, you Hellenes are never anything but children, and there is not an old man among you. Solon in return asked him what he meant. I mean to say, he replied, that in mind you are all young; there is no old opinion handed down among you by ancient tradition, nor any science, which is hoary with age. And I will tell you why.

> There have been, and will be again, many destructions of mankind arising out of many causes; the greatest have been brought about by the agencies of fire and water, and other lesser ones by innumerable other causes. There is a story, which even you have preserved, that once upon a time Phaeton, the son of Helios, having yoked the steeds in his father's chariot, because he was not able to drive them in the path of his father, burnt up all that was upon the earth, and was himself destroyed by a thunderbolt. Now this has the form of a myth, but really signifies *a declination of the bodies moving in the heavens around the earth*, and a great conflagration of things upon the earth, which recurs after long intervals; at such times those who live upon the mountains and in dry and lofty places are more liable to destruction than those who dwell by rivers or on the seashore. And from this calamity the Nile, who is our never-failing saviour, delivers and preserves us.

> When, on the other hand, the gods purge the earth with a deluge of water, the survivors in your country are herdsmen and shepherds who dwell on the mountains, but those who, like you, live in cities are carried by the rivers into the sea. Whereas in this land, neither then nor at any other time, does the water come down from above on the fields, having always a tendency to come up from below; for which reason the traditions preserved here are the most ancient. The fact is, that wherever the extremity of winter frost or of summer does not prevent, mankind exist, sometimes in greater, sometimes in lesser numbers. And whatever happened either in your country or in ours, or in any other region of which we are informed—if there were any actions noble or great or in any other way remarkable, they have all been written down by us of old, and are preserved in our temples.

We want to here make note of the fact that present day evidence suggests that—contrary to what the Egyptian priest above is saying—Egypt has been inundated and that it has—in the distant past—experienced a rainy climate. This leads us to question of whether or not this story being told by a real Egyptian priest of the Egypt we now know as Egypt? If it were about the Egypt we now know as Egypt, and if he had the knowledge of ancient Egypt that he is presented as having, then he would have known of the period of heavy rain and shallow seas in Egypt, by which the Sphinx and other monuments were eroded, and which deposited a layer of salt on the interior of the

---

[355] Plato, *Timaeus*, trans. Benjamin Jowett.

pyramids and other structures. And so we suggest, to reconcile this difficulty, not that the story is false, but rather that the dialogue is exactly as it is presented, but that the tellers of the story were fully aware that there was a more ancient Egypt that was not the Egypt of the pharaohs that we know as Egypt today and that this was even commonly known at the time.

> Whereas just when you and other nations are beginning to be provided with letters and the other requisites of civilized life, after the usual interval, the stream from heaven, like a pestilence, comes pouring down, and leaves only those of you who are destitute of letters and education; and so you have to begin all over again like children, and know nothing of what happened in ancient times, either among us or among yourselves. As for those genealogies of yours which you just now recounted to us, Solon, they are no better than the tales of children.

> In the first place you remember a single deluge only, but there were many previous ones; in the next place, you do not know that there formerly dwelt in your land the fairest and noblest race of men which ever lived, and that you and your whole city are descended from a small seed or remnant of them which survived. And this was unknown to you, because, for many generations, the survivors of that destruction died, leaving no written word. For there was a time, Solon, before the great deluge of all, when the city which now is Athens was first in war and in every way the best governed of all cities, is said to have performed the noblest deeds and to have had the fairest constitution of any of which tradition tells, under the face of heaven.

Again, let's interrupt the dialogue to point out that it is hardly likely that a priest of Egypt—as we know Egypt today—would have declared the Athenians to be "the fairest and noblest race of men," nor that they "performed the noblest deeds" and had the "fairest constitution [...] under the face of heaven"! This is completely contrary to what we know about the historical Egyptians. Is this another clue that the speaker is giving us that it is not a priest of the Egypt we now know as Egypt?

> Solon marveled at his words, and earnestly requested the priests to inform him exactly and in order about these former citizens. You are welcome to hear about them, Solon, said the priest, both for your own sake and for that of your city, and above all, for the sake of the goddess who is the common patron and parent and educator of both our cities. She founded your city a thousand years before ours, receiving from the Earth and Hephaestus the seed of your race, and afterwards she founded ours, of which the constitution is recorded in our sacred registers to be eight thousand years old.

Yet again, the Egyptian priest is giving *greater antiquity to the Greeks than to the Egyptians*! Another clue for the reader to understand that this is not an Egyptian story from Egypt as we know it today! Indeed, the worship of the goddess is the older form of worship in Egypt. But all of that came to an end, probably with the conquest of Narmer, the building of the temple to Hephaestus, the demoting of the goddess and the Moon calendar, and the instituting of the solar worship and the solar calendar of 365 days.[356]

> As touching your citizens of nine thousand years ago, I will briefly inform you of their laws and of their most famous action; the exact particulars of the whole we will hereafter go through at our leisure in the sacred registers themselves. If you compare these very laws with ours you will find that many of ours are the counterpart of yours as they were in the olden time.

Here, of course, we come to the idea that there was an ancient connection and communication between the true "old Egyptians" and the Northern peoples. Georges Gurdjieff once remarked that Christianity was taken from Egypt, a statement that might suggest that he agreed with the Pan-Egyptian school. But no: Christianity, he hastened to explain, was *not taken from the Egypt of history*, but from a "far older Egypt" which is unrecorded.[357]

> In the first place, there is the caste of priests, which is separated from all the others; next, there are the artificers, who ply their several crafts by themselves and do not intermix; and also there is the class of shepherds and of hunters, as well as that of husbandmen; and you will observe, too, that the warriors in Egypt are distinct from all the other classes, and are commanded by the law to devote themselves solely to military pursuits; moreover, the weapons which they carry are shields and spears, a style of equipment which the goddess taught of Asiatics first to us, as in your part of the world first to you.

The "classes" that are described here are very close to what are known from the most ancient of times as the Aryan class system that was imposed on India after the Aryan invasions about 1500 BCE, and continues to be a powerful influence in Indian society.

The remark that the right function of society was "first taught to the Asiatics" is most interesting. The reference to "Asiatics" in this context from an historical "Egyptian Priest" is extremely questionable because Asiatics were referred to by the real Egyptian priest, Manetho, as "vile". Nevertheless, even in historical times, it is indeed true that the Egyptians borrowed their military equipment and war strategies from the Asiatics, the Hyksos. The issue of who the "vile Asiatics" were is an ongoing debate, but it seems to devolve on such as the Hittites, Hyksos, and other Indo-European tribes that came down from the Steppes in various waves.

> Then as to wisdom, do you observe how our law from the very first made a study of the whole order of things, extending even to prophecy and medicine which gives health, out of these divine elements deriving what was needful for human life, and adding every sort of knowledge which was akin to them. All this order and arrangement the goddess first imparted to you when establishing your city; and *she chose the spot of earth in which you were born,* because she saw that the happy temperament of the seasons in that land would produce the wisest of men. Wherefore the goddess, who was a lover both of war and of wis-

---

[356] Which event may have been merely another of the cyclic events assimilated to an even earlier archetype.
[357] Geoffrey Ashe, *The Ancient Wisdom* (London: Sphere, 1979), 8-9.

dom, *selected and first of all settled that spot which was the most likely to produce men likest herself.* And there you dwelt, having such laws as these and still
better ones, and excelled all mankind in all virtue, as became the children and
disciples of the gods.

Again and again, this very strange "Egyptian" priest is saying things that
completely contradict the more "historical" Egyptian view that they are the
most "ancient and noble race". In the above remarks, he has said that the goddess imparted to the Greeks first all of the laws of health and those things
needed to preserve and prolong life. The Greeks are pronounced to have been
the "wisest of men", and those "most like the goddess" herself. And again
"excelled all mankind in all virtue", which is not very likely to have been
said by an Egyptian priest.

We are going to skip the part of the text that deals with Atlantis as a great
empire that came from across the Atlantic Ocean to make war against the
ancient Egyptians and Greeks and how the Greeks stood against them and
defeated them. Now is neither the time nor place to discuss whether or not
such an empire existed 9000 years before the time of Plato.[358] What we are
interested in is the idea that was being discussed as though it were common
knowledge, that there was a place called "Egypt" that is not what we currently know as Egypt. We are also interested in this story in relation to the
events surrounding the collapse of the Bronze Age which has been definitively linked to the eruption of the Volcano Thera on the island of Santorini.
It is highly likely that a great culture existed in Western Europe prior to the
collapse of the Bronze Age and that the freezing temperatures that fell upon
the earth after the eruption of Thera drove all these peoples East into Asia
and South, into the Mediterranean areas, bringing their stories and culture
and the names of their countries and cities with them. The idea that all of this
occurred either as a great war was in progress, or just after is suggested in the
text by Plato:

> But afterwards there occurred violent earthquakes and floods; and in a single
> day and night of misfortune all your warlike men in a body sank into the earth,
> and the island of Atlantis in like manner disappeared in the depths of the sea.
> For which reason the sea in those parts is impassable and impenetrable, because
> there is a shoal of mud in the way; and this was caused by the subsidence of the
> island.

Again, whether or not there was such an event 9,000 years before Plato and
a later event, or whether the eruption of Thera was mythicized to a time 9,000
years before Plato, does not concern us here. What we are concerned with is
the possible oral tradition of the Trojan War fought near the Gogmagog hills
in Britain:

> I have told you briefly, Socrates, what the aged Critias heard from Solon and re-
> lated to us. And when you were speaking yesterday about your city and citizens,
> the tale which I have just been repeating to you came into my mind, and I re-

---

[358] This is discussed at some length in *The Secret History of the World.*

marked with astonishment how, by some mysterious coincidence, you agreed in almost every particular with the narrative of Solon; but I did not like to speak at the moment. For a long time had elapsed, and I had forgotten too much; I thought that I must first of all run over the narrative in my own mind, and then I would speak.

Here we find another interesting clue. Critias has just told us that Socrates was discussing the very things that are included in this story—that everything Socrates had been saying the previous day "agreed in almost every particular with the narrative of Solon". Apparently, this story had been handed down via another line of transmission.

And so I readily assented to your request yesterday, considering that in all such cases the chief difficulty is *to find a tale suitable to our purpose*, and that with such a tale we should be fairly well provided. And therefore, as Hermocrates has told you, on my way home yesterday I at once communicated the tale to my companions as I remembered it; and after I left them, during the night by thinking I recovered nearly the whole it. Truly, as is often said, the lessons of our childhood make wonderful impression on our memories; for I am not sure that I could remember all the discourse of yesterday, but I should be much surprised if I forgot any of these things which I have heard very long ago. I listened at the time with childlike interest to the old man's narrative; he was very ready to teach me, and I asked him again and again to repeat his words, so that like an indelible picture they were branded into my mind.

As soon as the day broke, I rehearsed them as he spoke them to my companions, that they, as well as myself, might have something to say. And now, Socrates, to make an end my preface, I am ready to tell you the whole tale. I will give you not only the general heads, but the particulars, as they were told to me.

The city and citizens, which you yesterday described to us in fiction, *we will now transfer to the world of reality*. It shall be the ancient city of Athens, and we will suppose that the citizens whom you imagined, were our veritable ancestors, of whom the priest spoke; they will perfectly harmonise, and there will be no inconsistency in saying that the citizens of your republic are these ancient Athenians. Let us divide the subject among us, and all endeavour according to our ability gracefully to *execute the task which you have imposed upon us*. Consider then, Socrates, if this narrative is suited to the purpose, or whether we should seek for some other instead.[359]

And we come to the final understanding that conveys to us the secret of the story of Atlantis: that it did not actually come from an Egyptian priest of the Egypt we know today, but that this was a story that was created to "execute the task which you [Socrates] have imposed upon us", *which was to veil in fiction something that was Truth*. Does this mean that they were "making it up"? No, indeed. It means that they were attempting to find a vehicle for the history that would insure its preservation.

In any event, this dialogue was quite familiar in the time of Josephus who then decided to claim an antiquity and role for the Jews that simply has never been supported in the archaeological record, and considering the nature of

---

[359] Plato, op. cit.

Josephus himself, it is altogether likely that he created his fiction to give himself status.

Josephus was a contradiction. He presented himself as a devout Jew; his people as civilized, devout and philosophical, but he was never able to justify his own actions during the Jewish war. Many have asked the question why, for example, he did not commit suicide in Galilee in 67 CE with his compatriots; why, after his capture, he cooperated with the Roman invaders?

Many have viewed Josephus as a traitor and informer, and this has led to questions about his credibility as a historian. I think we all have encountered people like Josephus: cowards and traitors due to weakness and not necessarily meanness. And ever afterward, they try to "make it up" to those they know they have betrayed as well as to justify themselves. So, I think we can accept his descriptions of customs and certain ordinary matters, but we most definitely must be aware that anything he wrote about Jewish history or the events of the Jewish War are undoubtedly subjected to that particular spin of the guilty trying to make amends and trying to "buy their way" into being accepted, not only by those they have betrayed, but by those they betrayed them to who certainly know that anyone who betrays his own will betray everyone.

Against Apion

Josephus' work *Against Apion* is another two-volume methinks-he-protests-too-much defense of Judaism as a classical religion and philosophy, again stressing the antiquity of Judaism against what Josephus claimed was the relatively more recent traditions of the Greeks. Some anti-Judean allegations ascribed by Josephus to the Greek writer Apion, and stories about the "truth of the Exodus" accredited to Manetho, are quoted and denied as false.

Well, at this point, considering the fact that the Truth about the Exodus that was buried with King Tut was so damaging to the claims of the Jews to Israel that it was suppressed despite its enormous historical significance, I think we can figure out that Josephus' claims were more along the line of propaganda and apologia than truth. What's more, we are now more interested than ever to learn that Manetho said that the early "history of the Jews" was essentially false, that the Jews who came to Egypt were part of the 'Hyksos', a word meaning *foreign rulers* and who were an ethnically mixed group of Southwest Asiatic people who appear to have invaded the eastern Nile Delta and ruled lower and middle Egypt for about one hundred years. Manetho identifies the expulsion of the Jews both with the Hyksos and with the expulsion of a group of *Asiatic lepers*. Josephus states:

> These and the like accounts are written by Manetho. But I will demonstrate that
> he trifles, and tells arrant lies, after I have made a distinction which will relate to
> what I am going to say about him; for this Manetho had granted and confessed
> that this nation was not originally Egyptian, but that they had come from another country, and subdued Egypt, and then went away again out of it. But that

those Egyptians who were thus diseased in their bodies were not mingled with us afterward, and that Moses who brought the people out was not one of that company, but lived many generations earlier, I shall endeavor to demonstrate from Manetho's own accounts themselves.

Certainly, what interests us is that Josephus says that this story of the origins of the Jews was "what the Egyptians relate about the Jews."

It has been fairly simple for modern scholars to argue that perhaps Manetho didn't know what he was talking about because he lived so many years after the times of the histories he was recounting. And so, there is a strong tendency—especially amongst religious scholars—to take Josephus as the more authoritative source regarding the Jews, at least. However, it strikes me that if the papyri that were found in the tomb of King Tut confirm—even in part—what Manetho has said, then Josephus is soundly refuted along with everything else he writes about the "antiquities of the Jews".

THE TESTIMONY OF TACITUS

Tacitus wrote at the end of the first century and beginning of the second century CE. His concise style made his histories required reading from the 16th to the middle of the 19th century, and his influence can be detected in the works of Francis Bacon. Tacitus wrote for an educated audience, and thus his works reflect the prejudices of educated men of his time. We can discern from his writings that he lived in an era where the educated elite were rational and had a strong aversion to religious fanaticism of any kind. And so, it can be inferred that Tacitus' passage on the Hebrews is not so much a denunciation of religious zealots, but rather it is intended as a lesson on the evils of religious excesses. In our own day and time, particularly after September 11, 2001, we can see the dangers of religious fanaticism and delusion. Tacitus presents the various theories about the origins of the Jews that were commonly discussed in his time—obviously including Josephus—and he does not claim any one of them to be superior to the other, so his testimony is extremely valuable as to what ideas had been passed down.

> The Jews are said to have been refugees from the island of Crete who settled in the remotest corner of Libya in the days when, according to the story, Saturn was driven from his throne by the aggression of Jupiter.[360] This is a deduction from the name 'Judaei' by which they became known: the word is to be regarded as a barbarous lengthening of 'Idaei', the name of the people dwelling around the famous Mount Ida in Crete.

> A few authorities hold that in the reign of Isis[361] the surplus population of Egypt was evacuated to neighbouring lands under the leadership of Hierosolymus and Judas.

---

[360] This may refer to astronomical dating and the eruption of Thera.
[361] Probably a reference to astronomical dating.

Many assure us that the Jews are descended from those Ethiopians who were driven by fear and hatred to emigrate from their home country when Cepheus was king.[362]

There are some who say that a motley collection of landless Assyrians occupied a part of Egypt, and then built cities of their own, inhabiting the lands of the Hebrews and the nearer parts of Syria.

Others again find a famous ancestry for the Jews in the Solymi who are mentioned with respect in the epics of Homer: this tribe is supposed to have founded Jerusalem and named it after themselves.

Most authorities, however, *agree* on the following account. The whole of Egypt was once plagued by a wasting disease which caused *bodily disfigurement.* So Pharaoh Bocchoris went to the oracle of Hammon to ask for a cure, and was told to purify his kingdom by expelling the victims to other lands, as they lay under a divine curse. Thus a multitude of sufferers was rounded up, herded together, and abandoned in the wilderness. Here the exiles tearfully resigned themselves to their fate. But one of them, who was called Moses, urged his companions not to wait passively for help from god or man, for both had deserted them: they should trust to their own initiative and to whatever guidance first helped them to extricate themselves from their present plight.

They agreed, and started off at random into the unknown. But exhaustion set in, chiefly through lack of water, and the level plain was already strewn with the bodies of those who had collapsed and were at their last gasp when a herd of wild asses left their pasture and made for the shade of a wooded crag. Moses followed them and was able to bring to light a number of abundant channels of water whose presence he had deduced from a grassy patch of ground. This relieved their thirst. They travelled on for six days without a break, and on the seventh they expelled the previous inhabitants of Canaan, took over their lands and in them built a holy city and temple.

In order to secure the allegiance of his people in the future, Moses prescribed for them a novel religion quite different from those of the rest of mankind.

Among the Jews all things are profane that we hold sacred; on the other hand they regard as permissible what seems to us immoral.

In the innermost part of the Temple, they consecrated an image of the animal which had delivered them from their wandering and thirst, choosing a ram as beast of sacrifice to demonstrate, so it seems, their contempt for Hammon. The bull is also offered up, because the Egyptians worship it as Apis.

They avoid eating pork in memory of their tribulations, as they themselves were once infected with the disease to which this creature is subject.

They still fast frequently as an admission of the hunger they once endured so long, and to symbolize their hurried meal the bread eaten by the Jews is unleavened. We are told that the seventh day was set aside for rest because this marked the end of their toils.

In course of time the seductions of idleness made them devote every seventh year to indolence as well. Others say that this is a mark of respect to Saturn, either because they owe the basic principles of their religion to the Idaei, who, we

---

[362] Another astronomical date?

are told, were expelled in the company of Saturn and became the founders of the Jewish race, or because, among the seven stars that rule mankind, the one that describes the highest orbit and exerts the greatest influence is Saturn. A further argument is that most of the heavenly bodies complete their path and revolutions in multiples of seven.

Whatever their origin, these observances are sanctioned by their antiquity.[363]

The other practices of the Jews are sinister and revolting, and have entrenched themselves by their very wickedness. Wretches of the most abandoned kind who had no use for the religion of their fathers took to contributing dues and free-will offerings to swell the Jewish exchequer; and other reasons for their increasing wealth may be found in their stubborn loyalty and ready benevolence towards brother Jews. But the rest of the world they confront with the hatred reserved for enemies.

They will not feed or inter-marry with gentiles. Though a most lascivious people, the Jews avoid sexual intercourse with women of alien race. Among themselves nothing is barred.

They have introduced the practice of circumcision to show that they are different from others. Proselytes to Jewry adopt the same practices, and the very first lesson they learn is to despise the gods, shed all feelings of patriotism, and consider parents, children and brothers as readily expendable.

However, the Jews see to it that their numbers increase. It is a deadly sin to kill a born or unborn child, and they think that eternal life is granted to those who die in battle or execution — hence their eagerness to have children, and their contempt for death. Rather than cremate their dead, they prefer to bury them in imitation of the Egyptian fashion, and they have the same concern and beliefs about the world below. But their conception of heavenly things is quite different.

The Egyptians worship a variety of animals and half-human, half-bestial forms, whereas the Jewish religion is a purely spiritual monotheism. They hold it to be impious to make idols of perishable materials in the likeness of man: for them, the Most High and Eternal cannot be portrayed by human hands and will never pass away. For this reason they erect no images in their cities, still less in their temple. Their kings are not so flattered, the Roman emperors not so honoured. However, their priests used to perform their chants to the flute and drums, crowned with ivy, and a golden vine was discovered in the Temple; and this has led some to imagine that the god thus worshipped was Prince Liber, the conqueror of the East. But the two cults are diametrically opposed. Liber founded a festive and happy cult: the Jewish belief is paradoxical and degraded. [...]

While the Assyrian, Median and Persian Empires dominated the East, the Jews were slaves regarded as the lowest of the low. In the Hellenistic period, King Antiochus made an effort to get rid of their primitive cult and Hellenize them, but his would-be reform of this degraded nation was foiled by the outbreak of war with Parthia, for this was the moment of Arsaces' insurrection.

Then, since the Hellenistic rulers were weak and the Parthians had not yet developed into a great power (Rome, too, was still far away), the Jews established a dynasty of their own. These kings were expelled by the fickle mob, but regained control by force, setting up a reign of terror which embraced, among

---

[363] This comment strongly suggests that Tacitus was familiar with Josephus.

other typical acts of despotism, the banishment of fellow-citizens, the destruction of cities, and the murder of brothers, wives and parents. The kings encouraged the superstitious Jewish religion, for they assumed the office of High Priest in order to buttress their regime.

It seems pretty clear that something truly shameful and totally contradictory to the accepted story of the origins of the Jews occurred back then, and we guess that whatever it was, the true story may very well have been buried with Tutankhamun and then concealed again over 3500 years later.

WHO'S ON FIRST?

Now, let's take another look at something that Josephus wrote concerning the Judaism of his time:

> At this time there were *three sects among the Jews*, who had different opinions concerning human actions; the one was called the sect of the Pharisees, another, the sect of the Sadducees, and the other the sect of the Essens.
>
> Now for the Pharisees, they say that some actions, but not all, are the work of fate, and some of them are in our own power, and that they are liable to fate, but are not caused by fate.
>
> But the sect of the Essens affirm, that fate governs all things, and that nothing befalls men but what is according to its determination.
>
> And for the Sadducees, they take away fate, and say there is no such thing, and that the events of human affairs are not at its disposal; but they suppose that all our actions are in our own power, so that we are ourselves the causes of what is good, and receive what is evil from our own folly. [...]
>
> What I would now explain is this, that the Pharisees have delivered to the people a great many observances by succession from *their fathers*, which *are not written in the laws of Moses*; and for that reason it is that the Sadducees reject them, and say that we are to esteem those observances to be obligatory which are in the written word, but are not to observe what are derived from the tradition of our forefathers. And concerning these things it is that *great disputes and differences have arisen among them*, while the Sadducees are able to persuade none but the rich, and have not the populace obsequious to them, but *the Pharisees have the multitude on their side*. But about these two sects, and that of the Essenes, I have treated accurately in the second book of Jewish affairs. [...]
>
> However, this prosperous state of affairs moved the Jews to envy Hyrcanus; but they that were the worst disposed to him were the Pharisees, who were *one of the sects of the Judeans*, as we have informed you already. These have so great a power over the multitude, that when they say any thing against the king, or against the high priest, they are presently believed. Now Hyrcanus was a disciple of theirs, and greatly beloved by them. [...] [364]

And so we come to the idea that the Mishnah, a work by Tannaitic Rabbis under the leadership of Rabbi Judah Hanasi produced about 210 CE, must have been influenced by the pharisaic rabbis who, as Josephus reports, "have

---

[364] Josephus, *Antiquities of the Jews*, trans. William Whiston (Nelson Reference & Electronic Publishing, 30 Aug 2004).

delivered to the people a great many observances by succession from *their fathers*, which *are not written in the laws of Moses."*

We know that most of the Talmud—that which offends so many people—was completed about 500 CE. It is a collection of the discussions and decisions of the Rabbis from about 300 to 500 CE. These discussions were an elaboration and clarification of the laws of the Mishnah, which formed the basis of Talmudic debates.

We know from the evidence cited above that the Judaism of the Talmud that existed before the 9th century, after the conversion of the Khazars and the influence they brought to bear on it, changed again with the addition of the ideas of a "Jewish Kingdom on Earth" that necessitated the re-taking of Jerusalem.

We would like to add that this brief highlighting of the evolution of Judaism (or devolution, depending on how you look at it) is not a phenomenon exclusive to that faith. The same processes can be seen in both Christianity and Islam.

The point is, the idea of Jews as a nation or even as an ethnic group that should be "exclusive" does not seem to be original to the faith of the peoples of the short-lived state of ancient Israel.

As can be easily discerned, *the peoples who lived in what was then called Judea were from many different origins and nationalities and if there was an Exodus, it was the result of the eruption of the volcano Thera on the island of Santorini approximately 1600 BCE, an event which brought the Bronze Age civilization to its knees.*

Later, during the time of Josephus, Judea still was not strictly a "Jewish" state. The population again consisted of a hodge-podge of peoples and cultures. More than that, not all of the Israelites even lived according to the "ways of the Israelites" at any point in history. For example, in Josephus' time, many Jews were quite Hellenized, witness the apostle Paul.

One thing that is abundantly clear is that none of these peoples, once Jerusalem had been destroyed (apparently due mainly to Jewish rabble rousing as had been the case prior to the Babylonian invasion), had any idea that some great religious state had come to an end and that they should harbour hopes of its recreation in the future. That is purely and simply an evolution of thought produced by the Khazarian influence.

The Khazar people belonged to a grouping of Turks who wrote in a runic script that originated in Mongolia. The royalty of the Khazar kingdom was descended from the Ashina Turkic dynasty. In the ninth century, the Khazarian royalty and nobility as well as a significant portion of the Khazarian Turkic population embraced the Jewish religion. After their conversion, the Khazars were ruled by a succession of Jewish kings and began to adopt the hallmarks of Jewish civilization, including the Torah and Talmud, the Hebrew script, and the observance of Jewish holidays. A portion of the empire's population adopted Christianity and Islam.[365]

When the Khazarian Empire came under threat from hostile powers, *many* of them migrated deeper into Europe carrying the religion of Judaism with them into Hungary, Ukraine, and other areas of Europe.

Therefore it is evident that modern European Jews, while they practice a 1st century religion of the Pharisees which was established as Rabbinical Judaism after 70 CE, *have no connection whatsoever to the peoples who formerly occupied the area known as Palestine, given to "the Jews" by illegal acts of Britain, and turned into Israel.* They are, by definitions of the very Torah they claim to hold sacred, Gentiles. By the standards of the Essenes, who may very well be the followers of an ancient type of Judaism, the current day Jews aren't even Jews.

Furthermore, Judaism is a religious system, not a nationality or a race or even an ethnicity. The modern state of Israel came into being via imperial colonialism and genocide that continues to this very day.

So one should ask themselves if they are Jewish and practice Judaism: "Am I Jewish because I am Judean or Israelite by origin, or am I Jewish by being a descendant of a convert to the religion?" And if being Jewish today really is all about nationality, then why is it that anyone of any nation can convert to Judaism and become a Jew and Jewish?

And so, in the end, we discover that in the truest sense, anti-Semitism could be defined as "against Aryan/Indo-Europeans". Of course, if it is true that Abraham was a Hittite, then it could be said that the "Patriarch of the Jews" was truly a Semite, but the tribes who were assimilated to Judaism in those days were not, judging by the paternal affinity between the Sephardic Jews and the Palestinians.

As Koestler remarks, this history reduces the term "anti-Semitism" to meaningless jargon based on a misapprehension shared by both the Nazi killers and their victims.

It also reduces the Israeli-Palestinian conflict to the most meaningless and tragic **hoax** *which history has ever perpetrated.*

The Exodus was not the event claimed in the Bible, and the very thin justification for the Jewish claim to Palestine, that it had been given to them by their god, is as much of a complete fabrication as the rest of "the history of Israel".

Norman Finkelstein, in his book *Beyond Chutzpah*, brings us full circle to the Balfour Agreement:

> Another sort of justification conjured away the injustice inflicted on the indigenous population with the pretense that Palestine was (nearly) vacant before the Jews came. Ironically, this argument has proven to be the most compelling

---

[365] Kevin Alan Brook, *The Jews of Khazaria* (Jason Aronson Publishers, 1999).

proof of the injustice committed: it is a back-handed admission that, had Palestine been inhabited, which it plainly was, the Zionist enterprise was morally indefensible. Those admitting to the reality of a Palestinian presence yet functioning outside the ideological ambit of Zionism couldn't adduce any justification for Zionism except a racist one: that is, in the great scheme of things, the fate of Jews was simply more important than that of Arabs. If not publicly, at any rate privately, this is how the British rationalized the Balfour Declaration. For Balfour himself, "we deliberately and rightly decline to accept the principle of self-determination" for the "present inhabitants" of Palestine, because "the question of the Jews outside Palestine [is] one of world importance" and Zionism was "rooted in age-long traditions, in present needs, in future hopes, of a far profounder import than the desires and prejudices of the 700,000 Arabs who now inhabit that ancient land."[366]

At the time, British Cabinet Minster, Herbert Samuel, recognized that denying the Arabs majority rule was "in flat contradiction to one of the main purposes for which the Allies were fighting", but he then turned around and bought into the smokescreen belief propagated by religion, to wit "the anterior Jewish presence in Palestine [...] had resulted in events of spiritual and cultural value to mankind in striking contrast with the barren record of the last thousand years."

Winston Churchill testified before the Peel Commission saying that the indigenous population of Arabs had no more right to Palestine than a "dog in a manger has the final right to the manger, even though he may have lain there for a very long time". He further opined that "no wrong has been done to these people by the fact that a stronger race, a higher grade race, or at any rate, a more worldly-wise race, to put it that way, has come in and taken their place".

Finkelstein speaks of a fundamental paradox he ran across while writing his book:

> In the course of preparing the chapters of this book devoted to Israel's human rights record in the Occupied Territories, I went through literally thousands of pages of human rights reports, published by multiple, fiercely independent, and highly professional organizations—Amnesty International, Human Rights Watch, B'Tselem (Israeli Information Center for Human Rights in the Occupied Territories), Public Committee Against Torture in Israel, Physicians for Human Rights – Israel—each fielding its own autonomous staff of monitors and investigators.

> Except on one minor matter, I didn't come across a single point of law or fact on which these human rights organizations differed.

> In the case of Israel's human rights record, one can speak today not just of a broad consensus—as on historical questions—but of an *unqualified* consensus. All these organizations agreed, for example, that Palestinian detainees have been sytematically ill treated and tortured, the total number now probably reaching the tens of thousands.

---

[366] Norman G. Finkelstein, *Beyond Chutzpah* (London : Verso, 2005), 9.

Yet if, as I've suggested, broad agreement has been reached on the *factual* record, an obvious anomaly arises: what accounts for the impassioned controversy
that still swirls around the Israel-Palestine conflict? To my mind, explaining this
apparent paradox requires, first of all, that a fundamental distinction be made
between those controversies that are real and those that are contrived. To illustrate real differences of opinion, let us consider again the Palestinian refugee
question.

It is possible for interested parties to agree on the facts yet come to diametrically
opposed moral, legal, and political conclusions. Thus, as already mentioned, the
scholarly consensus is that Palestinians were ethnically cleansed in 1948.

Israel's leading historian on the topic, Benny Morris, although having done
more than anyone else to clarify exactly what happened, nonetheless concludes
that, morally, it was a good thing—just as, in his view, the "annihilation" of Native Americans was a good thing—that, legally, Palestinians have no right to return to their homes, and that, politically, Israel's big error in 1948 was that it
hadn't "carried out a large expulsion and cleansed the whole country—the
whole Land of Israel, as far as the Jordan" of Palestinians.

However repellant morally, these clearly can't be called *false* conclusions.

Returning to the universe inhabited by normal human beings, it's possible for
people to concur on the facts as well as on their moral and legal implications,
yet still reach divergent *political* conclusions.

Noam Chomsky agrees that, factually, Palestinians were expelled; that, morally,
this was a major crime; and that, legally, Palestinians have a right of return. Yet,
politically, he concludes that implementation of this right is infeasible and
pressing it inexpedient, indeed, that dangling this (in his view) illusory hope before Palestinian refugees is deeply immoral.

There are those, contrariwise, who maintain that a moral and legal right is
meaningless unless it can be exercised and that implementing the right of return
is a practical possibility.

For our purposes, the point is not who's right and who's wrong but that, even
among honest and decent people, there can be a real and legitimate differences
of political judgment.

This having been said, however, it bears emphasis that—at any rate, among
those sharing ordinary moral values—the range of political disagreement is
quite narrow, while the range of agreement quite broad.[367]

The paradox noted by Finkelstein is, in our opinion, a question of *conscience*.

The blatant disregard for the lives of hundreds of thousands of Palestinians
is a reality that we continue to live with today. We might ask ourselves what
it is about a person that makes them impervious to the pain and suffering of
another. Certainly we see such an attitude among the Zionists. We also see it
in the British, and, today, in the leaders of the United States of America. We
also see a disturbing pattern emerging in the relations between these groups,
as well as the leaders of other countries, who promote the hoax of the god-
given Israel. Somewhere, the moral compass of these people appears to break
down. Or perhaps, we can ask, if there is a moral compass at all?

---

[367] Finkelstein, 5-6.

The question remains, then, who is perpetrating this hoax? Is there a link between such a monstrous hoax and an inability to feel another's suffering, to act on true conscience? The answer, addressed in the next section, will lead us out of the labyrinth.

Out Of The Labyrinth

Political Ponerology

A science on the nature of evil adjusted for political purposes[368]

Ponerology: *n.* division of theology dealing with evil; theological doctrine of
wickedness or evil; from the Greek: *poneros* – evil.

WHAT is evil? Historically, the question of evil has been a theological one.
Generations of theological apologists have written entire libraries of books in
an attempt to certify the existence of a Good God that created an imperfect
world. Saint Augustine distinguished between two forms of evil: "moral
evil", the evil humans do, by choice, knowing that they are doing wrong; and
"natural evil", the bad things that just happen—the storm, the flood, volcanic
eruptions, fatal disease.

And then, there is what clinical psychologist, Andrew Lobaczewski, calls
Macrosocial Evil: large scale evil that overtakes whole societies and nations,
and has done so again and again since time immemorial.

The history of mankind, when considered objectively, is a terrible thing.
Death and destruction come to all, both rich and poor, free and slave, young
and old, good and evil, with an arbitrariness and insouciance that, when con-
templated even momentarily, can destroy a normal person's ability to function.

Over and over again, man has seen his fields and cattle laid waste by
drought and disease, his loved ones tormented and decimated by illness or
human cruelty, his life's work reduced to nothing in an instant by events over
which he has no control at all.

The study of history through its various disciplines offers a view of mankind that is almost insupportable. The rapacious movements of hungry tribes,
invading and conquering and destroying in the darkness of prehistory; the
barbarian invaders of the civilized world during medieval times, the bloodbaths of the crusades of Catholic Europe against the infidels of the Middle
East and then the "infidels" who were their own brothers: the stalking noon-
day terror of the Inquisition where martyrs quenched the flames with their
blood. Then, there is the raging holocaust of modern genocide; wars, famine,

---

[368] A discussion based on the work of Andrzej Lobaczewski, Ph.D, now published as *Political
Ponerology* (Red Pill Press, 2006).

and pestilence striding across the globe in hundred league boots; and never more frightening than today.

All of these things produce an intolerable sense of indefensibility against what Mircea Eliade calls the Terror of History.

There are those who will say that *now* this is all past; mankind has entered a new phase; science and technology have brought us to the brink of ending all this suffering. Many people believe that man is evolving; society is evolving; and that we now have control over the arbitrary evil of our environment—or at least we will have it after George Bush and his neocons have about 25 years to fight the Endless War against Terror. Anything that does not support this idea is reinterpreted or ignored.

Science has given us many wonderful gifts: the space program, laser, television, penicillin, sulfa-drugs, and a host of other useful developments which should make our lives more tolerable and fruitful. However, we can easily see that this is not the case. It could be said that never before has man been so precariously poised on the brink of such total destruction.

On a personal level, our lives are steadily deteriorating. The air we breathe and the water we drink is polluted almost beyond endurance. Our foods are loaded with substances which contribute very little to nourishment, and may, in fact, be injurious to our health. Stress and tension have become an accepted part of life and can be shown to have killed more people than the cigarettes that some people still smoke to relieve it. We swallow endless quantities of pills to wake up, go to sleep, get the job done, calm our nerves and make us feel good. The inhabitants of the earth spend more money on recreational drugs than they spend on housing, clothing, food, education or any other product or service.

At the social level, hatred, envy, greed and strife multiply exponentially. Crime increases nine times faster than the population. Combined with wars, insurrections, and political purges, multiplied millions of people across the globe are without adequate food or shelter due to political actions.

And then, of course, drought, famine, plague and natural disasters still take an annual toll in lives and suffering. This, too, seems to be increasing.

When man contemplates history, *as it is*, he is forced to realize that he is in the iron grip of an existence that seems to have no real care or concern for his pain and suffering. Over and over again, the same sufferings fall upon mankind multiplied millions upon millions of times over millennia. The totality of human suffering is a dreadful thing. I could write until the end of the world using oceans of ink and forests of paper and never fully convey this Terror. The beast of arbitrary calamity has always been with us. For as long as human hearts have pumped hot blood through their too-fragile bodies and glowed with the inexpressible sweetness of life and yearning for all that is good and right and loving, the sneering, stalking, drooling and scheming beast of unconscious evil has licked its lips in anticipation of its next feast of terror and suffering. Since the beginning of time, this mystery of the estate of man, this Curse of Cain has existed. And, since the Ancient of Days, the cry has been: My punishment is greater than I can bear!

It is conjectured that, in ancient times, when man perceived this intolerable and incomprehensible condition in which he found his existence, that he created cosmogonies to justify all the cruelties, aberrations, and tragedies of history. It is true that, man, as a rule and in general, is powerless against cosmic and geological catastrophes, and it has long been said that the average man can't really do anything about military onslaughts, social injustice, personal and familial misfortunes, and a host of assaults against his existence too numerous to list.

Macrosocial evil and everyday evil are, in a very real sense, inseparable. The long term accumulation of everyday evil always and inevitably leads to Grand Systemic Evil that destroys more innocent people than any other phenomenon on this planet.

The knowledge of Macrosocial Evil is also a survival guide; unless, of course, you are a psychopath.

"What does psychopathy have to do with personal or social evil?" you may ask.

Absolutely everything. Whether you know it or not, each and every day your life is touched by the effects of psychopathy on our world. Even if there isn't much we can do about geological and cosmological catastrophe, there is a lot we can do about social and macrosocial evil, and the very first thing to do is to learn about it. In the case of psychopathy and its effects on our world, what you don't know definitely can and will hurt you.

Nowadays the word "psychopath" generally evokes images of the barely restrained—yet surprisingly urbane—mad-dog serial killer, Dr. Hannibal Lecter of *Silence of the Lambs* fame. I will admit that this was the image that came to my mind whenever I heard the word; almost, that is. The big difference was that I never thought of a psychopath as possibly being so cultured or so capable of passing as "normal." But I was wrong, and I was to learn this lesson quite painfully by direct experience. The exact details are chronicled elsewhere; what is important is that this experience was probably one of the most painful and instructive episodes of my life, and it enabled me to overcome a block in my awareness of the world around me and those who inhabit it.

Regarding blocks to awareness, I need to state for the record that I have spent 30 years studying psychology, history, culture, religion, myth and the so-called paranormal.[369] I also have worked for many years with hypnotherapy, which gave me a very good mechanical knowledge of how the mind/brain of the human being operates at very deep levels. But even so, I was still operating with certain beliefs firmly in place that were shattered by my research into psychopathy. I realized that there was a certain set of ideas that I held about human beings that were sacrosanct—and false. I even wrote about this once in the following way:

---

[369] I have never received any academic degrees, so I am not a "professional", in that respect.

[…] My work has shown me that the vast majority of people want to do good, to experience good things, think good thoughts, and make decisions with good results. And they try with all their might to do so! With the majority of people having this internal desire, why the hell isn't it happening?

I was naïve, I admit. There were many things I did not know that I have learned since I penned those words. But even at that time I was aware of how our own minds can be used to deceive us.

Now, what beliefs did I hold that made me a victim of a psychopath? The first and most obvious one is that I truly believed that deep inside, all people are basically "good" and that they "want to do good, to experience good things, think good thoughts, and make decisions with good results. And they try with all their might to do so…"

As it happens, this is not true as I—and everyone involved in our research group—learned to our sorrow, as they say. But we also learned to our edification. In order to come to some understanding of exactly what kind of human being could do the things that were done to me (and others close to me), and why they might be motivated—even driven—to behave this way, we began to research the psychological literature for clues because we needed to understand for our own peace of mind.

If there is a psychological theory that can explain vicious and harmful behavior, it helps very much for the victim of such acts to have this information so that they do not have to spend all their time feeling hurt or angry. And certainly, if there is a psychological theory that helps a person to find what kind of words or deeds can bridge the chasm between people, to heal misunderstandings, then that is also a worthy goal. It was from such a perspective that we began our extensive work on the subjects of narcissism which then led to the study of psychopathy.

Of course, we didn't start out with such any such "diagnosis" or label for what we were witnessing. We started out with observations and searched the literature for clues, for profiles, for anything that would help us to understand the inner world of a human being—actually a group of human beings—who seemed to be utterly depraved and unlike anything we had ever encountered before. We found that this kind of human is all too common and that, according to some of the latest research, they cause more damage in human society than any other single so-called "mental illness". Martha Stout, who has worked extensively with victims of psychopaths, writes:

> Imagine—if you can—not having a conscience, none at all, no feelings of guilt or remorse no matter what you do, no limiting sense of concern for the well-being of strangers, friends, or even family members. Imagine no struggles with shame, not a single one in your whole life, no matter what kind of selfish, lazy, harmful, or immoral action you had taken.
>
> And pretend that the concept of responsibility is unknown to you, except as a burden others seem to accept without question, like gullible fools.
>
> Now add to this strange fantasy the ability to conceal from other people that your psychological makeup is radically different from theirs. Since everyone

simply assumes that conscience is universal among human beings, hiding the fact that you are conscience-free is nearly effortless.

You are not held back from any of your desires by guilt or shame, and you are never confronted by others for your cold-bloodedness. The ice water in your veins is so bizarre, so completely outside of their personal experience, that they seldom even guess at your condition.

In other words, you are completely free of internal restraints, and your unhampered liberty to do just as you please, with no pangs of conscience, is conveniently invisible to the world.

You can do anything at all, and still your strange advantage over the majority of people, who are kept in line by their consciences will most likely remain undiscovered.

How will you live your life?

What will you do with your huge and secret advantage, and with the corresponding handicap of other people (conscience)?

The answer will depend largely on just what your desires happen to be, because people are not all the same. Even the profoundly unscrupulous are not all the same. Some people—whether they have a conscience or not—favor the ease of inertia, while others are filled with dreams and wild ambitions. Some human beings are brilliant and talented, some are dull-witted, and most, conscience or not, are somewhere in between. There are violent people and nonviolent ones, individuals who are motivated by blood lust and those who have no such appetites. [...]

Provided you are not forcibly stopped, you can do anything at all.

If you are born at the right time, with some access to family fortune, and you have a special talent for whipping up other people's hatred and sense of deprivation, you can arrange to kill large numbers of unsuspecting people. With enough money, you can accomplish this from far away, and you can sit back safely and watch in satisfaction. [...]

Crazy and frightening—and real, in about 4 percent of the population. [...]

The prevalence rate for anorexic eating disorders is estimated a 3.43 percent, deemed to be nearly epidemic, and yet this figure is a fraction lower than the rate for antisocial personality. The high-profile disorders classed as schizophrenia occur in only about 1 percent of [the population]—a mere quarter of the rate of antisocial personality—and the Centers for Disease Control and Prevention say that the rate of colon cancer in the United States, considered "alarmingly high," is about 40 per 100,000—one hundred times lower than the rate of antisocial personality.

The high incidence of sociopathy in human society has a profound effect on the rest of us who must live on this planet, too, even those of us who have not been clinically traumatized. The individuals who constitute this 4 percent drain our relationships, our bank accounts, our accomplishments, our self-esteem, our very peace on earth.

Yet surprisingly, many people know nothing about this disorder, or if they do, they think only in terms of violent psychopathy—murderers, serial killers, mass murderers—people who have conspicuously broken the law many times over, and who, if caught, will be imprisoned, maybe even put to death by our legal system.

We are not commonly aware of, nor do we usually identify, the larger number of nonviolent sociopaths among us, people who often are not blatant lawbreakers, and against whom our formal legal system provides little defense.

Most of us would not imagine any correspondence between conceiving an ethnic genocide and, say, guiltlessly lying to one's boss about a coworker. But the psychological correspondence is not only there; it is chilling. Simple and profound, the link is the absence of the inner mechanism that beats up on us, emotionally speaking, when we make a choice we view as immoral, unethical, neglectful, or selfish.

Most of us feel mildly guilty if we eat the last piece of cake in the kitchen, let alone what we would feel if we intentionally and methodically set about to hurt another person.

Those who have no conscience at all are a group unto themselves, whether they be homicidal tyrants or merely ruthless social snipers.

The presence or absence of conscience is a deep human division, arguably more significant than intelligence, race, or even gender.

What differentiates a sociopath who lives off the labors of others from one who occasionally robs convenience stores, or from one who is a contemporary robber baron—or what makes the difference between an ordinary bully and a sociopathic murderer—is nothing more than social status, drive, intellect, blood lust, or simple opportunity?

What distinguishes all of these people from the rest of us is an utterly empty hole in the psyche, where there should be the most evolved of all humanizing functions.[370]

We did not have the advantage of Dr. Stout's book at the beginning of our research project. We did, of course, have Robert Hare, Hervey Cleckley, Guggenbuhl-Craig and others. But they were only approaching the subject of the possibly large numbers of psychopaths that live among us who never get caught breaking laws, who don't murder—or if they do, they don't get caught—and who still do untold damage to the lives of family, acquaintances, and strangers.

Most mental health experts, for a very long time, have operated on the premise that psychopaths come from impoverished backgrounds and have experienced abuse of one sort or another in childhood, so it is easy to spot them, or at least, they certainly don't move in society except as interlopers. This idea seems to be coming under some serious revision lately. As Lobaczewski points out in this book, there is some confusion between Psychopathy, Antisocial Personality Disorder and Sociopathy. As Robert Hare points out, yes, there are many psychopaths who are also "anti-socials" but there seem to be far more of them that would never be classified as anti-social or sociopathic! In other words, they can be doctors, lawyers, judges,

---

[370] Martha Stout, *The Sociopath Next Door* (New York: Broadway Books, 2005).

policemen, congressmen, presidents of corporations that rob from the poor to give to the rich, and even presidents.

In a recent paper, it is suggested that psychopathy may exist in ordinary society in even greater numbers than anyone has thus far considered:

> Psychopathy, as originally conceived by Cleckley (1941), is not limited to engagement in illegal activities, but rather encompasses such personality characteristics as manipulativeness, insincerity, egocentricity, and lack of guilt— characteristics clearly present in criminals but also in spouses, parents, bosses, attorneys, politicians, and CEOs, to name but a few (Bursten, 1973; Stewart, 1991). Our own examination of the prevalence of psychopathy within a university population suggested that perhaps 5% or more of this sample might be deemed psychopathic, although the vast majority of those will be male (more than 1/10 males versus approximately 1/100 females).

> As such, psychopathy may be characterized [...] as involving a tendency towards both dominance and coldness. Wiggins (1995) in summarizing numerous previous findings [...] indicates that such individuals are prone to anger and irritation and are willing to exploit others. They are arrogant, manipulative, cynical, exhibitionistic, sensation-seeking, Machiavellian, vindictive, and out for their own gain. With respect to their patterns of social exchange (Foa & Foa, 1974), they attribute love and status to themselves, seeing themselves as highly worthy and important, but prescribe neither love nor status to others, seeing them as unworthy and insignificant. This characterization is clearly consistent with the essence of psychopathy as commonly described.

> The present investigation sought to answer some basic questions regarding the construct of psychopathy in non forensic settings. [...] In so doing we have returned to Cleckley's (1941) original emphasis on psychopathy as a personality style not only among criminals, but also among successful individuals within the community.

> What is clear from our findings is that (a) psychopathy measures have converged on a prototype of psychopathy that involves a combination of dominant and cold interpersonal characteristics; (b) psychopathy does occur in the community and at what might be a higher than expected rate; and (c) psychopathy appears to have little overlap with personality disorders aside from Antisocial Personality Disorder. [...]

> Clearly, where much more work is needed is in understanding what factors differentiate the abiding (although perhaps not moral-abiding) psychopath from the law-breaking psychopath; such research surely needs to make greater use of non forensic samples than has been customary in the past.[371]

Lobaczewski discusses the fact that there are different types of psychopaths. One type, in particular, is the most deadly of all: the Essential Psychopath. He doesn't give us a "checklist" but rather discusses what is inside the psychopath. His description meshes very well with items in the paper quoted above.

---

[371] Salekin, Trobst, Krioukova, "Construct Validity of Psychopathy in a Community Sample: A Nomological Net Approach", *Journal of Personality Disorders* 15:5 (2001), 425-441.

Martha Stout also discusses the fact that psychopaths, like anyone else, are born with different basic likes and dislikes and desires which is why some of them are doctors and presidents and others are petty thieves or rapists.

"Likeable", "Charming", "Intelligent", "Alert", "Impressive", "Confidence-inspiring", and "A great success with the ladies". This is how Hervey Cleckley described most of his subjects in *The Mask of Sanity*. It seems that, in spite of the fact that their actions prove them to be "irresponsible" and "self-destructive", psychopaths seem to have in abundance the very traits most desired by normal persons. The smooth self-assurance acts as an almost supernatural magnet to normal people who have to read self-help books or go to counselling to be able to interact with others in an untroubled way. The psychopath, on the contrary, never has any neuroses, no self-doubts, never experiences angst, and *is* what "normal" people seek to be. What's more, even if they aren't that attractive, they are "babe magnets".

Cleckley's seminal hypothesis is that the psychopath suffers from profound and incurable *affective* deficit, that is, if the psychopath really feels anything at all, they are emotions of only the shallowest kind. He is able to do whatever he wants, based on whatever whim strikes him because consequences that would fill the ordinary man with shame, self-loathing, and embarrassment simply do not affect the psychopath at all. What to others would be a horror or a disaster is to him merely a fleeting inconvenience.

Cleckley posits that psychopathy is quite common in the community at large. His cases include examples of psychopaths who generally function normally in the community as businessmen, doctors, and even psychiatrists. Nowadays, some of the more astute researchers see criminal psychopathy—often referred to as anti-social personality disorder—as an extreme of a particular personality type. I think it is more helpful to characterize criminal psychopaths as "unsuccessful psychopaths".

One researcher, Alan Harrington goes so far as to say that the psychopath is the new man being produced by the evolutionary pressures of modern life:

> Certainly, there have always been shysters and crooks, but past concern was focused on ferreting out incompetents rather than psychopaths. Unfortunately, all that has changed. We now need to fear the super-sophisticated modern crook who does know what he is doing [...] and does it so well that no one else knows. Yes, psychopaths love the business world.
>
> Uninvolved with others, he coolly saw into their fears and desires, and maneuvered them as he wished. Such a man might not, after all, be doomed to a life of scrapes and escapades ending ignominiously in the jailhouse. Instead of murdering others, he might become a corporate raider and murder companies, firing people instead of killing them, and chopping up their functions rather than their bodies.
>
> [T]he consequences to the average citizen from business crimes are staggering. As criminologist Georgette Bennett says, "They account for nearly 30% of case filings in U.S. District Courts—more than any other category of crime. The combined burglary, mugging and other property losses induced by the country's

street punks come to about $4 billion a year. However, the seemingly upstanding citizens in our corporate board rooms and the humble clerks in our retail stores bilk us out of between $40 and $200 billion a year."

Concern here is that the costume for the new masked sanity of a psychopath is just as likely to be a three-piece suit as a ski mask and a gun. As Harrington says, "We also have the psychopath in respectable circles, no longer assumed to be a loser." He quotes William Krasner as saying, "They—psychopath and part psychopath—do well in the more unscrupulous types of sales work, because they take such delight in 'putting it over on them', getting away with it—and have so little conscience about defrauding their customers." Our society is fast becoming more materialistic, and success at any cost is the credo of many businessmen. The typical psychopath thrives in this kind of environment and is seen as a business "hero".[372]

The study of "ambulatory" psychopaths—what we call "The Garden Variety Psychopath"—has, however, hardly begun. Very little is known about sub-criminal psychopathy. Some researchers have begun to seriously consider the idea that it is important to study psychopathy not as a pathological category but as a general personality trait in the community at large. In other words, psychopathy is being recognized as a more or less a different type of human.

Hervey Cleckley actually comes very close to suggesting that psychopaths are human in every respect—but that they lack a soul. This lack of "soul quality" makes them very efficient "machines". They can write scholarly works, imitate the words of emotion, but over time, it becomes clear that their words do not match their actions. They are the type of person who can claim that they are devastated by grief who then attend a party "to forget". The problem is: they really *do* forget.

Being very efficient machines, like a computer, they are able to execute very complex routines designed to elicit from others support for what they want. In this way, many psychopaths are able to reach very high positions in life. It is only over time that their associates become aware of the fact that their climb up the ladder of success is predicated on violating the rights of others. "Even when they are indifferent to the rights of their associates, they are often able to inspire feelings of trust and confidence."

The psychopath recognizes no flaw in his psyche, no need for change.

Andrew Lobaczewski addresses the problem of the psychopath and their extremely significant contribution to our macrosocial evils, their ability to act as the *éminence grise* behind the very structure of our society. It is very important to keep in mind that this influence comes from a relatively small segment of humanity. The other 90 some percent of human beings are not psychopaths.

But that other, over 90 percent of normal people, know that something is wrong! They just can't quite identify it; can't quite put their finger on it; and

---

[372] Ken Magid and Carole McKelvey, The Psychopaths Favourite Playground: Business Relationships.

because they can't, they tend to think that there is nothing they can do about it, or maybe it is just God punishing people.

What is actually the case is that when that 90 some percent of human beings fall into a certain state, as Lobaczewski will describe, the psychopaths, like a virulent pathogen in a body, strike at the weaknesses and the entire society is plunged into conditions that always and inevitably lead to horror and tragedy on a very large scale.

The movie, *The Matrix*, touched a deep chord in society because it exemplified this mechanistic trap in which so many people find their lives enmeshed, and from which they are unable to extricate themselves because they believe that everyone around them who "looks human" is, in fact, just like them—emotionally, spiritually, and otherwise.

To give an example of how psychopaths can directly affect society at large, take the "legal argument" as explicated by Robert Canup in his work on the *Socially Adept Psychopath*. The legal argument seems to be at the foundation of our society. We believe that the legal argument is an advanced system of justice. This is a very cunning trick that has been foisted on normal people by psychopaths in order to have an advantage over them. Just think about it for a moment: the legal argument amounts to little more than the one who is the slickest at using the structure for convincing a group of people of something, is the one who is believed. Because this "legal argument" system has been slowly installed as part of our culture, when it invades our personal lives, we normally do not recognize it immediately. But here's how it works.

Human beings have been accustomed to assume that other human beings are—at the very least—trying to "do right" and "be good" and fair and honest. And so, very often, we do not take the time to use due diligence in order to determine if a person who has entered our life is, in fact, a "good person". When a conflict ensues, we automatically fall into the legal argument assumption that in any conflict, one side is partly right one way, and the other is partly right the other, and that we can form opinions about which side is mostly right or wrong. Because of our exposure to the "legal argument" norms, when any dispute arises, we automatically think that the truth will lie somewhere between two extremes. In this case, application of a little mathematical logic to the problem of the legal argument might be helpful.

Let us assume that in a dispute, one side is innocent, honest, and tells the truth. It is obvious that lying does an innocent person no good; what lie can he tell? If he is innocent, the only lie he can tell is to falsely confess "I did it". But lying is nothing but good for the liar. He can declare that "I didn't do it", and accuse another of doing it, all the while the innocent person he has accused is saying "I didn't do it", and is actually telling the truth.

The truth, when twisted by good liars, can always make an innocent person look bad—especially if the innocent person is honest and admits his mistakes.

The basic assumption that the truth lies between the testimony of the two sides always shifts the advantage to the lying side and away from the side telling the truth. Under most circumstances, this shift put together with the fact that the truth is going to also be twisted in such a way as to bring detriment to the innocent person, results in the advantage *always* resting in the hands of liars or psychopaths. Even the simple act of giving testimony under oath is a useless farce. If a person is a liar, swearing an oath means nothing to that person. However, swearing an oath acts strongly on a serious, truthful witness. Again, the advantage is placed on the side of the liar.

It has often been noted that psychopaths have a distinct advantage over human beings with conscience and feelings because the psychopath does not have conscience and feelings. What seems to be so is that conscience and feelings are related to the abstract concepts of "future" and "others". It is "spatio-temporal". We can feel fear, sympathy, empathy, sadness, and so on because we can imagine in an abstract way, the future based on our own experiences in the past, or even just "concepts of experiences" in myriad variations. We can "see ourselves" in them even though they are "out there", and this evokes feelings in us. We can't do something hurtful because we can imagine it being done to us and how it would feel. In other words, we can not only identify with others spatially—so to say—but also temporally—in time.

The psychopath does not seem to have this capacity.

They are unable to "imagine" in the sense of being able to really connect to images in a direct "self connecting to another self" sort of way.

Oh, indeed, they can *imitate* feelings, but the only real feelings they seem to have—the thing that drives them and causes them to act out different dramas for the effect—is a sort of "predatorial hunger" for what they want. That is to say, they "feel" need/want as love, and not having their needs/wants met is described by them as "not being loved". What is more, this "need/want" perspective posits that only the "hunger" of the psychopath is valid, and anything and everything "out there", outside of the psychopath, is not real except insofar as it has the capability of being assimilated to the psychopath as a sort of "food". "Can it be used or can it provide something?" is the only issue about which the psychopath seems to be concerned. All else—all activity—is subsumed to this drive.

In short, the psychopath is a predator. If we think about the interactions of predators with their prey in the animal kingdom, we can come to some idea of what is behind the "mask of sanity" of the psychopath. Just as an animal predator will adopt all kinds of stealthy functions in order to stalk their prey, cut them out of the herd, get close to them and reduce their resistance, so does the psychopath construct all kinds of elaborate camouflage composed of words and appearances—lies and manipulations—in order to "assimilate" their prey.

This leads us to an important question: what does the psychopath *really* get from their victims? It's easy to see what they are after when they lie and manipulate for money or material goods or power. But in many instances, such as love relationships or faked friendships, it is not so easy to see what the

psychopath is after. Without wandering too far afield into spiritual speculations—a problem Cleckley also faced—we can only say that it seems to be
that the psychopath *enjoys* making others suffer. Just as normal humans enjoy
seeing other people happy, or doing things that make other people smile, the
psychopath enjoys the exact opposite.

Anyone who has ever observed a cat playing with a mouse before killing
and eating it has probably explained to themselves that the cat is just "entertained" by the antics of the mouse and is unable to conceive of the terror and
pain being experienced by the mouse, and the cat, therefore, is innocent of
any evil intent. The mouse dies, the cat is fed, and that is nature.

Psychopaths don't generally eat their victims. Yes, in extreme cases of psychopathy, the entire cat and mouse dynamic *is* carried out—cannibalism has a
long history wherein it was assumed that certain powers of the victim could
be assimilated by eating some particular part of them—but in ordinary life,
psychopaths don't normally go all the way, so to say. This causes us to look
at the cat and mouse scenario again with different eyes. Now we ask: is it too
simplistic to think that the innocent cat is merely entertained by the mouse
running about and frantically trying to escape? Is there something more to
this dynamic than meets the eye? Is there something more than being "entertained" by the antics of the mouse trying to flee? After all, in terms of evolution, why would such behavior be hard-wired into the cat? Is the mouse tast-
ier because of the chemicals of fear that flood his little body? Is a mouse
frozen with terror more of a "gourmet" meal?

This suggests that we ought to revisit our ideas about psychopaths with a
slightly different perspective. One thing we do know is this: many people
who experience interactions with psychopaths and narcissists report feeling
"drained" and confused and often subsequently experience deteriorating
health. Does this mean that part of the dynamic, part of the explanation for
why psychopaths will pursue "love relationships" and "friendships" that ostensibly can result in no observable material gain, is because there is an actual energy consumption?

We do not know the answer to this question. We observe, we theorize, we
speculate and hypothesize. But in the end, only the individual victim can determine what they have lost in the dynamic—and it is often far more than
material goods. In a certain sense, it seems that psychopaths are soul eaters or
"Psychophagic".

In the past several years, there are many more psychologists and psychiatrists and other mental health workers beginning to look at these issues in
new ways in response to the questions about the state of our world and the
possibility that there is some essential difference between such individuals as
George W. Bush and many so-called neocons, and the rest of us.

Dr. Stout's book has one of the longest explanations as to why none of her
examples resemble any actual persons that I have ever read. And then, in a
very early chapter, she describes a "composite" case where the subject spent

his childhood blowing up frogs with fire-crackers. It is widely known that George W. Bush did this. The subject is also described as graduating college with a C average—which Bush did at Yale—so one naturally wonders...

In any event, even without Dr. Stout's work, at the time we were studying the matter, we realized that what we were learning was very important to everyone because as the data was assembled, we saw that the clues, the profiles, revealed that the issues we were facing were faced by everyone at one time or another, to one extent or another. We also began to realize that the profiles that emerged also describe rather accurately many individuals who seek positions of power in fields of authority, most particularly politics and commerce. That's really not so surprising an idea, but it honestly hadn't occurred to us until we saw the patterns and recognized them in the behaviors of numerous historical figures, and lately including George W. Bush and members of his administration.

Current day statistics tell us that there are more psychologically sick people than healthy ones. If you take a sampling of individuals in any given field, you are likely to find that a significant number of them display pathological symptoms to one extent or another. Politics is no exception, and by its very nature, would tend to attract more of the pathological "dominator types" than other fields. That is only logical, and we began to realize that it was not only logical, it was horrifyingly accurate; horrifying because pathology among people in power can have disastrous effects on all of the people under the control of such pathological individuals. And so, we decided to write about this subject and publish it on the Internet.

As the material went up, letters from our readers began to come in thanking us for putting a name to what was happening to them in their personal lives as well as helping them to understand what was happening in a world that seems to have gone completely mad. We began to think that it was an epidemic, and in a certain sense, we were right. If an individual with a highly contagious illness works in a job that puts them in contact with the public, an epidemic is the result. In the same way, if an individual in a position of political power is a psychopath, he or she can create an epidemic of psychopathology in people who are not, essentially, psychopathic. Our ideas along this line were soon to receive confirmation from an unexpected source: Andrew Lobaczewski, the author of *Political Ponerology: A science on the nature of evil adjusted for political purposes.* I received an email as follows:

Dear Ladies and Gentlemen.

I have got your Special Research Project on psychopathy by my computer. You are doing a most important and valuable work for the future of nations. [...]

I am a very aged clinical psychologist. Forty years ago I took part in a secret investigation of the real nature and psychopathology of the macro-social phenomenon called "Communism". The other researchers were the scientists of the previous generation who are now passed away.

The profound study of the nature psychopathy, which played the essential and inspirational part in this macro-social psychopathologic phenomenon, and distinguishing it from other mental anomalies, appeared to be the necessary preparation for understanding the entire nature of the phenomenon.

The large part of the work, you are doing now, was done in those times.

I am able to provide you with a most valuable scientific document, useful for your purposes. It is my book "Political Ponerology—A science on the nature of evil adjusted for political purposes". You may also find copy of this book in the Library of Congress and in some university and public libraries in the USA.

Be so kind and contact me so that I may mail a copy to you.

Very truly yours!

Andrew M. Lobaczewski

I promptly wrote a reply saying yes, I would very much like to read his book. A couple of weeks later the manuscript arrived in the mail.

As I read, I realized that what I was holding in my hand was essentially a chronicle of a descent into hell, transformation, and triumphant return to the world with knowledge of that hell that was priceless for the rest of us, particularly in this day and time when it seems evident that a similar hell is enveloping the planet. The risks that were taken by the group of scientists that did the research on which this book is based are beyond the comprehension of most of us.

Many of them were young, just starting in their careers when the Nazis began to stride in their hundred league jackboots across Europe. These researchers lived through that, and then when the Nazis were driven out and replaced by the Communists under the heel of Stalin, they faced years of oppression the likes of which those of us today who are choosing to take a stand against the Bush Reich cannot even imagine. But, based on the syndrome that describes the onset of the disease, it seems that the United States, in particular, and perhaps the entire world, will soon enter into "bad times" of such horror and despair that the holocaust of World War II will seem like just a practice run.

And so, since they were there, and they lived through it and brought back information to the rest of us, it may well save our lives to have a map to guide us in the falling darkness.

THE HISTORY OF PONEROLOGY

From the Author's Foreword:

In presenting my honored readers with this volume, which I generally worked on during the early hours before leaving to make a difficult living, I would first like to apologize for the defects which are the result of anomalous circumstances such as the absence of a proper laboratory. I readily admit that these lacunae should be filled, time-consuming as that may be, because the facts on which this book are based are urgently needed. Through no fault of the author's, these data have come too late.

The reader is entitled to an explanation of the long history and circumstances under which this work was compiled. This is the third time I have treated the same subject. I threw the first manuscript into a central-heating furnace, having been warned just in time about an official search, which took place minutes later. I sent the second draft to a Church dignitary at the Vatican by means of an American tourist and was absolutely unable to obtain any kind of information about the fate of the parcel once it was left with him.

This [...] history [...] made work on the third version even more laborious. Prior paragraphs and former phrases from one or both first drafts haunt the writer's mind and make proper planning of the content more difficult.

The two first drafts were written in very convoluted language for the benefit of specialists with the necessary background, particularly in the field of psychopathology. The irretrievable disappearance of the second version also included the overwhelming majority of statistical data and facts which would have been so valuable and conclusive for specialists. Several analyses of individual cases were also lost.

The present version contains only such statistical data which had been memorized due to frequent use, or which could be reconstructed with satisfactory precision. [...] I also nurse the hope that this work may reach a wider audience and make available some useful scientific data which may serve as a basis for comprehension of the contemporary world and its history. It may also make it easier for readers to understand themselves, their neighbors, and other nations.

Who produced the knowledge and performed the work summarized within the pages of this book? It is a joint endeavor containing not only my efforts, but also representing the work of many researchers. [...]

The author worked in Poland far away from active political and cultural centers for many years. That is where I undertook a series of detailed tests and observations which were to be combined within the resulting generalisations in order to produce an overall introduction for an understanding of the macro-social phenomenon surrounding us. The name of the person expected to effect this synthesis was a secret, as was understandable and necessary given the time and the situation. I would very occasionally receive anonymous summaries of the results of tests from Poland and Hungary. A few data were published, as it raised no suspicions that a specialized work was being compiled, and these data could still be located today.

The expected synthesis of this work did not occur. All my contacts became inoperative as a result of the secret arrests of researchers in the early sixties. The remaining scientific data in my possession were very incomplete, albeit priceless in value. It took many years of lonely work to weld these fragments into a coherent whole, filling the lacunae with my own experience and research.

My research on essential psychopathy and its exceptional role in the macro-social phenomenon was conducted concurrently with or shortly after that of others. Their conclusions reached me later and confirmed my own. The most characteristic item in my work is the general concept for a new scientific discipline named 'ponerology'. [...]

As the author of the final work, I hereby express my deep respect for all those who initiated the research and continued to conduct it at the risk of their careers, health and lives. I pay homage to those who paid the price through suffering or death. May this work constitute some compensation for their sacrifices." [...]

New York, N.Y. August 1984 [373]

As I read the book, *Political Ponerology*, I understood that I was holding the condensation of a very important work and that the man who had written it had suffered a great deal to assemble that information for the benefit of others. The manuscript had been translated at the University of New York in 1985, and I wondered why it had not been published.

As I continued to read the manuscript, the answer became apparent. Dr. Lobaczewski explains about his sojourn in the United States where he reassembled and wrote down his research after having escaped from Poland via Austria before Solidarity brought the downfall of communism in Poland:

Fifteen years passed, fraught with political occurrences. The world changed essentially due to the natural laws of the phenomenon described in this book, and due to the efforts of people of good will. Nonetheless, the world as yet is not restored to good health; and *the remainders of the great disease are still very active and threatening a reoccurrence of the illness.* Such is the result of a great effort completed without the support of the objective knowledge about the very nature of the phenomenon. [...]

The author was recognised as the bearer of this 'dangerous' science only in Austria, by a 'friendly' physician who turned out to be a 'red' agent. The communist groups in New York were then set up to organize a 'counter action'. It was terrible to learn how the system of conscious and unconscious pawns worked. Worst were the people who credulously trusted their conscious 'friends' and performed the insinuated activities with patriotic zeal. The author was refused assistance and had to save his life by working as a welder. My health collapsed, and two years were lost. It appeared that I was not the first who came to America bringing similar knowledge and, once there, treated in a similar way.

In spite of all these circumstances, the book was written on time, but no one would publish it. The work was described as 'very informative' but for psychological editors, it contained too much politics and for political editors, it contained too much psychology, or simply 'the editorial deadline has just closed'. Gradually, it became clear that the book did not pass the insider's inspection. [...]

The scientific value which may serve the future remains, and further investigations may yield a new understanding of human problems with progress toward universal peace. This was the reason I labored to retype, on my computer, the whole already fading manuscript. It is here presented as it was written in 1983-84 in New York, USA. So let it be a document of good science and dangerous labor. The author's desire is to hand this work into the hands of scholars in the hope they will take his burden over and progress with the theoretical research in ponerology—and put it in praxis for the good of people and nations."

Poland – June, 1998 [374]

---

[373] Andrew M. Lobaczewski, *Political Ponerology: A science on the nature of evil adjusted for political purposes*, trans. Alexandra Chciuk-Celt Ph.D. (Red Pill Press, 2006).

Dr. Lobaczewski left the United States and returned to Poland before September 11, 2001. But his remarks were prophetic:

> Nonetheless, the world as yet is not restored to good health; and the remainders of the great disease are still very active and threatening a reoccurrence of the illness.

Dr. Lobaczewski was not proposing a "theological" study, but rather a scientific study of what we can plainly call Evil. The problem is, our materialist scientific culture does not readily admit that evil actually exists, per se. Yes, "evil" plays a part in religious discourse, but even there it is given short shrift as an "error" or a "rebellion" that will be corrected at some point in the future, which is discussed in another theological division: eschatology, which is concerned with the final events in history of the world, the ultimate fate of humanity.

> Present-day philosophers developing meta-ethics are trying to press forward in their understanding, and as they slip and slide along the elastic space leading to an analysis of the language of ethics, they contribute toward eliminating some imperfections and habits of natural conceptual language. Penetrating this ever-mysterious nucleus, however, is highly tempting to a scientist. [...]

> If physicians behaved like ethicists and failed to study diseases because they were only interested in studying questions of health, there would be no such thing as modern medicine. [...] Physicians were correct in their emphasis on studying disease above all in order to discover the causes and biological properties of illnesses, and then to understand the pathodynamics of their courses. A comprehension of the nature of a disease, and the course it runs, after all, enables the proper curative means to be elaborated and employed. [...]

> The question thus arises: could some analogous modus operandi not be used to study the causes and genesis of other kinds of evil scourging human individuals, families, societies? Experience has taught the author that evil is similar to disease in nature, although possibly more complex and elusive to our understanding. [...]

> Parallel to the traditional approach, problems commonly perceived to be moral may also be treated on the basis of data provided by biology, medicine, and psychology, as the factors of this kind are simultaneously present in the question as a whole. Experience teaches us that a comprehension of the essence and genesis of evil generally makes use of data from these areas. [...]

> Philosophical thought may have engendered all the scientific disciplines, but the latter did not mature until they became independent, based on detailed data and a relationship to other disciplines supplying such data.

> Encouraged by the often 'coincidental' discovery of these naturalistic aspects of evil, the author initiated the methodology of medicine; a clinical psychologist and medical co-worker by profession, he had such tendencies anyway. As is the case with physicians and disease, he took the risks of close contact with evil and suffered the consequences. His purpose was to ascertain the possibilities of understanding the nature of evil, its etiological factors and to track its pathodynamics. [...]

---

[374] Lobaczewski, op. cit.

A new discipline thus arose: *Ponerology*. The process of the genesis of evil was called, correspondingly, 'ponerogenesis'. [...]

Considerable moral, intellectual, and practical advantages can be gleaned from an understanding of the genesis of Evil thanks to the objectivity required to study it dispassionately. The human heritage of ethics is *not destroyed* by taking such an approach: *it is actually strengthened* because *the scientific method can be utilized to confirm the basic values of moral teachings.*

Understanding the nature of macro-social pathology helps us to find a healthy attitude and thus *protects our minds from being controlled or poisoned by the diseased contents and influence of their propaganda.*

We can only conquer this huge, contagious social cancer if we comprehend its essence and its etiological causes.

Such an understanding of the nature of the phenomena leads to the logical conclusion that the measures for healing and reordering the world today should be completely different from the ones heretofore used for solving international conflicts. It is also true that, merely having the knowledge and awareness of the phenomena of the genesis of macro-social Evil can begin healing individual humans and help their minds regain harmony. [375]

There are quite a number of modern psychologists who are actually beginning to move in the direction of what Dr. Lobaczewski said and had already been done behind the Iron Curtain many years ago. I have a stack of their books on my desk. Some of them seem to be falling back into the religious perspective simply because they have no other scientific ground on which to stand. I think that is counterproductive. As George K. Simon, Jr. writes in his book *In Sheep's Clothing*:

[W]e've been pre-programmed to believe that people only exhibit problem behaviors when they're "troubled" inside or anxious about something. We've also been taught that people aggress only when they're attacked in some way. So, even when our gut tells us that somebody is attacking us and for no good reason, we don't readily accept the notion. We usually start to wonder what's bothering the person so badly "underneath it all" that's making them act in such a disturbing way. We may even wonder what we may have said or done that 'threatened' them. We almost never think that they might be fighting simply to get something, have their way, or gain the upper hand. So, instead of seeing them as merely fighting, we view them as primarily hurting in some way.

Not only do we often have trouble recognizing the ways people aggress us, but we also have difficulty discerning the distinctly aggressive character of some personalities. The legacy of Sigmund Freud's work has a lot to do with this. Freud's theories (and the theories of others who built upon his work) heavily influenced the psychology of personality for a long time. Elements of the classical theories of personality found their way into many disciplines other than psychology as well as into many of our social institutions and enterprises. The basic tenets of these theories and their hallmark construct, neurosis, have become fairly well etched in the public consciousness.

---

[375] Lobaczewski, op. cit.

Psychodynamic theories of personality tend to view everyone, at least to some degree, as *neurotic*. Neurotic individuals are overly inhibited people who suffer unreasonable fear (anxiety), guilt and shame when it comes to securing their basic wants and needs. The *malignant impact of overgeneralizing Freud's observations* about a small group of overly inhibited individuals into a broad set of assumptions about the causes of psychological ill-health in everyone *cannot be overstated.* [...]

Therapists whose training overly indoctrinated them in the theory of neurosis, may 'frame' problems presented them incorrectly. They may, for example, assume that a person, who all their life has aggressively pursued independence and demonstrated little affinity for others, must necessarily be 'compensating' for a 'fear' of intimacy. In other words, they will view a hardened fighter as a terrified runner, thus misperceiving the core reality of the situation. [...]

We need a completely different theoretical framework if we are to truly understand, deal with, and treat the kinds of people who fight too much as opposed to those who cower or "run" too much.[376]

The problem is, of course, that when you read all the books about such people as Dr. Simon is describing, you discover that "treatment" really means treating the victims because such aggressors almost never seek help.

Getting back to Dr. Lobaczewski, I wrote to ask for more details as to why this important work was generally unknown. He replied by mail:

[...] Years ago the publication of the book in the U.S. was killed by *Mr. Zbigniew Brzezinski* in a very cunning way. What was his motivation, I may only guess. Was it his own private strategy, or did he act as an insider of the 'great system' as he surely is? How many billions of dollars and how many human lives the lack of this science has cost the world. [...]

As for who else was involved in this work: in those times, such work could only be done in full secrecy. During the German occupation, we learned to never ask for names though it was well known among us that this was an international communication among some scientists. I can tell you that one Hungarian scientist was killed because of his work on this project, and in Poland, professor Stephan Bla-chowski died mysteriously while working on these investigations. It is a certainty that professor Kasimir Dabrowski[377] was active in the study, being an expert on psychopathy. He escaped to the U.S. and in New York, became an object of harassment as I had been. He went to Canada and worked at the university in Edmonton."

Learning that Zbigniew Brzezinski had read *Political Ponerology* and then suppressed it was a major piece of the puzzle. It became more and more obvious, as we read through Lobaczewski's work that we were seeing a description of exactly what was taking place in the United States—what had been

---

[376] Georg K. Simon, Jr, Ph.D., *In Sheep's Clothing* (Arkansas: A.J. Christopher & Co, 1996).

[377] Kasimir Dabrowski's development theories have particular applicability to understanding the life experiences of HSPs - Highly Sensitive People. The theory identifies inborn "overexcitabilities" (OEs) that can facilitate the achievement of higher levels of development via "positive disintegration", potentially leading individuals to develop higher levels of self-awareness and self-actualization. Dabrowski theory provides a hopeful way of understanding what can be painful and overwhelming experiences. See: http://www.hsperson.com/pages/hsp.htm

going on under the surface for a very long time—and which had been the energy driving those behind the events of September 11, 2001. It is in this context of Dr. Lobaczewski's work that we finally found the mechanism for how and why "grand conspiracies" can and *do* exist, but not necessarily in the way any of us ever imagined. They exist as a phenomenon of Nature and as such a phenomenon, deserve close and careful study.

We will now analyze certain aspects of September 11, 2001 using the tools put in our hands by a group of scientists, working in secret, under a regime similar to the one that organized and pulled off those attacks.

PATHOCRACY

We begin with a story told by Lobaczewski of his first encounter with the pathocracy when he was a university student. His first point is that the study of pathocratic behaviour must be done free from the moral interpretations usually used in understanding evil. It must be studied as a naturalist studies nature:

As a youth, I read a book about a naturalist wandering through the Amazon-basin wilderness. At some moment a small animal fell from a tree onto the nape of his neck, clawing his skin painfully and sucking his blood. The biologist cautiously removed it—without anger, since that was its form of feeding—and proceeded to study it carefully. This story stubbornly stuck in my mind during those very difficult times when a vampire fell onto our necks, sucking the blood of an unhappy nation.

The attitude of a naturalist—who attempts to track the nature of macro-social phenomena in spite of all adversity—insured a certain intellectual distance and better psychological hygiene, also slightly increasing the feeling of safety and furnishing a premonition that this very method may help find a certain creative solution. This required controlling the natural, moralizing reflexes of revulsion and other painful emotions this phenomenon provokes in any normal person when it deprives him of his joy of life and personal safety, ruining his own future and that of his nation. *Scientific curiosity becomes a loyal ally during such times.*

The importance of maintaining an objective point of view becomes clear in the following story:

May the reader please imagine a very large hall in some old Gothic university building. Many of us gathered there early in our studies in order to listen to the lectures of outstanding philosophers. We were herded back there the year before graduation in order to listen to the indoctrination lectures which recently have been introduced. [Under the new Communist regime] someone nobody knew appeared behind the lectern and informed us that he would now be the professor. His speech was fluent, but there was nothing scientific about it: he failed to distinguish between scientific and everyday concepts and treated borderline imaginings as though it were wisdom that could not be doubted. For ninety minutes each week, he flooded us with naïve, presumptuous paralogistics and a pathological view of human reality. We were treated with contempt and poorly controlled hatred. Since fun poking could entail dreadful consequences, we had to listen attentively and with the utmost gravity.

The grapevine soon discovered this person's origins. He had come from a Cracow suburb and attended high school, although no one knew if he graduated. Anyway, this was the first time he had crossed university portals—as a professor, at that! [...]

After such mind-torture, it took a long time for someone to break the silence. We studied ourselves, since we felt something strange had taken over our minds and something valuable was leaking away irretrievably. The world of psychological reality and moral values seemed suspended like in a chilly fog. Our human feeling and student solidarity lost their meaning, as did patriotism and our old established criteria. So we asked each other: 'Are you going through this too?' Each of us experienced this worry about his own personality and future in his own way. Some of us answered the questions with silence. The depth of these experiences turned out to be different for each individual.

We thus wondered how to protect ourselves from the results of this 'indoctrination'. Teresa D. made the first suggestion: Let's spend a weekend in the mountains. It worked. Pleasant company, a bit of joking, then exhaustion followed by deep sleep in a shelter, and our human personalities returned, albeit with a certain remnant. Time also proved to create a kind of psychological immunity, although not with everyone. Analysing the psychopathic characteristics of the 'professor's' personality proved another excellent way of protecting one's own psychological hygiene.

You can just imagine our worry, disappointment, and surprise when some colleagues we knew well suddenly began to change their world-view; their thought-patterns furthermore reminded us of the 'professor's' chatter. Their feelings, which had just recently been friendly, became noticeably cooler, although not yet hostile. Benevolent or critical student arguments bounced right off of them. They gave the impression of possessing some secret knowledge; we were only their former colleagues, still believing what those professors of old had taught us. We had to be careful of what we said to them.

Our former colleagues soon joined the [Communist] Party. Who were they? What social groups did they come from? What kind of students and people were they? How and why did they change so much in less than a year? Why did neither I nor a majority of my fellow students succumb to this phenomenon and process? Many such questions fluttered through our heads then. Those times, questions, and attitudes gave rise to the idea that this phenomenon could be objectively understood, an idea whose greater meaning crystallized with time. Many of us participated in the initial observations and reflections, but most crumbled away in the face of material or academic problems. Only a few remained; so the author of this book may be the last of the Mohicans.

It was relatively easy to determine the environments and origin of the people who succumbed to this process, which I then called 'transpersonification'. They came from all social groups, including aristocratic and fervently religious families, and caused a break in our student solidarity in the order of some 6 %. The remaining majority suffered varying degrees of personality disintegration which gave rise to individual efforts in searching for the values necessary to find ourselves again; the results were varied and sometimes creative.

Even then, we had no doubts as to the pathological nature of this 'transpersoni-fication' process, which ran similar but not identical in all cases. The duration of the results of this phenomenon also varied. Some of these people later became zealots. Others later took advantage of various circumstances to withdraw and reestablish their lost links to the society of normal people. They were replaced. The only constant value of the new social system was the magic number of 6 %.

We tried to evaluate the talent level of those colleagues who had succumbed to this personality-transformation process, and reached the conclusion that on av-erage, it was slightly lower than the average of the student population. Their lesser resistance obviously resided in other bio-psychological features which were most probably qualitatively heterogeneous.

I had to study subjects bordering on psychology and psychopathology in order to answer the questions arising from our observations; scientific neglect in these areas proved an obstacle difficult to overcome. At the same time, *someone guided by special knowledge apparently vacated the libraries of anything we could have found on the topic.*

Analysing these occurrences now in hindsight, we could say that the 'professor' was dangling bait over our heads, based on psychopaths' specific psychological knowledge. He knew in advance that he would fish out amenable individuals, but the limited numbers disappointed him. The transpersonification process generally took hold whenever an individual's instinctive substratum was marked by pallor or some deficits. To a lesser extent, it also worked among people who manifested other deficiencies, also the state provoked within them was partially impermanent, being largely the result of psychopathological induction.

This knowledge about the existence of susceptible individuals and how to work on them will continue being a tool for world conquest as long as it remains the secret of such 'professors'. When it becomes skillfully popular-ized science, it will help nations develop immunity. But none of us knew this at the time.

Nevertheless, we must admit that in demonstrating the properties of pathocracy in such a way as to force us into in-depth experience, the professor helped us understand the nature of the phenomenon in a larger scope than many a true sci-entific researcher participating in this work in one way or another.

This passage presents the essence of the pathocratic problem: its organized and self-conscious character, the ability of psychological deviants to manipu-late, control, and to a certain degree hypnotize others with their words and charisma, including the "special knowledge" they have of normal, non-pathological individuals, and their ability to influence and indoctrinate a cer-tain percentage of individuals and bring them under their sway. In other parts of the book, Lobaczewski discusses another sector of the population, forming about 12%, who make an alliance with the pathocrats, bringing the total per-centage of "ponerized" individuals to about 20%, a figure that gives the pathocracy more than enough members to completely control the govern-ment, business, law, and the media.

THE HYSTEROIDAL CYCLE[378]

An important aspect of the research of the Quantum Future Group is the study of cycles of history. Empires rise and fall. Those texts such as Revelations that are interpreted as prophecy may in fact be descriptions of past cataclysmic events—remember the discussion of Solon with the "Egyptian priest" referred to earlier—that were left as warnings for the descendents of the writers. Lobaczewski has also identified cycles in the ponerization of society. Writing over twenty years ago, he identified the cycle in which the United States was entering. It is relevant to our discussion of 9/11.

In building up to his discussion of the "hysteroidal cycle", he identifies a serious weakness of Western civilization that can be traced back to the notion of the individual in Roman law and its diversion into concern for *invented beings*, not real humans. Today, one particularly pernicious manifestation of this inheritance is the existence of so-called "legal persons", that is, corporations that can be used to avoid the personal responsibility of the owners.[379]

We will allow Lobaczewski to develop his argument at length:

> Three ancient systems coincided to form our Western Civilization: Greek philosophy, Roman imperial and legal ideas, and Christianity. The culture that we have inherited from these influences, consolidated by time and effort of later generations, is quite limited when dealing with aspects of psychology and spiritual life. It is stiffly anchored in materiality and law.

> Such a state of affairs has had a serious negative effect on our ability to comprehend reality, especially that reality that concerns human beings and society.

> With the imposition of Christianity, Europeans became unwilling to really study reality (i.e. subordinating their intellects to facts), preferring instead to attempt to impose on Nature their subjective ideational schemes. Not until modern times, thanks to the hard sciences which undertake to study facts by their very nature, as well as the willingness to study the apperception of the philosophical heritage of other cultures, has there been any clarification of our world of concepts.

What is troubling is to note that, just at the point in time when a quantum leap in progress along the line of combining scientific method with a recuperation of an understanding informed by psychology and spirit was possible and gaining energy every day, an event such as 9/11 took place, the aftermath of which has the potential of setting human progress back hundreds, if not thousands of years if the Armaggedon scenario being sold by the Christian hawkers is allowed to play out.

---

[378] Dr. Lobaczewski's manuscript is quite dense due to the academic language. I have slightly edited some of the quoted sections that I am including in this volume so that it will be easier to read by the layperson (including myself).

[379] For a trenchant analysis of this problem, as well as the psychopathic characteristics of the modern corporation, see the excellent film *The Corporation,* which looks at corporate behaviour through the lens of Dr. Robert Hare's checklist for psychopathic traits.

Greek culture included a rich mythological 'imagination' that was, apparently, developed in direct contact with nature. These conditions saw the birth of a literary tradition and philosophical reflections searching for essential content and criteria of values. The Greek heritage was rich and individual and primeval.

Rome was too vital and practical to reflect on the thoughts of the Greeks. They appropriated them, and subjugated them to administrative needs and judicial developments with 'practical priorities'. They thus used the 'idea' of philosophy as a means of developing the thinking process that could then be useful for the discharge of administrative functions and the exercise of political options.

In any imperial civilization, the complex problems of human nature are troublesome and only complicate the legal regulations of public affairs and administrative functions. This led to the Roman tendency to dismiss such individualistic human considerations in favor of developing a concept of human personality that was simple enough to serve the purposes of law. Roman citizens could have personal attitudes and follow their goals only within the framework set by 'fate' and legal principles having little to do with real, human, psychological properties.

Thus, cognitive psychology was diverted and left barren when Rome conquered Greece. This led to moral recession at both the individual and public levels.

Through Judaism, nascent Christianity claimed strong ties with the ancient cultures of the Middle East, including their philosophical and psychological ideas. This lead to a school of thought characterized by one's relationships to other people: one's neighbor. Understanding, forgiveness, and love opened the door to a psychological cognition which, often supported by charismatic phenomena, bore abundant fruit in the first three centuries of its existence.

One could thus expect Christianity to help develop the art of human understanding to a higher level than the older cultures and religions. One could hope that such knowledge would protect future generations from the dangers of speculative thought divorced from that psychological and profound reality which can only be comprehended through sincere respect for other human beings in all their shapes and sizes, and with all their differences honored and respected.

But that is not what happened.

In the second half of the fourth century, things went terribly wrong for Christianity.

Christianity adapted the Greek heritage of thought and language of philosophical concepts to its purposes. The Christian church appropriated Roman organizational forms and adapted to existing social institutions. As a result, Christianity inherited Roman habits of legal thinking, including its indifference to human nature and its variety. These two items were linked together so firmly and permanently that later generations forgot just how strange they were to each other. Roman influence deprived Christianity of its primeval psychological knowledge.

A civilization thus arose with a serious deficiency in the area which is supposed to protect societies from various kinds of evil, and we are the inheritors of this defect. This civilization developed formulations in the area of law—national, civil, and canon—which were conceived for *invented* beings, not human beings, and which gave short shrift to the total contents of the human personality and the *great psychological differences between individual members of the species Homo sapiens.* For many centuries, any understanding of certain psychological anomalies found among individuals was out of the question—even though such anomalies cause disaster.

Thus, *Western Civilization is insufficiently resistant to evil, which originates beyond the easily accessible areas of human consciousness* and takes advantage of the great gap between formal or legal thought and psychological reality.

In a civilization deficient in psychological cognition, individuals with dreams of imposing their power upon their environment and their society are not recognized as being fundamentally different, and they all too easily find a ready response in individuals with insufficiently developed consciousnesses. […]

We have earlier discussed the "legal argument". It is a direct consequence of the process described by Lobaczewski where the legal system deals with *invented beings* as opposed to human beings with their differences and individuality. Clearly, such a system where lying is rewarded and telling the truth is a handicap favours the psychopath.

Lobaczewski points out that much ink has been spilt by philosophers over the years discussing moral values, but he then goes on to look at the dearth of study on the origin of evil:

It is equally thought-provoking, however, to see how relatively little has been said about the opposite side of the coin; *the nature, causes, and genesis of evil.* These matters are usually cloaked behind the above generalized conclusions with a certain amount of secrecy. Such a state of affairs can be partially ascribed to the social conditions and historical circumstances under which these thinkers worked. Their modus operandi may have been dictated at least in part by personal fate, inherited traditions, or even prudishness. After all, justice and virtue are the opposites of force and perversity, the same applies to truthfulness vs. lies, similarly like health is the opposite of an illness.

The character and genesis of evil thus remained hidden in discreet shadows, leaving it to playwrights to deal with the subject in their highly expressive language, but that did not reach the primeval source of the phenomena. *A certain cognitive space thus remains uninvestigated, a thicket of moral questions which resists understanding and philosophical generalizations.* […]

The goal, then, is to look at the genesis of evil through the eyes of a scientist, or a naturalist as he put it above, not in moral terms. Evil must be studied clinically, dispassionately, and objectively.

Returning to the discussion of cycles, we know that societies and empires rise and fall, pass from good times to bad times and back again. There are certain psychological characteristics that are associated with "good times":

During good times, people lose sight of the need for thinking, introspection, knowledge of others, and an understanding of life. When things are 'good', people ask themselves whether it is worth it to ponder human nature and flaws in the personality (one's own, or that of another). In good times, entire generations can grow up with no understanding of the creative meaning of suffering since they have never experienced it themselves. When all the joys of life are there for the taking, mental effort to understand science and the laws of nature—to acquire knowledge that may not be directly related to accumulating stuff— seems like pointless labor. Being 'healthy minded', and positive—a good sport

sport with never a discouraging word—is seen as a good thing, and anyone who predicts dire consequences as the result of such insouciance is labeled a wet-blanket or a killjoy.

Perception of the truth about reality, especially a real understanding of human nature in all its ranges and permutations, ceases to be a virtue to be acquired. Thoughtful doubters are 'meddlers' who can't leave well enough alone. 'Don't fix it if it ain't broke.' This attitude leads to an impoverishment of psychological knowledge including the capacity to differentiate the properties of human nature and personality, and the ability to mold healthy minds creatively.

The cult of power thus supplants the mental and moral values so essential for maintaining peace by peaceful means. A nation's enrichment or involution as regards its psychological world-view could be considered an indicator of whether its future will be good or bad.

During good times, the search for the meaning of life, the truth of our reality, becomes uncomfortable because it reveals inconvenient factors. Unconscious elimination of data which are, or appear to be, inexpedient, begins to be habit-ual, a custom accepted by entire societies. The result is that *any thought processes based on such truncated information cannot bring correct conclusions.* This then leads to substitution of convenient lies to the self to replace uncom-fortable truths thereby approaching the boundaries of phenomena which should be viewed as psychopathological.

The facts are that "good times" for one group of people have been histori-cally rooted in some injustice to other groups of people. In such a society, where all the hidden truths lurk below the surface like an iceberg, disaster is just around the corner.

It is clear that America has experienced a long period of "good times" for most of its existence (no matter how many people they had to oppress or kill to do so), but particularly so during the 50 years preceding September 11, 2001. During those 50 years, several generations of children were born, and the ones that were born at the beginning of that time, who have never known "bad times", are now at an age where they want to enjoy the benefits they have accumulated. Unfortunately, it doesn't look like that is going to happen; 9/11 has changed everything so profoundly that it looks like there will be no enjoyment by anyone for a very, very long time.

How could this happen?

The answer is that a few generations' worth of "good times" results in the above described *societal deficits* regarding psychological skills and moral criticism. Long periods of preoccupation with the self and "accumulating benefits" for the self diminish the ability to accurately read the environment and other people. But the situation is more serious than just a generalized weakness of a society that could be "toughened up" with a little "hard times". Lobaczewski writes:

> The psychological features of each such crisis are unique to the culture and the time, but one common denominator that exists at the beginning of all such 'bad times' is an *exacerbation of society's hysterical condition.*

Here, Dr. Lobaczewski is referring to a precise psychological term. The hysterical person, or "histrionic personality disorder", is described as follows: People with a histrionic personality "conspicuously seek attention, are dramatic and excessively emotional, and are overly concerned with appearance. Their lively, expressive manner results in easily established but often superficial and transient relationships. Their expression of emotions often seems exaggerated, childish, and contrived to evoke sympathy or attention (often erotic or sexual) from others. People with a histrionic personality are prone to sexually provocative behavior or to sexualizing nonsexual relationships. However, they may not really want a sexual relationship; rather, their seductive behavior often masks their wish to be dependent and protected. Some people with a histrionic personality also are hypochondriacal and exaggerate their physical problems to get the attention they need" (The Merck Manual).

Lobaczewski then describes a society that eerily resembles the United States of today:

> The emotionalism dominating in individual, collective, and political life, combined with the subconscious selection and substitution of data in reasoning, lead to individual and national egotism. The mania for taking offense at the drop of a hat provokes constant retaliation, taking advantage of hyperirritability and hypocriticality on the part of others. It is this feature, *this hystericization of society, that enables pathological plotters, snake charmers, and other primitive deviants to act as essential factors in the processes of the origination of evil on a macro-social scale.*

Who, exactly, are the "pathological plotters", and what can motivate such individuals during times that are generally understood by others as "good"? If times are "good", why does anyone want to plot and generate evil?

Well, certainly, the current U.S. administration has come up with an answer: "They hate us because of our freedoms." This is a prime example of "selection and substitution of data in reasoning" which is willingly and gladly accepted as an explanation by the public because of their *deficits of psychological skills* and moral criticism.

Lobaczewski discusses the fact that "bad times" also seem to have a historical "purpose". It seems that suffering during times of crisis leads to mental activity aimed at solving or ending the suffering. The bitterness of loss invariably leads to a regeneration of values and empathy. He writes:

> When bad times arrive and people are overwhelmed by an excess of evil, they must gather all their physical and mental strength to fight for existence and protect human reason. The search for some way out of difficulties and dangers rekindles long-buried powers of discretion. Such people have the initial tendency to rely on force in order to counteract the threat; they may, for instance, become 'trigger happy' or dependent upon armies. Slowly and laboriously, however, they discover the advantages conferred by mental effort; improved understanding of psychological situations in particular, better differentiation of human characters and personalities, and finally, comprehension of one's adversaries. During such times, virtues which former generations relegated to literary motifs

regain their real and useful substance and become prized for their value. A wise person capable of furnishing sound advice is highly respected.

It seems that there have been many such "bad times" in the course of human history, and it was during such times that the great systems of ethics were developed. Reflection on such topics was necessary for survival, as we see again today in the post-9/11 world. Unfortunately, during "good times", nobody wants to hear about it. They want to "enjoy" things, to have pleasure and pleasant experiences, and so any literature that relates to such times is lost, forgotten, suppressed, or otherwise ignored. This leads to further debasing of the intellectual currency and opens the gap for bad times to come once again.

However, even if great systems of ethics have been developed in the past, there is a work that has yet to be written—*a scientific explanation of the origins of evil*:

> If a collection were to be made of all the books that describe the horrors of wars, the cruelties of revolutions, and the bloody deeds of political leaders and systems, most people would avoid such a library. In such a library, ancient works would be found alongside books by contemporary historians and reporters. The documentary evidence on German extermination and concentration camps, complete with dry statistical data, describing the well-organized 'labor' of the destruction of human life, would be seen to use a properly calm language, and would provide the basis for acknowledging the nature of Evil.

> The autobiography of Rudolf Hess, the commander of camps in Osweicim (Auschwitz) and Brzezinka (Birkenau), is *a classic example of how an intelligent psychopath thinks and feels.*

> Our library of death would include works on philosophy discussing the social and moral aspects of the genesis of Evil, while using history to partially justify the blood-drenched 'solutions'.

> The library would show to the alert reader a sort of evolution from primitive attitudes, that it is alright to enslave and murder vanquished peoples, to the present day moralizing which declares that such behavior is barbaric and worthy of condemnation.

> However, such a library would be missing one crucial tome: *there would not be a single work offering a sufficient explanation of the causes and processes whereby such historical dramas originate, of how and why human beings periodically degenerate into bloodthirsty madness.*

> The old questions would remain unanswered: what made this happen? Does everyone carry the seeds of crime within, or only some of us? No matter how faithful to the events, nor how psychologically accurate the books that are available may be, they cannot answer those questions nor can they fully explain the origin of Evil.

> Thus, humanity is at a great disadvantage because *without a fully scientific explanation of the origins of Evil, there is no possibility of the development of sufficiently effective principles for counteracting Evil.* […]

In the macro-social phenomenon where Evil runs rampant, 'Pathocracy', a certain hereditary anomaly isolated as 'essential psychopathy' is catalytically and causatively essential for the genesis and survival of such a State. [...] [380]

This last remark is the key to "grand conspiracies" that so many people reject as impossible. Dr. Lobaczewski discusses the kinds of individuals that form a "Pathocracy", or "psychopathic government", and further, he elaborates details about psychopaths based on his studies and the studies of those with whom he was associated that have never been openly discussed as far as I can tell after reading many thousands of pages of material on the subject generated here in the West. Dr. Lobaczewski, on the other hand, undertook his studies "in the belly of the beast", so to say, with live "specimens". The value of such a study cannot be overstated.

Dr. Lobaczewski tells us that out of a particular sample of 5000 psychotic, neurotic, and healthy patients, there were 384 that had behaved in a manner that seriously harmed others. His sampling was from a broad range of society, professions, and represented a cross-section of moral, social and political views. After administering a variety of tests, (medical and psychological), and taking detailed histories, both from the patients and those associated with them, he concluded that only about 15 percent of them did not exhibit any psychopathological factors. In other words, there were pathological factors involved in 85 percent of cases of "evildoers", which leads to the hypothesis that if a particular pathology did not exist in that individual, the individual would not have "gone bad". This is represented in the work of many scholars who suggest that evil in this world results from a kind of web of "mutual conditioning", a web of interlocking structures where one kind of evil feeds and opens doors for another.

Such a description of the "origin of evil" is generally accepted today and is often acknowledged by courts and public opinion. "He was abused as a child, and thus only knows how to abuse others." Or, "he was brain damaged at birth and has a brain lesion that causes him to act that way". Or "he is mentally retarded; he doesn't know right from wrong". That's the Freudian influence that has prevented us from seeing what we need to see about individuals whose fundamental existence is based on getting power over others.

Every person assimilates psychological characteristics throughout his or her life, but particularly during childhood. This can be via mental resonance, identification, imitation, and other means of communication. This assimilation is what *builds a person's personality and world-view*. If these types of influences are contaminated by pathological factors and malformations within those who interact closely with the individual in question, the development of that person may be likewise deformed. He will be unable to correctly understand himself or others, or to understand normal human relations and morals, and he or she will commit evil acts with no feeling (or a poor

---

[380] Lobaczewski, op. cit.

awareness) of being deformed relative to the rest of society. In such cases, our society rightly asks: can he or she be to blame for what they do not know?

> Such 'ponerogenic' processes as this are part of a complex network of causation which frequently contains feedback relationships. Sometimes, cause and effect are widely separated in time which makes it difficult to track. Ponerology should thus study the role of pathological factors in the origins of evil since conscious control and monitoring at a scientific, social and individual level could effectively disarm these processes and protect individuals and society.

For instance, in the course of psychotherapy, the patient can learn about the influences from some deformed person in his life who exhibited psychopathological characteristics and then, painful though it may be, the patient can develop the ability to liberate himself from the results of these influences, to improve his ability to understand himself, and to overcome his internal and interpersonal difficulties so as to avoid mistakes which hurt himself and others.

But we are still left wondering about the 15 percent of 384 people who hurt others and in whom there were no pathological factors found in their medical or psychological background. That is 1.15 percent of the total population of 5000 patients. Lobaczewski suggests that there may have been failures in the testing process. In other words, there might be pathologies, but they were not evident via the tests available at the time. We will return to them further on. For now, let's just consider the fact that pathological processes have historically had a profound influence upon human society at large due to the fact that many individuals with deformed characters have played outstanding roles in the formation of social constructs. It is helpful to have some background on this. Dr. Lobaczewski writes:

> Brain tissue is very limited in its regenerative ability. If it is damaged and the change subsequently heals, a process of rehabilitation takes place thanks to which the neighboring healthy tissue takes over the function of the damaged portion. This substitution is never quite perfect thus some deficits as regards skill and proper psychological processes can be detected, even in cases of very small damage, by using the appropriate tests. […]

> As regards pathological factors of ponerogenic processes, *perinatal or early-infant damages have more active results than damages which occur later.*

> In societies with highly developed medical care, we find among the lower grades of elementary schools that *5 to 7 percent of the children have suffered brain tissue lesions* which cause certain academic or behavioral difficulties. […]

This is actually a frightening figure. If we realize that an even higher percentage of the previous generations have suffered brain tissue lesions during a time when there was no highly developed perinatal and neonatal medical care, not to mention the damage that may be suffered among those populations today where such care is still primitive, we can understand that much of our own culture has been shaped by people with brain damage, and we are faced with dealing with a world in which brain damaged individuals have an important influence on the social constructs! Keep in mind that if your grandfather suffered perinatal or neonatal brain damage, it affected how he raised one of your parents, which affects how that parent raised you!

> Epilepsy constitutes the oldest known results of such lesions; it is observed in relatively small numbers of persons suffering such damage. Researchers in these matters are more or less unanimous in believing that Julius Caesar and then later Napoleon Bonaparte had epileptic seizures. The extent to which these ailments had a negative effect upon their characters and historical decision making, or played a ponerogenic role, can be the subject of a separate study. In most cases, however, epilepsy is an *evident ailment*, which limits its role as a ponerogenic factor.

In other words, because epilepsy is so evident, people who have it generally do not achieve positions of power. They are known to be sick, and often their sickness is so severe that they are limited in their activities.

> In a much larger part of the bearers of brain tissue damage, the negative deformation of their characters grows in the course of time. It takes on various mental pictures depending on the properties and localizations of the damage, their time of origin, and also the life conditions of the individual after their occurrence. We will call character disorders resulting from such pathology 'Characteropathies'.
>
> Some characteropathies play an outstanding role as pathological agents in the processes of the genesis of evil *on a large social scale*. [...]
>
> A relatively well-documented example of such an influence of a characteropathic personality on a macro-social scale is the last German emperor, Wilhelm II. He was subjected to brain trauma at birth. During and after his entire reign, his physical and psychological handicap was hidden from public knowledge. The motor abilities of the upper left portion of his body were handicapped. As a boy, he had difficulty learning grammar, geometry, and drawing, which constitutes *the typical triad of academic difficulties caused by minor brain lesions*. He developed a personality with infantilistic features and insufficient control over his emotions, and also a somewhat paranoid way of thinking which easily sidestepped the heart of some important issues in the process of dodging problems.
>
> Militaristic poses and a general's uniform overcompensated for his feelings of inferiority and effectively cloaked his shortcomings. Politically, his insufficient control of emotions and factors of personal rancor came into view. The old Iron Chancellor had to go, that cunning and ruthless politician who had been loyal to the monarchy and built up Prussian power. After all, he was too knowledgeable about the prince's defects and had worked against his coronation. A similar fate met other overly critical people, who were replaced by persons with lesser brains, more subservience, and sometimes, discreet psychological deviations. Negative selection took place.

Notice this last phrase: "negative selection took place". That is to say, a defective head of state selected his staff, his government, based on his own pathologically damaged worldview. I'm sure the reader can perceive how dangerous such a situation can be to the people governed by such a "negatively selected" cabal. The important thing to consider here is what effect this had on the social constructs under the rule of such individuals. Lobaczewski explains:

> The experience of people with such anomalies grows out of the normal human world to which they belong by nature. Thus, their different way of thinking, their emotional violence, and their egotism find relatively easy entry into other people's minds and are perceived within the categories of the natural world-view. *Such behavior on the part of persons with such character disorders traumatizes the minds and feelings of normal people, gradually diminishing their ability to use their common sense.* In spite of their resistance, *people become used to the rigid habits of pathological thinking and experiencing.* In young people, as a result, the personality suffers abnormal development leading to its malformation. They thus represent pathological ponerogenic factors which, by their covert activity, easily engenders new phases in the eternal genesis of evil, opening the door to a later activation of other factors which thereupon take over the main role. [...]

> [In the case of the effect of Wilhelm II], *many Germans were progressively deprived of their ability to use their common sense* because of the impingement of psychological material of the characteropathic type, **as the common people are prone to identify with the emperor.** [...]

> Many thoughtful persons keep asking the same anxious question: how could the German nation have chosen for a Fuehrer a clownish psychopath who made no bones about his pathological vision of superman rule? Under his leadership, Germany then unleashed a second war, criminal and politically absurd. *During the second half of this war, highly trained army officers honorably performed the inhuman orders, senseless from the political and military point of view, issued by a man whose psychological state corresponded to the routine criteria for being forcibly committed to psychiatric hospitalization.*

> Any attempt to explain the things that occurred during the first half of our century by means of categories generally accepted in historical thought leaves behind a nagging feeling of inadequacy. Only a ponerological approach can compensate for this deficit in our comprehension, as it does justice to the role of various pathological factors in the genesis of evil at every social level.

> Fed for generations on *pathologically altered psychological material*, the German nation fell into a state comparable to what we see in certain individuals raised by persons who are both characteropathic and hysterical. Psychologists know from experience how often such people then let themselves commit acts which seriously hurt others. [...]

> The Germans inflicted and suffered enormous pain during the first World War; they thus felt no substantial guilt and even thought they had been wronged, as *they were behaving in accordance with their customary habit without being aware of its pathological causes.* The need for this state to be clothed in heroic garb after a war in order to avoid bitter disintegration became all too common. A mysterious craving arose, as if the social organism had [...] become addicted to some drug. That was the hunger of pathologically modified psychological material, a phenomenon known to psychotherapeutic experience. This hunger could only be satisfied by another personality and system of government, both similarly pathological.

A characteropathic personality opened the door for leadership by a psycho-pathic individual.[381]

What is interesting at this point in Lobaczewski's discourse is his indication that this pattern repeats itself again and again in history: a pathologically brain-damaged individual creates circumstances that condition the public in a certain way, and this, then, opens the door for the psychopath to come to power. As I read this, I thought back to the last 45 or 50 years of history in America and realized that the "cold war", the nuclear threat, the assassination of JFK, the antics of Nixon, Johnson, Reagan, Clinton, the manipulation of Americans via the media, were just such characteropathic conditionings that opened the door for the neocons and their nominal puppet, George W. Bush, who can certainly be described as "a clownish psychopath who makes no bones about his pathological vision of super-American rule". We can even see in the cabal that is assembled around George W. Bush, the same "nega-tive selection" of advisors and cabinet officials as Lobaczewski described were assembled around Kaiser Wilhelm.

So, we begin to understand just how important this "science of evil adjusted for political purposes" may be and how much understanding we, as a society, lack.

ESSENTIAL PSYCHOPATHY

We now come to the most important pathology: psychopathy. Psychopathy is not, as many people think, so easy to recognize. The problem is that the term "psychopath" has come to be usually applied by the public (due to the influence of the media) to overtly and obviously mad-dog murderers. There is also some confusion regarding psychopathy *vis à vis* "antisocial personality disorder".

Nice words, aren't they? They sound so clean and clinical; just a person who is "anti-social". It almost suggests a hermit who never bothers anybody. But nothing could be further from the truth. Robert Hare, the current American guru on psychopathy, writes about this problem of terminology as follows:

> Traditionally, affective and interpersonal traits such as egocentricity, deceit, shallow affect, manipulativeness, selfishness, and lack of empathy, guilt or re-morse, have played a central role in the conceptualization and diagnosis of psy-chopathy (Cleckley; Hare 1993; in press; Widiger and Corbitt). In 1980 this tra-dition was broken with the publication of *DSM-III.*[382] Psychopathy—renamed antisocial personality disorder—was now defined by persistent violations of so-cial norms, including lying, stealing, truancy, inconsistent work behavior and traffic arrests.
>
> Among the reasons given for this dramatic shift away from the use of clinical inferences were that personality traits are difficult to measure reliably, and that

---

[381] Lobaczewski, op. cit.
[382] *Diagnostic and Statistical Manual of Mental Disorders*, Third Edition.

it is easier to agree on the behaviors that typify a disorder than on the reasons why they occur. The result was a diagnostic category with good reliability but dubious validity, a category that lacked congruence with other, well-established conceptions of psychopathy. [...]

The problems with *DSM-III* and its 1987 revision *(DSM-III-R)* were widely discussed in the clinical and research literature (Widiger and Corbitt). Much of the debate concerned the absence of personality traits in the diagnosis of ASPD, an omission that allowed antisocial individuals with completely different personalities, attitudes and motivations to share the same diagnosis. At the same time, there was mounting evidence that the criteria for ASPD defined a disorder that was more artifactual than 'real' (Livesley and Schroeder). [...]

Most psychopaths (with the exception of those who somehow manage to plow their way through life without coming into formal or prolonged contact with the criminal justice system) meet the criteria for ASPD, *but most individuals with ASPD are not psychopaths.* [...]

The differences between psychopathy and ASPD are further highlighted by recent laboratory research involving the processing and use of linguistic and emotional information. Psychopaths differ dramatically from non-psychopaths in their performance of a variety of cognitive and affective tasks. Compared with normal individuals, for example, psychopaths are less able to process or use the deep semantic meanings of language and to appreciate the emotional significance of events or experiences (Larbig and others; Patrick; Williamson and others). [...]

Things become even more problematic when we consider that the *DSM-IV* text description of ASPD (which it says is also known as psychopathy) contains many references to traditional features of psychopathy. [...]

The failure to differentiate between psychopathy and ASPD can have serious consequences for clinicians and for society. For example, most jurisdictions consider psychopathy to be an aggravating rather than a mitigating factor in determining criminal responsibility. In some states an offender convicted of first-degree murder and diagnosed as a psychopath is likely to receive the death penalty on the grounds that psychopaths are cold-blooded, remorseless, untreatable and almost certain to re-offend. But many of the killers on death row were, and continue to be, mistakenly referred to as psychopaths on the basis of *DSM-III, DSM-III-R or DSM-IV* criteria for ASPD (Meloy). We don't know how many of these inhabitants of death row actually exhibit the personality structure of the psychopath, or how many merely meet the criteria for ASPD, a disorder that applies to the majority of criminals and that has only tenuous implications for treatability and the likelihood of violent re-offending. If a diagnosis of psychopathy has consequences for the death penalty—or for any other severe disposition, such as an indeterminate sentence or a civil commitment—clinicians making the diagnosis should make certain they do not confuse ASPD with psychopathy. [...]

Diagnostic confusion about the two disorders has the potential for harming psychiatric patients and society as well.

In my book, *Without Conscience*, I argued that we live in a 'camouflage society', a society in which some psychopathic traits—egocentricity, lack of concern for others, superficiality, style over substance, being 'cool', manipulativeness, and so forth—increasingly are tolerated and even valued. With respect to the topic of this article, it is easy to see how both psychopaths and those with ASPD could blend in readily with groups holding antisocial or criminal values. It is more difficult to envisage how those with ASPD could hide out among more prosocial segments of society. Yet *psychopaths have little difficulty infiltrating the domains of business, politics, law enforcement, government, academia and other social structures* (Babiak). *It is the egocentric, cold-blooded and remorseless psychopaths who blend into all aspects of society and have such devastating impacts on people around them* who send chills down the spines of law enforcement officers. [383]

Read that last bit again:

> Yet *psychopaths have little difficulty infiltrating the domains of business, politics, law enforcement, government, academia and other social structures* (Babiak). *It is the egocentric, cold-blooded and remorseless psychopaths who blend into all aspects of society and have such devastating impacts on people around them who send chills down the spines of law enforcement officers.*

It makes you wonder whether the push to assimilate pyschopathy to ASPD wasn't the work of such "embedded" psychopaths. Regarding essential psychopathy, Lobaczewski tells us:

> Let us characterise another heredity-transmitted anomaly whose *role in ponerogenic processes on any social scale appears exceptionally great.* We should underscore that the need to isolate this phenomenon and examine it in detail became most evident to those researchers who were interested in the *macro social scale of genesis of evil* because they have witnessed it. I acknowledge my debt to Kasimir Dabrowski in doing this and calling this anomaly an 'essential psychopathy'.

> Biologically speaking, the phenomenon is similar to color-blindness and occurs with similar frequency (slightly above 0.5 percent), except that, unlike color-blindness, it affects both sexes.[384]

Here, Lobaczewski suggests a particular low frequency of occurrence of psychopathy which reminds us again of the 1.15 percent of Lobaczewski's total population that did not demonstrate any overtly identifiable pathology except that they performed actions that bring harm to other people for no explainable reason. If we consider what Dr. Hare has written above, that psychopaths "have little difficulty infiltrating the domains of business, politics, law enforcement, government, academia and other social structures [and] blend into all aspects of society", we must ask the question: is it possible that Lobaczewski's 1.15 percent of unidentified "evildoers" were this type of psychopath? As he pointed out, it could very well have been the diagnostic criteria that was lacking, and had he utilized Hare's psychopathy check-list, this group might very well have been identified as psychopaths. The point I wish to make is the number of psychopathic individuals likely to be found in

---

[383] Robert Hare, Ph.D., "Psychopathy and Antisocial Personality Disorder: A Case of Diagnostic Confusion", *Psychiatric Times* 13:2 (February 1996).
[384] Lobaczewski, op. cit.

any given cross-section sampling of society may be much higher than we suspect. Lobaczewski suggests that the occurrence of psychopathy is about the same as color-blindness: 0.5 percent. But if you add that figure to the 1.15 percent that he couldn't identify, the actual number may be closer to 1.65 percent.

Here I want to mention again that Harvard psychologist Martha Stout claims that 4 percent of "ordinary people" (one in twenty-five) often have an *"undetected mental disorder, the chief symptom of which is that the person possesses no conscience. He or she has no ability whatsoever to feel shame, guilt, or remorse* [and] *can do literally anything at all and feel absolutely no guilt.* "[385] That just happens to fit right in with Hare's description of psychopathy, though we are obviously dealing with an entire spectrum of manifestation, not to mention the difference between pathologies that are mechanical, i.e. brain damage, and pathologies that are inherited. If we add Stout's figure of 4 percent of undetected, "ordinary" people, to Lobaczewski's 0.5 percent, and include the 1.15 percent of people who had done harm to others with no evident pathology, we then have a figure of 5.65 percent—almost 6 percent of the population. Remember what Lobaczewski wrote about the influence of "indoctrination" on his peers?

> It was relatively easy to determine the environments and origin of the people who succumbed to this process, which I then called 'transpersonification'. They came from all social groups, including aristocratic and fervently religious families, and caused a break in our student solidarity in the order of some 6 %. [...]
>
> Even then, we had no doubts as to the pathological nature of this 'transpersonification' process, which ran similar but not identical in all cases. The duration of the results of this phenomenon also varied. Some of these people later became zealots. Others later took advantage of various circumstances to withdraw and reestablish their lost links to the society of normal people. They were replaced. The only constant value of the new social system was the magic number of 6 %.

This is an interesting thing, this coincidence of numbers. I have no explanation for it because we are certainly talking about many factors and not a single pathology. Moreover, the intensity also varies in scope from a level barely perceptive to an experienced observer to obvious pathological deficiency, that is, there is a range of manifestations of the various forms of psychopathy and these differences may be due deficits on the instinctive level:

> Analysis of the different experiential manner demonstrated by these individuals caused us to conclude that their instinctive substratum is also defective, containing certain gaps and lacking the natural syntonic[386] responses commonly evidenced by members of the species Homo sapiens. [...]

This defective instinctual substratum has an affect on the psychopath's ability to use language and understand abstract concepts:

---

[385] Stout, op. cit.
[386] From the Greek word "Syntony", to "bring into balance".

Our natural world of concepts then strikes such persons as a nearly incomprehensible convention with no justification in their own psychological experience. They think that normal human customs and principles of decency are a foreign convention invented and imposed by someone else ('probably by priests') silly, onerous, sometimes even ridiculous. At the same time, however, *they easily perceive the deficiencies and weaknesses of our natural language of psychological and moral concepts* in a manner somewhat reminiscent of the attitude of a contemporary psychologist—except in caricature.

As an example, imagine you had no sense of conscience, and therefore no feelings of remorse if you ever harmed another being. Because there was no inner voice guiding you on what is right or wrong, any rules would indeed appear ridiculous. If all you were concerned with was satisfying your own basic drives, without concern for others, and if this was what drove everything that you did, you would have no means of relating to rules that encouraged you to think about others. Moreover, the obvious hypocrisy of many people in their honouring of these rules would be readily apparent.

However, you would certainly develop your own set of rules and a special knowledge of the workings of the world, and the society of "normal people" in particular, that you would use to your advantage:

> The average intelligence of individuals with the above mentioned deviation, especially if measured via commonly used tests, is somewhat lower than that of normal people, albeit similarly variegated. However, this group does not contain instances of the highest intelligence, *nor do we find technical or craftsmanship talents among them.* The most gifted members of this kind may thus achieve accomplishments in those sciences which *do not require humanistic worldview or practical skills.* Whenever we attempt to construct special tests to measure 'life wisdom' or 'socio-moral imagination', even if the difficulties of psychometric evaluation are taken into account, individuals of this type indicate a deficit disproportionate to their personal IQ.

> In spite of their deficiencies as regards normal psychological and moral knowledge, *they develop and then have at their disposal a knowledge of their own,* something *lacked* by people with a natural worldview.

> **They learn to recognize each other in a crowd as early as childhood, and they develop an awareness of the existence of other individuals similar to themselves.**

> **They also become conscious of being different from the world of those other people surrounding them.** They view us from a certain distance, *like a paraspecific variety.*

> Natural human reactions—which often fail to elicit interest because they are considered self-evident—strike psychopaths as strange and therefore interesting, even comical. They therefore *observe us, deriving conclusions,* forming their different world of concepts.

> They become *experts in our weaknesses* and sometimes effect heartless experiments upon us. [...] Neither a normal person nor our natural worldview can perceive or properly evaluate the existence of this world of different concepts.

Consider the full implications of this passage. First, they are aware of each other. Second, they are aware of their difference from the rest of society. Third, they study us, deriving conclusions and becoming experts in our weaknesses. And what is the biggest of our "handicaps" according to the psychopath? That which they do not have: a *conscience*. Moreover, while they are aware of their differences from us, we are in complete ignorance, having no idea that there are individuals all around us, in positions of power and responsibility, who can do the most ruthless and harmful acts to others without a moment's remorse. And they continue to live amongst us and study us, putting up what Cleckley called "the mask of sanity"—that is, a sort of emulated humanity where they learn when it is proper to cry or show concern they do not feel, when it is necessary to express emotions they can only mimic:

> A researcher into such phenomena can glean a similar deviant knowledge through long-term studies of the personalities of such people, using it with some difficulty, like a foreign language. […] [The psychopath] will never be able to incorporate the worldview of a normal person, although they often try to do so all their lives. The product of their efforts is only a role and a mask behind which they hide their deviant reality.

> Another myth and role—albeit containing a grain of truth—would be the psychopath's brilliant mind or psychological genius; some of them actually believe in this and attempt to insinuate this belief to others. In speaking of the mask of psychological normality worn by such individuals (and by similar deviants to a lesser extent), we should mention the book *The Mask of Sanity*; the author, Hervey Cleckley, made this very phenomenon the crux of his reflections:

>> 'Let us remember that his typical behavior defeats what appear to be his own aims. Is it not he himself who is most deeply deceived by his apparent normality? Although he deliberately cheats others and is *quite conscious of his lies*, he appears unable to distinguish adequately between his own pseudo-intentions, pseudo-remorse, pseudo-love, and the genuine responses of a normal person. His *monumental lack of insight indicates how little he appreciates the nature of his disorder*. When others fail to accept immediately his 'word of honor as a gentleman', his amazement, I believe, is often genuine. The term genuine is used here not to qualify the psychopath's intentions but to qualify his amazement. *His subjective experience is so bleached of deep emotion that he is invincibly ignorant of what life means to others.*

When reading the above description, it is almost impossible not to think of the current U.S. president, George Bush. On many occasions where Bush has attempted to use words to demonstrate empathy with other human beings, he has failed miserably to convince. Applying Cleckley's analysis of the 'inner workings' of the psychopath, we see that, on these occasions, while realizing that he is lying, Bush is also convinced that he is accurately emulating the emotions that he observes in normal human beings and is bemused when he fails to convince. The problem, of course, is that people like Bush have no capacity to really understand what it is to feel positive emotions like empathy for another, and when they observe the display of such an emotion in other people, they cannot understand how it can be anything other than 'skin-deep':

His awareness of hypocrisy's opposite is so insubstantially theoretical that it becomes questionable if what we chiefly mean by hypocrisy should be attributed to him. *Having no major values himself, can he be said to realize adequately the nature and quality of the outrages his conduct inflicts upon others?* A young child who has no impressive memory of severe pain may have been told by his mother it is wrong to cut off the dog's tail. Knowing it is wrong he may proceed with the operation. We need not totally absolve him of responsibility if we say he realized less what he did than an adult who, in full appreciation of physical agony, so uses a knife. Can a person experience the deeper levels of sorrow without considerable knowledge of happiness? Can he achieve evil intention in the full sense without real awareness of evil's opposite? I have no final answer to these questions.[387]

If the psychopath is hiding behind a mask of sanity, how can he be recognized? Lobaczewski gives three characteristics:

All researchers into psychopathy underline three qualities primarily with regard to this most typical variety: the absence of a sense of guilt for antisocial actions, the inability to love truly, and the *tendency to be garrulous* in a way which easily deviates from reality.

A neurotic patient is generally taciturn and has trouble explaining what hurts him most. [...] These patients are capable of decent and enduring love, although they have difficulty expressing it or achieving their dreams. A psychopath's behavior constitutes the antipode of such phenomena and difficulties.

Our first contact [with the psychopath] is characterized by a *talkative stream which flows with ease* and avoids truly important matters with equal ease if they are uncomfortable for the talker. His train of thought also avoids those matter of human feelings and values whose representation is absent in the psychopathic world view. [...] From the logical point of view, the flow of thought is ostensibly correct.

[Psychopaths] are virtually unfamiliar with the enduring emotions of love for another person. [...] it constitutes a fairy-tale from that 'other' human world. [For the psychopath] love is an ephemeral phenomenon aimed at sexual adventure. However [the psychopath] is able to play the lover's role well enough for their partners to accept it in good faith. [Moral teachings] also strike them as a similar fairy-tale good only for children and those different 'others'. [...]

The world of normal people whom they hurt is incomprehensible and hostile to them. [...] [Life to the psychopath] is the pursuit of its immediate attractions, pleasure and power. They meet with failure along this road, along with force and condemnation from the society of those other incomprehensible people.[388]

The reader is referred to the growing literature on psychopathy for a better understanding.

Lobaczewski next gives us the most important clues as to how and why a truly global conspiracy can and does exist on our planet, though it certainly isn't a conspiracy in the normally accepted sense of the word. You could even say that such conspiracies arise simply as a natural result of the opposi-

---

[387] Hervey Cleckley, *The Mask of Sanity*, 4th edition (St. Louis: Mosby, 1983).
[388] Lobaczewski, op. cit.

tion between normal people and deviants. In a certain sense, understanding the view the psychopath has of "normal people", that they are "other" and even "foreign", helps us to realize how such conspiracies can be so "secret"—though that is not the precise word we would like to use. Lobaczewski describes it in the following way:

> In any society in this world, psychopathic individuals and some of the other deviants create a ponerogenically active network of common collusions, *partially estranged from the community of normal people.* Some inspirational role of the essential psychopathy in this network also appears to be a common phenomenon.
>
> They are aware of being different as they obtain their life experience and become familiar with different ways of fighting for their goals. Their world is forever divided into 'us and them'—their world with its own laws and customs and that other foreign world full of presumptuous ideas and customs in light of which they are condemned morally.
>
> Their 'sense of honor' bids them cheat and revile that other human world and its values. In contradiction to the customs of normal people, they feel non-fulfillment of their promises or obligations is customary behavior.
>
> *They also learn how their personalities can have traumatizing effects on the personalities of those normal people, and how to take advantage of this root of terror for purposes of reaching their goals.*
>
> This **dichotomy of worlds is permanent** and does not disappear even if they succeed in realizing their dreams of gaining power over the society of normal people. This proves that the separation is biologically conditioned.
>
> In such people a dream emerges like some youthful Utopia of a 'happy' world and a social system which would not reject them or force them to submit to laws and customs whose meaning is incomprehensible to them. They dream of a world in which their simple and radical way of experiencing and perceiving reality would dominate, where *they* would, of course, be assured safety and prosperity. Those 'others'—different, but also more technically skillful—should be put to work to achieve this goal. 'We', after all, will create a new government, one of justice. They are prepared to fight and suffer for the sake of such a brave new world, and also of course, to inflict suffering upon others. Such a vision justifies killing people whose suffering does not move them to compassion because 'they' are not quite conspecific.[389]

And there it is. Lobaczewski has said outright that psychopaths—from a certain perspective—are *a different type of human being*, a type that is aware of its difference from childhood. Put this together with his statement that such individuals *recognize their own kind*, and consider normal people as completely "other", and we can begin to understand why and how conspiracies can and do exist among such individuals. They do, indeed, collect together, with similar worldviews, like fat floating on a bowl of soup. When one of them begins to rant, others like them—or those with brain damage that makes them susceptible—"rally round the flag", so to say. Thus it is, when Robin Ramsay, editor of a conspiracy journal, *Lobster* magazine writes:

---

[389] Lobaczewski, op. cit.

Ultimately it comes down to how you see the world. The kind of conspiracy you are describing, or implying [regarding 9/11], is inconceivable to me: too big, too complex, too likely to go wrong or be discovered, ever to be mounted. What you are describing [...] is vastly much bigger—and more complex and more dangerous —than any known mind control/psy ops project. And there is no evidence for it.[390]

He may be viewing the world without full knowledge and awareness of psychopaths and their ponerogenic networks.

OTHER PSYCHOPATHIES

Political Ponerology includes a catalogue of different pathogical types, some of whom, like the essential psychopath, have a genetic predisposition, and others who become deviants through birth traumas or injuries, brain injuries while young, or from being raised in environments where they are shaped and formed by psychopathic ways of being. He discusses the way these various pathologies work together to form a complex system of ponerogenesis:

The cases of essential psychopathy seem similar enough to each other to permit them to be classified as qualitatively homogenous. However, we can also include within psychopathic categories a somewhat indeterminate number of anomalies with a hereditary substratum, whose symptoms are approximate to this most typical phenomenon. We also meet difficult individuals with a tendency to behave in a manner hurtful to other people, for whom tests do not indicate existing damage to brain tissue and anamnesis does not indicate very abnormal childrearing practices which could explain the state. The fact that such cases are repeated within families would suggest a hereditary substratum, but we must also take into account the possibility that harmful factors participated in the fetal stage. This is an area of medicine and psychology warranting more study, as there is more to learn than we already know concretely.

Such people also attempt to mask their different world of experience and play a role of normal people to varying degrees. [...] These people participate in the genesis of evil in very different ways, whether taking part openly or, to a lesser extent, when they have managed to adapt to proper ways of living. These psychopathies and related phenomena may, quantitatively speaking, be summarily estimated at two or three times the number of cases of essential psychopathy, i.e. at less than two per cent of the population.

This type of person finds it easier to adjust to social life. The lesser cases in particular adapt to the demands of the society of normal people, taking advantage of its understanding for the arts and other areas with similar traditions. Their literary creativity is often disturbing if conceived in ideational categories alone; they insinuate to their readers that their world of concepts and experiences is self-evident, also it actually contains characteristic deformities. [...]

Many people with various hereditary deviations and acquired defects develop pathological egotism. For such people, forcing others in their environment,

---

[390] Robin Ramsay, private correspondence with one of the authors.

whole social groups, and, if possible, entire nations to feel and think like themselves becomes an internal necessity, a ruling concept. Some issue a normal
person would not take seriously becomes an often lifelong goal for them, the
object of effort, sacrifices, and cunning psychological strategy. Pathological
egotism derives from repressing from one's field of consciousness any objec-
tionable self-critical associations referring to one's own nature or normality.
Dramatic questions such as 'who is abnormal here, me or this world of people
who feel and think differently?' are answered in the world's disfavor. Such egotism is always linked to a dissimulative attitude, with a Cleckley mask or some
other pathological quality being hidden from consciousness, both one's own and
that of other people. [...]

The importance of the contribution of this kind of egotism to the genesis of evil
thus hardly needs elaboration. It is a primarily societal resource, egotizing or
traumatizing others, which in turn causes further difficulties. Pathological egotism is a constant component of variegated states wherein someone who appears
to be normal (although he is in fact not quite so) is driven by motivations or battles for goals a normal person considers unrealistic or unlikely. The average person asks: 'What could he expect to gain by that?' Environmental opinion, however, interprets such a situation in accordance with 'common sense' and is prone
to accept a 'more likely' version of occurrence. *Such interpretation often results
in human tragedy.* We should thus always remember that the law principle of
cui prodest[391] becomes illusory whenever some pathological factor enters the
picture. [...]

Here, Lobaczewski is saying that we cannot take the results of the actions
of the psychopath at face value, or rather, assign normal interpretations to
such actions and their results. When a person lacks conscience and therefore
the ability to feel guilt, their understanding of the concepts of winning and
losing are very different from that of a normal person. The U.S. invasion of
Iraq in March 2003 resulted in an unwinnable quagmire, and anyone could be
forgiven for believing that it was a mistake on the part of the war planners,
that they essentially 'lost' the war and caused the fruitless deaths of thousands of U.S. military personnel and thousands more innocent Iraqi civilians.
We could also be excused for thinking that the planners of this misadventure
(from the point of view of normal people) experienced some negative emotion as a result. We might also wonder *cui prodest*—'who advances' or 'who
benefits'.

The simple fact however, is that for the psychopath, any negative 'emotion'
is limited to situations where he is prevented from doing what he desires to
do, and manipulating other human beings to serve his unadulterated self-
interest and lust for power and control over others is what the psychopath
desires. Of course, we can ponder further about what it is that creates this
desire—what is the core motivation? Perhaps in the final analysis we must
simply decide that psychopaths do what they do because *that is what they
are.* For example, if we look at why an animal does anything, we realize that

---

[391] Who "advances".

the main motivating factor is hunger. In the case of the psychopath however, it seems that they have a different kind of hunger: a 'psychic' hunger that plays out in material ways. If they can steal, hurt, destroy, they feel 'full'.

SPELLBINDERS AND PARAMORALISMS

One pathological type we would like to look at in particular is what Lobaczewski calls the "spellbinder", who, while statistically neglible, is highly active in the ponerogentic process:

> They are generally the carriers of various pathological factors, some characteropathies, and some inherited anomalies. [...]
>
> Spellbinders are characterized by pathological egotism. Such a person is forced by some internal causes to make an early choice between two possibilities: the first is forcing other people to think and experience things in a manner similar to his own; the second is a feeling of being lonely and different, a pathological misfit in social life. Sometimes the choice is either snake-charming or suicide.
>
> Triumphant repression of self-critical or unpleasant concepts from the field of consciousness gradually gives rise to [conversive thinking, i.e. paramoralism.]

The spellbinder is the charmer who can get up in front of a crowd and whip them into a frenzy. They are hypnotic and can "cast a spell" over a crowd. His drive comes from the need to convince others he is right, that his view of the world is the only one. As he is often fighting for his very existence, as Lobaczewski notes above, he is animated by a fire in his belly. But as his reading machine, his way of perceiving the world, is distorted and deviant, his discourse is too.

He casts his spell using *paramoralisms*:

> The conviction that moral values exist but that some actions violate moral rules is so common and ancient a phenomenon that it seems to have some substratum at man's instinctive endowment level, and not to be just a representation of centuries of experience, culture, religions, and socialization. Thus, any insinuation enclosed in a 'moral slogan' is always suggestive even if the 'moral' criteria used are just an ad hoc invention. Any act can thus be proved to be immoral or moral by means of using 'paramoralisms' through active suggestion and people who will succumb to this manipulation are plentiful.
>
> In searching for an example of an evil act whose negative value would not elicit doubt in any social situation, ethics scholars frequently mention child abuse. However, psychologists often meet with paramoral affirmations of such behavior in their practice.

To illustrate the ability of a paramoralism to turn even deeply held ideas and beliefs on their head, that is, to find a reason to explain them away, to justify that they hold in every case except the present case, Lobaczewski gives an example of a woman with prefrontal-field damage who was sadistically abusive to her child, but was supported in her abuse of the child by her brothers who were totally under her influence and convinced of her "exceptionally high moral qualifications". While child abuse in general was denounced by the brothers, the actual case of the abuse of their nephew was accepted. Particularly heinous examples of this type of thing often occur in a religious context where children have been beaten to death to "get the devil out". It is always done to "save their souls", and that is an example of "paramoralism" used in a conversive way.

A more recent example of a paramoralism would be the idea that the invasion of Iraq was undertaken to bring "democracy" to the country. Here the word "democracy" has been emptied of its original meaning and now means "the freedom for American capital to do what it wills". Paramoralism work because someone with a conscience will always interpret the saying of the spellbinder through his or her own worldview. They will always read a deeper meaning into the words, a meaning that they do not actually convey when used by spellbinders or other deviants.

> Paramoralistic statements and suggestions so often accompany various kinds of evil that they seem quite irreplaceable. Unfortunately, it has become a frequent phenomenon for individuals, oppressive groups, or patho-political systems to invent ever-new moral criteria for someone's convenience. Such suggestions deprive people of their moral reasoning and deform its development in children. Paramoralism factories have been founded worldwide, and a ponerologist finds it hard to believe that they are managed by psychologically normal people.

> The conversive features in the genesis of paramoralisms seem to prove they are derived from mostly subconscious rejection (and repression from the field of consciousness) of something completely different which we call the 'voice of conscience'. [...] Like all conversive phenomena, the tendency to use paramoralisms is psychologically contagious.

Returning to the subject of Spellbinders, Lobaczewski points out that "paramoralisms" stream profusely from such individuals so that they flood the average person's mind:

> To the spellbinder, everything becomes subordinated to their conviction that they are exceptional, sometimes even messianic. An ideology can emerge from such individuals that is certainly partly true, and the value of which is claimed to be superior to all other ideologies. They believe they will find many converts to their ideology and when they discover that this is not the case, they are shocked and fume with 'paramoral indignation'. The attitude of most normal people to such spellbinders is generally critical, pained and disturbed.

> The spellbinder places on a high moral plane anyone who succumbs to his influence, and he will shower such people with attention and property and perks of all kinds. Critics are met with 'moral' outrage, and it will be claimed by the spellbinder that the compliant minority is actually a majority.

> Such activity is always characterized by the inability to foresee its final results, something obvious from the psychological point of view, because its substratum contains pathological phenomena, and both spellbinding and self-charming make it impossible to perceive reality accurately enough to foresee results logically.

> In a healthy society, the activities of spellbinders meet with criticism effective enough to stifle them quickly. However, when they are preceded by conditions operating destructively on common sense and social order—such as social in-

justice, cultural backwardness, or intellectually limited rulers manifesting pathological traits—spellbinders activities have led entire societies into large-scale
human tragedy.

The consequences of having an entire media in the hands of such spellbinders— think Ann Coulter, Bill O'Reilly or the other mouthpieces of the
pathocracy in the United States—should be readily apparent. Anyone that
confronts their paramoralisms is denounced and marginalized.

> Such an individual fishes an environment or society for people amenable to his
> influence, deepening their psychological weaknesses until they finally become a
> ponerogenic union.

> On the other hand, people who have maintained their healthy critical faculties
> intact, attempt to counteract the spellbinders' activities and their results, based
> on their own common sense and moral criteria. In the resulting polarization of
> social attitudes, each side justifies itself by means of moral categories.

And we see just such a polarization going on in the U.S. today. The debate,
such as it is, goes in cirles over which side is "right" or "wrong". The only
way out of this infernal circle is to rise above such a moralistic debate and to
understand the true nature of the evil that had settled over the U.S. like a can-
cerous cloud.

> The awareness that a spellbinder is always a pathological individual should pro-
> tect us from the known results of a moralizing interpretation of pathological
> phenomena, ensuring us of objective criteria for more effective action.

> [A high IQ] generally helps in immunity to spellbinders, but only moderately.
> Actual differences in the formation of human attitudes under the influence of
> such activities should be attributed to other properties of human nature. The fac-
> tor most decisive as regards assuming a critical attitude is good basic intelli-
> gence, which conditions our perception of psychological reality. We can also
> observe how a spellbinder's activities 'husk out' amenable individuals with an
> astonishing regularity.

Could the decades old war on the public education system in the United
States, and now elsewhere in the world, be a conscious act on the part of the
pathocracy to eliminate the critical attitude necessary to see through them?

PONEROGENIC ASSOCIATIONS

We have identified several pieces of the pathocratic puzzle: the invisible
enemy amoung us, the psychopath; their recognition of their difference from
the rest of normal society at an early age; their special knowledge of normal
society and individuals that they can use to manipulate us and get what they
want; and their ability to recognize each other and work together. Next we
look at the question of ponerogenic associations, that is, associations of different pathological types working together to impose their vision and experience of the world on the rest of us. Some of these associations are ponerogenic from the start; others begin as associations of normal people working to

better the world, are taken over by deviants, and become the vehicle of pathocratic power:

> We shall give the name "ponerogenic association" to any group of people characterized by ponerogenic processes of above-average social intensity, wherein the carriers of various pathological factors function as inspirers, spellbinders, and leaders, and where a proper pathological social structure generates. Smaller, less permanent associations may be called "groups" or "unions".
>
> Such an association gives birth to evil which hurts other people as well as its own members. We could list various names ascribed to such organizations by linguistic tradition: gangs, criminal mobs, mafias, cliques, and coteries, which cunningly avoid collision with the law while seeking to gain their own advantage.
>
> Such unions frequently aspire to political power in order to impose their expedient legislation upon societies in the name of a suitably prepared ideology, deriving advantages in the form of disproportionate prosperity and the satisfaction of their craving for power. [...]
>
> One phenomenon all ponerogenic groups and associations have in common is the fact that their members lose (or have already lost) *the capacity to perceive pathological individuals as such*, interpreting their behavior in a fascinated, heroic, or melodramatic ways. The opinions, ideas, and judgments of people carrying various psychological deficits are endowed with an importance at least equal to that of outstanding individuals among normal people.
>
> *The atrophy of natural critical faculties with respect to pathological individuals becomes an opening to their activities, and, at the same time, a criterion for recognizing the association in concern as ponerogenic.* Let us call this the first criterion of ponerogenesis.

If we imagine a polarity with conscience at one pole and lack of conscience at the other, there will be a continuum between the two. There is a large area where the two are blending into each other, with pathological ideas subtly informing non-pathological ideas. An example that comes to mind is the issue of insults and provocations in professional sport. It is now commonly accepted by "everybody" that these taunts and personal attacks, verbal or physical, are "part of the game". However, if one can step back and brings one's critical attitude to bear on the question, it should be obvious that there is nothing about insults and provocations that are inherent to sport, either individual or team. It is a veneer laid over the game and the practice of the sport itself.

That such behaviour is now commonly accepted as being just the way it is, is a strong indicator of the ponerogenesis of sport. It is an example of our losing the ability to see pathological individuals and behaviour for what it is. We shouldn't be surprised, then, that scandal and criminal activity is also part of the world of professional sport.

> *Another phenomenon all ponerogenic associations have in common is their statistically high concentration of individuals with various psychological anomalies.* Their qualitative composition is crucially important in the formation of the entire union's character, activities, development, or extinction.

Groups dominated by various kinds of *characteropathic* individuals will develop relatively primitive activities, proving rather easy for a society of normal people to break. However, things are quite different when such unions are inspired by psychopathic individuals. [392]

Lobaczewski then describes the two basic types of ponerogenic unions: *primary and secondary ponerogenic*:

> Let us describe as primarily ponerogenic a union whose *abnormal* members were active from the very beginning, playing the role of crystallizing catalysts as early as the process of creation of the group occurred.
>
> We shall call secondarily ponerogenic a union which was *founded in the name of some idea with an independent social meaning*, generally comprehensible within the categories of the natural world view, but which later succumbed to a certain moral degeneration. This in turn opened the door to infection and activation of the pathological factors within, and later to a ponerization of the group as a whole, or often of its fraction.
>
> From the very outset, a primarily ponerogenic union is a foreign body within the organism of society, its character colliding with the moral values held or respected by the majority. The activities of such groups provoke opposition and disgust and are considered immoral; as a rule, therefore, such groups do not spread large, nor do they metastasize into numerous unions; they finally lose their battle with society.
>
> In order to have a chance to develop into a large ponerogenic association, however, it suffices that some human organization, characterized by social or political goals and an ideology with some creative value, be accepted by a larger number of normal people *before* it succumbs to a process of ponerogenic malignancy.
>
> The primary tradition and ideological values of such a society may then, for a long time, protect a union which has succumbed to the ponerization process from the awareness of society, especially its less critical components.

---

[392] Lobaczewski: Let us adduce the following example illustrating the roles of two different anomalies, selected from among actual events studied by the author.

In felonious youth gangs, a specific role is played by boys (and occasionally girls) that carry a characteristic deficit that is sometimes left behind by an inflammation of the parotid glands (the mumps). This disease entails brain reactions in some cases, leaving behind a discreet but permanent bleaching of feelings and a slight decrease in general mental skills. Similar results are sometimes left behind after diphtheria. As a result, such people easily succumb to the suggestions and manipulations of more clever individuals.

When drawn into a felonious group, these constitutionally weakened individuals become faint-critical helpers and executors of the leader's intentions, tools in the hands of more treacherous, usually psychopathic, leaders. Once arrested, they submit to their leaders' insinuated explanations that the higher (paramoral) group ideal demands that they become scapegoats, taking the majority of blame upon themselves. In court, the same leaders who initiated the delinquencies mercilessly dump all the blame onto their less crafty colleagues. Sometimes a judge actually accepts the insinuations.

Individuals with the above-mentioned post-mumps and post-diphtheria traits constitute less than 1.0 % of the population as a whole, but their share reaches 1/4 of juvenile delinquent groups. This represents an inspissation of the order of 30-fold, requiring no further methods of statistical analysis. When studying the contents of ponerogenic unions skillfully enough, we often meet with an inspissation of other psychological anomalies which also speak for themselves.

When the ponerogenic process touches such a human organization, which originally emerged and acted in the name of political or social goals, and whose causes were conditioned in history and the social situation, the original group's primary values will nourish and protect such a union, in spite of the fact that those primary values succumb to characteristic degeneration, the practical function becoming *completely different* from the primary one, because the names and symbols are retained.

Just because a group operates under the banner of "communism" or "socialism" or "democracy" or "conservatism" or "republicanism", doesn't mean that, in practice, their functions are anything close to the original ideology. The original ideology serves as a cover because ponerogenic associations that begin with pathological ideas aren't acceptable in normal society. And as long as the normal members continue to interpret the original ideals through their deeper understanding, they will be blind to the process of ponerogeneis taking place in their midst.

Lobaczewski then goes on to describe how the complentary deviations of different pathological types work together in such an association:

Ponerogenic unions of the primary variety are mainly of interest to criminology; our main concern will be associations that succumb to a secondary process of poneric malignancy. [...]

Within each ponerogenic union, a psychological structure is created which can be considered a counterpart or caricature of the normal structure of society or a normal societal organization. In a normal social organization, individuals with various psychological strengths and weaknesses complement each other's talents and characteristics. This structure is subjected to diachronic[393] modification with regard to changes in the character of the association as whole. The same is true of a ponerogenic union. Individuals with various psychological aberrations also complement each other's talents and characteristics.

The earlier phase of a ponerogenic union's activity is usually dominated by characteropathic, particularly paranoid, individuals, who often play an inspirational or spellbinding role in the ponerization process. Recall here the power of the paranoid characteropath lies in the fact that they easily enslave less critical minds, e.g. people with other kinds of psychological deficiencies, or who have been victims of individuals with character disorders, and, in particular, a large segment of young people.

At this point in time, the union still exhibits certain romantic features and is not yet characterized by excessively brutal behavior.

An example would be a paranoid character who believes himself to be a Robin Hood type character with a "mission" to "rob from the rich and give to the poor". This can easily transform to "rob from anyone to gain for the self" under the cover of "social injustice against us makes it right".

Soon, however, the more normal members are pushed into fringe functions and are excluded from organizational secrets; some of them thereupon leave such a union.

---

[393] Over time; employing a chronological perspective.

Individuals with inherited deviations then progressively take over the inspirational and leadership positions. The role of essential psychopaths gradually grows, although they like to remain ostensibly in the shadows (e.g. directing small groups), setting the pace as an *éminence grise*.[394] In ponerogenic unions on the largest social scales, the leadership role is generally played by a different kind of individual, one more easily digestible and representative. Examples include frontal characteropathy, or some more discreet complex of lesser taints.

A spellbinder at first simultaneously plays the role of leader in a ponerogenic group. Later there appears another kind of "leadership talent", a more vital individual who often joined the organization later, once it has already succumbed to ponerization. The spellbinding individual, being weaker, is forced to come to terms with being shunted into the shadows and recognizing the new leader's "genius", or accept the threat of total failure. Roles are parceled out. The spellbinder needs support from the primitive but decisive leader, who in turn needs the spellbinder to uphold the association's ideology, so essential in maintaining the proper attitude on the part of those members of the rank and file who betray a tendency to criticism and doubt of the moral variety.

The spellbinder's job then becomes to repackage the ideology appropriately, sliding new contents in under old titles, so that it can continue fulfilling its propaganda function under ever-changing conditions. He also has to uphold the leader's *mystique* inside and outside the association. Complete trust cannot exist between the two, however, since the leader secretly has contempt for the spellbinder and his ideology, whereas the spellbinder despises the leader for being such a coarse individual. A showdown is always probable; whoever is weaker becomes the loser.

The structure of such a union undergoes further variegation and specialization. A chasm opens between the somewhat more normal members and the elite initiates who are, as a rule, more pathological. This later subgroup becomes ever more dominated by hereditary pathological factors, the former by the after-effects of various diseases affecting the brain, less typically psychopathic individuals, and people whose malformed personalities were caused by early deprivation or brutal child-rearing methods on the part of pathological individuals. It soon develops that there is less and less room for normal people in the group at all. The leaders' secrets and intentions are kept hidden from the union's proletariat; the products of the spellbinders' work must suffice for this segment.

An observer watching such a union's activities from the outside and using the natural psychological world view will always tend to overestimate the role of the leader and his allegedly autocratic function. The spellbinders and the propaganda apparatus are mobilized to maintain this erroneous outside opinion. The leader, however, is *dependent upon the interests of the union, especially the elite initiates*, to an extent greater than he himself knows. He wages a constant position-jockeying battle; he is an actor with a director. In macrosocial unions, this position is generally occupied by a more representative individual not deprived of certain critical faculties; initiating him into *all* those plans and criminal calculations would be counterproductive.

---

[394] A powerful advisor or decision-maker who operates secretly or otherwise unofficially. This phrase originally referred to Cardinal Richelieu's right-hand man, François Leclerc du Tremblay, a Capuchin priest who wore gray robes.

In conjunction with part of the elite, a *group* of psychopathic individuals hiding behind the scenes steers the leader, the way Borman and his clique steered Hitler. If the leader does not fulfill his assigned role, he generally knows that the clique representing the elite of the union is in a position to kill or otherwise remove him.

We have sketched the properties of unions in which the ponerogenic process has transformed their original generally benevolent content into a pathological counter-part thereof and modified its structure and its later changes, in a manner sufficiently wide-scale to encompass the greatest possible scope of this kind of phenomena, from the smallest to the largest social scale. The general rules governing those phenomena appear to be at least analogous, independent of the quantitative, social, and historical scale of such a phenomenon.

The above description seems to be exactly the process that has occurred within the Republican Party in the United States, producing the so-called neo-conservatives. The same process is evident in the Democratic Party, though it has not come to full fruition. It might even be said that the Democratic Party, as it exists today, is merely "creature" of the neocons, though some democrats appear to still cling to the original ideology.

THE BIRD AND THE SERPENT

Speaking of networks, we need to take a closer look at how psychopaths affect other human beings whom they use to create the basis for their rule in macro-social dynamics. This highlights the fact that the lack of psychological knowledge among the general public, not to mention the general neurosis of most people, make them vulnerable to such predators. Lobaczewski writes:

> Subordinating a normal person to psychologically abnormal individuals *has a deforming effect on his personality*: it engenders trauma and neurosis. This is accomplished in a manner which generally evades sufficient conscious controls. Such a situation then deprives the person of his natural rights to practice his own mental hygiene, *develop a sufficiently autonomous personality*, and utilize his common sense. In the light of natural law, it thus constitutes a kind of illegality which can appear in any social scale although it is not mentioned in any code of law.[395]

We doubt there is a reader of this book who has not come under the influence of such psychologically abnormal individuals. Psychologist George Simon, in his book *In Sheep's Clothing,* discusses what he refers to as "covert-aggressive personalities" which reveal themselves to be members of the psychopathy spectrum. You may recognize the type. He writes:

> Aggressive personalities don't like anyone pushing them to do what they don't want to do or stopping them from doing what they want to do. 'No' is never an answer they accept.
>
> [In some cases], if they can see some benefit in self-restraint, they may internalize inhibitions [and become covertly aggressive].

---

[395] Lobaczewski, op. cit.

By refraining from any overt acts of hostility towards others, they manage to convince themselves and others they're not the ruthless people they are.[396] They may observe the letter of a law but violate its spirit with ease. They may exhibit behavioral constraint when it's in their best interest, but they resist truly submitting themselves to any higher authority or set of principles. [They are] striving primarily to conceal their true intentions and aggressive agendas from others. They may behave with civility and propriety when they're closely scrutinized or vulnerable. But when they believe they're immune from detection or retribution, it's an entirely different story. [...]

Dealing with covert-aggressive personalities is like getting whiplash. Often, you really don't know what's hit you until long after the damage is done. [...]

Covert-aggressives are often so expert at exploiting the weaknesses and emotional insecurities of others that almost anyone can be duped. [...]

Covert-aggressives exploit situations in which they are well aware of the vulnerability of their prey. They are often very selective about the kinds of people with whom they will associate or work. They are particularly adept at finding and keeping others in a one-down position. They relish being in positions of power over others. It's my experience that how a person uses power is the most reliable test of their character.[397]

Lobaczewski adds chilling detail that reminds of of basic predator-prey dynamics:

If a person with a normal instinctive substratum and basic intelligence has already heard and read about such a system of ruthless autocratic rule "based on a fanatical ideology", he feels he has already formed an opinion on the subject. However, direct confrontation with the phenomenon will inevitably produce in him the feeling of intellectual helplessness. All his prior imaginings prove to be virtually useless; they explain next to nothing. This provokes a nagging sensation that he and the society in which he was educated were quite naïve. [...]

When the human mind comes into contact with this new reality so different from any experiences encountered by a person raised in a society dominated by normal people, *it releases psychophysiological shock symptoms in the human brain with a higher tonus of cortex inhibition and a stifling of feelings, which then sometimes gush forth uncontrollably. The mind then works more slowly and less keenly because the associative mechanisms have become inefficient.* Especially when a person has direct contact with psychopathic representatives of the new rule, who use their specific experience so as to traumatize the minds of the "others" with their own personalities, *his mind succumbs to a state of short-term catatonia.* Their humiliating and arrogant techniques, brutal paramoralizations, and so forth deaden his thought processes and his self-defense capabilities, and their divergent experiential method anchors in his mind. In the presence of this kind of phenomenon, any moralizing evaluation of a person's behavior in such a situation thus becomes inaccurate at best.

Only once these unbelievably unpleasant psychological states have passed, thanks to rest in benevolent company, is it possible to reflect, always a difficult

---

[396] This echoes exactly what Cleckley said about psychopaths and their "mask of sanity", quoted above.

[397] Simon, op. cit.

and painful process, or to become aware that one's mind and common sense have been fooled by *something which cannot fit into the normal human imagination*.

Now, just imagine the 1 in 25 people mentioned by Martha Stout in *The Sociopath Next Door* being the very ones who seek and achieve positions of power and authority in just about any field of endeavour where power can be had, and you begin to understand how truly damaging this can be to an entire society. Imagine school teachers with power over your children who are "covert-aggressives". Imagine doctors, psychologists, "ministers of the faith"[398] and politicians—psychopaths all—in such positions.

Lobaczewski continues with his discussion of the effect of psychopaths on normal individuals:

> We have already discussed the nature of some pathological personalities—characteropathies—that may be 'created' by an individual's exposure to a person with a severe character deformation. *Essential psychopathy has exceptionally intense effects in this manner.* Something mysterious gnaws into the personality of an individual at the mercy of the psychopath, and it is fought like a demon. **His emotions become chilled, his sense of psychological reality is stifled.** This leads to decriterialization of thought and *a feeling of helplessness culminating in depressive reactions* which can be so severe that psychiatrists sometimes misdiagnose them as a manic-depressive psychosis. Many people evidently also rebel much earlier and start searching for some way to liberate themselves from such an influence.

> A social structure dominated by normal people and their conceptual world easily appears to the psychopath as a 'system of force and oppression'. If it happens that true injustice does, in fact, exist in that given society, pathological feelings of unfairness and suggestive statements can resonate among those who have truly been treated unfairly. Revolutionary doctrines may then find approval among both groups although their motivations will actually be quite different.

> The presence of pathogenic bacteria in our environment is a common phenomenon; however, it is not the single decisive factor as regards whether an individual or a society becomes ill. Similarly, psychopathological factors alone do not decide about the spread of evil.[399]

In other words, at the most basic instinctive level, the psychopath has an effect on normal human beings that is similar to the effect a serpent has on a bird or a small fuzzy creature: paralysis, a freezing of the mind, confusion, followed by an attempt to make sense of something that is just impossible to comprehend: something that looks human but behaves like a predator. Furthermore, they can play on the most noble of human ideals, that of working to make a better world, and turn those efforts to the construction of an even better trap.

---

[398] George Simon relates a case of a Christian minister in his book. It is a fascinating study of how Christianity is used to achieve power over others, subordinating them to psychologically aberrant ideas and thus, deforming their personalities.

[399] Lobaczewski, op. cit.

With this understanding, we begin to get a more precise idea of how psychopaths can conspire and actually pull it off: in a society where evil is not studied or understood, they easily "rise to the top" and proceed to condition normal people to accept their dominance, to accept their lies without question. As noted at the beginning of this section:

> Long periods of preoccupation with the self and 'accumulating benefits' for the self, diminish the ability to accurately read the environment and other people. [...] It is this feature, *this hystericization of society, that enables pathological plotters, snake charmers, and other primitive deviants to act as essential factors in the processes of the origination of evil on a macro-social scale.*

We see exactly this pattern of social development in the United States over the past 50 to 60 years or even more. The fact is, many people who may have been born "normal" have become what might be termed "secondary psychopaths" or characteropaths due to the influence of psychopathy on American culture from many fields—including science, medicine, psychology, law, etc.—where they are conscious of what they are doing to "normal" people!

MACRO-SOCIAL PHENOMENA

We have now looked at individual psychopathy as well as the formation of ponerogenic associations and unions. What happens when these organizations are capable of coming to power and wreaking their havoc over a society as a whole? We turn now to this question:

> When a ponerogenic process encompasses a society's entire ruling class, or nation, or when opposition on the part of normal people's societies is stifled—as a result of the mass character of the phenomenon, or by using spellbinding means and physical compulsion—we are dealing with macro-social ponerologic phenomenon. At that time, however, a society's tragedy, often coupled with that of the researcher's own suffering, are opening before him an entire volume of ponerologic knowledge, where he can read all about the laws governing such process if he is only able to familiarize himself in time with its naturalistic language and its different grammar.

It bears noting here that the similarities between what Lobaczewski is saying in the above paragraph about the effects of a "macro-social ponerologic phenomenon" and what is happening today in the U.S. (and around the world) are striking. It is also somewhat ironic that the publication of this book, which contains Lobaczewski's research on ponerology and the conditions surrounding the unveiling of "ponerologic knowledge", constitutes an *actual* unveiling of "ponerologic knowledge". As he noted in an earlier citation, it is during the "bad times" that this knowledge becomes necessary.

Next Lobaczewski describes the stages in the ponerogenesis of society as a whole, defining definite stages in the process. By understanding its development, we may become capable of discerning the underlying dynamic, helping us to predict future developments and obtaining the understanding necessary to effect change. But such understanding must be objective and not moralistic:

Studies in the genesis of evil, which are based on observing small groups of people, can indicate the details of these laws to us. [...]

In studying a macro-social phenomenon, we can obtain both quantitative and qualitative data, statistical correlation indices, and other observations as accurate as allowed by the state of the art as regards science, research methodology, and the obviously very difficult situation of the observer. [...] The comprehension of the phenomenon thus acquired can serve as a basis for predicting its future development, to be verified by time. Then we become aware that the colossus has an Achilles' heel after all. [...]

The difficulties confronted in abstracting the appropriate symptoms need not be insuperable, since our criteria are based on eternal phenomena subject to relatively limited transformations in time.

The traditional interpretation of theses great historical diseases has already taught historians to distinguish two phases. The first is represented by a period of spiritual crisis in a society, which historiography associates with exhausting of the ideational, moral and religious values heretofore nourishing the society in question. Egoism among individuals and social groups increases, and the links of moral duty and social networks are felt to be loosening. Trifling matters thereupon dominate human minds to such an extent that there is no room left for imagination regarding public matters or a feeling of commitment to the future. An atrophy of the hierarchy of values within the thinking of individuals and societies is an indication thereof; it has been described both in historiographic monographs and in psychiatric papers. The country's government is finally paralyzed, helpless in the face of problems which could be solved without great difficulty under other circumstances. Let us associate such periods of crisis with the familiar phase in social hysterization.

It is no stretch to see the current situation in the United States as fitting this description. While the world is burning, trifling matters are certainly dominating the minds of a great number of Americans.

The next phase has been marked by bloody tragedies, revolutions, wars, and the fall of empires. Historians or moralists' deliberations always leave behind a certain feeling of deficiency with reference to the possibility of perceiving certain psychological factors discerned within the nature of this phenomena; the essence of these factors remains outside the scope of their scientific experience.

An historian observing these great historical diseases is struck first of all by their similarities, easily forgetting that all diseases have many symptoms in common because they are states of absent health. A ponerologist [...] tends to doubt that we are dealing with only one kind of societal disease. [...] The complex conditions of social life [...] preclude using the method of distinction which is similar to etiological criterion in medicine. [...] We should then rather use certain abstractional patterns similar to those used in analyzing the neurotic states of human beings.

Governed by this type of reasoning, let us here attempt to differentiate two pathological states of societies; their essence and contents appear different enough, but they can operate sequentially in such a way that the first opens the door to the second. The first such state has already been sketched [as] the hysteroidal cycle.

We have already looked at this stage of Societal Hysterization in looking at the hysteroidal cycle. To recall:

> During happy times of peace, when social injustice also exists and grows in the background (which is natural when we consider that certain individuals among those who want to 'enjoy' what they have accumulated rapidly begin to oppress their fellows), children of the privileged classes learn to repress from their field of consciousness any of those uncomfortable concepts suggesting that they and their parents benefit from injustice. Young people learn to disqualify the moral and mental values of anyone whose work they are using to over-advantage.

> Young minds thus ingest habits of subconscious selection and substitution of data, which leads to a hysterical conversion economy of reasoning. They grow up to be somewhat hysterical adults who, by means of the ways adduced above, thereupon transmit their hysteria to the younger generation, which then develops these characteristics to a greater degree. The hysterical patterns for experience and behavior grow and spread downwards from the privileged classes until crossing the boundary of the first criterion of ponerology.

> When the habits of subconscious selection and substitution of thought-data spread to the macro-social level, *a society tends to develop contempt for factual criticism and to humiliate anyone sounding the alarm. Contempt is also shown for other nations which have maintained normal thought-patterns, and for their opinions.*

Here, we are reminded of the anti-French hysteria (complete with wine and cheese dumping and the proclamation of "freedom fries" on Captial Hill) that enveloped sections of the American population in 2003. That millions of Americans were moved to express such hysterical animosity towards another nation whose only 'sin' was to stand against the desires of the American elite to illegally invade Iraq and state the truth—that Saddam was no threat to anyone—is evidence that the ponerogenic transformation of the American people is well advanced.

> Egotistic thought terrorization is accomplished by the society itself and its processes of conversion thinking. This obviates the need for censorship of the press, theater, or broadcasting, as a pathologically hypersensitive censor *lives within the citizens themselves.*

In other words, pathocratic ideas are internalized. One learns not to step out of line, at first perhaps out of fear, and, eventually, because one has lost the capacity of discerning the pathological from the normal. When immersed in a sick society, there are no longer any healthy points of comparison.

> When three egos govern: egoism, egotism, and egocentrism; the feeling of social links and responsibility disappear; and the society in question splinters into groups ever more hostile to each other. *When a hysterical environment stops differentiating the opinions of limited, not-quite-normal people from those of normal, reasonable persons, this opens the door for activation of the pathological factors of various natures.*

Can you say "Fox News: Fair and Balanced"?

> Individuals governed by a pathological view of reality and abnormal goals caused by their different nature develop their activity in such conditions. If a

given society does not manage to overcome the state of hysterization [...] **a huge bloody tragedy can be the result.** One variation of such a tragedy can be a pathocracy. [...] The most valuable advice a ponerologist can offer under such circumstances is for a society to avail itself of the assistance of modern science, taking particular advantage of data remaining from the last great increase of hysteria in Europe.

A greater resistance to hysterization characterizes those social groups which earn their daily bread by daily effort, where the practicalities of everyday life force the mind to think soberly and reflect on generalities. As an example: peasants continue to view the hysterical customs of the well-to-do classes through their own earthy perception of psychological reality and their sense of humor. Similar customs on the part of the bourgeoisie inclined workers to bitter criticism and revolutionary anger. Whether couched in economic, ideological, or political terms, the criticism and demands of these social groups always contain a component of psychological, moral, and anti-hysterical motivation. For this reason, it is most appropriate to consider these demands with deliberation and to take these classes' feelings into account. [...]

Here, the question becomes: "Are there any such sectors still remaining in the American population?" The "good life" for so many decades seems to have removed even this protection. A good number of people who make their daily bread through daily effort have succumbed to the Christian fundamentalist virus. It is likely that until the average American is suffering in ways that they cannot yet imagine, they will not start looking for the answer of how things got that way.

Lobaczewski then describes what happens once pathocratic control is achieved in a country:

Pathocrats' achievement of absolute domination in the government of a country would not be permanent, since large sectors of the society would become disaffected by such rule and find some way of toppling it. Pathocracy at the summit of governmental organization also does not constitute the entire picture of the 'mature phenomenon'. Such a system of government has nowhere to go but down. Any leadership position—down to village headman and community cooperative managers, not to mention the directors of police units, and special-services police personnel, and activists in the pathocratic party—*must be filled by individuals whose feeling of linkage to such a regime is conditioned by corresponding psychological deviations, which are inherited as a rule.* However, such people become more valuable because they constitute a very small percentage of the population. Their intellectual level or professional skills cannot be taken into account, since people representing superior abilities with the requisite psychological deviations—are even harder to find. After such a system has lasted several years, one hundred percent of all the cases of essential psychopathy are involved in pathocratic activity; they are considered the most loyal, even though some of them were formerly involved on the other side in some way.

Under such conditions, no area of social life can develop normally, whether in economics, culture, science, technology, administration, etc. Pathocracy progressively paralyzes everything. Reasonable people must develop a level of patience beyond the ken of anyone living in a normal man's system, just to explain what to do and how to do it to some obtuse mediocrity of psychological deviant. This special pedagogy requires a great deal of time and effort, but it would otherwise not be possible to maintain tolerable living conditions and necessary achievements in the economic area or intellectual life of a society. However, pathocracy progressively intrudes everywhere and dulls everything.

Those people who initially found the original ideology attractive eventually come to the realization that they are in fact dealing with something else. The disillusionment experienced by such former ideological adherents is bitter in the extreme. The pathological minority's attempts to retain power will thus always be threatened by the society of normal people whose criticism keeps growing. On the other hand, *any and all methods of terror and exterminatory policies must therefore be used against individuals known for their patriotic feelings and military training*; on the other, specific 'indoctrination' activities such as those we have presented are also utilized. *Individuals lacking natural feeling of being linked to society become irreplaceable in either of these activities.* The foreground must again be occupied by cases of essential psychopathy, followed by those with similar anomalies, and finally by people alienated from the society in question as a result of racial or national differences.

We should note here that Lobaczewski's frame of reference for his analysis of the ponerological process is post World War II Eastern Europe, when Communist powers established their control. As Lobaczewski states, patriotic thinking and people with military training were singled out by the Communist pathocrats of the day as the biggest threat to the specific type of system (Communism) they sought to impose. It should also be noted however that both Communism and Capitalism seem to be equally suited to the establishment of a pathocracy. Over the past 50 years, it has been exactly patriotism and military training that have been the tools used to effect a ponerogenic transformation of Western nations, in particular America, with as much success as the apparently opposing Communist concepts employed in Russia and Eastern Europe 50 years ago. But as Lobaczewski points out, at a certain point, there is nowhere to go for the pathocrats but down:

> Pathocracy has other internal reasons for pursuing expansionism through the use of all means possible. As long as that 'other' world governed by the systems of normal man exists, it inducts into and within the strivings of the non-pathological majority, thereby creating a certain sense of direction. The non-pathological majority of the country's population will never stop dreaming of the reinstatement of normal man's system in any possible form. This majority will never stop watching other countries, waiting for the opportune moment; its attention and power must therefore be distracted from this purpose, and the masses must be educated and channeled in the direction of imperialist strivings. Such goals must be pursued doggedly so that everyone knows what is being fought for and in whose name a harsh discipline and poverty must be endured. This latter factor effectively limits the possibility of 'subversive' activities on the part of the society of normal people.

In Communist Eastern Europe, austerity formed the core of the Communist ideology that the Pathocrats forced upon normal people, and it was used, as Lobaczewski states, to limit the possibility of subversion. In modern-day

America on the other hand, while Americans also know what is being fought for—"freedom and democracy"—it is indulgence and extravagance rather than austerity that distracts the American people and limits the possibility of subversion on the road to the ponerogenic transformation of American society.

A normal person's actions and reactions, his ideas and moral criteria, all too often strike abnormal individuals as abnormal. For if a person with some psychological deviations considers himself normal, which is of course significantly easier if he possesses authority, then he would consider a normal person different and therefore abnormal, whether in reality or as a result of conversive thinking. That explains why such people's government shall always have the tendency to **treat any dissidents as "mentally abnormal".**

Operations such as driving a normal person into psychological illness and the use of psychiatric institutions for this purpose take place in many countries in which such institutions exist. Contemporary legislation binding upon normal man's countries is not based upon an adequate understanding of the psychology of such behavior, and thus does not constitute a sufficient preventive measure against it.

Within the categories of a normal psychological world view, the motivations for such behavior were variously understood and described: personal and family accounts, property matters, intent to discredit a witness' testimony, and even political motivations. Such defamatory suggestions are used particularly often by individuals who are themselves not entirely normal, whose behavior has driven someone to a nervous breakdown or to violent protest. Among hysterics, such behavior tends to be a projection onto other people of one's own self-critical associations. A normal person strikes a psychopath as a naive, smart-alecky believer in barely comprehensible theories; calling him "crazy" is not all that far away. […]

The abuse of psychiatry for purposes we already know thus derives from the very nature of pathocracy as a macrosocial psychopathological phenomenon. After all, that very area of knowledge and treatment must first be degraded to prevent it from jeopardizing the system itself by pronouncing a dramatic diagnosis (Ed: i.e. exposing the pathocrats), and must then be used as an expedient tool in the hands of the authorities. In every country, however, one meets with people who notice this and act astutely against it. […]

The pathocracy feels increasingly threatened by this area whenever the medical and psychological sciences make progress. After all, not only can these sciences knock the weapon of psychological conquest right out of its hands; they can even strike at its very nature, and from inside the empire, at that.

A specific perception of these matters therefore bids the pathocracy to be "ideationally alert" in this area. This also explains why anyone who is both too knowledgeable in this area and too far outside the immediate reach of such authorities should be accused of anything that can be trumped up, including **psychological abnormality**.

Here we should mention the 2006 case of Carol Fisher,[400] a 53-year-old American woman who was arrested by Cleveland police for the crime of

---

[400] http://lefti.blogspot.com/2006_05_01_lefti_archive.html#114738867749083229

posting a "Bush Step Down" sign on a utility pole. On arrival in court, in early May 2006, the judge made the outrageous decision to force Mrs. Fisher to undergo a state psychological exam as part of her pre-sentencing investigation. The need for such an exam, according to the judge, was evidenced by Mrs. Fisher's anti-Bush stance and that her opposition to the Bush regime makes her "delusional". Indeed, this is not an isolated instance but one of a growing number of cases where the American judicial system has taken a very dim view of any Americans exercising their constitutional rights.

Lobaczewski continues:

> **Psychopaths are conscious of being different from normal people.** That is why the "political system" inspired by their nature is able to conceal this awareness of being different. They wear a personal mask of sanity and know how to create a macrosocial mask of the same dissimulating nature. When we observe the role of ideology in this macrosocial phenomenon, quite conscious of the existence of this specific awareness of the psychopath, we can then understand why *ideology is relegated to a tool-like role: something useful in dealing with those other naive people and nations.* [...]

> Pathocrats know that their real ideology is derived from their deviant natures, and treat the "other"—the masking ideology—with barely concealed contempt. [...]

Consider the ideology of "freedom and democracy" that is espoused by the American government in the "war on terror". Clearly, the U.S. government is using these noble ideals as tools to "deal with" and deceive the population into supporting their plans. Given all that has occurred in Iraq and Afghanistan to date, the architects of the "war on terror" have obvious contempt for real freedom and democracy.

> The names and official contents are kept, but another, completely different content is insinuated underneath, thus giving rise to the well known double talk phenomenon within which the same names have two meanings: one for initiates, one for everyone else. The latter is derived from the original ideology; the former has a specifically pathocratic meaning, something which is known not only to the pathocrats themselves, but also is learned by those people living under long-term subjection to their rule.

Those members of the ruling pathocracy in the U.S. certainly use "double talk" when they speak of "fighting terrorism" and "promoting freedom" and, among themselves, they are certainly aware of the real meaning, as they define it, of these phrases: "fighting terrorism" means using terrorism to achieve their goals, and "promoting freedom" means crushing those people who aspire to true freedom.

> Doubletalk is only one of many symptoms. Others are the specific facility for producing new names which have suggestive effects and are accepted virtually uncritically, in particular outside the immediate scope of such a system's rule. We must thus point out the paramoralistic character and paranoidal qualities frequently contained within these names. The action of paralogisms and paramoralisms in this deformed ideology becomes comprehensible to us based on

the information presented previously. Anything which threatens pathocratic rule becomes deeply immoral.

For evidence of the twisted morality as promoted by the pathocrats we need only look to the morality of mainstream religion where to use contraception is to "sin". The U.S. and Israeli governments (among others) claim that the Iraqi insurgents are "immoral" in their tactics of resisting oppression and occupation and in their fight to safeguard the lives of their friends and families. Essentially, as Lobaczewski says, any resistance to the American government, be it by foreign insurgents or American 'disgruntled citizens', is immoral and must be crushed. The same attitude is shown by Israel to the Palestinians. Any action on the part of those people corralled into reservations on what was once their own land, starved, persecuted for simply being Palestinian, is taken as an act of "terror" on the part of Israel, justifying reprisals that far outweigh the initial act.

> *This privileged class of deviants feels permanently threatened by the "others", i.e. by the majority of normal people.* Neither do the pathocrats entertain any illusions about their personal fate should there be a return to the system of normal man.
>
> If the laws of normal man were to be reinstated, they and theirs could be subjected to judgment, including a moralizing interpretation of their psychological deviations; they would be threatened by a loss of freedom and life, not merely a loss of position and privilege. Since they are incapable of this kind of sacrifice, the survival of a system which is the best for them becomes a moral imperative. Such a threat must be battled by means of any and all psychological and political cunning implemented with a lack of scruples with regard to those other "inferior-quality" people that can be shocking in its depravity.

For evidence of the depths of depravity to which the ruling pathocrats have stooped to ensure their survival, we need only look at the events of 9/11 and all of the patriotic fervor, which amounted to psychological manipulation of the masses, that resulted. By the end of this book, you will have been presented with enough information to leave you in no doubt that the 9/11 event was just such an act of depravity carried out by the ruling pathocrats.

> Thus, the biological, psychological, moral, and economic destruction of the majority of normal people becomes, for the pathocrats, a "biological" necessity. Many means serve this end, starting with concentration camps and including warfare with an obstinate, well-armed foe who will devastate and debilitate the human power thrown at him, namely the very power jeopardizing pathocrats rule: the sons of normal man sent out to fight for an illusionary "noble cause". Once safely dead, the soldiers will then be decreed heroes to be revered in paeans, useful for raising a new generation faithful to the pathocracy and ever willing to go to their deaths to protect it.

The above paragraph is perhaps one of the most important and chilling things that Lobaczewski writes. The pathocracy ensures its continued hold on power by periodically engaging in reduction of the population of normal people—culling the herd—chiefly by means of manufactured war. As Lobaczewski says, the pathocracy uses "an obstinate and well-armed foe" at which to throw legions of normal people (in the form of the military) and thereby debilitate and subdue the normal peoples of the world—the only threat to the ruling pathocracy. It gives a whole new meaning to the massacres of the last 100 years, including the 60 plus million people that died in World War II.

Notice also the devilish manipulation whereby these soldiers, deliberately and needlessly sacrificed by the pathocrats, are then lauded as heroes to ensure future generations of cannon fodder. Notice the real life evidence of this where millions of American citizens cry "support our troops". What are they supporting but the futile sacrifice of their own sons and daughters, brothers and sisters, and all to serve the agenda of the psychopaths in power?

> Any war waged by a pathocratic nation has two fronts, the internal and the external. The internal front is more important for the leaders and the governing elite, and the internal threat is the deciding factor where unleashing war is concerned. In pondering whether to start a war against the pathocratic country, one must therefore give primary consideration to the fact that one can be used as an executioner of the common people whose increasing power represents incipient jeopardy for the pathocracy. *After all, pathocrats give short shrift to blood and suffering of people they consider to be not quite conspecific.*

It is obvious that the propaganda war waged in the U.S. media is aimed squarely at Americans—the internal front. Statements made by the Bush administration to the American people bear no relationship to the reality outside of the U.S. Armed with even a cursory awareness of the way the world really works, it is an easy task to see through such lies and propaganda. Sadly however, few Americans have anything close to a real grasp of the reality of the rest of the world. For this reason, when French workers take to the streets to defend their civil and employment rights as they did in 2005, the Bush government was able to portray the French demonstrators as whining ingrates and idiots who were unable to see the 'benefits' of free market policies and globalization. What should have been seen by the American people as an example of the exercising of real civil freedoms was instead ridiculed and understood as being backward and outdated.

> Pathocracy has other internal reasons for pursuing expansionism through the use of all means possible. As long as that "other" world governed by the systems of normal man exists, it inducts into the non-pathological majority a certain sense of direction. The non-pathological majority of the country's population will never stop dreaming of the reinstatement of the normal man's system in any possible form. This majority will never stop watching other countries, waiting for the opportune moment; its attention and power must therefore be distracted from this purpose, and *the masses must be "educated" and channeled in the direction of imperialist strivings. This goal must be pursued doggedly so that everyone knows what is being fought for and in whose name harsh discipline and poverty must be endured. The latter factor—creating conditions of poverty and hardship—effectively limits the possibility of "subversive" activities on the part of the society of normal people.*

The ideology must, of course, furnish a corresponding justification for this alleged right to conquer the world and must therefore be properly elaborated. Expansionism is derived from the very nature of pathocracy, not from ideology, but this fact must be masked by ideology. Whenever this phenomenon has been witnessed in history, imperialism was always its most demonstrative quality.

A clearer description of what is happening right now in modern day America is unlikely to be found. Expansionism has been made a virtue by the American pathocracy. Bush claims that the U.S. military is spreading "freedom and democracy" when in fact he is pursuing an imperialist agenda. Expansionism is sold and justified because without it, Americans will lose their comforts. Lobaczewski says:

> This goal must be pursued doggedly so that everyone knows what is being fought for and in whose name harsh discipline and poverty must be endured.

Reference the fact that Americans are being told that they must sacrifice their liberties in order for the government to better wage the "war on terror" and the clampdown on anti-Bush demonstrations because they "harm the war on terror". As regards "creating conditions of poverty" in order to limit the possibility of "subversive" activities on the part of the society of normal people, there is much evidence that the American economy is set for a major nose-dive. When it does, the effect on a large percentage of ordinary Americans (all those not part of the 'monied classes') will be a dramatic re-prioritization, leaving them concerned chiefly with their ability to feed themselves and their families.

NORMAL PEOPLE UNDER PATHOCRATIC RULE

We have seen the effect of the psychopathic mind on normal people, the temporary catatonic state that can be induced. Some people, however, are able to resist. They are able to reflect upon and learn from their experiences under pathocratic rule. As well, as Lobaczewski describes below, the hypnotic effects can transform into buffoonery after repeated exposure, leading to a process of immunization:

> I was once referred a patient who had been an inmate in a Nazi concentration camp. She came back from that hell in such exceptionally good condition that she was still able to marry and bear three children. However, her child-rearing methods were so extremely iron-fisted as to be much too reminiscent of the concentration camp life so stubbornly persevering in former prisoners. The children's reaction was neurotic protest and aggressiveness against other children.
>
> During the mother's psychotherapy, we recalled the figures of male and female SS officers to her mind, pointing out their psychopathic characteristics (such people were primary recruits). In order to help her eliminate their pathological material from her person, I furnished her with approximate statistical data regarding the appearance of such individuals within the population as whole. This helped her reach a more objective view of that reality and reestablish trust in the society of normal people.
>
> During the next visit, the patient showed to me a little card on which she had written the names of local pathocratic notables and added her own diagnoses—

which were largely correct. So I made a hushing gesture with my finger and admonished her with emphasis that we were dealing only with her problems. The patient understood, and—I am sure—she did not make her reflections on the matter known in the wrong places.

Parallel to the development of practical knowledge and a language of insider communication, other psychological phenomena take form; they are truly significant in the transformation of social life under pathocratic rule, and discerning them is essential if one wishes to understand individuals and nations fated to live under such conditions and to evaluate the situation in the political sphere. They include people's psychological immunization and their adaptation to life under such deviant conditions.

The methods of psychological terror (that specific pathocratic art), the techniques of pathological arrogance, and the striding roughshod into other people's souls initially have such traumatic effects that people are deprived of their capacity for purposeful reaction; I have already adduced the psychophysiological aspects of such states. Ten or twenty years later, analogous behavior can be recognized as well-known buffoonery and does not deprive the victim of his ability to think and react purposefully. His answers are usually well-thought-out strategies, issued from the position of a normal person's superiority and often laced with ridicule. Man can look suffering and even death in the eye with the required calm. A dangerous weapon falls out of ruler's hands.

We have to understand that this process of immunization is not merely a result of the above described increase in practical knowledge of the macrosocial phenomenon. It is the effect of a many-layered, gradual process of growth in knowledge, familiarization with the phenomenon, creation of the appropriate reactive habits, and self-control, with an overall conception and moral principles being worked out in the meantime. After several years, the same stimuli which formerly caused chilly spiritual impotence or mental paralysis now provoke the desire to gargle with something strong so as to get rid of this filth.

It was a time, when many people dreamed of finding some pill which would make it easier to endure dealing with the authorities or attending the forced indoctrination sessions generally chaired by a psychopathic character. Some anti-depressants did in fact prove to have the desired effect. Twenty years later, this had been forgotten entirely.

Here we draw the parallel with the increased use of anti-depressants in the western countries in the last fifteen years. Lobaczewski then tells a story about his own immunization:

When I was arrested for the first time in 1951, force, arrogance, and psychopathic methods of forcible confession deprived me almost entirely of my self-defense capabilities. My brain stopped functioning after only a few days' arrest without water, to such a point that I couldn't even properly remember the incident which resulted in my sudden arrest. I was not even aware that it had been purposely provoked and that conditions permitting self-defense did in fact exist. They did almost anything they wanted to me.

When I was arrested for last time in 1968, I was interrogated by five fierce-looking security functionaries. At one particular moment, after thinking through their predicted reactions, I let my gaze take in each face sequentially with great attentiveness. The most important one asked me, 'What's on your mind, buster, staring at us like that?' I answered without any fear of consequences: 'I'm just wondering why so many of you gentlemen's careers end up in a psychiatric hospital.' They were taken aback for a while, whereupon the same man exclaimed, 'Because it's such damned horrible work!' 'I am of the opinion that it's the other way round', I calmly responded. Then I was taken back to my cell.

Three days later, I had the opportunity to talk to him again, but this time he was much more respectful. Then he ordered me to be taken away--outside, as it turned out. I rode the streetcar home past a large park, still unable to believe my eyes. Once in my room, I lay down on the bed; the world was not quite real yet, but exhausted people fall asleep quickly. When I awoke, I spoke out loud: 'Dear God, aren't you supposed to be in charge here in this world!'

At that time, I knew not only that up to 1/4 of all secret police officials wind up in psychiatric hospitals. I also knew that their 'occupational disease' is the congestive dementia formerly encountered only among old prostitutes. Man cannot violate the natural human feelings inside him with impunity, no matter what kind of profession he performs. From that view-point, Comrade Captain was partially right. At the same time, however, my reactions had become resistant, a far cry from what they had been seventeen years earlier.[401]

CAPITALISM AND PSYCHOPATHY

As noted, the members of the Quantum Future Group have been engaged in studying psychopathy and pseudo-psychopathy for several years now. This has certainly prepared most of us to be able to see the man behind the curtain, or, in this case, behind the "mask of sanity". These studies led to the question: why does psychopathic behavior seem to be so widespread in the U.S. (But that is not to say that it doesn't exist everywhere—it does.)

Linda Mealey of the Department of Psychology at the College of St. Benedict in St. Joseph, Minnesota, has recently proposed certain ideas in her paper *The Sociobiology of Sociopathy: An Integrated Evolutionary Model.*[402] These ideas address the increase in psychopathy in American culture by suggesting that in a competitive society—capitalistic by definition—psychopathy is adaptive and likely to increase. She writes:

I have thus far argued that some individuals seem to have a genotype that disposes them to [psychopathy].

[Psychopathy describes] frequency-dependent, genetically based, individual differences in employment of life strategies. [Psychopaths] always appear in every culture, no matter what the socio-cultural conditions. [...]

Competition increases the use of antisocial and Machiavellian strategies and can counteract pro-social behavior. [...]

Some cultures encourage competitiveness more than others and these differences in social values vary both temporally and cross-culturally. [...] Across both dimensions, high levels of competitiveness are associated with high crime rates and Machiavellianism.

---

[401] Lobaczewski, op. cit.
[402] http://www.bbsonline.org/Preprints/OldArchive/bbs.mealey.html

High population density, an indirect form of competition, is also associated with reduced pro-social behavior and increased anti-social behavior.

The conclusion is that the capitalistic way of life associated in the United States with "democracy" and the "free market" has *optimized the survival of psychopaths* with the consequence that it is an adaptive "life strategy" that is extremely successful in U.S. society, and thus has *increased in the population in strictly genetic terms*. What is more, as a consequence of a society that is adaptive for psychopathy, many individuals who are *not* genetic psychopaths have similarly adapted, becoming "effective" psychopaths, or "secondary sociopaths" in the ways Lobaczewski has described.[403] Mealey continues:

> Of course, because they are not intellectually handicapped, these individuals [psychopaths] will progress normally in terms of cognitive development and will acquire a theory of mind. Their theories, however, will be formulated purely in instrumental terms [what can claiming this or that *get* for me?], without access to the empathic understanding that most of us rely on so much of the time.
>
> *They may become excellent predictors of others' behavior*, unhandicapped by the 'intrusiveness' of emotion, acting, as do professional gamblers, solely on nomothetic laws and *actuarial data* rather than on hunches and feelings.
>
> In determining how to 'play' in the social encounters of everyday life, they will use a pure *cost-benefit approach* based on *immediate personal outcomes*, with no 'accounting' for the emotional reactions of the others with whom they are dealing.
>
> Without any real love to 'commit' them to cooperation, without any anxiety to prevent fear of 'defection', without guilt to inspire repentance, *they are free to continually play for the short-term benefit*.
>
> At the same time, because changes in gene frequencies in the population would not be able to keep pace with the fast-changing parameters of social interactions, an additional fluctuating proportion of sociopathy should result because, in a society of [psychopathy], the environmental circumstances make an antisocial strategy of life more profitable than a pro-social one.

In other words, in a world of psychopaths, those who are not genetic psychopaths are induced to behave like psychopaths simply to survive. When the rules are set up to make a society "adaptive" to psychopathy, it makes sociopaths of everyone, emphasizing purely mechanical behaviour. The description given above of calculation sounds as if it could be carried out by a computer.

What makes the psychopath so frightening and dangerous is that he or she wears a completely convincing "Mask of Sanity". This may at first make such a person utterly persuasive and compellingly healthy, according to psychiatrist Hervey Cleckley. Cleckley was first to describe the key symptoms of the disorder.

---

[403] Many experts differentiate between primary and secondary sociopaths. The first is a sociopath because they have the "genes" and the second is more or less "created" by their environment of victimization. Other experts refer to these two categories as "psychopaths" for the genetic variety and "sociopaths" for the reactive variety. We prefer this latter distinction.

Psychopaths are experts at using people. They can ask anything of anyone without embarrassment and because of their outgoing seducing friendliness, their use of, "Poor innocent me! I am such a *good* person, and I have been treated so *badly*!", the victim invariably gets sucked into giving the psychopath what they ask for—no matter how outrageous.

Psychopaths are masters at faking emotions in order to manipulate others. One psychologist reported that if you actually catch them in the act of committing a crime, or telling a lie, "they will immediately justify their actions by self pity and blaming another, by creating a heart-rending scene of faked emotional feelings". These fake emotions are only for effect, as the careful observer will note. The psychopath considers getting their way or getting out of trouble using faked emotions as a victory over another person.

Indeed, using their "emotional performances", these individuals can be truly overwhelming. Their charisma can be so inspiring, their emotion so deep and sincere-seeming, that people just want to be around them, want to help them, want to give all and support such a noble, suffering being. What is generally not seen by the victim is that they are feeding an endless internal hunger for control, excitement and ego-recognition.

Psychopaths cannot feel fear for themselves, much less empathy for others. Most normal people, when they are about to do something dangerous, illegal, or immoral, feel a rush of worry, nervousness, or fear. Guilt may overwhelm them and prevent them from even committing the deed.

The psychopath feels little or nothing except that they want something and not having it is a sort of pain, a hunger, so to say.

As a result, the threat of punishment, even painful punishment, is a laughing matter for the psychopath. They can repeat the same destructive acts without skipping a heartbeat, as well as seek thrills and dangers without regard for possible risks. This is called "hypoarousal". That is, very little—if anything—really arouses them; they are more machine-like than human-like.

The psychopath seems to be full of something that our ordinary language can only describe as being akin to deep greed. They manifest this inner state in many ways. One of the most common ways is to steal something of value to their victim, or to hurt/slander the victim or something or someone the victim loves. In the psychopath's mind, this is justified because the victim crossed him, did not give him what he wanted, or rejected him (or her).

In general, the successful psychopath "computes" how much they can get away with in a cost-benefit ratio of the alternatives. Among the factors that they consider most important are money, power, and gratification of negative desires. They are not motivated by such social reinforcement as praise or future benefits or the well-being of others—even including those one would suspect them to care about, such as their own families. Studies have been done that show locking up a psychopath has absolutely no effect on them in terms of modifying their life strategies. In fact, it is shown to make them worse. Effectively, when locked up, psychopaths just simply learn how to be better psychopaths.

The psychopath is obsessed with control even if they give the impression of being helpless. Their pretence to emotional sensitivity is really part of their control function: The higher the level of belief in the psychopath that can be induced in their victim through their dramas, the more "control" the psychopath believes they have. And in fact, this is true. They *do* have control when others believe their lies. Sadly, the degree of belief, the degree of "submission" to this control via false representation, generally produces so much pain when the truth is glimpsed that the victim would prefer to continue in the lie than face the fact that they have been duped. The psychopath counts on this. It is part of their "actuarial calculations". It gives them a feeling of power.

Psychopathic behavior seems to be on the rise because of the very nature of U.S. capitalistic society. The great hustlers, charmers, and self-promoters in the sales fields are perfect examples of where the psychopath can thrive; the entertainment industry, the sports industry, the corporate world in the capitalist system, are all areas where psychopaths naturally rise to the top.

Since the psychopath bases their activities, designed to get what they want, on their particular "theory of mind", it is instructive to have a look at this issue. Having a "theory of mind" allows an individual to impute mental states (thoughts, perceptions, and feelings) not only to oneself, but also to other individuals. It is, in effect, a tool that helps us predict the behavior of others. The most successful individuals are those who most accurately predict what another person will do given a certain set of circumstances. In the present day, we have Game Theory, created by Nobel Prize winner John Nash, which is being used to model many social problems. This system is essential psychopathy in action.

When two individuals interact with each other, each must decide what to do often without knowledge of what the other is doing. Imagine that the two players are the government and the public. In the following model, each of the players faces only a binary choice: to behave ethically either in making laws or in obeying them.

The assumption is that both players are informed about everything *except the level of ethical behavior of the other.*[404] They know what it means to act ethically, and they know the consequences of being exposed as unethical.

There are three elements to the game. 1) The players, 2) the strategies available to either of them, and 3) the payoff each player receives for each possible combination of strategies.

In a legal regime, one party is obliged to compensate the other for damages under certain conditions but not under others. We are going to imagine a re-

---

[404] This seems to be the chief problem in the culturally rampant breakdown of human relations. Time and again people engage in dynamic interactions with others only to find that they are duped, tricked, cheated, hurt, or otherwise abused in physical or psychological ways that they *did not anticipate.*

gime wherein the government is never liable for losses suffered by the public because of its unethical behavior—instead, the public has to pay for the damages inflicted by the government due to unethical behavior.

The payoffs discussed in Game Theory are generally represented in terms of money, which is a metaphor for energy. That is, how much investment does each player have to make in ethical behavior and how much payoff does each player receive for his investment.

In this model (we will use an arbitrary set of numbers to make the example easy to understand), behaving ethically, according to standards of social values that are considered the "norm", costs each player $10.00. When law detrimental to the public is passed, it costs the public $100.00 (to represent a larger population than just a single individual). We take it as a given that such laws will be passed unless both players behave ethically, which is not likely based on historical precedent.

Next, we assume that the likelihood of a detrimental law being passed in the event that both the public and the government are behaving ethically is a one-in-ten chance.

In a legal regime in which the government is *never* held responsible for its unethical behavior, and if neither the government nor the public behave ethically, the government enjoys a payoff of $0, and the public is out $100 when a law detrimental to the public is passed.

If both "invest" in ethical behavior, the government has a payoff of minus $10 (the cost of behaving ethically) and the public is out minus $20 which is the $10 invested in being ethical *plus* the $10 of the one-in-ten chance of a $100 loss incurred if a detrimental law is passed.

If the government behaves ethically and the public does not, resulting in the passing of a law detrimental to the populace, the government is out the $10 invested in being ethical and the public is out $100.

If the government does not behave ethically, and the public does, the government has a payoff of $0 and the public is out $110 which is the "cost of being ethical" added to the losses suffered when the government passes detrimental laws. Modelled in a game theory bimatrix, it looks like this, with the two numbers representing the "payoff" to the people—the left number in each pair—and government—the right number in each pair.

		Government	
		No Ethics	Ethical
	No Ethics	-100, 0	-100, -10
Society/People			
	Ethical	-110, 0	-20, -10

In short, in this game, the government always does better by not being ethical, and we can predict the government's choice of strategy because there is a single strategy—no ethics—*that is better for the government no matter what choice the public makes*. This is a "strictly dominant strategy", or a strategy that is the best choice for the player no matter what choices are made by the other player.

What is even worse is the fact that the public is *penalized* for behaving ethically. Since we know that the government, in the above regime, will never behave ethically because it is the dominant strategy, we find that ethical behavior on the part of the public actually costs *more* than unethical behavior.

In short, psychopathic behavior is actually a *positive adaptation* in such a regime. The public, as you see, cannot even minimize their losses by behaving ethically. It costs them $110 to be ethical and only $100 to not be ethical.

Now, just substitute "psychopath" in the place of the government and non-psychopath in the place of the public, and you will have a form-game model of interpersonal relations between the psychopath and a normal person. This will help you understand why the psychopath will always win. If the "payoff" is emotional pain of being hurt, or shame for being exposed, in the world of the psychopath, that consequence simply does not exist just as in the legal regime created above, the government is never responsible for unethical behavior. The psychopath lives in a world in which it is like a government that is never held responsible for behavior that is detrimental to others. The psychopath has no conscience. It's that simple. And the form game above will tell you why psychopaths in the population, as well as in government, are able to induce the public to accept laws that are detrimental. It simply isn't worth it to be ethical. If you go along with the psychopath, you lose. If you resist the psychopath, you lose even more. We have seen a similar "game" when we look at the "legal argument" earlier.

Societies, too, can be considered "players" in the psychopath's game model. The past behavior of a society will be used by the psychopath (or ponerological network) to predict the future behavior of that society. Like an individual player, a society will have a certain probability of detecting deception and a more or less accurate memory of who has cheated them in the past. The society will also have a developed, or not developed, proclivity to retaliate against a liar and cheater. Since the psychopath is using an *actuarial approach* to assess the costs and benefits of different behaviors (just how much can he get away with), it is the actual past behavior of the society which will go into his calculations rather than any risk assessments based on any "fears or anxieties" of being caught and punished that empathic people would feel in anticipation of doing something illegal.

Thus, in order to reduce psychopathic behavior in society and in government, a society *must* establish and enforce a reputation for *high rates of de-*

tection of deception and identification of liars, and a willingness to retaliate. In other words, it must establish a successful strategy of deterrence.

Since the psychopath is particularly unable to make decisions based on future consequences, only able to focus attention on immediate gratification— short-term goals—*it is possible that such individuals can be dealt with by establishing a history of dealing out swift social retaliation.* That is, identifying and punishing liars and cheaters must be immediate and flawlessly consistent, thus predictable in its occurrence.

And here we come to the issue concerning real-world human social interactions on a large scale: reducing psychopathy in our leaders *depends upon expanding society's collective memory of individual players' past behavior.* Those who do not remember history are doomed to repeat it.

Any reasonable scan of the news will reveal that lies and cheating are not "covered up" as thoroughly as American apologists would like to think. Even the less well-informed Americans have some idea that there was certainly something fishy about the investigation into the assassination of JFK. In recent years, a man who participated on the Warren Commission, Gerald Ford, also a former President, admitted to "cheating" on the report when he admitted to changing the placement of one of the bullet wounds in the final report.

Then, there was Watergate followed by the Iran-Contra affair, not to mention "Monica-gate". Those seem almost naïve compared to the lies of the current criminal gang in power. The lies of the Bush gang, from stolen elections, to the 9/11 attacks, and through the infamous weapons of mass destruction in Iraq, have taken the art of lying to heights that would impress Hitler himself. And here we are just hitting some highlights, most familiar to all Americans.

What consequences did the cheaters of society suffer?

None to speak of. In fact, in nearly every case, they were rewarded handsomely with those things of value to the psychopath: money and material goods. If anyone thinks they were shamed by public exposure, think again!

But what is of *crucial* interest here is the fact that the American people have simply *not* responded to the revelations of lies in government with any outrage that could be considered more than token. At the present time, there isn't even "token outrage".

Don't you find that odd?

But we have already noted the reason: the American way of life has optimized the survival of psychopathy, and in a world of psychopaths, those who are not genetic psychopaths are induced to behave like psychopaths simply to survive. When the rules are set up to make a society "adaptive" to psychopathy, it makes sociopaths of everyone. As a consequence, a very large number of Americans are effective sociopaths (i.e. individuals who are not genetic psychopaths).

More than that, however, is the problem of denial.

In *States of Denial: Knowing about Atrocities and Suffering*,[405] Stanley Cohen discusses the subject of denial which may shed some light on why the American people do not seem to be able to do what is necessary to take back their republic. Cohen remarks:

> [T]he scientific discourse misses the fact that the ability to deny is an amazing human phenomenon [...] a product of sheer complexity of our emotional, linguistic, moral and intellectual lives.

He then says that denial is a "complex unconscious defence mechanism for coping with guilt, anxiety and other disturbing emotions aroused by reality."

Denial can be both deliberate and intentional as well as completely subconscious. An individual who is deliberately and intentionally denying something is "acting from an individual level of lying, concealment and deception". I don't think that we are dealing with this in the case of the American people. What we are dealing with is denial that is subconscious and therefore organized and "institutional". This implies propaganda, misinformation, whitewash, manipulation, spin, disinformation, etc.

Believing anything that comes down the pike is not the opposite of denial; it is simply one of its subtle forms. When people are actively aroused by certain information, they should assess the probability of a high level of truth about a given matter. It seems that today it is difficult to arouse many Americans at all, and so this assessment never takes place. They are in denial that a problem exists at all.

The information that we receive can be 1) factual or forensic truth; that is to say, legal or scientific information which is factual, accurate and objective; it is obtained by impartial procedures; or 2) personal and narrative truth including "witness testimonies". In both cases, they can be spun and twisted, distorted or even made up. A healthy mind will assess it all critically and come to its own conclusions.

I should add here that skepticism and solipsistic arguments—including epistemological relativism—about the existence of objective truth, are generally a social construction and might be considered in the terms of the hypnotized man who has been programmed to think that there "is no truth".

Denial occurs for a variety of reasons. There are truths that are "clearly known", but for many reasons—personal or political, justifiable or unjustifiable—are concealed, or it is agreed that they will not be acknowledged "out loud". There are "unpleasant truths" and there are truths that make us tired because if we acknowledge them—if we do more than give them a tacit nod—we may find it necessary to make changes in our lives.

Cohen points out that "[a]ll counter-claims about the denied reality are themselves only manoeuvres in endless truth-games. And truth, as we know, is inseparable from power." Denial of truth is, effectively, giving away your power.

---

[405] Stanley Cohen, *States of Denial* (Cambridge: Polity Press; Malden, MA: Blackwell Publishers, 2001).

The subject of denial then leads us to the issue of ideologies, those things used to mask evil activity.

IDEOLOGIES

Earlier we saw how ideologies can serve as a mask for the pathocratic take-over of social movements and political parties that may have begun as an expression of a just and noble desire to better the world. Over time, the meanings of the slogans change, assuming the character of double talk: one meaning for the initial adherents, and a second meaning understood by the new pathocratic leaders. Ideology is essential for the continued existence of such a ponerogenic association, as Lobaczewski discusses:

> It is a common phenomenon for a ponerogenic association or group to contain a *particular ideology* which always justifies its activities and furnishes motivational propaganda. Even a small-time gang of hoodlums has its own melodramatic ideology and pathological romanticism. Human nature demands that vile matters be haloed by an over-compensatory mystique in order to silence one's conscience and to deceive consciousness and critical faculties, whether one's own or those of others.

> If such a ponerogenic union could be stripped of its ideology, nothing would remain except psychological and moral pathology, naked and unattractive. *Such stripping would of course provoke "moral outrage", and not only among the members of the union. The fact is, even normal people, who condemn this kind of union along with its ideologies, feel hurt and deprived of something constituting part of their own romanticism, their way of perceiving reality when a widely idealized group is exposed as little more than a gang of criminals.* Perhaps even some of the readers of this book will resent the author's stripping evil so unceremoniously of all its literary motifs. The job of effecting such a "strip-tease" may thus turn out to be much more difficult and dangerous than expected.

He points out that ideology provides "an over-compensatory mystique in order to silence one's conscience and to deceive consciousness and critical faculties". We see this over and over again, be it in the ideology of communism, now pretty much relegated to the past, but also in the slogans of "democracy and freedom" and for "the free market" that are at the heart of the ideology driving the U.S. The crimes in Iraq are accepted by many in the U.S., as elsewhere, as necessary in the name of these code words. Support is given to the terrorists at the helm in Israel because "Israel is the lone democracy in the Middle East". Take this rhetoric away from the actions of the United States and Israel and "nothing would remain except psychological and moral pathology, naked and unattractive".

Lobaczewski then go on to describe how ideology takes on a double meaning:

> A primary ponerogenic union is formed at the same time as its ideology, perhaps even somewhat earlier. A normal person perceives such ideology to be different from the world of human concepts, obviously suggestive, and even primitively comical to a degree.

An ideology of a secondarily ponerogenic association is formed by gradual adaptation of the primary ideology to functions and goals other than the original formative ones. A certain kind of layering or schizophrenia of ideology takes place during the ponerization process. The outer layer closest to the original content is used for the group's propaganda purposes, especially regarding the outside world, although it can in part also be used inside with regard to disbelieving lower-echelon members. The second layer presents the elite with no problems of comprehension: it is more hermetic, generally composed by slipping a different meaning into the same names. Since identical names signify different contents depending on the layer in question, understanding this "doubletalk" requires simultaneous fluency in both languages.

Average people succumb to the first layer's suggestive insinuations for a long time before they learn to understand the second one as well.

People succumb because, without an understanding of psychopathy, they interpret the words and slogans according to a worldview that includes conscience. They give to the terms a meaning that they cannot have when welded by the pathocrats, for whom conscience is a laughable fiction. Those without conscience, or who have been infected by the pathocratic virus, will read the terms in a different way:

Anyone with certain psychological deviations, especially if he is wearing the mask of normality with which we are already familiar, immediately perceives the second layer to be attractive and significant; after all, it was built by people like him. Comprehending this doubletalk is therefore a vexatious task, provoking quite understandable psychological resistance; this very duality of language, however, is a pathognomonic[406] symptom indicating that the human union in question is touched by the ponerogenic process to an advanced degree.

The *ideology* of unions affected by such degeneration has certain constant factors regardless of their quality, quantity, or scope of action: namely, *the motivations of a wronged group, radical righting of the wrong, and the higher values of the individuals who have joined the organization.* These motivations facilitate sublimation of the feeling of being wronged and different, caused by one's own psychological failings, and appear to liberate the individual from the need to abide by uncomfortable moral principles.

In the world full of real injustice and human humiliation, making it conducive to the formation of an ideology containing the above elements, a union of its converts may easily succumb to degradation. When this happens, those people with a tendency to accept the better version of the ideology will tend to justify such ideological duality.

The ideology of the proletariat,[407] which aimed at revolutionary restructuring of the world, was already contaminated by a schizoid deficit in the understanding of, and trust for, human nature; small wonder, then, that it easily succumbed to a

---

[406] Specific characteristics of a disease.

[407] From the Communist Manifesto: "By proletariat [is meant] the class of modern wage laborers, who, having no means of production of their own, are reduced to selling their labor-power in order to live."

process of typical degeneration in order to nourish and disguise a macrosocial phenomenon whose basic essence is completely different.[408]

For future reference, let us remember: ideologies do not need spellbinders. Spellbinders need ideologies in order to subject them to their own deviant goals.

On the other hand, the fact that some ideology degenerated along with its corollary social movement, later succumbing to this schizophrenia and serving goals which the originators of the ideology would have abhorred, does not prove that it was worthless, false, and fallacious from the start. Quite the contrary: *it rather appears that under certain historical conditions, the ideology of any social movement, even if it is sacred truth, can yield to the ponerization process.*

A given ideology may have contained weak spots, created by the errors of human thought and emotion within; or it may, during the course of its history, become infiltrated by more primitive foreign material which can contain ponerogenic factors. Such material destroys an ideology's internal homogeny. The source of such infection by foreign ideological material may be the ruling social system with its laws and customs based on a more primitive tradition, or an imperialistic system of rule. It may be, of course, simply another philosophical movement often contaminated by the eccentricities of its founder, who considers the facts to blame for not conforming to his dialectical construct.

The Roman Empire, including its legal system and paucity of psychological concepts, similarly contaminated the primary homogeneous idea of Christianity. Christianity had to adapt to coexistence with a social system wherein *"dura lex sed lex"*,[409] rather than an understanding of human beings, decided a person's fate; this then led to the corruption of attempting to reach the goals of the "Kingdom of God" by means of Roman imperialistic methods.

The greater and truer the original ideology, the longer it may be capable of nourishing and disguising from human criticism that phenomenon which is the product of the specific degenerative process. In a great and valuable ideology,

---

[408] Fascism seems to be the diametric opposite of Communism and Marxism, both in a philosophic and political sense, and also opposed democratic capitalist economics along with socialism and liberal democracy. It viewed the state as an organic entity in a positive light rather than as an institution designed to protect collective and individual rights, or as one that should be held in check. Fascism is also typified by totalitarian attempts to impose state control over all aspects of life: political, social, cultural, and economic which accurately describes what was passed off under the name of Communism. The fascist state regulates and controls (as opposed to nationalizing) the means of production. Fascism exalts the nation, state, or race as superior to the individuals, institutions, or groups composing it. Fascism uses explicit populist rhetoric; calls for a heroic mass effort to restore past greatness; and demands loyalty to a single leader, often to the point of a cult of personality. Again, we see that Fascism was passed off as Communism. So, what actually seems to have happened is that the original ideals of the proletariat were cleverly subsumed to State corporatism. Most people in the west are not aware of this because of the Western propaganda against Communism. The word "Fascist" has become a slur throughout the world since the stunning failure of the Axis powers in World War II. In contemporary political discourse, adherents of some political ideologies tend to associate fascism with their enemies, or define it as the opposite of their own views. There are no major self-described fascist parties or organizations anywhere in the world. However, at the present time, in the U.S., the system is far more Fascist than Democratic which probably explains the existence of the years of anti-Communist propaganda. That would demonstrate an early process of ponerization of Western democracy which, at present, has almost completed the transformation to full-blown Fascism.

[409] The law [is] harsh, but [it is] the law.

the danger for small minds is hidden; they can become the factors of such preliminary degeneration, which opens the door to invasion by pathological factors.

Thus, if we intend to understand the secondary ponerization process and the
kinds of human associations which succumb to it, we must take great care to
separate the original ideology from its counterpart, or even caricature, created
by the ponerogenic process. Abstracting from any ideology, we must, by anal-
ogy, understand the essence of the process itself, which has its own etiological
causes which are potentially present in every society, as well as characteristic
developmental patho-dynamics.

And so we begin to understand how psychopaths can rise to power, how
they can use their special knowledge of the psychology of normal people—
particularly the tendency to denial—as well as their awareness of how their
own natures affect the human being with a normal instinctive substratum—
the Serpent and the Bird—to gain control and continue to bamboozle people
for a very long time have. People don't remember the lies because they don't
want to remember them! And the result is that we have George Bush and the
Fourth Reich calculating how much they can get away with by looking at the
history of the reactions of the American people to their lying and cheating
strategies.

There aren't any because the system is adaptive to psychopathy. In other
words, Americans support Bush and his agenda because most of them are
effectively *like* him. But that is not because they are *all* born that way. It is
because psychopathy is required to survive in the competitive, capitalist U.S.
Society.

As a society gets larger and more competitive, individuals become more
anonymous and more Machiavellian. Social stratification and segregation
leads to feelings of inferiority, pessimism and depression among the have-
nots, promoting the use of "cheating strategies" in life that then make the
environment more adaptive for psychopathy in general because those who are
suffering will respond positively to any sign of change, even if they don't
realize that the change is being proposed by those who will actually make
their lives worse.

Psychopathic behavior among non-genetic psychopaths could be viewed as
a functional method of obtaining desirable resources, increasing an individual's status in a local group, and even a means of providing stimulation that
socially and financially successful people find in acceptable physical and
intellectual challenges.

In America, a great many households are affected by the fact that work, divorce, or both, have removed one or both parents from interaction with their
children for much of the day. *This is a consequence of capitalistic economics.*

When the parents are absent, or even when one is present but not in possession of sufficient knowledge or information, children are left to the mercies
of their peers, a culture shaped by the media. Armed with joysticks and TV
remotes, children are guided from *South Park* and *Jerry Springer* to *Mortal
Kombat* on Nintendo. Normal kids become desensitized to violence. More-

susceptible kids—children with a genetic inheritance of psychopathy—are pushed toward a dangerous mental precipice. Meanwhile, the government is regularly passing laws, on the demand of parents and the psychological community, designed to avoid imposing consequences on junior's violent behavior.

As for media violence, few researchers continue to try to dispute that bloodshed on TV and in the movies has an effect on the kids who witness it. Added to the mix now are video games structured around models of hunting and killing. Engaged by graphics, children learn to associate spurts of "blood" with the primal gratification of scoring a "win".

Again, economics—capitalism disguised as "democracy"—controls the reality.

The fact is, it is almost a mechanical system that operates based on the *psychological nature of human beings*, most of whom *like* to live in denial or need to live in denial to please their parents, their peers, their religious leaders, and their political leaders. All they want to do is have some relaxation to enjoy the "American Dream". After all, "if ignorance is bliss, 'tis folly to be wise". This is most especially true when we consider the survival instinct of the ego. If the official culture says that wanton murder for the expansion of capital is "democracy", working through the inculcated belief systems, there is little possibility that the "subject" will be able to see the source of the ponerological phenomena in our world.

Consider all of the foregoing information now in relation to the 9/11 attacks and the fact that so many Americans find it almost impossible to believe that their government officials would wantonly sacrifice the lives of its citizens to further their personal agendas. More importantly, consider the fact that your government knows how you think only too well.

And then, also consider the issue of genetics. Is there a genetic marker for psychopathy that could be used to exclude psychopaths from death in the deployment of so-called "ethnic specific weapons"?

THE CULTURE OF CRITIQUE

Here we come to what may well be the most sensitive issue raised in this book: the influence of Israel and its supporters, be they Jewish or Christian Zionists, who believe the establishment of a Greater Israel is a necessary step in the process leading to the First, or Second, Coming of their Lord. The pro-Israel lobby is so powerful that it is forbidden to discuss its power and influence on U.S. politics and in the U.S. media. The imposed silence on this topic was highlighted with the publication in the spring of 2006 of the paper on the influence of the Israeli lobby on U.S. politics by Professors John Mearsheimer and Stephen Walt. Part of the problem is that it is often reduced to the question of the influence and power of "the Jews", which reduces it to a racial distinction. As the reader will see, our analysis is something else entirely.

The reader might wish to have a look at Kevin MacDonald's *The Culture of Critique: An Evolutionary Analysis of Jewish Involvement in Twentieth-Century Intellectual and Political Movements,*[410] where they will learn that ethnic Jews have a powerful influence in the American media—far larger than any other identifiable group. MacDonald concludes:

> The extent of Jewish ownership and influence on the popular media in the United States is remarkable given the relatively small proportion of the population that is Jewish.

It should be noted that, in saying this, neither we nor McDonald are talking about ordinary Jews, but rather the Jewish "elite" who claim to be acting in the interests of the Jewish people, but who, in reality, are using the lure of Judaism and its promises of a "safe homeland" for Jews to manipulate the Jewish people. We also wish to remind the reader of the comments of Dr. Lobaczewski concerning the influence of Schizoidal types and their writings on the preparatory stages of the inception of Pathocracy, and their statistically significant presence among Jews.

Israel, therefore, is in control of one of the most potent means of creating the "official culture" of America and can use these means to suit its own agenda, including making the terms "conspiracy theory" and "anti-Semitic" such horrible epithets that no one would dare to speak anything that might put them at risk of being so branded!

An examination of the mass media in the U.S. gives a chilling review of this influence:

> After World War II, television flourished. [...] Psychologists and sociologists were brought in to study human nature in relation to selling; in other words, to figure out how to manipulate people without their feeling manipulated. Dr. Ernest Dichter, President of the Institute for Motivational Research made a statement in 1941 [that] 'the successful ad agency manipulates human motivations and desires and develops a need for goods with which the public has at one time been unfamiliar—perhaps even undesirous of purchasing.'

> Discussing the influence of television, Daniel Boorstin wrote: 'Here at last is a supermarket of surrogate experience. Successful programming offers entertainment—under the guise of instruction; instruction—under the guise of entertainment; political persuasion—with the appeal of advertising; and advertising—with the appeal of drama.' [...]

> [P]rogrammed television serves not only to *spread acquiescence and conformity*, but it represents a deliberate industry approach.[411]

Allen Funt, host of a popular television show, *Candid Camera*, was once asked what was the most disturbing thing he had learned about people in his years of dealing with them through the media. His response was chilling in its ramifications:

[410] http://www.csulb.edu/~kmacd/books-Preface.html
[411] Quoted by Wallace and Wallechinsky in *The People's Almanac*, pp. 805, 807.

"The worst thing, and I see it over and over, is how easily people can be led by any kind of authority figure, or even the most minimal kinds of authority. A well-dressed man walks up the down escalator and most people will turn around and try desperately to go up also. [...] We put up a sign on the road, 'Delaware Closed Today'. Motorists didn't even question it. Instead they asked: 'Is Jersey open?'" [412]

Submission to minimal signs of authority; lack of knowledge and aware-ness; a desire for a quick fix and an easy way out. These, it would seem, are the characteristics of the average citizen on the planet today. Of course, none of it would be possible without the help of the mainstream media.

The careful observer with knowledge of history will note immediately that what we are describing is fascist style propaganda of the same sort that was instituted in Nazi Germany. [413]

On October 3, 2001, I.A.P. News reported that, according to Israel Radio (in Hebrew) Kol Yisrael, an acrimonious argument erupted during the Israeli cabinet weekly session between Israeli Prime Minister Ariel Sharon and his foreign Minister Shimon Peres. Peres warned Sharon that refusing to heed incessant American requests for a cease-fire with the Palestinians would en-danger Israeli interests and "turn the U.S. against us". "Sharon reportedly yelled at Peres, saying, *'don't worry about American pressure, we, the Jew-ish people control America'."*

On a July 1973 edition of CBS' "Face the Nation", Senator Fullbright, Chair of Senate Foreign Relations Committee stated:

"The Israelis control the policy in the congress and the senate."

On page 99 of Donald Neff's book *Fallen Pillars,* he quotes Secretary of State under President Dwight D. Eisenhower (from 1953 - 1959) John Foster Dulles as saying:

"I am aware how almost impossible it is in this country to carry out a foreign policy [in the Middle East] not approved by the Jews... [T]errific control the Jews have over the news media and the barrage the Jews have built up on con-gressmen. [...]

"I am very much concerned over the fact that the Jewish influence here is com-pletely dominating the scene and making it almost impossible to get congress to do anything they don't approve of. The Israeli embassy is practically dictating to the congress through influential Jewish people in the country."

We would like to stress again the very clear distinction between normal Jewish people and the psychopathic 'leaders' who claim to represent them. While there is strong evidence to suggest an Israeli government involvement in the 9/11 attacks, in recent years we have been concerned to see a growing

---

[412] Wallace, Wallechinsky, ibid.

[413] We would also like to point out that Fox News has been revealed by the events of 9/11 to be one of the main propaganda arms of neo-conservative power in Washington, though, certainly, the majority of the big media players thought that they had to "get in line" in order to survive. It is only in the past year that citizens of the US have begun "voting with their wallets", abando-ning major print media in droves.

tendency among some independent, mainly American, 9/11 investigators to fall into the trap of blaming the Jewish people *en masse* for the actions of their government.

Such authors should consider whether it would be fair to call all Americans, themselves included, "bloodthirsty war criminals that delight in the death of Iraqi children", because to talk about "Jews" being responsible for 9/11 is certainly unfair to the Jewish people. Instead of "Jews", a more accurate definition would be "Psychopathic Zionists". That is not to say that many Jews to one degree or another do not support the actions of the state of Israel, but the majority (like many American Christians) are manipulated by religions created by psychopaths; they are caught in the mesmerizing influence of "spellbinders" as Lobaczewski describes it.

In any case, by talking of "Jews" in this way, these authors are needlessly and wantonly exposing themselves and their fellow 9/11 truth seekers to attacks that *can* be justified in terms of the argument that most Jews, like most Americans, are not directly responsible for the crimes of their leaders, and any suggestion to the contrary is evidence of "anti-Semitism".

The simple fact is that most people are manipulated to bear responsibility for the crimes of their leaders. Do the authors in question not realise that by labelling all Jews as accomplices to the crimes of the elite cabal of psychopaths, they are helping this cabal in their ultimate goal: to create the right social conditions for a savage war in the Middle East where both Jews and Arabs may well be annihilated? That this war in the Middle East may explode on their own doorsteps if "ethnic specific weapons" designed to wipe out non-psychopaths don't get them first?

If such authors see themselves as true humanitarians and truth seekers, their goal should be to protect *normal* human beings—including ethical ethnic and religious Jews, ethical Christians, and ethical Muslims—from the predations and manipulations of the psychopathic elite few who use and abuse humanity over and over again, Jewish, Christian, and Islamic people alike. To this end their energy would be best used by focusing on and exposing the agenda of this "psychopathic elite", not by beating up on those who are least able to understand that they are being duped. The battle is fought between those from opposing sides of the fence who can See—what is being fought over is the soul and future of the human race.

Nevertheless, in considering all that we have covered so far in this volume, the issue of Jewish genetics studies and how they relate to the secret work on Ethnic Specific weapons must be brought forward.

THE NATURAL HISTORY OF ASHKENAZI INTELLIGENCE

In a paper written by Gregory Cochran, Jason Hardy and Henry Harpending of the Department of Anthropology, University of Utah, entitled *Natural His-*

tory of Ashkenazi Intelligence,[414] the authors elaborate the hypothesis that the unique demography and sociology of Ashkenazim in medieval Europe selected for (encouraged) intelligence. In the paper, it is said that there are two main clusters of Ashkenazi-inherited disease, the sphingolipid cluster and the DNA repair cluster. Among the other significant Ashkenazi disorders we find *idiopathic torsion dystonia* and non-classical *adrenal hyperplasia* which are known to elevate IQ.

In a paper entitled *Inborn Errors and Disturbances of Central Neurotransmission (with Special Reference to Phenylketonuria)*, M. Sandler mentions:

> A rather tenuous story of decreased adrenaline and noradrenaline production in the *Riley-Day syndrome (familial dysautonomia)* is on record (Goodall et al., 1971), despite normal dopamine generation with no impediment in the conversion of dopamine to noradrenaline. It is possible that any change in this disorder is secondary to some distortion of nerve growth factor disposition (Siggers et al., 1976; Schwartz and Breakefield, 1980).[415]

The paper in which this comment appears is mostly about Phenylketonuria, a genetic disorder that consists mainly of an inability of the body to utilize the essential amino acid, phenylalanine. *Classic PKU and the other causes of hyperphenylalaninemia affect mainly Caucasians and Orientals, and to a much lesser extent, Africans. Many of the infants who are born with this condition have blue eyes and fairer hair and skin than other family members.* The condition generally leads to severe brain problems such as mental retardation and seizures. So, what is the connection? *Riley-Day syndrome.* It is found almost exclusively in Ashkenazi Jews. The incidence is estimated to be 1 in 3,700 people, higher than the incidence of PKU.

> Infants with this condition have feeding problems and develop pneumonia caused by breathing their formula and food into their airways. Vomiting and sweating spells begin as the infant matures. Young children may also have breath-holding spells that produce unconsciousness, since they can hold their breath for long enough to pass out without feeling the discomfort that normal children would.

> A hallmark of Riley-Day syndrome is insensitivity to pain. This leads to unnoticed injuries or injuries that might not have occurred had the child sensed discomfort. Children do not feel the normal sensations that generally warn of impending injury, such as drying of the eyes, pressure over pressure points, and chronic rubbing and chaffing. Bone and skin pain, including burns, are also poorly perceived. However, they can feel visceral pain, like menstrual cramps.

> Seizures occur in almost 50% of affected children. They have acute problems with high and low blood pressure. They may have problems regulating their body temperature.[416]

---

[414] Gregory Cochran, Jason Hardy, Henry Harpending, "Natural History of Ashkenazi Intelligence", Department of Anthropology, University of Utah.
[415] M. Sandler, Bernhard Baron Memorial Research Laboratories and Institute of Obstetrics and Gynaecology, Queen Charlotte's Maternity Hospital, London W6 OXG.
[416] http://health.allrefer.com/health/riley-day-syndrome-info.html

Riley-Day syndrome is inherited as an autosomal recessive trait, which means that a person must inherit the defective gene from both parents in order to develop the condition.

> It is of interest that phenylethylamine possesses very similar pharmacological properties to amphetamine (Mantegazza and Riva, 1963), from which it differs only by the absence of a methyl group on the a-carbon atom. Amphetamine psychosis is almost indistinguishable from paranoid schizophrenia (Janowsky and Risch, 1979) and in accordance with the phenylethylamine hypothesis of schizophrenia (Sandler and Reynolds, 1976), it is not surprising that a high proportion of untreated phenylketonurics manifest with some of the stigmata of the disease which can be attenuated by reduced phenylalanine intake (Blyumina, 1975). These schizophreniform signs may well stem from the prolonged effects of phenylethylamine overproduction.[417]

Notice that PKU is a disorder that occurs mostly in very Aryan peoples, and Riley Day, a related disorder, only occurs in Ashkenazi. Both disorders seem to have some influence on intelligence. The conclusion is that this disease cluster that Ashkenazi are subjected to is seemingly a price they pay for their higher intelligence. Riley Day seems to be a disorder that embraces some of the known symptoms of psychopathy, a well. Let us now recall what Lobaczewski had to say about schizoidal psychopathy.

> Carriers of this anomaly are hypersensitive and distrustful, while, at the same time, *pay little attention to the feelings of others.* They tend to assume extreme positions, and are eager to retaliate for minor offenses. Sometimes they are eccentric and odd. Their poor sense of psychological situation and reality leads them to superimpose erroneous, pejorative interpretations upon other people's intentions. They easily become involved in activities which are ostensibly moral, but which actually inflict damage upon themselves and others. Their impoverished psychological worldview makes them typically pessimistic regarding human nature. We frequently find expressions of their characteristic attitudes in their statements and writings: "Human nature is so bad that order in human society can only be maintained by a strong power created by highly qualified individuals in the name of some higher idea." Let us call this typical expression the "schizoid declaration". [...]

> The quantitative frequency of this anomaly varies among races and nations: low among Blacks, the highest among Jews. Estimates of this frequency range from negligible up to 3%. In Poland it may be estimated as 0.7% of population. My observations suggest this anomaly is autosomally hereditary. [...]

> Their tendency to see human reality in the doctrinaire and simplistic manner they consider "proper"—i.e. "black or white"—transforms their frequently good intentions into bad results. However, their ponerogenic role can have macrosocial implications if their attitude toward human reality and their tendency to invent great doctrines are put to paper and duplicated in large editions. [...]

> An analysis of the role played by Karl Marx's works easily reveals all the above-mentioned types of apperception and the social reactions which engendered animosity between large groups of people. [...]

---

[417] Sandler, op. cit.

The conviction that Karl Marx is the best example of this is correct as he was the best-known figure of that kind. Frostig,[418] a psychiatrist of the old school, included Engels and others into a category he called "bearded schizoidal fanatics". The famous writings attributed to "Zionist Wise Men" at the turn of the century begin with a typically schizoidal declaration.[419] The nineteenth century, especially its latter half, appears to have been a time of exceptional activity on the part of schizoidal individuals, often but not always of Jewish descent. After all we have to remember that 97 % of all Jews do not manifest this anomaly, and that *it also appears among all European nations*, albeit to a markedly lesser extent. Our inheritance from this period includes world-images, scientific traditions, and legal concepts flavored with the shoddy ingredients of a schizoidal apprehension of reality.[420]

These papers are, therefore, suggestive of a genetic link between Ashkenazi Jews and certain pathologies.

In spite of the fact that psychopathy and schizophrenia are viewed as separate diagnostic entities, it has long been suggested that these two disorders may be related (Kraepelin, 1913; Kallman, 1938). It is only relatively recently however that a coherent argment in favour of this viewpoint has been advanced (Eysenck and Eysenck, 1976, 1978). These authors cite family studies of both schizophrenics and psychopaths/criminals as well as the theoretical accounts of Planasky (1972) and Gottesman and Shields (1973) in support of the notion that psychopathy and schizophrenia are genetically-related illnesses. Eysenck and Eysenck (1976) propose a polygenic model of psychoses, whereby the number of large- and small-value genes add up to determined degree of psychoses-proneness. On this continuum of diathesis psychopaths are argued to lie between non-psychotic individuals with subclinical symptoms and psychosis, and individuals who are clearly psychotic but without demonstrating the clear symptom pattern which, for example, characterizes paranoid or catatonic schizophrenics lying at the extreme of the continuum with large-value genes for psychosis.[421]

In other words, the story of the genetically enhanced intelligence of Ashkenazi Jews is very likely an anthropological description of the process of natural selection for not only intelligence but also for psychopathy. Lobaczewski

---

[418] Peter Jacob Frostig, 1896-1959. Professor of King John Kasimir University in Lwow (now Ukraine). Lobaczewski used his manual *Psychiatria*. Poland was then under pathocratic rule and his works were removed from public libraries as "ideologically improper".

[419] Ed. Note: The "Protocols of the Elders of Zion" is now well known to have been a hoax attributed to Jews. The could more accurately be called "The Protocols of the Pathocrats". However the contents of the Protocols are clearly not "hoaxed ideas" since a reasonable assessment of the events in the United States over the past 50 years or so gives ample evidence of the application of these Protocols in order to bring about the current neocon administration. Anyone who wishes to understand what has happened in the U.S. only needs to read the Protocols to understand that some group of deviant individuals took them to heart. The document, "Project For A New American Century", produced by the neoconservatives, expresses the same spirit as the Protocols.

[420] Lobaczewski, op. cit.

[421] Adrian Raine, (1986) Behavioural Sciences Section, Department of Psychiatry, Queen's Medical Centre, Nottingham, Notts. NO7 2UH, England, Psychopathy, Schizoid Personality And Borderline/Schizotypal Personality Disorders, Person. individ. Diff Vol. 7, No.4, pp. 493-501, 1986, Pergamon Journals Ltd

remarks that psychopaths are generally lower in intelligence than the populations of normal humans he has studied. We believe that this is due to the fact that the very intelligent psychopaths do not ever find themselves subjected to being studied. This certainly causes us to re-think the work being done in Ethnic Specific Weapons, the importance of mtDNA to that work, and, naturally, this:

> One of the earliest factual references to the Khazars occurs in a Syriac chronicle dating from the middle of the sixth century. It mentions the Khazars in a list of people who inhabit the region of the Caucasus. Koestler recounts that other sources indicate that *the Khazars were intimately connected with the Huns.* An interesting connection considering the legend that the Huns were a tribe of peoples that descended from Scythian witches who, cast out of their tribes, "mated with devils in the desert".

Finally, I would also like to draw your attention to certain remarks in the above quoted paper about the higher intelligence of the Ashkenazim:

> The suggested selective process explains the pattern of mental abilities in Ashkenazi Jews—high verbal and mathematical ability but relatively low spatio-visual ability. Verbal and mathematical talent helped medieval businessmen succeed, while spatio-visual abilities were irrelevant.

Put that together with certain remarks we have made earlier based on research in psychopathy:

> It has often been noted that psychopaths have a distinct advantage over human beings with conscience and feelings because the psychopath does not have conscience and feelings. What seems to be so is that conscience and feelings are related to the abstract concepts of "future" and "others". It is "spatio-temporal". We can feel fear, sympathy, empathy, sadness, and so on because we can **imagine** in an abstract way, the future based on our own experiences in the past, or even just "concepts of experiences" in myriad variations. We can "see ourselves" in them even though they are "out there" and this evokes feelings in us. We can't do something hurtful because we can imagine it being done to us and how it would feel. In other words, we can not only identify with others spatially, so to say, but also temporally—in time.
>
> The psychopath does not seem to have this capacity.
>
> They are unable to "imagine" in the sense of being able to really connect to images in a direct "self connecting to another self" sort of way.

And finally, connect the above with a series of remarks by Lobaczewski:

> As we have already pointed out, every psychological anomaly is in fact a kind of deficiency. Psychopathies are based primarily upon deficiencies in the instinctive substratum; however, their influence exerted upon mental development also leads to deficiencies in general intelligence, as discussed above. This deficiency is not compensated by the creation of the special psychological knowledge we observe among some psychopaths. *Such knowledge loses its mesmerizing power when normal people learn to understand these phenomena as well.* The psychopathologist was thus not surprised by the fact that the world of normal people is dominant regarding skill and talent. [...]

Since our intelligence is superior to theirs, we can recognize them and understand how they think and act. This is what a person learns in such a system on his own initiative, forced by everyday needs. He learns it while working in his office, school, or factory, when he needs to deal with the authorities, and when he is arrested, something only a few people manage to avoid. The author and many others learned a good deal about the psychology of this macrosocial phenomenon during compulsory indoctrinational schooling. The organizers and lecturers cannot have intended such a result. Practical knowledge of this new reality thus grows, thanks to which the society gains a resourcefulness of action which enables it to take ever better advantage of the weak spots of the rulership system. This permits gradual reorganization of societal links, which bears fruit with time.[422]

We end this discussion with a suggestive quote from the work of N.J. Danilevsky, a Russian historian in the nineteenth century. Danilevsky considered the classical conception of history to be erroneous. In its place he proposed a theory that spoke of different civilizing types of people. Without going into detail on his ideas, we think that the following quote cited by Boris Mouravieff in his paper *L'Histoire, a-t-elle un sens?*[423] opens an interesting field of study:

> Only the Creator peoples of these civilizations can be considered as agents of construction in human history. With each following its own role, placed in their own conditions, each developed the original element of its genius to bring it to the common cultural treasure chest of humanity.

> However, these historical types that we have just established as the positive agents of history do not cover the whole of the phenomena of this order. As in the solar system, next to the planets, we find comets that make their appearance only to lose themselves in the abyss of space for centuries, and as exist other cosmic matter that manifests under the form of shooting stars, airoliths and zodiacle light, there are as well, in the human universe, next to the positive and original agents of civilization, others that only intervene to bring trouble. Such is the case for the Huns, the Mongols, and the Turcs. Having filled their their destructive role as regards the agonizing civilizations, they return to their primitive state, a state without importance. We call them the negative agents of humanity.[424]

Keeping in mind Lev Gumilev's work on Ethnogenesis and the Biosphere that we cited above, we now see that it may well be that the three negative agents of humanity identified by Danilevsky are perhaps the same people, the psychopathic gene pool.

---

[422] Lobaczewski, op. cit.

[423] Boris Mouravieff, "L'Histoire a-t-elle un sens ?", *Revue Suisse d'histoire*, Tome 4, fasc. 4, 1954

[424] Ibid, 454.

THE CULT OF THE PLAUSIBLE LIE

Never ascribe to malice those things which may be explained by stupidity."
That is an important phrase, and a necessary one; it keeps people from being
paranoid. However, it has a corollary most people don't know: *One may ascribe
to malice those things which stupidity cannot explain.* – Robert Canup

The primary problem that we see humanity struggling with today is precisely delineated by psychologist Andrew Lobaczewski: it is an almost total
lack of adequate psychological knowledge on the part of the masses of humanity—the population of ordinary, normal people.

Unfortunately, after so long a time of being subjected to lies and disinformation, the likelihood of society being able to overcome the social and cultural programming is difficult, but not impossible. And that is where things
like COINTELPRO (Counter Intelligence Program) come into play: psyops
agents are masters of triggering emotional programs that put people back to
sleep. As a student on the subject, Robert Canup, has said, 99% of all of the
problems confronting mankind can be traced to a single cause: the problem of
the plausible lie. And the plausible lie is what COINTELPRO is all about.

Plausible lies are monstrous things propagated by evil people for the express purpose of deceiving good people into doing the will of those who do
not have their best interests at heart. It's that simple. The most powerful of
these lies are so plausible that nobody even dreams about questioning their
validity.

Now, even though I know I am little more than a David against the Goliath
of the well-funded arms of the National Security State, such as the many diverse and often contradictory sources of information and disinformation, including the mainstream media, many alternative media sources, so-called
"Truth-seeking groups" of all kinds, so-called New Age and Alternative writers and Impresarios of all shapes and sizes (most of whom are COINTEL-
PRO bogus organizations), I will continue to point out what can be observed
if your eyes are open and your neurons are firing, and what can be asserted
with some certainty based on collections of evidence, both material and circumstantial. Having said that, let me ask this: If there is such a thing as a
plausible lie, is it not also possible that there might be such a thing as an implausible truth? Here is Robert Canup's example:

Suppose that tomorrow when you walk out of your house, an alien spacecraft
lands in front of you. Aliens get out and assault you, leaving physical traces.
Next, imagine that this is not a hallucination, it is not dream; it really happens.
You are now in possession of an implausible truth. What chance is there of you
being able to convince anyone else of what happened to you? You know it is the
truth, but no one will believe you. And the root of the problem is the fact that
truth generally has a feeling of reality to it. However, that feeling of reality
which makes truth generally plausible is *not* the same thing as the truth itself.
Others who have not experienced aliens landing and assaulting them do not
have the same feeling of reality about what you are telling them. If everyone

else had experienced a similar event, with the attendant feeling of reality, the truth of that event would be accepted immediately. [425]

In short, people believe what is "familiar", or what is part of a careful, long term program of familiarization of lies that become plausible simply because they are familiar.

When science first discovered that solid matter was mostly empty space, many people reacted to this truth—this unfamiliar fact of our reality—with outrage. Debates over the "solidity" of matter and "kicking rocks" raged for years. It took a very long time, and a lot of work, to gradually make others aware of this truth in order to make this "implausible" fact part of our awareness.

Learning about evil in our society, how it operates on the macro-social scale, is considered by many to be "unpleasant". They don't want to go there. It is too disturbing and even frightening. More than that, talking about these things as I am here is not familiar. To talk about evil as though it were a *real* concept is something we have been programmed to *not* do!

We clearly need to study this problem of macro-social evil in our world in a systematic and scientific way. And we need to get over the idea that thinking only good thoughts, thinking about happy and "nice" things is the way to good psychological health.

As Canup writes, we face a particular, even monstrous, problem in our world: that most of what we know or think we know is based on plausible lies. A person who is sincere and speaks the truth really has almost no chance against a plausible liar. Yes, I know that goes against everything we have been taught from childhood in the "Land of the Free and Home of the Brave", but it is all too sadly true. We have been taught that "the Truth will always win" and that "anybody who believes a lie about you wasn't your friend to begin with", and a whole host of other platitudes that actually would work in a different world: a world run by people who tell the truth!

But since our world is run by people who lie for a living, you might expect that they have set things up so that liars will always win. And that is, oh so sadly, the case.

Our culture agrees on the signs of lying. Ask anyone how to tell if someone is lying and they will tell you that they can tell by "lack of eye contact, nervous shifting, or picking at one's clothes."

Psychologist Anna Salter writes with dry humor:

> This perception is so widespread I have had the fantasy that, immediately upon birth, nurses must take newborns and whisper in their ears, "Eye contact. It's a sign of truthfulness."[426]

---

[425] http://www.hal-pc.org/~rcanup/index.html

[426] Anna C. Salter, Ph.D., *Predators: Pedophiles, Rapists, and Other Sex Offenders: Who They Are, How We Can Protect Ourselves and Our Children* (Basic Books: 2004).

The problem is, if there is a psychopath—or those with related characteropathies—who doesn't know how to keep good eye contact when lying, they haven't been born. Eye contact is "universally known" to be a sign of truth-telling. The problem is that liars will fake anything that it is possible to fake, so in reality, eye contact is absolutely *not* a sign of truth telling. Anna Salter writes:

> The man in front of me is a Southern good-ole-boy, the kind of man I grew up with and like. If anything, I have a weakness for the kind of Southern male who can "Sam Ervin" you, the Southern lawyer who wears red suspenders in court along with twenty-five-year-old cowboy boots and who turns his accent up a notch when he sees the northern expert witness coming. A "northern city slicker" on the witness stand will elicit the same kind of focused interest that a deer will in hunting season. You can have some very long days in court with men who wear red suspenders and start by telling you how smart you are and how simple and dumb they are.

> I survey the man in front of me. I am not in court; I am in prison, and he is not an attorney but a sex offender, and he has bright eyes along with that slow, sweet drawl. He is a big man, slightly balding, and he has—I have to admit there is such a thing—an innocent face. [...]

> My Southern good-ole-boy certainly knows eye contact is considered a sign of truthfulness. He describes his manner in getting away with close to 100 rapes of adults and children.

>> "The manner that I use when I was trying to convince somebody—even though I knew I was lying—I'd look them in the eye, but I wouldn't stare at them. Staring makes people uncomfortable and that tends to turn them away, so I wouldn't stare at them. But look at them in a manner that, you know, "look at this innocent face. How can you believe that I would do something like that?" It helps if you have a good command of the vocabulary where you can explain yourself in a way that is easily understood. Dress nice. Use fluent hand gestures that are not attacking in any way.

>> "It's a whole combination of things. It's not any one thing that you can do. It's a whole combination of things that your body gestures and things that say 'Look, I'm telling you the truth, and I don't know what these people are trying to pull. I don't know what they're trying to prove, but I haven't done any of this. I don't know why they're doing this. You can check my records. I've got a good record. I've never been in any trouble like this. And I don't know what's going on. I'm confused.' [...]"

> As if reading my thoughts, he breaks off: "You don't' get this, Anna, do you?" he says. "You think that when I'm asked, 'Did I do it?' that's when I lie. But I've been lying every day for the last twenty-five years."

> The practiced liar: a category of liar that even experts find it difficult to detect.

> Problem is, even when dealing with people who are not practiced liars, such as college students who have volunteered for a research study of lying, most observers are not as good as they think in detecting deception. The research shows consistently that most people—even most professional groups such as police and psychologists—have no better than a chance ability to detect deception. Flipping a coin would serve as well.

"If you want to deny something, make sure you've got an element of truth in it. It sounds like its true, and there are elements of it that are very true that can be checked out, and try to balance it so that it has more truth than lie, so that when it is checked out, even if the lie part does come out, there's more truth there than lie."

This man was good enough that once he got away with stomping out of court in a huff. He was accused by his sister of raping her and molesting her daughter on the same day. He played it as a preposterous charge. His sister, he told the court, had once accused his uncle of abuse. She was well known in the family for making up crazy charges like this. He said he wasn't going to put up with such nonsense and walked out. No one stopped him, and no one ever called him back. The charge just disappeared somehow. He now admits that both charges were true.

It is likeability and charm that he wields as weapons.

The double life is a powerful tactic. There is the pattern of socially responsible behavior in public that causes people to drop their guard, and to turn a deaf ear to disclosures. The ability to charm, to be likeable, to radiate sincerity and truthfulness, is crucial to the successful liar—and they practice assiduously.

"Niceness is a decision," writes Gavin De Becker in *The Gift of Fear*. It is a "strategy of social interaction; it is not a character trait."

Despite the decades of research that have demonstrated that people cannot reliably tell who's lying and who isn't, most people believe they can. There is something so fundamentally threatening about the notion that we cannot really know whether or not to trust someone that it is very difficult to get anyone—clinicians, citizens, even police—to take such results seriously.

I stare at the child's statement in front of me. It is a report by a social worker of a four-year-old's account of sexual abuse by her father. […] [Excerpts of actual report not included; read the book.]

I consider the report carefully. It is filled with detail. The words are a child's words, the description exact. It is clear this child knows what oral sex is. It shows no signs of coaching. But why was this report sent to me with all the personal names and identifying information removed?

This report, I learn, surfaced in the middle of a custody fight. Dad was a wealthy businessman, successful, well respected, and well liked. Mom was an inpatient in a drug unit. My heart sinks. It does not matter how realistic this report is, how many signs of credibility, how few signs of coaching: In our system of justice, lawyers are for sale. Dad's money is going to buy some very good lawyers indeed. It isn't clear that Mom has either the money or the will to oppose him. And the child: she'll be lucky to be represented at all.

I've thought many times that if I were accused of a crime, I'd rather have the better lawyer than be innocent.

But it seems that the court responds appropriately and appoints two independent psychologists to make a recommendation. Two independent chances to get it right. Two people who are not beholden to either side and who can ask for any test, even a polygraph, as part of their decision-making. Two people whose job it is to know something about deception and to sort out the true from the false.

But both psychologists opt instead for what is termed an "interactional assessment." They simply watch the father interact with his daughter, looking for signs of bonding or, conversely, fear. They believe if he abused her, she will be afraid of him; if she loves him, he is innocent.

There is no research or theory to support this approach. Sex offenders are notorious for bonding with a child and using that relationship to manipulate the child into having sex with them. In addition, a child might be afraid for very different reasons; the man may have struck her mother, but never laid a hand on her, sexually or otherwise. What justification is there for believing that one can tell from the interaction between child and alleged perpetrator whether the abuse has occurred or no?[427]

Anna Salter stood up at a conference to challenge the "interactional assessment" approach and was silenced. This is a clear example of what Lobaczewski writes about in his discussion of how the sciences, particularly psychology and medicine, have been co-opted to the use of psychopaths.

In this child's case, the alleged perpetrator is her father. Surely she loves him, even if he did what she has disclosed. He has not used violence. She does not know that there is anything wrong with what he is doing. She is four years old.

One of the evaluator's notes: "Observations of father and daughter indicate a very happy, spontaneous and positive relationship." Salter writes:

I sigh. As if that had anything to do with anything. The fact that she loves him doesn't mean that he's innocent or guilty. Then I find something in the case file that makes me sit up straight. "Of concern are the admissions by Mr. Jones that earlier in his life he had engaged in sexually inappropriate behavior with three children... These were the children of the woman he was living with at the time."

I stare at the note. This psychologist knew he'd done it before—in identical circumstances. It is a damning admission and surely means the psychologist should take this latest disclosure seriously. But he does not. Mr. Jones, it seems, is too charming, too rich, too respected. Despite knowing he is an admitted child-molester, both psychologists recommend that full custody go to Dad.

And there the story ends—in most cases.

But, in this case, the father's attorney, so convinced that his client was innocent, sent him to a polygrapher. I know he thought he was innocent because he sent him to a very good polygrapher, not the one to whom an attorney would knowingly send a guilty client. This polygrapher is an unusually good interrogator and has a 98% confession rate. He tells his clients:

"Now the problem with the polygraph is that it can't tell the difference between a big lie and a little lie and I would hate, I would truly hate for you to mess up your polygraph with something little that don't amount to a hill of beans. So if there is anything, anything at all that you want to tell me before the polygraph, now's the time so we can get it out of the way."

Under these instructions, the polygrapher found that Mr. "Jones" had quite a few things to say:

---

[427] Salter, op. cit.

[I'm not including most of the confessions of this man, just selected and highly edited excerpts.]

> They shower together and fondle one another. Sometimes he masturbates while they are in the shower and he encourages the child to "assist," saying that this is "educational" for her. They sleep nude together and "sometimes things happen." This man bought a vibrator for his four-year-old daughter. And so on.

> All of these confessions were made *before* the polygraph. What is astonishing is that he fails the polygraph because he was withholding information on oral sex with his daughter.

> I find a handwritten note from the polygrapher in the file. He faxed the report to the attorney for the father. It was a private polygraph, after all, requested by the father's attorney and not one required by either of the independent evaluators (though they *could* have asked for it). Within five minutes of faxing the report, the phone rang, "I've worked with you for twenty years," the attorney said to him. "I hope I don't have to remind you what privileged communication means."

> What privileged communication means is that this report fell under attorney-client privilege and therefore was suppressed. What is means is that the father's attorney was under no requirement whatsoever to release the report to the court, and, by law, the polygrapher could not.

> What it means is that the only reports the court saw in this case were by the two psychologists who thought they could tell whether the father way lying by interviewing him and that they could tell if the child was abused by seeing if she loved her father. What it means is that, in 1996, full custody of this child went to her father where it has remained ever since.

> The polygrapher, anguished by the outcome, sent the case to me after removing the real names, with the hope that I can use it for "educational purposes."

> Mr. Jones was a well-respected member of the community with a crazy wife. And he was so sincere. Clearly, the child loved him dearly. Such a man is hardly likely to be a child molester, now is he?

Another similar case has a report about the father:

> Since the father denied the allegations, it is difficult to determine the identity of the perpetrator. In support of the father's truthfulness [...] he was very forthright during the interview and testing procedures. For example, he acknowledged having difficulty in his sexual relations at time, and he openly admitted that he had a possible drinking problem. [...] [428]

Because he admitted some problems, the psychologist concluded that he would not lie about other, more serious problems! Because he admitted problems that were legal, she concluded he would not lie about activity that was illegal! That is just rationalization; the truth is that the psychologist just simply believed the lies.

One clinical evaluator noted in a report about a sexual predator that he "stayed back to close one of the doors, a very solicitous gesture that, as it turned out, is consistent with his general pattern of behavior". The report

---

[428] Salter, op. cit.

went on to describe him as "kind, thoughtful, and considerate, a person who seemed to take pleasure in helping and caring":

> Instead of concluding that the man was good at creating a front, the psychologist concluded that the man was not a brutal, violent, serial rapist. Fortunately, there was considerable evidence that he was, and he was convicted. In this case, the court got it right even if the psychologist was out to lunch.
>
> In another case, a very well known psychologist evaluated a three month old infant with bite marks all over him. Only two people had the opportunity to inflict the bite marks in the specific time frame, and they were the parents. Suspicion centered on the father. The psychologist who was asked to evaluate him reported how tenderly he wiped the infant's nose in the evaluation, how carefully he held the baby. Based on the man's behavior in the interview, she exonerated him and recommended custody remain with the parents. Two years later, he killed the infant. [429]

This is an issue that will never die. It seems impossible to convince people that private behavior cannot be predicted from public behavior. Kind, non-violent individuals behave well in public, but so do predators, rapists, murderers, paedophiles and COINTELPRO agents who help to shape the culture in which we live. No, they weren't always called COINTELPRO, but the principle is the same. It has been used since time immemorial. The earliest written records we have are of "clappers" in the audiences of theatres in ancient Greece. What do you think the term "Greek Chorus" means? We have exactly that in the present day in the form of the mainstream media. Did you think that, with the power of the internet to reach millions of people that the "powers that be" would have ignored the necessity of installing a "Greek Chorus" on the net?

> The chorus offered background and summary information to help the audience follow the performance, commented on main themes, and showed how an ideal audience might react to the drama as it was presented. They also represent the general populace of any particular story.

Discussion boards are ideal formats for "Greek Choruses" as they can be vectored to "show how the ideal audience ought to react", and to "represent the general populace". In this way, the illusion can be created of a consensus when, in fact, such a consensus may not exist.

Polls are another example of Greek Choruses or Clappers.

Consider our legal system. Here you first have to ask yourself just what kind of people were in charge of the creation and shaping of our "social norms". Now sure, everybody will agree with the sayings that "you can't trust a politician", or "power corrupts" and so on, but have you ever really stopped to think about that and what it must really mean?

> Most people have heard of Ted Bundy; the serial killer who was executed in Florida several years ago. Not many people are aware of the fact that Bundy was studying to become a prosecutor, and that eventually he hoped to become a judge. Those that do know that fact see it as some strangely ironic twist—an in-

---

[429] Salter, op. cit.

explicable quirk in Bundy's bizarre makeup. It never seems to occur to most people that the perfect place for a psychopathic serial killer to hide in society is as a prosecutor or a judge; but I assure you that it occurs to the Psychopaths of the world. I would estimate that about 10% of the prosecutors and judges in the United States are in fact, S.A.P.s [Socially Adept Psychopaths]. The *only* difference between them and Ted Bundy is that they were able to control outward signs of their Psychopathy until they achieved their goal of being in a position of authority. [...]

John had one overriding dream; to become a judge. Here was the greatest reward possible for a psychopath: to put on the royal robes of the judiciary—to become a demigod—to have others plead to Him and beg His indulgence, to have everyone rise in awe and respect when He entered the room, for His word to literally be law, to be able to create an almost endless amount of human misery, just because He could, to punish summarily anyone who, quite correctly, displayed contempt for Him, to have the power of life and death over people, to be granted the only royal title available in the United States: "Your Honor".

How brilliant of his predecessors to slip that one past the watchful eyes of the founding fathers—who sought to establish an egalitarian society free of the mental disease of royalty. There are, he reflected, no "Your Majesties" or "Your Excellencies" in this country, but we quietly fooled everyone into accepting "Your Honors". [...]

'John House slept soundly. In his dreams he and his kind had finally succeeded in reshaping the world into the image they wanted: the dark ages had returned. Once more the plague swept unchallenged over the country side. John could hear the voice crying out in the mud street in front of his hovel: "Bring out your dead!"

'John was in his glory. This was life the way it was supposed to be. He was the new Torquemada: randomly selecting anyone who was unscarred by smallpox for a session on the rack; since anyone who had escaped disfigurement had obviously signed a pact with the devil. Here at last was an era where John and his kind could feel good by comparison: with so much misery around him John knew he was better off than those he could see dying in squalor and ignorance. John reveled in the suffering of all about him. He did what he could to make that suffering worse; no agony was so great that John House could not add to it.'

It is difficult to believe that huge parts of society have been built with the guidance of the mentally ill; but they have been. The average person is heavily invested in doing things the way Psychopaths want them done, and is unaware that the things that the S.A.Ps have them doing are psychopathic. [430]

Richard Dolan has pointed out that those at the top will *always* take whatever measures necessary to stay at the top, and when knowledge is power, that means that they will make sure that they are in control of what people know or think they know. As we noted earlier, as a society gets larger and more competitive, individuals become more anonymous and more Machiavellian. Social stratification and segregation leads to feelings of inferiority, pessimism and depression among the have-nots and this promotes the use of

---

[430] Robert Canup, *The Socially Adept Psychopath*: http://www.hal-pc.org/~rcanup/sap.html

"cheating strategies" in life which then makes the environment more adaptive for psychopathy in general. Such individuals may begin their lives in the lower socio-economic levels, but they often rise to the top. Robert Canup writes:

> By my estimates, about four percent of the population is evil—that is about one person in twenty five.
>
> The mental abilities of evil people closely echo those of the normal population; there is a bell shaped curve of intelligence in both good and evil people.
>
> Most good people are only aware of the least intelligent part of the evil distribution; those are the people who are obviously evil: criminals. The normal and intelligent ends of the evil distribution totally escape most good people's understanding. [Here] I will describe those undetected parts of evil.
>
> What does an evil person of normal intelligence look like? Most people are very familiar with them. An evil person of normal intelligence is a person who makes life difficult, painful, and unpleasant for the good people around them. The supervisor who creates a crises at work by trying to pour a cup and a half of coffee into a cup and then requires everyone to work holidays and weekends to clean up the mess—is an example of an evil person of normal intelligence. What distinguishes such people from criminals is that they are quicker learners; they figure out what will happen to them if they pursue the sort of obvious evil things that the least intelligent of the evil spectrum do.
>
> Evil people of normal intelligence are careful to do their best to blend into good society. This insulates and protects them from the angered reaction of good people; who would hammer them just as hard as they hammer the least intelligent of the evil. Indeed, evil people of normal intelligence are so successful at blending into good society that their statements, goals and culture have become 'normal' and 'accepted'. For example, the comic strip 'Miss Peach' is an example of the behavior and actions of evil people of normal intelligence. The 'Put Down', passive aggressive behavior, insults, 'back stabbing', these are all typical behaviors for evil people of normal intelligence. All of these things are so common that many good people adopt them as reasonable ways to behave; they are not, they are as evil as anything could be.
>
> By far evil people of normal intelligence are the most common type of evil person most people encounter. The stress in most good people's lives comes from interaction with evil people of normal intelligence. The goal of the average evil person is to make the lives of those around them as miserable as they can— without doing enough to attract the retribution they richly deserve.
>
> Next up the ladder is *the evil person of above average intelligence*. These people have a similar goal to evil people of average intelligence; the production of human misery. However these people see the opportunity to do something that evil people of normal intelligence don't see how to do; murder someone and get away with it. They understand that the way to murder someone and get away with it is to not care who they kill, how they kill them, or when they kill them. Such people set up conditions where someone will be 'accidentally' killed and wait for the circumstances to occur.
>
> For example, I once worked for an evil person of above average intelligence who built up a company which did about twenty million dollars a year of busi-

ness. He was only interested in his business as an instrument to his ends. He worked people long hours of overtime (without any extra pay)—he pushed people as hard as he could. What he was doing was setting up an environment as stressful as he could—secure in the knowledge that sooner or later—a death would be the result. Sure enough, a staff accountant driving home after a late night's work was hit by a drunken driver and killed. The boss was stunned; his life's goal had been accomplished—the guilt was obvious in his face the next day. He became very cheerful over the next several weeks, and lost interest in the company. Inside of a year and a half it was out of business.

Of course since he was cloaked in plausible deniability no criminal charges could ever be brought against him. But, he could see that the death had come as a direct result of his deliberately malicious behavior; he willed it, and it happened. Most industrial accidental deaths and injuries can be traced back to the malicious behavior of those who are evil and of above average intelligence.

That leaves us those who are evil and of high intelligence. Most good people are also familiar with these kind of people; we call them leaders—both of industry and of government. It is the goal of such people to get away with mass murder. An example will show how they work their agenda.

If you look at the Viet Nam War none of it makes much sense; not from a political standpoint, not from an economic standpoint, and certainly not from a military standpoint. Let us examine the well known case of 'Hamburger Hill'; a battle location in the Viet Nam war. In this engagement US forces fought their way up a hill against fierce opposition. Once the US forces had taken the hill they were ordered to **march back down** giving the hill back to the opposition. The action was repeated several times. The argument given was that the US forces were exhausting the enemy by forcing them to fight repeatedly. Of course the conventional military strategy is to exhaust the opposition forces by making them attempt to re-take the hill by force of arms—rather than by giving it back to them uncontested. The 'Hamburger Hill' strategy makes no sense whatsoever—unless you assume that very high up in the US government was an evil person of high intelligence whose goal was to murder ten's of thousands of people and get away with it. When thought of this way, the entire War in Viet Nam snaps into focus and makes sense—as far as I know, that is the **only** explanation of the war that allows it to be understandable.

If you are a good person you will meet many evil people in your life, you need to recognize them and their actions. More importantly you need to recognize which evil behaviors you have been conned into accepting as reasonable and to reject those behaviors—both in yourself and in others—as unacceptable.[431]

HOW THE GAME IS PLAYED

We repeat the awful truth: Psychopathic behavior seems to be on the rise because of the very nature of American capitalistic society. Psychopaths seek power over others, it's that simple, and they gravitate to any field where there is power: medicine, law, industry, politics. It has always been that way; this is nothing new. Indeed, they comprise a very small segment of the population

---

[431] http://www.hal-pc.org/~rcanup/evil.html

with an extremely large influence. It is due to this influence and the plausible lie that they can magnetize normal, decent people to follow them. They can make social conditions bad so that people feel oppressed and abused, and then they can easily blame it on someone else and agitate the people to go after and kill others based on such lies. Machiavelli discussed this sort of system plainly and openly and it has been the system of power since Cain killed Abel.

So, consider the idea that the ideas behind our social and cultural systems - including the legal system—were created by people whose agenda was to control society so that they could stay on top, and think about all the many ways they might go about doing that.

These are the same people who set up the legal system so that people would "get what they deserved".

Now, just think about that for a moment.

Imagine that you are a person at the top of the heap who knows that if you *really* set up a system where people got what they really deserved, you, yourself, would be instantly replaced—out the door in an instant! And so, if you are not just intent on staying on top and holding power, but cunning also, you will do everything in your power to insure that you and your kind are in charge of setting up that system, and that you remain in charge of it. You would make certain that evil was blended into the social and cultural concepts so seamlessly that nobody would ever notice.

And that is, quite literally, what happened. The individuals "at the top of the heap", who had gotten there by being the most vile and rapacious, then set about figuring out ways to deceive the masses, all the while keeping their favor and adulation. They knew they had to make laws to keep order, and they knew they had to make those laws seem fair and reasonable to the masses of people or they would lose control. Losing control was the thing to be feared as anyone who has read *The Prince* by Machiavelli realizes.

And so, Machiavellian manipulators at the top of the heap were deeply involved in the formation of our cultural and social norms, including our legal system.

As Canup describes, in the earliest days of this "legal system" there was a form of "justice" called "trial by ordeal". An example of trial by ordeal was holding a red hot iron to a defendant's tongue. The plausible lie used to justify this behavior was: if the defendant was telling a lie they would have a dry mouth and would be burned by the iron—while a truthful person would have a moist mouth and would be protected.

The fact is, a *normal* person who is telling the truth would most definitely have a dry mouth from fear, while a psychopath, who is incapable of feeling fear, would be the one with the moist mouth!

Now, just think about that for a few minutes.

Our current legal system is descended from "trial by ordeal"—and really isn't much different, though it is much cleverer and simply not as obviously evil as that one was. You have already read a few examples above of just how the system works. As Anna Salter said, if she was accused of a crime, she would rather have a good lawyer than be innocent. That is a truly sad statement on our reality. Here's a simple way to understand our legal system, adapted from the writings of Robert Canup[432]:

Suppose that you are on a team that is engaged in a game and you discover that:

1. The other team gets to make up the rules.

2. The referee plays for the other team.

3. One of the rules is that you are not allowed to score—the other team is at no risk.

4. Only you can be scored against.

That is precisely how our social, cultural, and legal systems operate.

The conditions of our world are designed to create the maximum chance that psychopaths will prevail and normal people will be punished by being good and telling the truth.

Punishing normal, decent, good people involves more than just creating a social system that acts against them. The system is designed to insure that these good people are subjected to as much pain as possible for the simple fact of being good and honest. An obvious example of punishing the innocent may be found in the way the victim in a rape case is treated; their reputations are dragged through the dirt—all in the name of justice of course. Note the case quoted above, of the fellow who raped his sister and her daughter and walked out of court after accusing her of being a mental case.

The system that controls our thinking is set up like the legal system. People are taught to assume that, in any conflict, one side is lying one way, and the other is lying the other way, and people can just form opinions about which side is telling the truth. They are taught that the truth will lie somewhere between two extremes.

That is a wonderfully plausible lie.

Moreover, none of the conditions conducive to finding the Truth prevail in a courtroom, even if we have been brainwashed to think that we have in the United States the "best legal system in the world". It is not much different than "Trial by Ordeal", only the hot poker has been replaced by a system that works as effectively to the advantage of liars.

Here then we see the worst feature of the law: it is designed to make the world safe for evil people. In effect the law serves to take the horns away from the bulls, while leaving the lions their teeth and claws. Massive, overwhelming advantage is placed in the hands of liars. Indeed, without the legal system insuring their safety, the world would be a much more difficult place for evil people.

Everyone knows somewhere deep inside, that there is something not right about our world. In fact, at the present moment, it could hardly be worse. But

---

[432] http://www.hal-pc.org/~rcanup/problem.html

most people spend their lives avoiding that fact at all cost. The brutal truth is that the our social, cultural, and legal systems are all about making people helpless then hammering them without mercy—all the while involving everyone in the illusion that right prevails.

THE SECRET CULT

"There exists in our world today a powerful and dangerous secret cult."

So wrote Victor Marchetti, a former high-ranking CIA official, in his book *The CIA and the Cult of Intelligence*. This is the first book the U.S. Government ever went to court to censor before publication. In this book, Marchetti tells us that there *is* a "Cabal" that rules the world and that its holy men are the clandestine professionals of the Central Intelligence Agency. Paraphrasing Marchetti:

> This cult is patronized and protected by the highest level government officials in the world. Its membership is composed of those in the power centers of government, industry, commerce, finance, and labor. *It manipulates individuals in areas of important public influence—including the academic world and the mass media.* The Secret Cult is a global fraternity of a political aristocracy whose purpose is to further the political policies of persons or agencies unknown. It acts covertly and illegally.

Others have had this to say:

> "The main threat to Democracy comes *not from the extreme left* but *from the extreme right*, which is able to *buy huge sections of the press and radio*, and wages a constant campaign to smear and discredit every progressive and humanitarian measure." – *George Seldes*

> "There exists a shadowy Government with its own Air Force, its own Navy, its own fundraising mechanism, and the ability to pursue its own ideas of national interest, free from all checks and balances, and free from the law itself." – Daniel K. Inouye, U.S. Senator

> "Some of the biggest men in the United States, in the field of commerce and manufacture, are afraid of something. They know that there is a power somewhere so organized, so subtle, so watchful, so interlocked, so complete, so pervasive, that they better not speak above their breath when they speak in condemnation of it." – Woodrow Wilson, *The New Freedom* (1913)

Remember: those who are at the top of the heap will always take whatever steps are necessary to maintain the status quo and the way this is done is via "official pathocratic culture" which is a product of COINTELPRO.

According to analysts, COINTELPRO was the FBI's secret program to undermine the popular anti-war and equal rights upsurge, which swept the country during the 1960s. Though the name stands for "Counterintelligence Program", the targets were *not enemy spies*. The FBI set out to eliminate "radical" political opposition inside the U.S. This was a high level psychological operation specifically set up to vector "ideological" trends—beliefs of the United States citizenry.

When traditional modes of repression (exposure, blatant harassment, and prosecution for political crimes) failed to counter the growing insurgency, and even helped to fuel it, the Bureau took the law into its own hands. Its methods ranged far beyond surveillance, and amounted to a domestic version of the covert action for which the CIA has become infamous throughout the world.

Usually, when we think of COINTELPRO, we think of the most well known and typical activities which include sending anonymous or fictitious letters designed to start rumors, publishing false defamatory or threatening information, forging signatures on fake documents, introducing disruptive and subversive members into organizations to destroy them from within, and so on. Blackmailing insiders in any group to force them to spread false rumors, or to foment factionalism was also common.

What a lot of people don't keep in mind is the fact that COINTELPRO also concentrated on creating bogus organizations. These bogus groups could serve many functions which might include attacking and/or disrupting bona fide groups, or even just simply creating a diversion with clever propaganda in order to attract members away so as to involve them with time-wasting activity designed to prevent them from doing anything useful. According to investigators, these FBI programs were noteworthy because all documents relating to them were stamped "do not file". This meant that they were *never filed in the system*, and for all intents and purposes, did not exist.[433] This cover was blown after activists broke into an FBI office in Media, Pennsylvania in 1971. The possibility of finding evidence for any of it, after that event, is about zero.

The COINTELPRO files that were retrieved during the above mentioned break-in showed that the U.S. Government targeted a very broad range of religious, labor and community groups opposed to any of its agendas. We can be certain that many groups formed for the ostensible purpose of "investigating 9/11" are of this type.

What seems to be certain is that the Powers That Be (PTB) have developed COINTELPRO to an all new level of social shaping, cultural brainwashing, and the main targets of this activity would include virtually anyone who is seeking the truth about the shifting realities of our world. The cases of COINTELPRO activities against political groups must be no more than the tip of the iceberg, given that the great bulk of COINTELPRO-type operations remain secret. By all indications, domestic covert operations have become a permanent feature of U.S. politics and Social Programming, and it is hardly likely, considering the evidence, that the 9/11 Truth groups are exempt.

It would be wrong to limit COINTELPRO to a specific period or manifestation of it. It is pervasive. One could think of the control of the media by the Jewish elite as a form of COINTELPRO.

---

[433] This, of course, makes us wonder just how much material relating to government activities is stamped: "Do Not File".

The implications of this are truly alarming. Those who manage to get close to the truth of these matters, despite the many obstacles in their path, face national covert campaigns to discredit and disrupt their research and reputations which certainly includes creation of the 9/11 Truth Movement itself in order to better control where it goes and what it uncovers. Clearly, COINTELPRO and similar operations under other names also work to distort academic and popular perceptions of the problems facing our world. They have done enormous damage to the search for the Truth.

"Terrorism is changing. New adversaries, new motivations and new rationales have surfaced in recent years to challenge much of the conventional wisdom..." wrote Dr. Bruce Hoffman, Director of RAND. And he was right. The only problem is, the reader is largely unaware of the definition of "new adversaries" that might be implied in his remarks. It doesn't take a genius to figure out that Dr. Hoffman may have been referring to "normal humans" as opposed to psychopaths in his remarks about "terrorism". The disclosures of George W. Bush spying on Americans can also be seen in this light. Undoubtedly, as Lobaczewski has written, to the psychopath, the world of normal people—even if they are the majority—must be rejected and destroyed.

The most effective weapon of COINTELPRO is ridicule and debunking. Notice that Marchetti mentions above that this is done via manipulation of individuals in areas of important public influence—including the *academic world and the mass media.* With the analysis of Lobaczewski, we easily understand how this is accomplished.

Bottom line is: if you have bought into the emotionally manipulated consensus of "official culture" that there are no conspiracies, it is very likely that you are being manipulated by a psychopath. You have been hypnotized by the suggestions of the holy men of the Secret Cult. And you have chosen to believe them over your own natural human observations and senses.

From an "Expert" on Lies:

> The size of the lie is a definite factor in causing it to be believed, because the vast masses of a nation are, in the depths of their hearts, more easily deceived than they are consciously and intentionally bad.

> The primitive simplicity of their minds renders them more easy victims of a big lie than a small one, because they themselves often tell little lies but would be ashamed to tell big ones. Such a form of lying would never enter their heads. They would never credit others with the possibility of such great impudence as the *complete reversal of facts.*

> Even explanations would long leave them in doubt and hesitation, and *any trifling reason would dispose them to accept a thing as true.* Something therefore always remains and sticks from the most imprudent of lies, a fact which all bodies and individuals concerned in the art of lying in this world know only too well, and therefore they stop at nothing to achieve this end. – Adolph Hitler, *Mein Kampf*

Government of, by, for Psychopaths

Totalitarianism in the guise of fascism was not defeated during WWII; it migrated to America thanks to the CIA. The totalitarian impulse is the fundament of psychopathy. The psychopathic governmental style is to impose dictatorial control of the masses for the benefit of a few. Total knowledge equals total control and is well represented by the Total Information Awareness program (led by the convicted felon, John Poindexter). Similarly, the Secret Government of psychopaths has spent decades extending its tentacles throughout society. Its plan was simple, first informers, then key positions, then control.

First they established their base in the Republican Party, co-opted the intelligence agencies, and then they took over the various officer corps. By 1963, the Secret Government felt confident enough to assassinate JFK in a stealth *coup d'état*. (He had just declared his intention to break the CIA into a thousand pieces, and was against Israel's plan to equip itself with nuclear weapons. The CIA, Mossad and their cronies got to him first.) Since 1963 they have had shadow government control over the U.S. But that is just the tip of the iceberg. As Lobaczewski points out, such a government—a Pathocracy— eventually attracts to itself all the deviants in a society and they "rise to positions of power in industry and local government until the infection has spread to every level of the nation".

Like a fungus, what you see of a Pathocracy is far outweighed by what you don't see. Not only is there a vast network of informers, the shadow government has been carrying out a decades long plan to infiltrate, monitor, and place individuals in strategically key positions, and then control all law enforcement bodies, major media outlets, and all political parties. If it seems that there is a high preponderance of Jews in such positions, it is only because Jewish psychopaths are smarter than any others.

In Lenni Brenner's book *51 Documents: Zionist collaboration with the Nazis*, Brenner presents historical documents that show that certain Zionist leaders assisted in "selecting" which Jews did or did not go to their deaths during WWII. I would like to speculate that this maneuver may very well have been predicated upon the psychopaths "special knowledge" and ability to recognize other psychopaths. Thus, a culling of the actual Jewish herd was first on the agenda in order to create a Master Race to control and direct the current psychopathic end game. It seems that this end game required the establishment of a Jewish homeland on Palestinian land, which was 'coincidentally' effected, in large part, by the Jewish Holocaust, which was aided and abetted by the psychopathic Zionist leaders. If this speculation is anywhere close to the reality—and there is good reason to believe it is—then that could very well explain the research into so-called "ethnic specific weapons" that can target everyone except genetic psychopaths.

If one considers the "model" of *Sayanim* mentioned previously, and simply uses it to describe a network of psychopaths as Lobaczewski observed in the totalitarian soviet dictatorship, the truth will become evident. Strategically key positions would be filled by psychological deviants selected by psychopaths at the top. Such positions would include county coroners (who can declare death squad murders to be suicides or natural deaths), federal judges (who can steer cases that endanger the psychopathic network to sympathetic psychopathic judges), law enforcement, both ordinary and leadership, story selecting editors, letters-to-the-editor editors, and archiving editors (to scrub the archives of dangerous breaking stories beyond the power of the selecting editors to squelch).

You ask: How could they keep such a structure secret?

The answer is also simple: the individuals making up this network have a much bigger secret, their own genetic deviance: psychopathy. Remember, they do not view normal humans—who, by the way, make up the majority of the population on the planet—as conspecific. This is also why, in any group or society, there are always despised "creatures" that can be found to betray their fellows in the most vile and inhuman ways. Why? Because they are psychopaths, and they occur in every group through the simple laws of genetic recombination.

They are nonhuman humans, predatory simulacrums of our own species' cheater strategists as Linda Mealey describes them:

> I have thus far argued that some individuals seem to have a genotype that disposes them to [psychopathy].

> [Psychopathy describes] frequency-dependent, genetically based, individual differences in employment of life strategies. [Psychopaths] always appear in every culture, no matter what the socio-cultural conditions. [...]

> Competition increases the use of antisocial and Machiavellian strategies and can counteract pro-social behavior. [...]

> Some cultures encourage competitiveness more than others and these differences in social values vary both temporally and cross-culturally. [...] Across both dimensions, high levels of competitiveness are associated with high crime rates and Machiavellianism.

> High population density, an indirect form of competition, is also associated with reduced pro-social behavior and increased anti-social behavior.[434]

Mealey, Stout, Hare, Lobaczewski, Simon and others seem to be trying to wake people up in a more or less gentle way. However, there are a few psychologists and psychiatrists out there who are so appalled by what they are seeing that they are taking a more direct method. Amos M. Gunsberg, a psychotherapist and trainer of psychotherapists in New York City and founder of the *School for Quality Being*, wrote the following article which was published in *PsychNews International*, Volume 2, Issue 5, and naturally a storm

---

[434] Mealey, op. cit.

of protest from psychopathic psychologists and psychiatrists blew up and hasn't died down since.

BEYOND INSANITY[435]

We used to call them psychopaths—these creatures that appear on our planet physically in human form, but are not human beings.

We noted they are amoral. That should have given us a clue.

We noted they do not *feel* feelings. That should have instructed us.

We noted they are heartless. That should have set off the alarm.

These creatures lack elements which distinguish the human being. They exhibit no connection with, no understanding of what we call "morality", "honesty", "decency", "fair play", etc. They lack the faculty we call empathy. They lack the faculty we call introspection.

Mankind has spent centuries trying to make sense of these creatures as some form of human being. All in vain. Not only in vain, but at enormous on-going cost to our civilization. These creatures are not human beings gone wrong. They are a different species dedicated to the murder of human values as a prelude to the murder of human beings e.g., the tactics used by Nazis, past and present.

They laugh at us. They say: "No one understands us. People can't put themselves in the minds of men who act without a conscience. They try to understand, but they can't."

These creatures do not *think* human. They do not *speak* human. They do not know what it is to *be* human.

We classify them as "humanoid".

Yes, they have human form. If we manage to resist their onslaught long enough, we will eventually develop technical scanning equipment which will measure how different they are from human beings, despite their similarity of form.

Here we would like to note that when Robert Hare submitted brain scans of psychopaths to a journal for publication with an article he sought to publish, the article was rejected because the editors did not believe the scans were human.

In the meantime, the quality of our lives—and often our very lives—depends on our recognizing these creatures for what they are, and taking steps to neutralize their attempts to destroy us.

Evidence of Humanoid Behavior

They make pronouncements without substantiation. To them, these pronouncements represent what reality is—pronouncement by pronouncement. The present pronouncement may contradict what they said a moment ago. This means nothing to them. They make no attempt to deal with the contradiction.

They demonstrate a total lack of understanding what we mean by a "fact". In their writings and in their speech, they do not use that word.

---

[435] *Psychnews International*, Volume 2, Issue 5 Oct-Dec 1997

We humans find this hard to believe. The use of facts is such a basic part of our lives. We base our conclusions and our actions on them. We go on from there to test things and establish more facts. When we debate, we present facts, and show how we derive our observations and our positions from them.

Without facts, all we have is what we call "fantasy".

Since these creatures have a human appearance, we assume they must think like us—be aware of what we are aware. We think they *must* know what facts are. When they don't address the facts, we say they are playing a game. We think they do know what the facts are, but don't want to admit it.

Not so! They don't know what a fact is. When we speak of facts and ask them to address the facts, they look at us with vacant eyes. They don't know what we're talking about.

They study us because their strategy is to pass as human. They hear us use the words—facts, evidence, substantiation. They lack the human capacity to understand what we mean. What they do is ignore our reference to facts, ignore our requests for them to supply facts, and hope we won't notice it's due to their lack of comprehension.

Let's look at examples of what *they* use for what *we* mean by "facts".

The Association for the Advancement of Gestalt Therapy (AAGT) held an open conference at which three "master" therapists worked with three volunteers. Dr. Jeffrey A. Schaler published a critique entitled "Bad Therapy" in which he cited examples not only of bad therapy, but also of systematic abuse of a volunteer by the "master" therapist. (*The Interpsych Newsletter*, Vol 2, Issue 9, Nov 95.) On their official Internet mail list (aagt@netride.com), members of the Association launched an attack on Dr. Schaler, culminating in their adoption of the slogan: "Saving Gestalt Therapy from Jeff Schaler", used as the subject line in a discussion thread. Under this heading they "saved" Gestalt therapy by sending in e-mails labeling Jeff Schaler as "arrogant, snide, hair-splitting, nit-picking, disturbed, mean-spirited, ranting, self-serving," etc.

When asked how this labeling "saved" Gestalt therapy, they ignored the question. When asked in what way Gestalt therapy was endangered by Jeff Schaler, they ignored the question.

It became clear they thoroughly believed their pronouncements erased not only the evidence presented but also erased Jeff Schaler himself. They "pronounced" him to be no longer in existence. For them, whatever they "declare" is what's real. What *we* call reality is not real to them. *They* "pronounce" what is to be considered real.

Here's another example. I asked a psychotherapy client to look at a chair which was situated about six feet away near a wall. I then asked her to describe the chair. She did, in rather complete detail, except for the legs. *The chair she described had no legs!*

I pointed this out, and asked how the chair could be suspended in air, with no legs to support it. She said: "I put it there." I asked: "If you look away, will it fall to the floor?" She said: "No. If I look away, the chair is no longer there." I asked: "If you look away—and it turns out the chair is still there?" She ignored the question.

Here's another example. During a discussion on CD@maelstrom.stjohns.edu earlier this year, the statement was made: "If enough people believe something to be true, then what they believe is what reality *is*."

A question was then asked: "There was a time when everyone, as far as we know, believed the sun revolved around the earth. Are you saying at that time the sun did, in fact, revolve around the earth—and it was only in obedience to a change in what people believed that the earth came to revolve around the sun?"

The question was ignored.

You might think their refusals to answer constitute an admission—an admission what they are saying is totally outlandish and indefensible. Experience has shown you would be wrong. Experience has shown they go right on making the same statements, even after evidence is produced to the contrary.

You see how different these creatures are? You see how far off their thinking and behavior are from human thinking and behavior?

Nothing of what *we* call reality is real to *them*.

I repeat.

Nothing of what we call reality is *real* to them.

When a human being mentions a chair, the reference is to a chair that sits there on its own legs. It's there whether anyone sees it or not, whether anyone mentions it or not, whether anyone "declares" it to be there or not. It's there *on its own*.

A basic element in the profile of humanoids is their lack of comprehension that anything exists on its own, separate from their say-so. They don't *see* it. The only objects humanoids see are the ones they "declare"... the ones they imagine.

Now, you may be thinking that the above description of a psychopath's very particular view on reality is an aberration, but consider the following comments to *New York Times* reporter Ron Suskin in 2002 by a "senior adviser" (probably Karl Rove) to George W Bush:

"[Ordinary people] are part of 'the reality-based community'. [These are] people who believe that solutions emerge from the judicious study of discernible reality. But that's not the way the world really works anymore, we're an empire now, and when we act, we create our own reality. And while you're studying that reality—judiciously, as you will—we'll act again, creating other new realities, which you can study too, and that's how things will sort out. We're history's actors [...] and you, all of you, will be left to just study what we do." [436]

Folks, this is not some fantasy, this is "reality", as defined by the psychopath, and when psychopaths rise to positions of power as they have done around the world, they possess the means to implement (or try to implement) their "world view", one that is defined by a complete and utter lack of empathy for other human beings. As you sit there right now, you have a very good explanation of why the world is currently sitting on the brink of annihilation and all-out war. Think about that, and think about who you can try and convey this information to. All of our lives may depend upon it.

---

[436] http://www.nytimes.com/2004/10/17/magazine/17BUSH.html?ex=1265346000&%2338;en=67e5 e499d9ce0514&%2338;ei=5088

Continuing with Gunsberg's paper:

We use the phrase "my perception" to mean an appraisal, a measurement of something separate from ourselves. We don't announce it as "fact". We are open to consider other views if given facts to consider.

Humanoids use the phrase "my perception" as a buzz word. They imagine what they choose, and tell us it is their "perception"—which, in their minds, *establishes* reality. What we call "facts" do not exist for them. That's why they whine and claim they are being attacked whenever substantiation is requested.

Humanoids claim their statements are valid simply because they make them! They elaborate on this: "I honor integrity in this regard. As an egoist, I make statements which are valid to me. Validity to my 'self' comes first. I grant other people this same respect assuming they say things valid to themselves."

Among human beings, for something to be deemed valid it has to be substantiated with facts. Nothing is valid simply because someone says it.

When humanoids are asked how they determine what someone says is valid to that person, and not something made up or imagined, they ignore the question.

Note the strange use of the word "integrity". Humans define integrity as uprightness of character; probity; honesty. We refer to sticking to the facts, sticking to the truth, not selling out. Humanoids use "integrity" to mean insisting what they imagine is what's real. No measurement. No evaluation.

When the demand is made for their pronouncements to be evaluated, they claim the confronter is the one who has no integrity [...] meaning the confronter is not upholding *their* position: what *they* imagine is what's real.

On what basis do they claim this? Humanoids treat the world as if it were their own private holodeck. They "declare" things into being. Everything is a hologram. They program the holograms. They interact with them in any way they choose. They have them under total control. When they decide to cancel a hologram, it vanishes.

A hologram is a hologram is a hologram. A hologram is not supposed to have the ability to think for itself. A hologram is not supposed to have the ability to measure, evaluate, appraise, etc. Most importantly, a hologram is not supposed to be able to break out of its holographic state and critique its master.

When this does happen, they first chastise it to bring it back into line. If that doesn't work, they "vanish" it. When that fails, they run for cover by abandoning the program and calling up another one.

Experience has shown no matter what we say, no matter what we point out, no matter how much evidence is given, it has no meaning for these creatures. They have one goal: to fool us into classifying them as human so they can concentrate on murdering our human values. Without human values, the next step is murdering human beings.

In the film "The Invasion of the Body Snatchers", aliens are shown to be taking over by occupying the bodies of human beings. The aliens take over not only the physical body but also the mind, memories, abilities, etc. In every way the people seem to be the same as always, except for one thing. They mention events, but with no feeling of them or about them. **They do not feel feelings**.

We see a child struggling to get away from what appears to be its mother. The next day they walk hand-in-hand. The child has been taken over.

The lovers in the film try to stay awake so they won't be taken over. She succumbs—and "she", now a creature, tries to fool him. When she doesn't fool him, she tries to betray him.

These creatures do not *feel* alive. They do not *feel* feelings. In order to pass as humans, they know they have to give the appearance of knowing they are alive. Their only recourse is to *declare* they are alive.

The declaration does not produce the quality of *feeling* alive. They still don't *feel* feelings. The only thing they have to go on, to refer to, is their own declaration. If "declaring" is shown to be insufficient—if they are called upon to discuss feelings, give evidence of feelings, distinguish between feelings, etc., they are lost. Their inner emptiness is apparent. Their un-human status is exposed.

Here's a final example. In the course of a discussion on psych-ci@ maelstrom.stjohns.edu some time ago, a humanoid said: "You hurt my feelings". The humanoid was asked to identify the exact statements, and explain in what way these statements caused hurt to what particular feelings. Answer: (Whining) "I've said you hurt my feelings. I don't know what else to say. ... You are attacking."

Question: "In what way do you consider a request for substantiation and clarification to be an attack?"

No answer.

An Oveview

Humanoids:

1. Make pronouncements without substantiation. These pronouncements are to be accepted as defining what reality is, moment by moment.

2. Ignore requests to provide the basis for their pronouncements.

3. Sneer at the human valuing of facts, honesty, decency, fair play.

4. Applaud the use of lies, deceit, etc.

5. Whine they are being "attacked" whenever they are questioned. Give no explanation of what the "attack" is or of what is being attacked.

6. Do not *feel* feelings.

7. View the world as their private holodeck.

8. Apply themselves to keeping humans in their place—namely, insignificance.

Further Considerations

Humanoids do not understand the distinction we humans make between good and evil. When they harm us, they do not understand why we call them evil. They do not understand why we have laws against murder. Their approach is to boast, even moralize over their victims.

Since they do not understand the reason for such laws, they argue they cannot be held accountable for their actions.

Not so. While they take the position the law does not apply to them, they do know the law was enacted to apply to everyone. Furthermore, if they try to claim they didn't know there was such a law, we respond with a firmly established principle: "Ignorance of the law is no excuse."

When they use those arguments, they make it clear they will continue to operate in accordance with their structure. We may look for remorse (a human capacity).

We find none. They do not think of themselves as promulgating evil. They are simply doing what it is in their structure to do. The rattlesnake does not think of itself as evil when it injects poison. It is simply doing what it is in its structure to do.

Experience has shown humanoids continue to behave in the ways of their species—murdering human values as a prelude to murdering human beings. Nazis demonstrate this graphically.

The issue as to whether to hold them "accountable", in our human sense of the word, has to be divided into two parts. We do not hold them accountable for *being* what they are. We do hold them accountable for the damage they *do*.

When a dog gets rabies, we don't hold the dog accountable for becoming rabid. What we do, as a matter of self-protection, is put the dog down *before* it bites us, *before* it infects us.

We do not hold the rattlesnake accountable for having poison fangs. What we do, as a matter of self-protection, is kill the rattlesnake *before* it kills us.

So with the humanoid. We need to be on our guard at the first sign of a murder of human values.

Those are pretty strong words, aren't they? I think that a brief survey of the conditions of our world easily support the view that something is terribly wrong, and we need to figure out what it is, and fast. The words of the experts I am citing here, along with your own observations and experiences ought to be sufficient to indicate that this is the best explanation we have.

Now that we have a better idea of who the real enemy of humanity actually is, let us turn to what they have in plan for the society of normal people.

THE SIXTH EXTINCTION

A gentleman named Joseph George Caldwell, a former contractor for a government think-tank, Lambda Corporation, has a website where he promotes the following idea:

"What is the sustainable human population for Earth?", I propose that a long-term sustainable number is on the order of ten million, consisting of a technologically advanced population of a single nation of about five million people concentrated in one or a few centers, and a globally distributed primitive population of about five million. I arrived at this size by approaching the problem from the point of view of estimating the *minimum* number of human beings that would have a good chance of long-term survival, instead of approaching it from the (usual) point of view of attempting to estimate the *maximum* number of human beings that the planet might be able to support. The reason why I use the approach of minimizing the human population is to keep the damaging effects of human industrial activity on the biosphere to a minimum. Because mankind's industrial activity produces so much waste that cannot be metabolized by "nature," any attempt to maximize the size of the human population risks total destruction of the biosphere (such as the "sixth extinction" now in progress).

Let's stop right here and ask the question: Who said that there was such a thing as the "*Sixth Extinction*", and that it was now in progress? Is this something that is generally "known" in the circles that do this kind of research? Is this why they are doing it? What do they know that the rest of us don't? Or better, what do they think that they aren't telling us? Caldwell writes:

> The role of the technological population is "planetary management": to ensure that the size of the primitive population does not expand. The role of the primitive population is to reduce the likelihood that a localized catastrophe might wipe out the human population altogether. The reason for choosing the number five million for the primitive population size is that this is approximately the number (an estimated 2-20 million) that Earth supported for millions of years, i.e., it is proved to be a long-term sustainable number (in mathematical terminology, a "feasible" solution to the optimization problem). The reason for choosing the number five million for the technological population size is that it is my opinion that that is about the minimum practical size for a technologically advanced population capable of managing a planet the size of Earth; also, it is my opinion that the "solar energy budget" of the planet can support a population of five million primitive people and five million "industrial" people indefinitely.[437]

Now, this is a guy who has been exposed to the government "think tankery" approach to global problems, and it seems that some government ideas about massive reduction of population have impressed themselves upon his mind. But there is more. On February 22, 2004, the UK *Guardian* reported:

> Climate change over the next 20 years could result in a global catastrophe costing millions of lives in wars and natural disasters.

> A secret report, suppressed by US defence chiefs and obtained by *The Observer*, warns that major European cities will be sunk beneath rising seas as Britain is plunged into a 'Siberian' climate by 2020. Nuclear conflict, mega-droughts, famine and widespread rioting will erupt across the world.

> The document predicts that abrupt climate change could bring the planet to the edge of anarchy as countries develop a nuclear threat to defend and secure dwindling food, water and energy supplies. The threat to global stability vastly eclipses that of terrorism, say the few experts privy to its contents.

> 'Disruption and conflict will be endemic features of life,' concludes the Pentagon analysis. 'Once again, warfare would define human life.'

> The findings will prove humiliating to the Bush administration, which has repeatedly denied that climate change even exists. Experts said that they will also make unsettling reading for a President who has insisted national defence is a priority.

> *The report was commissioned by influential Pentagon defence adviser Andrew Marshall, who has held considerable sway on US military thinking over the past three decades. He was the man behind a sweeping recent review aimed at transforming the American military under Defence Secretary Donald Rumsfeld.*

> Climate change 'should be elevated beyond a scientific debate to a US national security concern', say the authors, Peter Schwartz, CIA consultant and former head of planning at Royal Dutch/Shell Group, and Doug Randall of the California-based Global Business Network.

---

[437] www.foundationwebsite.org

An imminent scenario of catastrophic climate change is 'plausible and would challenge United States national security in ways that should be considered immediately', they conclude. As early as next year widespread flooding by a rise in sea levels will create major upheaval for millions.

[...] Already, according to Randall and Schwartz, the planet is carrying a higher population than it can sustain. By 2020 'catastrophic' shortages of water and energy supply will become increasingly harder to overcome, plunging the planet into war. They warn that 8,200 years ago climatic conditions brought widespread crop failure, famine, disease and mass migration of populations that could soon be repeated.

Randall told *The Observer* that the potential ramifications of rapid climate change would create global chaos. 'This is depressing stuff,' he said. 'It is a national security threat that is unique because there is no enemy to point your guns at and we have no control over the threat.'[438] (emphasis ours)

But is that all there is? Certainly if it were strictly an issue of energy, the technology exists to solve our problems, to reduce the population in a natural way by reducing the birthrate, and so on. Surely these "think tank" types can figure out how to do it.

But they don't. They have layers and layers of lies and disinformation. Terrorists are one layer, climate change is another, peak oil is the next, and none of it is the truth.

As it happens, at the same time I was following these research threads, I kept noticing some other factors that related to a series of ideas that had interested me for many years: the possibility that the earth periodically is bombarded by cometary bodies bringing the end of civilizations and reducing humanity to a Stone Age existence.

Until recently, impacts by extraterrestrial bodies (meteorites etc.) were regarded as, perhaps, an interesting but certainly not an important phenomenon in the spectrum of geological process affecting the Earth. The fact is, this has only been the case since Lyell, Laplace and Newton put a period to such speculations. What the collected evidence shows is that, through repeated cataclysms, man has been brought low, relegated to darkness regarding his history, and at the very point when he began to study and analyze his environment objectively, religion stepped in and put a period to such ideas.

There is in fact much evidence to support the idea that, in our recent history, parts of the earth have suffered cyclical natural catastrophes and cometary impacts. Such speculations, however, are relegated to the fringe of mainstream research and generally frowned upon and ignored and, in many cases, covered up.

The question, however, is why? What, in the name of all things reasonable, would prompt anyone to wish to hide these matters if they are true? What

---

[438] Mark Townsend and Paul Harris, "*Now the Pentagon tells Bush: climate change will destroy us*: Secret report warns of rioting and nuclear war; Britain will be 'Siberian' in less than 20 years; Threat to the world is greater than terrorism", (February 22, 2004): http://observer.guardian.co.uk/international/story/0,6903,1153513,00.html

kind of sick mind would divert the attention of humanity away from what is evident all over the planet to those with open eyes? What kind of sick mind would also promote, so assiduously, ideas that mislead, misguide, and generally placate the populace?

Well, we don't have to think too long to realise that keeping such matters from the general population serves a control agenda very well. But, Heavenly days! What kind of lunatics would want to keep everything under control in that sense if they have some idea that they, themselves, might be destroyed by the very processes they are concealing? Obviously, they don't think so. Obviously, they think they have a plan. And that suggests that, obviously, they know a lot more about what's going on, what the possibilities and probabilities are, than the rest of us.

The conclusion that the astute reader will have drawn from my book, *The Secret History of the World*, is that the inner solar system experiences swarms of comets/asteroids on a fairly regular schedule. One major swarm comes at 3600 year intervals, and there are minor swarms at other intervals, and these cycles are sub-cycles of even larger swarms at hundreds of thousands of year intervals, and even million year intervals. The massive bombardment of the East Coast of the U.S. around 12,000 to 12,500 years ago resulting in the Carolina Bays is evidence of the great number, and relatively small sizes of many of these bodies, indicating that they released their energy into the air above the ground, similar to the Tunguska event. Keep in mind, of course, that *the air blast of a single small body over Tunguska resulted in the devastation of 2000 sq. km of Siberian forest.* Heck, there was another Tunguska-type event just a few years ago, also in Siberia, as reported in 2003 by *Agence France Press:*

> A giant meteorite that struck the Irkutsk region of Siberia last September (2002) had the force of a nuclear bomb of medium power and devastated a huge area of taiga, Russian scientists reported Friday.
>
> A 10-strong expedition of scientists and doctors was unable to identify and reach the place where the meteorite landed until mid-May. It was finally located in the very remote, wooded semi-mountainous region of Bodaibo, northeast of Irkutsk and Lake Baikal.[439]

It seems that there is indeed something very mysterious going on all over the planet in terms of shaping the thinking of humanity via books, movies, and cultural themes, but at this point, we understand that most of what is promulgated is lies and disinformation. Those of us who do the research realize that there is, indeed, something to the ancient "prophecies" that are included in the so-called "holy writ", but that they have nothing whatsoever to do with this god or that god or any god, for that matter. It isn't a question of being saved or not saved or who owns what piece of real estate or any of the pathetic and childish beliefs into which most of humanity are inculcated. What are handed down to us as prophecies might be better understood as

---

[439] http://www.softcom.net/webnews/wed/bj/Qrussia-meteorite.RqyI_DlP.html

warnings from our ancestors. "It has happened before; it will happen again." If we date the last of the 3600 year cycles to the time of the eruption of Thera, discussed earlier, then we see that we are possibly due for another, and soon. It is quite simply a cyclical event in the very long lifespan of the planet and when understood correctly can be prepared for and accommodated.

But somebody doesn't want that to happen. Somebody—or a group of somebodies—seems to want to use the probable upcoming cataclysmic events to their own advantage. They want to be able to choose who gets in the lifeboat and who does not.

And this leads to a question: why is it that this kind of thing is going on in this day and age of modern—civilized—humanity when we not only have centuries of philosophers behind us, but also a long period of scientific expansion?

The fact seems to be that the *quality* of humanity has changed little in the past many millennia. Most human beings are still ruled by fear, hunger and sex in states of misery and chaos. There is something mysterious going on. It seems that there is some kind of disinformation machine that has worked very hard to keep this state of affairs intact, with great success. The nonsense propagated by the new-agers as "ascension" or by fundamentalist Christians as "the return of Jesus" is evidence of that fact.

We begin then to understand that members of the "elite" on our planet—psychopaths—having very likely been appraised of the secrets of cyclic cataclysm immediately went to work to discover the ways and means for their own escape and for the destruction of most normal humans, leaving only enough to be their slaves. As Lobaczewski writes:

> The following questions thus suggest themselves: what happens if the network [...] [of] psychopaths achieves power [internationally]? This can happen, especially during the later phases of the phenomenon. Goaded by their character, such people thirst for just that even though it would conflict with their own life interest. [...] They do not understand that a catastrophe would otherwise ensue. Germs are not aware that they will be burned alive or buried deep in the ground along with the human body whose death they are causing.

> If such and many managerial positions are assumed by individuals deprived of sufficient abilities to feel and understand most other people, and who also betray *deficiencies in technical imagination and practical skills* (faculties indispensable for governing economic and political matters), this must result in an exceptionally serious crisis in all areas, both within the country in question and with regard to international relations. [...]

> Pathocracy corrodes the entire social organism, wasting its skills and power. The effects of this more ideational wing of the party and its enlivening influence upon the workings of the entire country gradually weaken. Typical pathocrats take over all the managerial functions in a totally destroyed structure of a nation. Such a state must be short-term, since no ideology can vivify it. [...]

> One of the first discoveries made by a society of normal people is that it is superior to the [psychopaths] in intelligence and practical skills, no matter what geniuses they appear to be. [...]

The world of normal people is always superior to the other one whenever con-
structive activity is needed, whether it be the reconstruction of a devastated
country, the area of technology, the organization of economic life, or scientific
and medical work. "They want to build things, but they can't get much done
without us."[440]

We can theorize that this is why they funded Princeton and other institutions of higher learning to study these things, and why they imported all the
brains on the planet to put them to work to devise a method that could be
activated at a certain point in time to *ensure their survival and the exclusion
of everyone else.* This leads us to understand why they have made so concerted an effort to keep the masses of humanity deaf, dumb and blind.

We see around us, every day, the events that tell us that the events of Nazi
Germany were a "dress rehearsal" of sorts, for events that are to transpire in
our near future. In 9/11, we had the equivalent of the Reichstag Fire and now,
once again, the ordinary Jews, and their Semitic Arab brothers and sisters of
the Middle East, are in the cross hairs. Israeli right-wing groups make much
of the "never again" slogan, yet these very same groups are using the Jewish
holocaust to silence any criticism of the actions of the Ashkenazi state of
Israel and in doing so are helping to ensure that one of the worst episodes of
human history will happen all over again, only this time, it is undoubtedly
going to be much, much worse.

In the end, what we finally realize is that anyone who suggests that anything I have said about Jews is 'anti-Semitic' may well be serving the psychopathic supremacist agenda. In fact, what has become increasingly clear is
that the Ashkenazi Zionist agenda is truly psychopathic and thus anti-
Semitic.

When the time comes and the piper must be paid, will we have learned anything from history? Will we have been *allowed* to learn anything?

---

[440] Lobaczewski, op. cit.

Conclusion

So where Are We?

It is clear to us from all available evidence that the events of 9/11 were most likely organized and directed by Israeli intelligence agencies with the initial complicity, and later the forced complicity, of their "friends" in the United States. The goal was to galvanize the American government to wage a war of aggression and conquest in the Middle East that, while also serving the short-term aims of the Bush administration, was essentially for Israel, *on Israel's terms*, and to garner the support among the American population that would make it possible. However, while some of those involved on the Israeli side believe in the conquering mission of Greater Israel, it appears that the final outcome could well be the annihilation of Israel along with its Arab neighbors. This strong possibility leads us to surmise that the real power behind 9/11, even though it may have an Israeli or Zionist face, is interested in achieving what was left undone at the end of World War Two, the killing of the non-Ashkenazi Jews and their Semitic brothers and sisters in the wider Middle East.

We have given historical and genetic evidence that the Ashkenazi Jews are of Aryan descent; they are not Semites or true Jews at all. Zionism arose among these European or Ashkenazi Jews, and the Zionists showed in their dealing with Hitler that they were quite willing to allow Hitler to cull the herd if he allowed those willing to migrate to Palestine out of Germany.

We also note that although the proclaimed goal of the establishment of Israel was to create a state where Jews would be safe, the reality is that modern-day Israel is *the most dangerous place for Jews* at the present time, despite Zionists' claims of a new and rising tide of anti-Semitism in 'gentile' nations. In fact, the repeated claims by Israeli government apologists that "a new wave of anti-Semitism is sweeping Europe", while being entirely false, is a calculated maneuver to silence any opposition to the policies of the state of Israel, policies that, due to their provocative and belligerent nature, may ultimately lead to events that decimate the Middle Eastern Jewish and Arab populations alike.

In Palestine, the long-standing conflict with Israel appears as far as ever from resolution, and indeed, a state of affairs that Israel has done all in its power to achieve. By now it should be clear to all Middle East analysts that the main impediment to peace in the Israeli-Palestinian conflict is Israel and the right-wing Zionist extremists in leading positions in Israeli politics. Time and again the Palestinians have expressed their sincere desire to end the in-human conditions under which they are forced to live by the occupying IDF forces, yet every time that a peaceful settlement seems to be within their grasp, bizarrely, Hamas or Islamic Jihad decide to fire a few, usually harm-less, 'Qasam' rockets at an illegal Israeli settlement, or unknown "Palestinian gunmen" will murder an Israeli settler, inviting the IDF to retaliate with deadly and overwhelmingly superior force.

How to explain such repeated, apparently self-defeating acts by the alleged representatives of the beleaguered Palestinian people? It has been obvious for many years now that the Palestinians cannot win an armed conflict with the massively militarily superior Israel and any further attacks against Israeli forces, population, or interests simply provide Israeli politicians with the jus-tification to increase Israeli control and oppression in the occupied territories. And Israel's 200+ nuclear bombs ensure that no other Arab nation dare inter-fere. It is equally obvious that the international community has all but washed its hands of the conflict and is resigned to allowing it to play out to its final and surely tragic denouement.

On the subject of Palestinian (or general Muslim) "suicide bombings": Imagine a scenario where a Palestinian youth is arrested by the IDF, interro-gated and released on condition that he 'carry out a job' for Israeli intelli-gence. He is told to take a package in a backpack to a man at a certain Kebab stand in Tel Aviv on a certain day. The youth dutifully does so and when the security guard asks him to open his bag the Israeli intelligence agent, watch-ing from 50 yards across the road, pushes a button...boom! Instant Palestin-ian 'suicide bombing' with eyewitnesses to testify that the youth's bag ex-ploded.

Other likely scenarios involve the pre-placing of bombs somewhere in a restaurant or on a bus. The restaurant or bus is staked out until a likely sus-pect enters and again a button is pushed. In several purported 'Palestinian suicide bombings' in the past few years, Israeli authorities were forced to officially announce that they were "exploring the possibility that the bombing was the work of Palestinian suicide bombers dressed as an ultra-orthodox Jew". Why? Because the details of the attack involved nothing but a bus full of ultra-orthodox Jews and a bomb! But there just *had* to be 'Palestinian sui-cide bomber' in there somewhere, so they figuratively dress one up as an ultra-orthodox Jew and put him at the scene. Of course, the shadowy 'Islamic Jihad', 'al-Qaeda in Palestine' or some other mysterious 'Arab terror group' usually claims responsibility, but even here we have no way of verifying the authenticity of such claims which could easily come from some asset of the Israeli homeland intelligence agency 'Shin Bet'.

In the June 2005 summit between Sharon and PA authority Chairman Ab-bas, Abbas told the Israelis that he wanted "freedom of movement in and out of Gaza, air and sea ports re-opened, key Palestinian towns handed back to their control and the release of Palestinian prisoners." Such demands are widely understood to be a precursor to the formation of a Palestinian state, an eventuality that then Prime Minister Sharon had built his political career on ensuring never occurs.

On that occasion, the Israeli government agreed to Abbas' demands on the proviso that all Palestinian attacks against Israel must first stop. What is clear is that the only reason Sharon accepted Abbas' demands is because he was confident that he could ensure that the Palestinian authority would never be able to meet the condition of a cessation of all 'terrorist' attacks.

It is clear that Israeli government oppression of Palestinians has little to do with "security concerns" and everything to do with harassing and murdering Palestinian civilians and leaders in order to prevent them from establishing themselves as an independent people with a sovereign voice on the world stage.

Central to this goal is the continued portrayal of any Palestinian resistance to Israeli occupation as "terrorism", when in reality, resistance (including armed) to an occupying power is a fundamental right laid down in article four of the third Geneva Convention.

However, according to humanitarian law, in order to lawfully use force in a conflict you must first be designated a lawful 'combatant'. To be a 'combatant', you have to belong to an 'armed resistance group' and that group must belong to a 'party' to the conflict. It is in this fact that we find one of the chief reasons why Israel will *never* willingly allow the creation of a Palestinian state.

As long as Palestine does not have official state status, any Palestinian resistance group cannot claim to be a party in the conflict and must remain a simple independent resistance group, or "terrorist" group in modern parlance.

Not only did the developed world oversee the theft of Palestinian land in order to create the state of Israel in 1948, but in continuing to refuse to lobby for an independent Palestinian state, they ensure that any Palestinian resistance to Israeli aggression is 'delegitimised' in advance.

To the shame of the international community, in April 2006 it was an Israeli court that first officially ruled that the Palestinian Authority fulfilled all of the criteria to be classified as a state and that Israel had no jurisdiction over Palestinian lands. Of course, the ruling changed nothing and any opportunity that it contained to open international debate on the Israel-Palestine conflict was immediately crushed by a mainstream media blackout on the story. As I have said so often in the past, from the ruling Israeli right-wing's point of view, open and honest discussion, dialogue and debate on the Palestine issue must be prevented at all costs, because the day that ruling Israeli politicians engage in fair negotiations with the Palestinian Authority is the day that they lose their death grip on Palestine and its people. And that is the very last thing they are willing to do.

But how then can the Israeli government be so confident that the Palestinian dream of a state of their own will remain just that—a dream?

Israel controls all entrances and exits to and from the Gaza strip and the West Bank. It is Israel therefore—or more accurately Israel's military and intelligence apparatus—that decides who and what gets in and out of the occupied Palestinian territories. Without doubt, the Israeli army could, with relative ease, accomplish the goal of a cessation of all "terrorist" attacks that successive Israeli Prime Ministers have demanded of their Palestinian counterparts, yet the hard, cold fact of the matter is that Israel's present position as the dominant force in the Middle East is *dependent* on the continued existence of a terrorist threat. That this has been true for many, many years was made clear by Israeli commentator, Yoram Bar Porath, in the Israeli News outlet, *Yediot Aahronot* of July 14, 1972:

> It is the duty of Israeli leaders to explain to public opinion, clearly and courageously, a certain number of facts that are forgotten with time. The first of these is that there is no Zionism, colonialization or Jewish State without the eviction of the Arabs and the expropriation of their lands.

In attempting to ensure that the 'terrorism' that is the life-blood of the state of Israel is never vanquished, Sharon and his predecessors have gone to great lengths to infiltrate and co-opt various Palestinian resistance organizations. Indeed, there is much evidence to support the thesis that, far from being the victim of terrorism, Israel is in fact one of the prime instigators of terrorist attacks in Israel, attacks that are conveniently set up to look like the work of Palestinians. For example, consider the following excerpt from a UPI article from June 2002:

Hamas history tied to Israel

6/18/2002

In the wake of a suicide bomb attack Tuesday on a crowded Jerusalem city bus that killed 19 people and wounded at least 70 more, the Islamic Resistance Movement, Hamas, took credit for the blast.

Israeli officials called it the deadliest attack in Jerusalem in six years.

Israeli Prime Minister Ariel Sharon immediately vowed to fight "Palestinian terror" and summoned his cabinet to decide on a military response to the organization that Sharon had once described as "the deadliest terrorist group that we have ever had to face".

Active in Gaza and the West Bank, Hamas wants to liberate all of Palestine and establish a radical Islamic state in place of Israel. It is has gained notoriety with its assassinations, car bombs and other acts of terrorism.

But Sharon left something out.

Israel and Hamas may currently be locked in deadly combat, but, according to several current and former U.S. intelligence officials, beginning in the late 1970s, Tel Aviv gave direct and indirect financial aid to Hamas over a period of years.

Israel "aided Hamas directly—the Israelis wanted to use it as a counterbalance to the PLO (Palestinian Liberation Organization)," said Tony Cordesman, Middle East analyst for the Center for Strategic Studies.

Israel's support for Hamas "was a direct attempt to divide and dilute support for a strong, secular PLO by using a competing religious alternative," said a former senior CIA official.[441]

Of course, here, we are deep into conspiracy theory territory, yet when several current and former U.S. intelligence officials openly state that Hamas was established basically as a tool of Israeli intelligence, are we talking about a conspiracy theory, or simply the much-ignored standard operating procedure (SOP) of most of the world's spy agencies? Readers should also take note of the fact that, over recent years, Hamas or some other shadowy Palestinian resistance group that no one had heard of previously, has shown a unique ability to shoot themselves in the foot and appears to have played a significant role in thwarting Palestinian aspirations to independent statehood by way of their uncanny knack for launching attacks on Israeli interests precisely at junctures where Palestinians stand to benefit the least from such an attack. Such attacks generally only serve to provide Israeli political leaders with the justification they need to repeatedly renege on their hollow promises to recognise even the most basic rights of the Palestinian people.

Of course, Israel has a willing partner in its phony terror-crime in the American government. Vast sums (billions of dollars) in non-refundable loans are funnelled every year from the pockets of U.S. taxpayers into the coffers of the Israeli treasury for the purpose of "fighting terrorism". Israel, with the implicit support of the U.S. government, has been allowed to contravene or ignore dozens of UN resolutions, the Geneva conventions and Humanitarian and International law because it claims it is "fighting terrorism". Indeed, the role of the current U.S. government in facilitating the continued persecution of the Palestinian people can be clearly seen in its promotion of the phony "war on terror" and the equally phony 9/11 attacks that precipitated it, both of which have greatly benefited the extreme right despots in Tel Aviv and Washington.

Israel then, in its present configuration, is an illegal state founded on the unlawful theft of Palestinian land and the blood of the thousands of innocent Palestinian people that refused, and continue to refuse, to bow down to the murderous racism of their Israeli taskmasters. Every Israeli Prime Minister knew and understood this. They also knew that the day that an Israeli government allows Palestine to be officially recognised as an independent state, is the day that Israel will no longer have the right to bulldoze Palestinian homes or arbitrarily execute Palestinian school children and claim that they are "fighting terrorism". On that day, Palestinian resistance to a brutal occupying power will be legitimised and the actions of successive Israeli governments and the IDF will be recognised for the war crimes that they are.

---

[441] http://www.mathaba.net/0_index.shtml?x=508046

Please note here that all of my comments above refer to the state of Israel and the Zionists that control it. I hope I have made it clear enough that these psychopathic Zionists are *the real historical enemy of the Jews*, and that the psychopaths in power around the world are the historical enemy of normal human beings. Indeed, my chief concern here is for the Jewish people, and this book is, in essence, an attempt to sound the alarm bell that Jews—and everyone—must wake up and recognise their 'leaders' for what they are and where their plans are leading us.

It appears to us that the real goal of the invasion of Iraq, whether or not it was the intention of the Bush government when it ordered the attack, was to create the chaos needed to justify the division of the country through civil war and thereby push the greater Middle East closer to all-out war. Israelis and their supporters have been calling for such a strategy for over twenty years. Indeed, all the evidence suggests that Iraq is teetering on the brink of just such a manufactured 'civil war'.

In September 2005, several media outlets reported that two members of the British covert military group, the SAS, were arrested by Iraqi police and briefly imprisoned before being "rescued" by British troops who used a tank to break into the Iraqi prison where they were being held. The men were detained after they failed to stop at an Iraqi police checkpoint in the southern Iraqi town city of Basra and they shot and killed one policeman and wounded a second when confronted.[442]

The men were found to be wearing full traditional Arab dress. The car they were travelling in was loaded with weapons including allegedly, assault rifles, a light machine gun, an anti-tank weapon, radio gear and a medical kit ('standard' SAS issue according to the BBC). According to at least two reports, the car was also "booby-trapped" with a large quantity of explosives in the trunk. In essence this was to be a "suicide bombing".

The British government quickly spun the story claiming that the men had been handed over to Iraqi "insurgents" thereby necessitating their rescue. This spin was duly parroted by the mainstream press.

What was never addressed was exactly what these men were doing dressed as Iraqis driving what was essentially a car bomb. Not one mainstream media outlet discussed the most obvious explanation: that these were British "agents provocateur" sent into the relatively peaceful town of Basra to carry out a fake Iraqi "insurgent car bombing" in order to demonise and demoralise the real Iraqi resistance, to provide justification for the continued presence of coalition troops in Iraq to fight phantom 'terrorists' and to create the evidence that 'civil war' was brewing in Iraq.

In any modern pluralist society there are underlying religious, ethnic, political or social differences between the members of that society. Under normal circumstances, these differences would never lead to armed conflict between distinct groups unless a significant amount of effort is made by an

---

[442] http://www.signs-of-the-times.org/signs/signs20050920.htm

external force to highlight and inflame those differences and turn them into a plausible reason for conflict. It should be noted that major Western states with a history of invading foreign sovereign nations—Britain, America and Israel for three examples—have gained a lot of experience in what is known as 'counter-insurgency' tactics. Counter-insurgency strategy is the strategy used to neutralise the expected grass roots resistance that invariably springs forth in response to an invading army.

In Northern Ireland, for example, British army intelligence and MI5 dedicated significant resources to what was called the "Ulsterisation" of the conflict. The goal was to subvert the core reason for the conflict—the occupation of a sovereign nation by an aggressor state—and make it *appear* that the conflict was in fact the result of long-standing ethnic or religious divisions within the Ulster community, hence "Ulsterisation".

In the case of Northern Ireland, this was relatively easy given that there was indeed already a very clear religious divide between the Protestant and Catholic communities. But the fact remained that the IRA was not fighting a religious war against the Protestant community, but a war against the British government, its military and the biased state institutions that it had set up in the gerrymandered and then occupied 'statelet' of Northern Ireland. A major aspect of these biased institutions was the Northern Ireland police force, the Royal Ulster Constabulary ('RUC') that was comprised entirely of members of the Protestant community to the exclusion and detriment of Catholics.

The standard operating procedure of British civilian and military intelligence in Northern Ireland during 'the troubles' then was to provoke these divisions in Northern Irish society in order to turn the IRA's war against an occupying foreign power into a 'sectarian' conflict and, in doing so, diminish criticism of the British government for creating the conflict and afford it the opportunity to present itself as a peacekeeping force in an 'sectarian war' scenario. The ultimate aim was to deny the grass roots insurgency—the IRA—any chance to present their resistance to British occupation as a fundamental right as defined by the Geneva Convention, and therefore a just resistance.

Of course, the details of just how such a sectarian conflict was created are far from honourable and included the targeted assassination of members of the Protestant community and the detonation of bombs by British intelligence operatives, which were understood as the work of the IRA and 'evidence' that the conflict was internal and 'sectarian' in nature. Such acts would draw in Protestant paramilitaries who would respond by killing members of the Catholic community and thereby further mudding the real cause of the conflict and drawing the fire of the IRA away from their stated 'enemy'—the British military and members of the Protestant police force.

In Iraq, we see the very same counter-insurgency strategy being used against the legitimate Iraqi resistance, albeit on a much larger scale. Few readers will be unaware of the thousands of murders of Iraqi civilians and the many shrine bombings and alleged 'suicide bombings' that have occurred in Iraq more or less since the beginning of the U.S. invasion of that country, but which reached new heights in the 2nd and 3rd years of the occupation. As mentioned, there exists clear evidence that the vast majority of these attacks are actually the work of U.S. and Israeli-funded and directed 'death squads' working out of the Iraqi interior ministry as reported in the mainstream press.[443] However, the mainstream press attempted to present these death squads as evidence of "terrorist" infiltration of the Iraqi government. The plain fact, however, is that the Iraqi interior ministry is 100% controlled by the CIA (as is the Iraqi government), and if there are death squads working out of the Iraqi Interior Ministry, then they are working for the CIA and the American government.[444] As might be expected of such psychopaths, the Bush government, via mainstream media reports, has also utilised these mass murders to spread the lie that the entirely fictitious 'Islamic terror group' 'al-Qaeda in Iraq', is alive and well and trying to spread their extremist doctrine around the world. At the same time, we are told that Iraq is "on the brink of civil war". Missing from all such reports, however, is any explanation of why Iraqi Shia and Sunni groups, who have lived together and intermarried in relative peace and harmony for centuries, would suddenly, in response to a U.S. military invasion of their country, decide to attack and kill each other.

The simple fact is that they are not attacking and killing each other, and if a real civil war breaks out, it will be the result of a deliberate and protracted campaign by British, American and Israeli covert agencies to destroy a formerly cohesive Iraqi society. The ultimate goal appears to be to create the situation where the international community calls for the physical break up of Iraq along religious lines into three separate and easily manageable state-lets—the Kurds in the north, the Sunnis in the center and the Shia in the south. Such a division of Iraq has been the goal of Israel for many years in order to render Iraq politically impotent, ensure Israel's continued hegemony in the Middle East and thereby facilitate the Zionists final solution for all Semitic peoples of the Middle East, Jews and their Arab brothers alike.

With the planned U.S. and Israeli attack on Iran or Syria, the Middle East tinderbox is set to be fully ignited, creating the necessary conditions wherein the Jews and Arab, genetic brothers, can be annihilated. This, at least at the highest level of planning, appears to be the ultimate goal of the political madness currently unfolding on our planet. The deeper question of "why" is further discussed in *The Secret History of the World*.[445]

The political agendas being played out on the world stage are, however, but one part of what appears to be a very ominous future for humanity as a whole. We need only reference the alarming vigour and general strangeness that we see in the world's weather and geological conditions over the first

---

[443] http://www.washingtonpost.com/wp-dyn/content/article/2006/05/13/AR2006051300843.html
[444] http://www.brusselstribunal.org/DiyalaFuller.htm
[445] http://www.qfgpublishing.com

years of the 21st century. Hurricanes, earthquakes, and volcanoes are all rearing their heads in unpredictable ways, increasing in number, frequency and violence.

One must remember when looking at the current situation that there are many players with different, overlapping, and, sometimes, conflicting agendas. The hierarchy of power is a pyramid. Only those at the top have a complete understanding of the real plans. Those below are given only as much information as they need to do their jobs. For some, it is the excuse that "we" are running out of oil (all evidence would suggest that this is not the case). For others, it is the necessity for Israel to carve out a permanent place for itself from the shores of the Mediterranean to the banks of the Tigris in modern-day Iraq to act as a front line against "militant Islam", which by all accounts, of course, is the creation of the intelligence agencies of the U.S., Britain and Israel. For others, it is support for Israel to bring on Armageddon and the Second Coming of their Lord. For others it is knowledge of the coming cataclysmic events and a promise of safety if they cooperate. The American people are told that they need the oil to run their SUVs, while those higher up may believe they need the oil to get through the oncoming weather and geological disasters. Both are in support of doing whatever is necessary to secure oil supplies, but their justifications are different. Those wanting oil for the cataclysm believe that many of those who support the war to keep their SUVs on the road will be killed, and the others won't have any roads left on which to drive. While psychopaths are able to cooperate, that doesn't mean that different groups don't have their own interests.

Indeed, it seems that, at the highest level of the pyramid, the prime motivating factor is to conceal certain knowledge from humanity—that our planet goes through cyclical catastrophes and that our modern Western society has been created and is being led by our intra-species predator, the psychopath.

The conflicting agendas and goals easily add to the confusion, if one is not aware of their existence. The war in Iraq can be explained away by the need for oil, and Dick Cheney and his oil industry cronies are then given the blame. Certainly, they carry some of the blame, but when one recognizes the other agendas at play, one sees that there are other players who also have an important, and, sometimes, preponderant role.

Many analysts and commentators recognize the pyramid of power, but they mistake it for what they excitedly term the 'One World Government' that will be imposed upon the planet, particularly, the free, American people, through the auspices of the UN or the Bilderbergers, or the Council on Foreign Relations, or the Vatican, or the bankers of the City of London. However, when one understands the true nature of our reality, it is clear to see that this one world government exists already. It is here. There is nothing left to impose; there are only the windows to be shut, the shutters pulled, and the doors permanently locked. We see this happening with greater restrictions on travel, the growing imposition of biometric identity cards and chips, and with the increased policing and monitoring of the Internet, including the use of search engines such as Google and services such as PayPal to manipulate what can and can't be found or bought and sold. What we see are burgeoning police states in many countries that still claim to be the last line in the defence of "freedom and democracy". It doesn't get any more devious than that.

The United States of America, far from being the beacon of freedom and liberty in the world today, is the center of a cancer that seeks to engulf us all. The myth of the free, American people dies hard. The shocks necessary to awaken Americans to their true situation will be proportional to the depth of their illusion—and the illusion is very deep indeed. The facts of the self-enslavement of the American people to the mythology of the 'land of the free and home of the brave', the ideological cover for the work of the pathocrats, are there for all to see. It is indeed a dastardly maneuver: to exploit honourable, human values such as freedom, equality, justice and prosperity in order to con millions of people into supporting their diametrical opposites—slavery, greed, injustice, poverty.

As we have demonstrated, the conspiracy within which we are all experimental subjects has been unable to completely cover its tracks. Bits and pieces of the truth *do* come to the surface, only to quickly disappear beneath the flotsam of disinformation. But for the observant spectator, the signs are there.

Daily, we notice that the psychopathic Powers That Be are circling the planet, closing off alternatives, and battening down the hatches for their own survival while they consign the majority of humanity to probable death and destruction. Georges Gurdjieff commented:

> There are periods in the life of humanity, which generally coincide with the beginning or the fall of cultures and civilizations, when the masses irretrievably lose their reason and begin to destroy everything that has been created by centuries and millenniums of culture. Such periods of mass madness, often coinciding with geological cataclysms, climatic changes, and similar phenomena of a planetary character, release a very great quantity of the matter of knowledge. *This, in turn, necessitates the work of collecting this matter of knowledge which would otherwise be lost.* Thus the work of collecting scattered matter of knowledge frequently coincides with the beginning of the destruction and fall of cultures and civilizations.[446]

It seems that Gurdjieff knew only too well the effect that global upheaval exerts on the illusion-seeking majority of humanity. When confronted with the ever widening gap between the reality being presented to them and the facts before their eyes, and at some point unable to reconcile the two, those that attempt to cling to the lie as truth are driven mad.

Yet Gurdjieff also understood the *opportunity* that such an outpouring of fear and madness presents for those that seek the truth to finally see and know it. We cannot ignore the fact that our own civilization at present ap-

---

[446] As quoted by P. D. Ouspensky, *In Search of the Miraculous* (Harcourt, 2001), 38.

pears to be on the edge of a precipice. In a very natural way this may act as a "wake up call" to those that have an inner desire to seek and know the truth.

Gurdjieff continued:

> This aspect of the question is clear. The crowd neither wants nor seeks knowledge, and the leaders of the crowd, in their own interests, try to strengthen its fear and dislike of everything new and unknown. The slavery in which mankind lives is based upon this fear. It is even difficult to imagine all the horror of this slavery. We do not understand what people are losing. But in order to understand the cause of this slavery it is enough to see how people live, what constitutes the aim of their existence, the object of their desires, passions, and aspirations, of what they think, of what they talk, what they serve and what they worship. Consider what the cultured humanity of our time spends money on; even leaving the war out, what commands the highest price; where the biggest crowds are. If we think for a moment about these questions it becomes clear that humanity, as it is now, with the interests it lives by, cannot expect to have anything different from what it has.

And we see the truth of this in the current state of our planet. Yet truth was rarely, if ever, the domain of the people. Since the dawn of modern civilisation, the truth has been withheld and used to control rather than liberate. At present, it appears that we are living at the tail end of this grand millennia-long deception. As our world stands on the brink of all-out war and cataclysmic destruction, the masses continue to perform the most complex of mental gymnastics to enable the continuance of their illusions about themselves, their world and the psychopaths that rule over us. The masses will believe anything, as long as it is not the reality that their very existence hangs in the balance. Yet none can claim that justice is not being served, for what can be more equitable than to give that which is asked for?

As a result of their insatiable appetite for illusion, it is very likely that the sleeping masses, so enamoured of illusion, will receive exactly what they have asked for—they will be the victims of the greatest deception of all at the hands of those in whom, against all logic and reason, they have placed their trust.

Our published books, and the considerable body of information on our web sites, are a result of the collecting of the knowledge described by Gurdjieff and its presentation for the benefit of those that understand its application. While we attempt to facilitate an understanding of the application of this knowledge, we can only go so far. Definite and real steps must be taken by the earnest Truth Seeker in order to make clear that they understand that which they are choosing. If we choose to commit to the search for knowledge, it must be by *doing* something, not by showing a vicarious interest from the sidelines and expecting that knowledge will simply fall into our laps.

As Gurdjieff said:

> But the acquisition or transmission of true knowledge demands great labor and great effort both of him who receives and of him who gives. And those who possess this knowledge are doing everything they can to transmit and communi-

cate it to the greatest possible number of people, to facilitate people's approach to it and enable them to prepare themselves to receive the truth.

He who wants knowledge must himself make the initial efforts to find the source of knowledge and to approach it, taking advantage of the help and indications which are given to all, but which people, as a rule, do not want to see or recognize.

Knowledge cannot come to people without effort on their own part. And yet there are theories which affirm that knowledge can come to people without any effort on their part, that they can acquire it even in sleep. The very existence of such theories constitutes an additional explanation of why knowledge cannot come to people.

Our goal is to be useful to creation, to create, to *align ourselves with that which is real*, to reject lies and deceit at every turn, both in the world "out there" and within our own beings.

People that consciously believe in and accept lies as truth are making a statement to life, to the *real objective universe*, that they do not desire to exist in such a universe where truth is valued over lies. While very often we do not get what we desire in life, we can be sure that, in the end, we will get back that which we give to life. *For those people that align themselves with illusion, with that which is not real, they will become just that—"a dream in the past"*. Those who pay strict attention to objective reality right and left, become the reality of the 'future'.

The fact is that the conditions of the present day are ideally suited to the acquisition of real knowledge. But why, you might ask, do we consider discovering the closest approximation of the truth of our past to be a worthy occupation?

It's quite simple: in a universe where the observer is as important as the observed, the closer they are in *alignment*, the more order is possible from the side of the universe which—being unimpeded by the barriers of lies—allows creation to manifest unlimited possibilities. When there is great disparity between the observer and the observed, it naturally creates disorder, chaos and destruction due to this conflict. This is why all the efforts of the New Age to have "harmonic convergence" that focus on "peace and brotherhood"—while the true foundation of our civilization is based on lies and greed—has only served to add to the chaos and disorder. It is also the reason why those who turns their backs on the horrors of the world, hoping that if they only "focus on the positive", they will be spared, will be one day confronted with a very rude awakening.

The universe—what is being observed—*is as it is* and operates based on certain principles that are little known despite millennia of claims by this or that group to "know the secrets". When you observe the universe, you are, in a certain sense, observing "God". When you attempt to impose your subjective ideas, notions, beliefs, on this vast primal consciousness, you are acting "in opposition" to *what is*, to "God". You are therefore, not "in alignment" with the observed, and contribute to the chaos.

It is only in purity, with the mind of the curious and creative child that does not impose beliefs or subjective opinions on the cosmos, that objectivity can be achieved.

From our position of millennia of cultural and religious brainwashing, the only possibility we have of achieving the mind of the child that observes and does not judge is to strip away as many lies and illusions as possible about our reality as a whole. And the only effect we can have on the future is to "allow it to manifest" *according to our present "observational state"*. That is: objectivity does not limit creation while subjectivity attempts to limit, constrain and inhibit that which is limitless. The previously-mentioned senior advisor to George Bush who claimed "we create the reality" is a perfect example of an attempt to constrain and inhibit a limitless reality. It will never work!

For each of us, our observational state determines the shape of our future, individually and collectively. If it is in alignment with objective reality—*what is*—then "order" results. If our "observer status" consists in a "belief" that has nothing to do with *what is*, "chaos" results because of the conflict between *what is* and what is "believed" that is not true. It then follows that if our present observational state is based on ideas that have nothing to do with what may have objectively occurred in the past, then our "now" is delusion, and that creates a future of "chaos".

The only thing we have to practice this observation on is the past and the present. We cannot "observe the future" that has not yet manifested. What's more, we cannot observe the 'now' objectively if our observations are based on lies of the past. We must confront reality, which includes the clear evidence for degenerative psychopathic control of the political and financial powerhouses on the planet.

As mentioned, these psychopaths in power believe themselves to be the "creators of reality", but they are not gods; objective reality does not bend to their will. As they push for ever greater control over their subjective and brutal faux "reality", they bring ever closer the day when the True objective reality of the universe will be forced to reassert itself in order to bring back balance. On that day, each of us will want to be in a position where we have, to the greatest extent possible, aligned ourselves with the Truth of our world.

Such an alignment is achieved by genuine, honest and open Seeking of the Truth, whatever it turns out to be.

Finally, let us conclude with some additional words from Lobaczewski. You see, we are quite sure that a number of "experts" will crawl out of the woodwork to declare the facts collected together in this book to be "outrageous lies" or "perversion of science" or sheer madness. We expect that. After all, Lobaczewski observed just that sort of thing and wrote about it. Here is what he said in part:

> When I came to the West, I met people with leftist attitudes who unquestion-
> ingly believed that communist countries existed in more or less the form ex-

pounded by American political doctrines. These persons were almost certain that psychology and psychiatry must enjoy freedom in those countries referred to as communist, and that matters were similar to what was mentioned above. When I contradicted them, they refused to believe me and kept asking why, "Why isn't it like that?"

What can politics have to do with psychiatry?

My attempts to explain what that other reality looks like met with the difficulties we are already familiar with, although some people had previously heard about the abuse of psychiatry. However, such "whys" kept cropping up in conversation, and remained unanswered.

The situation in these scientific areas, of social and curative activities, and of the people occupied in these matters, can only be comprehended once we have perceived the true nature of pathocracy in the light of the ponerological approach. Let us thus imagine something which is only possible in theory, namely, that a country under pathocratic rule is inadvertently allowed to freely develop these sciences, enabling a normal influx of scientific literature and contacts with scientists in other countries. Psychology, psychopathology, and psychiatry would flourish abundantly and produce outstanding representatives. What would it result in?

This accumulation of proper knowledge would, within a short time, enable undertaking investigations whose meaning we already understand. Missing elements and insufficiently investigated questions would be complemented and deepened by means of the appropriate detailed research. The diagnosis of the state of affairs would then be elaborated within the first dozen or so years of the formation of pathocracy, especially if the latter is imposed. The basis of the deductive rationale would be significantly wider than anything the author can present here, and would be illustrated by means of a rich body of analytical and statistical material.

Once transmitted to world opinion, such a diagnosis would quickly become incorporated into it, forcing naive political and propaganda doctrines out of societal consciousness. It would reach nations who are the objects of the pathocratic empire's expansionist intentions. This would render the usefulness of any ideology as a pathocratic Trojan horse doubtful at best. In spite of differences among them, countries with normal human systems would be united by characteristic solidarity in the defense of an already understood danger, similar to the solidarity linking normal people living under pathocratic rule. This consciousness, popularized in the countries affected by this phenomenon, would simultaneously reinforce psychological resistance on the part of normal human societies and furnish them with new measures of self-defense.

Can any pathocratic empire risk permitting such a possibility?

In times when the above-mentioned disciplines are developing swiftly in many countries, the problem of preventing such a psychiatric threat becomes a matter of "to be or not to be" for pathocracy. Any possibility of such a situation's emerging must thus be staved off prophylactically and skillfully, both within and without the empire. At the same time, the empire is able to find effective preventive measures thanks to its consciousness of being different as well as that specific psychological knowledge of psychopaths with which we are already familiar, partially reinforced by academic knowledge.

Both inside and outside the boundaries of countries affected by the above-mentioned phenomenon, a purposeful and conscious system of control, terror, and diversion is thus set to work. Any scientific papers publishing under such governments or imported from abroad must be monitored to ascertain that they do not contain data which could be harmful to the pathocracy. Specialists with superior talent become the objects of blackmail and malicious control. This of course causes the results to become inferior with reference to these areas of science. The entire operation must of course be managed in such a way as to avoid attracting the attention of public opinion in countries with normal human structures. The effects of such a "bad break" could be too far-reaching.

This explains why people caught doing investigative work in this area are destroyed without a sound, and suspicious persons are forced abroad to become the objects of appropriately organized harassment campaigns there.

Battles are thus being fought on secret fronts which may be reminiscent of the Second World War. The soldiers and leaders fighting in various theaters were not aware that their fate depended on the outcome of that other war, waged by scientists and other soldiers, whose goal was preventing the Germans from producing the atom bomb. The Allies won this battle, and the United States became the first to possess this lethal weapon. For the present, however, the West keeps losing scientific and political battles on this new secret front. Lone fighters are looked upon as odd, denied assistance, or forced to work hard for their bread. Meanwhile, the ideological Trojan horse keeps invading new countries.

An examination of the methodology of such battles, both on the internal and the external fronts, points to that specific pathocratic self-knowledge so difficult to comprehend in the light of the natural language of concepts. In order to be able to control people and those relatively non-popularized areas of science, one must know or be able to sense what is going on and which fragments of psychopathology are most dangerous. The examiner of this methodology thus also becomes aware of the boundaries and imperfections of this self-knowledge and practice, i.e. the other side's weaknesses, errors, and gaffes, and may manage to take advantage of them.

In nations with pathocratic systems, supervision over scientific and cultural organizations is assigned to a special department of especially trusted people, a "Nameless Office" composed almost entirely of relatively intelligent persons who betray characteristic psychopathic traits. These people must be capable of completing their academic studies, albeit sometimes by forcing examiners to issue generous evaluations. Their talents are usually inferior to those of average students, especially regarding psychological science. In spite of that, they are rewarded for their services by obtaining academic degrees and positions and are allowed to represent their country's scientific community abroad. As especially trusted individuals, they are allowed to not participate in local meetings of the party, or to even avoid joining it entirely. In case of need, they might then pass for non-party. In spite of that, these scientific and cultural superintendents are well known to the society of normal people, who learn the art of differentiation rather quickly. They are not always properly distinguished from agents of the political police; although they consider themselves in a better class than the latter, they must nevertheless cooperate with them.

We often meet with such people abroad, where various foundations and institutes give them scientific grants with the conviction that they are thereby assisting the development of proper knowledge. These benefactors do not realize that they are rendering a disservice to such science and to real scientists by allowing the supervisors to attain a certain semi-authentic authority, and by allowing them to become more familiar with whatever they shall later deem to be dangerous.

After all, those people shall later have the power to permit someone to take a doctorate, embark upon a scientific career, achieve academic tenure, and become promoted. Very mediocre scientists themselves, they attempt to knock down more talented persons, governed both by self-interest and that typical jealousy which characterizes a pathocrat's attitude toward normal people. They will be the ones monitoring scientific papers for their "proper ideology" and attempting to ensure that a good specialist will be denied the scientific literature he needs.

Controls are exceptionally malicious and treacherous in the above-mentioned psychological sciences in particular, for reasons now understandable to us.

Written and unwritten lists are compiled for subjects that may not be taught, and corresponding directives are issued to appropriately distort other subjects. This list is so vast in the area of psychology that nothing remains of this science except a skeleton picked bare of anything that might be subtle or penetrating.

A psychiatrist's required curriculum contains neither the minimal knowledge from the areas of general, developmental, and clinical psychology, nor the basic skills in psychotherapy. Thanks to such a state of affairs, the most mediocre or privileged of physicians become a psychiatrist after a course of study lasting only weeks. This opens the door to psychiatric careers to individuals who are by nature inclined to serving such an authority, and it has fateful repercussions upon the level of the treatment. It later permits psychiatry to be abused for purposes for which it should never be used.

Since they are undereducated, these psychologists then prove helpless in the face of many human problems, especially in cases where detailed knowledge is needed. Such knowledge must then be acquired on one's own, a feat not everyone is able to manage.

Such behavior carries in its wake a good deal of damage and human injustice in areas of life which have nothing whatsoever to do with politics. Unfortunately, however, such behavior is necessary from the pathocrat's point of view in order to prevent these dangerous sciences from jeopardizing the existence of a system they consider the best of all possible worlds. [...]

This makes it possible to realize that this may be one of the roads via which we can reach the crux of the matter or the nature of this macrosocial phenomenon. The prohibitions engulf depth psychology, the analysis of the human instinctive substratum, together with analysis of man's dreams. [...]

We return once more to this system's peculiar psychological "genius" and its self-knowledge. One might admire how the above mentioned definition of psychopathy effectively blocks the ability to comprehend phenomena covered therein. We may investigate the relationships between these prohibitions and the essence of the macrosocial phenomenon they in fact mirror. We may also observe the limits of these skills and the errors committed by those who execute this strategy. [...]

In that other reality, the battlefront crosses every study of psychology and psychiatry, every psychiatric hospital, every mental health consultation center, and the personality of everyone working in these areas. What takes place there: hidden thrust-and-parry duels, a smuggling through of true scientific information and accomplishments, and harassment. Some people become morally derailed under these conditions, whereas others create a solid foundation for their convictions and are prepared to undertake difficulty and risk in order to obtain honest knowledge so as to serve the sick and needy. The initial motivation of this latter group is thus not political in character, since it derives from their good will and professional decency. Their consciousness of the political causes of the limitations and the political meaning of this battle is raised later, in conjunction with experience and professional maturity, especially if their experience and skills must be used in order to save persecuted people.

In the meantime, however, the necessary scientific data and papers must be obtained somehow, taking difficulties and other people's lack of understanding into account. Students and beginning specialists not yet aware of what was removed from the educational curricula attempt to gain access to the scientific data stolen from them. Science starts to be degraded at a worrisome rate once such awareness is missing.

We need to understand the nature of the macrosocial phenomenon as well as that basic relationship and controversy between the pathological system and those areas of science which describe psychological and psychopathological phenomena. Otherwise, we cannot become fully conscious of the reasons for such a government's published behavior. [...]

On the other hand, any system in which the abuse of psychiatry for allegedly political reasons has become a common phenomenon should be examined in the light of similar psychological criteria extrapolated onto the macro-social scale. Any person rebelling internally against a governmental system, which shall always strike him as foreign and difficult to understand, and who is unable to hide this well enough, shall thus easily be designated by the representatives of said government as "mentally abnormal", someone who should submit to psychiatric treatment. A scientifically and morally degenerate psychiatrist becomes a tool easily used for this purpose. Thus is born the sole method of terror and human torture unfamiliar even to the secret police of Czar Alexander II.

The abuse of psychiatry for purposes we already know thus derives from the very nature of pathocracy as a macrosocial psychopathological phenomenon. After all, that very area of knowledge and treatment must first be degraded to prevent it from jeopardizing the system itself by pronouncing a [...] diagnosis, and must then be used as an expedient tool in the hands of the authorities. In every country, however, one meets with people who notice this and act astutely against it.

The pathocracy feels increasingly threatened by this area whenever the medical and psychological sciences make constant progress. After all, not only can these sciences knock the weapon of psychological conquest right out of its hands; they can even strike at its very nature, and from inside the empire, at that. A specific perception of these matters therefore bids the pathocracy to be "ideationally alert" in this area. This also explains why anyone who is both too knowledgeable in this area and too far outside the immediate reach of such authorities should be accused of anything that can be trumped up, including psychological abnormality.

We began this book by pulling on the threads of the attacks of 9/11. The facts on the ground led us to the conlusion that the perpetrators came from Israel and within the United States government, military, and intelligence services. From there we entered the labyrinthine pseudohistory of the Jewish people, a story concoted long ago and given new life by a Catholic Church in need of validation. We have seen how the Ashkenazi Jews are not in fact descendents of the original Jews at all, being descended instead from the Khazars. We have looked at Ashkenazi genetics and seen suggestive evidence of links between long inbreeding within that community and diseases that may be related to the genetic underpinnings of psychopathy. We then looked at the question of political ponerology and the complex system of pathocratic rule based upon the self-awareness of various deviants and the war for survial in a world of normal people. This study has given us a scientific basis on which to reinterpret what are disargaingly known as "conspiracy theories", showing that he who laughs may well be sealing his fate. We have gone over some of the literature on psychopathy and have seen that this almost human is humanity's invisible enemy, invisible because he is found in every culture, speaking every language, serving every god, and wearing every color of skin. Finally, we have sketched out the final goal of the pathocrats, the elimination of normal society as a whole as the only means of ensuring their own survial.

Indeed, the experts will denounce our findings as lies. It is up to each reader to do the work to decide for him or herself whether what we say is an accurate reading of our reality or not. Your life, and the lives of your children, may well depend upon your answer.

APPENDIX

A Window On Their World

The following contains some excerpts adapted from an anonymous essay posted on the internet back in 2003. It is shocking in its frankness, so brace yourself to read the Ultimate Truth.

To understand the world of the psychopath, imagine an orphan looking through a window at a happy family during the holidays. An orphan, normal instincts in place, would understand exactly what he/she saw and was missing. A psychopath on the other hand, would be truly puzzled. They'd recognize what others say is a desirable state, everyone laughing and happy. But when they ask, "What is this thing called love", they really mean it. They can't comprehend the emotional attachment between individuals.

This awareness of being looked down upon for being different is one point where they turn from a "just don't care" amorality (which can still be devastating to those who try to be close to them) to an active evil and desire to cause misery. The realization represented here by the hypothetical window scene can cause them to say, "What is this warmth and happiness when I, a god, have only a heart so cold?" This makes them feel inferior and thus angry. To get back at the world, some then dedicate their lives to destroying happiness, whenever, wherever possible. Many others become "home wreckers", either as seducers or whispering Iagos.

Many people ask me what life satisfactions do psychopaths have; how do they emotionally overcome the disappointments of life?

What disappointments? If there are no emotional attachments what are the disappointments?

Well then, what are the rewards?

Sadly, it's all chemical. I believe nature soaks their brains in feel good, "ain't I grand", chemicals. Somewhere in their psyches, I think they unconsciously know this. To combat this realization (and the deep paranoia that accompanies it, *this paranoia is actually one of the ways to recognize them)* they are driven on a lifelong quest to prove that their felt superiority is real.

Thus they con and manipulate again and again without thought of consequences.

For example, an employee might seduce both the boss's wife and girlfriend despite the almost certainty of being fired (at the least). It is that important to him to prove his superiority. Many just *cannot stop* conning.

At the very heart of their psyche, where you and I have a soul, they have only a pit of despair; despair at having been cheated of the human experience. But this is a despair they cannot acknowledge. I have no doubt that the Soulless Ones, Rumsferatu and Cheney, Prince of Darkness, would, and very well might, kill millions to protect themselves from this awareness. It is very important that one not make the vast neediness of a psychopath one's own. The world is full of women who have dedicated their lives to fulfilling the needs of a psychopathic spouse. They would have more success filling the Grand Canyon with a teaspoon—at least the results could be measured by science.

Psychopaths do not experience their neediness *as neediness*, rather they see it as a great tool for the manipulation of others, particularly women.

Also, one must be careful not to expect reciprocity. Ask Moises Ghiroldi, a Panamanian general. Well actually you can't. In return for his sparing the psychopath Noriega's life in an abortive coup, Noriega turned around and killed him.

To a psychopath, the expectation of reciprocity is the sign of a fool, of a sucker. It should be noted, that Noriega (H.W.'s once good friend) was a graduate of the army's School of the Americas, also known as S.O.A. or, as I call it and as it really is, S.O.A.P., School of American Psychopaths. I am very serious. S.O.A.'s mission is the discovery, training and installing in leadership positions of mutant psychopaths throughout Central and South America. The hell on earth that many of these countries have become is a gift from the United States' CIA and a window on what the CIA could bring to our country and the rest of the world. Concerning Ghiroldi, it should also be noted that the General in charge of the Southern Command just sat on his hands during the coup, saying he thought it might have been a setup.

A DIFFERENT PSYCHOLOGY

Their psychology is not like ours. A psychopath can prostitute his own wife, considering it the equivalent of found money. A mother can prostitute her children for drug money without second thought. Or a psychopath mother can hold onto her marriage by pushing a daughter towards the incestuous embrace of a psychopathic or otherwise corrupt father.

Psychopaths see nothing wrong whatsoever with incest or child molesting. Indeed, the objection to it is utterly beyond their understanding. Dyncorp's mutants actually traded in eleven and twelve year old sex slaves after the Yugoslavian conflict (don't take my word for it, look it up). Dyncorp is a CIA contract company, like Air America was during the Vietnam War. I believe these companies should simply be considered as part of the CIA, not as separate at all. They're set up to keep the crime (and the money) within the family. They also enable the CIA to get around U.S. laws of what the CIA is allowed to do

The degeneracy of Dyncorp employees is simply the degeneracy of psychopathy.

If people see psychopaths in their true light, I have no doubt they will turn against them. How many people sided with the sister-desiring mutant psychopath emperor in *Gladiator*? Not many, I'm sure. (Incidentally, such films remind us that illegal pretenders to the throne, murdering usurpers and powers behind the throne are nothing new.)

Let's not forget Sante Kimes, grifter and serial murderer. She wedded her own son to her criminal schemes by bedding him.

Now there is no denying that the perverse and the unusual carry a certain fascination. Does that mean that Jerry Springer has proven that we are all like him? I don't think so.

EMPIRE OF PSYCHOPATHS

The degeneracy of psychopathy is at the very core of the CIA and other intelligence agencies that support the shadow government that has—since 9/11 and by 9/11—come out into the open. Any words of patriotism, anti-communism, virtue, or piety are just that, words; doubletalk; words used as tools to scam the taxpaying, voting citizens of America. The current U.S. administration is simply a vast organized criminal enterprise that has co-opted the U.S. government and is now attempting to create a worldwide Empire of psychopaths.

The psychopaths have been joined in this attempt by non-psychopath moral degenerates [Characteropaths]. The 'normie' children of psychopaths often end up either corrupt, e.g., Michael Powell, F.C.C. chairman and son of Colin Powell, or demoralized and disturbed, e.g., the daughter of B.F. Skinner, behaviorist and psychopath totalitarian theorist, who committed suicide (amazingly he had used her for psychological experiments from infancy).

DEUTERONOMY 21:18-21

Deuteronomy 21:18-21 instructs the ancient Israelis to bring stubborn and rebellious children incapable of obeying wisdom to the elders to be stoned to death. Likewise certain of our early colonies asked parents of teenagers unamenable to the Word of God (i.e., incapable of respecting and acting on the concepts of right and wrong) to put them to death publicly in the town square.

So-called primitive people often describe individuals who shirk their responsibility to hunt, yet excel at freeloading and who lack respect for the institution of marriage. Not surprisingly, such individuals often die early as a result of a hunting "accident", a fall off a cliff or being in the wrong place when a tree falls. (This is a psychopath's life in the state of nature, a rush to procreate before being recognized and killed.)

So the ancients, our forebears and so-called primitive people all recognized psychopaths and their danger.

Why don't we? What is the difference?

Well, they believed in evil, they trusted their own observations, their own judgment, and they were willing to act on this judgment.

We rely on "experts" (many of whom are psychopaths), think most people are good "deep down inside", and would never take matters into our own hands. Most of us probably can't imagine believing, saying and acting upon the phrase "slay the monster". I disagree. I believe you could, given enough provocation. But don't take my word for it, please read *In Broad Daylight* by Harry MacLean (or see the excellent Brian Dennehy movie version). It's the true story of a long-suffering town rising up and killing a law-twisting, rampaging psychopath in front of dozens of witnesses, none of whom talked. They rarely show this movie on TV, I wonder why?

HOMO SAPIENS NORMALIS VS. HOMO SAPIENS PSYCHOPATHICUS

All of us must have wondered how we would have done in one of the great tests of the past, the Revolutionary War, the Civil War, WWI and WWII. Well this is our chance to find out; this is our time, our test. Greatness calls. We face the struggle of the ages, the battle for evolutionary supremacy between normal humans and psychopaths. If we lose, slavery will be our lot. Some of us might enjoy it however. No doubt there'll be 500 channels of Springer TV, a new Britney Spears every 3 years, a new Jeff Gordon every 5, Super Prozac and Super Viagra. Perfect slaves believe they are free.

Let me make this very clear, your enemies are not individuals of any particular race or religion but rather the psychopaths of all races and religions.

You want to defend your kind? OK, 'normies', that's your kind.

That said, let me make a controversial point. There are several peoples who historically have lived as outsiders among a host society. The host societies have often reviled them for their too predatory trading and/or money lending practices. Among these peoples are the Indians (from India), Overseas Chinese and the Jews. Now, if you look at these three cultures you'll note, among other things, that they have traditionally promoted—and still often cling to—arranged marriages.

The relationship between a husband and a wife is a gift from God. Normal people who turn their backs on this gift (either through choice, psychological blocks or biology) pay a huge psychological or spiritual price. Psychopaths, however, are unscathed. Marriages of convenience were made by and for psychopaths.

RECOGNIZING PSYCHOPATHS

This is extremely difficult.

When I tell people that most media personalities, doctors, lawyers, judges, etc., are all psychopaths, they usually don't believe me. If they do believe me, they then usually assume psychopathology is a mild condition since these often seem like such nice people.

If psychopaths were obviously monstrous, then there'd be no problem, would there?

The monstrousness of psychopathology stems from the facade of normalcy and niceness. Don't take my word for it, read the research.

Are psychopaths physically recognizable? Not really. But "not really" means yes, sort of.

Psychopaths often say they can recognize other psychopaths by sight.

Some people describe some psychopaths as being hollow or shallow eyed. But what does that mean objectively? Almost nothing, two people could use the same terms very differently.

Before one can hope to "recognize" psychopaths, one must first be able to look at someone and ask oneself, "What is looking out of that person's eyes?" This is beyond the imagination of most people. Most people would say, "Why, a person much like myself". The ability to entertain other possibilities comes with age or great emotional cost (such as recognizing a marriage to a psychopath), or a psychopathic betrayal by a psychopath parent (such as a parental affair with a child's spouse). Usually, however, people never recognize a psychopath spouse or parent. It's too painful to acknowledge. A DNA test would be very convenient.

To recognize psychopaths you need to use all your senses, all your instincts. If you say, "I'm too rational and mature to pay attention to the hairs on the back of my neck prickling, I need rational reasons for my opinion of other people", then you might as well put a sign on your forehead saying, "The sucker is in, psychopaths step right up."

Psychopaths are in every walk of life, they are everywhere. I'm sure many of you have ended up calling betraying acquaintances "snakes". I'm also sure a majority of theses "snakes" were psychopaths. Many people say, "Oh, I could never be fooled by a psychopath, I can just tell." Nothing could be further from the truth

Both my livelihood and my professional reputation depend on my knowledge of psychopaths, and I get fooled all the time. [447]

As a hypothetical, if you asked a top rank psychopath a question such as, "Where did the story, 'Why did the cow jump over the moon,' come from," you might get the reply, "Oh, that's a true story, the cow was trying to steal the Man in the Moon's cheese, but missed." Then walking away you might say to yourself, "Oh, I see, sure, that makes sense." Ten steps later, "Hey, wait a minute!"

It's that second thought you should pay attention to.

Just watch "junk science" psychopath experts testify in trials. They are extremely convincing. I have come to think that it is more than just their ability

---

[447] This suggests that the writer of this piece is a professional in the field of psychology or perhaps the law who is afraid to express his views publicly with his real name attached.

to turn on sincerity and con. I believe they are stuck in a child's sense of reality. The world makes no sense to them; they are like children who go to bed saying, "But Daddy, Daddy! What if they turn off gravity while I'm asleep? I'll float away!" They never learn to internalize day to day physical laws. So even when they speak of reality it makes no sense to them, thus it's easy for them to speak pure nonsense while making it seem realistic. Speaking *as though they understand* what they are talking about is essentially normal practice to them, one they can easily apply to the sheerest nonsense. This "frozen child" aspect is central to a psychopath's personality development and characteristics. It is central to their lack of moral development. It is also a way to recognize them.

Psychopaths lack adult judgment and reasoning powers. I have no doubt many have kept their Green Lantern Decoding Rings from childhood.

(Actually "to wonder if someone's a psychopath" is a safer concept, "recognize" sounds too certain, we might be wrong and we don't want to attack the merely odd. On the other hand, if criminal conduct is involved and the diagnosis is certain, then the situation is different.) We all have different life experiences and are attuned to different senses. You need to use all your experience, abilities, instincts, intuitions and reasoning to protect yourself and your family from psychopaths.

For me, female psychopaths are a deeper source of mystery. They may be much more different from normal humans than the male psychopaths. I usually find them much harder to recognize, even when their behavior makes it obvious. Some however are still immediately obvious to me, even in a still photo (though they have to be looking straight into the camera). Look at pictures of Diane Zamora, naval midshipman and murderess, and Kyra Phillips, CNN anchor and CIA propagandress. If you see any qualities in common, run if you ever see the same in daily life. These two are full blown psychopaths, having only the appearance of humanity.

Actually a number of important men have psychopath wives/fiancees: George W. Bush, Laura Bush; James Carville, Mary Matalin; Alan Greenspan, Andrea Mitchell; William Bratton, Rikki Kleiman; Rudy Giuliani; Rupert Murdoch; William Colby.

Considering Colby's fate, maybe these guys should worry.

When I look at the faces of Laura Bush, Condi Rice and Andrea Mitchell I see a strange mask-like quality. I have come to believe that this is because there simply is *no human soul inside* pulling the face muscles, even more so than is typical for most psychopaths.

THE SHAPE OF THINGS TO COME

Normie police commanders, how can you recognize CIA psychopath officers? They're the ones who went away for national training (FBI, CIA or military) and came back with attitudes. Actually they probably had attitudes to begin with; psychopaths have a natural arrogance and hatred of authority. They're the ones who have to denigrate their opponents even if their opponents are actually very able, maybe especially in that case. They're the ones who view all human interactions as competitions they must win. (This is true in all spheres, psychopaths don't really care who sleeps with whom, who marries whom, who keeps the kids after the divorce, just that they come out the winner.)

Normie police commanders, this is more than just a theoretical discussion, in the case of a breakdown of law you will be eliminated in order for the psychopaths to take operational control.

How do psychopath police officers view their comrades? Well, we can't ask the New Orleans cops, Antoinette Frank, or her partner, Ronald Williams. She was executed after murdering him and others in a robbery at a restaurant where he was moonlighting as security. With true psychopath chutzpah, she even showed up later in uniform as one of the investigating officers. We can, however, see the movie *Training Day*, which I recommend.

It is interesting to note that identifying psychopaths is central to an advancement in scientific policing. Psychopaths always corrupt the groups they are in, a bad seed as it were. Thus a group of young toughs may become misdemeanour-minded delinquents, a social gang might take up drug dealing, drug dealers might take up murder, etc. If law enforcement could identify the psychopathic evil core, it would be very helpful. Often after group crimes, parents will say such things as, "Oh, no. Joey's not like that. It can't be." I believe them—rather I believe that normally Joey wouldn't do such things. Under the influence of a psychopath corrupted social group, however, he might. A group of G.I. Joey's found out the hard way, just what they were capable of, if conditions were just wrong and if leadership, formal or informal, was pathic. The place was My Lai.

Some people say that the best way to recognize psychopaths is to think of them as odd-looking, wide-eyed harmless kids. Okay, imagine wide-eyed kids stepping on frogs, now imagine them stepping on the Wellstone family, now imagine them stepping on your family.

After throwing "communist suspects" (not so incidentally, they were turned in by an early CIA designed Neighborhood Watch program in Vietnam) out of helicopters to their deaths, our mutant Phoenix Program operatives would go out drinking, laughing and joking.

While making one of the recent CIA movies, Ben Affleck was given a tour of the Agency. He said that the members reputed to have done "the really bad things" actually looked harmless, just a little odd. Yeah, I bet they did, Ben.

Having said all the above, I believe readers new to psychopathology should focus on *recognizing psychopathic behavior* not the psychopaths themselves.

Be on the lookout for behavior that exceeds the bounds of humanity. One problem is that this is also beyond the imagination of most people. They will deny or excuse such behaviors, not only that they hear of, but even what they witness. Psychopaths know this. I have often heard, both from the victims and psychopaths themselves, that psychopaths will taunt their victims, telling them that no one would believe them anyway.

We need science to develop a DNA test.

Also, please bear in mind that the higher-level psychopaths are the hardest to recognize.

I would say that hitting the Pentagon with a cruise missile-laden drone and calling it a Boeing 757 would be beyond the bounds of normal human behavior (to say nothing of allowing thousands to die in order to cow a people, whip up a war fervor and impose a police state). Rumsferatu and Cheney, Prince of Darkness, are protected *because most people cannot imagine evil this inhuman.*

These Pathocrats, however, have utter faith in our lack of imagination. They even have a name for us; they call us "sheeple".

SHEEPLE NO MORE

Most people resist thinking of themselves as ever having been brainwashed sheep. On one hand I naturally understand this, but on the other hand I don't understand this at all. We've all been fooled in daily life, lied to and manipulated by those we considered friends. If we hadn't realized this when we had the evidence, what would that have made us?

Exactly.

My friends, I'm afraid there is no way around it. We have to face the fact that we've been bamboozled, conned, tricked, hornswoggled, lied to, snookered, fooled in every way imaginable. Join us, those who say "sheeple no more!"

THE MIRROR WORLD, THE SHADOW SOCIETY

I stated earlier that the Pathocracy has extended its tentacles throughout society creating a virtual shadow society, not simply a shadow government. The CIA has scattered its minions across the ideological spectrum to fool us into thinking we have a political voice, a media outlet. What does win-win mean to you? If the CIA controls both sides of the playing field, how can they lose? My friends, it's as though we're playing poker, not realizing there's a hidden team at the table. As our losses mount, all we can do is look at each other in confused bewilderment. The psychopaths: the enemy within, the fifth column, human doppelgangers, the killers of our heroes, the stealers of our history, traitors to America and the world. It's not confusing at all.

With control of media voices and leadership positions across the ideological spectrum, it's no wonder that they thought they could get away with the 2000 and 2004 theft of those elections. With their elementary-school-minds they're used to living like pouting kids, pouting kids who sooner or later have to get back on the bus. They thought we too would have no choice but to fall in line.

In their heart of hearts they think we are just like them, that we only pretend to care about others, to have spiritual convictions and deep beliefs, to have inner personal strength.

Their positioning across the ideological spectrum is designed to make us feel we are represented politically and have a voice in the media. The truth comes out only at crunch time or the end game.

Thus Mario Cuomo, with his sad beagle eyes, goes down to Florida in 2000 to tell Gore that the time has come to put the country first, to preserve the fabric of civil society and faith in the law by conceding. (I consider Mario Cuomo to be a 'voice of reason' type psychopath. They come across so reasonable, even shedding alligator tears, so simpatico; however, pay attention only to their suggestions and the results of these suggestions, that is their true self and true message.)

Similarly, Jesse Jackson, who I do not believe is a psychopath but is definitely CIA (he was picked as the new "Black Leader" before they assassinated MLK), raced down to Florida, ran to the front of the Gore demonstrations, turned them around, and shut them down in defeat.

Similarly the *Washington Post* and the *NY Times* put a lie to their liberalism by calling on Gore to concede.

Our Constitution wasn't written by idiots. There are provisions for resolving deadlocks (forgetting for now, the fact that accurate post-election recounts showed that Gore had actually had the most votes in FL and Kerry in Ohio). Nobody had to "do the right thing" by conceding, just let the process work. Gore, little boy in short pants, didn't have the stomach for a fight, neither did Kerry, because they are part and parcel of the same group of elite psychopaths in power.

Those on the right may have felt much of the same betrayal at the Bush TIA database plan. The next time you have a turkey shoot to raise money for the local volunteer fire department; you had better have everybody bring their own shells. If not, the purchase may be flagged by TIA computers as matching a terrorist pattern. You could even be thrown in Gitmo, as an enemy combatant, deprived of an attorney. Just wait until the Republi-psychos outlaw cash. You can be sure they want to.

If you think that someone is an anti-government investigative journalist, better analyze their writings closely.

Seymour Hersh wrote an investigation of My Lai called *Coverup*, which is what it was (clever, clever!).

Alexander Cockburn writes anti-government diatribes that describe conspiracies and horrible atrocities. However, they are unprovable. Show him a provable conspiracy, such as the Warren Commission, and he takes the government line faithfully (this is part of the public record, please look it up).

The Pathocratic strategy is to establish their journalist sleeper agents' anti-government bona fides as a means for derailing true investigations by true journalists.

Michael Moore wrote an otherwise excellent anti-Bush book called *Stupid White Men*. What's the real message being conveyed here? No matter what is inside the book, the majority of white males who did in fact vote for Bush are not going to read it. This is its true purpose, solidifying the white male support for Bush (clever, clever!).

Are they capable of using the "song of truth" in the cause of a lie?

Hell, this is one of their specialties.

Can they get too clever?

Certainly, it happens all the time.

It's hard to say, but Moore's book may very well have done more good than harm. (Incidentally, I consider Michael Moore to be one of the "too-ugly-to-be-psychopaths" corrupt normies who serve the mutant psychopath CIA. Psychopaths, themselves, can always turn on the charm and attractiveness.)

Other such servants of the mutants include Alan "Torture Warrants" Dershowitz, Jerry Falwell, and Al Sharpton. These are all hideously corrupt and evil individuals who have chosen to serve the enemy. In their own lives and careers they are also very closely associated with psychopaths (for example, Claus Von Bulow, Pat Robertson, Alton Maddox and Vernon Mason of the Tawana Brawley hoax, respectively).

One example where they definitely did more good than harm was Vincent "Never-met-a-government- crime-I-didn't-like" Bugliosi's pamphlet in *The Nation* on the 2000 stolen election. Impassioned and accusatory, it gave voice to and raised the morale of those devastated by the Bush rape of the electoral process. However, when the results of the media recount came out (the NORC study), he claimed, "Oh well, it's all moot. Bush would have won anyway."

This was an absolutely dishonest, intentional misreading of study results. The Pathocracy's intention was that those upset over Florida would follow Bugliosi into acquiescence at the results. Actually, the aggrieved just ignored his second opinion as being some kind of inexplicable accident. In fact, neither of his opinions were any kind of accident, they were both part of a thoroughly planned propaganda stratagem that just didn't work.

I view the truth of post-WWII history as a trail up a broad mountain with innumerable side trails. Starting at the foot of the mountain then posted at various heights are psychopathic (CIA and other agencies) disinformationists. At the foot they say, "Oswald acted alone. Anyone who climbs this mountain is a conspiracy nut. Here, stay on level ground with all the people with common sense."

As you travel up the mountain, the spooks speak the truth for that height on the mountain but then lead you astray on a side trail. Thus they might say, "Sure there was a JFK assassination conspiracy, it was the Mafia or Castro."

Further on they say, "it was rogue elements in the CIA." Further still, "here's the JFK truth, plus everything you want to know about UFOs", and on and on.

Finally, you come to the 95%+ true disinformationists, such as Fletcher Prouty and Greg Palast. Obviously, you can learn a lot from the 95%+ truth spooks. If you can discover their lies, what it is that they are protecting, essentially you have the entire picture.

The smarter psychopaths behind the CIA realize that the truth is out there to be found. By having their own reveal it, they are able to spin the truth and continue to mislead at every level of investigation. I believe that the CIA has used all intelligence agency stratagems that they ever used against the KGB, against America, its political parties and media and other institutions, including disinformation, moles, sleeper agents, double agents, "honey traps," blackmail, agent provocateurs, criminal free agents freed to follow their own interests and much more.

WHY THE COUP?

OK, let's say I'm right. Let's say that the psychopaths in the CIA did have a brilliantly successful fifty year plan (perhaps McCloy's and Gehlen's brainchild) to create a Stealthtalitarian political system enforced by and rewarding to psychopaths, a genius level Punch-and-Judy puppet show that still has the vast majority of the population fooled, a society-wide Game of Charades. Why then throw over such shadow control through the daylight robbery that took place in Florida (Jeb Bush's state)?

What would make it worth it?

CONTROL OF THE HUMAN GENOME

Quite simply they need to control the human genome *and the public reaction to the open establishment of the government most suited to psychopaths.* [448]

My friends, we are all caught in a Twilight Zone episode in which the mutant children have seized power through their lethal toys. In this case, the lethal toy is the U.S. military. It is time for us adults to take it away from them.

Do we have enough knowledge to start DNA testing of psychopath suspects? Well, we certainly have enough to start serious research. In my opinion, a good place to start would be the officer corps of the service branches. The military with its essentially captive subjects and extensive personnel records is an excellent platform for psychological research.

Normie officers, how do you recognize psychopath officers, in the absence of a DNA test? They're the ones who treat their fighting men as soulless automatons. When the killing is over, warriors have to go back home and sleep peacefully next to their spouses and infants. Psychopath officers have

---

[448] This remark suggests to me that this individual must have read Lobaczewski's work which was published in the West in a limited academic edition back in 1985.

no understanding of this, no understanding that the warrior's own soul is never more than microns away from the cross hairs.

South and Central American officers, you have it easier. You simply need to know who attended S.O.A.P., almost as good as a DNA test in identifying psychopaths. Once we have a reliable and proven DNA test, then I believe we may need to test all politicians, all military officers, all judges, all law enforcement personnel, all employees of the Justice Department. Note that I don't include the CIA/NSA here. Their tests will no doubt be part of their crimes against humanity trials.

Federal psychopath path judges, if you want to head off this future, I suggest you rule consistently for the Constitution. Let me make this simple for you. Whatever lets you live out your life unmolested is good, whatever puts you on trial for your life is bad. When Patriot Act, Homeland Defense, electoral issues come before you, rule for the Constitution. If you shut down the Bush/CIA, now we may never get to the point of widespread testing, let alone a shooting war. Testing could still be restricted to those convicted of felonies.

SO WHERE DO WE STAND?

On shifting sands, Bizarro World, House of Mirrors, Puzzle Palace, Endless Maze, the Grand Charade, use whichever image you wish. My friends, we are all lost in a tall grass swamp, not knowing which paths lead to solid ground, we can hear other lost parties but not see them through the tall grass. My friends, we need to put aside past differences, ideological, political, religious. We are all patriots now. We must pool our efforts, our knowledge to defeat the psychopaths.

George Washington: "We have, therefore, to resolve to conquer or die."

WHAT DO WE DO?

For the time being, we must all be on our own. Any organization or leadership will be snuffed out immediately. We must educate ourselves and spread the word. Bear in mind that all organizations will be thoroughly infiltrated. Study psychopathology, study the CIA crimes of the past. Tape the news channels, saving the tapes of acts of terrorism and suspicious accidents. Study famous psychopaths of the past. Rasputin was a historical psychopath who had the Tsar and Tsarina of Russia under his spell. He was one of the reasons, one of the many reasons, that the Tsar's government was not able to respond effectively to the rise of the Bolsheviks. The result was that the Soviet Union spent 70 plus years as a communist totalitarian prison camp the size of a continent. Read Orwell's *1984* and Huxley's *Brave New World*. You can be sure that 'Rovesputin' has. The CIA has studied all the propaganda of the past. Read *Mein Kampf*. Study propaganda techniques. Become a poll watcher. Believe me the CIA has.

BIBLIOGRAPHY

9/11

Ahmed, Nafeez Mosaddeq. *The War on Truth*. Olive Branch Press, 2005.

Burke, Jason. *Al-Qaeda: The True Story of Radical Islam*. London: Penguin Books, 2004.

Der Spiegal. *Inside 9-11, What Really Happened*. St. Martin's Paperbacks, 2002.

Griffin, David Ray. *The 9/11 Commission Report: Omissions and Distortions*. Olive Branch Press, 2005.

Griffin, David Ray. *The New Pearl Harbor*. Olive Branch Press, 2004.

Hopsicker, Daniel. *Welcome to Terrorland*. Mad Cow Press, 2004.

Marrs, Jim. *Inside Job: Unmasking the 9/11 Conspiracy*. Origin Press, 2004.

Matier, Phillip, and Andrew Ross, Chronicle Staff Writers. "Early Warning: State Department memo warned of terrorist threat." *SFGate.com*, September 14, 2001.

McGowan, Dave. Many articles found at http://www.davesweb.cnchost.com/. McGowan has written an excellent series of articles demolishing the "Peak Oil" being promoted by Mike Ruppert.

Meyssan, Thierry. *Pentagate*. London: Carnot Publishing Ltd., 2002.

Meyssan, Thierry. *The Big Lie*. London: Carnot Publishing Ltd., 2002.

Piper, Michael Collins. *The High Priests of War*. American Free Press, 2004.

Ruppert, Mike. *Crossing the Rubicon*. New Society Publishers, 2004.

Selwyn, Manning. *The Scoop*, April 22, 2004, http://www.scoop.co.nz/mason/stories/HL0404/S00176.html

Stinnett, Robert. *Day Of Deceit: The Truth About FDR and Pearl Harbor*. Touchstone Books, 2001.

Thompson, Paul, and the Center for Cooperative Research. *The Terror Timeline*. Regan Books, 2004.

Tremblay, Rodrique. *The New American Empire*. Infinity Publishing, 2004.

History, Israel, the Ashkenazim, and Genetic Research

– , "New Carbon Dates Support Revised History of Ancient Mediterranean." *Science* 312, April 28 2006.

Ashe, Geoffrey. *The Ancient Wisdom*. London: Sphere, 1979.

Ashe, Geoffrey. *The Book of Prophecy*. London: Blandford, 1999.

Augstein, Rudolf. *Jesus Menschensohn*. Munich.

B. Dugdale. *Arthur James Balfour,* Vol I. 1939.

Baillie, Mike. *Exodus to Arthur*. London: B.T. Batesford Ltd., 1999.

Beres, Judit, and C. R. Guglielmino. "Genetic Structure in relation to the history of the Hungarian ethnic group." *Human Biology* 68:3 (June 1996): 335-356.

Boyd, Robert S. "Comets may have caused Earth's great empires to fall." *Knight Ridder Washington Bureau* (August 17, 1999).

Breasted, James. *Ancient Records of Egypt*, 1906-7, 5 Vols. London: Histories & Mysteries of Man Ltd., 1988.

Brook, Kevin Alan. *The Jews of Khazaria*. Jason Aronson Publishers, 1999.

Budge, E. A. Wallis. *Tutankhamen: Amenism, Atenism, and Egyptian Monotheism*. Cambridge: Polity Press; Malden: Blackwell Publishers, 2001.

Cluckman, John. "Footprints in the Dust." *CounterPunch*, March 11, 2002, http://www.counterpunch.org/chuckmanfootprints.html

Cochran, Gregory, Jason Hardy, Henry Harpending. "Natural History of Ashkenazi Intelligence." Department of Anthropology, University of Utah.

Collins, Andrew, and Chris Ogilvie-Herald. *Tutankhamun: The Exodus Conspiracy*. London: Virgin Books, 2002.

Crabitès Collection, Newspaper clipping, Mss. 73-85, Scrapbooks 1919-1939. New Orleans: University of New Orleans.

De Espinosa, Alonso. *The Guanches of Tenerife*, trans. Sir Clements Markham. Nendeln/Liechtenstein: Kraus Repring, 1972.

Diodorus of Sicily, trans. C. H. Oldfather. Loeb Classical Library, Vols. II and III. London: William Heinemann, 1935, and Cambridge: Harvard University Press, 1939.

Dolan, Richard. *UFOs and the National Security State*. Revised Edition. Hampton Roads, 2002.

Egyptian Gazette, February 16, 1924.

Egyptian Gazette, February 18, 1924.

Egyptian Gazette, February 21, 1924.

Egyptian Gazette, March 7, 1924.

Eschenburg, J. J. *Manual of Classical Literature from the German of J. J. Eschenburg*. Kessinger Publishing, LLC, 2005.

Norman Finkelstein. *Beyond Chutzpah*. London: Verso, 2005.

Friedman, Richard Elliot. *Who Wrote the Bible*. New York: Harper & Row, 1987.

Geoffrey of Monmouth. *The History of the Kings of Britain*, trans. Lewis Thorpe. 1966.

Gorenberg, Gershom. *The End of Days: Fundamentalism and the Struggle for the Temple Mount*. New York: Oxford University Press, 2000.

Graves, Robert. *The Greek Myths*. London: Penguin, 1992.

Gumilev, Lev. *Ethnogenesis and the Biosphere*. Moscow: Progress Publishers, 1990.

Ouspensky, P.D. *In Search of the Miraculous*. Orlando: Harcourt, 2001.

Halsell, Grace. *Forcing God's Hand*. Amana Publications, 1999.

Herodotus. *The Histories*, Book IV, trans. Aubrey De Selincourt, revised John Marincola. London: Penguin, 1972.

Higham, Charles. *Trading with the Enemy: An Expose of the Nazi-American Money Plot 1933-1949*. New York: Delacorte Press, 1983.

Hoving, Thomas. *Tutankhamun*. Cooper Square Press, 2002.

Jones, Steve. *In the Blood: God, Genes, and Destiny*. Harper Collins, 1996.

Joseph, Frank. *The Lost Pyramids of Rock Lake*. Lakeville, MN: Galde Press, Inc., 1992.

Josephus. *Antiquities of the Jews*, trans. William Whiston. Nelson Reference & Electronic Publishing, 2004.

Koestler, Arthur. *The Thirteenth Tribe*. New York: Random House, 1976.

Le Journal du Caire, February 16, 1924.

Le Journal du Caire, February 25, 1924.

Le Temps, February 17, 1924.

Le Temps, February 24, 1924.

Lindbergh, Charles. *Speech in Iowa*. September 11, 1941.

Marrs, Jim. *Alien Agenda*. New York: Harper Collins, 1997.

Mearsheimer, John and Stephen Walt. "The Israel Lobby." 2006.

Mouravieff, Boris. "L'Histoire a-t-elle un sens?" *Revue Suisse d'histoire*, tome 4, fasc. 4 (1954).

New York Times, March 13, 1924.

New York Times, March 20, 1924.

New York Times, February 22, 1924.

Ostrovsky, Victor. *By Way of Deception*. Toronto: Stoddart, 1990.

Parkinson, Brian. Doctoral Thesis of Department of History, Florida State University, August 4, 2005.

Plato. *Timaeus*, trans. Benjamin Jowett.

Redford, Donald B. *Egypt, Canaan, and Israel in Ancient Times*. Princeton: Princeton University Press, 1992.

Reeves, C. N., John H. Taylor, Nicholas Reeves. *Howard Carter: Before Tutankhamun*. Harry N. Abrams, 1993.

Schecter, Bruce. *My Brain is Open*. New York: Touchstone, 1998.

Schwartz, Regina M. *The Curse of Cain*. Chicago: The University of Chicago Press, 1997.

Shanks, Hershel. "The Exodus and the Crossing of the Red Sea, According to Hans Goedicke." *Biblical Archaeology Review* 7:5 (September/October 1981).

Sykes, Bryan. *The Seven Daughters of Eve*. W.W. Norton & Company, 2001.

The Courier, September 15-17, 1977.

The Times, December 18, 1922.

Thomas, Mark G., Michael E. Weale, Abigail L. Jones, Martin Richards, Alice Smith, Nicola Redhead, Antonio Torroni, Rosaria Scozzari, Fiona Gratrix, Ayele Tarekegn, James F. Wilson, Cristian Capelli, Neil Bradman, and David B. Goldstein. "Founding Mothers of Jewish Communities: Geographically Separated Jewish Groups Were Independently Founded by Very Few Female Ancestors."

Times of London, February 14, 1924.

Times of London, February 19, 1924.

Times of London, February 22, 1924.

Times of London, February 23, 1924.

Townsend, Mark, and Paul Harris. "Now the Pentagon tells Bush: climate change will destroy us." *The Observer*, February 22, 2004, http://observer.guardian.co.uk/international/story/0,6903,1153513,00.html

Wade, Nicolas. "DNA, New Clues to Jewish Roots." *New York Times*, May 14, 2002.

Wagner, Donald. "Christian Zionism." *The Daily Star*. Beirut.

Washington Times, September 10, 2001.

Wilkens, Iman. *Where Troy Once Stood*. Rider, 1990.

Ponerology and Psychopathy

Assagiolli, Roberto. *Dynamic Psychology and Psychosynthesis*. New York Research Foundation, 1959.

Becker, Ernest. *The Structure of Evil*. New York: The Free Press, 1968.

Black, Donald W., M.D. with C. Lindon Larson. *Bad Men, Bad Boys: Confronting Antisocial Personality Disorder*. New York: Oxford University Press, 1999.

Blair, James, Derek Mitchell, and Karina Blair. *The Psychopath, Emotion and the Brain*. London: Blackwell Publishing, 2005.

Buhler, Charlotte Malachowski. *The Course of Human Life: A Study of Goals in the Humanistic Perspective*. New York: Springer Publishing Co., 1968.

Campbell, Philip. "The nature of belief systems in mass publics" in David Apter, ed., *Ideology and Discontent*. New York: Free Press, 1964.

Canup, Robert. The Socially Adept Psychopath. http://www.hal-pc.org/~rcanup/sap.html

Chirot, Daniel. *Modern Tyrants*. Princeton, New Jersey: Princeton University Press, 1994.

Cleckley, Hervey. *The Mask of Sanity*. 4th Edition. St. Louis: Mosby, 1983.

Dabrowski, Kazimierz. *Psychoneurosis is Not an Illness*. London: Gryf Publications Ltd., 1972.

DeMause, Lloyd. *Foundations of Psychohistory*. New York: Creative Roots, 1982.

Diagnostic and Statistical Manual of Mental Disorders. 3rd Edition.

Doren, Denis M. *Understanding and Treating the Psychopath*. New York: J. Wiley & Sons, 1987.

Drewa, Gerard (ed.). *Podstawy genetyki*. Volumed. Wroclaw, 1995.

Edwards, Paul (ed.). *Encyclopedia of Philosophy*. New York: MacMillan Publishing Co., Inc. & Free Press, 1972.

Ehrlich, S. K. and R.P. Keogh. "The psychopath in a mental institution." Archiv neurol. *Psychiatr*. vol 76 (1956): 286-295.

Freud, Sigmund. *Basic Writings*. New York: Modern Library, 1955.

Freud, Sigmund. *Studies in Hysteria*. New York: Basic Books, 1957.

Goertzel, Ted. "Generational Conflict and Social Change." *Youth and Society* (1972).

Gordon, Thomas and Max Morgan-Witts. *Pontif*. New York: New American Library, 1964.

Granovetter, Mark. "Threshold Models of Collective Behavior." *American Journal of Sociology* 83 (1978): 1420-1443.

Gray, K.C. and H.C. Hutchinson. "The psychopathic personality: a survey of Canadian psychiatrists' opinions." *Canadian Psychiatric Association*. J. vol. 9 (1964): 452-461.

Greenfield, Susan (ed.). *The Human Mind Explained: An Owner's Guide to the Mysteries of the Mind*. New York: Holt, 1996.

Hartau, Frederyk. *Wilhelm II*. Lublin: Median s.c., 1992.

Hare, Robert, Ph.D. "Psychopathy and Antisocial Personality Disorder: A Case of Diagnostic Confusion." *Psychiatric Times* 8:2 (February 1996).

Hare, Robert. *Without Conscience: The Disturbing World of the Psychopaths Among Us*. New York: The Guilford Press, 1993.

Herling-Grudzinski, Gustav. *A World Apart*. New York: Penguin, 1996.

Hoess, Rudolf. *Commandant of Auschwitz: The Autobiography of Rudolph Hoess*. World Pub. Co., 1960.

Horney, Karen. *Neurosis and Human Growth*. New York: W. W. Norton & Company, 1950.

Horney, Karen. *The Neurotic Personality of Our Time*. New York: W. W. Norton & Company, 1959.

Irving, David. *Secret Diaries of Hitler's Doctor*. London: Grafton Books, 1991.

Jenkins, Richard. *Social Identity*. Routledge, 1996.

Jenkins, Richard. "The psychopathic or antisocial personality, J. nerv. Ment." *Disease,* vol 131 (1960): 318-332.

Keller, Morton. "Reflections on Politics and Generations in America." In *Generations,* edited by Stephen Graubard, 123-135. New York: Norton, 1979.

Koestler, Arthur. *Darkness at Noon.* Bantam Books, 1966.

Klinberg, Frank. "The historical alternation of moods in American foreign policy." *World Politics* 4 (1952): 239-273.

Kraupl Taylor, Frederick. *Psychopathy: Its Causes and Symptoms.* Baltimore: Johns Hopkins University Press, 1979.

Kretshmer, E. *Physique and Character.* Routledge, reprinted 1999.

Klinberg, Frank. "The historical alternation of moods in American foreign policy." *World Politics* 4 (1952): 239-273.

Łobaczewski, Andrew M. *Political Ponerology,* trans. Alexandra Chciuk-Celt, Ph.D. New York: University of New York, 1984.

Łobaczewski, Andrew M. *Political Ponerology: A science on the nature of evil adjusted for political purposes.* Red Pill Press, 2006.

Magid, Ken, and Carole McKelvey. *"The Psychopaths Favourite Playground: Business Relationships."*

Maher, Brendan, ed. *Contemporary Abnormal Psychology.* Harmondsworth, Middlesex, England: Penguin Books Ltd., 1974.

Mannheim, Karl. *Essays on the Sociology of Knowledge.* London: Routledge and Kegan Paul, 1952.

Marias, Julian. *Generations: A Historical Method.* University of Alabama Press, translation, 1970.

McCord, W. and J. *Psychopathy and Delinquency.* Grune & Stratton, 1956.

Miller, Alice. *Am Anfang war Erziehung.* Frankfurt am Main: Surkamp Verlag, 1951.

Nasar, Sylvia. *A Beautiful Mind.* Simon & Schuster, 2001.

Neumayr, Anton. *Dictators in the Mirror of Medicine: Napoleon, Hitler, Stalin,* trans. David J. Parent. Bloomington, Illinois: Medi-Ed Press, 1995.

Psychnews International 2:5 (Oct-Dec 1997).

Psychotherapy: Journal of the Division of Psychotherapy of the American Psychological Association.

Raine, Adrian. "Psychopathy, Schizoid Personality and Borderline/Schizotypal Personality Disorders, Person. individ. Diff." Vol. 7, No.4, Pergamon Journals Ltd., 1986.

Russell, E.S. *Form and Function: A Contribution to the History of Animal Morphology.* Univ of Chicago Press, 1982.

Salekin, Trobst, Krioukova. "Construct Validity of Psychopathy in a Community Sample: A Nomological Net Approach." *Journal of Personality Disorders* 15:5 (2001): 425-441.

Salter, Anna C., Ph.D. *Predators: Pedophiles, Rapists, and Other Sex Offenders: Who They Are, How We Can Protect Ourselves and Our Children* Basic Books, 2004.

Schlesinger, Arthur M., Sr. *Paths to the Present.* New York: MacMillan, 1949.

Simon, Georg K., Jr, Ph.D. *In Sheep's Clothing.* Arkansas: A.J. Christopher & Co, 1996.

Simonton, Dean Keith. "Does Sorokin's data support his theory? A study of generational fluctuations in philosophical beliefs." *Journal for the Scientific Study of Religion* 15 (1976): 187-198.

Sommerhoff, G. *Analytical biology.* Oxford University Press, 1950.

Sorokin, Pitirim. *Social and Cultural Dynamics, Volume Four: Basic Problems, Principles and Methods.* New York: American Book Company, 1941.

Sorokin, Pitirim. *Social and Cultural Dynamics, One Volume Revision.* Boston: Porter Sargent, 1957.

Stout, Martha. *The Sociopath Next Door.* New York: Broadway Books, 2005.

Stout, Martha. *The Myth of Sanity.* New York: Penguin Books, 2001.

Taylor, Frederick K. *Psychopathology in Causes and Symptoms.* London and Baltimore: Johns Hopkins University Press, 1979.

Ziskind E., Somerfield-Ziskind E. Peter Jacob Frostig, 1896-1959. *Am J Psychiatry* 117 (November 1960): 479-80.